BACK TO FRANK BLACK

BACK TO FRANK BLACK

A Return to Chris Carter's *Millennium*

Edited by
Adam Chamberlain & Brian A. Dixon

Fourth Horseman Press

Back to Frank Black
Edited by Adam Chamberlain & Brian A. Dixon
Published by Fourth Horseman Press

First Edition, September 2012

All Materials Copyright © by the Individual Authors

Cover Artwork: "Frank Black" by Matthew Ingles

Interior Illustrations by James McLean

ISBN: 978-0-9883922-8-1

No part of this publication may be reproduced, stored in or introduced into a retrieval system, or transmitted, in any form, or by any means (electronic, mechanical, photocopying, recording, or otherwise), without the prior written permission of the copyright owner.

Fourth Horseman Press
http://www.fourthhorsemanpress.com/

TABLE OF CONTENTS

	Foreword Lance Henriksen	15
	Foreword Frank Spotnitz	17
	Introduction Chris Carter	21
I.	Frank Black and America's *Fin de Siècle* Joseph Maddrey	25
II.	Painting Away the Darkness: A Conversation with Chris Carter	39
III.	Enemies Within: Season One of Chris Carter's *Millennium* and America's Suburban Apocalypse John Kenneth Muir	49
IV.	The Mystery Guest: A Conversation with Lance Henriksen	57
V.	The Story of Lance Henriksen and the Fable of Frank Black Paul Clark	77
VI.	The Good Wife: A Conversation with Megan Gallagher	89

VII.	Make-Believing in Jordan Black Brittany Tiplady	101
VIII.	98% Less Serial Killers: A Conversation with Glen Morgan & James Wong	107
IX.	This is Who We Are: Secret Society and Family Redefined Gordon Roberts	127
X.	Here's My Thing: A Conversation with Kristen Cloke	163
XI.	Darren McGavin's Cat: A Conversation with Erin Maher & Kay Reindl	175
XII.	Snakes in the Grass and Snakes in the Open: Animal Symbolism in *Millennium*'s Second Season John Kenneth Muir	195
XIII.	Bigger than the Beatles: A Conversation with Mark Snow	201
XIV.	The Evil Earworm: Popular Music in *Millennium* Joe Tangari	215
XV.	The Devil's Liege: A Conversation with Sarah-Jane Redmond	241
XVI.	Seeing Evil: Lucy Butler as Legion Through the Eyes of Frank Black Alexander Zelenyj	249
XVII.	Heart of Darkness: A Conversation with Frank Spotnitz	273
XVIII.	Evil Has Many Faces: The Darkness in the World of *Millennium* Adam Chamberlain	283

XIX.	Avatar Unmasked: A Conversation with Michael R. Perry	323
XX.	Second Sight: Profiling, Prophecy, and Deductive Reasoning in Chris Carter's *Millennium* Brian A. Dixon	341
XXI.	Out of the Master's Shadow: A Conversation with Thomas J. Wright	383
XXII.	The Painter of Light: A Conversation with Robert McLachlan	397
XXIII.	Bardo Thodol: The Third Season and a New, Unified Theory of *Millennium* John Kenneth Muir	405
XXIV.	Rushing Toward an Apocalypse: A Conversation with Chip Johannessen	415
XXV.	Hard Graft: A History of the Back to Frank Black Campaign James McLean	421
XXVI.	The End of Innocence: A Conversation with Klea Scott	445
XXVII.	Back to Frank Black: A New *Millennium*	465
	Appendix	477

Illustrations by James McLean

FOREWORD

by Lance Henriksen

So much has happened in the world since *Millennium*. I feel like Luther nailing his manifesto to the doors of the powers that be to get their attention, surrounded by the fans of the show that have grown in such numbers. They have become a tribe from seventy-five countries.

Back in the day, I was so honored that Chris Carter trusted that Frank Black could live with me in the role. That I trusted his explanation of the yellow house.

9/11, the Patriot Act, wars, the Arab Spring, bank fraud, the Fed printing trillions... Overwhelming complexity in control of a few. The Constitution describes tyranny as fatiguing us into compliance. The disconnect between the average American and our government has become dangerous, as with many other countries and their governments. It has created a situation where the value of life is diminished. A mountain of people split off, full of rage. Acts of violence with no bounds. A glut of information hammering us from every corner of the globe, establishing a "take your pick" scenario of conspiracy and confusion, leaving us high and dry.

The man alone, Frank Black, a person with the chess player's eye for detail, stringing a thousand random pieces of information into a scenario like beads on a string, would need a gift. The Truth...

FOREWORD

by Frank Spotnitz

Chris Carter knows how to surf. In the fall of 1995, he was riding the growing wave of ratings success that was *The X-Files*. It wasn't surprising Twentieth Television would want him to create a second series—per his contract—to bolster the still-young Fox network. But what kind of series would Chris dream up? How do you follow *The X-Files* without repeating it? And how do you not repeat it without disappointing the network, critics, or fans?

It wasn't like Chris had a lot of time to think about it. Producing twenty-four episodes of *The X-Files* was already more than a full-time job. During the week, Chris's mud-splattered Toyota Land Cruiser was the first car you'd see parked outside the office in the morning and the last one to leave at night. If Chris wasn't in the office on a Saturday or Sunday, he was at his house writing or rewriting, looking out his window at the ocean waves he doubtless would've been surfing before *The X-Files* swept into his life, taking all his free time with it.

Although I worked closely with Chris—easily eighty or a hundred hours a week—I don't remember him ever discussing the genesis of *Millennium* with me. I knew he was somehow finding the time to write it, of course. But—and I'm only speculating here, because we've still never talked about it—I imagine he felt this idea so deeply and personally, he didn't want anyone else's opinions or ideas to tempt him to stray from whatever voice was calling him to this new territory in his imagination.

Finally, early in December 1995, he invited me into his office to read the first draft of the *Millennium* pilot on his Toshiba laptop. I was utterly transfixed. It was for me the single greatest hour of television Chris had ever written—and that was saying a lot, even in those relatively early days of the *X-Files* run.

After standing from his desk, I asked Chris what inspired him to write it. He cited a Season Two episode of *The X-Files* called "Irresistible," about a serial killer named Donnie Pfaster. Although Donnie sometimes appeared to those who saw him as a devil, in fact there was nothing supernatural about him.

The studio obviously wanted a show that fans of *The X-Files* would want to watch. But rather than mimicking *The X-Files*, Chris had gone deeper into the idea at the heart of it—the things that scare us in the night. The darkness that we fear in the real world. Frank Black's ability to see into this darkness. To understand the horror of it. By giving Frank this gift (and curse), Chris was saying something that—with the exception of "Irresistible"—*The X-Files* wouldn't have said. That there is nothing supernatural about evil—that it resides in each of us. Which makes it all the more terrifying, because there is no escaping it.

For me, the single most beautiful and moving scene in that first hour is when Catherine confronts Frank about keeping his work secret from her.

> FRANK
>
> I don't keep secrets, Catherine. I'll tell you anything you want.
>
> CATHERINE
>
> You think you're protecting me but you make it worse, Frank. You can't shut the world out for me. You can't ask me to

FOREWORD

> pretend that I don't know what you do.
>
> FRANK
>
> Everyone pretends. We all make believe. These men I help catch - make us.
>
> CATHERINE
>
> We're raising a daughter, Frank. The real world starts to seep in. You can't stop it.
>
> FRANK
>
> I want you to make believe that I can.

We make believe. We erect psychological boundaries to protect us, from the evil without and within. *But we are not safe.* As dark as the horrors in *Millennium* were, Chris knew that life is not worth living without light. Hence the beauty and simplicity of the yellow house where Catherine and Jordan lived, the little island of domesticity that Frank sought to protect despite the darkness that he saw in the world and in himself.

Chris had a wish list of actors to play Frank Black, and he managed to land his top choice, Lance Henriksen. Lance was already well known for his long and distinguished film career. But he'd often been cast as the heavy, not the hero. Yet Chris saw in Lance a man with the intelligence and the humanity to embody Frank Black. You can't help looking into Lance's eyes and feeling *this man has seen things.* Of course he could be believable as a bad guy. Which is what made the fact that he was a good guy—on our side, protecting us from all the real-life monsters out there—even more powerful.

I like to say that to be successful in television, you have to do everything right—and then, *get lucky.* In devising the pilot for *Millennium*, Chris did everything right. He hired the incomparable pilot director David Nutter and surrounded Lance with an amazing cast of actors, starting with Megan Gallagher, Terry O'Quinn, and Bill Smitrovich, then going on to include Klea Scott and Sarah-Jane Redmond. Mark Snow wrote a theme every bit as haunting and perfect as *The X-Files*'s classic main title music, and many other talented directors, producers, writers, and artists brought the series to life.

Despite the undisputed excellence of *Millennium*, it never did match the popular success of *The X-Files*. And after three seasons—the victim of declining ratings, an industry-wide trend misunderstood by the network as the fault of the series—it was canceled, before the actual turn of the millennium. And yet...

The monsters in *Millennium* were driven by ideology and destructive psychology. These are the sorts of real-life monsters who have given so many of the nightmares in the post-9/11 era. And in that way, perhaps, *Millennium* proved more prescient than Chris could have imagined.

To this day, I often meet people who liked *The X-Files* but who *loved Millennium*. I understand this. To these fans, and to me, *Millennium* touched on something profound, a truth that many find too dark to look at. But I believe by shining a light on that darkness, *Millennium* helped bring a little more light into our lives.

INTRODUCTION

by Chris Carter

I couldn't have imagined—sitting down to write the script that became the pilot that became the T.V. show—that almost twenty years later I would be sitting down to write an introduction for a book about this same show that never died in the dark hearts and minds of a group of fans who still want to believe that the final episode remains to be written. And God bless 'em. Who cares? They care. A whole lot, apparently.

As a T.V. concept, *Millennium* is really a so-called non-starter; not a genre show exactly, not a procedural exactly, decidedly not a family show, and certainly not a melodrama. It was a bit of all those things, and more. While the concept sprang from the dread of the approaching Y2K and from the loins of *The X-Files* (it never would've happened without Mulder and Scully), it really was about a man dealing with an existential problem. Namely: living in horror that something terrible is going to happen, the clock is ticking and, Atlas-like, the responsibility is all on him.

He was right, of course, making Frank Black prophetic and wise, even if he didn't live to see the ball drop himself. (On cable T.V., Frank would've been staring into the grim shadows of Season Seventeen, asking Peter Watts in his gruff baritone what it was like to work on a T.V. show that shoots in sunny Hawaii rather than moody Vancouver.)

Ironically, I'm writing this from sunny Vancouver, not but a stone's throw from where the show was filmed at the North Shore Studios. I'm reminded how many talented people came to work on it, how beautiful the series looked, and how weird it is I chose to make such a creepy show in such a cheerful place. Everywhere I go here, I'm reminded of a scene where we killed someone, buried someone, or burned someone alive. It's not necessarily a pleasant thing.

I'm often asked about shows akin to *Millennium*—*Dexter*, for instance—and I have to admit I don't watch them because I've grown weary of serial killers, of murder and mayhem generally. I think about Tom Wright, who directed so many excellent episodes, talking with a group of us about what we were all doing with our summer breaks. (Two weeks!) Some were going camping, some fishing, some on one adventure or another. Tom, who'd served in Vietnam, was going to sit by a pool with a drink in his hand. Now I understand.

A T.V. show is more than one person's idea. It's a product of its various influences, its physical location, its social construct—as the literary critics call it. If it's good, it's a reflection of the time it was created in and captures our hopes and fears, our dreams and aspirations. Period shows often depict the timelessness of many of these things.

I believe *Millennium* captured the anxiety of an age that didn't know how anxious it was about to become, after 9/11. I write in the wake of the Aurora shootings and also court proceedings for the gunman who killed six and wounded Gabby Giffords. This morning the headlines told of a gunman who'd walked into a Sikh temple in Oak Creek, Wisconsin, and killed six worshippers.

These are schizophrenic times. Gun control has evaporated from the political debate, and while crime statistics have gone down, mass murder looms large in our psyches. My friends at the F.B.I. talk about another terrorist attack on American soil not in terms of if, but when. We all live free here, but not from fear.

Bring back Frank Black? Has his time come around again? Even I could imagine it.

FRANK BLACK AND AMERICA'S *FIN DE SIÈCLE*

by Joseph Maddrey

> *"A man sees further looking out of the dark upon the light than a man does in the light and looking out upon the light."*
>
> —William Faulkner

I. THE CALL

In a 1996 issue of *Xposè*, Chris Carter explained the genesis of the television series *Millennium* (1996-99): "The inspiration for the show was that there were certain stories I couldn't do on *The X-Files*... They had to do with psychological terror, the real world with real criminals, and truly human monsters" (Brooks 54). The creator's bias is apparent.

The X-Files (1993-2002) is speculative horror, rooted in conspiracy theories and conjecture about the existence of aliens. Carter once said that the characters of Mulder and Scully were easy for him to write because, like Scully, he doesn't believe in the paranormal—but, like Mulder, he wants to believe (Schuster 6). This tension does not exist in the world of *Millennium*, which is firmly rooted in the real-life horror of 1990s America. In another 1996 interview, Carter asserted, "In most neighborhoods you can't go on a walk alone; certainly a woman can't walk alone at night. So I'm reacting to the darkness in the world. The show is a response to the times" (Brooks 55). His goal, he says, was to create an ideal hero, "a person who was behaving selflessly and heroically to solve the kind of violent crimes we read about in the papers all too often" (Castner 50). That hero was Frank Black, one man's answer to America's *fin de siècle*.

The term "*fin de siècle*" is French for "end of the century" and is often used to designate the cultural climate of western Europe at the conclusion of the nineteenth century, a time when urban Gothic literature was thriving with the publication of works like Robert Louis Stevenson's *The Strange Case of Dr. Jekyll and Mr. Hyde* (1886), George du Maurier's *Trilby* (1894), and Bram Stoker's *Dracula* (1897). Literary critic and cultural historian Mark Edmundson designates 30 March 1991 as the beginning of "America's fin de siècle" (Edmundson 3). That was the night when Jonathan Demme's *The Silence of the Lambs* (1991) swept the Academy Awards—incontrovertible proof that Gothic fiction had gone mainstream. Edmundson interprets this critical and commercial success as evidence of an underlying tenor of fear in pre-millennial American society. "Terror Gothic," he says, "insists that there is surely something rotten at the top, especially when the leaders are devoted to parading their virtues. Paranoia is sanity; what you don't know will hurt you; what you do know probably will too" (Edmundson 21). He could also have been summing up the essence of *The X-Files*.

Chris Carter has cited numerous influences for the creation of *The X-Files*. In addition to *The Silence of the Lambs*, he points to several political thrillers of the 1970s: *The Parallax View* (1974), *Three Days of the Condor* (1975) and *All the President's Men* (1976) (Schuster 4). The last of these films revolves around the Watergate scandal and the subsequent resignation of President Richard Nixon, an event that Carter identifies as "the most formative event of my youth" (Lowry 12). It was only natural that he, like so many members of his generation, grew up with a deep-seated mistrust of authority. In the early 1990s, Carter began ruminating on the theory (popular among U.F.O. hunters) that the American government orchestrated a massive cover-up after an alien ship crash-landed in Roswell, New Mexico, in the summer of 1947. This alleged cover-up became the basis for what he imagined as a scary television series in the tradition of *The Twilight Zone* (1959–64), *The Outer Limits* (1963–65) and *Kolchak: The Night Stalker* (1974–75).

The X-Files debuted in the fall of 1993. By the spring of 1995, it was a cultural touchstone. Its creator observed, "The show's original spirit has become kind of the spirit of the country—if not the world." He also offered an opinion about why that was true: "With the Berlin Wall down, with the global nuclear threat gone, with Russia trying to be a market economy, there is a growing paranoia, because as somebody once said, there are no easy villains anymore" (Meisler 9). Bestselling authors like Whitley Streiber (*Majestic*) and popular conspiracy theorists like William Cooper (*Behold a Pale Horse*) were among the first to tap into that "spirit of the age" by writing narratives about a secret plan, hatched at Roswell, to unite humanity under a global power elite. Cooper boldly states, "George Bush is not a loyal citizen of the United States but instead is loyal only to the destruction of the United States and to the formation of the New World Order" (Cooper 90). If Bush was a Gothic master villain for half of the American population, Bill Clinton quickly morphed into a Gothic master villain for the other half. Throughout the course of his presidency (1993–2001), critics eagerly vilified Clinton as a liar, a cheat, and even a murderer.

Bush and Clinton certainly weren't alone. Cooper maintained that Bush was in league with many other world leaders and members of a power elite including Pope John Paul II. To find liars, cheats, and murderers a little closer to home, Americans had only to turn on the television (or log onto the internet) for endless news coverage of pop criminals Jeffrey Dahmer, the Menendez Brothers, Tonya Harding, Lorena Bobbitt, O. J. Simpson, Susan Smith, Timothy McVeigh, Ted Kaczynski, et al. Mark Edmundson reminds us that these were necessary evils: "Once there was only one Gothic master-villain in our lives… With the dwindling of the Soviet Union we need many" (Edmundson 66).

The idea of a legion of Gothic master-villains—literally a "serial killer of the week"—became the foundation of Chris Carter's

Millennium series. The show offers variations on the real-life cases of New York bomber George Metesky ("522666"), sexual predator Jerome Brudos ("Loin Like a Hunting Flame"), alleged child abuser Virginia McMartin ("Monster"), and the Zodiac Killer ("The Mikado"), among many others. The "serial killer of the week" formula, however, quickly began to grow tired. Just as the writers of *The X-Files* had expanded beyond its "U.F.O. of the week" concept and established an elaborate series mythology, so the writers of *Millennium* began to reinvent its mythology in the second half of its inaugural season.

Edmundson suggests there is a point when "terror Gothic" no longer meets the needs of a culture in crisis. When that happens, the genre slips into another mode. "Apocalyptic Gothic," he writes, "is collective Gothic: as terror Gothic would haunt the individual, so exercises in apocalyptic Gothic would haunt the society at large" (Edmundson 23). An early example of apocalyptic Gothic is Mary Shelley's novel *Frankenstein* (1818), in which Nature itself wreaks havoc on mankind. Carter's series finds its parallel in the first season episode "*Force Majeure*," a story that introduces the idea of a ticking clock—a countdown to an impending natural disaster on the scale of the Great Flood. End date: New Year's Eve 1999. A subsequent episode, "Lamentation," inserts the Devil into the series mythology and hints that the dawn of the new millennium could be the Christian "end times." *Millennium*'s so-called "Legion myth-arc" also fits Edmundson's description of apocalyptic Gothic. He writes, "Comprehensively informing the fin-de-siècle culture of apocalyptic Gothic is the religious fundamentalists' belief in a very real and impending apocalypse. To the premillennarian fundamentalists, we are in the midst of a dark dispensation; the present age is ruled by Satan, the lord of this world" (Edmundson 29).

In an effort to boost ratings in the "back nine" of the first season, Chris Carter once again successfully tapped into the spirit of the age. Although he played a relatively minor role in the development of the series mythology in Season Two, Carter's staff of writers and producers followed his lead into an irreducibly complex world of angels and demons, natural disasters and shadowy organizations "too big to fail." *Millennium* became a show about a world that is infinitely capable of reducing the common man to an impotent pawn and replacing his hope for the future with Gothic despair. Against this backdrop, Chris Carter asks the most vital question. It appears, simply stated, in the series' opening: *Who cares?* The creator explains, "It's really, who will care? Who is strong enough to care? Are we going to allow these things to run out of hand or are we going to take action?" (Schuster 43).

II. THE RESPONSE

The popular alternative to Gothic despair in 1990s American culture, according to Edmundson, was the "facile transcendence" found in angel stories, new car commercials, twelve-step programs, Prozac, and *Forrest Gump* (1994) (Edmundson 93-94). Chris Carter went a different route, immersing audiences in a world as dark and disturbing as the nightly news. When critics accused him of celebrating ugliness and violence, he responded as follows: "If you just deal with goodness and selflessness, it means nothing—unless it is in jeopardy" (Schwed 16). Carter is not simply talking about the necessity for dramatic conflict and the requirements for genuine catharsis, but about the responsibilities of the *fin de siècle* storyteller. Series star Lance Henriksen agreed: "On television, where it goes into people's homes, everything is sanitized reality. That's not good. When a bullet hits a human being... it turns them to pink mud that no longer has a defense or a life or anything. And that's the reality. We're dealing with the underbelly of the world in the sense that, if you [commit acts of violence], you can't live in denial about it" (Castner 51). His message is simple: we cannot get beyond violence and fear (and "Gothic despair") until we are willing to seriously confront them.

This message might just as easily have come from the fictional hero that Henriksen portrays onscreen. It is Carter's "appropriate response to the world we live in" (Brooks 54). Frank Black's main goal is to understand the causes of violence. He doesn't fight criminals in the conventional sense, with handcuffs or a gun. Instead, he looks for the causes of criminal behavior. One obvious template for this type of character is Sherlock Holmes, Sir Arthur Conan Doyle's response to the urban Gothic fiction of the Victorian era. Doyle defines his hero as an intense, laconic scientist who knows "every detail of every horror perpetrated in the century" (17). Holmes himself explains his method for criminal detection as follows: "There is a strong family resemblance about misdeeds, and if you have all the details of a thousand at your finger ends, it is odd if you can't unravel the thousand and first" (18).

In addition to Sherlock Holmes, Frank Black has a real-life template. (One imagines that Chris Carter, so seriously dismayed by the "darkness" in 1990s America, could not have presented that darkness onscreen if he hadn't also found a corresponding light in the real world.) The series creator found his inspiration after *The X-Files* achieved celebrity status, when he first gained personal access to the Federal Bureau of Investigation headquarters. His first impression of Quantico was revelatory: "You go there and you realize that these people are protectors of the world" (Schuster 33). He was particularly taken with the Behavioral Sciences Unit, which provided the inspiration for *The Silence of the Lambs*. Later, Carter also gained access to a "mysterious" group of retired F.B.I. agents who were working as private consultants. He used The Academy Group as the real-life basis for the Millennium Group (Brooks 55).

In his autobiography *Not Bad for a Human* (2011), Lance Henriksen writes that initially he struggled to internalize the character of Frank Black. He had Carter's advice and the Academy Group as points of reference, but he felt like he needed more than an intellectual understanding of the character to make Frank Black genuine. Ultimately, he looked inward to find what he needed. "I used my most primitive instincts to play the most sophisticated character," he says, explaining that Frank Black's "basic nature is what gives him the strength: his intuition gives him strength, his caring gives him strength, his nonjudgmental nature gives him the strength to do what he has to do and to survive" (Henriksen 234).

Just as Sherlock Holmes draws on a vast body of knowledge about crimes and criminals, so Henriksen intuitively drew on a vast body of acting roles and personal experience to bring Frank Black to life. Certainly, he had plenty of experience playing onscreen cops. One of Henriksen's earliest significant roles as a law enforcement officer was a featured role in a 1984 episode of the television series *Cagney & Lacey* (1981-88) entitled "Heat." Henriksen's character, King, was a hostage negotiator tasked with saving one of the series regulars from a dangerous thug. King displays all of the traits and skills of a reliable negotiator. When he begins communicating with the hostage taker, he projects the calmness and confidence of a seasoned professional. (Henriksen's baritone voice alone conveys the integrity and authority that every hostage negotiator needs.) Even more importantly, King proves himself to be an active listener. Once he establishes a trusting rapport with the hostage taker, he tries to broker a mutually beneficial compromise between the cops and the criminal. Years later Henriksen remains proud of the episode, noting that "the government used it as a hostage negotiation training film" (Henriksen 104).

In the years that followed, the actor brought the same professionalism to more nuanced roles. In *Jennifer Eight* (1992), he played a cop who is both world-weary and warm-hearted. In his autobiography Henriksen presents his character, Freddy Ross, as a complicated man who is quite literally hardened by his experiences on the job. "A cop's body is a little bit like a boxer's body," the actor explains. "They have so much fear about getting hit that their muscles are always tense" (Henriksen 182). Nevertheless, Ross remains endlessly compassionate with his friends and family. The dichotomy between hardened cop and compassionate family man is even more explicit in *Powder* (1995), a film that features Henriksen as small town sheriff Doug Barnum. Barnum is alternately intimidating and vulnerable, world-weary and childlike in his role as a literal and figurative father.

Frank Black exhibits these same characteristics in the first season of *Millennium* when he is torn between his "yellow house" and "a thousand points of darkness." In an oft-discussed scene from the pilot episode, he delivers his profile of a serial killer to a room of skeptical cops. Here we see the evolution of King, Freddy Ross, and Sheriff Barnum into Frank Black. Like King, Frank speaks calmly and confidently, without using his hands. (After all, what good are gesticulations to a hostage negotiator, who usually does his work over the phone?) Like Ross, he wears two faces: one he shows at work and one he shows at home. There's a conversation later in the episode in which Frank's wife insists that he "can't keep the job out of our personal life." He responds, "I want you to make believe that I can." When he's with his daughter, Frank Black "makes believe" that it is a beautiful world. Then again, maybe that's not a fair statement. In those rare and beautiful moments between Frank Black and his daughter, it seems that the character—and the actor—knows beyond a shadow of a doubt that it is a beautiful world. Chris Carter knew that Henriksen could convey this wholehearted emotion, because he had witnessed Barnum's revelatory transformation at the end of *Powder*—from debilitating fear to profound hope. That was precisely the transformation that Carter needed Frank Black to negotiate for America's *fin de siècle*.

From the beginning, Carter perceived his profiler as different kind of hero than *X-Files* seeker Fox Mulder. Mulder fights lies; Frank Black fights Evil. Mulder is driven by personal obsession; Frank is driven by a sense of obligation to the world around him. Carter explains, "He has a wife and a child and, certainly in the beginning, he loved them unconditionally, and he wanted to make the world a better place for them. He wasn't a person driven by ego as much as by duty, by the powers of his abilities, and the responsibilities that they set up for him" (Simpson 22). Henriksen agrees that Frank's strength comes from his devotion to his family. In his autobiography, he says flatly, "I was basing all my strength [as that character] on family" (Henriksen 263). This was not the first time the actor had approached a role in that way.

One of Henriksen's earliest paternal roles was in Don Coscarelli's film *Survival Quest* (1989). In the film, Henriksen plays an outdoorsman named Hank Chambers who leads a group of city dwellers into the heart of nature. Hank treats all of his wards—especially an orphaned teenager—like family and teaches them that "survival in the wilderness is a matter of heart, not hardware." When a ragtag group of military trainees threatens his family, Hank tries to talk sense into them rather than resorting to violence himself. He understands, implicitly, that violence perpetuates violence. In the end, he's even willing to take a bullet to protect his family.

Henriksen brought the same nonviolent nature to the character of Bishop, his breakthrough role in *Aliens* (1986). Bishop doesn't try to talk sense into the aliens, but nor will he take up arms against them—because he holds all life sacred. The actor explains, "Anything that's really organically alive is fascinating to Bishop. There's no good or evil—just this ultimate respect for anything living" (Rafferty 52). Bishop's love for his surrogate family is so strong that he willfully risks his life for them and, in the end, saves them. "The Father," Henriksen's character in *No Escape* (1994), embodies the same philosophy. Once again, the philosophy came mostly from the actor, who decided that his character's sole purpose in life should be to bring purpose and hope to the members of his "family" of rehabilitated criminals and political prisoners. Henriksen even tried to convince the film's director that "The Father" should ultimately sacrifice himself to save his "family." The actor explains, "I felt like that really gave dignity to my character, because the greatest gift you can give is to give up your life for other human beings" (Henriksen 197). He did not get his desired ending, but the selfless and caring nature behind all of these paternal roles found their way into the altruistic soul of Frank Black.

In "Kingdom Come," a first season episode of *Millennium*, writer Jorge Zamacona dances around the question of whether or not Frank's altruism is based on Christian belief. The episode puts the hero in dialogue with a murderer who has renounced his faith. "There is no peace," the killer claims, "There is no forgiveness... Just lonely nights spent in empty houses." In the same breath, he accuses Frank of the same unbelief. According to Henriksen, the script called for Frank Black to confirm that he was an atheist. The actor refused to deliver his lines as written. He did not want to simplify the hero's response to such a complex and important question (Henriksen 243). It becomes clear, over the course of the series, that Frank's quarrel is not with God but with organized and fanatical religion. The hero, as written by Chris Carter, has an essential faith that is continually challenged and continually strengthened by the horrors of the everyday world. "If I see in the darkness," Carter's hero says resolutely in a third season episode, "it is because there is a light."

Lance Henriksen had grappled with the same subject matter years earlier, in an episode of the T.V. series *Darkroom* (1981-82). In "The Benediction," the actor played a priest who loses his faith when he is tormented by nightmares. Disillusioned, he wonders why we are "given so many signs of evil and so few signs of good?" His fellow priest has no answer. Henriksen's character, Father Frank MacLeod, comes to the haunting conclusion that there is no such thing as good and evil, that "we are living in a great void." Instead of making him angry, this makes him despondent. Only when he finally confronts a manifestation of evil does he regain his belief in the battle between good and evil and return to his parish.

Henriksen is dismissive of this early role, believing that his decision to "play that priest with no anger" made the character weak and uninteresting (Henriksen 105). Certainly, Father Frank doesn't exhibit the emotional fortitude of many of Henriksen's most memorable characters, but that's precisely what makes this character's journey interesting within the context of the actor's career. Frank Black, as embodied by Lance Henriksen, is a man who has been through that great void and come out the other side. Season Two of *Millennium* (at least up to the episode "Luminary") retraces that journey through the dark night of the soul, admittedly with a lot more vigor than "The Benediction."

The most important character trait of Frank Black is what Henriksen calls his "nonjudgmental nature." Elaborating on an earlier comparison of a cop to a boxer, the actor explains, "If you judge, you run out of energy. It's like a boxer holding his breath when he's throwing a punch" (Ferrante 37). This is the basis for the central conflict of the *Millennium* series, a conflict that is set up as early as the second episode. In "Dead Letters," Frank warns a fellow profiler that "if you make every one of these [cases] personal, you'll go crazy." Frank has to heed his own warning as his cases become increasingly personal; he himself is targeted in the episodes "522666" and "Blood Relatives," and episodes throughout the season hint that an unknown criminal is stalking his family. The central conflict of the series becomes a full-blown crisis in the season finale, when Frank's wife is abducted. The main question is not whether Frank will get her back but what her abduction will do to his spirit. After this, will he be able to remain nonjudgmental and nonviolent? Will he still be Chris Carter's ideal hero?

In an interview with *TV Guide* during the making of first season, Lance Henriksen told a reporter, "I've never killed anybody on the show and I'm not going to" (Schwed 16). The actor had to eat his own words at the beginning of Season Two, when Frank dispatches the man who abducted his wife. His actions temporarily redefine him and cost him his family. His wife plainly explains, "You lost something." In the next episode, a strange old man frames Frank Black's struggle in mythic terms, telling him that he must overcome his fear in order to rediscover himself. Fear, the old man cryptically asserts, "shrinks the world." In subsequent episodes, the hero learns to let go of the things he cannot control. Like Hank Chambers in *Survival Quest* or Sheriff Barnum in *Powder*, he has to "push beyond the boundaries" of hope and fear, faith and doubt. It is a journey that reaches its lowest point in "The Curse of Frank Black," when the hero nearly succumbs to Gothic despair, and subsequently ascends to the spiritual peak of "Luminary," when he rediscovers his heroic identity and his place in the world and returns—in a sense—to his parish.

This is the end of one narrative, but it is not the end of Frank Black's life or of the *Millennium* series. The God of *Millennium* (which is to say, the writers) continues to move the main character by pains and contradictions, challenging his heroic nature at every turn. First, they kill his wife. Repeatedly, they threaten his child. Ultimately, they turn his friends, Peter Watts and the Millennium Group, against him and against his ideals. Carter's original concept of the Millennium Group clearly allied them with Frank. "They believe," he explains, "that [in] all this random violence we see these days, that there may actually be some order in the chaos. There may be something out there, and these guys think that, if they care enough, that they can stem the tide of this thing" (Schuster 42). Over the course of Seasons Two and Three, the Millennium Group appears to become more dedicated to promoting fear of the future than to fighting it.

Henriksen opines that the "idea of a cultish kind of Millennium Group... just about destroyed the show" (Spelling 50). Certainly, it pushed Frank Black back to the brink of despair and threatened to overload the central conflict of the series... but perhaps that was inevitable. The tension between darkness and light is the crux of the show, and the reality is that one man cannot single-handedly eradicate the "thousand points of darkness." He can only point the way; others will have to take up where he leaves off. At the end of Season Three, this has not yet happened. Even his protégé, Emma Hollis, has seemingly been corrupted. The hero apparently succumbs to violence once again and flees with his daughter into an uncertain future. For *Millennium* viewers, this is (so far) the final outcome of the battle between Chris Carter's ideal hero and the forces of darkness in contemporary America. Is it reassuring? Certainly not. Is it honest? Perhaps.

Chris Carter once suggested that *X-Files* hero Fox Mulder's quest for truth was doomed to failure. "I don't think that you can ever know the truth," Carter explains. "There is no truth. The truth is a hundred, a thousand, a million different things. The truth is like *Rashomon*. For every person, there's a different truth" (Schuster 9). Obviously, for the creator, there are no easy answers. And who can argue with him? The millennium has come and gone. America's *fin de siècle* is over, but the battle against the "thousand points of darkness" is still being waged. That said, there are plenty of people who continue to believe that Carter's ideal hero, realized by Lance Henriksen, can still embody the "appropriate response" to the world we live in:

How should we fight violence? With understanding.

How should we face the future? Without fear.
How can we change the world? One person at a time.
This is who we are.

WORKS CITED

Brooks, James. "Mister MM." *Xposè* December 1996: 52-57. Print.

Castner, Michael. "Through a Lens Darkly." *Entertainment @ Home* Fall 1996: 50-51. Print.

Cooper, William. *Behold a Pale Horse*. Flagstaff: Light Technology Publishing, 1991. Print.

Doyle, Sir Arthur Conan. *The Complete Illustrated Sherlock Holmes*. Chatham: Omega Books Limited, 1986. Print.

Edmundson, Mark. *Nightmare on Main Street: Angels, Sadomasochism, and the Culture of Gothic*. Boston: Harvard UP, 1997. Print.

Ferrante, Tim. "Lance Henriksen: Millennium Man." *Videoscope* Winter 1996: 37-40. Print.

Henriksen, Lance and Joseph Maddrey. *Not Bad for a Human*. Los Angeles: Bloody Pulp, 2011. Print.

Lowry, Brian. *The Truth is Out There: The Official Guide to The X-Files*. New York: HarperPrism, 1995. Print.

Meisler, Andy. *I Want to Believe: The Official Guide to The X-Files, Vol. 3*. New York: HarperPrism, 1998. Print.

Rafferty, Jane Gael. "Lance Henriksen: Call Him Chameleon." *Starlog* August 1987: 52-54, 71. Print.

Schuster, Hal. *The Unauthorized Guide to The X-Files*. Rocklin, CA: Prima, 1997. Print.

Schwed, Mark. "*Millennium*." *TV Guide* 16 November 1996: 14-21. Print.

Simpson, Paul. "Dark Visionary." *Dreamwatch* April 1998: 20-22. Print.

Spelling, Ian. "Black and Fright." *Fangoria* April 2000: 48-50. Print.

Joseph Maddrey is a freelance writer and television producer. He is the author of *Nightmares in Red, White and Blue: The Evolution of the American Horror Film* (2004) and *The Making of T.S. Eliot* (2009) and the co-author of *Not Bad for a Human* (2011). He is also co-creator of the Dark Horse comic *To Hell You Ride* (2012), with Lance Henriksen and Tom Mandrake. Maddrey lives in Studio City, California, with his wife Liza.

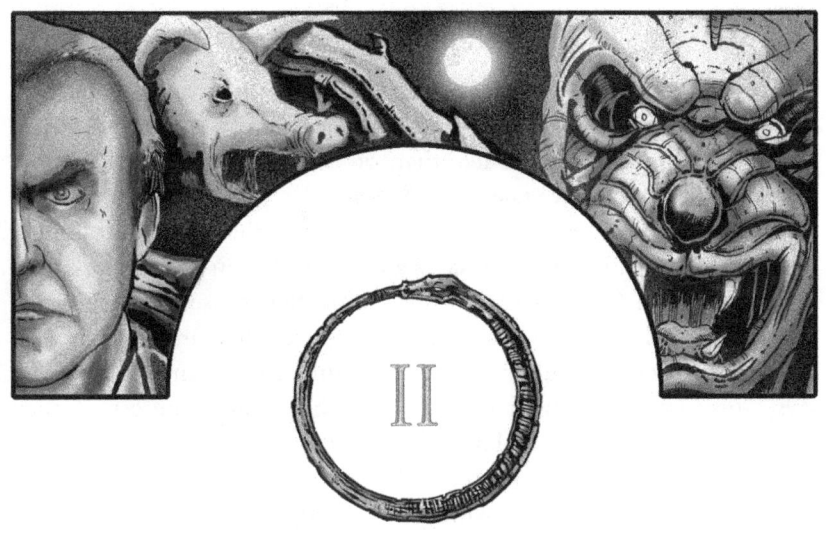

PAINTING AWAY THE DARKNESS:
A CONVERSATION WITH CHRIS CARTER

Interview by James McLean & Troy L. Foreman
Written by Adam Chamberlain

It is fair to say that Chris Carter has grown accustomed to the darkness. Across nine seasons of *The X-Files* (1993-2002) and two feature films, as well as three seasons of *Millennium* (1996-99), he has written, directed, or produced over two hundred and seventy hours of drama exploring mythology-driven conspiracy, horror, and evil of every shape and form. Prior to that first crucial meeting of Agents Mulder and Scully in an F.B.I. basement or the Black family's fateful relocation to Seattle, however, his career found him inhabiting a very different world. Carter spent thirteen years working as a journalist and an editor for *Surfing* magazine before moving on to Walt Disney Studios in 1985 to begin his career as a professional screenwriter. Venturing back still further, he traces the self-discovery of his potential to his school days. "I had written in high school and I had written in college," he recalls in his quietly authoritative tone. "I had two classes, and in one of them I had gotten very good feedback. I had a professor who got up and read one of my blue book essays in front of the class and had said he wished all his students would write like that. So that was a first glimmer that maybe I had some native talent."

It was during *The X-Files*'s second season, as the series was building its audience and assuring its place as a mainstay hit on the network, that Fox approached Carter with the suggestion that he seek to repeat his success. Initially, he was wary of the responsibility and demands of running two series simultaneously. "Fox came to me with an idea," he says, "because it was hard enough work just doing one series, then setting out to do a second. Then we did a movie kind of between those two things. It was more work than anyone should really take on."

Millennium premiered with the expertly crafted "Pilot" on 25 October 1996 to a massive audience of nearly eighteen million viewers. It is, at times, challenging to watch due to its intense subject matter and strong imagery. Having been immersed in the creative process for some time, including a month for filming alone, Carter's own reaction to the finished episode was somewhat divorced from that of the viewers at home. "It's funny," he explains, "when you make a T.V. show you sit and you get a chance to watch it with friends, colleagues, and everybody has been in on the process, usually, or if they aren't then they are close to the process, so it's more like, 'Wow, we pulled this off.' It doesn't scare us, and even though you get immediate feedback on the internet it's rare that you got to sit in a room with people you didn't know or people who were coming at it fresh."

Speaking further to the tone of the pilot, Carter relates one of his key influences in creating the series. "One of the inspirations was the movie *Seven*. These were all dark, dark images and stories, and it was interesting to try to tell those stories for television. It's almost like how far could you go before the censors stop you. But I think what happens, or at least what happened to me, is that you get tired of that milieu and you get tired of the genre, and you want to write something else. The darkness affects you." Indeed, Carter's copious research into serial killers eventually took its toll. "Accumulatively it did, and just doing that kind of show where we had the Millennium Group that were research based, you are always talking to people about the most grisly things. I think it catches up with you, and I think naturally—and I think that I can speak for most of the writers—that you just want to write away from the darkness."

Nevertheless, the first season of *Millennium* features a slew of distinctively diabolical antagonists and events that separate the series from all other crime dramas. Asked to explain his creative wellspring, Carter pauses for a moment's reflection—as he often does throughout the interview—before offering a typically considered reply. "I think you just read a lot," he suggests. "You find something that strikes you, you write it down, you save it for a rainy day, and you go back and you look at those things. I think, really, you're working so hard to produce a television show, you take every moment you can to input information, since you're outputting so much information. So you just look for those stories—things that appeal to you, things that scare you—and try to incorporate them."

Millennium boasts an unconventional set-up for a television series, beginning with its protagonist. Frank Black is a middle-aged family man with a wife and daughter, a far cry from the more familiar personality of the younger, sexually available male lead. For Carter, the family life of Frank Black was integral to the concept for the series, even if it posed creative challenges. "It just felt right for *Millennium*. It felt right for the concept and the character. For me, it was what it was all about. It was his protection of that yellow house, painting away the darkness and having something to go home to and a reason to do what he did. It felt right to me, but I think that especially if you look at procedurals on T.V. now—*CSI*, for example—they dispense with all of that. It's a caper, pure and simple. In the end it became something of an impediment to the storytelling, because you had to service the family stories, and it was really the capers that everyone wanted. I think that that—unfairly and unfortunately for Megan Gallagher—foretold [Catherine's] death."

How did Carter address such challenges in his storytelling, especially given the grueling schedule of working on two series and a film simultaneously? "You have to remember that you are also surrounded by creative people, so you've got people to bounce things off of. It's a competitive environment, everybody wants to do the best episode, but it is stressful because you only have a certain amount of time to finish an episode. You have to think of an airdate, the real deadline. If you don't work as hard as you can then it's not going to be as good as it can be, so the schedule and the process are a built-in system to perpetuate itself."

During the course of *Millennium*'s first season, an emerging mythology explores evil in various guises, often via criminal investigations into human monsters but increasingly hinting at more elemental forces conspiring against Frank Black. This trend peaks with "Lamentation," scripted by Carter, an episode that introduces the Devil's liege herself, Lucy Butler (Sarah-Jane Redmond), one of the show's most popular antagonists. "I think that there was a struggle in the first season to come up with what was this amorphous, looming threat," Carter says, "and I think that we played with it through characters, villains. And I think that it was kind of an adventure, poking around in the dark." This characterization of the creative process evokes Frank Black's own disturbing investigations. Were these two manifestations of evil—the human monsters and the more mythological agents of evil—planned to coexist in the series from its conception? "Yes, and hence the title *Millennium*, that we were heading towards something, that it was coalescing and we didn't know what it was, but Frank sensed it. When he's going after the Frenchman, when he's reading Nostradamus or Yeats or whatever he's doing, he's using those sources—be it poetry, mysticism or psychic forecast. That, I think, is built into the concept early on."

Also part of Carter's carefully considered design for the series was the casting of its lead, with the role of Frank Black written specifically for actor Lance Henriksen. Carter had courted Henriksen for a role on *The X-Files* on a number of occasions, and once, when the actor was in town, he had a note slipped under his Vancouver hotel room door in order to express a desire to work with him. Henriksen rejected these overtures, categorically refusing to work in television. Ultimately, it was the strength of the script for "Pilot" and a conversation with its writer that changed the actor's mind. Thus Frank Black was realized, just as Carter had intended from the outset. "It was so interesting," says Carter of his collaboration with Henriksen. "I remember the 'Pilot' experience and the first day of filming. I had been working so carefully and closely with David [Duchovny] and Gillian [Anderson on *The X-Files*] and I had gotten used to their approach as actors and how they worked, and working with Lance was a completely difference experience. Lance worked much more from his gut and less from the page. I'm not taking anything away from anyone, just that the way he processed the story and the material was different from David and Gillian."

Henriksen often relates an anecdote, telling that he was directed by *Millennium*'s creator during the filming of the pilot not to use his hands whilst speaking, something that—as a New Yorker—went against all of his instincts. "That was my note," confirms Carter. "I said that that represents salesmanship, and you're not a salesman. You're not presenting this material trying to impress people—you're presenting it as fact. Your hands get in the way. Your face and your voice are the beauty of you as an actor. That really goes back to what I was saying too about working from the gut. With Lance, everything seemed to come up right through his voice."

Another aspect of the depiction of Frank Black on screen has given viewers much cause for reflection: the nature of his "gift." Whilst its representation would vary throughout the series, developing in sometimes surprising ways, Carter shares his perspective on how he originally envisaged its true quality. "Well, I never wanted it to be a psychic ability per se," he affirms. "I wanted it to be almost empathic, that the problem was that he could see into the darkness. It was not something that came to him paranormally or supernaturally but came to him naturally."

If this perspective seems to imply—as has often been suggested—that Carter did not appreciate the more supernatural approach to the series favored by Glen Morgan and James Wong in Season Two, nothing could be farther from the truth. Asked to cite episodes from *Millennium* that represent the series at its best, he states, "Of course I loved the second season Darin Morgan episodes. I think that those are standout episodes, as are his episodes on *The X-Files*. And I think that there was interesting work done in the second season, particularly in light of the fact that it was, in a way, a new approach to the show. The credits changed, the support group changed, among other things—some cast members came in—and it was just a new angle on what had worked, to an extent, in the first season."

He also points to the further shifts wrought upon the series by another set of changes in the creative team for *Millennium*'s third year of production, following Morgan and Wong's exit. At the season's outset, this new lineup faced the challenge of resolving the previous year's apocalyptic season finale. "Some of the same writing staff came back and helped a lot with trying to figure out that transition," Carter

43

recalls, "and we had some new writing staff as well. I can't remember exactly how it went because, once again, we were very involved at that point with the sixth season of *The X-Files*, and all of a sudden *The X-Files* was in Los Angeles and *Millennium* was up in Vancouver. It was a trick going back and forth if you wanted to be hands on, which we tended to be. But I think that we were given—as you always are at the beginning of a season—a series of situations, and it is how you resourcefully solve the problems and resolve those situations." Part of that resolution to a large extent side-stepped the dramatic events of Season Two finale "The Time is Now" altogether, jumping forward eight months and placing Frank back in Washington, D.C., working once more for the F.B.I. "I think that if the second season was a reaction to the first, the third season was somewhat of a reaction to the second," Carter suggests. "We didn't have Catherine anymore. We had this character Lucy Butler. If you watch the show properly chronologically I think it has many personalities through the course of the changing staff and changing cast."

The third season was to be the series' last, and Carter has been forced to acknowledge that his subsequent property for Fox, the virtual reality thriller *Harsh Realm* (1999-2000), might, at least in part, have been responsible for *Millennium*'s untimely demise. "It's funny, because in the end I think you could really look at it as we knocked ourselves out of the box on *Millennium* with *Harsh Realm*. *Harsh Realm* took *Millennium*'s time slot, and I think that if there wouldn't have been a *Harsh Realm*, *Millennium* would have come back for a fourth and who knows how many more seasons, because—compared with shows now—the ratings were still quite high and respectable. I don't want to blame myself, exactly, because we were just trying to do good work, but looking back I think we may have shot ourselves in the foot."

Frank Black was to make one further appearance in a Ten Thirteen production, guest-starring in a Season Seven installment of *The X-Files* titled for his own series. The episode notably eschews *Millennium*'s own mythology, although it does offer a continuation of sorts for the personal stories of Frank and Jordan Black. According to Carter, no further crossovers were considered after that episode ushered in the new millennium. "I think we played out that *X-Files/Millennium* connection with the appearance of Lance in that episode." Did it fulfill his expectations in terms of offering a measure of closure for Frank Black? "I think it did, in a way, because it needed to be an *X-Files* first and anything to do with *Millennium* second. I think that it worked in that way. It incorporated Lance in probably one of the best ways we could: tongue-in-cheek and self-referential."

In considering a filmic return for Frank Black, a suitable reference can be found in *The X-Files: I Want to Believe* (2008), directed by Carter and co-written with Frank Spotnitz. An intelligent, character-led, and often beautiful film exploring themes of science and faith, this second big screen outing for Mulder and Scully nevertheless met with a muted response, in part due to the fact that it premiered during the summer blockbuster season just one week after the release of the box office-busting *The Dark Knight*. Carter is self-critical in appraising the reasons for the film's reception. "I think that what people were looking for, coming back six years later, may have been something other than exactly what we gave them," he suggests. "That's not to take anything away from the movie," he quickly adds, "that's just to say that if there were expectations and anticipation it may have been for another mythology show or alien show. In a weird way, we took the second movie and scaled it way back from the first movie. We had a much smaller budget. We told a much more conventional *X-Files* story, a procedural of sorts, and then we had this relationship with Mulder and Scully which had evolved. I don't know if we, in the end, satisfied expectation, by which I think people were expecting—and I can see why—a bigger movie than the first."

The creative team took great pains during filming to ensure that no spoilers regarding the movie's content were leaked, even employing deliberate misdirection in order to preserve the storyline as a secret. How do such efforts further complicate matters, in terms of both production and promotion? "It's very stressful and it takes a lot of work. In the end, I think it was somewhat counter-productive. It tends to limit the press that you get during the production, it tends to play against the run-up to the premiere date. I think that it had a detrimental effect."

Nevertheless, *I Want to Believe* retains a strong following among many fans of *The X-Files*, not least for the truthfulness embraced in the evolution of the franchise's two charismatic leads. "We had to imagine where Mulder and Scully were six years after we last saw them, and we came up with what you saw in the last movie," says Carter. Where, then, does Frank Black's creator think our favorite forensic profiler might find himself today? "It's really hard to say. I would imagine that his responsibility would be the same to his daughter, to his new family if he happened to go there, but also to solving the cases that he did. That's what made him tick."

Gillian Anderson has remarked that it took her some time to slip back into her role when filming for *I Want to Believe* commenced. As a writer, would it be difficult to slip back into scripting a familiar character such as Frank Black after so long away? "It's hard to say at this point in my life," he muses. "I'm sure if the villain were interesting enough and his psychology were interesting enough, then I am sure that you could find some place to make a connection. And since the stories were always about taking down the villain, I think that would play into something appealing. When we did the second *X-Files* movie, I thought we had found something that was so grisly as to be science fiction. I had found something on the internet that I couldn't believe. A man had done experiments on dogs. He had actually put two heads on one body. It seemed just horrific, but it also seemed like it was right for a standalone *X-Files* episode." Significantly—and notably so, given that the film featured a number of *Millennium*'s recurring cast members in supporting roles—he suggests that the subject matter might well have played better as the foundation for a tale featuring Frank Black instead: "Now I think maybe it was more suited to a *Millennium* approach."

Such statements raise the all-important question: is Carter interested in revisiting Frank Black? "If someone called up and said, 'Would you consider doing this?' I certainly would consider doing it. I would talk to Lance and find out how he's doing, what he thinks." He teases the fact that he has already given the concept some consideration, although he is determined not to give anything away. "I've always had an idea about who should be in that movie—and I won't tell you who that is! As time passes we all change, evolve, so it would be a sitting down with Lance and figuring out how he felt."

With so many crime dramas having evidently been influenced in both tone and content by *Millennium* and its themes seemingly even more relevant today than they were when the series first aired, does he agree with the prevailing assessment that the series was ahead of its time? "No," he responds, although he does acknowledge its impact upon the genre. "I look at some procedurals on T.V. today and I see elements of what writers on *Millennium* were doing before those procedurals were started."

PAINTING AWAY THE DARKNESS

A recurring theme evident in interviews with other Ten Thirteen alumni is their overwhelming praise for Chris Carter's creative vision. For each and every one, their collaborations with the man represented a defining moment in their careers. Everyone wants to be remembered to him, and to thank him for the opportunities that he offered them. "It's also nice to be able to say hello to them through this process," he responds in kind. "You work so hard with people and then when you wrap up a project everyone goes on their merry way. You see each other, hopefully, at award shows, but you lose track, so that's nice."

There is one final question in the minds of Ten Thirteen fanatics the world over, dedicated viewers left wondering if the *Millennium* and *X-Files* universes could collide again in the future. Chris Carter takes another of his characteristic pauses, wordlessly pondering the possibilities for Frank Black's return, before teasingly replying, "Never say never."

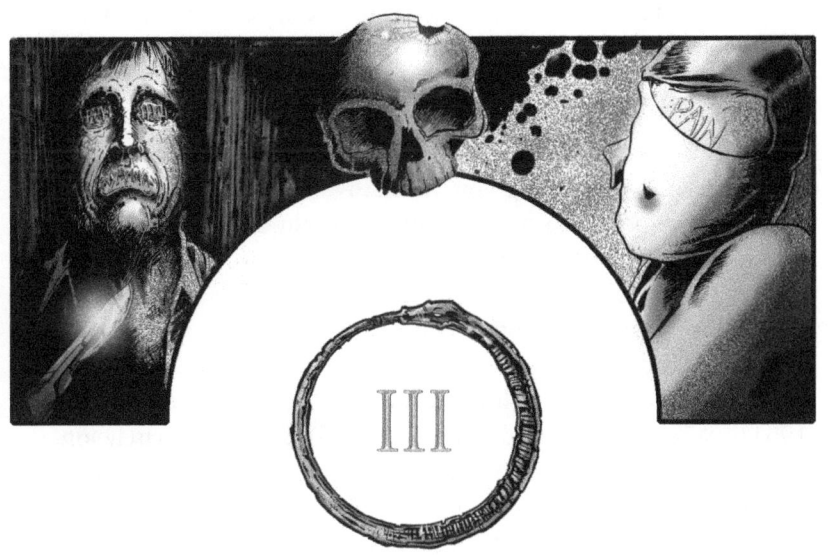

ENEMIES WITHIN:
SEASON ONE OF CHRIS CARTER'S *MILLENNIUM* AND AMERICA'S SUBURBAN APOCALYPSE

by John Kenneth Muir

In the first season episode of *Millennium* (1996-99) entitled "Wide Open," violent crime consultant and dedicated family man Frank Black (Lance Henriksen) sits pensively on the front porch of his idyllic yellow house on Ezekiel Drive—a symbol first of paradise, then of paradise lost. There, he laments the American culture of the 1990s, one "besieged by our own fear." His wife, a beautiful therapist named Catherine (Megan Gallagher), counters "if you're not afraid... you're in denial."

As Chris Carter and the writers of *Millennium* might succinctly state the matter, "This is who we are."

Or, at least, this is who we *were* during the Age of *Millennium*, pre-Y2K. The question then becomes, *why* is this "who" we were? As always, we find our answer in historical, cultural context. As *Millennium* commenced its freshman season on Fox in 1996, our nation prepared to send President Bill Clinton back to the White House for a second term of four more years. His first term had witnessed a Federal siege gone tragically awry in Waco, Texas, the Oklahoma City bombing by Timothy McVeigh, societal unrest following the O. J. Simpson murder trial, and the gathering of intolerant forces on the Right, forces that were now unified for the first time in American history by one factor: an irrational, overwhelming hatred for Clinton, whom many considered morally corrupt, a philanderer and perhaps even a murderer.

Culturally, popular films including *The Silence of The Lambs* (1991), *Se7en* (1995), and *Copycat* (1995) focused squarely on the presence of serial killers—insane, malevolent bogeymen—prowling America in virtual anonymity and freedom. On television, *The X-Files* (1993-2002) sometimes cast its investigative gaze on society's human monsters, too, in classic episodes such as "Beyond the Sea" and "*Unruhe*," among others. Mainstream television "news" magazines, especially the sensational *Dateline* (1992-) and *48 Hours* (1988-), seemed to feed America a never ending diet of "true" horror stories starring serial killer.

The ascent of the serial killer to a position of prominence in the American Imagination, and perhaps in the American Reptilian Brain, was the result of several important factors. First, there were high profile serial killers actually making news as the 1990s began. Jeffrey Dahmer (1960-1994) of Milwaukee murdered seventeen people and practiced, among other things, necrophilia and cannibalism. His heinous crimes captured the imagination of a fearful nation. So did those of Ted Bundy (1946-1989), who was a sociopath and serial killer executed by Florida state officials in 1989.

Almost as important as the crimes themselves, however, was the non-stop coverage given by the expanding, ratings-seeking mainstream media. The just-born 24-hour news cycle made Dahmer's horror show in Milwaukee a nightmare for all Americans, no matter the region of the country they inhabited or even the considerable distance from the real life crimes. From Florida to Rhode Island, from Dallas to Seattle, people were afraid of other monsters like Dahmer—monsters bred in secret, waiting to pounce. It was not merely the tabloid cable news that fed this burgeoning fear, either. The internet—booming into the mainstream of 1990s life—provided predators a new "in" to the private lives of innocent Americans at the same time that it allowed them to remain secretive and dishonest about their true identities and perverse agendas.

But there were other factors, too, that made the serial killer America's trademark ghoul during the 1990s. In particular, the ability of Americans to travel cheaply and easily cross-country after the 1970s resulted in a nation whose traditional roots became scrambled. Due to the affordability of air flight and easy access to interstate highways, the communal hearth of old America—the small town where everyone knew you, your parents, and your grandparents—was shattered, perhaps permanently. In its stead arose the suburbs, new, young, affluent communities in which neighbors had no shared history with other neighbors, in which virtual strangers lived across the street, over the next driveway.

As it is so in all great horror (and, indeed, all great art), *Millennium* reflected the culture in which it was created. The series selected as its central setting the new hunting fields of the serial killer: suburban America. And though it was and today remains tempting for blinkered critics to dismiss *Millennium* as simply "the serial killer of the week," it became evident on a close viewing of the series that there was something deeper—something philosophical—happening in Chris Carter's new creation. In particular, Frank's experiences with serial killers of various stripe in Season One served a distinctly didactic purpose: to tell us not so much about the monsters hiding beyond the white picket fences but to share with audiences something about ourselves, about the world we've built.

In the final analysis, *Millennium* is not about these monsters; it is about our response to the monsters. I have often likened the series and its first season, serial killer conceit to Gene Roddenberry's *Star Trek* (1966-69). There, each week, the starship *Enterprise* visited another alien world and saw the crew's values reflected, challenged, and often affirmed by the planet or civilization of the week. The serial killers on *Millennium* during the first season served the same purpose for Frank Black and the audience who watched. They were examples to learn from.

In "Wide Open," Frank investigates the case of a serial killer who attacks families that have installed high-tech alarm systems in their fancy suburban homes. The alarm keypad's display notes comfortingly in telling close-ups that the house is "ALL SECURE," though this is plainly not the truth. While the homeowners are away, the killer enters the house lawfully, during a real estate open house. Then, he waits until the family returns home—alarmed-up—to strike with brute force. The family never sees what's coming: the enemy within.

This killer, Frank informs us, is "teaching us a lesson about our pretensions to safety... about how vulnerable we are." Similarly, *Millennium* teaches the audience that very lesson. An alarm system keypad does not guarantee safety when you drop your guard, when you do not know who has been inside your home, when visitors or strangers enter and leave. In the suburbs, when you do not really know people, any "monster" could lurk.

Accordingly, by episode climax, an imperiled family is rescued by a more traditional, old-fashioned "security system:" the family dog. The canine does away with the home invader, pitching him over a second story ledge and onto (and through) a glass table in the foyer below.

The serial killer appearing in "Wide Open" gives himself the name "John Allworth," a name that provides him with a sense of value and importance in a society that does not value him. And, desiring his fifteen minutes of fame (equal to that achieved by Dahmer), Allworth utilizes other convenient technologies—not just the alarm—to get attention and make his point. He leaves messages for the police on their voicemails and sends a videotape of the murders to the real estate agent showing the house/crime scene. At the same time he is teaching people "a lesson," Allworth is also becoming "famous." In no other previous decade could the killer utilize this *modus operandi* (outsmarting the alarm systems) or connect with his victims (via videotape) in this intimate fashion. He is a creature of the technological nineties, of the suburban lifestyle.

Notably, one victimized family in "Wide Open" carries the name "Highsmith." *Highest of all Smiths*. In other words, they are the typical American family. The name Highsmith simultaneously indicates "importance" (high) and the quality of being "average" (Smith is a common name). This is *Millennium*'s tactic, perhaps for revealing to us that any one of its viewers—even the Smiths, even us—could be the next victim of this particular criminal. The episode also features some subtle imagery that suggests the suburbs themselves actually bred this particular monster. There are messages of violence everywhere in the culture. One real estate company is advertised with the motto, "Killer

Views. Killer Prices." The camera lingers on this catchy motto. As engaged viewers, we become aware of the double meaning.

The serial killer's profession in "Wide Open" is another important factor in understanding the didactic purpose of *Millennium*. Allworth is a school crossing guard, one who is "helping children to safety" by his own definition. This line of dialogue serves as a direct contrast to the episode's opening quotation ("The children are far from safety. They shall be crushed at the gate without a rescuer.") There is an easy translation: the children are the future, and if they are killed or corrupted, all our tomorrows die with them. Allworth believes he is teaching the children a lesson when, in fact, he is perpetuating a cycle of violence. (He was an abused child, and his crime spree has left a shattered orphan behind, one who may pick up his tricks in the years to come.)

As Frank notes, "tragedy begets itself."

Speaking of "gates" and "rescuers," Frank Spotnitz's "Weeds" is another first season episode of *Millennium* that focuses squarely on a 1990s development and/or trend: the rise of the affluent gated community. Here, a deranged serial killer prowls a rich suburban development despite the presence of 24-hour private security, despite perimeter walls, despite a community watch group. We see images of the entrance gates closing, but what use are gates when the enemy is already within?

In "Weeds," a homegrown madman kidnaps the children of immoral homeowners and makes the children (again!) suffer for the sins of the father. Ghoulishly, the perpetrator makes the youngsters drink his blood because he considers himself a holy "purifier." Though acting far outside the bounds of the law, this killer successfully exposes to Frank (and to the audience) the sick underside of affluent America. In every home dwells an adulterer, a fraud, a hit-and-run driver, or some other corrupted personality. Expensive homes and a private police force do not make up for or excuse sin.

One scene in "Weeds" is set inside a fancy home. Playing on the T.V. in the background is a clip from Irwin Allen's sci-fi series *Land of the Giants* (1968-70). This particular clip reveals a diverse group of people (of varying color and sex) being physically trapped inside an oversized cage by a giant. It is not hard to discern that the "cage" in "Weeds" is the affluent gated community itself and the malevolent giant the secret "sins" that keep residents in a state of perpetual fear, alienation, estrangement, and self-loathing.

Another sequence, set at the community's conference center, makes the point about "strange" neighbors explicit. The episode cuts to close-ups of various residents as if to ask, "Who are you? What secret do you cloak?" Just as these people do not know their neighbors, we do not recognize them as either friend or foe.

Any one of them could be the killer...

The title "Weeds" also explicitly suggests that something undesirable has sprouted up in suburbia, and the killer this time is a man driven by deep feelings of disillusionment. He hates the hypocrisy he sees all around him and wants to root out sin. The view of the suburbs proffered by "Weeds" is absolutely merciless, then. Accordingly, when we see through the killer's eyes, we view all the residents of the community as old, decaying hags, their souls filthy and contaminated. It is not too far a leap to suggest this is how many Americans saw President Bill Clinton, as a sinner in the highest office of the land, contaminated by moral corruption. Never mind that those who led the charge against him were also adulterers and hypocrites. (Newt Gingrich, Henry Hyde, and Bob Livingston—Republicans all—had engaged in extra-marital affairs and held high office too.) Perhaps this example makes the point. Everyone has a skeleton in his closet, and everyone is a hypocrite.

In other episodes of *Millennium*'s first season, Frank returned to the suburbs of America again and again only to unearth more horror and immorality. He uncovered it in Ogden, Utah, in "Covenant" while attempting to determine if a man—a police officer—had actually murdered his wife and children in cold blood. The accused killer had lived by the motto, carved on a sign hung in his workshop, "If a man fails at home, he fails in life." And yet, as Frank learns, the man did fail at home. His wife was the true murderer, driven to such horrible crimes by an act of infidelity. Again, the sins of the father were passed to the children, who were killed for his trespasses.

Child molestation ("The Well-Worn Lock") and domestic violence ("The Wild and the Innocent") also came home to the suburbs in various installments of *Millennium*'s first, sterling season. It was not just the crime of the week, as some asserted, it was the *immorality* of the week, and *Millennium*—in strongly didactic terms—provided suburban America a bracing look in the mirror. Sometimes our new technologies (home alarm systems or the internet) bedeviled us, sometimes new cultural trends (gated communities) achieved the same end.

Always, *Millennium*'s first season came down not merely to the predator in our midst but the failures of our society that gave rise to that predator in the first place. Frank understood this and suggested that those who did not see it were willfully avoiding the truth, living in denial. This is a powerful message about what America had become on the eve of the twenty-first century, presenting a look in the mirror much more significant than simply "seeing what the killer sees."

THE MYSTERY GUEST:
A CONVERSATION WITH LANCE HENRIKSEN

Interview by James McLean & Troy L. Foreman
Written by Brian A. Dixon

Lance Henriksen is a compulsive potter. "I make thirty-six-inch platters," he says, contentment in his voice. His dedication to making earthenware platters and bowls reveals a great deal about his commitment to other crafts as well. Over the years, it has offered him the opportunity to work with some of the most noteworthy sculptors and potters in America. "I have another world of friends who are all potters. They put me on the board of the American Museum of Ceramic Art in Pomona. It's the only museum in California devoted to pottery and they have all the great artists from all over the country come to the museum and have shows there.

"I'm sitting on the board with the founder and five other people. We went around the table and introduced ourselves. Four or five said how they went to Stanford or to Berkeley and they were great at business, and they came to me and I said, 'Hi, my name is Lance Henriksen. I am a compulsive potter. That's all I have to say! That's it. That's me. And I have no idea what use I'll be on this board with you but I'll give it my best.' Talk about dropping their jaws! And I said that only because that's the truth, I'm telling the truth. You can have all kinds of degrees and all kinds of business degrees, but what are you going to do with it?"

As a celebrated actor who has played a role in nearly two hundred films and boasts one of the most recognizable faces in movies, Henriksen has accomplished a great deal with the lessons he has learned from working in clay. Indeed, he believes that it is his background as a potter, a painter, and an artist, not an actor, that enabled him to imbue the character of Frank Black with such a noble and commanding presence in television's *Millennium* (1996-99). Henriksen put all that he had into becoming the iconic criminal profiler and, in turn, the character changed his life.

"Listen, I have a lot of flaws as a human being," Henriksen confesses, offering us a glimpse of the heartfelt honesty that is instinctual to him. "Everybody has a certain amount of character defects. One of the reasons I got into this industry in the first place was because, really, in a lot of ways, it was the only place I could go. I've been a painter and an artist. I love the arts and all I know is working from my intuition and that's where I'm at and why the role of Frank Black was so good for me. It was a role that required a lot of restraint and observation. Those are things that are natural to me anyway. In the arts, like in making pottery, you're basing your pursuit on an observation you've made after a firing and you pursue it until something else comes up and then you pursue that, so it's a lifelong thing. Because you're one person, it's coming from a very private source, from you alone. Everyone has a gift, whether they see it coming to fruition or not, and that's the place I like to work from. I really don't know any other way."

After Chris Carter convinced an initially hesitant Henriksen to take the lead in *Millennium*, the actor chose to approach this remarkable role by starting fresh and letting the character come naturally. "I'm a bit of a primitive so when I do a new job I really try to start from zero again, like I've never really done it, to stay open. If I ever get bored with this, I'll stop. I'll just quit and make pottery the rest of my life. What really happens is, if you do that, you open your heart and your senses to what's going on. It's a new thing and it's a new challenge, then you start building it. When I first read the script I remember thinking, 'I have to read this thing maybe fifty times without making a choice or decision.' Just keep reading it over and over again, and suddenly you absorb it. So the lines you have, you're not trying to memorize them, you absorb them. It's just a way of working. I'm too primitive to work any other way. I have to work that way."

Henriksen's performance on *Millennium* was instantly captivating, offering a presence unique to primetime television. In the aftermath of a record-breaking series premiere on Fox, *The New York Times* would refer to him as an "actor's actor, the American Max von Sydow, the scariest voice in show business," noting that to many, including the actors and directors who have had the privilege of working with him, Henriksen is "one of the best in the business, a versatile and dedicated character actor who always gives vivid, edgy performances." During the time that *Millennium* was on the air, he would earn three consecutive Golden Globe Award nominations for Best Performance by an Actor in a Television Drama.

For Henriksen—who famously once said, "I'm hoping I never get caught acting"—the power of a performance is in the life that has been lived by the artist. "I love boxing," he says, selecting an apt metaphor. "I'm a real boxing fan. In real championship fights—like a Pacquiao-Hatton fight, for instance—you could cut the tension with a knife, but you could also feel how high the stakes were. When those two guys got into the ring you knew that this was not going to be a tomato can fight, this was going to be life or death with all of their skills. Everything in their life had bled into that moment. It really was something, and in a sense acting should really be that way."

Henriksen believes in this philosophy so strongly, in fact, that he eschews the very term. "It's not acting. That's an odd phrase for it. Acting implies that you're going to fake this. The thing that really works is that you get into a scene and you live it. Then when the scene is over you say to yourself, 'I don't remember a thing I did.' And likewise, in life you don't remember everything you did every day—you just do it. And that's the exciting part about it. It really is a wonderful experience. Because, frankly, what I really feel is that to play a character that is as bright, educated, and experienced as Frank Black is a gift, because I'm not that guy. I'm only an instrument, and doing that guy, to live him for a while—for a few years, or to do a movie—what a gift that is. I'm experiencing something that I would never have experienced any other way."

On the set of *Millennium*, Henriksen, a true Method actor, *became* Frank Black, metamorphosing into the world's greatest criminal profiler. The character's assets and anguish became his own, and he was compelled to contemplate those perceptual talents that distinguish the show's embattled protagonist from other onscreen heroes. Frank's gift, his unique ability to "see what the killer sees," is a concept that has become a point of much contention. As the man who had to convey singular insight and react to such appalling visions, squinting and wincing his way through the fiercest of murder reenactments, Henriksen possesses a unique understanding of the nature of that gift. "Well, let me say this: you know how a great chess player works, right? They study, they study, they study. They know all the moves of different great chess players. I always felt Frank Black had morphed into a person who put abstract loose ends together in his head in a way that other people couldn't. He could take threads of an idea and they would suddenly appear to him, almost as a linear story. In other words, walking into a room he would see pieces of a puzzle like a great chess player and he would string them together. And that's what I always thought—that the gift was intellect and intuition, not psychic."

Like Carter, Henriksen disputes any interpretation of the hero's remarkable abilities that relates to psychic phenomenon. "I don't know how you would describe a psychic, actually. I couldn't describe one, except a gift from God, like Moses talking to him, or a luminary or some stuff. To me, it was something much more pragmatic. I always felt Chris understood that I didn't want to judge anybody. I didn't want Frank Black to be a judge or a puritan who sat on the edge of whether something is good or bad. No gift would work in your brain if you had judgments going on. The gift was only about discovering the intent and the function of what was happening."

Is it this trait, the open-minded refusal to judge others, that separates Frank Black from other crime fighters? "Right, because I read all the books on what different kinds of serial killers there are and the things they go through, how they cover their tracks and all these things. I always felt the art that would come out of this is in the impartial acceptance. In a way it's like raising a child. You don't ever want to break the self-esteem of a child. You want to nourish and nurture them, right? In a sense, in pursuing someone doing terrible things you really want to know why, to stop them from happening again. Because these people are not well, they're really not well. You do know they have to be put away, but that's somebody else's job. That's not [Frank's] job, his life. There is a great phrase: 'I don't really like religion so much because it's for people who are afraid to go to hell; spirituality is for a person who has already been there.' And I think that's more about what Frank Black is. He's already been there."

On a very human level, the actor has found that he can identify with the empathy so essential to the character in spite of the differences between the man and the legend. "Listen, if you just watch the news on any given day, one of the things you'll see is almost a social trend going on. Like in the States, we have had some terrible things happen to children. Children, to me, are probably the most important thing in the world because they're really defenseless." The strength in this conviction can be seen in Henriksen's ongoing efforts to support charities such as the Los Angeles-based Children of the Night, dedicated exclusively to rescuing children from prostitution. "We have a job to do to nurture them and have them grow up to be independent, quality people, if we can manage that. You don't try to force them, you just try to entreat them. And the reason I'm bringing that up is that when you see things like that happen, there are certain elements in life that really bother you and you want to solve them.

"A homeless person, someone living in their car: you want to change that. You want to get to the bottom of it. What happened to make that happen, and is there something I can do? And that's the same thing as Frank Black. He's a guy that, when he starts seeing a scenario laying itself out at his feet, he can see elements that other people can't see, and he's obligated in a sense to take it on, to move in that direction, to see where it goes. And I understand that. I can understand it on my level, and I can understand it on his level. You can be on vacation watching killer whales do their thing in a big tank and suddenly get hit with a scenario, like a chess player. The chess player sees all the pieces on the board, and when one moves he has a response and it's almost an automatic response. And I see that as what Frank Black does."

In spite of its inspiring hero, it took some time for Henriksen to come to terms with the often oppressive darkness that dominates *Millennium*. The show's creator attempted to allay his fears by continually pointing to the series' central symbol of hope. "While we were doing *Millennium* we were a little ahead of our time. Chris had a real vision for the show in what he wanted to do and how he wanted to do it. When I met with him I said, 'This is very dark. Where is the light? How is this going to work?' He was very cryptic. He said, 'The yellow house.' I said, 'What?!' And he said, 'Yeah, Lance, the yellow house. Trust me, this is going to really work.' The guy had the vision and so I went along with it. He was very convincing to me."

Carter's vision for *Millennium* was both bold and brilliant, launching an undeniably dark but deeply reflective drama series that stood apart on primetime network television. Did Henriksen enjoy a particularly collaborative relationship with Carter during his time on the series? "To be blunt, no," Henriksen admits. "One of the things that I kept asking Chris for was, at the end of every year, let's have dinner together and I just want to tell you what I learned this year after all those hours, days, weeks, and months on a set. And the guy is pretty shy so he wasn't very receptive to that. But then he surprised me one year by bringing all the Academy Group out from Manassas, Virginia, to Fox Studios, and we sat for a day talking about what the year had been. He was intense, so he did it in his own way." Henriksen would come to understand and appreciate the way in which Carter's creative mind works. "I think that the way to talk about Chris is that he sets the tone. He's a great tone-setter, he knew what he wanted and he moved it in the direction that he wanted it to go."

It is *Millennium*'s format that most frustrated him, Henriksen explains, hinting at the sort of stories he might have suggested if he had been granted the opportunity for one of those collaborative year-end meetings. "If you notice, *Millennium* differed from *The X-Files*. *The X-Files* would never wrap anything up. It was ongoing, with a lot of loose threads, and he did the opposite with *Millennium*. He would wrap the show up on the hour with somewhat of a solution, and I never thought that that would be a good idea. I thought the idea would be that some cases last ten years before you can solve them, but you inevitably will. The truth shouts no matter how long it takes, so as long as Frank was alive there would be these ongoing cases in his mind. I always wanted to interrupt the case I was working on with a sudden Eureka and go in another direction, because I solved another piece of another case that just suddenly hit me. It could be a waitress at a counter putting her order in to the cook and the way she did made me realize something about another case, and I could've cracked it. It's an interesting thing."

THE MYSTERY GUEST

Indeed, this very approach to storytelling now dominates during an era of television in which network and cable dramas spin increasingly complex season-long story arcs. Is this the future of the medium? "In a way, yeah. I think it's closer to life. Back when we were doing *Millennium*, Chris had started with *The X-Files* and had worked his way into something that was originally his. The next show to come along that did it that way was *The Sopranos*. That thing would just go in any direction; you didn't know where it was going to go. That's what made it interesting, but that's exactly what I thought *Millennium* ought to be.

"I listened to a cop today on television. There was a mother and father who had sixteen kids and who had been murdered in their house and the kids were stolen. The cop was standing there saying, 'These people weren't the kind of people who put themselves into jeopardy by being somewhere they shouldn't have been, like a neighborhood.' And I thought, 'There you have it. That's framing it right there.' There are all kinds of opinions about where the jeopardy is going to come from in life, and we all try to walk the straight and narrow and try to stay among friends. But the mystery guest in all of this to me was always Frank Black. He would be arriving when we least expected him to. So, again, you've got these elements of conflict and danger, but you've also got the poetry of it. That's what I always liked about that role, because he was non-judgmental. He was just looking at the world the way it led him and the way it was."

Frank may have been the "mystery guest" intervening in *Millennium*'s tragic tales of cruelty and violence but much of the hope found in the series came from the Black family, particularly Jordan. "Oh, I loved her!" Henriksen exclaims at the mere mention of his young co-star. "Brittany Tiplady, what a wonderful child. Oh my God, I fell in love with her. She was like my daughter, she really was! She was such a giving and wonderful child." Asked how he would characterize his onscreen relationship with her, Henriksen utters without hesitation, "It was genuine."

Tiplady was just five years old when shooting began on *Millennium* and, as Henriksen explains, her presence on the set demanded a degree of sensitivity. "Her family were the nicest people in the world and we had earned their trust. One of the things that we never wanted to do—and this was very important to Chris, too—was to overwork her, scare her, or treat her in any other way than she was a child. Because the danger on a set is that if you start giving the wrong kind of attention to children it twists their brain, it really does. They're always trying to please, they're always trying to do what you want them to do. I remember when we did the pilot… There was a moment in that pilot that I will never ever forget. She was sitting in my lap and I was showing them the yellow house for the first time, and she got so excited that she licked my face like a puppy! She licked my nose and up my face and I went, 'Sweetheart, you like it, don't you? You like the house.' She just completely accepted me, and me likewise. I bought her a rabbit. I wanted to make sure that she felt safe. She's very, very talented. If you met us, it was all genuine. We weren't acting, we were genuinely liking each other. I miss her greatly. It would be great to have her in the movie. I really have nothing but love and respect for that girl. She was really something, and her family—really great people."

As Henriksen describes it, Brittany Tiplady's emotional responses were driven by "pure instinct," demonstrating the sort of candor any dedicated actor should take note of. "If you lied in your acting to her or you acted, so to speak, rather than be completely present, I don't think it would've worked. If you are very present with her and really care about her and really feel wonderful with her, she really picked up on that. That's what she was picking up on. With her, you couldn't fake it. You had to be really doing it. I remember when she started, I think she was four, so talented. When I bought her that dog, we were bonded forever. That was it—she was so happy to see that dog. I had just won the jackpot. It was like, 'Wow! You are the greatest daddy that ever lived!' It was a cute little puppy too, it really was."

The emotional grounding of the family was special to Henriksen, as was the philosophical approach of the series as a whole. He knew *Millennium* was unique right from the start of production as thought-provoking scripts, such as that written by Ted Mann for "The Judge," focused on sometimes challenging subject matter. "There was a line in the first season that fascinated me: 'There's an unusual element of mindfulness associated with the violence.' I thought, 'Oh my God, what does that mean?'" Clad in a tuxedo, accepting a 1996 People's Choice Award for Favorite New Dramatic Series, the actor recited the line at the podium in front of a gathering of Hollywood's elite. "That was one of things I said, and I could see the audience jaw drop. They didn't know what the meaning was any more than I did when I first heard it! I loved [Ted], who wrote it, and he thanked me for saying the line. It was funny!"

THE MYSTERY GUEST

On stage at the People's Choice Awards, Henriksen was recognized by all in attendance as the stalwart hero of Carter's *Millennium* but, prior to being cast as Frank Black, the actor was not known for such roles. Quite the opposite, in fact. Henriksen has spent decades bringing substance to nefarious characters somewhat less considered than the role of Frank Black. In films such as *Stone Cold* (1991) and *Hard Target* (1993), Henriksen is unforgettable as an unconventional antagonist. "Playing a bad guy in a movie, often you have a piece of work that is written where the guy is bad in a bit of a cliché way. It's obvious stuff. What I try and do with those roles is build a real dense character that has a life to him, and that world of bikers' clubs in *Stone Cold* is a very dark place. What I tried to do with that character was to be very unyielding in terms of the lifestyle the character was living, absolutely unforgiving. And it worked. I don't know if the movie worked, but the character really worked."

His approach to such parts in horror and action films continues to this day. "I've just finished a movie called *Cyrus*. It's an independent film and I'm playing a guy who is the best friend of a serial killer. When I say best friend what I mean is he's an enabler. He's a real thick enabler who has a tow truck and crushes cars somewhere in the Midwest. He has a psychopathic edge, has no feelings. He has affection for this one person because he can enable him and it was fun to play, it really was. It was almost like playing a sixty-year-old teenager who had that feeling, you know, the one where you can never be hurt in any way? That's who this guy is, I suddenly realized when I started playing him. I had a lot of fun playing him because the character didn't actually hurt anyone personally, and I thought, 'Wow, this is sick shit! Really, wow.' But it was so much fun to do him. I even found a hat that a member of the crew was wearing and I thought, 'Oh shit, yeah!' I felt like I was on a shopping spree and found all the little pieces of this guy! I grabbed this hat from this guy's head and I said, 'Hey, can I use that?' and he said, 'Yeah.' I brought my own boots because I had my instincts tell me that, being a tow truck driver, he'd have a certain pair of boots and so I brought mine. Anyway, it was putting together pieces of a character and I love that. Believe me, I love acting, otherwise I wouldn't do it, I'd stop."

Emmett in *Cyrus* (2010) is, no doubt, the sort of character that Frank Black would be driven to apprehend. "Exactly," Henriksen says with a nod. "Remember, as a person I've never killed anybody or hurt anybody in any way. It's a piece of entertainment where you investigate these types of characters and make audiences believe it, just what's going on, and lead them down unusual paths. But I don't only want to do the Hollywood bad guys or good guys. It's about playing characters that have a full range of emotions. I find a lot of inspiration in acting just comes in a flash and then, if you pursue that inspiration, you expand it and you see its effect on the whole world. We're not a usual creature, humans.

"You know, last night I was with a group of people and suddenly I was thinking that we were like a pod, a pod of whales—we can't survive without each other. Whenever I'm in an airplane and look down, we're like algae, we really are, algae on a planet." Perhaps. But intelligent algae, yes? "Yeah, well, we think anyway! I mean, the chickens in the chicken yard think they're the hot shit. They walk around and there's a pecking order and they can be nasty, but they probably think they are the shit! If you have a snow leopard up in the mountains, it's so mysterious and nobody knows what it's thinking or its behavior. I'm a believer that animals are really, really misunderstood."

Equally misunderstood are many broken human beings, of course, and Henriksen believes that *Millennium* was audacious in its attempts to consider just what separates violent offenders from those they abuse. "Most men that work in the F.B.I. really just want to know why, and for years they have been trying to work out why these things happen. They know enough to know, no matter what the reason is, we've got to get them off the street, because there are some dysfunctional people out there who will do terrible things and you can't let them keep doing it. That's all there is to it."

On set, working with his fellow actors, Henriksen was constantly stressing the need to express respect for the victims of violence depicted on the series. He wanted *Millennium* to be different among crime dramas. "Not enough is made of the victims. In most things you hear all about the bad guy: what he's done, why he did it. You don't hear anything anymore about the victims and the outcome for the families. I'm not talking about a soap opera. There are real consequences that happen when somebody has to live their life after becoming the relative of a victim. Nobody has cracked that one either. They just glorify the concept. Some terrible thing happens with this terrible person, the police come and sweep up the mess, and then they go, 'Hurrah—we got them,' and that's it."

THE MYSTERY GUEST

Henriksen's sensitivity can be seen in his performance. Frank Black possesses a profoundly empathic gift, one that allows him to connect with even the darkest and most damaged of human souls. The hero isn't quite suave, however, and he wasn't always sophisticated. Take, for instance, the rather awkward way in which he interacts with technology. The world's greatest criminal profiler understands people, but machines? As fans of the series are fond of pointing out, he was particularly brutal in his approach to using a mouse and keyboard. Does this tell us something about the actor's conception of the character? "That's me! It took me years to get a computer. It scared me to death. I thought it was going to steal my soul! I didn't know what it would do. I just slammed that baby around. If it can't take it then it's not worth it. They had to bring me into the digital world kicking and screaming, even thought my heart was open. My heart *was* open, but my feet didn't want to go. Whenever they gave me something on the computer I went, 'Oh, man. This is tough stuff.' Because I always thought of the computer as being a mask, like a mask that somebody is wearing but I don't know what's behind it, and the deeper you look the more mask you find. I've always been threatened by the idea of a whole world that is based on ones and zeroes. There's nothing's tangible yet it keeps sucking money out of our bank accounts. It's only information."

Far more than sets or technology, Henriksen enjoyed working with the many talented actors who appeared throughout *Millennium*'s three-year run. "One of the most important things I tried to do every time was that every guest actor that was on the show, it was so important to me to make them feel at home. I would always say to them, 'If you have any ideas, please share them.' It was a gift to me, because I love working with different people, meeting them, and watching them struggle and do their thing. Privately, I had a good environment for myself. I really loved it."

Among the most outstanding of those guest performers, Henriksen recalls, was actress Sarah-Jane Redmond. Her performances as Lucy Butler, *Millennium*'s ultimate evil, exude a seductive menace that is not easily forgotten. "She was really something else! I did a movie with her. They asked me to do this little movie up in Canada called *The Invitation* and she was in it too. She's some actress, she really is. I always loved it because she was so seductively devilish. If the Devil was going to appear he would be as beautiful and as seductive as her, no doubt about it. A lot of people try to do that but she really did it. She had a mystery about her. I was married at the time. I had to block all that out!"

Butler's return appearances during each season of the series established her foremost among Frank Black's many demonic nemeses. "She was almost like my opposite, like if you say that there is a good and an evil. In a sense, when I got around her she started sapping all my energy. I felt like she would slowly deteriorate me, and I had to fight her and fight it. It was as if she was a succubus. There are certain wasps that will lay an egg in an animal or another insect, and it would feed at it until there was nothing left of its victim. I always felt that she was like that. Remember back in the old days in slasher movies, if two kids made love you knew they were going to be victims? It's the same thing with Lucy Butler. If you get involved with her in any way you're going to pay the ultimate price, so it was like a throwback to that, in a funny way. I would always try to understand the map of her schemes. She's showing me her left hand, but what's her right hand doing?"

Sarah-Jane Redmond's three appearances as Lucy Butler, each distinct in tone and subject matter, are illustrative of larger creative shifts that occur on the series. Frank Black remains a constant and unfaltering figure but the shadowy world he inhabits and the conspiracies he fights, like Butler, constantly change shape under the direction of various showrunners. The changes instituted by Glen Morgan and James Wong during Season Two were particularly controversial, as far as Henriksen was concerned. At times, his resistance to this deviation from the show's original format has been quite vocal. "It wasn't hated," he states before broaching the subject. "We felt the second season was subversive to the show. The first thing that happened was Glen Morgan and James Wong put out a t-shirt saying, '98% less serial killers!' What?! The whole premise of the show was solving crimes that were almost impossible to solve. We felt it was subversive in a real way!" Henriksen's opinion of the epic stories told by Morgan and Wong has shifted somewhat in the years since those episodes were shot, however. "Remember, I couldn't watch the show while I was doing it! I couldn't, I didn't have the time. I didn't see the shows themselves until the box sets were coming out. As I got deeper into Season Two, I felt that the writers were trying out some very unusual work, some very strange events! I started to see one or two of the episodes were very creative! That took the sting out of my original feelings."

THE MYSTERY GUEST

The second season brought its pleasures, too, as in satirical episodes such as Darin Morgan's "Jose Chung's *Doomsday Defense*." "There was this scene where they had me play the detective in the book," the outrageously optimistic private eye Rocket McGrain. "I had a blue trench coat on and blond hair, like Kirk Douglas, and I punched a guy in the nuts! To me that was one of the funniest scenes I'd ever done in that show, where suddenly the guy is out of control. It was hilarious. I had such a good time doing that scene."

Henriksen seems to smile more often during "Jose Chung's *Doomsday Defense*" than he did during the whole of *Millennium*'s first season. "Absolutely. I used to get letters from fans saying, 'Why don't you smile? Why don't you ever tell a joke?' I would say, 'I wish I could!'" As the typically reserved *Monsieur Noir*, however, Henriksen was cut off from his usual modes of expression. "I'm from New York originally, so New Yorkers talk with their hands to emphasize, and I remember when we did the pilot I was doing this long profile and Chris said to me, 'Lance, here's one rule for the whole show. Don't move your hands.' I said, 'Oh, no! You've got to be kidding me! I'm from New York, man, what are you doing to me? Why not put a straitjacket on me!' He said, 'When somebody talks with their hands it looks like they're selling something.' His other peeve is that he never wants actors to put their hands in their pockets, so as soon as *Millennium* was over, the first film, I did the whole thing with my hands in my pockets! That's my rebellious nature."

Another second season installment that stands out for Henriksen—in part because it appeals to that rebellious nature—is "Luminary." He remembers it vividly. The actor describes that he felt "relieved" when the script for the episode, written by Chip Johannessen, was delivered. "I understand that," Henriksen says of the journey of discovery undertaken by teenager Alex Glaser. "If you've ever been married, there's a moment after every divorce where you feel like, 'I'm just going to take everything and leave it and walk off into the woods.' So I understand it, basically. You just want to curl up into a ball and heal yourself. We need to hear that inner voice, we really do.

"Everybody does it in a different style and everybody's going to see it in a different way because of their own life experience. The only thing that changed it was when he broke his leg. If he hadn't broken his leg he probably would've gone on and on, and maybe lived to be sixty. You don't know. But the point was that he risked everything in that terrain, to go out there in that terrain with nothing—or very little—and shed everything. To the outside world it would appear insanity, but to him it was more like, 'How far can I push this, and what's the road leading me to? Am I on the road, or am I angry at the road, or is the road coming to me?'"

In "Luminary," Alex's grief-stricken parents don't seem willing or able to understand this. "No, and when I tried to hand them the diary they didn't even take it. It was as if they were in so much denial that it was unbelievable, and I had sympathy for them because you've missed something. The sympathy I had for them was about that. They missed an opportunity."

Indeed, one of the episode's messages seems to be that, for each child, there is something beyond the family to be embraced and explored. "I have a ten year old and sometimes, quietly, I look at her when she is doing something of her own and she's not watching me watch her, and I say, 'I brought you into this world, and someday you're going to die.' And it's a very sad thought. It just comes to me as a thought. And it's almost like I'm asking myself to have to surrender her, because she's already in the process of pushing away from the table as a person. When you think about that, one of the things is we don't choose our family. We suddenly arrive, and then somewhere along the line we have got to get in contact with ourselves, in our own ways. Sometimes that's workaholism, it can be arts, it could be trying to dive into another woman's life to try to find yourself through a woman, then that doesn't work and you have to find yourself through being alone and meditating. Who knows? There are a myriad of issues involved in becoming a human being that you are searching for. So there is a cycle of life."

The reflective scenes of "Luminary," in which the always straightforward Frank struggles to understand an ambiguous evaluation from the typically secretive Millennium Group, offered Henriksen a chance to reevaluate his character and the series as a whole. "At the beginning of this, when I was sitting with the Millennium Group, I felt like I was lost," he remembers. "Everybody was lost. It's almost like, 'Who are we, what are we doing, and why are we doing it?' So it really did set the trend, but in a lot of different languages." His unfriendly meeting with the Millennium Group inspires Frank to act independently, to be more proactive. "I really wanted more of that in the show. I never got to smile, there were so many things they took away from me, including using my hands. It was a good direction to go in. The 'trick bag' reference was my own line; that wasn't in the script. That came from my wife. She used to say that to me: 'You're putting me in a trick bag.' I knew we were into a new direction, and one of the things is when all the people you thought were your friends are now becoming your enemies. It's a very despairing moment."

In spite of the trials endured by his character, or perhaps because of them, Henriksen has nothing but praise for Johannessen's work on the standout script, inspired by John Krakauer's heartbreaking *Into the Wild* (1996). "The other part of this is that this was a little ahead of *Into the Wild*, in the sense of a kid going out and risking his life to pursue this dream, or to find out what a dream is, even. It was a really good script. They had some really good writers on that show. There was a scene where he fell into the river off of the thing that I was dragging him on, and I remember that river was so cold. We could hardly breathe, let alone pull somebody out of a river. As soon as they said, 'Cut!' there were five guys who came in to drag us out of the water because we were so numb. Man, it was cold. But when you finally string it all together it really told a story."

"Luminary," like so many installments of *Millennium*, is a painfully sad story that also proves to be surprisingly uplifting. "Life, in a lot of ways, is a sad story, really, when you get down to it," Henriksen reflects. "We're born, we live, and we die. That's a given. So there's poetry in the struggle, and when I found that kid's diary that scene really got me. Because I opened the diary and somebody had actually written it—I don't know whether Chip did, or the kid did—but it was very touching, really."

Season Three, in which Johannessen became an executive producer on the series, initiated further changes for *Millennium* and its storytelling and brought with it greater challenges for Henriksen. Asked to reflect on the hardest episode he ever had to shoot, mentally or physically, the actor answers, "I think the last episode, where I went after [Peter Watts] and you assume that I shot him with a .45. That was really bad, when they got into the shows where suddenly I didn't like him anymore. That was the hardest, because Terry [O'Quinn] and I really worked beautifully together and when they got into that betrayal stuff it really bothered me a lot. So that last show was really painful. It was against everything that I believed about Frank Black."

Indeed, Frank is a very angry man during the third season of *Millennium*, as his violent confrontation with Peter Watts in "Goodbye to All That" proves. "I know, and I didn't want that. I never wanted that. I never wanted to see him with a gun in his hand, because it's so mundane. It's like cop, cop, cop, and I didn't want to do that... I don't think anything can be solved with that violence. Certainly war is like a protracted, disastrous, futile, wasteful thing in every way. Why haven't we been able to crack the issue of communication instead of manipulation? It's just unbelievable."

Frank and Jordan escape to the open road and a fresh start during the final frames of the series finale. At the time of *Millennium*'s cancellation, Henriksen had his own ideas of where the series might have headed in future seasons, inspired in large part by those real life heroes driven to analyze violent crimes. "I was really thinking about it in a more philosophical way, but I thought what needed to happen was that more cases were being worked on at one time. It was never one case. After speaking to the guys from the Academy Group, the first thing they said to me was, 'I wish I could see those movies when I touched some part of a crime scene. I wish I had those flashbacks.' I said, 'I don't like them very much.' I never did." Nevertheless, living as Frank Black for three years during production of the series imbued Henriksen with something of the profiler's gift.

"Let me tell you a quick story. They came with a bunch of slides of crimes and one in particular was of a girl who was found dead, strangled, under a comforter on the floor in an empty apartment. They gave me some information but not very much, but as they looked into her life she had about four boyfriends at the same time. Two of them were very rich playboys and all of that and they would take her everywhere and do everything with her, another one was a Navy sailor, and the other was a neighbor. And I sat there and said, 'I don't think it was the rich guys and I don't think it was the neighbor. I think it was the sailor, because he was very much in love with her.' And what gave me the clue to it all was that he had covered her naked body, because when she was found he didn't want anybody to see that intimacy that he had shared with her. And that was exactly right. So over the period of the few years and all the books I had been reading I was able to figure that case out, and they were surprised because I did it in two minutes.

"The reason I'm saying that is because we can absorb from all of the stuff that's going on in the world that we're seeing on a daily basis."

THE MYSTERY GUEST

Our lives, as Henriksen suggests, bleed into all that we do, and those things that touch us are absorbed and internalized. Speaking with Henriksen, touching on ever-shifting subjects ranging from pottery to boxing to social unrest, one is continually reminded of a complex interconnectivity at work in the world. "Here's how they get you with the news," he warns, just to drive the point home. "The news comes on, you have a real life event happen. The next thing that happens, somebody is selling you insurance, they're selling you medical equipment, or they're selling you a car. You're inundated with that stuff, so they're bridging the gap between your needs as a human being that they're trying to peddle you and your fear. Your fear of getting ill, your fear of having no money—all of these things, they are linking directly to the news."

It all ties back to the larger idea of what *Millennium* might have become had it reached the year 2000. "What I'm saying is, if we did more than one case going on at the same time, they interrelate. There are only seven original story structures, and Frank has a way of simplifying and absolutely seeing it. There's a book that some of this was related to, where there was a profiler who was in the F.B.I. who was working on over a hundred cases at one time and his workload was so heavy that he was in a hotel room and he had a stroke." In December of 1983, consulting on almost one hundred and fifty cases without backup, John Douglas was in a coma, hovering between life and death. The famed serial killer profiler describes the terrifying ordeal in his first memoir, *Mindhunter* (1995). "He barely survived it. He did survive it and he went back to work, but he could've died. But imagine that workload. I was never playing Frank like he was tired or any of that stuff. He *was* tired, his workload was heavy... Like a great boxer, you know how to use your energy. You use as little energy as possible knowing it's going to be twelve rounds, it's going to be a lifetime."

Frank Black was undoubtedly prepared for a lifelong battle against evil and, as far as Henriksen is concerned, he isn't down for the count. The actor's response is the same whenever he is asked to comment on the character's return. "I would absolutely love to do it and I really think it is a possibility, but it's really up to Frank Spotnitz and Chris Carter." Ideally, he would like to see such a project take the form of a film. "A movie would be very different. With a movie you have an end in sight—you can gear your energy for it—but when you have a series that goes on for ten and a half months there is no way to really have that end in sight because you know you'll be coming back next year. It's very tiring."

Henriksen, of course, in spite of a number of recent television appearances and increasing voiceover work for videogames and animation, has worked far more extensively in film. He contrasts the endless possibilities inherent to the medium with those countless limitations imposed on television production. "The reason I've always believed [*Millennium*] should be a movie on the big screen or a channel like HBO is you have more freedom with language and the things that can happen. You are allowed to talk about more, and that's more natural to me as opposed to being kind of the sanitized guy. I'm not very good at that." In general, the actor's films do not tend to reflected a sanitized subject matter. "No, I don't go for it," he agrees. "I've tried everything you can try in films, having fun, and it's a wonderful expression. To be locked into a thing like T.V. is really tough. I don't mean to whinge about it. Believe me, I loved every minute of *Millennium*, but it was tiring. It was like despair, it was so tiring. I was so tired, but everyone in T.V. has felt that. I don't feel very special about it."

Millennium's visionary hero continues to live on in the hearts and minds of its dedicated fans. Today, it is one of those legendary roles that audiences around the world instantly associated with Henriksen's distinctive visage. What does it take, as an actor, to create a role as iconic as that of Frank Black? "A friend of mine has a great phrase: 'If you're having bacon and eggs for breakfast, a chicken was involved in laying the egg, but the pig was committed.' I think commitment is something that an actor like Heath Ledger had. Man, he really tried. You see it a lot when you see him in [*The Dark Knight*]. This guy really went somewhere! He dug deep. There are a lot of actors out there like that, there really are, but you can't hit a home run without a bat. If you are given a role that requires that type of commitment and a director and producer want to support you in that pursuit, then you can do that kind of work. But often they'll give you a job that is in a style that they're not willing to let you go there; they're asking for more a surface style that doesn't lend itself to that pursuit of commitment."

Frank Black remains a figure of hope. In the third millennium, Henriksen suggests, the wave of violence and strife forecast by Carter's *Millennium* has become tidal. We need his greatest hero now more than ever. "When you look at what's going on in the world right now—

extreme people causing destruction—it's more like what everybody thought it would be when the clock ticked to midnight. And here we are, and there is a lot of terrible shit going on, there really is. But weaving through that there are a lot of people really trying to have a good life and do the right thing. There are lot of these people, more than the others causing destruction! Of course, governments are a pain in the ass, but the thing to remember is that there are people trying to have a life, and from that there's a lot of beauty. I think children are the only heaven I'll ever know when you really get down to it; my children are the only heaven I'll ever know. They're incredible to watch and they are the best of what we are." Cometh the hour, cometh the man; such times call for a champion such as Frank Black. "He's not another James Bond—he's the opposite of James Bond—and he's not a Partridge family. There is a reality to it so, yes, there's a place for Frank Black in the twenty-first century, and I think there is room for a guy like me doing it!"

Imagining *Millennium* as a film, be it on the big or small screen, conjures countless creative possibilities previously unrealized. Modern cinema is dominated by C.G.I., for instance, and Henriksen suggests that computer graphics might be employed to depict Frank's gift in striking new ways. "I've always thought that Frank Black should go to a country like Bulgaria where everything is in Cyrillic and he doesn't understand the language. He has to come there and solve something, and then you see these finite concepts rolling around him. It would really be great. I just think the more conflict you give a character like Frank Black the more interesting it becomes." As an actor who feeds off the emotions of fellow performers and best responds to that which is genuine or real, would it prove challenging to perform in a C.G.I. environment? "No. Let me tell you why it's not a problem. I did about nine years of theater, Off-Broadway. I was at the Guthrie Theater in Minnesota and the Boston Theater Company, and sometimes all you had was a stage that was painted black. It was all black and there were maybe a few sticks of furniture, and the rest was all language. It was creating the whole world that you were doing in the play. And all that has changed is the color of the set. It's the same thing. I guess the statement that can be made is that nobody does this alone, and there are a lot of skills coming in from all directions."

Henriksen is ready and willing to assume the mantle of Frank Black once more, and there are audiences across the world clamoring for such a comeback. Critically acclaimed and still highly regarded within the industry itself, *Millennium* continues to find new viewers and to enthrall the old, years after it aired its final episode. It is a phenomenon Henriksen is acutely aware of. "I think, to be honest, *Millennium* has taken a life of its own, which is why I really want to talk to you. If a thing like this is happening, it should be done! I hope that Chris and Frank take the lead and say, 'This will happen.' Sometimes it's a sociological event. If this is something the fans really want, they can certainly get it." The fans of Carter's dark drama are out there, and they are forever finding new ways to make their voices heard.

The actor continues to appear at conventions—genre gigs that keep him cross-crossing the globe, from the Long Beach Comic Con in Long Beach, California, to the annual Rock & Shock in Worcester, Massachusetts, to Collectormania in Milton Keynes, England—where he enjoys interacting with his fans. "I love meeting people and talking, even if it's for a brief few moments. At least I'm making contact and I've had some really good conversations around the hotel. It is really worth doing, really fun. I live with that kind of attitude of gratitude, believe me. That's how my life really wants to be and to be accepted in the industry like I have been, it's been wonderful. I have nothing to complain about at all."

Thirteen years later, after the end of *Millennium*, is Henriksen surprised by the response he continues to see from fans of the series? "Very surprised. I'm very surprised that it caught fire like that. If we do the movie, I'm going to tour the world and meet all these fans. I really am, and just sign pictures and get connected with them, hear their ideas and things. And the movie should be good enough to make them feel satisfied. If I do it, it really is going to be a good one." There can be no question that Henriksen would still give his all to the character. As he suggests, the mystery guest remains Frank Black, a man of hope and compassion who enters our lives when he is least expected but most needed.

"It's the most absurd quote I've ever said, but I said to my wife—now my ex-wife—I said, 'I believe in myself more than you believe in my excuses.'" Lance Henriksen believes in himself, and he genuinely believes that *Millennium*'s hero will return. "If they don't make this movie, something's really wrong with the universe. I really believe that."

THE STORY OF LANCE HENRIKSEN AND THE FABLE OF FRANK BLACK

by Paul Clark

"Far off the silent, changing sound was still, with the black islands lying thick around."

—Edwin Muir
"Childhood"

In 1940, the Scottish poet and essayist Edwin Muir wrote his autobiography, *The Story and the Fable*. In 2010, Lance Henriksen and Joseph Maddrey collaborated to offer us the actor's autobiography, *Not Bad for a Human*. In both works, the same truth becomes boldly apparent: the story can only ever chronicle the events and the people that surround a person's life whereas the fable will always present us the deeper realm of meaning that undergirds that same person's life. Henriksen drew upon his own fable in order to intuit and then create the character of Frank Black. Why does Frank Black continue to matter so much to so many? It is because—thanks to Henriksen—we became witnesses to the creation of a life-affirming myth that will not go away. This essay will offer some preliminary reflections on how this came to be.

In his autobiography, Henriksen offers a story from his early life that helps us to understand the symbolic grounding of the entire first season of *Millennium* (1996-99). Maddrey defines this moment as an "epiphany," a breakthrough to some deeper recognition of both the self and the world.

> Here I was—this kid, with no clue who the fuck I am and what I wanted to do. I felt completely lost. It was the loneliest feeling in the world. I hadn't eaten for a very long time, and I remember just walking out into the desert as the sun was starting to set... Suddenly, I realized that all around me—from horizon to horizon—the ground was covered with these yellow flowers. I hadn't seen them before because the sun was the same color they were, but now I could see them everywhere. Suddenly, I felt connected somehow. It was just my own personal feeling of being *connected*. I had never experienced anything like that before. It was like everything else just melted away: who my father was, who my mother was, and what my life had been like. All of that was just gone. And I suddenly felt like: *I've got to make myself. I've got to become myself...* That's when I realized I wanted to be some kind of artist. I really felt like that was going to be my salvation. (48)

Surrounded by those yellow flowers, Henriksen found a new and clearer connection to both himself and to a world that often seemed extremely hostile.

At this point, we can begin to see how Henriksen's story feeds into the fable of Frank Black. Walking in that desert among those yellow flowers, walking over a terrain where life and death are both equally real, Henriksen could feel what Frank would later feel walking into that yellow house for the first time with his wife, Catherine, and his daughter, Jordan. We learn early on that Frank is recovering from a nervous breakdown. He was imprisoned within his own mind by the intense fear and dread of the menace that surrounded him and his family. It is this darkness that overwhelms Frank and carries him into the strange rooms and corridors of a mental institution. Frank Black is coming from a place of profound disorder and disorientation into this new geography of life, this new connection, and hopeful possibilities and this is a breakthrough that Henriksen had lived.

Those who know *Millennium* appreciate that the central grounding of the first season is the yellow house, which—like those little yellow flowers—connects Henriksen on a powerful unconscious level to the reality of Frank Black. It is, in fact, what all of us continue to experience when we revisit those early episodes of *Millennium*. There is a sense of hope that permeates the entire first season as we descend toward "Paper Dove." In his autobiography, Henriksen explains, "Whenever I was in the yellow house, it was part of a support system. The people in it—Megan Gallagher [who plays Frank's wife Catherine] and Brittany Tiplady [who plays his daughter Jordan]—they were my support. We were each other's support. When we did those scenes together, it wasn't about the writing—it was about each other... I did love them, I really did. At times I felt childlike with them. I wasn't always expressing it, but I was feeling it. That's what Chris was right about—about the yellow house" (232).

"At times I felt childlike with them." With these few words, Henriksen is able to beautifully bring together his story and Frank's fable. The sad, wandering child within Henriksen has finally come home to the yellow house. Neglect has been replaced with a sense of support and belonging. Inside that new emotional space, Henriksen is able to breathe deeply and give birth to Frank Black. A new hope is created in us as we watch this happen.

Hope, however, should never be confused with a sentimental optimism. Hope is not the radiant glow that "all is well." From the moment the first set of Polaroids is delivered to Ezekiel Drive right up to the brutal murder of Lt. Bob Bletcher in the basement, the yellow house is constantly under assault by what William Stringfellow once called "the power of death at work in the world." Frank Black offers us hope not because he triumphs but rather because he resists that power of death and despair. Could that truth have convinced any of us if

Henriksen had not affirmed the power of life at the deepest human level so many years before?[1]

There is a sense of hope, yes, but there is also great sadness, because without that intense grief neither Henriksen nor Frank could offer us anything real. As the series turns the corner into Season Two, it is that very sadness and the loneliness of Henriksen's early life that allows him to navigate the dreamscape of these episodes. Once again, Henriksen's story helps him to create the fable of Frank Black. Frank is now cut off from the yellow house, from Catherine, and—most importantly—from Jordan. He now drifts and wanders through the dreams and nightmares of a profound loneliness that was once defined as "the closest you can get to death without dying." Bill Sienkiewicz's evocative cover artwork for *Not Bad for a Human* expresses such emotion. That strong—yet haunted—look in many ways captures the spirit of the second season, the sadness and the loneliness.

What event in Lance Henriksen's story made it possible for him to find the interior myth of Frank Black in this set of dream stories? *Not Bad for a Human* makes it apparent that no single moment in Henriksen's life could have prepared him for this. In truth, the entirety of his life made this act of creation possible.

Two very clear images stand out in the actor's narrative. Firstly, we see a fierce and frightened young boy sitting in a movie theater alone, imagining a world that had a different shape, feel, and quality to it than the one that existed outside that dark theater. Throughout the second season of *Millennium*, we see Frank Black—also alone—sitting inside that other house, waiting, waiting for things to make sense once again. The second image is very stark indeed. Henriksen explains the reality of being incarcerated in a brig at Portsmouth Naval Prison in Maine. "I was really down, doing hard time, and getting angrier by the minute. Remember I wasn't sitting in a cell, reading. I was sitting in a cell, sitting in a cell. Staring out through those fucking bars. I had no escape" (43).

This short section of descriptive narrative beautifully and truthfully defines for us one of the most compelling aspects of *Millennium*. What does it mean for Frank Black—or any human being—to sit and to wait on this hard edge of reality that separates hope and despair with the expectation that life will break through at some point? Both Henriksen and Frank knew on a deeply felt level that life expected something from them. And, so, they waited—and invited us to wait with them.

"Luminary" represents that moment in the second season when the hard waiting comes to an end.

But what "hard waiting" has come to an end? When I teach "Luminary" in the classroom, I always subtitle the episode "The Receiving of Wisdom." (This is the caption beneath the illustration of Petrarch on Mt. Ventoux.) In "Luminary," a mythic journey takes place and, in the context of such a journey, the "hard waiting" can only cease when a new wisdom, a new understanding has been mysteriously apprehended and then consciously comprehended. We can believe this is happening to Frank Black because Henriksen has lived both the "hard waiting" and "the receiving of wisdom."

In his book *Beyond the Hero* (1995), Allan Chinen outlines the mythic journey that proves central to *Millennium*. Although the book was published a year prior to the broadcast of the series, the conceptual framework of the text opens up incredible possibilities for yet another way to explore the series. Chinen's area of study is the analysis of fables and fairy tales from all over the world. He seeks to discover the pattern of meaning and myth that emerges from them. In *Beyond the Hero*, Chinen offers this conclusion: the mythic geography of masculinity takes men from the "Masculine," through the "Inner Feminine," and then into the "Deep Masculine."

In order to better understand Chinen, however, it is important to know that his work grows out of the psychological school of thought created by C. G. Jung, an early follower of Freud. One of Jung's greatest contributions is found in his fierce determination to explore the Unconscious Mind—especially the Collective Unconscious—and the Archetypes that represent the defining manifestations of the Self. Thus, when Chinen uses the terms "Masculine," "Inner Feminine," and "Deep Masculine," he is embarking on his own investigation of this archetypal interior world.[2]

For the purposes of this essay, a brief examination of the three terms might prove useful in understanding the fable of Frank Black. The Masculine represents that early stage of a man's psychological development in which the exterior world still remains a mystery, when the ground beneath a man's feet is shaky at best and breaking apart at worst, when the illusion of controlling one's surroundings and other human beings is still alive and well. At some point, a man discovers a simple fact: this state of existence is unreal and help is required to change. It is the journey into the wilderness of the Inner Feminine that becomes the necessary transition, the healing of these great wounds. The Inner Feminine is always found in some manifestation of "wilderness." Some examples of wilderness in fable are the desert, the forest (often enchanted), the mountain, or an ocean voyage. Lastly, having endured the pain and confusion of the Masculine as well as the struggle and transformation of the Inner Feminine, a man has survived the rapids and the waterfall to land finally in the peaceful stream of authentic courage, compassion, and commitment to life.

Let us return to *Millennium* in general and to "Luminary" in particular. Frank Black arrives at the yellow house in a state of imbalance. Fear, anguish, and confusion are still his companions as he makes a fresh start in Season One. According to Chinen's model, this disorientation perfectly exemplifies the Masculine stage of the mythic journey. In this phase, the Masculine struggles to come to terms with the exterior reality that surrounds him. We are drawn back to the image of a young Lance Henriksen, wandering the mean streets of an often unfriendly world, searching sadly and desperately for a meaning and a purpose to his life. For either Henriksen or Frank to be trapped in the Masculine represents a true dead end for their lives. Something must change.

As we know, neither journey ends in this "Masculine cage." The metaphor of a cage directs our attention back to Season Two. From the moment Catherine and Jordan leave the yellow house and Frank is exiled into the loneliness of that new "dark house," conceived of by Glen Morgan and James Wong, we know that something different is now necessary for Frank Black to develop. The second phase of the mythic journey begins with Frank alone, surrounded by wild dogs, and moving toward his first enigmatic meeting with the Old Man; "Beware of the Dog" underscores Frank's lack of control and his sense of being lost.

Henriksen's gift to us at this moment in the series is his ability to tap into both his conscious and unconscious mind in order to make us feel the menace and the madness of this dark wilderness experience. After reading *Not Bad for a Human*, we can imagine Henriksen at the age of twelve, surrounded by the "wild dogs" of southern racism.

> When I was about twelve, I was hitchhiking through the Bible Belt. All day long I was riding with rednecks and every time I got into a car, the driver would know that I

THE STORY OF LANCE HENRIKSEN

was from the North and they'd start talking about "niggers," and saying all these hideous things about how you've gotta hang 'em and kill 'em. I never thought that way, because I didn't grow up in a racist environment. Everybody in New York was too busy dealing with poverty. (61-62)

How does a young boy survive this kind of nightmare? In struggling to feel an answer to that hard question, we begin to know how Henriksen made Frank so real.

If Season Two depicts numerous instances of Frank Black locked inside a cage of dark "wilderness" experiences, "Luminary" represents Frank's jailbreak. As we think back to the episode we remember clearly that caged-in opening sequence, in which Frank is interrogated by the Millennium Group in an interview that Frank wisely and accurately identifies as "a trick bag." Neither Frank, nor Henriksen, nor any of us can move forward until we acknowledge the truth about where we are. In his autobiography, Henriksen asserts his belief "that the truth shouts, and that the truth can heal things" (344). In this "trick bag" moment, Frank Black shouts the truth, begins to heal himself, and continues his journey toward freedom.

In "Luminary," Frank travels deeper into the wilderness—not only for Alex Ventoux but also for himself. In that wilderness, he reaches out to Alex and finds a new opening to life. In fact, in that wilderness—anointed by those amazing Northern Lights of the "Inner Feminine"—Frank reaches out to Alex as Lance Henriksen simultaneously reached out his hand to that frightened young boy sitting alone in the dark of a movie theater, saying, "I'm not going to let you die, kid." Frank kept his promise, and so did Henriksen.

Near the end of the episode, we are offered one of the most powerful moments in the series. After Frank Black hands Alex's injured body over to Peter Watts, he chooses to remain behind in order to complete the second phase of his mythic transformation. Wrapped in a simple woolen blanket, grounded in the Earth itself, focused outward at his own "glassy sea" of revelation, Frank Black—after the hard waiting and a hard struggle—knows that he has crossed into a new place within himself: the Deep Masculine, that place where "the truth shouts, and that truth can heal things."

This journey from the Masculine through the Inner Feminine and into the Deep Masculine does not mean that life is suddenly easy or devoid of dark experiences. After all, it is after this mythic transformation takes place that Frank must face an intense confrontation with the Millennium Group, a profound betrayal by the group, the loss of his wife, Catherine, and his own psychic and spiritual unraveling. Without the "Receiving of Wisdom" that leads him into the "Deep Masculine," Frank would likely have disappeared within himself, never to be seen or heard from again.[3]

In Season Three, Henriksen takes all the betrayal, sadness, and loss in his own life—as well as the courage, commitment, and creativity that saved him—and uses it to reshape and redefine the fable of Frank Black once more. All false hopes are gone, all delusional prophecies are put to rest, and all that remains is a loving father (something Henriksen understands very well indeed) and a human being who is determined to be authentic, responsible, and free. There are moments in the third season that are simply electric as we watch Henriksen's story and Frank's fable fuse before our eyes. Three unique episodic examples illustrate the point.

After the terrible loneliness and sadness of loss have been experienced, both Henriksen and Frank move back into the world to reclaim self, life, and compassion. In the episode "Through a Glass, Darkly," Frank Black meets Max Brunelli (Tom MacCleister) by a rusting swing set in a desolate park. This single scene captures with amazing clarity the journey Frank has made from the innocence of the yellow house, through the nightmarish descent of loss and betrayal, to this moment, a demonstration of the compassionate presence that dominates the third season. Frank confronts Max but then confesses, "I know what it is to suffer." With those words echoing in the air, we understand that we have arrived at the intersection of Henriksen's story and Frank's fable. For both Henriksen and Frank, if the suffering cannot lead us toward compassion, then what would any of it mean? In moments like this throughout the third season, the heart of *Millennium* is revealed to us; Henriksen's pain and hope create the haunting and truthful reality of Frank Black.

The episode "Bardo Thodol" includes many beautiful scenes. The sadness and the beauty of life and death encountering one another can be seen as Frank Black bends over the dying Japanese scientist Steven Takahashi (Tzi Ma), meeting him face-to-face, touching his deformed and death-ridden presence with both of his hands. With a gun held against the back of his own skull, Frank speaks words of comfort and hope: "Forget the Group. They've stood everything on its head. Because they don't trust the clear voice you heard inside you. Trust that voice. Listen to that voice. They have no hold over you. Recognize them for what they are and they cannot defeat you."

In the wasteland of Lance Henriksen's own childhood and adolescence, he learned what it was to die inside and, yet, still to live and to seek out those same words of comfort and hope from others and from art. Why do we believe Frank Black in this scene? It is because—in those words spoken by Frank to the dying Takahashi—we hear Henriksen reflecting back on those he needed as a child—his father, mother, and others. They were not there. From that personal pain and suffering, Henriksen learned compassion—and then embodied it in the character of Frank Black.

In the final episode of the series, "Goodbye to All That," we experience one more example, an example that represents the culmination of the compassionate arc of Season Three. One of the final scenes depicts Frank Black's encounter with Lucas Barr (Jeff Parise) in a claustrophobic kitchen. The tormented Barr, a drill in hand, wants only one thing: to end his life. With the drill bit to his temple, Frank pleads with Barr not to add his own death to all the others he has seen throughout a hard life. The power of death and despair claim Lucas Barr. There is nothing that Frank can do to stop the act, and once again there is a profound sense of helplessness. It is the same helplessness that Henriksen felt so often as a child and a young man. Whether he was walking away from his father's house after yet another rejection, standing by the bedside of a mother who only understood what she needed, or roaming the roads on dark nights in America, Henriksen learned of the helplessness that causes Frank to cry out in that kitchen.

Importantly, the scene does not end with Barr's death. It is not over until Frank Black kneels down next to him, cradles his bloody head and body in his arms, and whispers two words: "Oh, Christ." Looking into the face of a desperate and terrible death once again, Frank Black chooses to stay and to offer compassionate human comfort to this broken young man. Frank has the last word: life is most real when we suffer with others. Lance Henriksen knows this powerful truth, and Frank Black embodies it for us.

If we are fortunate, we all will find a way to move from story to fable in our lives. Lance Henriksen made that strange, wonderful, and difficult journey, and in the process he broke through to us by creating the character of Frank Black. The shaping of such powerful myths help us to define the world we live in. These myths move us from desolation to redemption. In silence, we give thanks for such a gift.

NOTES

1. No one reading believes that great art is a haphazard occurrence. Notice, therefore, that Frank Black lives on Ezekiel Drive. Ezekiel, one of the four major prophets in the Bible, is asked a very crucial question by the divine. In the valley of dry bones, in the presence of the power of death, God asks Ezekiel: "Can these bones live?" Do we really think that a similar question was not posed to both Lance Henriksen and Frank Black again and again? This question can break our hearts, but the content and actions of our lives can bring us back to hope.

2. Just as these mythic categories enable men to examine who they are, so the language of "Feminine," "Inner Masculine," and "Deep Feminine" allows women the same chance to journey inward and down into the Self. In the context of *Millennium*, both Lara Means and Emma Hollis offer exciting opportunities for such discussion.

3. As noted, some future examination of the fable of Lara Means—especially in the context of her final episode, "The Time is Now"—would only serve to sharpen the contrast between Frank and Lara in particular and Frank and the Millennium Group in general. When we allow the myth to dominate us, we disappear. When we integrate the myth into our own story, fable, and truth, then we transform and live.

WORKS CITED

Henriksen, Lance and Joseph Maddrey. *Not Bad for a Human: The Life and Films of Lance Henriksen.* Los Angeles: Bloody Pulp, 2011. Print.

Chinen, Allan B. *Beyond the Hero: Classic Stories of Men in Search of Soul.* New York: G. P. Putnam's Sons, 1993. Print.

Paul Clark is a poet, teacher, and activist. He is an ordained minister in the United Church of Christ and is presently serving as the Chaplain and Director of the Multifaith Center at Albright College in Reading, Pennsylvania. His wife, Susan, shares both his life and his love for *Millennium*.

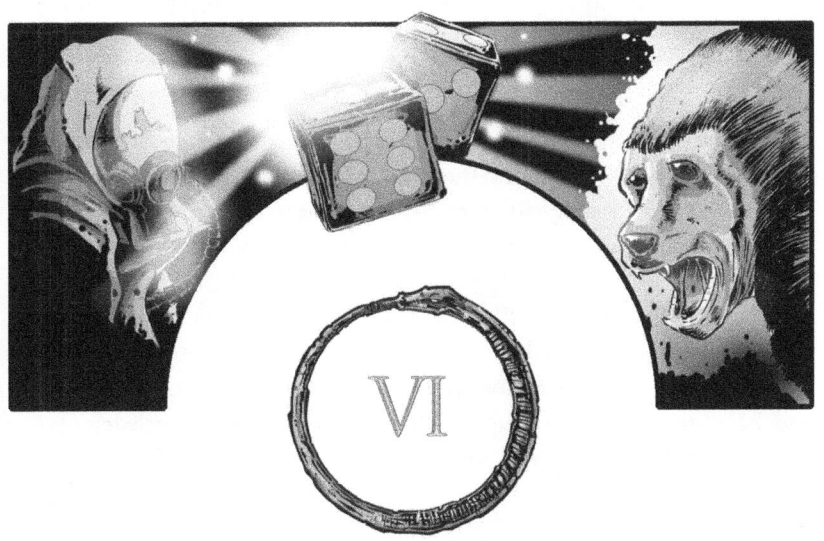

THE GOOD WIFE:
A CONVERSATION WITH MEGAN GALLAGHER

Interview by James McLean & Troy L. Foreman
Written by Adam Chamberlain

Megan Gallagher, the actress who would ably project such kindness and strength as Frank Black's wife Catherine, recalls with a smile one particular meeting during the process of winning the role. Sat across from creator Chris Carter and director David Nutter, what could have been a nervous industry audition fraught with tension quickly turned toward laughter. "I asked a few questions about the script," she recalls, "and then I said, 'Do you have any questions for me?' Chris said, 'How could you sleep with Hank Kingsley?' That was from *The Larry Sanders Show*, and that was hilarious because they were big Larry Sanders fans! So we talked about that and that episode; it was just a great meeting and a huge surprise."

The role of Catherine Black, so central to the family dynamic that serves as the emotional foundation of *Millennium*'s (1996-99) pilot, proved a pleasant surprise in and of itself for the in-demand actress. "It was such a gift," says Megan. "It was just sort of this thing that fell out of the sky. It was pilot season and I was making the rounds and going to various things, and I remember I had a meeting at Paramount that day, and it was a very different kind of character. And then I had a meeting all the way across town with Chris and David."

The launch of this intriguing new series from the acclaimed creator of *The X-Files* (1993-2002) was both hotly anticipated and, in production, a well-guarded secret. "I had gotten the script the night before, and it was one of those that was delivered at ten o'clock at night and I had to sign something they had faxed over on the privacy. There wasn't that much back and forth dialogue for me to really read, but I could tell that it was going to be an important role because it was [Frank Black]'s wife and the mother of the show. I was excited to go in; I was a huge *X-Files* fan from the very beginning of that series. I thought, 'Wow, Chris Carter! This is his new thing, that's great!' That particular day was a crazy day as I had to be at a meeting for something that Kelsey Grammer was producing at Paramount, and that was also a hot project. Then I'm in an hour and a half later—and it's a good hour's drive—and I had to be at Fox for this thing with Chris Carter and David. I ended up changing my clothes in the car, because there was no place for me to change! I just had to do a little change, but I did!"

Fortunately, none of this chaos spilled over into her first meeting with *Millennium*'s creator. In fact, as with Frank Black and Lance Henriksen, Carter had written the role of Catherine specifically for Gallagher. "I went over there and then was delighted. Chris was very funny. I asked them a couple of questions about it. They did not have me read, they just wanted to talk to me, and what I learned was that he had written this with me in mind. He was a fan of mine and he wrote Catherine Black thinking of me, and David Nutter felt the same way and he, of course, was going to direct it, and they were sort of meeting me to make sure I wasn't a jerk!

"They didn't ask me to read the words but they wanted a chat, so it was very flattering; it was great. There's nothing better than finding out that people that you admire think that your work is great too."

THE GOOD WIFE

Indeed, it is as if Megan was fated to step into the role of Catherine Black. "When you are going to do a television series, and certainly when you are going to be the female lead in a series, you have to test at the network. Well, Peter Roth—who at the time was the head of the network at Fox—was also a fan. So it was just this wonderful thing where a bunch of people who liked my work were all involved in this thing. I had done an episode of *Picket Fences*, which was just Peter's favorite thing ever; he loved this episode. He was at the studio then, and now he was the head of the network. They decided that I didn't have to test, which was just the most extraordinary thing. I did not expect that at all. I absolutely expected to have to test, but Peter just said, 'Let's try and work this out.' The fact was I was not able to test, because I was recurring at the time on a show called *Nowhere Man* with Bruce Greenwood, and we were shooting in Oregon. So I was in Portland on the day that this test was to occur, and from what I understand they actually did test a couple of actresses, but they decided in the room just to go with me because I was the one they wanted in the first place. I literally just got a call on the set saying, 'You got the job.' And I had to go from Portland straight to Vancouver to start doing the pilot, so it really knocked my socks off. It was the best possible way to get a job and the easiest job I ever got!"

Asked what first put her on the path to becoming an actress, Megan replies, "Probably my mother, because she had been an actor when she was young and it remained something that she loved to do throughout her life. She took a break because she had six children, so I think that got in the way of the career path for her, and now that I have two kids I understand why. I can't even imagine having six! She just had a great love for theater and a great sense of fun, and we saw lots of things when I was a kid. My big birthday present was going to see shows on Broadway, so she certainly nurtured that. But I also think that there's just something in you that makes you want to do that. You almost don't have any other choice, because you're going to find that thing, one way or the other."

Were there any screen stars that served to inspire her? "Mary Tyler Moore, actually. I thought she was amazing, and I continue to think she's amazing. Also, people told me when I was younger that I looked like her, and when she was younger I think that's actually kind of true."

Another iconic actress had a more direct influence. "Katharine Hepburn probably [inspired me] more than anybody else," Megan reveals, "and then I got to meet her. In fact, she played a significant role for me a couple of times. I met her once; she came to see a play I was doing in New Haven, Connecticut, and was very complimentary. She knew one of the cast members really well; in fact, I think she was her godmother. It was at the Long Wharf, a wonderful theater in New Haven, and it was a play that was very much the kind of play that she might have done. It was a Paul Osborn play from 1936 called *Oliver Oliver*, and I was playing the young heiress in it, so I was sort of playing her part. The fact that she came back, liked it, and was complimentary was really special."

Hepburn would play a more active part in the young actress' career when Gallagher was cast as Lieutenant Commander JoAnne Galloway in the Broadway production of Aaron Sorkin's *A Few Good Men*, which premiered at New York's intimate Music Box Theatre in November of 1989. "She came to see that on the opening night. In those days Frank Rich ruled the roost in terms of critics and real criticism that was going to affect your play in New York and on Broadway, and if he didn't like something then it was probably not long for this world. He said that he liked all the actors but he wasn't that wild about the play. It was a wonderful play and it was a very successful film, so whatever—I suppose it's all completely subjective—but it was a lukewarm review and it was an extensive production. I was the only woman in it and then there were nineteen men, so twenty cast members for a straight play is a lot of people to have on the payroll, and if you don't have an expectation that you're going to completely sell out then it's an expensive undertaking. The producers, I think, were really on the fence about it, and yet before we opened we did a few weeks of previews and the audiences were crazy happy with it: standing ovations every night.

"There was huge enthusiasm built in the city for it and then we got a lukewarm review from Mr. Rich and they were thinking about closing it. Then Katharine Hepburn called Robert Whitehead, who was one of our producers, just this great producer. He produced Tennessee Williams plays and so on. We had this amazing group of people putting this play together. She said, 'That's just ridiculous, Bob. I loved that play. It's marvelous!' And she came back, and she complimented all of us, and so I got to meet her again and it was a lot of fun. He said, 'Kate, could I quote you on that?' And she said, 'Yes, yes. Let me think about exactly what I want to say, and I'll call you back.' So they hatched this plan. It used to be that quote ads were always quotes from critics, especially for a play on Broadway, but the quote was from her and it was from a person who actually saw the production. So they tried to counteract the lukewarm review by doing this thing, which also got its own attention, and she gave us this wonderful quote. That got its own publicity, and I think in certain ways she single-handedly kept that play open in the first few months. It was crucial to build the audience and make it a success, so she did that. She formulated a quote, they ran a big ad in the *New York Times*, and that was it! So instead of quoting Don Simon and Frank Rich and whoever else, they quoted Katharine Hepburn and it was a really big deal. It was a full circle fan experience with her for me. It was really amazing to encounter her and have her affect my life. It was very cool."

Fast-forward to 1996 and, having made the move from Portland to Vancouver, Gallagher immediately began work on *Millennium*'s ambitious pilot. She cites a striking example from the filming of the episode to illustrate a key aspect of her approach to her craft. In a particularly naturalistic scene, Frank brings home a puppy as a surprise gift for Jordan—to both her and Catherine's obvious delight. Representing a sharp contrast with much of the episode's dark tone and content, it is a moment of pure joy captured on film. "I knew it was going to happen; Brittany [Tiplady] did not," Megan reveals. "Acting, for me—even though I trained—I've found the better part of it is hopefully about being in the moment, letting it go and not thinking about what the moment is going to be, but letting it play and wash over you. That's the deal. Technique aside, that's sort of what I'm going for."

Is this easier to accomplish in television than in theater? "Yeah, it's more necessary in television because the camera is right on your face. If you have a contrived moment, the camera is going to pick it up. If you look like you're acting, it's just going to be dreadful, because they're right there. You are literally telling stories sometimes just with your eyes, little tiny aspects of your face, whereas in theater it is a different thing."

As Megan explains, the inherent differences between the two mediums can have a profound effect on performance. "Theater actually feeds all of it, because you get to live through entire moments so, even though you've done them over and over again, because of the familiarity you get to be really loose. The challenge is different. You can just sort of play with something because you're not at all thinking about what this moment is all about. You've had a longer time to think about how you're going to tell the story, and so there is a certain freedom in that, because you are used to doing it. You can find the play in that, because you know what the structure is. You're playing against the structure, whereas with film it's a different kind of structure and it works in a more intimate way. Hopefully, in both venues the work is really intimate and personal and real, but you do get to that in a different way." Such intimacy, such plain honesty, was often shown in the interplay of the Black family at home in their yellow house.

"Television and film is really quick, which can help you with the spontaneity. There have been times where I have asked actors to change something or do something to surprise me when the camera is on me, because sometimes you'll shoot something so many times. You will do so many takes just because of the set-up or because it's a complicated scene; there are a lot of people in it and everybody has to repeat what they are doing over and over again. You're repeating this tiny little moment or a few lines in the overall picture and so I'll say, 'Surprise me! Just screw around with me if you want.' Because it will just freshen it up. But real is always what you are going for, and it does feel real. It's fun."

Whilst some actors would undoubtedly find it challenging to play so many scenes with a child—not to mention a boisterous Border Collie pup—for Gallagher, performing alongside her onscreen daughter was a highlight of her involvement in the series. "I was [worried] initially but it was dispelled because, for one thing, kids are so great. W. C. Fields used to say he would never work with children or dogs, but I completely disagree with Mr. Fields because they are so real. It's not that they upstage you, but they give you something really fresh. And when you can react to something fresh, I think it's great. It's really fun, because if your focus is really on them—as it should be on any actor, always on the other actor in the scene—then it's going to be new and very real and very spontaneous. The thing about Brittany in particular is that she is the sweetest girl."

In a personal gesture evocative of the aforementioned scene in "Pilot," Megan later gave her young co-star a puppy as a gift. "I got her a dog when I left the series. I used to talk about my dog, Henry, all the time and she really wanted a dog. So, of course, I went to her parents and said, 'I would love to get her a dog. Would that be okay with you? You guys have to pick it out, but I want it to be a present from me.' So we did that when I was leaving the show. But she was just a delightful little girl: just the loveliest person, so sweet and very bright and just had the best attitude. We had a really natural rapport; it was just so easy. What a doll baby! She was the best."

Brittany Tiplady's performance as Jordan Black touched the hearts of many in the audience, but the effect upon Gallagher's own personal life was to be quite profound. "I have to say, I credit her with actually making me kind of want to have kids. At that point I was in my late thirties and I was thinking if I wanted to have kids, and being around her all the time and playing her mom gave me this other really rich experience with a little person, and I think it encouraged me to allow that to happen in my life. She's a sweetie pie, so sweet and so natural and very down-to-earth. I also credit her parents with that too because they were also just very nice people, and some of that comes from the home environment and the fact that they were very down-to-earth and very sweet, not like showbiz parents at all, just nice people."

Of the actor portraying her onscreen husband, Gallagher reveals she was already very taken with his previous work. "One of the many things I had been impressed with was *Aliens*," says Gallagher, recalling Henriksen's legendary role as the android Bishop. On set, her appreciation for the actor grew. "He was just as nice as could be. David [Nutter] wanted to do some rehearsal days before we started to shoot, which is good especially when you are playing husband and wife and you have to have some kind of a rapport. You don't want to just meet and do it; you want to spend a little bit of time around a person. He was just really great, charming and kind. I told him I was a big fan. I think that showed, that he's a really good guy. My husband had also met him years before, literally on an elevator. They were both up in Vancouver shooting different things and he met Lance and told him he was a big fan, and he was just as nice as could be."

Somewhat unusually for the male and female leads of a television series, Frank and Catherine's relationship was portrayed in a subdued and natural way. The fact that they were a married couple allowed their relationship to eschew the dramatic clichés of sexual tension and instead center upon the maturity of their partnership. "It's an interesting perspective in terms of what came across and what we were doing and what that relationship was about because there was a lot that was in the ellipse; it was very elliptical in many ways. It was a real relationship. As anybody knows who has been in a real relationship for a long time, it does become much more about the friendship and the relationship and your priorities in life, and not that other stuff that they put on, which is silly and a little too light for real life."

There was, however, a marked and deliberate contrast between the two characters. "My character was supposed to represent the potential for healing. He had to deal with the crazy, psychotic, serial-killing, dark people that were the monsters that live in the abyss, and I was supposed to represent the other side, which was hopefully healing and overcoming. She was a psychological social worker and hopefully able to help people, so they were meant to be diametrically opposed. I think that can provide good balance in a relationship too—I mean in life."

Chris Carter has spoken of the importance and the challenges of ensuring that Catherine—and by extension Megan—had an active involvement in the series beyond simply serving as a spouse to Frank Black. Gallagher is able to situate such concerns in a wider context. "I think every show tries to find the ways in which it can branch out, and I think the concern in the first season was that it was going to be a freak-of-the-week show, that Frank was out there and that he would solve these things, but that essentially it would go through the same emotional loop over and over again.

"They were trying to find other ways to involve these people and what they were capable of doing. What was their position, what was this character bringing to the table? Because otherwise it was the guy who drank blood, the guy who did this, the guy who hid inside the open houses... To me, that episode ['Wide Open'] was the most terrifying—apart from the pilot, of course, which was one of the most deeply scary, haunted things I have ever seen! I remember I took a bunch of friends to a screening in Hollywood before it premiered, and the mouths-sewn-shut thing was horrifying! My friends, who love that sort of thing, and my husband—who is a big horror aficionado—thought it was great, but I have some friends for whom the show was just too dark. I loved *Seven*, and there was a lot about the show that was similar. It has a similar style, from the credits to the set decoration and the look of the show, and that was a pretty popular movie. So I was more on that side; I could appreciate it. It was talked about early on and I thought, 'Cool, I remember that.' So I was glad. But at least my head didn't end up in a box; I wasn't beheaded!"

What was the biggest challenge in filming the series? "Just in general, the schedule was really rough because we shot a lot of nights. The hardest thing to play emotionally, certainly, would have been the goodbye, at the end [of 'The Time Is Now.'] It's not hard, but when you have to do those really intense, emotional moments… That and the day that I was tortured [in 'The Beginning and the End.']

"Along those lines, those were the difficult times, but just in general, in terms of the show, we shot a lot of nights. We would finish very often around five-thirty in the morning on the Saturday morning and then would have to be back at six on Monday morning. So to go home on Saturday, sleeping until one or something, get up, have some dinner or lunch… You just feel like you are in a fog for the day. You try to get in bed on Saturday night, because you didn't really have a real Saturday because you were so wiped, then try to flip your schedule back to going back to work on Monday. That was the tough thing, just the rigors of the schedule.

"I wasn't in every single episode, but there were these very heavy episodes, and we had a very generous shooting schedule, which was great. Fox gave us eight days with the regular first unit, then two more days of second unit. The two days of the second unit would overlap into the first unit of the next episode, so sometimes you were doing catch-up stuff from past episodes while you were also shooting the next episode. It was rigorous—that was challenging, physically—but, again, I didn't have kids then. I could just exist to do the work. I had a bunch of pets, but they are a lot simpler than human beings! I could just be there for that, and I had a pet nanny back in California so I had help even with that, and I was living in a hotel."

Season Two brought about some dramatic changes in the Black family dynamic, including a separation for Frank and Catherine in the wake of her abduction by the Polaroid Stalker. Gallagher welcomed this new direction. "I was interested in going some other places and doing some other stuff," she says, "because, as an actor, it's more interesting to do. They didn't want to replicate that same emotional loop too many times, and so you always want to go and do some more stuff. So I was happy to go along and do what they wanted to do. And then there was of course my abduction with Doug Hutchison, and that was fun! In real life, of course, I went to Europe and I did a press tour for the show. They said, 'Okay, you have a few episodes off, so we'll send you off and you can do some press,' which was great. I was happy to try whatever they wanted to do."

Another brief but striking change to the dynamic of the series occurs in the second season episode "Anamnesis," which saw Catherine take center stage alongside Lara Means, as played by Kristen Cloke, in the only episode of the series that does not feature Frank Black. "I liked Kristen—she was fun. We got along really well." The actress is quick to dispel any lingering controversy concerning *Millennium*'s sometimes dramatic second season creative shifts, as evinced by episodes such as "Anamnesis," insisting that such trials are only natural for a television series. "Again, every show goes through this. When you look at the growth of pretty much anything, you can look at the pilot and it can almost seem like a completely different series. You are setting up basic elements that are hopefully going to carry through for seasons and seasons, so you have to move with it in order for it to grow. It really has to happen. That was when Glen [Morgan] and Jim [Wong] had taken over the show. That episode was a lot of fun; I liked working with Kristen."

Would she have liked to have been involved in more episodes focusing upon Catherine's own work? "A few more episodes like that might have been interesting, but again I felt like that show fell out of the sky. I got to work with wonderful people for a long time, so I feel like that would be complaining. It's not my business to second guess or to say that I want it to be something that it wasn't. What it was was great, and I was lucky to be there. So that's my perspective on what might have been or wasn't. Sure, that episode was fun, there were other episodes that were fun, but the fact is that it's tricky to find what path to go on. For a while I remember there was a lot of feedback from people saying, 'Is he just psychic?' and that's not what they meant to project about Frank, because that's too simple. There's a lot of really complex stuff that they were taking on in those episodes. There's no easy trick in branching characters out and having them grow, and I think they did a perfectly fine job."

If Gallagher has any regrets regarding her experiences on *Millennium*, chief amongst these seems to be missing the opportunity to work alongside her husband, "Thirteen Years Later" guest star Jeff

Yagher. "My husband had to go on the show the year after I was gone, so I was no longer a regular," she explains. "I had died, and he played a character who had to imitate Lance. He was obsessed with Frank Black and he had to do that voice. He said it was so embarrassing to do that in front of him, because he loves Lance and thinks he's just awesome, and he didn't want Lance to think he was making fun of him in any way. He was just trying to get as close as he could to it. But the character—who turns out to be this psycho killer guy—was obsessed with Frank and he had to imitate him. I was doing another play, and of course he got that episode and was shooting it exactly when I was having my opening night. So he was doing my old show, the show I had just left." Fortunately, the amiable actress is able to laugh about this: "They couldn't cast him while I was there; we couldn't be together on the show—no!"

Despite Catherine's tragic death during the apocalyptic climax to Season Two, Megan Gallagher was able to return to the series for one final performance in the celebrated "The Sound of Snow," a deeply resonant story that depicts Frank Black mourning the loss of his wife. "It was fun," the actress says, recalling her days of filming the episode in a nostalgic shoot that stirred fond memories. "It was very cold, I remember. We were in this area called the Greater Vancouver Regional District, and it was very cold and wet up there in that shack. It was bittersweet, because you get to see everybody who you've been working with, and it was great to see Lance and Brittany again. I was off doing some other stuff, and we get used to that as actors—you do something for a while, and then you don't and you move on to something else. I think bittersweet would be the best way to describe it, but fun. It was great to see everybody again."

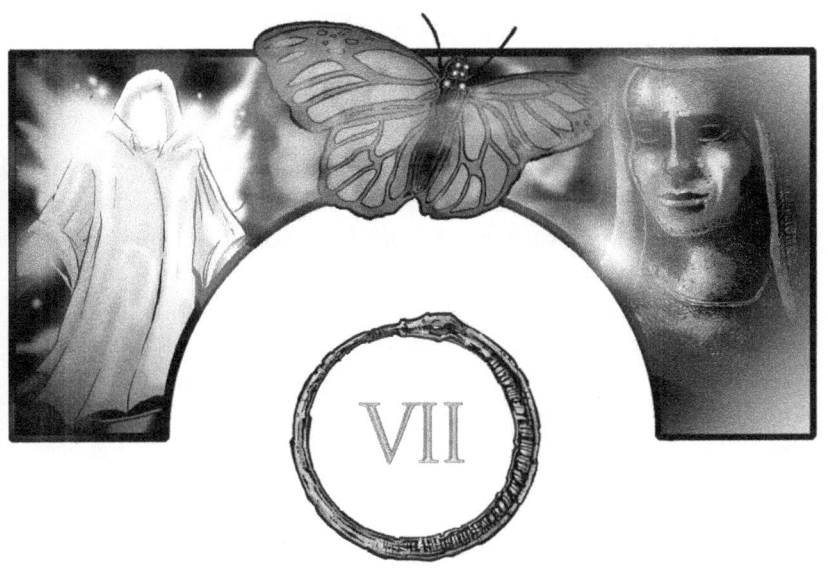

MAKE-BELIEVING IN JORDAN BLACK

by Brittany Tiplady

At five years old, I didn't know what "acting" was. I didn't know the magnitude of what I had delved into and what it meant for my future. All I knew was that I liked being around the funny, kind people that made up the cast and crew of *Millennium*, answering to the name "Jordan," and playing with the Border Collie puppy who would be my onscreen dog.

My first memories are cloudy. I remember walking into a room of smiling faces with a puppy in a cage and squealing so loudly that I hardly had to pretend to act the scene. I remember getting a phone call very late that kept my parents up all night talking in hushed voices in the next room. What I didn't know was that I had just been cast as Jordan Black in the new Fox series *Millennium*, and my life was about to get a lot different.

The next months of my time on *Millennium* jump in waves of opaque memory. I sharply recall shooting my opening scene for the pilot. Lance's voice—sharp and familiar like gravel—still resonates in my ears. I can remember my mom standing out of the shot as I peered out at her through the window of the red jeep. She waved at me with a smile from ear to ear. During the dialogue I, completely out of nowhere, decided to lick Lance's nose. Horrified at my mistake, for a split second I thought I might be in trouble. My ad-lib moment ended up being what the world first saw of Jordan Black.

When I think of my first season on *Millennium*, I think of my "fake daddy," Lance Henriksen, my "pretend mommy," Megan Gallagher, and the amazingly fun ladies in the makeup and hair trailer who did the Spice Girls dance with me relentlessly, day after day. I think about the craft services table with all the goodies my mom wouldn't buy at home, the catering trucks with hot food that never disappointed, the A.D.s shouting "stepping" before they walked up the trailer stairs, and costume fittings with clothes I wanted to take home. To me, showing up to set at 6 a.m. was the best time I could possibly have. Each new day of shooting meant time with the people who became my second family, people who treated my family as theirs.

Anything frightening, gruesome, or gory on set was hidden from me very well. I waltzed around without the knowledge that I was actually an actor on a very dark show, and that was something to be thankful for. I remember on one occasion a crewmember left a dummy in the open on set, and I saw it. I wasn't scared. To be honest, I was completely oblivious and unbothered, but that poor crewmate got in a lot of trouble. Being the only kid on set meant that I was made to feel more special than gold. I still can hear myself squealing as Bill Smitrovich—who played Bob Bletcher—would hang me upside down by my feet. I remember the redheaded camera guy—whose name sadly escapes me—who used to crack jokes so funny that my mom and I would both be doubled over, crying with laughter.

When the show aired Friday nights on Fox, my parents did the watching. I sat in the rec room, watching *TGIF* on ABC and waiting for my parents to call, "Brittany, you're on!" so I could have just enough time to dash to their T.V., watch a couple minutes of myself, and then trot back to my own set to watch what was, in my opinion, a far more interesting episode of *Sabrina the Teenage Witch*. This was the weekly routine for three years, and I was okay with it. I knew I was on a "scary, adult show," and that was fine by me. I would get asked for autographs every so often. People in the grocery store would recognize me and ask me to sign my name on little pieces of napkins found in the bottom of their purses. I never felt this was uncomfortable or weird; it was different, but so was my life and I knew all along that this sort of thing came with the territory. If anything, people's kind comments were encouraging.

But, of course, there was negativity and controversy that followed me, considering I was so young and involved in such a dark show, a show that dealt with the heaviest and most bizarre storylines to air on the Fox network. Once, my mom and I were at a pottery shop when some people in the store recognized me from *Millennium* and the discussion of my role in the show began. One lady interjected into an otherwise positive conversation with a burst of accusations, questioning how my mom could "allow" me to be on such a scary show. "I would never allow my child to be exposed to that," she ranted. It hurt. It also hurt my mom. I was acting. I was playing a role. It was T.V., make-believe, fantasy; nothing about *Millennium*'s storylines were tangible to me, except for the memories I took home with me every day from the family I had built on set.

During the first season, *TV Guide* interviewed me for a promotional piece on the show. From my memory, it was my first interview for any kind of publication and I answered each question with honesty. I was five; of course I was honest. And now, as a journalism student and newly working journalist, I have learned all about the power of a single interview and what journalists can do with the questions they ask and the answers they receive. When the piece came out a few days later, my words had been entirely manipulated. At five years old, you would be surprised to know that manipulation is something that can still be recognized. The writer had woven into the story the notion that I was haunted by nightmares after my time on set, that I clutched my doll every night for comfort so that I would not be scared. What? I remember clearly telling the interviewer that I slept with my blanket and doll every night. No mention of fear or the need for security from nightmares due to *Millennium* was said or suggested. After the piece came out, I recall speaking to my grandpa on the phone, furious. My grandpa is an incredibly smart man with a lot of knowledge on media and he told me to let it go, that it may not be the only time something like that would happen. Thankfully, it was.

The three years I spent on *Millennium* brought me so many things. Even as I'm writing, I run into more momentous events that I had locked away in my memory bank. I can still feel myself sitting at the Young Artists Awards of Hollywood when I was five or six, after my first nomination. I wore a green dress and was accompanied by my dad and grandparents, but I didn't take the award home that time. Hot tears poured down my face as my dad tried to comfort me. I wasn't usually the type of kid to be a sore loser but I think the excitement of flying to L.A., having pictures taken on a red carpet, and wearing a brand new emerald green dress would leave most five or six year old girls worked up if their name wasn't called. After the second season I was nominated again, but we decided not to attend and the award was not to be given for Jordan Black that year either. The third time was the charm in 1998 when I posed back in our L.A. hotel room in a burgundy dress, smiling from ear to ear and holding my first Young Artist Award.

Hearing my name being called was a strange. My stomach jumped into my throat as I hopped off my mom's lap and dashed up to the stage. My knees felt wobbly as I recited my planned speech to thank my mom, my dad, and my agent, Gary. I was eight; I had just wrapped three seasons of a high-profile television show, and I had just won a big award for youth in the film and television industry. That little statue still sits on my mantel.

As the show progressed, so did my role, and so did my relationships with the cast, the crew, the writers, and the directors. Playing Jordan Black became something more notable to me. I honed my role in a more mature way as the lines became longer, my storylines became deeper, and the show began to increase in popularity. Shows like the Halloween episode, or the second season episode in which Megan was getting sick and the virus was spreading, gave me more responsibility as an actress. I wasn't just the cute Jordan Black with easy scenes and lots of giggling. I had real lines and real performances to give, and I was ecstatic to accept the challenge. I wanted to spend my time rehearsing with my on-set tutors. I never had much trouble with memorization, but I always wanted to be sure that once I stepped a foot on set for blocking that I knew what I was doing. And in the last two seasons, when I began to find myself as Jordan, I fell in love with the intricacy of performance.

MAKE-BELIEVING IN JORDAN BLACK

The day I found out that Megan wouldn't be returning for the third season of *Millennium* was a sad one. My mom and Megan went off and spoke for a while, and I was desperately anxious to find out what they were talking about and why I hadn't been invited. In the car on the way home that night, my mom told me that Megan was going to be written off the show. I was furious. I loved Megan. We had the same curly hair, everyone told us we looked alike, and she had the most soothing, buttery voice, a voice that consistently put me at ease after long days of hearing, "One more take!", take after take. But her parting brought me the gift of my first dog, Lucy, and for that generosity I couldn't be more grateful.

To me, Lance truly was my "second dad" and Megan was my "second mom," and I thrived on their continuous positive energy. We were an onscreen family unit, and any rifts that formed on set were hardly visible to me. Going to "work" was like going to hang out with really fun adults who became my friends and also my mentors. As I grew a little older I cherished more and more what I had on *Millennium*. The American Doll Lance gave me one Christmas, or the gift baskets from Fox, the way everyone smiled as soon as I was in my trailer and ready to go. It was the best learning environment for a young kid breaking into the T.V. industry and I consider myself incredibly fortunate to have had that experience.

I think what surprised me the most about working on *Millennium* was how fans viewed the show. Once every week or two, my parents and I would sort through the pile of fan mail I had received and, using special pens we had bought specifically for writing on photos, sign pictures with "Best Wishes" and "All the Best," then send them off to the people who had written me letters of encouraging words. Fandom wasn't something I really questioned. Every now and then I would get grumpy after my left hand was smudged with ink and I had signed more photos than I had bargained for, but my parents were adamant that it was the polite thing to do. They said if people are kind enough to send you nice letters, it is your responsibility to answer. They were right.

There were times when I would receive mail that wasn't of the sort that should be answered. Letters arrived from male penitentiaries throughout the years which, of course, we ignored. However, those were the letters that really put into perspective the power of being on T.V.—who's watching, who's listening, who remembers your face. It is a different feeling to know that every Friday night millions of people saw my name flash onscreen as the show started, and millions of people heard my nasally little voice recite lines as Jordan Black. I don't think I really grew into that concept until much later in life.

It has been some time since I said goodbye to the cast and crew of *Millennium* and I packed up my specially made, monogrammed director's chair, but I was able to relive some of those moments while writing this piece. Participating in the highly emotional podcast reunion with Lance and Megan and the Back to Frank Black crew last Christmas was like opening a time capsule that flooded me with so much memorable joy. My time on the show opened doors of experience and fortune, and it took me and my family on a once in a lifetime adventure. My life as Jordan Black is preserved in countless framed photographs and that little statue on my mantel, objects that remind me that I am lucky to have been given the opportunity by Chris Carter fifteen years ago to play Jordan on such an impactful show.

98% LESS SERIAL KILLERS:
A CONVERSATION WITH
GLEN MORGAN & JAMES WONG

Interview by James McLean & Troy L. Foreman
Written by Adam Chamberlain & Brian A. Dixon

Millennium (1996-99) is a television series that underwent an unexpected but remarkable evolution. From the moment Frank Black and his family step foot into their yellow house on Ezekiel Drive, their lives begin to change. Dramatically. During its second and third seasons, the series received criticism from some quarters for straying from its original concept. Many claimed the series was continually gravitating towards territory arguably more appropriate to *The X-Files*. Glen Morgan, one half of the creative team that stepped in to executive produce Season Two, argues that, in fact, any inspirational link between the two series was mutual. "I think that *Millennium* had influences on *The X-Files*," says Morgan, at once turning the suggestion around. "I think that some of the graphic nature of *The X-Files* got more intense once Chris and we all started doing *Millennium*. They had an influence on each other."

Indeed, just two weeks before the premiere of *Millennium*, in October of 1996, an episode aired that is arguably the single most graphic of *The X-Files*'s entire run. Written by Glen Morgan and his longtime collaborator James Wong, "Home" features the repulsive Peacock family, inter-breeding mutants who live in isolation from the world and mete out brutal, primal violence upon any they perceive as a threat. Airing in the Friday 9 p.m. timeslot that *Millennium* was to inherit from *The X-Files* a fortnight later, the installment provoked a sharp response. "We got in big trouble for that," recalls Wong. "I remember it was really quite controversial, even though we didn't think that at the time we wrote it."

The writer goes on to reveal the unusual origins of the episode. "We had four ideas for that season of *The X-Files*—or, actually, we were obligated to do four episodes—so we came out with four ideas and we thought about which one we should do first. We decided we should do 'Home' because it's the most straightforward, down-the-middle episode. I remember I was in Hawaii, sitting by the pool, and I met this gentleman who was a dentist, and he told me a story about one of his patients, who was bald but whose head was blackened. The patient said, 'You don't have to do any Novocain for me—there won't be any pain.' He said this gentleman literally went through a very painful procedure that would normally have a person squirming in their seat even with Novocain, but in this case this gentleman didn't feel anything. He came back three months later and this time he had hair, and the dentist realized that his patient was one of those few people who literally could not feel any pain, and that usually when those people get injured they don't really know that they are injured. So from that we got one of the attributes of the Peacock family, that they would feel no pain.

"Then, in a Charlie Chaplin biography, he describes going to a town and [visiting] a friend's family who gave him a meal at their home, who liked him so much that they were going to show him a very special family member. He went to a room and they just slid this kid out from underneath the bed, and he was just a stump—he had no legs and no arms—and they stood him up and they started singing and clapping, and this kid was from his own generation. So that became the Peacock's mom. Then I think Glen was reading about nature: how cruel and sadistic nature could be, that nature is not this 'live and let live' world. All those forces combined to make that show."

Having been immersed in the creative process of pulling the episode together, Morgan and Wong were unprepared for the outraged reaction it would provoke. "We did it and we thought it was pretty straightforward," says Wong, "and then we started getting phone calls from executives saying, 'You guys are sick! What is wrong with you?!' We said, 'What's the matter?' They said, 'You have incest! You kill babies!' And I just said, 'Well, I guess that is kind of sick.' I thought it was a cool episode, but they hated it. It became such a controversial show that they ran it with something else on Halloween and advertised it as a show that had never been re-run before, and then they didn't re-run it for a couple of years. They never showed it again."

In spite of the network's misgivings, "Home" remains a fan favorite, so much so that the Peacock family was considered for a return outing a year later, during Season Two of *Millennium*, once Morgan and Wong were in charge of the series. "We thought it would be a great Halloween sweeps episode," reveals Wong. Morgan explains, "I approached Fox and said, 'What if Frank Black came across the surviving members of the Peacock family?' and Peter Roth said yes. So we started working that out, I checked the actor Karin Konoval's availability, we were ready to go, and then the lobbyists in Washington for Fox or News Corp. or whoever it was called up and said, 'Those characters never appear on television again!' So that was that."

The Peacocks may have never crossed over to trouble Frank Black on *Millennium* but viewers would continue to seek out points of comparison between the series and its precursor on Fox's Friday nights. Wong insists, however, that the two series are distinctly different. "When you compare *The X-Files* to *Millennium*, with *The X-Files* you could always do something funny even though it was creepy and scary. Mulder's funny—you could always do something quirky, and at the end it didn't always have to be these horrific things that people do. With *Millennium* you had to go much darker than *The X-Files*, so it was harder to get into. Or it was easier to get into, but harder to get out of, I think."

In Morgan's opinion, any similarities between the series owe more to a style inherent to the work he produces with Wong than to any intentional cross-contamination between the two Ten Thirteen properties. "I remember at the time people said we were just trying to do that," he recalls, "but what Jim, Darin [Morgan] , and I did on *The X-Files* is what we do. You can see what Jim and I did in *The X-Files* is in *Final Destination* and *Willard*, and the other stuff we have done is what we like to do. So some of the tone and some of the humor—they thought we were trying to do the Lone Gunmen with the character of Roedecker—is just what we did." There was, of course, one deliberate crossover: "Specifically with 'Jose Chung's *Doomsday Defense*,' Darin had really hit it off with Charles Nelson Reilly and so he said, 'I want to do this.'"

Morgan goes on to attribute much of the style of *Millennium* to those crewmembers who were integral to realizing its trademark tone and style. "I really believe that *Millennium* has a great deal to do with Rob McLachlan, the director of photography, and Mark Freeborn, the production designer. At that time, people were copying what *The X-Files* did, which was a very cold, blue-gray color scheme, and for what Rob and Mark could do working hand-in-hand with blacks, browns and ambers—which weren't really seen as horror at the time—I thought that *Millennium* had such an incredible look. It was warm and yet their art work helped so much to imply that there was something going on with Frank Black, with the Millennium Group. I couldn't say enough about those crewmen."

The partnership between Morgan and Wong was established long before they took control as executive producers on *Millennium*'s second year. "Jim and I met at El Cajon Valley High School," remembers Morgan, "about fifteen miles north of Qualcomm Stadium in San Diego. I think we met in Mrs. Brooks's Honors Advance Placement English. We both wrote a short story, and he liked mine, and I liked his. Jim went to Loyola as an engineering major, I went there as a film student. He saw that my final exams had questions on *Annie Hall* and he goes, 'Forget it. I'm not an engineering major anymore.'"

Naturally, Glen Morgan also grew up alongside his brother Darin, the acclaimed writer of such singular *Millennium* installments as "Jose Chung's *Doomsday Defense*" and "Somehow, Satan Got Behind Me" and a slew of equally remarkable episodes of *The X-Files*. "I'm four years older," Morgan points out, "so with everything I would venture into—say playing Little League baseball—Darin would come along and be the greatest Little League player ever. Then I did drama in high school, and he came along and was the greatest actor ever. So I can't get rid of him."

Together, Morgan and Wong's first job in entertainment was serving as ushers for a movie theater in San Diego. "I got fired for sneaking people in to see *The Wiz*," Morgan remembers with a laugh. "I saw the first half of *Beatlemania* forty-five times, I think. But then the first real one was when we went to Loyola Marymount University. Our friend Patty Whitcher, who is a huge producer now, got a job at Sandy Howard Productions, and she brought along a lot of people from Loyola... We were all hired to be runners. I was actually hired to answer the phones, and that was a bad mistake on Patty's part. She told me, 'If you can't answer the phones by noon, I'm gonna fire you.'"

The duo's involvement with Chris Carter's creations was the result of a decisive career choice made just as the Ten Thirteen universe was beginning to take shape. "Jim and I had been at Steve Cannell's company and we were on *The Commish*. We were leaving that series, and Peter Roth had been the president at Cannell, and he had gone over to run Twentieth [Century Fox]'s television studio. He had this show, I read the script, and it didn't really register with me. Jim and I were going to go onto a show called *Moon Over Miami*, which was a romantic comedy, and we hadn't seen the pilot but that was what we wanted to do. Columbia was going to do that and we were all but signed on, and our agent said, 'Peter Roth is begging you to watch this pilot.' Of course we had to do that as Peter really did a lot for our career. We went into the Creative Artists Agency and we watched *The X-Files* pilot and we thought, 'Wow, that was really good! We'll go this afternoon and watch the *Moon Over Miami* pilot, and that will be that.' And we went and watched the *Moon Over Miami* pilot and we went, 'Uh-oh,' and so we decided to go onto *The X-Files*. Columbia just yelled at us, and everyone wondered why we would do that because *Moon Over Miami* was expected to be the hit show. Then Peter introduced us to Chris, and Howard [Gordon], and Alex [Gansa], and that was that." Beginning with the unsettling "Squeeze," Morgan and Wong would script some of *The X-Files*'s most distinctive and celebrated installments, episodes that unquestionably influenced the hit series and its supernatural storytelling.

Their talents as screenwriters would not go unrecognized. Within two years of the debut of *The X-Files*, the duo had their own series on Fox, the science fiction wartime saga *Space: Above and Beyond* (1995-

96). Of all their projects, this is the one Morgan values the most: "*Space: Above and Beyond* will always be the closest to my heart." During that year, the two began to work out a division of responsibilities that made their heavy workload more sustainable. Wong recalls, "We were there until ten o'clock at night every day on *Space*, and it was really stressful all of a sudden." Their respective roles would often vary, although the duo was content to have all of their work co-credited. "Every project, it changed for the most part," says Morgan. "We'd go, 'Here's this idea,' and then we'd work it out. In *Space* it was so insane—I wrote a lot of the episodes and Jim would go cut them, but not all the time. And the same with *Millennium*—he was writing or cutting while I was doing the next thing. So it varied, and I think we had always been not secretive but private about how we went about things. Sometimes partners get into, 'I did this, he did that,' but we never did."

After the cancellation of *Space: Above and Beyond* after just one season, Morgan and Wong felt a responsibility to the series' ensemble of talented actors, including James Morrison, Tucker Smallwood, Rodney Rowland, and Kristen Cloke. "We all know that it's a business and it can get cancelled," Morgan acknowledges, "but we went back to do a few *X-Files* episodes the next year and I told Chris, 'I'm writing four episodes, and each episode is for one of the actors of *Space*.' That was the deal, and I thought that could get them exposure to a wider audience. I think James Morrison actually did 'Dead Letters' on *Millennium* instead of *The X-Files*. Chris had said, 'Do you want to do both?' and we said, 'Okay.' I focused a lot on those four *X-Files* episodes and Jim was a little more focused on the first year of *Millennium*."

In retrospect, James Wong is quite self-critical about their initial contributions to *Millennium*. "I felt like we didn't do a superb job," he admits. "I felt Season One was flawed in some ways. We didn't really concentrate on it that much. We had to write two episodes, I think. To me it was really a lot of serial killing. It was pretty straightforward in that regard. We did an okay job, but I don't think we really had a grasp of what the show could be or what we would do with it. We were just following the lead: here's Frank Black, he can sort of flash on images."

Wong does, however, recall the inspiration for their very first contribution to the series. "We went to a crazy place in Culver City in L.A. called the Museum of Jurassic Technology. We were just walking around, and I found the 'Dead Letters' idea there. The really tiny images that the serial killer was leaving behind were inspired by an exhibit where there was an artist who was carving on a grain of rice, and he was also writing messages, either a sentence or a short poem. We thought that was really cool, and that was how that particular killer was leaving his imprint."

Whilst Morgan in particular bemoans the loss of *Space: Above and Beyond*, Wong remains more philosophical, recalling a pilot that never came to fruition and which may be more directly related to their opportunity to act as showrunners for *Millennium*. "We did another pilot called *The Notorious Seven*. I really loved that pilot and I think it would've made a very interesting show. It was basically that you take Michael Corleone from *The Godfather*, he comes home and he's framed for the Godfather's death. You had seven families in this city that were [led by] mob bosses, and so Michael's character—his name wasn't Michael—was sent to jail, and in jail he was mentored by this guy. The Michael character was really into magic and all that stuff, so he would go into disguise and go undercover into the bottom of each mob family, and destroy the family from within."

"So we had this pilot that we really loved," continues Morgan, "and Fox [thought], 'I don't know, it's kind of weird. We like it, but it's not on T.V.' And they said they would put it on the air for six episodes in March, which was basically a way of saying, 'Here's your six episodes—forget anything more.' *Millennium* had premiered to huge ratings, and the ratings had decreased slowly and had stabilized. The people running the network at the time wanted to ease off on the serial killers and have a little more humor and things like that. Chris had talked to us and we said maybe we would do it, and he was onboard with it. My memory is that he wanted to go back and be a little bit more focused on *The X-Files*. That's how that came about." Though the pilot for *The Notorious Seven* never did air, Morgan notes that sharp-eyed viewers can catch a glimpse of its rousing opening credits sequence during an installment of *Millennium*. "Actually, *The Notorious Seven* is on T.V. in 'The Curse of Frank Black'—he's walking by and there's a show on!"

"It was something crazy where this carrot was dangled at the same time as they were quashing our next show," suggests Wong, "and then they gave us a lot of money for *Millennium*. So for me it wasn't a reaction to *Space* being cancelled. There were other circumstances involved."

Lance Henriksen has said that when they assumed the role of executive producers on *Millennium*, Morgan and Wong's first duty was to issue cast and crew t-shirts bearing the tongue-in-cheek slogan, "98% Less Serial Killers." Indeed, it is the deviation from the so-called "serial killer of the week" format that most significantly marks their take on *Millennium* as different from what had come before. Their season-long reinvention of the series begins by tracing a comet's trail across the sky and ends with an apocalyptic tide of blood bringing pestilence and death to America.

Morgan goes on to talk about the reasons for the significant shift in direction for the series when the two stepped in. "The network had said, 'The serial killer thing is killing us.' We looked at it, Jim and I talked, and what was really interesting was the Millennium Group." Wong agrees, "It was always the conspiracy, the Millennium Group. There's a part of you asking, 'Are these really a good group of people? Why are they doing all this stuff?'"

The duo's interest in such enigmatic subjects was further piqued when they began to investigate the dramatic possibilities offered by real-life precedents in more detail. "When you start doing some research, there are always conspiracies about these types of groups, with the masons and the Bilderberg and all that kind of stuff, and that hadn't been on T.V.," Morgan states. "We were approaching the millennium and, when you started looking at it, every religion had this kind of apocalyptic literature. Maybe it wasn't really well known, because a lot of it was embarrassing to them, but it was really fascinating. Also, there was an anxiety about the approach of the millennium—which I think didn't really come to fruition until after the year 2000 had passed—but that was something interesting as well. To me, I didn't want to bail upon what they did in the first year with the serial killers—there are still serial killer episodes in year two—but there was an approaching anxiety about the next century, and it wasn't on T.V. It was a thing that if you went and pitched it and tried to set that up, no network would have bought it, so it was this great opportunity to incorporate these elements that weren't on television."

In spite of their intentions, their desire to diversify the storytelling rather than completely cast aside the tenets of *Millennium*'s first season, not everyone was happy with this new creative mandate. "It was intentional to put all that stuff in," Wong explains, "and then of course once you do it then there are complaints of, 'Hey, how come you didn't stick to what was the core of the show?'" Wong isn't interested in dwelling on any criticism, however. There was a consensus, he maintains, at the time that these decisions were made. "You can always go back and criticize afterwards, but everyone agreed on the path that we were going to take before we took it. We weren't just going in there and saying, 'We're going to change everything, and we're not going to tell anyone what we're doing.' Everyone said, 'Yeah, this sounds good, let's do it' before we did it. It was only afterwards that people felt like we went too far. I got to the point where I didn't really listen to that because I think everyone is entitled to their opinion, and lots of times I disagree, so I can't get into listening to it."

Morgan does acknowledge some stylistic oversights. "What I will admit to not knowing is that I remember Ken [Horton] coming to me at the beginning of Season Two and he said, 'What happened to the *cha-koom*?' And I said, 'The what?!' He said, 'Every act starts with the Polaroid picture thing and the *boom-boom*!' I said, 'It does?! Do we have to do that?' He was adamant. I was looking at some of these recently and I'm not sure I followed it to the tee, but for the most part the '*boom-boom*' openings were just so Ken would be happy. I think we lost the quotes for the most part. Year one had a quote at the beginning of every episode and I didn't know if that was feeling pretentious or if we should save that feeling for a really heavy duty episode, and they got mad at that. So they might have gotten mad at some of the little tweaks that we did and just disregarded everything."

Such disagreements over minor stylistic details were unfortunately often indicative of greater creative strife on the series, as Morgan reveals. "Ken and Chip [Johannessen] were less than thrilled with what we were doing. There were arguments and fights back then but—and I'm not just saying this to patch things up or sound like a good guy— the hatchet has really been buried. Chip and I walked the picket line together [during the Writers Guild of America strike in 2007 and 2008], and Ken and I had a flight back from Vancouver where we talked about all kinds of stuff, so everybody's friends. But at the time the guys who had been there the first year wanted to keep it that way, and Jim and I had a new way of going."

Morgan draws a parallel with his brother's work on *The X-Files*, observing that outlandish episodes such as "Humbug" helped open the series up to the breadth of its potential. "When Darin wrote his first *X-Files* episode with the circus freak, there was chaos! What was he doing to the show?! It was Chris Carter that trusted him, and it really opened up what *The X-Files* could do and made a lot of room for Vince Gilligan's work. So, when Darin did 'Jose Chung's *Doomsday Defense*' on *Millennium*, Lance especially despised it, but Chris understood what Darin had done on *The X-Files* and said, 'Okay, we're going to try it here.' And I think it did open things up for stuff that Michael R. Perry did in Season Three."

Darin Morgan's rollicking satires stand out, largely because they offer such a vivid contrast to the dominant tone of the series as a whole. As other writers for the series have expressed, *Millennium* wreaked an emotional toll on those who were working to realize such dark subject matter. "I remember, when we were told we were running *Millennium* Season Two, doing a lot of research right away because we were so behind already," recalls Wong. "I remember reading a lot of John Douglas books, basically a lot of research on serial killers and people who do horrible things. I remember reading all that stuff and that I just threw myself at it. I remember finishing at about three o'clock in the morning, crawling into bed with my wife, and thinking to myself, 'Okay, tomorrow I must get a gun,' because I was so freaked out by all these people and how they come upon their victims—people who, if your house is unlocked, would see that as an invitation to come in and kill you. I came to my senses the following morning after a good night's sleep. That's an effect that *Millennium* and the research I had to go into had upon me. It was a very dark show and in order to get there you had to wallow in that darkness yourself when you were running a show like that. Much later we did a pilot for Showtime that didn't get picked up, but they liked our work and they sent us *Dexter*, the book, to see if we wanted to write the series. I remember talking to Glen and saying, 'Do you really want to go there again?' It's a great series, but at that point at least I wasn't ready to revisit that darkness."

As a screenwriter, Wong compares his relationship to that darkness with the troubling connections that Frank Black makes using his gift. "I think it's interesting that Frank has this power. Often, I'm not sure he was interested because it has ruined his life, when you think about how he was afraid his daughter would have the same powers. We had alluded to that, and then Catherine was kidnapped, and there was all that crazy stuff." The origins for those plot threads that would prove so integral to *Millennium* in its later mythology can be found in hints and whispers during even its earliest episodes.

As it turns out, however, not all stories take shape in a strict linear fashion. "Some shows are crazy like that," Wong observes. "For instance, an *X-Files* we wrote was called '*Die Hand Die Verlezt*.' That idea came from talking to Howard Gordon a long time ago and we said, 'You know, Howard, you should really do a show where a snake eats a guy!' And he goes, 'What?!' We said, 'A snake eats a guy.' And he said, 'That's the end of Act Three, that's gold!' Howard never used it. He probably thought we were crazy—which we were. So when we came to the episode, we came up with that story from that image, as to how do we get to a snake eating a guy. But it's interesting that we started with a scene that ends Act Three and then we built the story around it."

Another of the duo's first season installments of *Millennium*, largely written by Wong, began with more cerebral musings. "I remember reading Norman Mailer's book about Gary Gilmore, [*The Executioner's Song*,] and I think 'The Thin White Line' was inspired by that." Each of Morgan and Wong's contributions to Season One—"Dead Letters," "522666," and "The Thin White Line"—offers something of a variation upon more straightforward serial killer themes. "I think that was our attempt to do different things," Wong concurs. "I think everyone realized, or at least we felt, that Season Two couldn't follow the same path, because you would run out of interesting things to say. I think that's why they brought us in to do it, because we had a very different angle on it that they were willing to try. It was courageous for Fox to try it. I guess they had nothing to lose, really, if they liked us."

Among those elements of the series that Morgan was most eager to reconsider was Frank Black's gift, which progressively grows more mystical with each new interpretation. For Morgan, the mystery inherent to that gift was something inherited from *Millennium*'s first year. "That was a constant issue. What is that? Is he psychic? Chris would sometimes say it was sort of an intense intuitiveness, but then they would use it in a way that seemed to imply that it was psychic, and we just went back and forth on that. There's also a scene in 'Gehenna' where he's seeing the devil, so that's more than just logging into a crime scene and getting an energy from it. I think that we approached it instinctively. Darin made great fun of it in 'Jose Chung's *Doomsday*

Defense,' and you just kind of knew when it was over the line or when it wasn't enough. Bringing in that Lara Means is seeing angels and things like that seemed to be a way to suggest, 'Could it be this or could it be that?' I think if anyone tells you definitively, 'This is what it was,' they are lying! I think it becomes a thing that it's neat that no one really knows."

The bold move toward a more mystical, supernatural, and open-ended storytelling is a quality that leaves Season Two open to multiple interpretations and ongoing debate. According to Morgan, some of the seemingly far-out concepts explored onscreen are more rooted in fact than many viewers realize. "I think if there's a mistake, we had done a lot of research. The Owls and Roosters were not just made up. There's actually that kind of stuff out there. My memory is that there was Hebrew apocalyptic literature that is just not talked about, and I think that we had touched upon a lot of these things that the audience doesn't know about. You probably don't know about it unless you've read about it. So that was our mistake, such that a lot of this stuff just seemed like it was crazy writers making stuff up. But, in actuality, I believe that it didn't hit or it causes confusion because a lot of people weren't aware of these obscure things that we were drawing upon."

At the same time, he welcomed the creative freedom afforded the duo, allowing them to explore such varied and obscure subjects in the first place. "I knew it at the time, but both *The X-Files* and *Millennium* were really lucky situations in that Fox left us alone. What happens more and more with a lot of these shows is that the network wants everything to be answered and tied up, not to be serialized, and then all this stuff becomes boring because it's getting back to the way it was in the Sixties, that it all had to be wrapped up in an episode. And the good ones don't, the good ones leave a lot of room for talk. So I'm thrilled that people are still talking about it."

Wong agrees with this outlook on television narrative. "I remember being very proud of the work we did in Season Two because it really felt like we were stretching the bounds of that T.V. show. I loved the fact that we could do an act with Kristen that was basically a music video of her going crazy, and that people allowed us to do it. We were given an opportunity to do some crazy stuff and they let us do it, which I'm always surprised and happy with."

Such commentary references another signature aspect of Morgan and Wong's work—the use of popular music to complement or enhance particularly intense onscreen action. Which creative choice tends to come first: the scene in which the music will be used, or the song itself? "It depends," Wong muses. "I think what we did for *The X-Files* [episode 'Home'] was we found that after the 'Wonderful! Wonderful!' thing happened we loved the effect of that. It was not only a juxtaposition of the standard emotion of a song like that with the contrast—that was what we were going for. Sometimes we would choose a song because you know the effect that you want for the scene already, or sometimes you think you need something, but you can't get the song so you have to go for [another song with] the same tone. But I believe at the time we really felt like the schmaltzy contrast between the songs and the images was what made it work."

If reactions to their efforts on *Millennium* were mixed, the creative partners were unaware of it whilst they were actually doing the work. "I wasn't as aware of it until after we had finished Season Two," says Wong. "I guess you just put blinders on when you are doing it, but I thought we did some good work, and I thought some of those episodes were amazing, particularly Darin's episodes. I thought they were fantastic. Not too many T.V. shows could have done those and done them so well, I thought, and 'The Curse of Frank Black' was terrific.

"I remember being very proud of some of the work that we did. In a season of shows, not every episode can be super. You do your best, but the schedule of shooting for television is this huge train rushing down the tracks towards you, because it never stops. You try to start ahead of time, getting some shows banked, but by the time it gets towards the end of the first third of the season you have to do all this work, and sometimes the stories get short-changed or the scripts are not as wonderful as they could be. So, not every show could be great, but I'm pretty happy and proud of the work that we did. I thought we put some really interesting ideas out there and told stories in different ways, so that you weren't just following the procedural from the scary thing in the teaser. I really feel like we were experimenting with the form as well as the content. I was happy with that."

Wong's pride in what he and Morgan accomplished on *Millennium* is evident in his voice and entirely well earned. "I just think we did some great stuff, so I was surprised. At least while we were doing it I didn't feel like people were unhappy with it, but I think afterwards, I guess, people felt it strayed too far from the origins of *Millennium*. And we were leaving again, so I think they felt, 'Let's put it back on track.'"

Some of the most extreme reactions to their artistic approach to the *Millennium* mythology were provoked by the fallout from the tumultuous finale of Season Two, the epic two-part story that unfolds in "The Fourth Horseman" and "The Time is Now." A thrilling, unique, and superlative segment of television, the second installment features one of the most inspired sequences of *Millennium*'s entire run, with the entire third act devoted to Lara Means's descent into insanity. The sequence contains surreal, frightening, and spell-binding imagery unlike anything else seen on network television before or since, all set to the strains of the Patti Smith song "Land." Glen Morgan talks about the inception of the sequence. "That was a thing from the time my roommate at Loyola listened to that Patti Smith album [*Horses*] over and over. One night in 1980 or whenever I thought, 'Man, I'd love to do a short film where someone goes crazy to this,' and it just sticks with you for all those years. Then one day you go, 'Well, here's this,' and you had an actress that you trusted, and I think we had worked Lara Means to that point that we could do that act just totally to that Patti Smith song. I always saw Means as [akin to the character Sam Lowry] in *Brazil*—the only way to escape was within her own insanity. I listened to the song over and over, and I scripted it out a lot."

The idea may have been Morgan's own, but he gives great credit for the sequence to one of *Millennium*'s most prolific directors as well as a veteran editor. "I had great trust with Tom Wright, the director, who we'd met on *Space*. When you get into the Directors' Guild you have to be sponsored by two members of the Guild, and his card was signed by Robert Wise and Alfred Hitchcock! He did the storyboards for [Alfred Hitchcock's final film] *Family Plot*, and I would just hound him with Hitchcock stories. Also, there was a Rod Serling series, *Night Gallery*, which began with these paintings that introduced the stories. Tom Wright did those paintings. So when we did that sequence I had a lot of it scripted, but there was a part where you'd just say to Tom, 'Shoot weird stuff!' There was one overhead shot of Kristen lying there in roses—and that came out a year before *American Beauty*—and then Rob McLachlan and camera operator Mike Wrinch would get these squishy lenses and all kinds of stuff and just torture her! They put her in jet-black water and threw stuff at her, and had her throw stuff at them, and when it was all done you just had this sequence and Tom and I and the editor, George Potter, got all this footage.

"George Potter had been an editor in the old *Mannix* days, the Quinn Martin type of deal, 'two shot, close-up, wide shot, out-of-scene' kind of cutting, and George had been working as a runner because of ageism. He was this really good editor who was just driving around getting post-production people coffee. We brought him onto *Space: Above and Beyond* and he cut 'Who Monitors the Birds,' which is an odd episode for T.V. We got all this footage and all this stuff with Kristen losing her mind, and the Patti Smith song, and George Potter literally took his shirt off in this hot editing room and just did this kind of weird music video."

"The Time is Now" subsequently inspired a segment on NPR's *Morning Edition*, in which host Barbra Bradley vividly describes that Means's vision "careens through images of natural apocalypse—fires and hurricanes and floods—then lurches through scenes of man-made destruction: an atomic plume, black helicopters and SWAT teams, the scream of a monkey with Ebola virus." Given the chaos and sheer insanity of this imagery, on a first viewing one might miss the dramatic achievement inherent to the hallucination. Morgan stresses that the sequence is not only visually striking, it also advances the episode's story. "When you watch it, there's information coming through. The horses come through: one is red, and then it cuts to the Iraq war, because in Revelation there would be war and pestilence and disease. So then the yellow horse could come through, and you would cut to the Marburg virus and the jungle. There was a lot of information going through." Though this be madness, yet there is method in it. "It wasn't like we were just throwing any weird shit we could up there. It could've been better if we'd had more time, but I was really extremely proud of that, the way that everybody came together for that. That was my favorite moment of *Millennium*."

The episode also ends in dramatic fashion, with Catherine presumed dead from the Marburg virus, the outbreak seemingly out of control, and Frank Black having suffered a breakdown. His hair has turned gray overnight and he is slumped, staring into space and apparently suffering internal flashes of static. Morgan discusses the origins of that unforgettable final scene. "I like a cliffhanger. Lance, all year long, had been less than thrilled about dying his hair—he wanted to go gray. Here's how these creative things come about. He wanted to have his hair go gray, and I was trying to figure that out. I knew that my grandfather apparently broke his back, and that night in the hospital his hair turned gray. So there are cases of a catastrophic event that can turn a person's hair gray. Then Darin and I were coming back from a Chargers game, and we were upset that Fox had not given us any promo in the championship game or Super Bowl or something. We were so mad, thinking, 'Couldn't we get a thirty second promo in the Super Bowl?' We said, 'Okay, for every second that we believed we should have had a promo on the Super Bowl we are going to show static.' So that's how that came about."

"The Time is Now" makes for one of the most dramatic season finales of all time, but it also posed a formidable creative challenge for the incoming producers that were to replace Morgan and Wong. The duo denies that there was any question of the series' cancellation, that they deliberately tried to paint the series into a corner, or that they were seeking to return the following year. "No, never," confirms Morgan. "Chip, Ken, and Lance were less than thrilled with us. We did what we were brought in to do—the ratings went up a bit and it brought it back for a third season. It just seemed like it was time to move on. With *Space: Above and Beyond* I knew that it was done and so I killed them, and we did a series after *Millennium* called *The Others* that was on NBC, and I knew that was going to be cancelled, and Kristen killed everybody! I knowingly thought this is going to be a thirteen-part story and this would be a mind-blowing way to end it, and if by some miracle it came back there were ways to get it back. So those two times I knowingly killed everybody off. But no, [in the case of *Millennium*] there were escape hatches that would have led you into year three from year two."

The incoming producers ultimately decided to downplay this apparent Armageddon, addressing the events only indirectly at the start of *Millennium*'s third season. "Well, they did what they did," Morgan says, shrugging it off. "They were so angry with us, or just didn't like what we were doing, or were unhappy that they would be unable to return to Season One, that they never came into the office and said, 'What are you doing?' I would've said, 'Okay, here are your escape hatches that are written into these episodes. Here's how you can get out of it.' But that's cool too, I'm not saying they should have done year two [again]. Jim and I left, and they were there and they had a great passion for that series. But it wasn't like we had tied this huge knot that we didn't know how to get out of. We never really talked about it, so it was weird to watch some of Season Three where there was this plague, and then we just forget about it. There were a couple of ways you could go. I just watched *The Road*, and that was kind of one of the ideas that we had—the show would just kind of become that."

For many, the analysis of Morgan and Wong's work on *Millennium* has benefited from the passage of time and the opportunity to take a step back and reflect upon their work. This includes star Lance Henriksen, whose schedule made it impossible for him to watch most episodes when they originally aired, but he has had the chance to do so since their release on DVD. Revisiting the second season has led him to a much deeper appreciation of its complexities, something he had been unable to attain during the punishing shooting schedule. "I sensed that at the time," affirms Morgan. "If you have somebody like David Duchovny taking issue with a scene, it's a totally different discussion. They're very different actors. They both have great instincts, but David is a paper away from a Ph.D. in English; Lance is extremely instinctive. Also, it's not that he wasn't getting it. I think that he was distrustful that we were making fun or trying to sabotage what they had done in the first year, when we were really trying to expand what the show could do. Lance had it tough. It was a hard show, really a difficult series to make, and there was a lot going on."

In retrospect, it can also be argued that *Millennium* gains a great deal, artistically, from its differing approaches over three distinct seasons. "Yeah, I agree," Morgan says with a nod. "I think it's tough, when you get a show on. The BBC and the British do it more often, for instance, with a show like *Alan Partridge*. The first year is this talk show, then the second year [shifts to a comedy about the character's ailing career]. I wish we could do it all the time, but here the network say, 'There's your format. Stick with it. Don't change it.'" He applauds "what Chris was able to do with those two series, to have such a variation from episode to episode based on the writer that wrote it or the director."

After so much controversy and creative conflict, is it fair to say that both Morgan and Wong have maintained a professional distance from the audience? "Well, you can't help it," says Morgan, "when you're away from your family, and it's twelve hours a day, and that series is in

Vancouver, and the cast and crew up in Vancouver are your family, and you are so dismissed." Wong agrees, adding that many in the audience lack an appreciation for the politics involved. "I actually do keep away from that most of the time, because there was that frustration that people don't really know how it works. When you do a T.V. show or a movie, you don't do it in a vacuum. There are all kinds of executives, there's all these people telling you what you need to do, but at the end of the day you take the brunt of the complaints. Nobody knows the executive's name who says, 'You've got to do this.' But then you do it and people say, 'Well, that really sucked!' But we had, really, no choice. We had to do it that way. Sometimes we really do suck—you make a mistake when something didn't work at all that you thought would work. But if you take the accolades of random people then you have to take the criticisms of random people. So I've found it easier just not to look at it, and go on with my business because yes, I take responsibility for the things that have my name on them, but it's not as simple as everyone seems to think it is."

That said, Morgan notes they would try to offer nods to their previous work whenever possible, much to the delight of their dedicated fans. This included having a Chig—one of the alien adversaries from *Space: Above and Beyond*—make a fleeting appearance on Halloween night in "The Curse of Frank Black." "I loved our *Space: Above and Beyond* fans," he beams, "and there were just little things that you could do. You didn't want to interfere with that tale that was being told of *Millennium* and Frank Black, but if it was just an inside joke and it didn't really interfere then we were going to go for it, just to acknowledge that Jim and I appreciated that they were out there."

Some of these incidental references—such as the aforementioned bursts of static seen in "The Time is Now"—were directed at Fox or other controlling parties. "Well, they enjoyed their digs, I bet," says Morgan. "There was Darin's little sequence with the Standards and Practices guy [in 'Somehow, Satan Got Behind Me'] and they loved it! We were really good friends with the Standards and Practices executive, Linda Shima-Tsumo, and she had taken a lot of grief for 'Home.' We were close with her, so from that sequence that Darin did where the guys look up at the traffic signs—'No Testicles,' 'No Butt Jokes'—she has all of those."

Television has changed a great deal since *Millennium* had a home on Fox's Friday nights and, Morgan and Wong have observed, the once strict boundaries of censorship have since shifted. "I think it has changed quite a bit," says Wong. "Watching television I will think, 'Oh my God—can they say that? Can they do that?!' I remember, going through Fox's Standards with *Millennium* and *The X-Files*, that there were so many things that we had to cut out. On *Space: Above and Beyond*, there's a gag that Wang says where he uses the word 'testicles,' and they wanted us to cut it out. We refused to cut it out, and they actually cut it themselves and left a hole in the show. So that was then, and now I am just shocked at what they can show and say. Also on *The X-Files* there was an episode about vampires, [Season Two's '3,'] that David Nutter directed, and there's a shot in a garage where gasoline is poured all over the place, and they light a match and the lodge goes up in flames. They made us cut out the shot were the match ignites when it strikes against the book, because that was too demonstrative. They felt like if they didn't show how to light a match then kids won't know how to. I don't know what the heck their thinking was, but that was the sort of thing they refused to let us show back then. But you flash forward to now and it's completely crazy what they allow." He ascribes much of these changes to the trail blazed by cable channels such as FX, Showtime, and HBO. "I think those things have made the broadcast channels decide they'd better catch up, otherwise they're going to be left behind."

Following the apocalyptic tumult of *Millennium*, both Morgan and Wong's careers have led them in a variety of directions in both film and television as producers, writers, and directors. Do they have a preference, for either a medium or production role? "That depends which film or T.V. show you're doing," answers Morgan. "I could have done *Space* forever, I really enjoyed *The X-Files*, the *Final Destination* movies are really difficult to make but they are fun to make. Randy Stone—the guy who had moved to Bucksnort—was the airline host in *Final Destination*. He had cast David and Gillian in *The X-Files*, and Kristen and I met in his office. He passed away last year—he was just a great friend—and guys like that had so much influence over those shows."

For Wong, both the disciplines of writing and directing appeal. "I like both of them, for different reasons. Writing I like because you get to spend the time at home with your family, and when you're writing almost anything is possible. And then directing, you find that not everything is possible—the restrictions of the world come in. But that's also a challenge at the same time, so that comes at you in a different way. When you're directing, you're working with a lot of people and I like that also. So they are great in different ways. The fact that you can write anywhere by yourself is great, but at the same time it can be really frustrating, in particular when it's not going well, and you say to yourself, 'I hate this!' When you are directing you are with a lot of people, and so it's fun, and it's social, and you're getting creative ideas from other people. So that part is really great but then there's all the pressure too, because you have very limited time and money just pouring out every moment that you are working on the film, so there's all this pressure. I think they're both great."

Do the two ever go back to look at their work on *Millennium*? "I watch 'Jose Chung's *Doomsday Defense*' probably once every three months with my kids," confesses Morgan. "Man, I love that episode. And it's a third of what it was, because he was long. There was so much more to it. If you listen to it, you can hear Charles Nelson Reilly talking really quick because they had to cram so much into it. The original version was really great. Otherwise, here and there but not so much. Sometimes, if I'm working on something now, I don't want to inadvertently steal or repeat something, so I'll go back and look at it to make sure that something I'm working on now is not just a memory from a show."

The duo, whose names will forever be linked in the minds of Ten Thirteen devotees everywhere, are clearly and justifiably proud of their work on *Millennium* in spite of the challenges it presented. James Wong credits the Back to Frank Black campaign, dedicated to seeing the return of the series' singular protagonist, with helping *Millennium* to endure. "You guys have really kept the flame lit on the show. That, I think, deserves attention. It would be cool to see something come of it. And I'm glad to have been a part of it."

THIS IS WHO WE ARE:
SECRET SOCIETY AND FAMILY REDEFINED

by Gordon Roberts

group (ˈgrüp) • individuals who share some relationship.

fam·i·ly (ˈfam-lē) • a domestic or social group.

se·cret so·ci·e·ty (ˈsē-krət sə-ˈsī-ə-tē) • a group or organization involved with secret knowledge or hidden activities that is concealed from nonmembers.

Much has influenced and changed the traditionally accepted definition of the family. As a society we have moved a considerable distance from the ideal of the Cleavers on *Leave it to Beaver* (1957-63) or the Robinsons on *Lost in Space* (1965-68). Those were traditional nuclear families—a father, mother, and child who shared a home.

Family has assumed a much different complexion above and beyond the emergence of combined families, as seen on *The Brady Bunch* (1969-74). Our understanding of family has assumed far more complex designs and now includes a mix of multi-racial members, gender-specific families, adopted children, and even divorced and remarried spouses, as reflected in the ABC sitcom *Modern Family* (2009-). Today, the family is seemingly beset with innumerable external challenges. Television's *Millennium* (1996-99) offers its own traditional family under siege in the Black family.

On *Millennium*, criminal profiler Frank Black (Lance Henriksen) is the patriarch of his own nuclear family, comprised of his wife Catherine (Megan Gallagher) and daughter Jordan (Brittany Tiplady). It is small in size and in keeping with the times. Throughout the series Frank is lured by an outside family, the fictional Millennium Group. The Group, an endlessly fascinating creation of creator Chris Carter, would evolve beyond the scope of its initial design. The series gradually reveals the push-and-pull dynamic of the family subjected to the whims of the secret society as central to the protagonist's life over three substantial seasons of television.

At the heart of Carter's series is Frank and his family. Outside of that union stands the shadowy, external influence of the Millennium Group, a variant of the secret society similar to the Mafia that redefines the concept of family for Frank as much as the concept of family has been redefined by social mores and norms over passing generations. This essay will consider the effect of the secret society as a family group, like the *Cosa Nostra*, on the traditional family establishment as presented in *Millennium*.

On its surface, the Millennium Group is essentially innocuous in the first season of the series. There is a heroic component to the mysterious unit, a unit that would ultimately function as something of a surrogate family to Frank. It serves to ground our profiling hero along with his own family unit for a common good, offering a stronghold for hope. The Group is a representation of security and strength that complements those ties to family which reinforce Frank internally. The Millennium Group, while covert in nature, symbolically represents those elements of the nuclear family that grant us resolve and fortify us. On an almost mythic level, the Group serves Frank in this fashion. It is a cornerstone to the series mythology as much as Frank's family was the keystone to his own character. These are foundations.

THIS IS WHO WE ARE

In his book *Freemasonry and its Image of Man: A Philosophical Investigation* (1989), Giuliano di Bernardo considers the social function of Freemasonry, writing, "The society of masons consists of men who have partial anthropology in common... which can however be integrated with other anthropologies" (5). Those bound by blood, or not, shall find common union. It is by our very biology, our anthropology, that we form social groups organized for security or other common purposes.

Frank is drawn to the Group based on a desire to protect his family. His gift of second sight allows him to see evil in its true form. Placing his family out of harm's way is his greatest desire. It is the reason for his geographical relocation at the very start in "Pilot." Frank moves his family to what he believes to be a safer harbor. That is his hope. An upper middle class home painted yellow with white trim, surrounded by flowered gardens, represents the family ideal, an ideal that Frank requires. Inside the safety of those walls is a place for the family to be nurtured and to flourish. The protection of wife and child, of family, is a natural human aspiration.

Fictional mobster Tony Soprano (James Gandolfini) of HBO's *The Sopranos* (1999-2007) faces similar concerns as he balances the family with his Mafia responsibilities in the pilot episode of the series. "It's the link—a connection. I'm afraid I'm gonna lose my family... That's what I'm full of dread about. It's always with me." Frank understands dread. It surrounds him, too. Even Michael Corleone (Al Pacino) wonders in Francis Ford Coppola's *The Godfather: Part II* (1974) if his responsibilities in running the "family" will result in the loss of his own family. He asks his mother if his late father, Vito, ever worried he could "lose his family." There is significant stress on those walking the line between these worlds. *Millennium* offers a constant struggle between light and darkness. Frank's life is one of balance between good and evil, yin and yang, and his two families inevitably represent and symbolize the elements of that struggle.

By the time of *Millennium*'s second season, Frank philosophically ponders, "Which am I?" He asks if his existence is of consequence or to be lost among the meaningless, broken rubble of evil that drifts across the universe like so much stardust. Keeping evil at the gates is part of Frank's internalized struggle for survival. Keeping evil restrained and his own heart of darkness controlled is a part of who he is. Alone, Frank is lost, but through his family he is defined. Amidst a swirling potential apocalypse, Frank looks to family and, for a time, the Millennium Group.

The family as a unit of security defines who we are. Before the Group, Frank is a husband and father. This is the foundation of his unflappable strength, his inner calm. He does everything within his power to love, protect, and serve the family. In turn, the family returns that devotion. Amidst dark forces, the family fortifies Frank's identity. The yellow house is a symbol of protection and that strength. The inevitable loss of that house symbolically represents the dissolution of that which he aims to protect—his ideal of the family.

The apocalyptic atmosphere surrounding Frank is only magnified by his compelling gift of second sight, which in turn fortifies his instincts to secure family. While he is not a religious man—as evidenced in the conversations of "Kingdom Come" —Frank is endowed with a spiritual gift of faith. Frank is at war and that faith in family merely magnifies his ability to ward off evil. He is compelled to do battle with the other side, driven by the instinctual need to protect his child. That other side understands Frank, too. It is instinctively hell-bent on finding and engaging Frank as one of its greatest adversaries. A restrained Lance Henriksen conveys a character that served as one of television's strongest and most subtle symbols of faith and family.

Frank explicitly understands the nature of the war. His brother senses it, too. In "Sacrament," Thomas Black (Philip Anglim) pleads with Frank out of frustration: "You don't see it, do you, Frank? You bring it upon yourself. It's a sickness. You can't just keep it locked away in the basement." The basement of the yellow house could easily be interpreted as a metaphor for the soul. Frank knows he is doing all he can to maintain control and this underscores that which fuels him: "I would do anything to protect you and yours." He is maintaining control in the only way he knows. After all, the world-weary Frank is a measured man. This man of measure takes information, dissects it, breaks it down, and articulates solutions. This is who he is. Without understanding evil, without his innate gift to break it down, Frank would lose control. This sense of clarity elucidates his clearly defined sense of family. In a sobering moment for Frank, his brother calls the big picture into perspective. "You can't keep them from us, can you, Frank? You can't keep them from any of us." Inevitably, it is his engagement with forces of evil that strengthens Frank's need to fortify the fabric of what matters—his family.

THIS IS WHO WE ARE

In a rare moment, Frank illustrates his uninhibited, unchecked, potentially explosive nature at the start of Season Two. "The Beginning and the End" sees the character abandon those traits that have defined him, control and measure, when his family is jeopardized. Colleague, friend, and Group brother Peter Watts, played with steady affirmation by Terry O'Quinn, is drawn closer to Frank. Peter assures Frank that he is not alone. Frank is lifted by the support of the Millennium Group family. The men connect and the Group makes efforts to bridge their connection to Frank in a moment of personal weakness.

Season Two offers a radical departure from the rhythms of Season One, especially in its approach to the Millennium Group, its intentions, and its impact on the Black family. In "The Beginning and the End," Frank is rattled by the Polaroid stalker, who infects his world. His circle of trust is violated by an infiltration of evil. He speaks to Jordan with some degree of anger and reacts to her with frustration for the first time. This is the same world his brother Tom warned he could not conceal or constrain. Frank is uncharacteristically shaken by these events. "I've known this dangerous level of anger," he bemoans. "I've never felt so helpless." Peter comforts Frank, assuring him, "That's why the Millennium Group is here, Frank, why it always has been." The Group is a conduit, an instrument through which Frank can channel his gift and protect his immediate family. Likewise, the Group acts as an extension of that family. Di Bernardo writes that "the idea of Brotherhood dates back to the remotest times in the history of mankind. It can be supposed that the bond that first tied one man to another was that of blood and that subsequently this was extended to the tribe or community" (26). The Millennium Group is a brotherhood to Frank and, like Freemasonry, has a rich history of assembly, as we discover.

When Catherine is abducted, the failure weighs heavily on Frank's heart. That time-worn face has been hardened by relentless wickedness. Family relationships require work and Frank wonders what he must "sacrifice" to see Catherine returned to him safely. He confides in Peter, who in turn makes a deeper connection with Frank, sharing his own family story, explaining how he came to be the father of three daughters with a deeply personal revelation. Peter acknowledges he was drawn to seek justice in a war against unrelenting evil. "I'm starting to wonder if you can sacrifice one thing to get another," he confides. "I know there's a price to be paid." In that painful, heartfelt exchange between Peter and Frank lies a cautionary tale of consequence. Nevertheless, Frank is drawn in by the promise of the Group, and the bond of the Millennium family strengthens.

In "Gehenna," Peter is accompanied by Mike Atkins (Robin Gammell), a Group member who would return in "Powers, Principalities, Thrones and Dominions." There is a significant hit taken personally by Frank and by the Group itself in the latter entry with Atkins's brutal death. The impact is like losing one's own; it is like a death in the family. In "Lamentation," Frank's family is the target of Lucy Butler. The walls of familial security appear to be cracking as the first season nears its end. This reality becomes all the more apparent when Frank loses his close friend Lt. Bob Bletcher (Bill Smitrovich). The threat is compounded when evil targets Atkins. The apocalypse is coming and the deaths of Atkins and Bletcher are a direct violation of Frank's personal security and family code. They mark the loss of non-traditional family members. These are deeply affecting losses. We observe the traditional reaction of law enforcement to losing one of their own. The notion that "he was family" proves to be a reality within such circles. Frank's bond to both of these family units is in question as Season Two develops. Frank confides in his wife Catherine as a lover and the matriarch of his family. He confides equally in Peter as his Millennium Group partner, his professional support system. In fact, the image of family strength that is found in Frank, Catherine, and Jordan as a unit is mirrored beautifully in parallel by visuals of Frank, Peter, and Atkins conferring as associates in "Powers, Principalities, Thrones and Dominions."

For Season Two, Chris Carter handed the reins of *Millennium*'s mythology-building to showrunners Glen Morgan and James Wong. Combining law enforcement elements with a deeper, secret society-like culture merely hinted at in Season One, Morgan and Wong took the Millennium Group in a far more complicated direction. Family relationships are always complex and Season Two takes Frank's connections with Catherine and Peter to new heights. Relations are dynamic things always subject to change. They are not static. Even the best of families endure hardships. Some break apart, but even those separated remain family. *Millennium*'s second season subjects Frank, our moral center, to new stresses, new challenges, and greater self-examination.

THIS IS WHO WE ARE

In any family, there is the potential for dysfunction. As we know, members associate for a mutually beneficial purpose. Despite dysfunction, this is why groups prosper for decades. Sadly, Season Two presents Frank Black with his own familial adversity and dysfunction. Until "The Beginning and the End," Frank remains on the periphery of the Millennium Group family. Only the incident of Catherine's abduction allows Frank greater influence and input within the clandestine organization. Trust is opened to him. Time is required to gain trust and acceptance.

Peter indicates unapologetically that the Group had prior knowledge of Catherine's abductor. Frank is alerted to this information after the fact. Family secrets have the potential to fracture any group. These revelations have a psychological impact on Frank and affect his relationship with the Group. It is information. It is there. It cannot be undone. Such disclosures can have resounding consequences within families. If secrets and lies remain unattended, demands unanswered, they can fester and damage longstanding relationships, causing dysfunction. Frank understands membership is required for full access, but the seeds of uncertainty have been sown. The dysfunction within Frank's own family also reverberates throughout Season Two, running parallel to the dysfunction within the Group organization. This runs contrary to the established relationships that were markedly different for Frank in each case during Season One.

The Millennium Group is based upon the Academy Group, Inc. (A.G.I.), founded in 1989 by Dr. Roger L. Depue, a former chief of the F.B.I.'s Behavioral Science Unit at the F.B.I. National Academy in Quantico, Virginia. The Academy Group is comprised of former law enforcement professionals. The first season of *Millennium* remains true to this original template. Of the transformation of the Academy Group into the Millennium Group, Carter has said, "They think what I'm doing is actually quite responsible, [though] of course... they think that I took a little bit of dramatic license with the vision" (Endrst).

That original outline or model would become wholly different as the Millennium Group was later twisted beyond Carter's original plan. Morgan and Wong took the organization into territories of intrigue. The Group later exemplifies an amalgamation of both law enforcement and criminal elements. In the second season, there is something more nefarious at play within. The fictitious creation moves into more ambiguous territory, more of a secret society than a law enforcement entity. These changes suggest facets often attributed to a score of societies in the show's evolving Group dynamic.

The marked contrasts evident within the Millennium Group, the distinction between its benign portrait and origins and the more malevolent designs established in the second season, is dramatic. The myth-building approach for the second season separated this organization from the first season's criminal profilers. The development of the Millennium Group initiated by Morgan and Wong would incite controversy. In his autobiography, *Not Bad for a Human* (2011), co-authored with Joseph Maddrey, a baffled Henriksen would later decry, "How can you call the Academy Group evil?" (261). Henriksen took issue with the direction the series took. In particular, in one of *Millennium*'s greatest missteps, Peter, Frank's "best friend," is progressively transformed into a foe. The move left Henriksen stunned at script readings and prompted an intense response: "Oh fuck, why did you do that? Why?!" (261).

Writer Michael R. Perry has stated that Morgan and Wong were shooting for a "substantially different thing" than Carter. They were looking for "far-reaching world conspiracies and, if not a Masonic conspiracy... something like that" ("Turn of the Tide"). This certainly presented a far richer, more complex fusion of family and secret society. Wong himself explains, "I was doing research on the Knights of Templar and the Masons, and it seems like all those groups had other groups who were against them and betrayed them. There was so much intrigue. I realized that is how groups act and I thought, why shouldn't the Millennium Group have the same thing?" (Vitaris 22). "The Hand of St. Sebastian," "Owls," and "Roosters" would illustrate this approach. Henriksen captures the essence of the threat the Group would come to signify: "Any secret organizations that you know something about—you become a danger to them if they want to remain secret" ("Turn of the Tide"). The Millennium Group was headed down dark roads.

"The Beginning and the End" throws down the gauntlet. Morgan and Wong had planned a different path for Frank. Following Frank's murder of the Polaroid stalker, Catherine draws a line in the sand over her husband's connection to something darker. While Frank wants nothing more than the warmth and assurance of family for his own peace, the lures of evil and his connection to the intricate world of the secret society as a surrogate family would prove undeniable. Frank was about to embark on "a long series of trials and temptations," placed squarely between the Group and the yellow house—*Millennium*'s powerful symbols of family (Henriksen 249).

During the course of "The Beginning and the End," Peter reaches out to Frank, attempting to control the handling of the Polaroid stalker. Frank is seething with Peter given he has confided in his surrogate with the very meaning of family itself. Peter is instructed by another voice from within the Group: "He's only doing what we should have done by now. Help him." This aid withheld initiates a significant turning point for the hero as he aligns his focus on the nuclear family and rescuing Catherine. In the final minutes of the episode, Frank is reunited with his family and his control, but at what cost? His relationship with Catherine and Jordan has been irreparably altered by allowing the Group into the yellow house. Speaking with her husband, Catherine says, "I feel like you lost something, sacrificed something for the safety of Jordan and me and I need time. You need time and distance to know if we can ever get it back again." Lives are changing and the paradigm of family is in question.

There was always an element of mystery to the Group, but here the plan alters radically. Frank's relationship with Peter and the Group is irrevocably changed, as any relationship would be altered through betrayal. An imbalance creeps into the tonality of the series and into those things Frank once placed his faith in.

In "Beware of the Dog," Frank's family dreams continue to dismantle with Catherine's request to sell the yellow house and her stated intention to move in with a friend. Frank's desire for stability is indeed being shaken to its foundation. Returning to their former home, Frank removes a "FOR SALE" sign from the lawn, insisting to Catherine that they will move back "when it's a home again." Frank never gives up on the dream. Evil serves as a wedge, and a family rift is evidenced with Catherine and in continuing tensions with Peter.

Confronted with his latest case, Frank is directed to Bucksnort, a town symbolizing the character's immersion into a world of secrets. He meets the Old Man—the spiritual guide of the Millennium Group, a version of the Mafia *consigliere*, an advisor, *Millennium*'s answer to Tom Hagen (Robert Duvall) of *The Godfather* (1972)—who confirms that Frank has a gift. "I don't have the gift anymore," Frank insists, directly addressing his turmoil and imbalance. The Old Man lectures, "Neither good nor evil can be destroyed, and both will always be here.

It's meant to be. 'The Lord hath made all things for himself, yea, even the wicked for the day of evil.' Our role is to achieve equilibrium. And as we do that we must respect evil and we must make evil respect us. But, at times such as now, events indicate that we're losing balance. And time is running out." The Old Man assures Frank that his gift will return "greater than before." Balance and harmony is what moves us. It is that which nurtures a thriving family, yet Frank's world is fractured.

As Frank strikes out on his own, a lone wolf, to work independently on a case in "Sense and Antisense," it serves to aggravate the Group. Parallels to the secret society as family become more pronounced. "Why didn't you tell me?" asks a wounded Peter. Frank insists, "I'm trying to feed my family, Pete." He is an associate rather than an integral part of the inner circle. Frank explains that since his separation with Catherine he has "two of everything." Family and the Millennium Group are in essence the social component of Frank's own personal sense and antisense. Peter returns the focus to the Group as a support mechanism—"We work together, Frank. You should have come to us."—assuring Frank he is going to become an important part of the Group. "You and I, the Group, we don't walk away." Peter suggests that a family sticks together. These are people that are tied not by traditional family responsibility but by a code of loyalty and tradition built into their society. Of course, there is a dark side, and the suggestion that one cannot walk away speaks to the silent oath made by one's unification with such groups. At the close of "Sense and Antisense," Peter alludes to a deeper knowledge of Frank's psyche. "It's in all of us if the switch gets flipped." He adds, "But you know that." Peter speaks in ambiguities. He understands the importance of maintaining secrets within.

The attraction and allure of the Group to someone like Frank is that of an extended family who shares resources and responsibilities. The collective group makes for a generally more secure group. What is the Millennium Group if not a cooperative of blood and non-blood related members assuming the form of an extended family? These notions are reinforced in "Monster," in which Frank meets Lara Means (Kristen Cloke), a fellow Group investigator. He continues to invest time in the Group in the hopes of establishing that connection. The Group monitors its candidates. "It's a test," Frank observes, a test to find evil, "and we passed." Their investigation in Arkansas is demonstrative of many recurring tests candidates must face to join a given group. Potential members are always subjected to tests. When a young Henry Hill (Ray Liotta) is brought to court but refuses to rat on his Mafia brethren in director Martin Scorsese's *Goodfellas* (1990), he is released. Hill is then rewarded, greeted by his Mafia family with congratulations for passing their first test. His ties to them quickly begin to replace his blood ties.

In "Monster," Catherine begins to suspect displacement following her separation from Frank. She suggests an affair. In the case of Frank Black, however, there is not another woman but another family. With Frank in trouble, accused of a crime he has not committed, Peter intervenes to ask for Catherine's help. These two representatives meet to present evidence. They converge, a patriarch and a corresponding matriarch. Catherine suggests there is something extramarital at work in her husband's relationship with the Millennium Group: "I feel like I'm meeting with the other woman." With humor Peter replies, "I don't know exactly how I should take that." Catherine confesses her feelings, stating, "In my mind, he had an affair. He hid the truth. He had a life other than his family." Peter points out that her partisan view of things suggests the actions of a selfish man when, in fact, Frank's actions were intended "to protect his family—that is his life." Peter tells Catherine point blank, "There are people in this world who have a gift and, no matter how hard they try to ignore it, they know its true purpose, what that gift must be used for. This is who we are." Peter makes it clear that the other woman, the Group, is a family with a greater purpose, one that cannot simply be discounted or brushed aside.

In *The Godfather: Part II*, at a congressional hearing, a soldier of the Mafia speaks before an investigative committee. He is confronted with an inquiry: "You were a member of the Corleone crime organization?" He replies, "No, we called it the Corleone family, Senator. We called it the family." This is the perception from the inside. A similar pronouncement takes place in *Goodfellas* when Karen Hill (Lorraine Bracco), the wife of Henry Hill, says of her husband, "It was like he had two families." Peter and the Group are part of Frank's life and thus part of Catherine's life by extension. This is Frank's family. Peter pleads with Catherine, "He needs your help." Catherine, the proverbial wounded wife, wonders, "Frank needs my help? Or the Group?" She openly questions Frank's loyalty by questioning Peter's motives. Peter understands the need to protect the family, because even he has misplaced loyalty to the traditional family by twisting his priorities and trusting in the Group. This is the cost of Peter's compromised position, placing those he should protect in jeopardy.

The Millennium Group family's role as a secret society becomes increasingly evident during *Millennium*'s second season. The American Mafia or *Cosa Nostra* is defined as "our thing" or "this thing of ours." The loosely structured, secret organization comprised of families and non-family members lives by a strict code of conduct. This code of secrecy or silence is dubbed *omertà*. Both the *Cosa Nostra* and the Millennium Group keep their share of secrets. It is ironic the two should prove to be so comparable considering Carter's original intention was to model the Group after the Academy Group, a criminal-profiling entity. Nevertheless, though features taken from various secret societies are notable in the Millennium Group, included Freemasons, the Mafia offers a fascinating point of comparison.

The Millennium Group shares a similar approach in keeping their activities private. When Catherine asks to learn more about the Group in "Monster," Peter refuses to answer. "I can't tell you that and I never will," he barks, urging her not to get "too close to what we do." The open discussion of "family" business with non-member affiliates is not advised in either organization. A distinct facet of the secret society that is the *Cosa Nostra*, *omertà*, a Sicilian term for the code of silence, calls for members not only to remain silent on family matters but to actively avoid cooperation with law enforcement entities. *Omertà* speaks to the heart and fabric of that intersection between family and secret society—keeping the society secret. In the Third Season of *Millennium* Frank tells his partner, Emma Hollis (Klea Scott), "I don't know much about organized crime." Frank is far too close to the Group to consider the organization in this way. It is patently appropriate that *Millennium* should turn to a Mafia hit story to further illustrate these thematic concerns in the third season's "Omerta," an episode that explores the idea of the underground society on a more intimate level.

On the matter of cooperation, the furtive Millennium Group works with regional law enforcement agencies on federal, state, and local levels as befitting its own ends. The Mafia generally commits to the opposite approach, but there have been instances historically wherein the Mafia has cooperated with law enforcement. Beyond cooperation with U.S. Naval Intelligence during World War II, the Central Intelligence Agency established a relationship with the Mafia in the early 1960s in its efforts to eliminate Cuba's Fidel Castro, if the opportunity should present itself. Such historical events lend a palpable sense of reality to *Millennium*.

A hierarchy exists in the Group in much the same way a hierarchy exists within the *Cosa Nostra*. Though not identical, the structure suggests an order to these surreptitious societies. A flowchart of the Mafia would reveal a boss and an underboss, with a third, a powerful *consigliere*, as spiritual advisor. The boss and underboss oversee a number of *caporegimes* or "made men" who manage crews encompassing soldiers. In the effort to bring Frank into Group membership, having him speak with the Group's spiritual advisor or work with candidates as associates reveals a specific hierarchy.

The Millennium Group offers a fascinating, law enforcement-based parallel to the criminal syndicate and operates in a style not atypical of a host of secret societies. Prospective members of both groups are carefully considered and tested before formal admission is granted. Most such organizations have very specific traditions of admittance. Candidates for Skull and Bones, for instance, the student secret society of Yale University, are physically "tapped" out of a crowd of hopefuls during the annual selection ceremony known as Tap Day. Initiation is much more severe and grueling within both the Mafia and the Millennium Group. Initiation rituals for members of the Mafia sometimes involved the smearing of blood on a sacred image, preferably a saint. In "The Fourth Horseman," an enlightening backstory for Peter Watts is shared. He makes a blood oath, drawing a knife across his hand. Lara Means, as well, would undergo a unique entry ceremony.

Made men or men of honor are often required to carry out murders or contract killings to gain acceptance within the *Cosa Nostra*. The exact reverse is true for members of the Group. Candidates are rigorously tested for their gifts and law enforcement acumen and they are challenged with solving cases and finding killers. Individuals like Frank are serially tested. The Group family is bound by a sacred oath to "find the evil," as Peter implores. "This is who we are." Like members brought into the *Cosa Nostra*, once you are admitted to the Group you are a part of the family, given responsibilities as a soldier. Peter assures Frank that he is looking to induct him into the ranks: "I'm working on making you more than officially a consultant, because you and I, the Group—we don't walk away." A made man within the Mafia family is protected, untouchable, a part of that family until death, untimely or otherwise. Harm to a made man may result in retaliation. Henry Hill aptly describes the arrangement in *Goodfellas*. "It's the highest honor they can give you. It means you belong to a family and a crew. It means that nobody can fuck around with you. It also means you can fuck around with anybody just as long as they aren't also a member. It's like a license to steal. It's a license to do anything."

A member of the Group receives similar support, as Peter describes to Frank. The *Cosa Nostra*'s identification as "this thing of ours" in many ways mirrors the Millennium Group's own identification or calling card, "This is who we are." Both organizations possess extraordinary resources and shield their organizations accordingly. Tactically, segments remind us of a group working outside the accepted and established precepts of law. "We'll take care of it," Peter says, invoking the Group's ability to fix a problem in "19:19." It speaks to the influence and power of the secret society as an operation.

Members of the *Cosa Nostra* were not permitted to grow facial hair. This was an element of the Mustache Pete rule invoked by older Sicilian Mafia who came to the United States at the beginning of the twentieth century. It is ironic that the Millennium Group should have its own mustached Peter, a made man to render that rule a moot point.

Even the forces of evil closing in on Frank Black and opposing the efforts of the Millennium Group seem to assume the structure of a crime family in *Millennium*. In "The Curse of Frank Black," a vision from Frank's past, that of Mr. Crocell (Dean Winters), comes to him like a family underboss representing dark forces. "He's been watching you," Crocell warns. Speaking as a member of a sort of supernatural crime family, Crocell gives it to Frank straight. "Here's the deal, kid. Give up the fight, sit it out. Forget about this Millennium Group." Crocell cannot believe Frank has not been offered a better contract by his "boss" given Frank's innate talent: "I don't know why you're not being offered a sweeter deal." Deals represent a part of Mafia bargaining. In effect, Frank is asked to walk away from the battle with evil. It is suggested he turn his back on his Group family, which lives by the oft-mentioned code of refusing to walk away from such a fight. At its core, to this point, it is a group in direct conflict with the Devil himself. The Devil advises Frank to rejoin his true family, to return to Catherine and Jordan. Frank wishes that he could, but Crocell is a representation of Frank's imbalance, of his confusion between both families. Thus, Frank must continue his journey of discovery regarding the Group.

THIS IS WHO WE ARE

From a historical perspective, the Millennium Group as a cause dates back to 100 A.D. and the beginnings of Christianity. The writers cut their group from the kind of historical tapestry associated with the likes of Freemasonry, which dates back to the sixteenth century. The Millennium Group began to splinter around 998 A.D., beginning in Monti Sabatini, Italy, according to "The Hand of St. Sebastian," and this is an important component of *Millennium*'s myth arc. The Sicilian Mafia, while not as historic, can be traced back to the early nineteenth century in Sicily, following Italy's shift away from feudalism.

With "The Hand of St. Sebastian" we find that within the Millennium Group, like the *Cosa Nostra*, and despite the appearance of unity in any family or social group, there exist differences of opinion. There are factions. There are alternate agendas. There are traitors. And, as with the Mafia, there are rats. In "The Hand of St. Sebastian," Peter is working independent of the Group to determine "who we are." He initially meets with the Elder of the Millennium Group, the equivalent of the boss within the Mafia, like Vito Corleone (Marlon Brando) in *The Godfather*, further illustrating the Group hierarchy. Peter asks Frank to assist him in his quest based on faith alone. Faith and trust in partnerships are at the heart of any functioning family. Like any associate of a group or family, Frank is intentionally kept in the dark about many things. He is working for the Group, carrying out responsibilities, but he is not yet receiving the protection of a soldier within the Group's circle of trust. Partnerships are fragile, and schisms within begin to be revealed.

As they arrive in Germany to pursue their quest, Peter and Frank escape what is clearly meant to be a hit when their car detonates. These events recall some of the most horrific moments of *The Godfather*, *The Sopranos*, or *Goodfellas*. We are reminded of the fate of Tommy DeVito (Joe Pesci) in *Goodfellas* or Santino "Sonny" Corleone (James Caan) in *The Godfather*. When cracks in the family trust begin to appear, it rarely ends well.

More emblematic still is the legendary dinner sequence highlighted by a David Mamet-penned monologue for Al Capone (Robert De Niro)—in which he discusses the concept of a team before a room filled with gangsters—in director Brian De Palma's *The Untouchables* (1987). Capone lectures about "teamwork" and the value of the "team" before crushing the head of one of his lackeys with a wooden bat. The baseball analogy is thought-provoking. Why do we so passionately support our teams? What is family but teamwork? Al Capone expresses these ideas to his criminal family, proving the point that disloyalty results in expendability at the barrel of not a gun but a bat. In no other context are the consequences of disloyalty to the family hammered home more viciously. As *The Untouchables* illustrates, "rival gangs compete for control," whether in a turf war staged in contemporary Los Angeles or in the struggle for control over a "billion dollar empire of illegal alcohol" during the Prohibition era of the 1930s. These unconventional families thrive on teamwork. If you are not a team player then, in a manner of speaking, you are benched.

In "The Hand of St. Sebastian" Frank asks Peter, "Can I trust you?" How much do we actually know about our extended family? Frank has been a friend to Peter since the pilot, yet he is still uneasy and must ask this essential question. Lives depend on trust. Consider Liotta's Henry Hill at the diner with De Niro's Jimmy Conway in the final moments of *Goodfellas*. Trust was certainly the order of the day, but it was not on the menu between these men when Hill decided to turn rat and, for reasons of self-preservation, chose to protect the lives of his family.

As members begin to acknowledge one another with the refrain "this is who we are," *Millennium* begins to expresses the cult-like nature of the Group. But, as with members of the *Cosa Nostra*, there are rules. While in Germany, Frank meets in a clandestine location with another member, Cheryl Andrews (CCH Pounder), who, with verbiage likened to Mafia code, expresses her mission targeting Peter. "The Group brought me over here to bring him in. He's been acting totally on his own, under the auspices of Millennium, without authorization, without consultation… It's jeopardizing your candidacy." Andrews claims to be enforcing a "hit" on Peter. Betrayal within the family can lead to schisms, as is suggested in the episode's conclusion. Clan war is a legitimate reality as families jockey for power and control. In *The Godfather*, war is declared between the Corleone family and Barzini, Tattaglia, and others. It is no surprise the saga was drawn from writer Mario Puzo's own real life experiences. Outside of popular culture, violence inside of the Sicilian Mafia escalated into the First Mafia War of the 1960s as well as the Second Mafia War of the 1970s and 1980s.

There is little question the conspiratorial nature of the mythology-building that began to take shape in Season Two of *Millennium* grew out of the shadowy world of its equally intelligent sister series, *The X-*

Files (1993-2002). Scriptwriters Morgan and Wong adopted cues from their work on the previous series and intentionally upped the ante for *Millennium*. The duo took the Group from painstaking profiles of criminal procedure to the layered framework of a dark, serialized mythology. The seeds for their makeover were certainly sown in *Millennium*'s first season. In fact, while episodes like "The Thin White Line" delve deeply into the paralyzing darkness of evil, Season Two examines the dysfunctional forces fighting that battle against evil and considers the darkness within their own hearts. Forces working for the alleged good demonstrate something wicked in their own right. The Group family, entrenched in a morass of secret machinations and family strife, proves a far cry from the Academy Group mold.

The dual nature of Frank's loyalties to his own family and the Millennium Group is drawn out in "Midnight of the Century" at his daughter's Christmas pageant. The focus on his estranged father and his fractured past works in strange parallel to his own contemporary troubles at home and within the Group. Frank's gift is directly correlated to confrontations both past and present. Frank and Catherine argue over Jordan's inheritance. "She's got a gift. You can't suppress it," he insists. Catherine argues, "Your gift gave you a nervous breakdown. This gift makes you see horrible images. It's turned you away from your family—from your daughter. It's caused you to turn toward the Millennium Group. You don't see yourself withdrawing from your family."

The *Cosa Nostra* and the Millennium Group serve as family when the conjugal or nuclear family is shaken. Spousal eruption is familiar within the Mafia and, evidently, within the Millennium Group. On Christmas Eve, the night Frank lost his mother in 1946, he is torn between love for one and loyalty to another. This kind of internal friction within the nuclear family certainly is not uncommon in fictional portraits of the Mafia on television and in film. Family turmoil was a consistent reality for Tony and Carmela Soprano (Edie Falco) on HBO's *The Sopranos*, Michael Corleone in *The Godfather*, and Henry Hill in *Goodfellas*, and it is a reality for Frank Black on *Millennium*.

In "Luminary," Frank's worlds continue to collide. Peter escorts Frank to a secret location to meet with the Group. Frank is seated at the center of a circle. The surreal moment is reminiscent of *The Star Chamber* (1983) as an unlawful, secret organization holds direct judgment over the fate of men. The Group asks Frank if he remains a "viable candidate" for membership. The members present emphasize his flash of violence and his estrangement from Catherine. With his family fragmented they ask if Frank can commit "strength" to the family without jeopardizing their own secrecy. Surrounded by ten members, the Representative Board, Frank is pressed for answers. The matter of Frank's lone wolf approach to his wife's abduction is called into question. Loyalty is in question. One member inquires, "Is that how this works? Now you're with us, now you're not?" The society's safety, security, and survival, as in any family, are always the larger issues. Frank shoots back, "You know, I could have quietly retired from the F.B.I., and I'd be a father and then I'd have a wife and family, but I sacrificed that for the Group. I have done everything the Group has asked me to do." "Luminary" sheds light on the Group's required sacrifices, Frank's family conundrum, and the intensifying pressure from both sides.

The Mafia serves as a superb example of a secret society when compared and contrasted organizationally with the Millennium Group. The Representative Board itself is reminiscent of an internal unit within the Sicilian and American Mafia referred to as the Commission, an organized body of bosses that resolves disputes, offers consultation, and presides over various clan matters. The collective units differ in responsibilities but the spirit of the mission is there and the correlation is intriguing. Further, the group's board, in addition to considering initiations, serves to suggest comparisons outside of the Mafia. One of the landmarks of Freemasonry, according to the Grand Lodge of Connecticut, is the law that "no candidate may be received unless unanimously voted, after due investigation into his merits" (di Bernardo 62). The board must ask pertinent questions about the candidate out of a sense of self-preservation; they must safeguard the group.

Maddrey writes that Frank "explicitly rejects the Millennium Group" at this juncture (252). While agents within the family utter the collective code "this is who we are," the decisively independent Frank declares "this is who I am," refusing to utter the identifying phrase of the Group. The distinct difference between an associate to a criminal syndicate and Frank to the Group is that Frank is the reluctant candidate. Associates often look to their non-nuclear collectives for prestige and power, acting out of the need to belong. Frank, too, desires the family connection for a greater good, and his gift has paved the way for a natural association with the Group. His intentions are righteous and noble. The Group's intentions are far more ambiguous and perhaps crooked in their unyielding, unbending beliefs. This is why Frank never consummates his connection to the Group. He desires membership for the right reasons but never compromises his virtuous principles. There are too many strings attached. Frank cannot find the hope he requires within the Group, as much as he might desire it.

Frank's odyssey to Alaska in "Luminary" is undertaken without the Group's blessing. As a result, his access to the Group's computer files is terminated. Ultimately, his journey of self-discovery does not compromise the Group and thus he is not excommunicated, but therein lies the pitfall of a non-connubial family. Even if you are not married to it, you are. You are subject to the consequences of your decisions as in any family. At his request, Catherine goes to Frank's home to make contact with his Millennium Group computer account. Without warning Peter breaks into his home and subsequently removes his hard drive. Frank is considered a risk. The scene illustrates the treacherous, covert world of the society. How far is his new family willing to go? In the Mafia, nothing is entirely secret when it comes to the family interest.

Catherine, like Frank, appears lost as a result of their splintered union. The two are searching for answers. Catherine visits Peter at his home. He, too, is a man navigating a balance between family and his secret world. The stress of such effort by members is significant. Every day spent within the organization takes an emotional toll. Catherine asks Peter questions, but he continues to conceal understanding out of his loyalty to the Group. In truth, even Peter has questions, as "The Hand of St. Sebastian" establishes. In the end, Peter offers an overture towards Frank in a written note acknowledging that Frank is on his way to membership.

In Freemasonry, an approved candidate permanently becomes mason. "The constitutive act of the Worshipful Master gives the mason a dimension that only death can dissolve. Even if circumstances in life lead him to stray from Masonic principles, he would be considered sleeping. This means the Masonic dimension will never leave him and he will never be able to reject it," records di Bernardo (35). This concept epitomizes Peter's quandary and ultimately exemplifies the reasons that lead Frank to refuse membership. He knows he will never be free.

Moving from the concept of the candidate and once again focusing on the Millennium Group's overarching hierarchy, it is worth noting that, while decentralized, that hierarchy is comprised of individuals or candidates with unique allegiances to specific schools of thought, like the Owls and the Roosters. These divisions operate like Mafia crews led by *caporegimes*, whereby members or, in the Mafia's case, soldiers are often unrelated by blood but bonded by common purpose.

Just as there are schisms between families, we soon learn of these divisions within the Millennium Group. How fitting that one such division within the Group, revealed in "Anamnesis," should be dubbed the Family. This cell divided from the Group over specifics of mission and purpose. "Owls" reveals there are international implications for the Group just as there are international connections between the *Cosa Nostra* of Italian descent and the American Mafia, as posited in *The Godfather* and documented historically. "Only twice in two thousand years has the Millennium Group been so divided, but this is our darkest hour," a Group member declares. "I never thought members would kill members." He suggests a fraternal, benign relationship within the Group reminiscent of the Freemasons. Di Bernardo observes the non-confrontational code of the Freemasons, writing, "It follows that masons cannot cause conflict amongst themselves from their individually shared anthropologies" (5). Of course, historically, there have been schisms regardless of blood or bond in any group. This certainly holds true for the Mafia and the Millennium Group, which has been the subject of much past internal strife, as the mythology discloses.

The theft of the crucifixion cross from Damascus, Syria, and its later seizure at an airport in Jordan serves as the triggering event for the latest schism within the Group. The Group is comprised of Owls and Roosters. They represent a theological perception of apocalypse in direct conflict with a secular, naturalist, and scientific view; faith and belief (Roosters) oppose applied science (Owls). It is made to appear as if the Owls have stolen the cross to weaken the Roosters' faith—and make themselves invincible. Peter, a Rooster, insists, "I will not fight against our own unless we have proof." He also believes Lara and Frank are associates ready to become official members of the Group. Members of the divided family seek to acquire Lara and Frank, bringing them within their own ranks or faction. Like a crime boss reaching out to his advising *consigliere*, Peter and the Roosters reach out to the Old Man.

Wong and Morgan infuse elements from a number of societies into their modified Academy Group. Religious, Christian elements reflect such organizations as the Knights Templar, who protected elements of the faith as the Group protects the cross. Morgan says, "What was really interesting was the Millennium Group." His research concluded "there are always conspiracies about these types of groups, with the masons and the Bilderberg and all that kind of stuff, and that hadn't been on T.V., and we were approaching the millennium. And when you started looking at it, every religion had this kind of apocalyptic literature."

Millennium is occupied with secret political implications as much as it is with religious associations. Season Three's "Matryoshka" revisits U.S. history and J. Edgar Hoover's association with the Millennium Group within the *Millennium* myth arc. Interestingly, Hoover, the founder and first director of the Federal Bureau of Investigation, was a devoted Freemason. Historically, Hoover is a controversial figure. His tenure in the F.B.I. led to ongoing battles with gangsters in the 1930s both during and after Prohibition. In a scenario mirrored in the perversion of the Academy Group into the fictional Millennium Group, Hoover was a noted, dedicated law enforcement official who ultimately corrupted his own criminal justice innovations and perverted the process he created to varying degrees. The connection in *Millennium* is a fitting one.

In "Owls," Catherine is lured by a private company, Aerotech International, a front for a secret unit dubbed ODESSA. Could the shadow world of *Millennium* become any more shadowy? ODESSA, like those groups bound by a common symbol, reveals its associations to the Nazis in the use of a Germanic rune. The Freemasons utilize a square and compass. The Millennium Group employs the ouroboros, an amulet of a snake eating its own tail. These ciphers are accurately summed up by di Bernardo, who states that this is "symbolism as an instrument of the initiatic secret, and the oath as a commitment not to transgress it" (41). In *Millennium*, ODESSA defeated communism, the greatest threat to Nazi power, and now it has set its sights on the Group. ODESSA's roots trace back to the Nazi *Schutzstaffel* (SS), a secret unit in and of itself. The SS was eventually banned as a criminal organization in Germany after World War II.

ODESSA, like any subversive power block, works to generate a schism within the Millennium Group. This is a logical and perfectly realized fiction. The Nazis' rise to power epitomized the rising power of fascism. By the 1920s, Benito Mussolini made every effort to isolate and destroy the Sicilian Mafia from existence. The Mafia threatened governmental power and authority, and the controlling weight of a fascist hand was the ultimate weapon in crushing the crime family. Similarly, Freemasonry was assaulted by Mussolini during the rise of fascism in Italy. Mussolini gave a speech concerning the association of such societies: "To my friends, all my heart, to my enemies, all that is evil! Therefore, I will fight to the end against Freemasonry" (148). The fact that ODESSA, replete with its Nazi iconography, engages in efforts to destroy the Group reflects true history. Such ideologies were at odds with secret societies across Europe in the build-up to World War II.

Plenty of controversy circles the inner workings of the secret society. "There have always been those who've opposed the Group's methods and philosophy," admits Peter in "The Hand of St. Sebastian." In "Owls," ODESSA hit man Helmut Gunsche (Bob Dawson) operates specifically to incite a war within the Group by killing Gordon Johnston (Malcolm Stewart). He would later kill the Group's *consigliere* by terminating the life of the Old Man in "Roosters." Gunsche is an assassin working on behalf of ODESSA mastermind Rudolph Axmann (Ernest Lenart). Their relationship recalls that between enforcer Luca Brasi (Lenny Montana) and Vito Corleone in *The Godfather*. Such figures are triggering devices for violent conflicts. Gavrilo Princip, the assassin responsible for the death of Archduke Franz Ferdinand of Austria in Sarajevo in 1914, served to trigger World War I.

Persistent political and religious elements influence the stability of the traditional family as well as that of governments. Aerotech's vice president, Clear Knight (Kim Patton), interviews Catherine for a position. Clear has performed a thorough background check on Catherine, informing her, "You're perfect for us." She declares, "We only want the kind of people we want." These arms that reach out to the candidates, Catherine and Frank, continue to disrupt the traditional concept of family first established in *Millennium*. At one point Catherine looks to Frank, after weeks of separation, and tells him that it "felt like family there for a minute again." The traditional family in

Millennium is certainly an unstable proposition in Season Two, continually under assault by external forces.

As Aerotech continues to court Catherine, Frank reaches a boiling point with Peter in regard to the Group's influence on his life. He has respected the Group from a distance but it has become more than he could have anticipated. Frank feels misled and, to a degree, he blames Peter and the Group for his separation from his family. Peter takes exception, proclaiming, "You left your family, but you didn't leave us." Indeed, Frank has come to "accept" but not necessarily embrace their methods. Peter offers the Freemasons as an example of brotherhood, noting the organization's historical ranks included signers of the Declaration of Independence. He reveals that the seal of that order adorns the one dollar bill. Di Bernardo confirms Peter's points. "The authors of the Revolution for the freedom of the American people were nearly all masons. Fifty out of the fifty-six men who signed the Declaration of Independence were masons." He further lends evidence to the idea of a conflict from within the group: "Not all masons supported Washington and many continued to be loyal to the British Crown" (18).

Inevitably, Frank becomes uneasy about Aerotech, a company with no record of existence. Frank thanks Clear for helping Catherine. Towing the party line, Clear assures, "We're so pleased to have both of you in our family." Images adorning her office linked to Nazi Germany and the artwork of Adolf Hitler immediately alarm Frank. Evil is at the very threshold of his traditional family's door once again.

The political intrigue of Morgan and Wong's two-part thriller continues to unfold. In classic fashion, Mr. Johnston, an Owl, is strangled and set on fire in a hit by Gunsche of ODESSA. The supposed segment of the original crucifix is placed inside Johnston's burning vehicle as part of a setup to implicate him and the Owls. Burned beyond testing, the cross cannot be properly identified. By the end of "Owls," men arrive at Frank's home, guns are drawn, and an all-out war erupts within the Millennium Group family, manipulated by ODESSA.

By the time we reach "Roosters," we have veered well into the territory of *Goodfellas* and *The Godfather*. Trunks are popping, weapons are drawn, and conspiracy is the order of the day. A full-fledged war between families is brewing, Roosters versus Owls, comparable to events found in real or theatrical mob wars. Even the cinema of the

Japanese clan war is suggested. Takeshi Kitano's *Outrage* (2010) is an example of Asian cinema's dramatization of the traditional organized crime family blood feuds in Japan. In Japanese and American cinema, family wars fuel drama. The fear of igniting another Mafia war dominates *The Godfather: Part II* as Michael Corleone meets with Hyman Roth (Lee Strasberg). The events on *Millennium* emphasize the potential for war.

Peter visits with the Group Elder, a soldier visiting with a boss. He has been conflicted since his unfortunate parting of ways with Frank. Peter is empathetic to Frank's concerns about the Group and his place in the organization. The Group Elder understands Peter's affection for Frank and the relationship of a soldier to his associate. The Elder suggests that Frank "was always reluctant to join the Group—period." He points to Frank's already fragile connection to the Group, suggesting he has been a "lost" candidate. There is a familial undertone in Peter's desire to reach out to Frank despite their soured affiliation. The Elder underlines the realities of these bonds: "You empathize with your candidate's doubts. You console their fear. You elate at their revelation. You can't experience these emotions with another person and not feel close to them. But until the candidate becomes initiated and comprehends the secrets that we accept, the affinity is a one-way street."

These relationships can be tenuous. Take real life F.B.I. Agent Joseph Dominick Pistone, alias Donnie Brasco, who, in the late 1970s, infiltrated the Bonanno crime family in New York, one of the five dominant families, ultimately betraying them. The film *Donnie Brasco* (1997) was based on Pistone's book. His tale represents one of the great examples of a cultivated relationship, the establishment of trust in an association, ultimately leading to a betrayal of the family. Ironically, Pistone placed his real family at great risk in his effort to gain inside access. His transformation affected his relationship with his nuclear family significantly and placed them in great danger.

As bullets fly at the opening of "Roosters," Frank manages to come out of the hit attempt unscathed. Catherine returns to him. As the fracture within his clandestine family grows it draws his nuclear family closer. The healing process is delicate and difficult as Frank attempts to gather the facts, certain the truth is out there. In *Goodfellas*, a hit placed on Henry Hill leads to his only recourse—to protect his family from certain death. Henry would become the proverbial rat against those he once trusted and who trusted him. The only way out once you are in is to run, hide, or die. Nicholas Pileggi, author of *Wiseguy: Life in a Mafia Family* (1985), the basis for the film, bluntly explains, "Once you join it, you can't leave" ("Getting Made"). The British gangster film *Sexy Beast* (2000) offers an alternate example. Gary "Gal" Dove (Ray Winstone) would love to retire to a Spanish villa for the remainder of time but he is doggedly pursued by vicious criminal associate Don Logan (Ben Kingsley), who answers to crime boss Teddy Bass, played with relish by Ian McShane.

There is an interesting juxtaposition between families as Catherine and Frank attempt to establish what is true and what is false. In *Millennium*'s version of history, sixteen Millennium Group members died in an effort to prevent the Nazis from seizing power. ODESSA perceives Frank as a weak link within the Group, resulting in their exploitation of Catherine to access Frank. Frank's explanation of these facts and the exposure of these truths brings Catherine closer to her husband. For their relationship to be grounded and stable there must be trust. Their scenes of reconciliation are intercut with Peter and the Group Elder underscoring these same values. Lies and deceit cannot be the foundation for any group or family, but the reality for both is often another matter.

At a meeting between Owls and Roosters, Peter discusses the political, religious, and ideological fracturing of Catholics and Protestants in Northern Ireland to a reunified Millennium Group. He points to the schisms that can splinter a people through religious or political ideology. "It's become about who controls who and that's what's happening here and this is not who we are!" His speech articulates Frank's concerns. Control and power are central to the crime family. The differences between Owls and Roosters are significant and the tensions between them are heightened despite the family attempt to quell internal struggles. The Old Man fears the Millennium Group might inevitably tear itself apart from within, regardless of external forces. Internal fracturing through mistrust is one of the greatest threats to any family.

With Group disharmony on the brink of all-out war, a peace enters the Owl and Rooster union through the words and actions of Peter. Survival is at the fore and the Group is resolute in meting out its own distinct form of justice. Peace must come if the Group is to survive. Peter declares "the Group must destroy them," it must destroy

ODESSA. One is reminded of the ruthless and unmerciful actions undertaken by Michael Corleone to protect the Corleone family at the conclusion of *The Godfather*. There is a sense of poetic retribution. In the manner of warring, dysfunctional crime families, the Owls and Roosters unite by placing hits on the members of ODESSA. *Millennium*'s soundtrack and the music of Wagner's *Parsifal* (1882) grant the final scenes of "Roosters" an added sense of apocalyptic verse and a finality reminiscent of the best in mob cinema. The approved assassination of targets by families takes on a Mafia aesthetic. Justice is twisted when evil is met by evil. The crucifix is repossessed by the Group in the end, a group influenced by religious and spiritual principles not foreign to the likes of the Freemason.

In the first part of the second season finale, "The Fourth Horseman," Frank is approached by yet another external group, the Trust, and is invited to leave the Group and become a partner. The Trust is a "corporate security dream team" comprised of former members of the K.G.B., Mossad, and the F.B.I., a conglomerate of agents lending it a curious pedigree. It denotes another Academy Group aberration. The Trust's invitation is a power play initiated by another family competing for business. During his meeting with Trust representative Richard Gilbert (Glenn Morshower), Frank is notified of his father Henry's passing. His daughter, Jordan, stands by his side at the cemetery and asks him, "Are you lonely without your mommy and daddy?" She steps away and Frank whispers, "I'm very lonely." Seeking out others is a natural form of sociological identity. It is Frank's continued search for understanding, for his place outside of his immediate family, that leads to the mysteries of the secret society.

Frank later accepts Richard's offer to join the Trust, an acceptance prompted by his growing distrust of the Millennium Group. Richard extends, "The Trust understands the danger you're in. We've heard about the Millennium Group." Like anyone loyal to those they care about, Frank insists, "There are people involved. I can't leave them behind. I've got to get 'em out." Frank, a principled man, is willing to turn on the Group. To the Mafia, such an individual would be identified as a rat, such as Joseph Valachi, who testified against the American Mafia in 1963, exposing the *Cosa Nostra* before the U.S. Senate. Formerly a member of the Genovese crime family, a price was placed on Valachi's head but the hit was never completed. Frank, a family man, understands the menace of the Group. Richard observes,

THIS IS WHO WE ARE

"Investigating the Millennium Group will be the most difficult case you've ever had. They don't tolerate enemies." Disloyalty is intolerable, and Frank understands what is at stake.

Catherine and Frank continue their argument regarding the influence of the Group on their family. "Look at what they have done to you," Catherine accuses. "You care more about their concerns than your own daughter." These are caustic words, but he is alone in this fight. He realizes, like many who live and bond within their secret fraternities, that the Group is a cult. He must leave the Group and shield his family from the repercussions. "We'll go back to the yellow house as a family," he assures Catherine, "as a family!"

Questioning the Millennium Group and its motives more than ever, Frank approaches Peter and asks that he assist in investigating the organization. Frank makes his case: "Ceremonies and secrets that only certain members can understand, collecting the cross of the crucifixion, ancient texts for future prophecies. It's all a diversion, sleight of hand, distraction from the problems they're trying to control. This is not about the end of the world. It's about controlling the world, and that's not who I am." Peter understands the consequences for a good soldier turning on a trusted group. "If they found out that I was doing that—a made member investigating the group—they would kill me."

The subsequent episode, "The Time is Now," opens with the image of Frank, Catherine, and Jordan reunited, standing before the fence of their bright, yellow home, a symbol of the nuclear family ideal. Following the previous episode's earthquake, Frank points out the home's "foundation is cracked," a fitting symbol for the assault on the family. Catherine notes the family has "found our way back to the yellow house." Frank believes a change is in order, perhaps "a different yellow house." It is a proposal of adaptation. He informs his wife he "can't walk away" from his "responsibility," however misguided the Group's larger intentions. Frank cannot simply walk away from one family to protect the other. He is tied to his principles. Any progress toward reconciliation is hindered by Frank's allegiance to the Group and his efforts to halt evil.

Peter is left with doubts planted in his mind by Frank. Frank meets with Richard Gilbert in a secret location under the shroud of darkness. He informs Richard he must remain with the Group and is unable to join the Trust. Again, Richard cautions, "Any Group that so closely monitors their own members should be feared." Upon his departure, four representatives of the Millennium Group meet Frank. "Our responsibility—and remember that word, it'll come up again—our responsibility is to the life of the whole of mankind," lectures Mr. Lott (Stephen Macht). Frank would undoubtedly be required to take lives to protect a greater cause. He would embrace danger to his person and his beloved, compromising his principles, by becoming a part of this family. "This is who we are." Again, we are reminded of the oath of membership for "this thing of ours." As the Group confronts Frank, Richard is conveniently killed in a car explosion. Frank is made to understand his own family is secondary according to the Group philosophy.

As the deadly Marburg virus spreads at the end of the second season, Peter informs Frank that only members of the Group will ultimately be protected. Personal relations are not included. Ironically, the Group family, which Frank joined to protect his wife and daughter, is linked to the dissolution and destruction of his own nuclear family as Catherine dies of exposure to the Marburg variant. The risk of the association comes full circle. Season Two reveals a Millennium Group that, for better or worse, deviates markedly from the original concept of the Academy Group. This is a family gone awry. As a character, Frank would remain true to the Carter ideal, abandoning the machinations of the Group going forward.

When Season Three began, showrunner Chip Johannessen, with Michael Duggan, took the reins from Morgan and Wong. Frank moves away from the Millennium Group and takes residence within the F.B.I. again, the agency that once served as his working family. He is joined by Special Agent Emma Hollis (Klea Scott). Meanwhile, Frank's relations with the Group have chilled considerably, and the nature of his relationship with them becomes markedly different. As Maddrey writes, Frank "no longer needs validation from the Millennium Group" and "he cannot rely on the Millennium Group" as one relies on a family (255-56). This need for validation or desire to belong, whether it be with the *Cosa Nostra*, the Freemasons, the Hell's Angels, or an urban gang, is always a defining factor. These groups often attain new members as a counter to the breakdown of family, out of a need to belong, a need for security, or for mutual benefit. The underlying reasons for membership are familiar.

In "Exegesis," Peter Watts returns, to the ire of Frank, discussing the Group with F.B.I. Assistant Director Andy McClaren (Stephen E.

Miller). McClaren perceives the Group as it was originally conceived: "They're ex-F.B.I., family men, people you and I worked together with for years. We have a relationship with them." He cannot see the true nature of the Group, as Frank does. As a former insider, Frank knows the reality: "The Group killed my wife. They're dangerous people." Frank is later greeted by Peter at Jordan's school, igniting a volatile, patriarchal response. Like a lion protecting his cub, Frank is now at odds with Peter. "Are you threatening me again?" Frank asks. The Group is watching, but he vows to protect his sole source of strength. Peter is very much the soldier for the Group even McLaren likens to "family." The Millennium Group is responsible for a string of deaths, the targeted killings of a family of cloned women. The final remaining clone, in custody, assures Frank, "They won't let you go." It serves as a reminder that former members can never be free.

The title for "Skull and Bones," a clear double entendre, references the substantive aftermath of unearthing the dead and once again alludes to the notion of the secret family. It pays direct homage to the series' own Millennium Group by alluding to the secret Yale University order founded in 1833, a secret society often tied to American political conspiracy. "Skull and Bones" serves as both a prequel and follow-up to the events seen in "The Hand of St. Sebastian." The title specifically links Frank to his lost Group family through Victim 38, former member Cheryl Andrews. "People," like Cheryl, "can be erased!" This is the frightening reality facing a former associate such as Frank. "Skull and Bones" speaks directly to the only alternative for lifetime membership: death. In the episode, Franks explains the Group to Emma. "Watch your back," he warns. Emma questions, "Is this how you live, wondering if it'll happen to you? To your daughter?" In the aftermath of the second season, all that is important to Frank is in jeopardy.

Like the Mafia, the Millennium Group has its own version of the hit man in Mabius (Bob Wilde). Former candidates or associates are in danger as long as the Group employs its own version of *The Godfather*'s Luca Brasi. The Group's assassination tactics are demonstrated throughout the third season, as in "Bardo Thodol," when Frank spots men turning up dead and dubs their deaths "Millennium Group executions."

In "Skull and Bones," an observer named Ed (Arye Gross) learns too much about the Group, and the F.B.I. considers placing him in the witness protection program. Witness protection is always an option for the F.B.I. when seeking to safeguard information on criminal organizations. Henry Hill, formerly with the Lucchese crime family, became such a witness, entering into the U.S. Marshals' Witness Protection Program in 1980. For Ed, Frank knows the man will be safer "on his own" since the organization Ed fears is directly tied to the F.B.I. Unfortunately, Frank, too, is a loose end and another potential victim.

In "Collateral Damage," the dichotomy of loyalty between family and secret society is blurred more than ever through the conundrum faced by Peter Watts. Peter's daughter, Taylor, is abducted. Could this be the work of enemies of his Millennium Group family? Could it be the Group itself? When the F.B.I. convenes a search for Taylor, McLaren declares before his agents, "This is family." He is not referring to the fact that Taylor is Peter's blood, instead emphasizing that he will engage all of the agency's resources on the case in the aid one of their own—Peter Watts. Again, the Group is working in collaboration with the F.B.I. Frank immediately suspects the abduction was planned by an enemy of the Group. He also questions Peter's loyalty to the organization. His loyalty to this second family supersedes blood. The duality of these connections is amplified by Peter's own family troubles. HBO's *The Sopranos* poetically captured the blurring of these family lines through similar struggles weighing on its protagonist, Tony Soprano. The same confusion of loyalties evident in the mob drama is very much at in play on *Millennium*.

Of course, the Group is one step ahead of the F.B.I. and controlling the flow of information. Frank knows this. Peter knows this. He pleads for Frank's assistance. Living by the code of *omertà*, Peter is steadfast in remaining tight-lipped for the good of the Group, even with his daughter's life on the line. The violation of loyalty to the nuclear family is not an unreasonable expectation within the secret family. Peter insists that he cannot answer certain questions. Frank questions whether he cannot or will not. Frank values the traditional family and the life of his own daughter and works to save Peter's girl out of honor for his belief in the traditional family. Peter admits, "The Group can't know." Commitment to the organization demands sacrifice and the lives of self and family are placed in jeopardy, always.

When Andy asks Frank how he received certain information, he deceives those around him out a desire to protect Taylor Watts and out of respect for Peter's immediate family. In spite of all this, when the end comes, Peter ultimately uses Frank. Peter and the Group quickly brush him aside. "We'll take it from here." Frank is no longer of use. In the final moments, joy is quickly replaced with questions of loyalty and trust as the Watts family sits around the dinner table. Peter and Taylor stare at one another. The final seconds are sobering as Peter looks away, overcome by the horror of knowing the willing sacrifices he would make for the Group at the expense of his own family. As Hyman Roth declares in *The Godfather: Part II*, "This is the business we chose." The collateral damage alluded to in the episode's title is the family.

A family peace arrives for Frank in the form of the bittersweet "The Sound of Snow." In the episode, *Millennium* tackles issues of guilt and considers Frank's decision to separate himself from the Group, a decision that ultimately led to the premature death of his wife. He wonders if a different decision might have led to her survival as he considers the fate averted by Peter's daughter. Taylor Watts is alive, sitting at the family dinner table, as a result of Peter's sacrifice, his deal with the devil. "They wanted me to join them. They wanted me to join the Group, and then you'd be saved," Frank tells a ghostly vision of Catherine. "Peter Watts's family is alive. His daughters have a mother. They set the table and she sits down to eat with them." Cathartically, the spirit of Catherine assures Frank, "You chose me—not them." Frank suffers from her loss, but his dedication was always to family. His guilt is long-lasting, but she reassures him, "They had already taken too much of you. We beat them." Frank is comforted as she tells him, "You chose me. We chose each other." He refused to compromise his principles and thus has lost his "center," as Giebelhouse describes her. "I can't let go," Frank admits, for Jordan is always there to remind him of her. Through Jordan, his family ideal will always be with him. In the end, Frank understands the Group. He refers to the villain of this entry as a force the Group will either "appropriate" or destroy." Frank severs his ties with the Group for the health of his sole remaining source of love—his daughter. Ironically, Frank believes it is the Group itself that has offered closure concerning his wife. "They gave me my wife back," he considers.

In "Matryoshka," a former member of both the F.B.I. and the Group, Michael Lanyard, is found dead. Reporting to the group Elder, Peter discusses his personal guilt over the loss of Frank from the Group. "He was my candidate. I recruited him at his time of need." Peter internalizes a sense of failure. He tells the Elder, "You told me once that the Group didn't choose its members, that the members chose the Group." Frank is evidence of this reality. The third season explores the repercussions of the decision made by Frank to ultimately take back his family and move away from the Group.

Frank's influence on Peter resonates in the final moments of "Matryoshka." "Are we afraid of the truth?" Peter asks the Elder. The boss quashes such insubordination. "This is no time to question your faith," he declares. In the epilogue, a long held promise is fulfilled when a woman receives a letter addressed to her in 1945. The Group has manipulated her inclusion. Her decision to join was not her decision. At last, she is allowed to discover the truth of her own family, her father, thanks to Peter. We begin to consider the possibility of redemption for Peter Watts.

In "*Via Dolorosa*," with Frank steadfast in his conviction to move forward with Jordan, Peter makes his Machiavellian play to tap Frank's partner, Emma Hollis, on behalf of the Group through the instrument of her greatest affection—her father. Like those candidates that preceded her, Emma is vulnerable to the intangibilities of the Group. Love for family informs our decisions. Emma concedes to her interest in the Group. The circle of the ouroboros continues. Di Bernardo describes the serpent eating its tail as "an expression of eternity" (42). This is the perpetuity of the ancient Millennium Group—a seemingly unending, ancient family tree.

In *Not Bad for a Human*, Henriksen declares "a father is most vulnerable through his daughter. That's a very pure relationship" (294). In this instance the actor is not referring to his role in *Millennium*, but the sentiment speaks directly to Frank's own vulnerabilities. Frank has been the recipient of much painful discord, evident in Emma's move toward the Group, the duplicity of the Group itself, and the unfortunate disconnect with his wife, Catherine. "These betrayals take an emotional toll" (264), but clarity begins to take hold for Frank Black.

In the final *Millennium* hour, "Goodbye to All That," Frank is informed that someone has entered his home and videotaped his sleeping daughter. Pushed to the brink of rage, Frank visits Peter's home, crashing into his dining room, where his family is joined for dinner. Peter denies the Group's involvement. "I came here to put a bullet in you, but I don't have to," growls Frank, "the Group will do it for me." Frank knows the Group cleans up its loose ends. Peter subsequently meets with Frank in an isolated location. He wants to know if the Group truly is involved. "Think about who they are," says Frank. Peter admits that he has been protecting Frank from the Group since his departure as a candidate.

Elsewhere, Emma's father tells his daughter she should not have assented to the Millennium Group's demands. The price was too high. "You shouldn't have done what they asked." How far would you go for your family? Would you compromise principle?

A leather satchel with personal profiles on Frank and Jordan Black is returned to Frank's jeep, a case file previously held by Peter. Symbolically, Peter has set Frank free. Peter must pay a price for his betrayal of the group. Emma has replaced him and the cycle continues, reminding us of the symbol of the ouroboros.

The theme of family has comes full circle like the ouroboros itself. The promise of the yellow home is gone, but Frank retains that symbol of eternal hope and the family dream through his daughter, Jordan. Mark Snow's score plays as Frank spontaneously retrieves his daughter from school, unannounced. They proceed to run down the halls, their hands held tight. In a memorable final shot, the rays of the sun that penetrate the clouds in the distance shine down upon Frank and Jordan as they make their escape. The light represents Frank's continued hope and the strength and warmth of that which he holds dear and true—his daughter, his family. He is breaking free for his daughter. While the future is certainly unclear, the end brings the potential for that hope that inspired Frank's character for three seasons as he rides off, secure in the fact his daughter is by his side. When they are together, Frank is home.

At the end of the series Frank's world has crumbled, decimated by plague, conspiracies, and evil. For a time, he lost the joy, purity and union of the nuclear family symbolized in the yellow house. He lost those allies closest to him in the Millennium Group family. He stands where he has always stood, heroically alone, and were it not for the love of his daughter he would be powerless. When Frank reaches the decisive finale it is his daughter that sustains him—his sole family connection. Henriksen himself recalls the character's motivations: "I was basing all my strength on family" (263). Both his wife and the nuclear family, along with the Group, nurtured his mission. By the end of a sustained journey of betrayals, Frank survives. The loss of these support systems results in a battle-hardened road to the future, but it is his daughter that pulls him back from the edge of darkness. "She saved me" (263).

The duality of two parallel family lines—the blood family and the secret family of the Millennium Group—is complex throughout the series. Frank Black repeatedly questions whether the Millennium Group is a force for good or evil as an influence in his life and on his family. This is the question that remains with Frank as he navigates between worlds, between family and secret society, throughout *Millennium*. Frank works tirelessly, a fact evinced in his very face, to protect that which is true from chaos. It is within the arms of family and love that we find safety and order, as Frank finds through Jordan. He does everything in his power to protect the potential for life, for family, and for goodness. Through family we find strength. This was at the core of *Millennium* and it is a truth that speaks to all of us.

We all seek the love and strength of family in whatever form it finds us in, and that love and support protects us and nurtures us. It is what drives us as a people and it is what compels Frank Black. Undeniably, the truth is, this is who we are—all of us.

WORKS CITED

"Chasing the Dragon: A Conversation with the Academy Group." *Millennium: The Complete First Season*. Prod. Jon Mefford. Twentieth Century Fox Home Entertainment, 2004. DVD.

di Bernardo, Giuliano. *Freemasonry and Its Image of Man: A Philosophical Investigation*. Worcester: Freestone, 1989. Print.

Donnie Brasco. Dir. Mike Newell. TriStar, 1997. Film.

Endrst, James. "Prepare for *Millennium*." *Hartford Courant*. Hartford Courant, 21 October 1996. Web. 14 August 2012.

"Getting Made: The Making of *Goodfellas*." *Goodfellas*. Prod. Stephen Altobello and Jeffrey Schwarz. Warner Home Video, 2004. DVD.

The Godfather. Dir. Francis Ford Coppola. Paramount, 1972. Film.

The Godfather: Part II. Dir. Francis Ford Coppola. Paramount, 1974. Film.

THIS IS WHO WE ARE

Goodfellas. Dir. Martin Scorsese. Warner Bros., 1990. Film.

Henriksen, Lance and Joseph Maddrey. *Not Bad for a Human: The Life and Films of Lance Henriksen*. Los Angeles: Bloody Pulp, 2011. Print.

Morgan, Glen. Interview by James McLean and Troy L. Foreman. *The Millennium Group Sessions*. Back to Frank Black, 28 February 2010. Web. 14 August 2012.

"Order in Chaos." *Millennium: The Complete First Season*. Prod. John Mefford. Twentieth Century Fox Home Entertainment, 2004. DVD.

Sexy Beast. Dir. Jonathan Glazer. FilmFour, 2000. Film.

The Sopranos: The Complete First Season. HBO Home Video, 2000. DVD.

"The Turn of the Tide." *Millennium: The Complete Second Season*. Prod. John Mefford. Twentieth Century Fox Home Entertainment, 2004. DVD.

The Untouchables. Dir. Brian De Palma. Paramount, 1987. Film.

Vitaris, Paula. "*Millennium*: TV's Best Kept Secret Improves in its Sophomore Season." *Cinefantastique* October 1998: 18-22, 125. Print.

Gordon Roberts has written for various independent publications, including *The Lexicon*. He is the author of the website *Musings of a Sci-Fi Fanatic*. Roberts is a husband to his wife, Candace, and the proud father of two children, Owen and Róisín, who love and patiently support his passion for analyzing all things science fiction in film and television.

HERE'S MY THING:
A CONVERSATION WITH KRISTEN CLOKE

Interview by James McLean & Troy L. Foreman
Written by Adam Chamberlain

For fans of *Millennium*'s second season, the developing relationship between forensic psychologist Lara Means and Frank Black remains a lingering preoccupation. Some sentimental devotees even perceive an unspoken romantic link between the two during the period that Frank and Catherine are separated. Kristen Cloke, the actress who played Means, is quick to reject such a notion. "I don't think Frank and Lara had romantic feelings for each other," she states resolutely, "but I do think they shared something that was completely unique to only them. To feel really understood by someone is very powerful. Lara was a mirror for Frank. I think her purpose was to help Frank and the audience better understand Frank's gift."

The actress, of course, possesses a unique understanding of the character's tragic arc. "She was there to play a part in that she and

Frank had a simpatico, because they had a similar thing that they really identified with each other," Cloke explains. "Any time you meet somebody who can see the world in a similar way that you do it is very gratifying, or comforting, in a weird way. So she was put there to be a reflection of him and help him solve the mysteries of that season and the Millennium Group. The character was put there almost as a device for the Frank Black character. She could mirror him and also allow him to go on by giving him her antidote for the virus. She sacrificed herself to him, and I think that's what the arc of that character was. She reflected the overall arc of the series, and went into madness, and reflected Frank in that way."

Cloke's career path, forged many years before finding common ground with the visionary hero of *Millennium*, contains its own sage lessons—this time for aspiring actors seeking to mirror her vocation. "I was an English major in college," she recalls. "I was interested in acting, and I enrolled in some theater classes. I had done acting as a kid a little bit. I had done some theater in town, and I had always been one of those kids who performed for anybody who would watch. I did as much theater as I could do when I was in college without claiming it as a major or even a minor. Then I got one of the leads in a play with just three or four leads, and I wasn't a theater major, and it was a scandal at the time. 'How could they cast someone who's not a theater major?' Then, in my third year, I got a letter from the English department asking me to join the Honors English program. At the same time my boyfriend—who was a writer/director and just a really lovely man—had introduced me to his agent, who was making a transition from one agency to another. She landed at an agency called the Susan Smith Agency, which was one of the great boutique agencies of its time. It had a lot of really special actors, and she said she would take a chance on me."

The exceptional career opportunity forced the young actress to weigh a potentially momentous decision. "My boyfriend was much older and he was a very salty guy and had been around for a long time, and he said, 'You can't do both. You've got to be an actor or be a student.' I said, 'Well, I'll have nothing to fall back on if it doesn't work out.' He said, 'If you create fallbacks, you'll always fall back.' In some ways he was right, because I was a very serious actress in the sense that I worked out, I went to acting classes, I did other artistic things, I went to therapy—which I think is very important—and I really spent a lot of time being about Kristen. Making sure that I was always in shape so I could do any part that I wanted, that I was taking acting classes, that I was going on auditions—I was really just about that. In that respect, he was right. I needed to focus. I was just twenty-one when I got my Screen Actors Guild card, so I was still kind of a kid. That's what any twenty-one-year-old needs to do. You've got to be into what you're into, whether it's your school, your study, your music, or whatever. At twenty-one, that's what you need to be about."

The twenty-one-year-old Kristen followed the advice and was rewarded with immediate success. "I quit school, and I got the first audition I went out on, which was a movie with Billy Zane," the science fiction thriller *Megaville* (1990). "It was the lead, a small movie, and it was right after he had done *Dead Calm*. It seemed like it was going to be something special, and it was in its own way. I got my Screen Actors Guild card and I really supported myself as an actress, for the most part. Billy was a big name at that point, and it was just a little independent sci-fi movie."

In spite of her early success, however, Cloke offers cautionary and somewhat contrary advice for aspiring artists of any kind seeking to carve out a career from their craft. "I wouldn't advise anybody to become a professional artist," she says. "I think that when you take money for your art, it changes it. If you're really passionate about something, you love something, you have to do two things. You need to either keep that art sacred, and do something else to earn money, or know that when you're going in to do that art for money that it changes the art. I don't think there is one way to go about it. I don't know that the path that I took was necessarily successful in terms of the business side of it.

"I think that I really wanted to be a serious actress. I earned a living playing the girl parts—the chick parts—but the parts that I really liked, those where I really became very attached to the people, were parts where I wasn't necessarily playing that part. I'm not really the best person to ask about that. I think there are a lot of different paths, but I certainly, most definitely, feel that when you're an actor you're not always in control of whether you work or not, or even what you do when you do get the job. You're earning money for that thing, you can have some opinions, and if you happen to be lucky to work with someone who cares what those opinions are and they're collaborative, that's a really fantastic place to be. But that's not always the case, so I don't know if I'm the best person to ask, but I certainly think that everybody should always have their lives and then their passion projects. We all have the capacity to be lots of different things, and we shouldn't be defined by any one of those things. I certainly am not defined at all by having been an actor. That doesn't really play that big a part of my life today, so I think we have to have lots of things that turn us on that are creative and interesting, and everything leads back to it and fills your passion. I think that everybody has to pick their own path, but to know that everything leads to everything." Her view on even the most conflicted of creative endeavors is refreshingly philosophical. "It's surprising how much stuff you can carry on your back in this world."

For all her misgivings, Cloke's career would connect her with her future husband, none other than *Millennium* writer and executive producer Glen Morgan. Two years previous, in 1993, the actress had guest starred in the final season of *Cheers* (1982-93), appearing as a secretary and short-lived love interest for Dr. Frasier Crane (Kelsey Grammer) in an episode entitled "Sunday Dinner." Cloke's brief guest spot caught Morgan's eye. "When I auditioned for *Space: Above and Beyond*, it was one of the first things that Glen ever said to me, as I was walking out," she says with a smile. "People who have auditioned for Glen and Jim don't really like it, because they're pretty taciturn guys. They're pretty quiet. They play everything close to their chest. I walked out, and this little voice went, 'I liked your *Cheers*.' I said, 'What? Who are you? What are you talking about?!' I think those were probably the first words that Glen ever said to me. I don't remember—they were so quiet. I thought, 'There's no way I got this job, because they said nothing. They had no words. These people don't like me.'"

She did, in fact, land the role of Captain Shane Vansen, leader of the United States Marine Corps Space Aviator Cavalry's 58th Squadron, in Glen Morgan and James Wong's gritty science fiction war drama *Space: Above and Beyond* (1995-96). The collaboration was to have a profound and lasting impact upon the actress' life, both personally and professionally. "It was a strange and wonderful show in so many ways because so many of the people that we worked with on that show have become such huge parts of our lives. That show was so deeply special for many reasons, but partially just because it was a convergence of all these truly special people in our lives." As a result, her role on *Space* has forever remained with her. "Those were great characters—full, rich characters. I think that part of the reason that it's hard for me to even be an actress anymore is Shane Vansen. I'm not sure that it really gets much more rich than that. I'm not even sure that I knew it, because there's a lot of pain involved, but that was a great time."

In addition to allowing her to collaborate with her future husband, *Space: Above and Beyond* had Cloke working alongside another celebrated *Millennium* alumnus, the director Thomas J. Wright. "He used to call me the 'Maybelline Marine!' He used to get mad, because I think that one of the things that made Shane a little bit special is that I think a female that is strong can also be a lot of things. I like that. I didn't want Shane to be pigeonholed as the tough chick. I didn't necessarily want her to be the Maybelline Marine. I wanted her to have a lot of facets. I wanted her to be very complex and layered. You always wanted to know more about her because, just when you thought you kind of knew who she was, she was sort of something different, and I loved that about her. She was a pretty layered character."

Shane Vansen, a fighter pilot and squadron leader boasting the call sign "Queen of Diamonds," stands as a prime example of a strong female character—as, in many ways, does the understanding and intuitive Lara Means. Did the actress perceive any emergent trend in television roles for women during the 1990s? "I think there've always been a lot of strong women," claims Cloke, "especially if you go back and watch all those *noir* movies. They were just depicted differently. Then, of course, you had the *Alien* movies and *Terminator 2: Judgment Day*, and so you're beginning to see that brawny, strong female character come out. Shane was part Barbara Stanwyck tough guy and part Ripley. She was a little bit of all those things, but she was unique. She came from a very sad place, a very tortured place, so she had all of that going on. I really tried not to have her be a stereotype. I really tried to make Shane very unique, not in-the-box. Maybe that show would have been more successful had she fit a little better into what was seen as a modern, tough guy box in that way, but I tried to keep her pretty layered. I wanted her to be a girl, but I wanted her to be strong. She carried all that baggage with her. She was very much a mother to the other people in the show. I don't think anybody really paid that close attention to the show, so I'm not really sure that she changed anything, but it was certainly a great opportunity. I can't name that many other actresses who got to do that for twenty-two episodes, so I feel really lucky. That was a great part."

After the cancellation of *Space: Above and Beyond*, Cloke took on another challenging and rather remarkable role during the fourth season of *The X-Files*, portraying a woman recalling past lives in the emotional "The Field Where I Died," written by Morgan and Wong. It was shortly after this introduction to Ten Thirteen Productions that she was offered the recurring role of Lara Means in *Millennium*. What were her initial reactions to the character? "She was pretty unraveled. She wasn't unraveled at the beginning, but she was a great character. She was also somebody who had all this stuff that was always brimming right towards the top, and she had to work so hard to keep it together. I felt really lucky—she's a great character. I'm always happy to work with Glen. I know that some people feel that it's nepotism—and I suppose, in some ways, it is—but we really have a good time working together. It's a really good collaboration."

Cloke has appeared in more than a half dozen of Morgan's productions, from *Space: Above and Beyond* to *Black Christmas* (2006). How do collaborations between the two tend to work? "We don't really talk that much about it. He writes it—Glen and I have a sort of shorthand—and it's just very easy for him. I am his biggest fan and greatest supporter. I'm just there to exercise his vision of what he's writing. I feel like I'm just more of a Glen Morgan tool than really an actress in some ways. I know that people sometimes don't always like the fact that Glen always works with his wife, but it's a great collaboration and it makes it very easy for both of us. He's not going to get something that he necessarily didn't want, and if there's a question about it, then we talk about it. Glen often creates a character for me in his scripts that serve as a storytelling device for him. We have a lot of trust, and he knows I really want to serve his purpose as a storyteller."

Naturally, it is difficult for a wife to view her husband's work without being in some way partisan. "I can't watch Glen's stuff with a lot of objectivity," Kristen confesses, "because I know all the parts that went into it, and if something doesn't work I would see the pain of how he got some note and the note doesn't work, because the executives who are working on that are not seeing it the same way that he is. I know that hurts him—when it doesn't work and he could have done it—so that's hard to watch. It's hard to see Glen feel not victorious, because I get what he's trying to do. I think that's why we have a great time working together, that I see where he's going with something. We're very close. We talk about every single thing. There's not much that I don't know about what's going on with something that he's working on or something that he's writing. We talk about it—we're really good friends. We talk about almost everything. I'm almost too close to Glen's stuff to really watch it at the time. I can look back—like some of *Space: Above and Beyond*—and really appreciate it, but also I know Glen and I know his writing. He writes so much and he's written so much that his writing has even evolved since then. It's different. I'm not really the greatest person to ask about Glen's work!"

Setting aside her self-confessed bias for a moment, was she aware of any behind-the-scenes conflict over the creative direction of *Millennium*'s second season under the aegis of her husband and James Wong? "I'm sure that there were issues," Cloke concedes, "but Glen was doing what he was asked to do. I know that Fox wanted to take the show into a different area in the second season. I think they felt like they didn't want it to be a serial-killer-of-the-week show anymore, that it was too gruesome, that it would turn off a big part of what they felt their potential audience was. They asked Glen to switch it around, and they did. They turned it into something else. The goal was that Glen and Jim would go in there for a year, change the course of the show, and get it brought back for a third season. They achieved that goal. I'm sure that some people didn't like it—they liked the show as it was in the first season and they wanted it to stay the same, which I totally understand and respect—but Glen and Jim were hired to do a job and I felt like they did that. I felt like they did it really well." Those viewers who were captivated by the show's explosion of religious intrigue or enthralled by the ensuing apocalyptic action would undoubtedly agree.

The epic mythology that Morgan and Wong were drafting for *Millennium* was, in fact, as Cloke notes, highly original. "All that stuff was done before *The Da Vinci Code* was published," she points out, "and that was huge, so I think they did a really good job. I think those episodes are really interesting, and especially all the Owls and Roosters stuff—I loved all that. I thought they were really interesting, really dark, strange, interesting episodes. There's just a lot of dark, strange stuff that was pretty innovative."

The actress also highlights the experimental nature of brother-in-law Darin Morgan's scripts, suggesting that *Millennium*'s second season pushed boundaries in its effort to tell unforgettable tales. "Darin's episodes are classic television in and of themselves, outside of the arc of that season. They're great standalones. Nothing good on T.V. comes from being safe. Nothing. There's no good safe T.V.—you've seen it all. You've seen the elevator episode. You've seen the lead guy and the lead girl kiss. You've seen those. You've got to have your comfort food television. Everybody needs that. Everybody wants to come home from work and see the same stuff that they see all the time, and that makes them feel happy and comfortable. They know the characters and make them feel that they're not going to do anything really strange. But it's nice to see something dark, different, and crazy that keeps you looking at the world in a different way. I think there's a place for all of that. Glen, Jim, and Darin are really creative storytellers. I think they approach stories in a unique way. That is who they are as writers, and it is reflected in the show."

Lara Means was introduced on *Millennium* without much by way of a backstory. Slowly, however, as the season progresses, more is revealed about the character's motivations and hardships. Cloke cites the year's Christmas installment as an example of a story that significantly expanded our understanding of Means. "Dwight Little directed 'Midnight of the Century'—he's a great director—and I was happy to have that episode because I think it's one of the first times that you really understood what her deal was, that you saw her as a sympathetic person, someone who is very troubled and trying to keep it together. I believe they were talking about how [Frank's] daughter saw things, and she could sympathize. She talked about it, and you could see that there was a little trouble there. I was appreciative of that, because I was able to verbalize a lot of the things that I knew I was starting to play, the arc of which was coming up. So I was grateful to be able to have that character talk about it a little bit. I guess I felt that I knew what her story was, so I never really thought about whether it was talked about [earlier in the season]."

Another standout episode is "Anamnesis," the sole episode in *Millennium*'s entire run not to feature Lance Henriksen as Frank Black, instead presenting an investigation into the religious visions of a teenage girl led by the series' opposing leading ladies: Lara Means and Catherine Black, as played by Megan Gallagher. "That was fun," recalls Cloke. "Megan and I got to work together. It was a fun episode to do, and it was a little out of the Lara Means thing. She was partnered up with Catherine. It was a little departure and I enjoyed it." How did Kristen perceive her role amidst the troubles between Frank and Catherine? "I like to see the Lara character as being a sort of Band Aid to a lot of that," she offers. "Not necessarily the character, but that whole season you got to see [Catherine] as more than the wife with the worried face. She got to really do some great acting in that season. Her ending was very sad. Everybody was very sad when she was not there. 'Anamnesis' shows that we represent two different emotional pieces of that chorus—Frank Black being the main person, and then everybody else being part of the chorus that supports that story. We were, in some ways, part of that chorus, but we were different voices for that and I never saw it as someone replacing her character. Frank and Lara didn't have that kind of a relationship. They really understood each other. They saw themselves in each other in a certain way, but I think that Frank Black loved his wife."

For the most part, Means was partnered with Frank. What was working with Lance like? "It was great," Cloke beams. "He is an actor who puts his whole self into his roles. Lance was, on any given day, what Frank Black was on any given day. You weren't really sure which Frank Black was going to show up that day, because he was very involved. He did take it all very seriously. I don't think that he really separated himself from that character at all when he was working. But he really did make me laugh, I remember that. He was very funny. I don't know if anybody ever talks about that. Sometimes, he and Terry [O'Quinn] together could really make me laugh. The two of them were hilarious, because both are these men with a very strong presence and gravitas, then when they were goofy it was very funny."

The most memorable scene to star Lara Means, of course, remains one of the most famous moments in the whole of the series. Shortly after being inducted into the Millennium Group in "The Fourth Horseman," season finale "The Time is Now" sees Means suffer a full-blown mental breakdown after the true extent of the Group's knowledge and influence is revealed to her. An entire act is devoted to depicting her staggering descent into insanity in a stunningly artistic sequence inspired by the symbolic imagery of the Book of Revelation and set to the roaring tones of Patti Smith's "Land."

Cloke recalls filming these classic scenes, exclaiming, "That was a long day! It was hard to do, because Tom Wright—who is a dear friend, a lovely man and a very talented person—had taken me through the storyboards of what it was going to be. I don't know that there was much in the script—I think a lot of it is what Tom came up with. It was really created in the editing room. The song had been picked and

Glen knew what he wanted, and he and Tom had talked about it. Tom directed me very much through his storyboards. 'Here's what this piece is going to be, here's what that piece is going to be.' But there's no dialogue. You're just sitting on a set, you've seen a picture, and you know what they want it to look like, then it's just, 'Action!' and you lose your mind! It had to all happen completely in your head, so that was a very grueling time. I had to fill in all of the blanks to make it work emotionally for that cut. It was really a challenge and fairly painful. That was a time when it was hard to come in and out of it for sure. It was the kind of thing that took a lot of trust on everyone's part."

The nerve-wracking sequence may have been difficult to film, but the challenge of inhabiting characters such as Means is one to which the actress has become accustomed thanks to her collaborations with her husband. "Glen has written me a lot of those," she says. "I had *The X-Files* the year before, and it took me a long time to come out of that character [from 'The Field Where I Died,'] because the impetus for all those character changes was sadness. Lara Means was always fighting these visions. She did feel crazy, and yet she was trying to operate in her brain as if she was completely together, and she just wasn't. By the time you see her in that last episode where she loses her mind, it lets you know. That's all happening inside her head, and it was brimming—that she was having her own personal millennium, her ending, her apocalypse. It was hard, so I did bring it home. I'm not the kind of actor who can just waltz onto a set, have a breakdown, and walk off. I have to get into it and come out of it. It's very difficult for me. It's been one of the things about being a mother and trying to be an actor that doesn't work for me. I put my whole self into almost everything that I do, and it's very hard for me to separate. I have to completely go there."

Did the actress have any wish to return the role after the tumultuous events of the second season finale? "I don't think Lara Means was thought of again after that season," she says. "I had resigned to the fact that I knew she was going into the hospital and probably wouldn't come out. I didn't expect that they would revive that character in Season Three, because Glen wasn't there. Glen prepared me for that, that they were going to put her far, far away because you can't leave that open-ended, because it probably never would have been closed in Season Three. I think he put Lara Means away in the Season Two box, in a loony bin somewhere, and that's probably where she needed to be. I was prepared for that, and I didn't expect to come back, so I had resigned myself to that ending and was fine with that. I have yet to work with Glen where I did not die or simply go insane, never to be heard from again! But I liked Lara Means a lot." Fans still share an appreciation for the character, one whom many would like to see return in a continuation of Frank Black's story. Cloke is both pleased and surprised to learn of Means's enduring popularity with audiences. "It's so shocking to me when you say that, because you did it and you moved on and you went away, and you don't think that anybody really still remembers it. It's very flattering and kind that people do. I'm very touched, and very surprised."

Does she ever revisit her work for herself, and, if so, how does she relate to it in retrospect? "A couple of summers ago, Glen's kids—who are teenagers now—wanted to watch all of the *Space: Above and Beyond* episodes. I would come in and out of those, and those were fun to watch. It was like seeing old friends. Even those characters are like old friends now. Occasionally you would have to put a reel together and you would watch all of your scenes, but I don't like to watch myself very much. I like watching my friends' work, and I work with a lot of friends, so that part is certainly fun. I like watching Glen's work, so in that I would watch my own, but I don't really go looking for it necessarily." She goes on to reveal that her focus in life remains, for the moment, very much with her family rather than in further acting. "I really loved acting. I did not care if it was in television or film. It is most important to me to feel helpful and useful as an actress and as a human. I really pour my whole self into acting when I do it, so I don't do it much anymore. My children need me now, and I truly love being a mother to them."

Kristen closes our interview with a final revelation intended to set the record straight on a key point—Lara Means's trademark catchphrase is not a mere line in a script, not some droll snippet of dialogue dreamt up by Glen Morgan. "'Here's my thing' was stolen from me," she divulges. "I just want you to know that Glen took that from me. That's something I actually say. It was stolen from me. I don't know that I'm saying it—it's a wind-up. When I get very wound up about something, I'll say, 'Here's my thing—blah, blah, blah.' So when Glen put it in the show, when I would be in the middle of saying it, I would be, 'Oh, now it seems like I'm quoting my character, and I feel like an idiot!' It's a complete habit. It's one of those speech things that's my own that Glen lifted from me. He's a thief! People should know that he has stolen from me. When I say it I know it looks like I'm a complete nut ball, because it's something that I can't separate—it's part of my person. I can't remove it from my personal vernacular, so at least if I run into somebody and 'here's my thing' blurts out they won't think that I've lost my mind completely and over-identified with this part that I played ten years ago!"

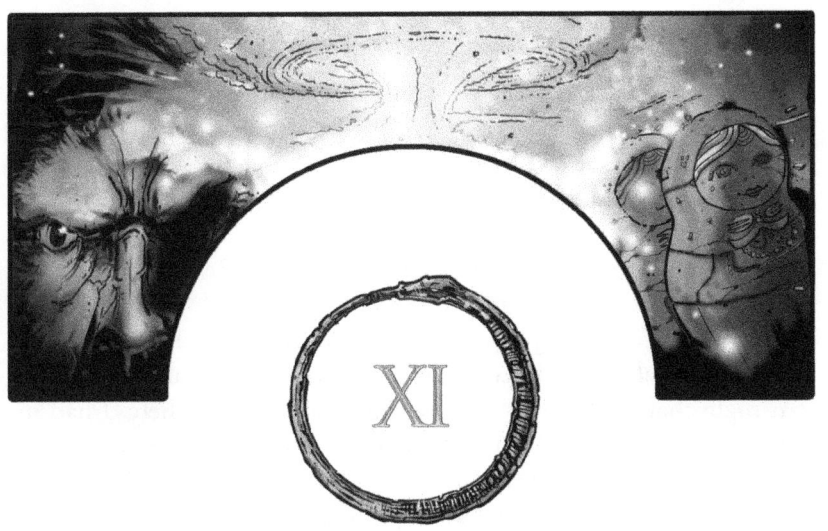

DARREN McGAVIN'S CAT:
A CONVERSATION WITH ERIN MAHER & KAY REINDL

Interview by James McLean & Troy L. Foreman
Written by Adam Chamberlain

Erin Maher is eager that her writing partner, Kay Reindl, should tell the cautionary and somewhat embarrassing tale of her first meeting with writer and producer Glen Morgan. "This is a story that we didn't tell anyone," confesses Reindl, "and then when we would have meetings people would say, 'Now, didn't you and Glen fight on the internet?' We realized that he'd been telling people, so then we thought we could tell people too.

"On *The X-Files* message boards on AOL, back in those beautiful, horrible days, they were doing 'The Field Where I Died,' which had not aired yet, and everyone was talking about what the idea was. And I said, 'Oh, it just sounds like they're going to screw it up!' Glen was posting on the message boards every now and then, and he posts a really nasty message at me, like, 'You don't know what you're talking about!' Then he emails me as well, because you could do that on AOL, and basically in a longer way said, 'You don't know what you're talking about!' I was mortified."

"She really was," pitches in Maher, "because even then she was the hugest fan of Glen and Jim."

"At the thought of pissing him off," continues Reindl, "I just went, 'Oh my God. This was not my intention,' and I wrote him this incredibly long, weeping, apologetic email about how horrified I was. We had mutual friends in common and I was going to an awards thing that night that I knew he was going to be at. So I got there, I had my two gin and tonics—which is what I need to talk to strangers—and found him, and said, 'Hey, I'm a really big fan of yours. By the way, you slapped me online earlier today!' He had this physical reaction where he kind of jumped backwards, as if he thought, 'She's come to kill me!' And he just went, 'Oh my God, I am so sorry about that. I knew after I sent that email that I shouldn't have sent it.' I said, 'No, don't be silly. I was the idiot!' So that's how I met him."

Luckily for all concerned, the indiscretion did no lasting damage, as Maher notes. "Then they hired us right onto their show!"

In conversation, Reindl and Maher have an uncanny habit of finishing one another's sentences, a rapport that surely serves them in their work together. How did their writing partnership come about? "We actually met when we were working at Universal Pictures in the story department," says Reindl. "If any of you kids out there want to get into film or T.V., working at the studio or a network and learning that process is really valuable. We met there, and we were just filing scripts and coverage and things like that. Assistants were writing and we thought, 'Hey, we think we can do that,' and that's kind of how we started."

"But it's funny too," adds Maher, "because our paths had actually crossed about three or four times before that. I'm from Fresno, California, and Kay moved up to Fresno right when I was moving away. We both went to Cal State Northridge, but we didn't meet there. We were interested in some of the same bands, and I had actually read some of her music stuff and had never met her. So it was weird. When we met we realized we had been in the same room at the same time a lot, so it was sort of like we were meant to get together and work together, in a way."

"We'd been at some concerts at the same time," Reindl confirms.

"Small concerts, though, like the Alarm played at Cal State Northridge and we were both there, and I actually remember seeing Kay there but I didn't really know her yet. She was a big U2 fan and did some work on fanzines and stuff, so I knew her work from that. When we finally met I was talking about a U2 cartoon that I had seen—this really cute little piece of artwork—and I asked her if she had seen it. She just looked at me and said, 'That's mine!'"

The duo benefited from evolving a writing process together from the outset, as Reindl explains. "It was actually kind of easy for us, because we hadn't written scripts on our own. I think if you ask a lot of writers would they consider writing with somebody else, they just want to shoot themselves in the head because the thought of having to change their process to accommodate somebody else is literally unthinkable. We didn't really know what we were doing, so it was easier for us to sit down and figure it out together. We created a process together, as opposed to two processes coming together to fight against each other and then one of them eventually winning out. Also, we really like the same kinds of things, so that makes it a little easier. It's not like one of us always wants to write stuff about war, because neither one of us is a boy, so there's that. We have an idea, and one of us says, 'Hey, where should we put the ancient manuscript in this story?' And the other one will say, 'Well, in Act Three.' We have the same kind of likes and dislikes when it comes to story, so there's never really been an issue with that."

But what happens on those few occasions when there is a difference of opinion? "If there ever is a problem, if one of us feels really strongly about something they'll usually win out," answers Maher. "I don't think we've ever really had a huge fight about anything. We may have had minor disagreements about stuff, but it eventually comes down to the person who feels more strongly. You go, 'Okay, I see your point. You have an emotional investment in this and you see it very strongly, and I don't.' It usually tends to work out okay."

From "A Single Blade of Grass" to "Matryoshka," the writing team of Maher and Reindl contributed some of *Millennium*'s most eclectic tales, stories that reconsider everything from ancient religious mythology to modern American history. Story concepts "come from everywhere," says Reindl, "especially now because I look at everything as a potential story. I don't consciously say, 'I'm looking for a story,' but you'll read something and you'll go, 'Oh, that's interesting. I don't know how that would be a complete story, but there's a kernel of something there.' You put stuff away sometimes, or something will leap out at you right away and you have to work on it right then. So it kind of works that way, but there's always a story hanging around, lurking somewhere."

"I get a lot of ideas driving for some reason," muses Maher. "I think it's because you're in the car and you don't really have anything to do, you're on the same freeway that you're on all the time, so it's very routine and it's a good time to let ideas pop into your head. I'm always getting ideas in the car and going, 'Oh, I've got to pull over and write this down.'"

Reindl's offhand reference to the fact that she and Maher never "write stuff about war" because neither of them is a boy is uttered with a laugh, a distinctly tongue-in-cheek statement, but it has the ring of truth about it, especially since their scripts do stand out as being particularly character driven. Would it be a crass generalization to suggest that women writers are naturally more drawn to character over action than their male counterparts? "I think they can," considers Reindl, "but I don't think they necessarily have to, and I think it becomes a problem when you assume that they will. I think, for example, that Morgan and Wong are tremendously good at writing female characters, but I think part of the reason for that is that they don't approach them as female characters; they approach them as characters who happen to be female. I tend to respond to writers who write that way as opposed to writers who say, 'Okay, we have to create a female character here.' I think there are definitely male writers who just want to gut people, but we like to gut people too! We have! We've sewn some people back together in episodes!"

"But we're definitely not generally drawn to big action pieces unless there's a good character story that goes along with it," Maher suggests.

"Yeah," says Reindl, "or some really cool genre element to it. That's kind of our catnip too, as opposed to just a big action thing."

"I love to go and see big action movies because they're really fun, especially if they're really well done. It's not the first thing that we would think of to write, but I know there are women who write them very well."

The holiday-themed "Midnight of the Century" is Maher and Reindl's most character-led installment, offering viewers a somber glimpse into the private family life of Frank Black. Reflecting on the inception of the episode, Maher recalls, "I think Glen actually came to us to tell us that they were going to give us the Christmas episode."

"And then we all laughed for about five minutes about the idea of a *Millennium* Christmas episode!" Reindl interjects.

"But we were really intrigued by that idea, because there is so much mysticism around the Christmas season, and we are both demons for doing research. So we just dove in and did a lot of research about the mythology of Christmas. Not just Christian mythology, but ghosts and fetches—which come up in the episode—and the veil between the worlds, and the solstice, and all of those things. We found so many things that we wanted to pack in, and we did pack in a lot. We probably could have packed in even more if we'd been allowed to. It was kind of fun because we really got to do a little character driven Christmas journey for Frank, and we didn't have to have a case. We really didn't have to have anything except Frank exploring his own past."

The Christmas installment also stands out due to a memorable guest star performance by Darren McGavin as Henry Black, Frank's estranged father. "We were so excited," beams Maher. "Originally, though, they were trying very hard to get Johnny Cash. Because, as Glen said, 'The Man in Black' as Frank Black's dad would have been great. He was ill at the time and ended up not being able to do it, but we were over the moon to get Darren McGavin. We didn't think we would be able to get him, because I think he had already turned down *The X-Files* at that point, so they weren't sure that he would say yes. We had a lot of really great older male actors come in and audition for it. We felt horrible that so many great actors were there who wanted to play this part and that we couldn't cast, but when Darren McGavin said he would do it, obviously we just leapt at that. And he was wonderful.

"I remember a story about him. They were shooting it over the Thanksgiving holiday, and he was going to be staying up in Vancouver, obviously, and he wanted to take his cat. There was this whole big thing about taking the cat. I think that they didn't want to pay, because there was an extra fee at the hotel for having his cat, and the production didn't want to pay for it. So finally Jim Wong said, 'Take it out of my *per diem*. I'll pay for the cat.' And they actually did take it out of Jim's *per diem* so that Darren McGavin could have his cat with him over the Thanksgiving holiday." She pauses mischievously before adding, "We wanted to start a band called Darren McGavin's Cat, but that never happened either."

The scenes between Frank and Henry are some of the most poignant and powerful of the entire series. Reindl gives both actors their due. "I don't think I've seen Lance play a scene the way he plays that scene. It's just a different kind of performance for him, and it's so specific to his relationship with his dad. And Darren McGavin is just so spectacular—the way he plays it, where he realizes the mistakes and doesn't really know how to fix them, and finally gets handed this chance to at least explain himself. His performance is just beautiful."

"It just makes me cry every time I see it," agrees Maher. "They elevated that scene so much. Watching that again, the way it holds up, for us it is just the honor of having these two actors do it. It was the second thing we'd ever written for television, and we were so pleased. It remains one of the best experiences that we've ever had. I think we didn't really know how lucky we were."

"I kind of feel like we had a pretty good idea, then later you realize you were even luckier than you thought you were. At the time, though, we knew that it was an amazing opportunity. I feel good about that, never taking it for granted."

"Midnight of the Century" continues a tradition of holiday-themed *Millennium* episodes initiated by Morgan and Wong's "The Curse of Frank Black," in which Frank Black is haunted by memories of his past on All Hallows Eve. Reindl explains that "Midnight of the Century" was originally intended to be the second in a trilogy of holiday installments for Season Two. "Really, when Morgan and Wong decided to do the Halloween episode—'The Curse of Frank Black'—it was supposed to be three holiday episodes for Frank. Then, of course, Easter didn't happen, because I think everybody went, 'Oh God, we can't let them do an Easter episode—it could be a disaster!' We said, 'No, come on—it'll be a great idea!' So that was really the idea, and having watched the Halloween episode again recently, it's just one of the best hours of T.V. I've ever seen. It is fun to see how they fit together, leading Frank back into his past and the way that his gift can be helpful. We really loved that idea, and to be able to do it in a Christmas episode was super fun."

The festive theme is also one that allows a little humor into *Millennium*, as Frank frantically seeks a suitable gift for Jordan, and that lighter touch often appears in the duo's episodes, even "A Single Blade of Grass." The production of the episode, however, their first for television, suffered a number of difficulties. "There were some problems for various reasons with that episode," Maher admits. "I'm still pretty pleased with it, but there were definitely some things that could have gone better, or possibly been written better."

Reindl agrees, although those very problems also granted the writers some valuable insight into the post-production process. "It didn't quite come together the way we hoped it would. But it was a good experience for us, because we did have some trouble with it, [as it gave us the opportunity] to be able to be in the editing room."

"And watch Jim Wong and the editor fix it!"

"When we first saw our dailies we went, 'Erm, is it supposed to be like this?'" recalls Reindl.

"We were so new at it—we had never worked in television before and had no idea how any of it worked—and we were horrified. They were like, 'No, no, this is great! This is fine. Don't worry.' It's really weird for the first time watching dailies and not really knowing yet how everything is going to come together."

The episode was also subject to budgetary restrictions, and Maher discusses how one such cut posed the two writers quite a challenge, albeit not such an uncommon one. "The night before they were going to shoot the big museum sequence they cut the budget, and we had to basically rewrite Act Three overnight, which is one of the problems with the episode. 'Okay, you can't do this whole giant sequence that we had planned, so you guys need to rewrite this by nine o'clock.' As you work more in television, that's something that you find can happen and you just kind of have to be ready for it. We've done a lot of rewriting episodes in twenty-four hours. It just happens, but that was our first episode and we weren't as prepared for it. There was a huge thing with a wolf, and things coming alive, and we couldn't do it."

"It was going to be really cool!" vouches Reindl.

"I know Morgan and Wong were very good about staying on budget, but I think that the things that we wanted to do in the episode wound up costing more."

"I don't think it was any mistake anyone had made—it was just a last minute decision."

"It was, 'Oh, I don't think we're going to be able to pull this off.'"

Unfortunately, the resulting rewrite served only to present a further complication. "We wound up rewriting it and our episode almost ended up short, which is why—if you count—Frank has twenty-one visions in the episode. If you think sometimes it looks like he's not reacting to a vision, it's because Lance had no idea he was having one at the time! It's not his fault. Do not do a drinking game with it!" Sound advice for *Millennium* fans.

The visions of "A Single Blade of Grass," inspired by the symbolism of Native American lore and possessing a distinctly mystical quality, are also radically different to those seen elsewhere in *Millennium*. "They're very beautiful," says Maher. "One of my favorite things that the effects people did was the crows flying into the longhouse. I thought that just was absolutely beautiful. Now I can probably do it on my phone, but I was super happy with that. There's a lot of nice stuff in there, but there was a lot of rebuilding and creating visions just because we needed it for time."

Regardless of the reasons for adding those sequences to the episode, their appearance makes some bold suggestions regarding Frank's gift. "It was very risky," agrees Reindl, "and we just kind of went, 'Hey, this would be a cool idea!' without really thinking about it. But Morgan and Wong were extremely supportive, so we never saw it that we were reaching too high. I think we did reach too high, but I think that's okay. I think it's okay to reach too high and not succeed sometimes. At least you've tried. And there is that nice moment in the middle when he's talking to the anthropologist about what he's seeing and, having watched it again, I had forgotten that Lance has this really emotional moment in it. It's kind of unexpected, and that's really nice."

Maher seizes this opportunity to single out Henriksen's unique presence: "There's really nobody like Lance on a show now, and it's so nice to see someone of his stature and the type of actor he is. He's pretty wonderful in the series, and I kind of miss having somebody like that. What's interesting too—and people don't realize—he had a huge following among women, and among older women, such that the show had a really big female following. I think a lot of people didn't really realize that, but there's just that appeal that he has to a lot of people: his voice and his presence. He's a pretty fascinating actor."

Given such praise, it is ironic, then, that the duo penned the only episode of *Millennium* not to feature Frank Black. Maher recalls that the series' producers were not looking forward to breaking this news to their lead actor as "Anamnesis" was preparing to enter production. "They were really worried about telling Lance that he wasn't going to be in the episode, because they thought that he would get freaked out and think he was going to be fired or something," she says.

Reindl chimes in. "Remember, at first, that he was only going to make a phone call? He was going to make a phone call to keep him present in the episode. We were talking about this phone call, and Darin [Morgan] thought it was the funniest thing he had ever heard. He was hysterical about, 'Oh, I can't wait to hear the phone call that Frank is going to make!' We just kind of realized that the episode would work better without him."

"So then they had to go and tell him that he wasn't going to be in the episode," Maher continues, "very trepidatiously. And he said, 'Great—I'm going to Hawaii!'"

The duo relished the opportunity to write an episode featuring Catherine in the leading role, as Maher recalls. "We had really wanted to do something for her, because she's so wonderful."

In spite of all apprehensions, Henriksen's reaction to the news that he would not be involved in the episode would prove to be the least controversial aspect of "Anamnesis." "You remember, of course the whole part in 'Somehow, Satan Got Behind Me' with the censor?" asks Reindl. "That is specifically from our arguments with our censor over 'Anamnesis.'"

"Our Standards and Practices person," clarifies Maher, "who was actually terrific."

It was not that Standards and Practices executive Linda Shima-Tsumo had personal objections to the religious ideology on display in the episode. "She was fantastic," Reindl explains. "With her it was not about what she thought, it was about how she was going to defend the episode to people who were going to complain."

"But it was really funny," adds Maher, "because Glen Morgan and Kay and I were on speakerphones with her for three hours! Darin kept wandering in and out, hysterical, and writing things down, and that's where the line, 'I am Network Standards and Practices!' in 'Somehow, Satan Got Behind Me' came from. She actually said that."

With its focus on Apocrypha, "Anamnesis" is rife with controversial religious themes. The episode's script is the sort of document that might inspire a network censors to break out in a cold sweat. "They were very concerned," Reindl remembers, "not really so much about offending people but about being able to back up that we had a legitimate reason for telling the story. I think at one point she asked us, 'Do you have research?' And of course we had the same research as Dan Brown, we just didn't steal it word for word like he did! But we sent her over this huge stack of research. Basically what they wanted to know was, 'That you guys did not come up with the idea of Jesus and Mary Magdalene getting together and having a child, that it did not spring from your head.' And we said, 'No, it didn't. Here's centuries of people talking about this stuff.' We sent it over and, when she looked at that, she said, 'Okay, go ahead.' But they didn't even realize until the second time through the script, because they were focused on the fact that we had a kid who was going to kill somebody. It was the second time through the script, we're on the call, and she says, 'Wait a minute. Are you saying that Jesus and Mary Magdalene got married and had a kid?' We said, 'Yeah!' And she said, 'You guys can't say that!'"

"I remember Glen just said, 'Why not?' And then I think we had two more hours."

The fact that this thread of the script was only picked up on a second read-through only compounded the issue, as Reindl explains. "We were just sitting there going, 'We're shooting tomorrow. There's nothing we can do.'"

Having one of their executive producers on hand, however, helped to diffuse the situation. "It was so funny because Glen was conducting the conversation," says Maher, "and if we would start to say something and it was the wrong moment he would stop us, and then at other times he would beckon us: 'Say something now! Say this!'"

"It was pretty masterful," agrees Reindl.

Ultimately, Shima-Tsumo proved very supportive. "She was great," says Maher, "once we were able to persuade her that there was some sort of scholarly background to this."

Describing "Anamnesis" as scholarly may, however, be something of an exaggeration considering at least one of their source texts, which was less than rigorous in building its argument. "We sent her Xeroxed pages from *The Holy Blood and the Holy Grail*," reveals Reindl. "The interesting thing about that book is that there actually is a lot of interesting research in the back half of it. It's just that the first half of it is so insane! It will say, 'Hey, have you ever thought about the possibility that this might be true?' Then they go, 'Okay, so that's true' and continue on with the book. And you think, 'No! You can't just say that!'"

Nevertheless, the hypothetical-driven *The Holy Blood and the Holy Grail* (1982) made for inspired source material on *Millennium*. "It was great," says Maher. "That was another episode where we had just done tons of research with the Black Virgins and all of these things that we managed to cram in. But I remember the first letter that we got after that episode aired. Somebody sent a letter or an email, and the title of it was, 'Why blasphemy, Mr. Carter?' And we went, 'Yay!'"

"Our job is done!" cheers Reindl.

The potential for viewer offense was, however, not an issue for the duo as they developed the episode, as Maher explains. "We went to Glen and Jim and said, 'We have this idea about this girl having [visions].' We originally came up with the Virgin Mary, and then we came up with Mary Magdalene because we were reading all the research."

"We started doing the research on visions of the Virgin Mary and you wind up at the various spots that you always wind up at, and we kind of got sidetracked. I think we found *The Cult of the Black Virgin*. We read that book and we went, 'Oh, wait a minute. This is actually even more interesting.'"

The text prompted the writers to reconsider the role played by Mary Magdalene in Christian mythology. "You start really seeing Mary Magdalene as this amazing forgotten figure," says Maher, "for what she actually stood for at one point, which is this very strong female character in the Christian religion who ended up getting sidelined and branded as a prostitute and all of these things, which she clearly was not. It was really fun to think about that. What if someone was having a vision of her? What would that mean? Glen and Jim were great, because you would take them an idea and they would just either go, 'No' or they would go, 'Okay, yeah—go break it.' That was one where they just thought that was really interesting, and they said, 'Go break it.' They would say something like, 'Just keep in mind that Lara's going to go crazy three episodes later, so start seeding that in.' So we got to have her having her visions, and you could see her breakdown starting to happen."

As well as incorporating the ongoing character arc for Lara Means, her interactions with Catherine help to define and explore opposing viewpoints in relation to the case. "I think that's what the series does," says Reindl. "It does it with the Owls and the Roosters, it does it with Watts and Frank, with Frank and Catherine. I think it presents two sides with all the characters really."

Some viewers would argue that the conflict between Lara and Catherine is, at its deepest level, focused foremost on Frank, a perspective which Maher vehemently rejects. *Millennium*'s characters, she argues, are above such petty interpersonal politics. "I remember somebody at the time getting very upset because they thought that the two women should be fighting more about Frank. That was really upsetting to hear, because not all women are fighting over the guy. That's not what this is about, and that's not something that Catherine's worried about. There is something deeper going on here. I think we were lucky because we had such strong characters that we got to write to, and that had been established as being really strong characters, and never really got into any of that silliness. For some shows it works; for this show that's so not what the show is about, and that's not where these people's insecurities lay."

When *Millennium* returned after the climactic events of its second year, Erin Maher and Kay Reindl became story editors on the series. Reindl explains what this meant in practice. "It's not really the way it works everywhere else. Story editor is just really a level. You start out in T.V. as a staff writer, and that's the lowest rung, then the next level up is story editor. So it really doesn't mean that we had necessarily more to do as story editors, because it was really just our level; we got promoted up to the next level. It means different things in different countries, and it means different things in animation than it does in live action—because a story editor is more like a showrunner in animation—so we were basically just responsible for our episodes, although we were involved at the beginning of the season in trying to figure out what the show was going to be. The whole staff was involved in that."

The transition was not easy, and Reindl goes on to offer some insight into why that was. "It was really tough, because Morgan and

Wong weren't there anymore. They had hired Michael Duggan, who had worked on *Law & Order*. So the idea was—or at least our understanding was—we're going to go back to doing more crime stuff. But it just never really came together, and then he wound up leaving and Chip [Johannessen] and Ken [Horton] ran the show. I think by the time they started to right the ship we were already several episodes down the line into production. Then all you're doing really is playing catch-up. So I think there are some really good episodes in Season Three, but as a whole Season Two is a more cohesive season of television than Season Three. I think with *Millennium* it's tricky, when you're doing a show that has that much mythology. You really want to be able to plot where your big moments are going to be. I think that kind of hurt Season Three a little bit, with not being able to do that. So there was a lot of, 'Okay, we're breaking this episode but we also have to think about where we are in the mythology.' When you're doing it at the same time it's just harder to step back from it."

Maher agrees. "With Ken and Chip getting the show thrown in their laps a little bit, they were not expecting to be in that position. Whilst they rose to the occasion and did a great job—because they're both really good—it wasn't a position they expected to be in, and there was a lot of pressure on them too, not only to get their own stuff done but now to be running the whole thing and sort of rethinking the way maybe they wanted the whole season to go."

Maher and Reindl's sole produced script in Season Three is the singular installment "Matryoshka," aptly named for the Russian nesting dolls that suggest secrets within secrets *ad infinitum*. The concept at the core of the episode, Maher explains, was first sparked by the writings of Robert Louis Stevenson. "That was another one where we came upon it because we had been doing a lot of research for something. We just got really intrigued by the idea that we had always wanted to do a Jekyll and Hyde kind of thing, and we had also been reading a lot about Los Alamos and atomic weapons, and somehow it all just tied together. I think we pitched that one to Ken and he liked the idea, so we went away and worked on it. That was actually a tough episode. We did a lot of rewriting on it."

"We did," agrees Reindl, "and there was a ton of research. And we didn't have the internet way back then—we had books! We had a terrific research department at Fox; they were unbelievable."

"They don't get enough credit."

"They don't. They would get anything for us. They were fantastic. We had a lot of research that we got from them, a lot of it just on how it worked at Los Alamos and what it looked like. I thought the way it was shot, it looked fantastic. It felt just like Los Alamos."

The episode features a memorable teaser sequence, as a retired F.B.I. agent commits suicide to the sentimental strains of the Mills Brothers song "Till Then," a romantic tune that enjoyed great success upon its release in 1944. "We always loved to have a song in the teaser," Maher says, "and that was something where we actually did a lot of looking into music from that period, and trying to find the exact right song that felt like it would really fit there. I think that song really worked. We were really happy when we came up with that. Everybody was so great on that show. We would go to them and say, 'Okay, we want this!' and generally they would get it for you. We said, 'We really want to get this song,' and we had it. It was great. It was always really challenging, but really fun and exciting. I could not praise the crew highly enough. It was an amazing bunch of people who would just go that extra mile on a daily basis. You would just have these little ideas. I remember how hard they worked to get us the little angel [in 'Midnight of the Century']. [Production designer] Mark Freeborn kept bringing us one."

"We would be in somebody's house," Reindl recalls, "and he would come up and go, 'What about this angel? Is this right?'"

"The attention to detail was just fantastic. It's not something that always happens, and I think everybody who worked on that show was really proud of the show and really wanted to make it great. It really did feel like a family."

"Matryoshka" significantly expands upon the existing mythology underpinning the Millennium Group by implying that J. Edgar Hoover influenced the organization whilst he was the feared, all-powerful Director of the F.B.I. How do Maher and Reindl correlate this development with Season Two's assertions regarding the Group's more ancient roots as a religious cult? "Our interpretation was that it was still the same Group that we saw in the second season, but that Hoover was a part of it," Reindl expounds, recalling mythological developments that began to be seeded as far back as "Beware of the Dog."

"He latched onto an already existing, very old motivation and turned it into something else."

"Because if anyone was going to do that, it was going to be Hoover. That's where we got that idea, and we kind of liked the idea of different branches of the Group."

"And people using it for their own ends."

Reindl suggests further context: "At Los Alamos, they really all thought they were going to blow up the world; they thought they were going to ignite the atmosphere. That, to us, felt like an end of the world scenario, so that's why we wanted to do that, and we liked the idea of going back and bringing in crazy Hoover." With a laugh she adds, "I'm disappointed that Leonardo DiCaprio did not have an ouroboros tattoo on him in *J. Edgar*, because that would have been fantastic!"

The duo was well matched with the aspirations of Morgan and Wong in terms of their interest in detailing the Group's mysterious background, as Reindl explains. "When we met with them to be on the show and they asked us what we would do with it, we said, 'Well, we really liked the Millennium Group stuff. We would like to explore that.' And that's what they wanted to do. I think Season Two explores the beginnings of the Group, going all the way back to the bog people, and its ancient origins. Then in Season Three you get into more governmental stuff. But that would make sense—if something's been around for a thousand years, it's going to lead elsewhere."

"People seize on it and use it to their own ends," adds Maher, emphasizing the realism of their approach to the mythology, "and that was our interpretation. We loved the idea of it going back for God only knows how long. [Season Three] really doesn't rewrite [the mythology of Season Two]; it just takes it and runs in another direction."

"It never says, 'This didn't happen.' I think that maybe if you're watching it you think that's what it's saying, but I don't think that it's saying that at all, and we never heard that at all from anybody on the show."

"No, definitely not."

"I think it's one of the fun things about the show," Reindl goes on, "and one of the things that we loved about the fans, that people were really willing to do some work themselves and try to figure things out and expand upon things themselves. I thought that was kind of exciting, that you could actually get people thinking about these things and wanting to know more. After 'Anamnesis,' we got a lot of mail from people wanting to know a lot more about Gnosticism and wanting to know about what research we had done and what books we had read. So that was pretty cool, that people wanted to explore that stuff further."

Season Two and, in particular, Season Three arguably offer up the ambiguity in a number of episodes, leaving *Millennium*'s challenging stories open to interpretation. Reindl attributes this quality in the series to writer and executive producer Chip Johannessen. "He loves to do that. If he weren't a writer I think he would be a thought experiment guy, because that's what he loves doing. He just loves to pose questions like that. And I love that that exists on television, because usually everything is all tied up at some point, if not at the end of an episode then at the end of a season or series."

Maher recalls Johannessen's creative process as being unique. "It's really interesting the way he jumps into stories. He's really different from anybody else. He comes in a lot of times with a visual that he wants to play with. I remember him coming in one day and saying, 'I have an idea for an episode I want to do. It's about the Tibetan Book of the Dead and five little severed hands.' We all went, 'Okay.' And we figured Chip would figure out what to do with that! Nobody else came into stories the way he did, and it was always really interesting to see what he would come up with and then how that would turn into a story.

"It's funny, too, because then you look at a show like *Lost*, which did a lot of the same things that *Millennium* did—but we did them first! A lot of people got so angry at the end of *Lost* because every question wasn't answered or it didn't wrap up the way that they wanted it to, and they had expectations. But I think they didn't want to answer every question. You don't want to answer every question. You don't want to spoon-feed people. Especially with a show like *Lost*, which gave you so much to think about. I think there's no way to answer every question. You're going to have an hour of someone just sitting there explaining it. I think there are times when you have to go, 'Look, this is what the showrunners wanted to do. This is what the creator of the show wanted to do.'"

Alongside Johannessen, the writers sing the praises of Glen Morgan and James Wong. "I believe Glen and Jim should be running television," proclaims Maher. "It upsets me that they're not together anymore running great shows. They're both great separately, too, but I just want to work with them again, together or separately. Those guys are just geniuses."

"There is nobody like them," Reindl agrees. "It's funny watching Season Two of *Millennium* again, having had the distance. I miss the way they write, I miss the way they edit episodes—which was better than anyone else does it."

Given Maher and Reindl's love of music, it is unsurprising that the relished the opportunity to work with composer Mark Snow. "He's amazing," Maher raves. "I remember going to meet him and actually getting to talk to him about the scoring. I saw him not that long ago. He was signing the CDs for the *Millennium* soundtrack in Burbank, and I went down to buy some copies and reintroduce myself to him. He was just really excited. To see him and talk to him again and to remember just how incredible the music from *Millennium* was, and watching 'Midnight of the Century' again and seeing what he did, it just knocks me out. It's so beautiful."

"He was allowed to just be free as a composer," Reindl explains, "and he created so many different themes. The episodes all have different little touches."

Maher offers some notable examples: "'A Single Blade of Grass,' the things that he found to do there, and then 'Anamnesis,' where he got really influenced by some of Peter Gabriel. He was another one of those guys where you just feel like he could do anything. He has such a great knowledge of different types of music, and he could just bring all these different points of view and really elevate each episode. I really feel like his score for 'Midnight of the Century' just notches everything up so much higher. That ending kills me, and the music is a huge part of it, the camera going up and that music. Shaun Cassidy actually once told us that was the most depressing Christmas episode in the history of television! I disagree, because Frank reconciles with his Dad kind of at the last minute, and that was definitely meant to be uplifting. That was something that had been hanging over him all of these years, and he got that closure and a new relationship with his father, and an explanation for what was going on at the time. So to me that's all really very uplifting and very moving."

Does music ever play a role in their writing process? "Not coming up with ideas necessarily," Reindl replies, "but I always like to have a soundtrack to a story. Even if you don't have one right away, the music comes to it, and that's something that we really responded to with Morgan and Wong, because they worked that way too. If you notice, in *Millennium* there's a lot of music. It's funny, because we had wanted to do the teaser for 'Anamnesis' to a song, and we had tried to get a Sinead O'Connor song, but she would not give us the time of day!"

"We worked really hard," bemoans Maher, "and we wrote her this letter about how this was a very feminist story about the suppression of women in the church, and she still said no. We still love her, though!"

"She didn't care. We just thought she was full of it," jokes Reindl. "But then we settled on this Patti Smith song, and we went to Glen and said, 'Hey, we want to use this song instead.' And he went, 'Oh, Patti Smith. That's great. That actually works out, because we're going to make Lara go crazy to Patti Smith.' So we were on the same wavelength in a scary way with those guys. I love using music for things and, even if you don't use music, having the song kind of there. I really like that."

Erin Maher and Kay Reindl are overwhelmingly positive in reflecting upon their experiences on *Millennium*. "There was just something about being allowed to be so creative with the show," says Maher. "It was amazing to go to Glen and Jim and pitch these crazy ideas and have them go, 'Okay, go do that.' That just doesn't happen. Also, the studio and the network were very supportive. It's really different now, with the documentation that you have to come up with to pitch an idea—six pages of how we would do it. In those days, you would send six loglines over to the studio and the network, and they would go, 'Okay.' It was a lot easier then. You kind of had to please fewer people. On recent shows we've been on, you're on a notes call with six people from the studio and five people from the network, and it's hard to get a consensus on anything. We didn't realize, in a way, how easy we had it, in terms of being allowed to be the creative ones and not having to fight with people who thought that they should be the creative ones, even though that's what they were kind of paying us to do. Although we've also worked with some great executives who do have some great ideas."

Reindl is quick to reinforce this point, offering a more positive outlook on show business. "That's important to note too, because a lot of writers in particular will just complain about all the suits and everything, but there are some smart executives, smart producers, and great people who you will want to work with all the time. And I think if a lot of these people were actually given the power to make decisions, you would see some different things happening. But some of them are just really fantastic. We've been kind of lucky."

"*Millennium* was our first show; it was our first experience," reflects Maher. "We have such a soft spot for that show, and looking at it again now has been amazing, because it really does hold up."

All this from a fateful first meeting that followed on from an insult leveled at one of their future producers. Reindl is quick to caution anyone who is considering imitating her behavior to think again. "Kids, I do not recommend picking a fight with people on the internet!"

Once again, Maher completes the thought: "I don't think anyone else has ever gotten a job that way!"

SNAKES IN THE GRASS AND SNAKES IN THE OPEN:
ANIMAL SYMBOLISM IN *MILLENNIUM'S* SECOND SEASON

by John Kenneth Muir

During the second season, *Millennium* (1996-99) shifted perspective, narrative focus, and tone in many dramatic ways. The resulting change of focus shepherded by producers James Wong and Glen Morgan led to a rather dramatic "opening up" of Frank Black's (Lance Henriksen) world, one that would change the very nature of both the Millennium Group (now rather definitively a cult, right down to the use of secret code words) and the bizarre threats Frank would be called upon to investigate.

Gazing back across the second season today, one can see how the series regularly deployed animals—or animal symbolism—to fill the didactic role previously held by the human serial killers in Season One, though serial killers did appear in episodes such as "The Beginning and the End" and "Mikado."

Why animals?

Animals have been a vital element in the development of mythological systems throughout history, across virtually every culture imaginable. In Western societies of the Middle Ages, in particular, animals represented specific traits and could therefore be utilized as symbols to convey moral and religious lessons in works of art. Animals can represent victims of technology, industrialization, or war. Also, animals sometimes equate with the concept of "purity," existing in a wild, natural state and therefore utterly free of man's sins and vices. Some passion plays and other didactic forms of theater utilized animal imagery to represent specific modes of behavior, including human vices.

Considering *Millennium*'s heavily didactic qualities, it was only natural that the drama would marshal animals and symbols of animals to help us in the 1990s to understand "who we are." This shift from serial killers to animal symbols was apparent almost immediately during *Millennium*'s sophomore season, commencing with the second episode in the queue, "Beware of the Dog."

In this tale, Frank Black is ordered by the Millennium Group to visit the remote town of Bucksnort, an isolated burg where a couple of elderly vacationers have been murdered in a vicious animal attack. Upon arrival, Frank uncovers an entire town dreading sundown, the span in which a pack of wild dogs consistently emerge to terrorize the citizens. What Frank soon discovers is that these dogs in fact "represent evil" and are overrunning the town of Bucksnort because the world—in the lead up to the millennium—is losing its sense of balance in favor of an encroaching evil.

In the apocryphal Acts of Andrew, the apostle Saint Andrew is called upon to expel demons in the form of dogs from an imperiled city, and that is the role Frank explicitly takes on in this second season installment (Elliott 274). This leads us to another obvious reference: hellhounds. In Celtic myth, hellhounds are believed to be the Devil's dogs, and similar canine beasts called *cadejo* also turn up in Central and South American folklore.

In "Beware the Dog," Frank first meets "The Old Man" (R. G. Armstrong), the leader of the Millennium Group, a figure who warns him "you have no idea about true Evil." Though this may be a bit of an exaggeration since Frank has been around the block with Evil quite a few times (he *did* battle Lucy Butler in "Lamentation"), it is nonetheless a line of dialogue that resonates throughout the remainder of the season.

Indeed, Frank frequently finds himself countenancing different mythologies that concern the apocalypse or end of the world, mythologies implicitly about Evil. Already, "Beware of the Dog" harks back to the apocryphal texts of Saint Andrew and the aforementioned devil dog legends.

Just two episodes later, in "A Single Blade of Grass," Frank again faces a myth of "end times," one explicitly connected to animals or involving animal symbolism. Here, Frank travels to New York City to learn the identity of a corpse found on a construction site. Before long, he is enmeshed in a Native American ritual, one that is meant to forge a contact with the spirit world and spur an Indian version of the apocalypse. A sign that this apocalypse has begun in earnest is the return of an animal—the buffalo, in particular. What the buffalo represents, in terms of abstract symbolism, is that thing which was "taken" by the white man's colonization of America: both the land and the wildlife.

In the final scene of the episode, Frank escapes a ritual involving human sacrifice and—on the streets of Manhattan—sees several buffalo miraculously running nearby, just feet from him. The prophecy was true; the buffalo have returned to their home, as the cult believed, but the sign does not mean what they hoped it would mean—an end to white man's dominion. Instead, the buffalo are quickly followed by the clowns of a circus, a sign that belief in this legend is foolish, silly, or misplaced. Frank notes the irony and wonders if the things we wish to come true will do so in the way we would like.

What else does the return of the buffalo represent? One might make the argument that the presence of buffalo in the urban, technological jungle of the Big Apple is a sign—like the dogs of Bucksnort—of a world disordered and unbalanced, of wildlife shattering or otherwise violating man's carefully organized world. If we began to add up these bizarre animal occurrences, a pattern emerges, and we see it clearly in the last episode of the year, "The Fourth Horseman" and "The Time is Now."

"The Hand of St. Sebastian" also explicitly trades in animal symbolism. The episode begins in 998 A.D. with a fledgling Millennium Group in Eastern Europe battling evil, divisive forces. One

Millennium Group member is shot and killed in a bog. A thousand years later, Peter Watts (Terry O'Quinn) and Frank Black exhume the warrior's preserved corpse and discover emblazoned on his back a tattoo of the Millennium Group's symbol: the dragon or snake forever devouring its own tail. The Ouroboros. This Gnostic symbol represents the ephemeral, self-devouring nature of our terrestrial, material existence, a direct contrast to a spiritual life.

More than that, the Ouroboros represents *a cycle*, and, going back to "Beware of The Dog," the Old Man speaks to Frank of the "divine life" (a spiritual existence), "cyclical systems," and "birth and death." Even before Ronald D. Moore utilized the concept in the reimagined *Battlestar Galactica* (2004-09), we have an example in science fiction television of the idea that "this has all happened before and it will all happen again."

This idea of the cycle captured so beautifully by the snake image of the Ouroboros is reinforced thematically in an important manner. Specifically, "The Hand of St. Sebastian" makes viewers privy to two *fin de siècle* moments of an identical nature, even though they are separated by centuries. In 998 A.D., Millennium Group members face betrayal from enemies within ("the snake in the grass," one says) and enemies outside ("the snake in the open," the term utilized to describe the Catholic Church). This is the cycle that Peter and Frank unconsciously repeat—down to identical dialogue—in 1998 A.D. The point should be emphasized: Peter specifically makes note of the snake in the grass and the snake in the open. History repeats. The Millennium Group Members of 998 A.D. prevented the end of the world, and that is what Peter Watts claims to be achieving a millennium later. The two men in the past are balanced with the two men of the "now," and the Ouroboros is the symbol that ties them together, explaining that this is a cycle which will repeat forever and forever, perhaps next in 2998.

One of the most important episodes in *Millennium*'s second season is the two-part epic "Owls" and "Roosters," which depicts a growing schism inside the Millennium Group. Both of the warring factions—as can be plainly seen—are named after animals. The "Owls" are a secular group, a faction of atheist non-believers who are certain that a scientific, cosmic (meaning astronomical) apocalypse is due in sixty years. The "owls" moniker is important because, traditionally, owls represent Evil and Satan in Christian myth. They are associated with a lack of faith.

Outside of Christian tradition, by contrast, owls—in Greek myth, for example—represent something else entirely: wisdom, knowledge, and scholarship (thus science or secularism). Also, as the episode indicates, owls are a symbol of nighttime and sleep, which is critical since the Owls in the Millennium Group believe it is not yet the dawn of the apocalypse, that we are in a sixty-year "night" until that dawn.

By contrast, the "Roosters" in the Millennium Group believe in a Christian, religious apocalypse that will arrive in the year 2000 or 2001. They believe it is already the Dawn of the End, and thus—like roosters—are crowing rather loudly about it.

In Christian myth, roosters tend to represent prescience (advance knowledge), reliability, watchfulness, and faith. They are also, in some circles, a sign of "spiritual resurrection," and that is an end that this group of devout believers wants to "force," in some sense. In China, a red rooster is reputed to ward off flames or fire while white roosters are known for chasing ghosts. Both of these ideas find resonance in *Millennium*. The Roosters inside the Millennium cult do indeed want to ward off the fires of the end times and, in some sense, we know they are chasing ghosts as the world did not end at the turn of the century. Y2K was a bust.

Finally, it is impossible to ignore that it is an animal that brings forth the apocalypse in *Millennium*'s season ending two-parter, "The Fourth Horseman" and "The Time is Near." The manmade plague called known as the "Marburg variant" begins its reign of terror in chickens. Again, not coincidentally, the Four Horsemen of the Apocalypse are often linked directly with animals, at least according to visions in Ezekiel (Holy Bible, Ezekiel 1-10). Given that the end times begin with animal-bred disease on *Millennium* (a forecast of avian flu?), one can gaze across the breadth of Season Two and see its episodes— from "Beware of the Dog" to "A Single Blade of Grass," from "The Hand of St. Sebastian" to "Owls" and "Roosters"—as ominous forecasts, with the animal allusions as token indicators—warning signs—of the impending end times.

Animal symbols are truly crucial to a deeper understanding of this season of *Millennium* in another important respect: the explanation and definition of the Group's nature. The "conspiracy" episodes of *Millennium*—those involving the Group—almost all involve animals of some variety. From the introduction of the Old Man in "Beware of the Dog" to the Group's civil war in "Owls" and "Roosters" to the fruition of the Group's secret agenda to force the end in "The Fourth Horseman" and "The Time is Now," animal mythology and symbols pervade the narrative.

Whether the animals are meant to reveal nature disordered, reveal human vice, or represent spiritual evil and eternal cycles, "when animals attack" on *Millennium*, they are—like the serial killers that preceded them—showing us who we are.

WORKS CITED

Elliott, J. K. *The Apocryphal New Testament.* Oxford: Oxford UP, 1993. Print.

The Holy Bible: King James Version. London: Cambridge UP, 1945. Print.

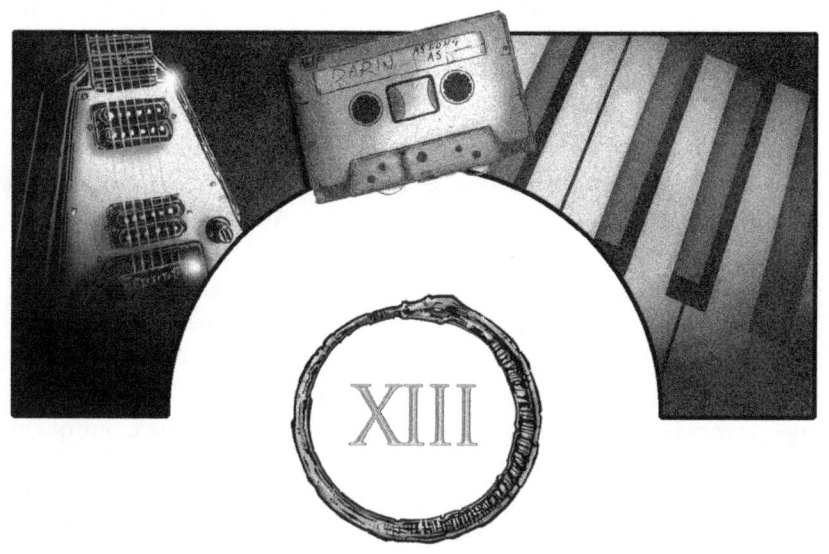

BIGGER THAN THE BEATLES:
A CONVERSATION WITH MARK SNOW

Interview by James McLean & Troy L. Foreman
Written by Adam Chamberlain

Fans of Mark Snow's distinctive, atmospheric soundtracks for the likes of *The X-Files* (1993-2002) and *Millennium* (1996-99) might be surprised to learn that the composer once enjoyed a burgeoning career as a rock star alongside one of his equally illustrious peers. "When I was at Juilliard I had this roommate, Michael Kamen, a very famous film composer. We were both actually oboe players, and we decided one day to put a band together. It was called the New York Rock & Roll Ensemble, and everyone in the band played two instruments. I played the drums that I had kind of learned from my dad—I was a very good rock-and-roll drummer, but that was about it, I couldn't really play jazz or anything too complicated, but I could lay it down pretty good—and I played the oboe. That was one of the more unusual doubles around. Michael played oboe and keyboard, the bass player played cello, and the guitarist played all kinds of guitars: mandolins, twelve-strings, and so forth and so on. We worked together for two weeks, and my now-wife's sister had a boyfriend who was an engineer at Atlantic Records. It was during the Sixties, and that was the time of Aretha Franklin, Cream, Buffalo Springfield, the Rascals, and early Bee Gees, and we went in and cut three original songs from twelve midnight to six in the morning. The engineer fellow played these for Ahmet Ertegün, who was a big shot record mogul at the time and said, 'You guys are great! You're going to be bigger than the Beatles!' So I went home and told my parents to start packing, because we were going to move out of the apartment and get a couple of jets—the whole bit, right?!"

It certainly seemed as if it might turn out that way for a time, as the New York Rock & Roll Ensemble were rubbing shoulders with the musical elite. "What happened was that we were a big time band in New York for social events for the real rich and famous," Snow continues. "We started to play gigs at college, and then all the venues like Fillmore East and West and all the other places like that. We played with a host of people from Jefferson Airplane, Janis Joplin, Grateful Dead, Eric Clapton with Cream, Eric Clapton with Delaney & Bonnie, Ten Years After, Alice Cooper, all these British bands, Sly and the Family Stone, the Turtles. It was just an amazing time. We had five albums, the thing lasted five years, and then it looked like we weren't going to be one of these big bands and so we disbanded. Michael Kamen went off to England and met up with the Monty Python guys and that's where he got his big career started, and the guitar player and I had a record deal in New York, where we were producing records."

Ultimately, the sun set on this phase of Snow's career, but new horizons beckoned. "That didn't work out, but it was a nice time for a year-and-a-half, and then my wife said, 'We're going to California, and you're going to write music for T.V. shows and movies.' I said, 'Okay, and who's going to teach me how to do that, and who's going to give me those jobs?' She said, 'Well, you're smart, you're good, I've got relatives out there—they can introduce you.' And I said, 'Okay.' We had a thousand bucks, a station wagon, two kids, and off we went. We went to California, found this place in Malibu for three hundred a month that was a shack but was overlooking the beach. After six months, I had a meeting with someone and they gave me a job writing music for an episodic show called *The Rookies*, which was an Aaron Spelling show. It just took off from there."

Music evidently runs in the blood for Mark Snow. "My dad was a drummer in Broadway pit orchestras, and there was a piano in the house," he recalls. "My mother was a kindergarten teacher, and she had to play the piano for the kids to do their eurythmic exercises. So they wanted me to take piano lessons, and I really didn't want to, but there was a famous T.V. show, *I Love Lucy*, and I wanted to see it, and they said, 'Well, we'll let you stay up and see it if you take piano lessons.' So I said, 'Okay,' and that's where it started.

"It wasn't that much of a thrill, but it was okay. I sort of picked up drumming from my dad, and I thought, 'Gee, I don't want to schlep around drums, and I don't want to be one of the eight zillion piano players. Let's find an instrument that's unusual or different that I could carry with no problem,' so I chose the oboe. I started taking lessons on that, and I auditioned for this high school in New York called the High School of Music and Art, which now is at the Lincoln Center building area, but then it was way up town in Manhattan. I was from Brooklyn, and I had to travel up there for that. But that opened my whole world, because if I had gone to a high school in Brooklyn I probably would have been—I don't know! But there were so many creative people at this school from all over the city lumped into this one place. After that, I had a private teacher who was also a teacher at Juilliard, and I auditioned for Juilliard and got into there. It looked like that was what was going to happen to me. Somehow I would be an oboe player in some orchestra."

Fate had other plans, however, and after five years playing with the New York Rock & Roll Ensemble and a move to California, Snow's composing career took off. Over a period of nearly two decades, he built up a lengthy list of credits for television, including stints on shows such as *Starsky and Hutch* (1975-79), *Hart to Hart* (1979-84), *T. J. Hooker* (1982-86), *Cagney & Lacey* (1981-88), and *Dynasty* (1981-89). It is for his subsequent collaborations with Ten Thirteen Productions, however, that he remains best known. "The idea that *The X-Files* came along when it did was just this lucky chance type thing," he recollects.

"There were five guys up for the composer job. Chris Carter—luckily for me—didn't have a friend or relative who was a composer, and apparently I lived the closest to him, and he thought, 'Oh, this would be convenient,' to go to my place to listen to music. So he came over a couple of times, and we listened to whatever projects I was working on. He liked it, but he didn't say much." Carter, as others have confessed, takes some getting used to. "To this day, he's a very just-the-facts man, not terribly outwardly exuberant or emotional. A brilliant guy, obviously, and friendly and sweet and decent, but a little bit difficult to read what he's thinking. So these two visits were, 'Thank you very much. I appreciate it. We'll get back to you.' I thought nothing of it—just another gig. Two weeks later I got a call from my agent saying, 'Well, they want you to do the thing.' And I said, 'Okay.' Then they sent the pilot, and I watched it with my wife. They took tons of music and just laid it in for a temp track, and that really set the tone for the idea that there was a lot of music in these shows."

Most iconic of all, of course, is Mark Snow's theme for *The X-Files*, featuring a simple but haunting melody that has become synonymous with tales of alien intervention and shadowy conspiracy. Its composer recalls how a lengthy exchange with the show's creator led to its inception. "It was time to come up with a theme and, luckily for me, this was just a little bit before the time when these shows were looking for songs from bands, so I had a shot. Chris sent me eight tons of CDs—everything from classical to punk to new age to country to pop to this, that, and the other thing—and he said, 'I like the drums here, I like the singing here, I like the guitar sound here.' I did one thing that sounded to me kind of like what you would expect on a show like this. He came over and he said, 'Gee, that's really great, but it's not quite [what I'm looking for].' And then this happened four times! Luckily he didn't seem to lose enthusiasm. I said, 'Look—let's try something. Let me just wipe the slate clean here and come up with something completely fresh.' He says, 'Okay,' and he leaves. And this is true: about an hour and a half later I wrote this theme.

"I was learning the kinds of things he liked. He was very clear not to over-produce it, not to make a big deal, but just something so simple. Whether it was loud, soft, fast, or slow, that was up to me. So I put my hands on the keyboard in my studio and I had this echo effect on the piano sound I had at the time, which made this repeat sound. I thought, 'Oh, that's pretty cool. Well, how simple can you get? You can use that as an accompaniment, and just put some paddy, dark, sustain stuff underneath and then come up with the melody.' So that all happened pretty quick, the melody came, and then it was time to find the right sound for it—the right instrument. That actually took the longest, because I thought, 'Let's try a flute, let's try a marimba, let's try a vocal sound, let's try the trombone, let's try the sax, let's try guitar.' Onward and onward, and then in this bunch of sounds and noises, this collection I had, there was this whistle thing. I played that and I said, 'Whoa, that's pretty cool.' My wife was outside the studio, and she came in and said, 'Wow, that's pretty great. That's really different. That's interesting. Especially for the show where you think it's going to be some big ass sound.' I called Chris Carter, and he turned around and he came right back, heard it and he said, 'Yeah, that's good. Just take out a little of this and a little of this. That's good.' He wasn't jumping up and down, but he said, 'I like it. That's good.'"

This was, however, just the first stage in finalizing the iconic theme. "The next step was to play this thing for executives at Fox," Snow goes on. "Chris said, 'I'll meet you at so-and-so room and we'll go in with the boom box. You bring your little CD copy of the thing.' So we go there, and just as we're going in he says, 'I've got a meeting. I've gotta go. You can handle this. You'll be fine.' I'm thinking, 'Oh, yow, I'm all alone with the guys in suits!'" Indeed, Fox Mulder himself would face less stressful trials in skirmishes with alien monsters and creatures of the night.

"Four guys. I walked in—very nice—I put the thing on, and these guys are completely baffled! They don't have a clue, but they're being polite. No one says anything. One guy says, 'Well, y'know, this sound... Bill?' They pass it over to the next guy, and then Bill would say, 'You've got... I'm thinking... I... Jim?' This went around and they kind of looked at each other and they seemed uncomfortable, because it was something unexpected. The thing comes on and in about a month or two, all of a sudden, there was this reaction like, 'Wow, this is this cool theme. What the hell?! Where did this come from?! This is so crazy, and it's perfect for the show. It's simple, you've got your six little notes there.' Then these guys called me up, one by one, to say, 'Didn't we tell you how fabulous this was?!' And what you do—if you're smart, like I hope I was—is say, 'Y'know, you guys were great! Thank you for your support! It wouldn't have gone on without you!'"

When the pilot for *Millennium* was being produced in 1996, given his well-established success with *The X-Files*, Snow was the natural choice to take on composing duties for this highly anticipated new series from Chris Carter and Ten Thirteen Productions. "I remember that David Nutter was the director," Snow recalls, "who is the 'Pilot King'—most pilots this guy does are sold—and he did a bunch of *X-Files* episodes, a very talented guy." In comparison to those seemingly endless developmental trails that led to the theme song for *The X-Files*, the birth of *Millennium*'s melancholic theme was fairly straightforward. "David and Chris found this Irish rock band where there was a violin solo in it which was slightly Celtic, and they said, 'We really love this sound.' I said, 'Okay,' so then I wrote that theme and they thought, 'Whoa, that's pretty cool.' So that went out, and that was pretty good because there was just one pass on that."

Was it easier the second time out, given Snow had worked with Carter for some time and had acquired a feel for what he liked? "Oh, yeah. It must be the same with John Williams and Steven Spielberg. Sometimes he'll say, 'We really need it to be something-or-other,' but it's all shorthand. The language, the respect, and the relationship is there, so now it's, 'Hi. How are you doing? Are you going to do a good job?' 'Yeah, I'm going to do a good job.' 'Okay, I need you to do a good job. I didn't do such a good job in directing this part of it, so can you help me out here?' 'Yeah, I'm gonna help you out here.' Or, 'Don't help me out here, this is brilliant over here. Just complement it. You know what to do, right?' 'Right.' You'd think after all these years that's how it should be, and that is how it is."

If the composer's score had become a significant part of the tone and character of *The X-Files*, then the same was very much true of his work on *Millennium*. Snow feels a particular affinity for the music he composed for the series, especially in terms of how it complements the character of Frank Black. "The music I wrote for that show I felt so completely personally involved with, because I loved ethnic and folk music. Here was a chance to play these simple, sort-of ethnic, folky melodies, and there was this heartbreaking, deep, profound melancholy with Frank Black and with his voice. He was the ultimate prisoner of fate with this 'gift' that he had. Everyone thought the music sound was just a great marriage with him and all the hijinks that he got involved in, and certainly there were some wonderful [examples of that]—'Jose Chung's *Doomsday Defense*' and 'Somehow, Satan Got Behind Me' and other moments—but the meat of it was that it felt so great to play these simple, dark melodies using the violin as the main instrument. I couldn't use it every time—it would get a little monotonous."

The composer picks out his work on *The X-Files* and *Millennium* as an all-time creative highlight in his career. "I thought *The X-Files* was a dream job come true," he beams. "It certainly was in terms of success, but also they let me do what I wanted to do. When I was at Juilliard I was a huge fan of *avant-garde*, atonal, twelve-tone music, and a lot of that appears in some of those *X-Files* scores. I remember getting calls from certain classical composers who wrote that thing for legit concert audiences to say, 'Did they really let you do that?' I said, 'I guess they did.' Because they didn't know what it was—they just knew they liked it. That was all they cared about. So between that and *Millennium*, I would have to say those were the times when I got to do a hundred percent of what I wanted."

Was it a challenge to compose for the two series simultaneously whilst ensuring a distinct tone for each? "Well, right. *Millennium* did have real super dark moments, more sort of serial-killer-does-this, the-Group-does-this. I knew that as long as I kept that darker, sad, sort-of heavy tone with *Millennium* I'd be okay. I knew there was a similarity, just as the composer of both of them, but I didn't think of it too much when I would see the episodes. I would just react to them at the time, knowing where the theme started and came from. So there were times where people might say they sounded a little close, but I always thought the best of the *Millennium* music were these melodies—almost like sad Appalachia, in a funny way. I wish I could say I had stayed up for months trying to figure this all out. I guess because I was so busy with it all it just fell right out of me. Again, it was stuff that I really related to and liked, and the good luck that these producers were into it."

Snow's body of work for *Millennium* was granted a limited edition two-disc release by La-La Land Records in 2008, which quickly sold out. It at once charts the distinctive tone of his work for the series and a degree of diversity and development of the music over the series' three seasons. "Well, that's a very nice thing to say," Snow responds with a smile, "and makes me feel that I was successful in doing that. I listened to all the *Millennium* CDs and sometimes thought, 'This is not something you want to play at a wedding' but, nevertheless, it's a mood and a real simple and perhaps direct, unfettered, uncluttered thing that is very definitive in its sound." The collection of such music on CD for public consumption is, however, necessarily far from his thoughts when composing a score. "You can't think of the CD, because that's not the job at hand. The first thing is to write the music for the picture and the show. Especially with *The X-Files* and *Millennium*, it wasn't like, 'Oh, now I have to really work hard to make this fit.' There was nothing like that about these experiences. All this music felt so natural. That's why two years out of the three of *Millennium* where both shows were going on at once it seemed like, 'Wow, this is a lot to do,' but because I felt so comfortable with those styles it wasn't particularly weighty or uncomfortable. It really was okay. I've done shows since and before where you've got to work harder to make these things work.

"Just as an overview—and this is kind of interesting—I never thought for me, personally, that vast chase music is as interesting as these melodic pieces or these mood pieces. Certainly I think I am probably known more for the ambient mood pieces rather than balls-out action stuff. There are a lot of people who can do that well, and it was hard to find something that had a real distinct personality and character, whereas in the moody stuff there seemed to be much more room to be able to say something. I remember one of the great action pieces was James Newton Howard in *The Fugitive*, which was just amazing. He's one of my favorite film composers working now."

Reflecting on his work for the series, Snow singles out the influence of one of *Millennium*'s most characteristic musical motifs. "I forgot about that double hit drum thing—that '*boom-boom*'—which was these real big ambient things. You go listen to the *Pirates of the Caribbean* score, or any Hans Zimmer score, and you'll hear those things all over the place. But that seemed to be the theme in itself—the '*boom-boom*'—with that dark of the devils coming up here, the bells tolling and we are done for, and hopefully Frank Black is not going to be knocking on your door with some information."

Writer and producer Michael R. Perry has commented that one of the most enjoyable aspects of writing an episode of *Millennium* was being taken to Snow's house to hear his compositions and offer feedback. Is it unusual for writers to be included in the process in this way? "It is," says Snow, "but here's a good experiment. Turn on a popular T.V. show and watch the beginning, then watch the credits. Writers, in the last five to ten years, get credits as producers, whether they are executive producers, co-executive producers, associate producers, producers, consulting producers, and some of these shows have twenty people listed. So, as time went on with the agents for writers, they would figure out this way to give them a producer credit."

If that sounds like a recipe for too many cooks spoiling his delicious melodic broth, then Snow is quick to reassure that this was never the case on *Millennium*, particularly given the isolation in which a composer mostly operates. "I loved all these guys on the show because they knew it was about coming over, listening to the stuff and it was never, 'Oh, that's terrible. Change it. Take this out.' It was just, 'Hey, what do you think about maybe we need more bang when the monster jumps out of the closet,' or something like that—the collaborative thing. I'm an only child, but the work I do is pretty isolating. You're alone in your studio, and that's it for hours a day. When someone comes over, it's 'Hi! Come on in! You want something to eat? Can you stay awhile? Oh, great! What are you doing later?' So when these guys came over I thought it was fun for them, because they could get out of the studio and be in a world where they could just sit back and relax and check out how the show all of a sudden got even more fleshed out with the music added, and say their comments—but very few—and it was just a great time. People would say, 'Isn't that annoying? Don't they trust you?' They'd come over literally for every episode—for nine years of *The X-Files* and three years of *Millennium*, somebody was there. It was incredible. It was welcome. It was fun. It was like a little party—sometimes it was three or four people. It was really great, actually."

Speaking with Mark Snow, it becomes clear that he not only welcomes the feedback of writers and producers, he thrives upon it. "I have colleagues of mine who can't stand that," he confides, "and find it intrusive and arrogant and obnoxious. But part of the job is collaborative. I remember one time I was able—because of a friend—to watch a screening of *Home Alone*, for which John Williams did the score. I'm there, and there's John Williams. I'm not sitting next to him, I don't know him—I'm in the back somewhere. They screened the movie for him, and then the lights go on and he said, 'Gee, guys, this movie is fantastic. I love it! Would it be too much to ask if we could have the projectionist stay so I could watch it again? It's just wonderful.' They're all flipped out: 'The great John Williams loves our movie! This is fantastic!'"

Snow has great respect for the work of John Williams. "The other day there was a re-run of *E.T.*, and the very end scene where E.T. goes back in the craft and away he goes and all that, the music there is just unbelievable. I'm telling you, there is nobody alive who can do it as well as John Williams for that kind of sound. The idea that there is this one person who is still doing it, it's the eighth or ninth wonder of the world, this guy, it really is. It's remarkable. James Horner, Hans Zimmer, James Newton Howard, guys like that are wonderful and brilliant, but I can say to myself, 'Well, if I had a big budget and a chance, I could come close to that or do that.' John Williams, nobody can come close to. I went to a couple of recording sessions of his, and he would turn around to Spielberg or George Lucas and say, 'How do you like that?' And they said, 'Well, it's just brilliant but maybe…' 'Oh, absolutely!' So, no matter who you are in the business, you're working for someone, and it is collaborative."

It is a spirit of open and egoless collaboration, Snow explains, that is vital to forming working relationships. "I have to say that as time went on I got more respect, and when that happens it's really kind of fun. People come over, and usually a lot of people say the first thing, right off the bat, 'Hey, I'm no musician but… I don't know anything about music, but…' To me, that's a welcome comment, because they don't care about the techniques of writing music, they care about what it does for their movie and their show and the emotion behind it. That, to me, is important. If I've done something that is a little too complicated and they want to simplify it, we can do it. Obviously, having the technology that there is today, someone can come over and say, 'It's just too busy. It's just too loud. Can you try to thin it out?' All you have to do is push some buttons and boom—there goes the bass, there go the strings, there goes something else, whatever it is. It's like, 'Wow.' And they say, 'Yes, that's great. Now put back the strings and take out the trombones.' And they'll say, 'Is that okay musically?' I'll say, 'Yes, it's really great, actually. I didn't think of this the first time.' I just love that stuff, and sometimes guys will talk and talk and talk and you want to try to get them to, 'What are you trying to say here? Just get to the point!' But I've really loved the collaborating."

Occasionally, a particularly unusual installment of *Millennium* would call for a composition quite different in tone from the music written for other episodes. An example Snow holds up as a highlight of such an approach is "Omerta," an offbeat episode in which a Mafia hit man finds himself under the protection of two mystical women. "I loved that," he exudes. "I found there's this library of vocal things, actually from London. The big heading is the London Symphony Orchestra and Chorus, and they have these solo little bits of opera. I figured out a way to incorporate these in the show and just write some accompaniment under it, and making sure I stayed in the right key of the singing. There was a male and a female part and I thought, 'Wow, this is kind of charming.' It sounded like opera, but not heavy duty and not ethnic and not African or Chinese. I thought, 'Wow, I haven't heard that, ever.' That was a ton of fun and I remember when the writers or producers came over we had a great time with that."

As with many of the other members of the cast and crew, Snow points to the creative freedom granted to the series that enabled everyone to produce their best work. "It seemed to me as if not only myself but the writers and the producers were given this wonderful freedom to come up with this stuff. Some of the ideas were so inventive and out there and almost experimental, and it feels as time has gone on shows have gotten safer and safer. The stuff I was involved in, and the writers and producers of *Millennium*, really had this amazing freedom. To come up with things, I thought, was remarkable, and the idea that it didn't go on was really sad." Enthused by the Back to Frank Black campaign, he also joins the ranks of those eager to see the character return. "Here's the deal. You guys have got to get this thing going where we force the powers that be to make a movie about this. That would be a dream come true."

In the meantime, Snow remains in great demand. Does he get the chance to do much just for his own musical enjoyment? "I don't have the time because when you're doing these shows it's so intense that, when it's over for the season, that's it—you just want to go fishing, or some version of that. One of these days it will slow down enough where I'll have that time. I'm trying to think of what I could do musically for my own personal enjoyment. That would be really a joy, to not think I'm working for anyone but myself."

Alongside his ongoing scores, Snow has also invested some time as an educator. "I've had some really great experiences teaching at New

York University in New York and Yale with an old friend, so that's fun and interesting, actually," he says. "So many of these high end schools have theme scoring programs, which never happened in my day and have only happened in the last fifteen years or something, but now they're becoming more prevalent all over the place. But still, in all the thrill of writing one piece of music and having it go out there some way and having it become such a big deal in the world, with *The X-Files*, that was amazing. I could lie in bed at night and think about how it became number two [in the British singles chart], it was number one in France... All these foreign places, getting comments and emails, and excuse me for not getting too modest about it, but wow—for six little notes! It wasn't even like some big rock and roll song like 'A Whiter Shade of Pale.' I would've liked that too!"

Despite having never surpassed the pop music success of the Fab Four, as had once been prophesied, Mark Snow continues to enjoy a career as a film composer now entering its fifth decade. During this time he has received a multitude of awards, eleven of them for his work on *The X-Files* alone. What advice does the composer have for anyone who might dream of following in those legendary footsteps? "I think it's a two-part thing. If somehow you can write music that you are passionate about, that you feel an incredible personal involvement with, and at the same time understand that you're a collaborative piece of this puzzle—just one of the elements that go into a film, like the editor, the director, the acting, the cinematography, the set design, and the script—if somehow you can combine those two things, that is the key. And not to approach a particular project with, 'I'm going to do what they want. I have to find out exactly what they want, and what I want to do doesn't matter.'

"First things first—you've got to get the gig. When I do all this teaching stuff, these kids come up to me and say, 'Would you take my CD and listen to it, and help me get a job? How do you get a job?' That part is completely abstract and luck, and I always tell everyone it's not like being a lawyer or a doctor—if you go to school and you're very good then you are almost guaranteed that you will be successful—because the ladder going up in those worlds is pretty simple and pretty automatic. I know a lot of the people who write music for T.V. and film, and each one of them has an individual story about how they have gotten into it. It's not like, 'I did this, and then I did this, and then I followed the book *How to Get Work as a Film Composer*.' It just doesn't exist. Certainly to network like crazy and any student film, anyone who's got a cousin or a brother who's making a documentary or anything, to try to take advantage and exploit those relationships. But I remember there's a composer now named Michael Giacchino, who's absolutely killing it, absolutely gigantic with *Star Trek* and Pixar movies. He's got T.V. shows like *Fringe* and *Lost*. He was at a conference and someone asked him the same question: 'What would be your advice?' He said, 'Well, try not to get involved in anything you don't really like or feel.' And everyone just sat there dumbfounded, thinking, 'Now wait a minute.' If someone comes along with a project about the making of *The Brady Bunch* or something, you're going to take it! When you're starting, it's a no-brainer. I was just surprised he didn't add, 'After you get established, do this.' 'Michael, I've got a wife and kids, and I've got to pay the goddamned rent! Come on!'"

The importance of Mark Snow's contributions to the body of work of that is *Millennium* cannot be overestimated, and the composer pauses before the interview is over to express that *Millennium* remains deeply important to him. "Y'know, it's one thing to be interviewed for things and shows that were okay," Snow reflects, "but for *Millennium* especially the idea that you guys are out there, keeping the flame alive with the show, is very touching and moving. If there was anything—just a T.V. special—that came back with this cast and crew, it would be such a thrill. The time to be able to reminisce and talk about this has been great. So many people [just talk about] what's current and what's new and what's hot, and so it makes me feel really great to be able to think, 'That was great. That was a great time in my life.'"

THE EVIL EARWORM:
POPULAR MUSIC IN *MILLENNIUM*

by Joe Tangari

Music is not like other art. In a world where technology makes recorded sound nearly ubiquitous in our society, there is no need to travel to hear it, though you may go to specific places at specific times to hear specific music played live. We experience music by choice and we have it imposed on us nearly every time we go out in public; it is in the air our society breathes, and it gets inside of us very easily. What song is stuck in your head right now? You likely have an answer.

Ask yourself: how did that song get there? Do you even *like* the song stuck in your head?

Songs work their way into people's heads in an astonishing variety of ways. You might hear a song in the morning and be unable to shake it until evening. You might suddenly and inexplicably be struck by the chorus of a song you have not heard in years and have not consciously thought of. You might get a fragment of a song that you cannot identify out of context stuck in your head and it will bother you for days as you struggle to figure out what it is. Two songs may stick in your head at once, and you might find they go pretty well together.

One of the reasons those songs from years ago, the ones we have not heard in forever, come back to us without beckoning is that, somewhere in the tangle of neural pathways in our brain, a connection was forged between it and something else. It is a deeply subconscious connection, so much so that even when the song comes back, we often cannot pinpoint the connection or determine why it came back when it did.

Researchers in the fields of neurology and psychology have explored the existence and persistence of earworms (referred to by neurologist Oliver Sacks as "involuntary musical imagery") in a variety of studies. However, certain limitations of existing research have prevented the development of a complete understanding of the way earworms work in everyday life. Musical imagery can be induced in a laboratory setting, but the very act of inducing it places a buffer between the mental activity observed in the lab and that which would occur under normal circumstances (Liikkanen 2). Further, many studies rely on retrospective reporting rather than real-time data gathering to examine the phenomenon (3).

In their 2010 paper "Earworms ('Stuck Song Syndrome'): Towards a Natural History of Intrusive Thoughts," the University of Reading's C. P. Beaman and Tim I. Williams found that attempts among their study subjects to block or eliminate the song stuck their heads were less successful than passive acceptance (16). D. M. Wegner calls this phenomenon ironic control; attempts to block out aural imagery or particular thoughts actually lead people to pay far more attention to the thoughts than they otherwise would (34).

In his 2008 book *Musicophilia*, Sacks documents extreme cases in which, for example, a man who hears Frank Sinatra singing "Love and Marriage" over the opening credits of *Married with Children* (1987-97) becomes nearly paralyzed by the song's incessant repetition in his head over a ten-day span, affecting his ability to think and even his gait when he walks (45). The stories told by Sacks reveal just how little is known about the scientific underpinnings of our propensity for getting songs stuck in our heads. Medication that reduces one patient's musical hallucinations has no effect on another patient's similar internal concert. The nature of what becomes stuck in one's head and the frequency with which earworms come and go is highly individual.

Particularly in its second season, *Millennium* (1996-99) took great advantage of the subconscious and conscious ways music integrates itself into our lives. Before we get too far into examining the ways in which the show enriched its storytelling through the use of music, let us be clear that this article does not consider the score, written specifically for each episode by Mark Snow. Instead it focuses upon pre-existing, externally sourced music that was used to dramatic effect on the show. This music appears in two basic ways. Sometimes, it is diegetic. This means that it emanates clearly from some onscreen source. Other times, it is more clearly a soundtrack, played over a scene to influence mood or audience expectations. At its best, *Millennium* often blurred the line between these two methods, introducing music diegetically and changing the way it was applied as the scene progressed.

NINE INCH NAILS AND BLOOD RUNS DOWN THE WALLS

The challenge for any new television series is to pull viewers into its world and give them reason to stay. In its earliest episodes, *Millennium* made heavy use of music to establish the mood and tone of the series. The first two episodes in particular employ pop music loudly to help make their points.

The grinding beats of Nine Inch Nails's "Head Like a Hole" seem natural, supporting the grinding motions of the peep show dancers in the "Pilot" teaser, and this is perversely reinforced later when we see what the killer sees—blood running down the walls and over the body of a dancer. Here is a show establishing the darkness and horror of its world swiftly and without much subtlety. There is never any question that we are in a bad place where bad things are going to happen.

There is more going on in the music of "Pilot" than a simple confirmation of what we see onscreen, however. Consider that when the Frenchman gets his private session at the Ruby Tip, as blood runs down the walls and fire flares behind the dancer in the booth, the music shifts gears. Portishead's "Roads"—a down-tempo trip-hop song sung by a woman—plays here and again later, when Frank Black (Lance Henriksen) sits in the same booth to question another dancer who knew the victim.¹ Here, the music is more audible, and there is a lyric that stands out: "Ohh, can't anybody see / we've got a war to fight." This is, in effect, the very first shot fired in the battle of good and evil that would eventually move to center stage in the series and it slips right by on the soundtrack, unnoticed. This is likely a coincidence, but it is a happy one—Frank does not yet see the war at this point, but he will in time. (The plague would eventually come to the maritime city, too, though not until the end of season two.)

If anything, "Gehenna" is even more on-the-nose with its musical selections. Three Cypress Hill songs are used diegetically as initiates to a Satanic telemarketing firm are dosed with L.S.D. and tormented, and the songs are all pointedly about getting high: "Hits from the Bong" and "I Wanna Get High" advertise it in their titles. The third and best known Cypress Hill song used in the episode, "Insane in the Brain," clearly has lyrical parallels to the actions of the boys on screen, including one direct reference to a serial killer in the first verse: "Damn, I feel like the Son of Sam."² Cypress Hill's drug of choice was weed, but there remains a clear connection between song and scene here. It could only be more obvious if "How I Could Just Kill a Man" had been chosen as a fourth Cypress Hill title.

This approach to soundtracking is well established, and for good reason. At this point, the show is still building its world, and the aggression of the music—and the posse mentality elucidated within it—are important analogs to the storytelling. A funny thing happens over the next string of episodes, however. Outside of the necessary (and generic) techno score to the club sequences in "The Wild and the Innocent," the music very nearly disappears as the show pursues other means of fleshing out its themes. When the music returns, it is used very differently.

The return occurs in the teaser sequence of "Weeds," the eleventh episode. As Edward Petey (Josh Clark) drives through his gated community, he sees flashes of decay interspersed with the reality of children playing and people on their lawns. As he drives, his visions are accompanied by an almost grotesquely antiseptic easy-listening instrumental. The music, playing on the minivan stereo, belongs to a certain lineage of popular recording designed to be as gentle and harmless as possible. When I was a child, my grandparents used to watch *The Lawrence Welk Show* (1951-82), and this is the kind of music that soundtracked the brightly colored, wholesome dance routines and set pieces of the show.³ It was a homogenous, squeaky-clean vision of America, where all the bad things of the world were kept at bay, a sort of televised gated community. There is a natural disconnect between sound and image at work here that serves as an early, isolated embryo for the direction the show's soundtrack would take in its second season. The music suggests comfort and security, but there is none to be found.

SWINGING DURING WARTIME

"Weeds" is not among the best episodes of the first season but its brief nod to a Lynchian juxtaposition of idyll and horror may be the clearest premonition of the shape the show's music-soaked second season would take.⁴ Glen Morgan and James Wong took over showrunning duties during the second season, and their vision for *Millennium* took it in a wide variety of unexplored directions. The two had worked together since the mid-1980s, and their contributions to *The X-Files* (1993-2002) included some of that show's finest episodes. Two stand out as clear precedents for the approach they would take with *Millennium*. The first is "Beyond the Sea," in which Bobby Darin's song of the same title plays an integral role in developing the relationship between Agent Dana Scully and serial killer Luther Lee Boggs. The second is the notorious "Home."

"Home" aired near the start of *The X-Files*'s fourth season. It centers on an inbred family that lives on the outskirts of Home, Pennsylvania, an idyllic rural town watched over by a sheriff named Andy Taylor.⁵ The episode's most memorable scene features the troglodytic Peacock brothers jumping in their Fifties-era convertible and driving to Sheriff Taylor's home, where they brutally beat him and his wife to death. During this scene, Morgan and Wong, working with director Kim Manners, heavily blur the line between diegetic and extra-diegetic music.

When the brothers start the car, a soundalike take on Johnny Mathis's "Wonderful! Wonderful!" begins playing. (Mathis refused to let his own voice soundtrack the scene.) What is cinematically interesting is what happens next. As the direction collapses time to show the Peacocks departing and arriving without depicting the entirety of their trip, the song does not skip forward, instead playing as though no time has been lost, and at a volume that suggests it is not coming from the car stereo. Yet, when the brothers arrive, Sheriff Taylor hears the song outside. The song moves back and forth across the fourth wall, jumping from the stereo to the foreground as the drama of the scene requires.

From nearly the moment they took over *Millennium*, Morgan and Wong pushed the use of music as a narrative device. In the highly charged first act of the second season premier, the Polaroid Man makes his escape with Catherine to the tune of the *Stop Making Sense* (1984) version of Talking Heads's "Life During Wartime." As Frank runs between the cars stopped at the checkpoint on Route 509 we hear the song, faintly in the distance, emanating from the Polaroid Man's car, and it becomes our signal that Frank is close but not nearly close enough. As the song slips away, so does Catherine. That war going on—the one Beth Gibbons sang about in the Portishead song a full season ago—is now explicit in the title of the well-known track playing on the car stereo of a kidnapper.

The song here has the right message, delivered with a spiky bounce that is slightly incongruous with Frank's growing panic. War is strange and confronts us with strange situations, and Morgan and Wong knew this. When Frank commits his shocking murder of the Polaroid Man to save Catherine, he is not acting as a civilian, he is acting as a soldier in an army he does not even know that he has joined. The Millennium Group, his army, apply the rules of war to his actions when the ordeal is over, treating him as though he has killed an enemy combatant and not a fellow citizen.

The evil in Frank's world is not always so clear-cut, however. Consider the Kevorkian-like doctor of "Goodbye, Charlie." Portrayed by guest star Tucker Smallwood—who also played the doomed sheriff in "Home"—Ellsworth Beedle believes he is ending the suffering of his informal patients, but his euthanasia sessions are given a surreally homicidal twist by the fact that the hands of his victims are bound at the time of their deaths, and especially by the fact that he sings karaoke to them as they die. Somewhere along the tangle of emotional and intellectual pathways that brought Beedle to this point, the idea of music as a soother entered his mind and became part of his assisted suicide routine. The amount of comfort one might derive from hearing Terry Jacks's "Seasons in the Sun" vocalized by a man with a marginal singing voice as they lie taped-up on a motel bed with Sodium Pentothal racing toward their heart remains open to debate.

This is where the ambiguous morality of Beedle's actions is thrown into relief. He truly believes he is gently removing a burden from these terminally ill men and women, singing them off to another plane of existence where they will not hurt anymore. His victims may not be victims at all—at some point in the process, each was a willing volunteer, and some remain willing to the end.

The choice of music is, in some respects, obvious. "Seasons in the Sun" is known for being saccharine and depressing at once, delivering the line, "Goodbye, my friend, it's hard to die" over an almost comically buoyant bass line. It is also very familiar; Jacks, an obscure Canadian singer-songwriter, self-released the song on his own record label and licensed it to Bell when it took off, reaching number one on the singles charts in the United States and Britain. This exposure cemented the song's place in the popular conscience, though Jacks would never come close to repeating its success.[6]

It is the Bobby Darin song that Beedle sings to poor Eleanor (Deanne Henry), "Goodbye Charlie," that is the really inspired choice. For one, the song has appeared on the show before, in the episode "Monster," when Frank listens to it to pass the time aboard a flight. This creates a connection between killer and investigator, one that is even born out in interrogation, when Beedle uses the story of Darin's tragically short life and his decision not to undergo a final surgery to prolong that life as the means to justify his actions without admitting to them.

Beedle's assertion that Bobby Darin opted not to have a final life-saving surgery is not quite correct. Darin, born Robert Walden Cassatto, lived only thirty-seven years, dying after heart surgery in 1973. He had long suffered from a heart condition induced by childhood bouts of rheumatic fever and had received artificial heart valves in 1971. The surgery that killed him was meant to address damage to these valves caused by an infection. The circumstances of Darin's childhood were odd—he was raised by his grandmother, believing her to be his mother. At the age of thirty-two, he learned that the woman he had thought all along was his much older sister was actually his mother. Though he is best remembered for his hit-making musical career, Darin was multi-talented, appearing in several films and hosting his own television show.

Bobby Darin was chosen to be Frank Black's favorite artist for a multitude of reasons, not least of which is that Glen Morgan and James Wong like his music. Glen Morgan's brother, Darin Morgan, the writer and director of two *Millennium* episodes, is named for the singer. The match with the show's subject matter is striking. Darin's earliest pop hits, "Splish Splash" and "Dream Lover," were heavily rooted in rock-and-roll, but as he gained more creative control he pushed his music in a big band direction. His best known hit today is "Mack the Knife," an English-language version of Kurt Weill's "*Die Moritat von Mackie Messer*," which was written for Weill's 1928 stage work *The Threepenny Opera*. The song relates the story of a serial killer in an exceedingly boisterous big band arrangement. Black's affection for Darin is one element of Morgan and Wong's season-long endeavor to turn Frank Black into more of a man and less of a symbol—giving him art to appreciate points to an inner life (and a past life) to which the audience is not always privy while watching. The tragedy of Darin's life is icing on the cake. Darin had a way of swinging through the most horrific stories without betraying so much as a care.

The song "Goodbye Charlie" was composed by André and Dory Previn for a musical, also called *Goodbye Charlie*, as a send-off for a doomed philanderer.[7] Listen to the song and check Darin's phrasing throughout. This is not a lament. It is spirited, almost joyful. Putting aside which songs were heard on *Millennium* and which were omitted, we can look at Darin's wider catalog and find many songs that follow this pattern. His version of "Mack the Knife" just about congratulates the serial killer of the title, "Artificial Flowers" is a bounding rave-up about a poor little girl that freezes to death trying to make a little money, and even "Beyond the Sea" is casual about love and longing.

One of the central themes of *Millennium*—particularly during the first two seasons, when Catherine was still alive and the hope for a normal family dangled always just out of reach—is the struggle to rise above evil, to hold back the dark and live well. The way in which Darin bursts through the sadness of the songs he sings corresponds strongly to the way in which Frank tries to paint over the darkness with a coat of yellow but cannot quite hold it back. The sadness is still there in those songs, even as Darin swings.

The use of "Goodbye Charlie" in the episode of the same name also nicely parallels the use of "Beyond the Sea" in *The X-Files* episode of the same name—the song becomes the connection between the killer and the hero who does not want any such connection to exist. As modern people build their identities, popular culture and the elements of popular culture they reject or embrace become part of those identities. To find that a portion of your self-created identity is shared with someone you consider monstrous can shake your confidence in how well-built your identity really is.

Discussing "Goodbye Charlie," the episode's writer, Richard Whitley, has noted the remarkable confluence of factors that led to the song's use during the suicide/homicide scenes. Some of them were mechanical. For instance, he was given a list of Bobby Darin songs that the series' producers had the rights to use, and "Goodbye Charlie" was on the list. Others were more thematic. Whitely explains, "It was funny because I got the list of the Bobby Darin songs, and I had made a list of all the phrases for dying, like 'checking out'—slang and all that. One of the things for dying was 'goodbye Charlie,' and then I see that it's a Bobby Darin song!" Darin's biography played well into the planned interrogation scene, and so the show gets its cake and devours it too.

THEY LONG TO BE CLOSE TO YOU

In "Home," that notorious installment of *The X-Files*, there is a shot wherein Sheriff Taylor, in bed next to his wife, is awakened by the arrival of the Peacock brothers. What he hears is not just the noise of their car pulling up but also "Wonderful! Wonderful!" blaring from its stereo. The fanfare for Taylor's brutal murder is not Wagner's "Ride of the Valkyries" or something nasty. It is easy listening schmaltz. And it is terrifying.

There are a host of reasons why setting murder scenes to such ostensibly innocuous music works to make things infinitely more creepy than they might otherwise be. Consider the use of the Carpenters in the "Beware of the Dog" teaser. "(They Long to Be) Close to You" is the height of innocuousness. Almost everybody watching the episode knows the song, perhaps from their childhood—chances are it played somewhere you visited. "Close to You" is not supposed to be threatening; "Close to You" is secure nights in your parents' wood-paneled den, the kind of music teenagers rebel against because of its cultivated blandness.

"Close to You" was written by the enormously successful songwriting team of Hal David and Burt Bacharach. It was originally recorded in 1963 by Richard Chamberlain, and also recorded by Dionne Warwick and Bacharach himself over the course of the 60s, but it remained obscure until A&M Records co-founder Herb Alpert brought it to the Carpenters. Their 1970 version was number one on the Billboard Hot 100 in the United States for four weeks and became a soft-rock touchstone, a song so emblematic of its era that the creators of *The Simpsons* (1989-) chose to make it Marge and Homer Simpson's song.

With lyrics such as "on the day that you were born / the angels got together and decided to create a dream come true" delivered conversationally and in pillowy harmonies over Richard Carpenter's soft-hued piano, the song embodies a whole range of romantic clichés. Its rhythm never approaches a sitting heart rate, and Alpert's trumpet solo is recorded to sound roughly like syrup. At a time when rock was getting louder and heavier, this created an island people left out of the edgier trends of the day could retreat to.

Morgan and Wong use the track to accompany a scene in which two nice old people are mauled to death by German Shepherds in their R.V. Let us consider what this accomplishes. In the series premiere, we were treated to images of evil set to a soundtrack of music meant to be edgy, to challenge. It was music you would expect to find in a place like the Ruby Tip, and the Ruby Tip was a place where you might expect bad things to happen. It is creepy and terrible, but what does it have to do with you and me?

In the universe of *Millennium*, evil is alive and active in the world. It is not terribly surprising when it rears its head in strip clubs and abandoned dry cleaning supply factories. Pairing "Close to You" with the grisly and unexpected death of a retired couple effectively brings evil home. Suddenly, evil is not something you can avoid by skipping the strip club and staying out of abandoned factories. It is right there, over your shoulder, in the wood-paneled den of your childhood, where you first listened to the Carpenters with your parents close by.[8]

Evil must be everywhere when even the Carpenters can be party to a bloodletting.

LOVE IS BLUE: THE EVIL EARWORM

At the start of this article, I asked what song was stuck in your head. Over three thousand words later, and after discussing a variety of mainstream hits, the answer may well be different. Consider this: what if it was always the same song? This essentially represents the experience of the boys imprisoned by Lucy Butler in "A Room with No View."

Paul Mauriat's sap-coated instrumental "Love is Blue" loops *ad infinitum* in the cells where Butler keeps her prisoners, and every time that little harpsichord figure at the beginning comes back around, the song burrows in a little deeper. It is a song stuck *outside* of these poor kids' heads and in some ways it sees the Carpenters and raises them; now, the music is not simply a signal that evil is everywhere, it is the very messenger of that evil, breaking down the defenses of the prisoners further with each play.

Return to the case of Tim, the man Oliver Sacks wrote about who was debilitated for a week by the incessant repetition of "Love and Marriage" in his head. Tim found the song crowding out other thoughts and, as mentioned, affecting the way he walked as his pace conformed to its tempo. The music had a powerful suggestive capacity, even though it was only in Tim's head. In *Musicophilia*, Sacks documents many cases of people driven to distraction by music or internal sounds that arrived unbidden. "A Room with No View" merely externalizes that process. Under Wegner's theory of ironic control, the boys' very attempts to ignore the music cause them to fixate upon its presence, just as their attempts to escape only draw Lucy further into their personal space.

In this case, the music also plays into Butler's disturbing message to Landon Bryce (Christopher Masterson), that he should abandon his exceptional qualities and embrace ordinariness. Mauriat's recording throws its arms wide around ordinariness and seeks to fit into the background. The recording is inoffensive to a fault, but this did not hurt its commercial prospects. In 1968, his instrumental version of "Love is Blue" became the only recording by a French performer ever to top the Billboard Hot 100 in the United States. (The song has many versions, including the original vocal version with French lyrics, written by André Popp and Pierre Cour. There is an English-language version of these lyrics as well.) It is elevator music.[9] When I was young, my barber used to play this stuff in his shop for all the old ladies who came in to get their hair dyed. Ten or so songs might play while I waited to have my hair cut, but they might as well have been one big, long, creamy pile of orchestral mush. They were designed not to step on anyone's toes—which, by Lucy's reckoning, is pure evil.

Lucy's use of "Love is Blue" echoes another important concept at the heart of *Millennium*, which is the contagion of evil. This is a theme first explored in depth in "The Thin White Line," in which a killer Frank once apprehended literally passes on his murderous ways to his longtime cellmate.[10] In the third season, the Millennium Group even pioneers a way to medically transfer one man's proclivity for murder to another, keeping the murderous spirit of the infamous Ed Cuffle alive in the body and mind of Lucas Wayne Barr. Butler's methods are more obtuse but also more frightening because of the insidiousness of the approach. No one notices ordinariness. It is expected. In "A Room with No View," Lucy and her guidance counselor accomplice personify the banality of evil, reinforcing the idea that you never quite know where temptation lies.

FIVE SONGS, FIVE USES
TRACING THE ARC OF A MYTH

An effective overview of the various and powerful ways in which *Millennium* uses pre-existing music to bolster its storytelling can be seen in the two relentlessly paced myth arc two-parters of season two. The first occurs in "Owls." When Mr. Johnston (Malcolm Stewart) switches his stereo from inane talk radio to America's "Horse with No Name," the song, completely independent of its content, immediately becomes a foreshadowing device—we know something big is going to happen. Here again, Morgan and Wong blur the line between diegetic and extra-diegetic music, introducing the song through the radio and stopping it when the car suddenly malfunctions and stops. When the car re-starts, the song comes back and grows steadily more disembodied from the radio as Johnston struggles for his life with Helmut Gunsche's (Bob Dawson) rubber tube around his neck. Finally, the song survives the car's explosion, fading out as the episode pauses for a commercial break.

One of the things this accomplishes is a boost in the drama of the scene, but the mechanics of how this works are hard to grasp firmly.

THE EVIL EARWORM

One of the unique abilities of music is to wordlessly express a great deal of emotion and feeling. It can often say what we cannot, and very eloquently at that. Beyond this, the presence of a certain piece of music at a certain time and place can have the strange effect of making the moment feel more charged than it otherwise should. I have a peculiar memory of my time as a summer custodian at my hometown's middle school, for instance. I was listening to Radiohead's *The Bends* (1995) on a boombox while straightening out the gym and adjacent locker rooms and, as the album came to its last song, "Street Spirit," I was organizing a scattered assortment of brightly colored soda cans. I have a vivid audio-visual memory of the way my hands moved and the way the cans fit together as the song's hypnotic guitar part played, a memory I almost certainly would not have retained had I not been listening to the song while I organized those cans.

This right-fit situation is easily achieved in the "Horse with No Name" sequence, but it is bested in the second half of the two-parter, during which Richard Wagner's prelude to Act One of his 1882 opera *Parsifal* plays over nearly a quarter of the episode, with one small break, tying together a series of beautifully understated events that bring this portion of the show's myth arc to a meditative close. The Old Man (R. G. Armstrong) plays it for Lara Means as he explains to her the history of the Nazis's fascination with religious ephemera, but it carries over to Frank explaining the very same to Catherine. Thomas J. Wright's direction tells the story through two simultaneous conversations united by this simple orchestral theme, bringing visual and situational variety to what might otherwise be fairly boring exposition. Then, after two scenes in which no music at all is present, either from Mark Snow's score or an outside source—the Old Man's murder and Peter Watts's reconciliation with Frank and Lara—the prelude returns.[11]

The next six minutes are played with an astonishingly light touch, considering that they include both a car explosion and the incendiary bombing of a mansion in Paraguay. We cut back and forth between the ritualistic funeral for the Old Man and the fiery murders of both the Old Man's killer and the oldest surviving member of Adolf Hitler's inner circle, but the prelude to *Parsifal* never fades or disappears. Frank and Lara rejoin the Group, the Elder becomes the new Old Man, and what may or may not be a piece of the True Cross finds its way to the Old Man's home, where it is stowed behind books for future use.

Parsifal, conceived by Wagner in 1857 but not completed until 1882, centers on a group of holy knights who protect the Holy Grail, and the parallels to the Roosters, who seek to possess and guard a piece of the Cross of the Crucifixion, are clear. There is vigorous debate among historians as to whether the opera reflects Wagner's anti-Semitism in its content, though there is no explicit mention of Judaism in the opera.

"Roosters" does double duty as a sort of reclamation project for Wagner's music from the heavy historical tarnish of Hitler's devotion to it. (Wagner wrote anti-Semitic articles and correspondence, but Hitler's use of Wagner's music was still a grotesque distortion of its purpose and meaning.) There is a satisfying twist of irony to watching a blood-spattered Nazi flag burn to the strains of Wagner. While the talk in the episode of Hitler turning *Parsifal* into a religion is not quite true—Hitler indeed co-opted Wagner's work into his national heroic mythology but himself thought that the occultism of many of the other Nazi leaders was ridiculous—the existence of ODESSA, the Nazi-sheltering organization that the Group destroys in the episode's *denouement*, is true to life.

One could also say that using Wagner to drive propulsive pacing is ironic in itself. *Parsifal* is, after all, five hours long. But it works, and the relatively slow pacing of the music itself is one of the reasons it so easily ties all of the disparate images together—the same texture hangs across all of the images.

It is different in effect, and offers a much less subtle message, but the use of Zager and Evans's "In the Year 2525" similarly serves as a sort of through-line between "The Fourth Horseman" and "The Time is Now." This song is not explicitly apocalyptic. Rather, it jumps ahead in time by millennia, speculating on what human beings might be like at each juncture. By the time we reach the seventy-sixth century, God is weighing the timing of Judgment Day, but it sort of slips by, and Man ends himself by taking all the world can give him while returning nothing. This is pretty bleak subject matter for a one-hit wonder, and that is what Zager and Evans were. "In the Year 2525" sold two million copies in 1968 and was number one in the United States for six weeks, including the week that Man landed on the Moon for the first time. The Nebraska-based duo released a few follow-ups but never came close to having another hit.[12] The song is often thought of as a novelty hit for its commitment to its theme of Man erasing himself through his own progress, but that theme is particularly appropriate to the subject matter of this season finale. The Marburg variant killing people in the Greater Seattle area is man-made, and the Group's vaccine exists only in pathetically small amounts.

The song plays on radios during an autopsy and in the Blacks' yellow house, nagging at the viewer with its hints of something awful on the way, and as people begin to die and the virus spreads, the song becomes part of the frenzied urgency of Frank's need to get his family away from this horrible plague. In a way, the song embodies Frank's helplessness to stop the outbreak or protect his wife from it as the music whisks along from verse to verse, changing keys as it leaps a thousand years in a few seconds with each new verse. When it comes in for the final time, creeping up through the static in Frank's visions, the "if man is still alive" of the opening verse seems very much an open question.

In the midst of all of this are two of the show's most important set pieces: the death of the Davis family and the collapse of Lara Means into catatonic insanity. The first of these is among the most demented scenes in any network television show. The Davis family's Mother's Day gathering is almost supernaturally cheerful, and the use of Dionne Warwick's "I'll Never Fall in Love Again," with its cornball brass arrangement and lyrics comparing love to the common cold, heightens the sense that this is a visit to another world, like a commercial for some family friendly product that got swallowed by the episode and turned into some kind of sweat-inducing nightmare. The juxtaposition of horror and harmlessness here harks back to the Carpenters and the German Shepherds. The deaths of the family members may be horrifying, but this is nothing the show has not done to us before. The opening fanfare of the song is practically a signpost for viewers indicating that we are only seconds from disaster. Much less conventional, and unprecedented for a network drama, is the sequence in which Lara Means loses her mind.

The scene is essentially a music video set to Patti Smith's harrowing, nine-minute depiction of heroin addiction, "Land, Part I: Horses, Part II: Land of a Thousand Dances, Part III: La Mer (De)"—colloquially known as "Horses." This is a raw, poetic song that addresses its subject matter with a mix of abstract and visceral imagery, and as such it makes a good accompaniment to what we are shown on screen, which is a bizarre tangle of apocalyptic imagery and Means's own disintegration, which is itself shown with a mix of symbolic images and straightforward shots of her losing control.

Loss of control is the central theme of "Horses." As the characters in the song spiral through heroin abuse, Smith moves back and forth between hellish drug imagery and a deconstruction of the popular dance tune "Land of a Thousand Dances." Her free verse lyrics are spoken and never coalesce into a sung chorus. The whole piece is as loosely structured as the visual collage that accompanies it in "The Time Is Now." Not only was this something that had not been done before on television, it is something no one has really tried since. Such a sequence is challenging to execute, in part because it is expensive and difficult to edit a scene like this on a weekly television schedule. Glen Morgan himself has mentioned in interviews that putting the sequence together was a trial. "Editing was really difficult... Music videos probably have a budget close to what one of our entire episodes costs, and we had only three days to put it together. I don't think we competed very well with the kind of imagery you see on MTV but I felt that this hasn't been done on a primetime, network drama. I'm glad we did it but it was really, really hard" (Vitaris 125).

The greater difficulty for an executive producer, however, is putting yourself in a position where you can justify devoting almost ten of your forty-four minutes of screen time in a season finale to a music video featuring a secondary character cracking up. The show's creative team earned its way to this point through storytelling and the inventive use of music, no small feat.

AFTER THE END OF THE WORLD

Millennium's third season is the year that most divides fans, and it is easy to understand why. It is difficult for anything to feel climactic after you have just witnessed the end of the world. One of the ways in which the show dealt with this problem was to retreat to more familiar ground, moving Frank back to the F.B.I. and to Washington, D.C., and giving him a down-to-earth foil in Agent Emma Hollis (Klea Scott). There are a few examples of the show using what it learned during the second season about the ways in which popular music and dramatic narrative can dovetail. To quickly address the most obvious use of music in a season three episode, it must be said that one of those examples is not "Thirteen Years Later," which features Kiss playing "Psycho Circus" during a scene in which Frank searches for a murderer.

When Kiss appeared on *Millennium* in October 1998, they were promoting their album *Psycho Circus* (1998)—they play the title track during the concert scene. *Psycho Circus* was the first album by the band's complete original lineup of Ace Frehley, Peter Criss, Gene Simmons, and Paul Stanley since 1980, and it was preceded by a massive world tour, replete with elaborate stage sets and pyrotechnic displays. The following year, the band appeared as themselves in the feature film *Detroit Rock City* (1999) and also collaborated with the World Wrestling Federation to create a wrestler with a persona based on Gene Simmons's "Demon" stage persona. "Thirteen Years Later" takes its place in history as a single ingredient in a concerted four-year promotional blitz designed to re-establish Kiss as a top-draw live act.

This is an episode in which nearly every element, from the characters to the plot to Frank's ridiculous visions of the members of Kiss in their stage make-up, is a caricature. The concert scene, part of the film being shot in the episode, is as much a caricature of filmmaking convention as any other element. It is evocative of the sequence in Michelangelo Antonioni's *Blow-Up* (1966) in which David Hemmings chases Vanessa Redgrave into a Yardbirds concert and loses her in the crowd. This sort of sequence has been done in many other contexts, too, but the comedic tone of "Thirteen Years Later" makes it feel as if there is very little at stake as Kiss nakedly promotes its mediocre new album.

There are much better uses of music in the third season. Blur's "Trimm Trabb" is used fairly conventionally to soundtrack the teaser sequence of "Darwin's Eye," but it is still very effective at ramping up the sense of peril as Cassie Doyle (Tracy Middendorf) makes her break from the asylum. In particular, there is a moment wherein Cassie grabs Deputy Joe Doherty's (Peter Simmons) gun and holds it on him, and the song shifts from an acoustic arrangement to a much louder electric arrangement soaked with heavily distorted guitar. It pushes the energy level much higher than Doyle's voiceover ramblings about evolution possibly ever could and, more importantly, it lets us know that this moment sets the entire rest of the episode in motion. Here are our players, and here is the essence of their relationship. Everything else that happens in the episode preserves this dynamic, even when it appears not to. Doherty never holds the upper hand over Doyle.

The Percy Sledge cover of James Carr's "The Dark End of the Street" is similarly used to amplify the script in "The Sound of Snow." The episode focuses on the deaths of two people who are sent audio tapes containing nothing but white noise. Frank also receives one of these tapes. The episode is never really clear about how the tapes affect the relationship between perception and reality. This ambiguity leaves it to us to read what we will into the tapes, as it is suggested the recipients do. When "The Sound of Snow" originally aired, the internet was still a marginal source of music and other audio entertainment, and even CD burners were not yet commonplace. The medium of exchange for these things between friends and (importantly) lovers was the blank cassette. Many people have deep associations with the cassette tape and the people they exchanged tapes with.

Because mixtapes were shared between people, each one has two stories surrounding it, one devised by the maker of the tape, the other by the recipient. The maker could attempt to encode messages into the song and sound clip choices and it was up to the receiver to perceive them. In "The Sound of Snow," Alice Severin (Jessica Tuck) distills this approach by forgoing recognizable content altogether, allowing people to hear into the tape what they will. If death is the result, she appears to feel that it is out of her hands.

Listening to his own tape sends Frank on a life-threatening trip through visions of the departed Catherine. "The Dark End of the Street" plays while Frank, back in Seattle investigating this mystery, drives to see the yellow house, which the new owners have painted white (though Frank's visions prevent him from seeing this at first). There is an interesting inversion of expectations while Frank is driving. He removes one cassette from the car's tape deck and puts in another. The audience assumes he is going to subject himself to more of the white noise, but instead Sledge's "Dark End of the Street" comes on. The implication seems to be that, without closure on Catherine's death, Frank will have visions of her no matter what he's listening to. Frank gets his closure during the course of the episode but nearly at the cost of his life.

"The Dark End of the Street" makes a powerful scene more poignant but it does not comment much on the story. The final third season example, however, does. This is the use of Nazareth's "Love Hurts" in "Skull and Bones." As Emma Hollis, gun drawn, apprehensively begins to search the foul-smelling house of Homer B.

Pettey in search of clues to the origin of the skeletons in the path of a new highway, a radio clicks on and begins playing the song. As diegetic music goes, this is extremely creepy. She presses into Pettey's dissection room, which has not been cleaned at all (the smell of so much fetid tissue and old blood would be overwhelming) and the song follows her, its gentle guitar and exaggeratedly pained vocals adding a surreal layer to her hideous discoveries.

Nazareth hailed from Dunfermline, Scotland, and their core sound was hard rock, epitomized by their hit single "Hair of the Dog" (identifiable from its chorus, with its "now you're messing with a son of a bitch" refrain). "Love Hurts" was nevertheless the band's biggest hit, and their 1975 version of the song remains the best-known, though it was not the first successful version. Originally performed by the Everley Brothers in 1960, the song first became a hit in Australia a year later in a version by Roy Orbison (it was issued as a B-side in the United States). There was a second hit version of "Love Hurts" in 1975, by former Traffic drummer Jim Capaldi. It reached number four in the U.K. Nazareth's version peaked at number fifteen in the U.K. and number eight in the U.S. There is something about the big-budget earnestness of this rendition of "Love Hurts" that makes it an especially weird accompaniment to the carnage in Pettey's shabby back room. Nazareth was primarily a hard rock band, and vocalist Dan McCafferty doesn't modulate his delivery for the softer song, so the song has its own kind of built-in disconnect as he wails and the band practices studied restraint behind him.

This is an instance in which it would be easy to simply assume that the show was aiming for a disturbing juxtaposition of sound and image, but it is likely not so simple. The Millennium Group, which ultimately seeks out Hollis as a member, seems to be sending her an early message here: "love hurts." The Group wants her to know that what she has discovered is a sign of the Group's love for the country and the world. (Love hurts, Emma. Once you accept that, we'll tell you more.) We have heard this message before: certain lives need to be sacrificed for the greater good.

LITTLE DEMONS

There is one final episode whose use of music must be addressed, and it may be my favorite of all the various examples. Not coincidentally, "The Curse of Frank Black" is my favorite *Millennium* episode—it is the episode with the deepest silences and the darkest blacks. It is also the episode that has the most fun exploring evil's place in the world and how it introduces itself when it wants to formally make its presence known.

In Frank's world, evil makes itself known when it wants to make a deal, and the agreement it offers to Frank is tempting: inaction in exchange for a place in the more desirable afterlife for his family. Frank, however, knows that inaction itself would be a damnable offense. This foreshadows "A Room with No View," in which Lucy Butler attempts to awaken the ordinariness of her prisoners, tamping down their exceptional qualities. Frank Black has a gift, one that sometimes appears to him to be a curse, and to deny it, to go on living as though there were no evil in the world, is unacceptable to him. This is a theme deeply embedded in the character's backstory, the story of the man who left the F.B.I. to escape his calling and then found himself right back at the scene of the crime, using his tremendous gift to catch the killer.

When Frank speaks to the apparition of Mr. Crocell (Dean Winters) in his attic, Crocell tempts him with the Devil's offer, to be sure, but beyond that, it is not clear which side Crocell is really on. The warning he delivers to Frank, that the investigator is becoming Crocell, the man who didn't care, is certainly clear enough. Perhaps hidden in his advocacy for the Devil is a subtle pitch for redemption. Frank hears Crocell's pitch, rejects the temptation but heeds the warning, and he goes to clean the egg off the yellow house.

Before any of this can happen, the Devil has to introduce himself, and what better way to do this than in a song? As Frank's Jeep Cherokee approaches 28,006 miles on the odometer, the Devil lets Frank know he is watching through the voice of Screamin' Jay Hawkins. Screamin' Jay's "Little Demon" is a masterpiece of marble-mouthed rockabilly, and the scrambled syllables he puts in his demon's mouth may be gobbledygook but they're *boisterous* gobbledygook—the Devil may not ever come right out and say what he wants but he is confident you will get his message anyway.

There is another running theme at work here, one that runs in the background of the series, which is that evil is perfectly happy to play tricks, to riddle, and to fake people out. If you head down what appears to be the righteous path, you may soon find that you have taken an invitation to a wrong turn. Consider Crocell's pitch to Frank. We know that the Devil promises to leave Frank and his family alone—forever—if Frank will only walk away from the fight. The man feels obligated to his family—couldn't taking the path that ensures a future for his loved ones be the right thing to do? Staying in the fight has threatened to destroy the goodness in him and led him to kill without mercy. Is this a catch-22? Is his soul bound for the Devil's back pocket either way?

"Little Demon" offers no answer to this question, acting only as its title character would, as the foot soldier of the Devil, hounding Frank and letting him know that he will not be left alone until the boss gets a chance to make his offer. The song is perfectly pitched to fit Frank's ghoulish Halloween, and when it pops back up, completely unbidden, after Frank returns home and has to fight to keep the stop-motion devil off his television screen, it provides a startling message to Frank that his night is not over yet. This is a rare instance of a song functioning as a kind of character, even if that character is just a front for someone else.

Could it be that the Devil understands the power of an earworm to drive a person to distraction? Perhaps "Little Demon" makes a better first impression than a physical demon with a full complement of horns and pitchfork tines. The man downstairs has a sense of humor. Further, the devil surely knows of evil's power in the world of *Millennium* to infect through exposure; his use of a catchy song to presage his offer to Frank may serve the secondary purpose of softening his target.

"Little Demon" gains its power to startle in "The Curse of Frank Black" from a simple fact: Mark Snow leaves great, yawning silences in his score where the sound of the wind and the rustling leaves becomes a soundtrack. The score is present in small, mood-setting islands and is at one point used beautifully to set up a false scare, but Screamin' Jay's main competition is the foley.[13] For Frank, visits from the little demon are like having an uninvited song stuck in his head. It does not matter that he did not press play. The song still plays for him—and only him.

NOTES

1. One of the most interesting things about the choice of Portishead here is that it offers such a sharp shift from music of male aggression to a song sung by a woman, Beth Gibbons. Gibbons issues no threats and exhibits no lust. Her lyrics are a warning and call to action issued by a woman.

2. David Berkowitz, born Richard David Falco and popularly known as "Son of Sam" or "The .44 Caliber Killer," confessed to the murder of six people and the wounding of several others in New York City between July 1976 and August 1977. He has been imprisoned ever since but has subsequently given two explanations for his crimes. The first is that he was commanded to kill by a demon that possessed his neighbor's dog. The second, a partial recantation of his original confession, is that he only directly committed two of the shootings, and the others were carried out by members of a satanic cult to which he belonged. While the veracity of his subsequent explanations has never been supported by physical evidence, the case remains open. The name "Son of Sam" comes directly from a letter written by the killer to police

3. Lawrence Welk's life spanned nearly the entire twentieth century, from 1903 to 1992. He hosted *The Lawrence Welk Show* from 1951 to 1982. It was broadcast across the United States on ABC from 1955 until 1971. From there, it was produced for first-run syndication until 1982. It has been syndicated sporadically by public broadcasting channels ever since, and several generations of Americans can recall it playing on the television at their grandparents' houses. Many of its primary sponsors were the manufacturers of items such as denture cleaners, laxatives, aftershaves, fruit juices, and vitamins.

4. A striking example of director David Lynch's penchant for juxtaposing the mundane or even enjoyable moment with horror can be found in the opening sequence of *Blue Velvet* (1986), in which a man watering his lawn on a beautiful, sunny day has a sudden heart attack. We see roses in front of a white picket fence, a crossing guard helping children across the street, an old-fashioned fire engine, and the man's wife watching a movie inside, a movie in which someone wielding a pistol is stealthily moving through a building. Bobby Vinton's 1963 soft-pop hit "Blue Velvet" plays the whole time. As the man lies unconscious (or possibly dead), hose still in hand, a dog drinks from the hose and a child approaches. The camera plunges into the grass, panning forward through the blades to a scene of insects horrifically killing each other. This idea that horror is happening all around us, even on a beautiful day when all seems right, lies deep at the core of *Millennium*, and the use of soft, friendly music in this sequence is a direct antecedent to the use of music in the series, particularly during season two.

5. Sheriff Andy Taylor's name in "Home" is a reference to *The Andy Griffith Show*, an American sitcom broadcast from 1960 to 1968. Griffith played Taylor, a widowed father and the sheriff of a small town in North Carolina called Mayberry. Sheriff Taylor and his bumbling deputy, Barney Fife (Don Knotts), mostly contend with community disputes, hayseed moonshiners, and criminal elements from out of town hoping to exploit the community's

sleepiness. The show launched the career of Ron Howard, who played Taylor's son, Opie, and has since gone on to a distinguished career as a movie director.

6. "Seasons in the Sun" was not originally by Terry Jacks. The English-language version of the song was written in 1965 by Rod McKuen, based on Jacques Brel's "*Le Moribond.*" Brel, a Belgian, has a large catalog of French-language songs celebrating sex and death, often in gleefully ironic ways. The fact that Jacks himself recorded the song at all was something of a fluke. He was originally scheduled to produce a version by the Beach Boys but wound up recording it himself when the group decided to drop it.

7. The Broadway version of *Goodbye Charlie* flopped, but it was later made into a feature film starring Tony Curtis and Debbie Reynolds. The film also flopped.

8. Though they were known for their squeaky clean public image, the story of the Carpenters is not entirely wholesome. The group was a duo made up of brother Richard Carpenter and sister Karen Carpenter. Richard was the primary writer/arranger, and on stage, could be found at the keyboard of a piano or Wurlitzer. Karen was a drummer and also the group's vocalist. She considered herself a drummer foremost, and her gradual transition to appearing on stage solely as the lead singer was quite difficult, leading to body image issues and *anorexia nervosa*. Karen died of heart failure in 1983 at the age of 32. Richard suffered through addiction in the 1970s but overcame it and has spent much of the intervening years curating the group's recorded legacy.

9. "Elevator music" is often used synonymously with "Muzak," and this is no accident. The Muzak Holdings Corporation, founded in 1934, was established to provide music in public spaces. The company conducted extensive research, leading to publications that showed how music could increase worker productivity, and aggressively sold its product to businesses. The original music produced for these public music systems was made intentionally nondescript so that it would not distract people from their tasks, be they employees or patrons. In the 1980s, Muzak moved away from its elevator music model and began offering channels that played selections of popular music. It has since expanded its offerings into satellite broadcasting.

10. Jacob Tyler (Scott Heindl), the killer contaminated by the contagion of evil in "The Thin White Line," memorably preps for his first kill while listening to the Bee Gees's "How Deep is Your Love," a direct nod to his relationship with Richard Alan Hance (Jeremy Roberts), the killer who inspired him.

11. The silence on the soundtrack during the scene in which Lara, Peter, and Frank lament the passing of the Old Man is essential to making the scene work. If the conversation had to contend with a score pushing the viewer's emotions in a particular direction, it would lose most of its power. Mark Snow's restraint here deserves credit and recalls another instance in which restraint constituted an important musical contribution: King Crimson's "Trio." "Trio" is a short, placid instrumental that the band improvised in the studio. The instrumental is credited to all four band members, including drummer Bill Bruford, in spite of the fact that Bruford chose not to play anything while his bandmates created the song. The rest of the group found his silence contributed so much to the piece that he deserved a composer credit for having the good taste to do nothing.

12. Denny Zager now runs his own custom guitar company, Zager E-Z Play. Rick Evans kept writing and performing after the success of "In the Year 2525" died away but maintained a low profile for the rest of his career.

13. Though popular music is frequently featured on the soundtrack of *Millennium*, Mark Snow's original score avoids engaging with it directly; he declines to quote or sample from the selections, instead scoring around them in his unique style. The single instance in which Snow directly references and incorporates a pre-existing piece of music into his newly composed score for an episode of *Millennium* occurs in "Midnight of the Century." Snow subtly uses the melody of the Christmas standard "We Three Kings" many times over as a running, morphing motif in the episode's score. While popular music never found its way directly into his compositions, Snow did frequently build off his theme song for *Millennium* in his episode scores, using small, altered phrases from the main melody. According to Snow, the inspiration for the theme's melancholy violin is actually a pop song, and an unlikely one at that. Australian pop star Kylie Minogue's "Confide in Me" features a very similar-feeling violin during its introduction, though the melodic material it plays is quite different.

WORKS CITED

Beaman, C. Philip and Tim I. Williams. "Earworms ('Stuck Song Syndrome'): Towards a Natural History of Intrusive Thoughts." *British Journal of Psychology* 101.4 (2010): 637-653. Print.

Carpenters, The. "(They Long to Be) Close to You." A&M, 1970. 45 rpm single.

THE EVIL EARWORM

Cypress Hill. "Insane in the Brain." *Black Sunday*. Ruffhouse/Columbia, 1993. CD.

Jacks, Terry. "Seasons in the Sun." *Seasons in the Sun*. Goldfish Records, 1973. 45 rpm single.

Liikkanen, Lassi. "Inducing Involuntary Musical Imagery: An Experimental Study." *Musicae Scientiae* 16.2 (2012): 217-234. Print.

Portishead. "Roads." *Dummy*. Go! Beat, 1994. CD.

Sacks, Oliver. *Musicophilia: Tales of Music and the Brain*. New York: Vintage Books, 2007. Print.

Smith, Patti. "Land, Part I: Horses, Part II: Land of 1,000 Dances, Part III: La Mer (De)." *Horses*. Arista, 1975. CD.

Vitaris, Paula. "*Millennium*: TV's Best Kept Secret Improves in its Sophomore Season." *Cinefantastique* October 1998: 18-22, 125. Print.

Whitley, Richard. Interview by James McLean and Troy L. Foreman. *The Millennium Group Sessions*. Back to Frank Black, 16 November 2011. Web. 14 August 2012.

Wegner, D. M. "Ironic Process of Mental Control." *Psychological Review* 101.1 (1994): 34-52. Print.

Zager and Evans. "In the Year 2525." RCA/Victor, 1968. 45 rpm single.

Joe Tangari is an American writer. He has lived in several states and currently calls Michigan home. He has written about music for *Pitchfork, Down Beat, One More Robot*, and *The Thread* and talked about music for ABC News. Life has been good to him, on balance: he has a wonderful wife and two fantastic cats to support him while he earns a master's degree, and he serves on the board of a small animal rescue organization.

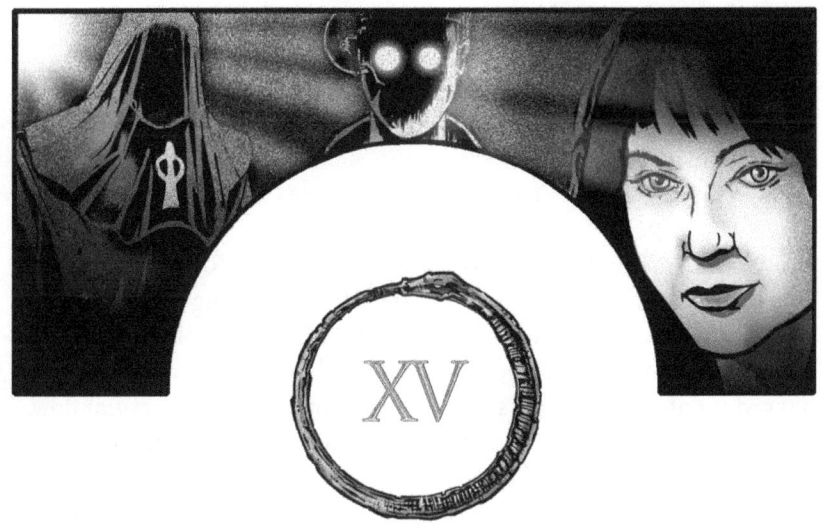

THE DEVIL'S LIEGE:
A CONVERSATION WITH SARAH-JANE REDMOND

Interview by James McLean & Troy L. Foreman
Written by Adam Chamberlain & Brian A. Dixon

As Lucy Butler, actress Sarah-Jane Redmond can lay claim to having starred in what may be the single most memorable scene in all of *Millennium*. The moment in which Butler descends the stairs of 1910 Ezekiel Drive, allowing Lieutenant Bob Bletcher to see the Devil incarnate lit by lightning in his final moments, is seared forever into the memories of all who have seen the seminal "Lamentation," written by series creator Chris Carter. The scene is paralyzing and it is dominated by Redmond's presence. A similar experience of heightened drama and anticipation awaited the actress when she first read this and, indeed, every script. "It was so good," she recalls. "One of the most fun things of being involved in the show was reading the scripts for the first time. I'd sit down and I'd just sort of look at the first page and take my time with it and always wonder what was going to happen, and it was never disappointing. It was always incredible to turn each page." What Redmond was able to achieve so effectively as a performer was to imbue that character on the page with an allure both sinful and enticing, transforming the devilish Lucy Butler into *Millennium*'s most celebrated villain.

Unlike many in her profession, Sarah-Jane Redmond did not harbor the dream to become an actress from a young age. "I think it just sort of grew on me," she says. "It was never really a decision I made. I traveled quite a bit when I was a kid, and I got into dance. I danced for about eight years, and it just seemed to be the natural flow. I don't ever recall making a decision that that's what I wanted to do; it just seemed that was the natural path of evolution for me." She was, however, influenced to take to the stage by a famous singer-songwriter. "This is very strange," she admits. "I remember watching a John Denver concert on television when I was six or seven. I was glued to it, and I thought, 'Wow, that's what I want to do! I want to be up there on stage!'"

Redmond is British by birth, and that childhood spent traveling was a result of her father's career in the Royal Air Force. "I was born in Cyprus, Greece, where we were stationed. Then we moved back to England—Lincolnshire and the Lake District—and then we ended up moving to Canada." She was to return to England before studying to be an actress. "I traveled and I had a really good time in London. I did go there to go to theater school, and I ended up coming back to Canada to study, but I was in London for a year. It was a feeling of coming home."

Having completed her studies abroad, Redmond took the bold step of launching her own theater company. "You're kind of sitting around, you've done all your studies and then you're thinking, 'Okay, what now? How do I get a job?' The people that I had graduated from theater school with were sitting around as well and I thought, 'Let's do something.' It's one of those things where, had I known how much hard work it was, I don't know if I would have done it! But we all got together and the first couple of shows were horrendous and we were really bad, but they got better and better and [I] ended up doing theater for a couple of years, and really great shows. You get to a place where doing it for nothing is okay, then you start making money and it all changes things. But I loved the theater, I really loved doing live theater, and I haven't done much since."

It was Ten Thirteen Productions—specifically, a role on *The X-Files* in the second season episode "Aubrey"—that provided Redmond with what she describes as "the really wonderful launch" for her acting life. "I owe so much to Chris for being such an instrumental part of my career," she explains. Her guest appearance on *The X-Files* proved fateful for the connections she made there would set her on a path to a role that would forever change the status quo of *Millennium*. "I had auditioned for David Nutter for a day player on *Millennium*. It was a really nice role, but it was one of those days where everything kind of lined up. I went into the room and David Nutter was there, Chris Carter was sitting in the corner, and a couple of other producers were there. You just never know sometimes how auditioning is going to go, and it was one of those days where everything felt right, and it was a great audition. The next day Coreen Mayrs called me at home. In Vancouver she's one of the biggest casting directors and it was very odd that she was calling me at home, and she said, 'I'm calling you to let you know two things. One, you didn't get the part—they ended up writing the part out—but two, Chris has a character that he'd like to write for you. It's a recurring role, and they'd like to know if you'd like to take the role.' I remember it was one of those moments where I couldn't help but scream on the phone! She was saying, 'I guess I'll let them know that that will be a yes.'"

Redmond believes that one of the strengths of Carter's writing is the way in which he allows his actors the space to make their own choices about their characters. "I think that's one of the really magical things that Chris has about him," she says, "that he doesn't give a lot away, and I think he writes for the people that play the roles. He leaves a lot up to the performer to create in their own imagination. When things are spelled out too clearly it doesn't leave a lot to the imagination of the viewer, and so when you're given [the space], your own inventiveness can kick in and create a background and not spell too much out—and you'll notice in his writing he leaves a lot to the imagination. There were things where you just go by instinct that you're not going to give away as a performer and you don't give away in interviews, but a lot of it is left unsaid. There's a lot of trust that he gives the performers."

What influenced these creative choices in her approach to playing Lucy Butler beyond what appeared in the script? "There were things that I pulled, but mainly it was from the writing. Mainly it was from what Chris alluded to. There are always various aspects of human nature that I think everybody has inside of them, that you can pull from within, and this just seemed to be one of those characters that things could come from within, as opposed to looking outside for inspiration. A lot of times it's really great to look outside—I think Johnny Depp's a really great example of that in [*Pirates of the Caribbean*], what he does—but sometimes you can just go inside. That was a really scary thing about the character, and liberating."

The reasons for Lucy Butler's success as a recurring antagonist on *Millennium* aren't difficult to discern. She is cruel and also changeable, wicked and enigmatic, and Redmond's nuanced performance grants the villainess a seductive menace with which to oppose the rugged determination of Frank Black. She changes her shape as often as she changes her mood, and each episode featuring the character considered her evil in a striking new context. In one scene during the third season episode "Antipas," Butler appears as a demon, her feminine features replaced by horns and a monstrous visage. This offered Redmond the chance to explore the character in an altogether fresh way. "I remember the first time we worked with the special effects and they were incredible, the stuff that they did. It was over the Christmas holidays that they started working on the special effects for the whole mask, hands, and chest plate. When I had it all on the very first time I had quite a few hours to go back into the trailer and explore it. It was very interesting and an experience like no other. When you get to do that, but with that kind of talent in terms of the special effects, you can really lose yourself in it—in a good way!"

The changeable nature of Lucy Butler allowed for an evolving representation of the character across each of her appearances. One aspect of this evolution involved the character becoming more overtly sexual in both "A Room with No View" and "Antipas." The trend became a recurrent element of the scripts. "I think that again there were aspects of that in the writing and it just sort of naturally came out. There were never really any big discussions; I think there's a lot to be said for if you're doing something wrong, they'll let you know. It just came out in where the writing was taking it, and so I just ended up following that." Though she is quick to praise the writers of

THE DEVIL'S LIEGE

Millennium, the basis for this aggressive sexuality is undoubtedly to be found in Redmond's chemistry with her onscreen nemesis. "It was also really fun to play with Lance in that realm, too. I remember the scene [in 'Lamentation'] when we're in the interview room. I'm sitting on the edge of the desk and he's gotten me in the police station. That was when it just first started coming out and it might have inspired the writers to go in that direction, but I just remember really toying with Frank Black in that scene, and it was kind of the spark of that. Lance is so much fun to play with because he's quite intimidating, and so to be able to play with him on that level was really exciting."

Butler is at times represented by a male alter ego, the so-called Long-Haired Man, played in "Antipas" by actor Scott Heindl. In this context, Redmond believes that the two performers benefited from not collaborating at all. "We actually kept ourselves very separate," she reveals. "I think that was an unconscious/conscious decision, and we just were both on the same page. We pretty much avoided each other, which was really neat. The danger is when you want to talk too much and you want to get the story down, and again it comes back to giving the viewer the respect and the responsibility to play with their own imagination."

Butler's Season Two appearance in "A Room with No View" defines a haunting episode in which she keeps teenagers of some promise captive and submits them to a terrifying psychological ordeal in order to break their spirits. The tense audience expectation of a confrontation between Lucy and Frank never materializes on this occasion and, once again, she evades capture. "That was the really neat thing about the two lines that episode had. There is an element of the brainwashing and trying to take what is unique and special about people and take it out of them. I think that's what the episode was [about]. It's very interesting, and there's a lot of reality to that."

Despite the grim heart to this and other storylines involving Lucy Butler, the actress found herself able to resist being adversely affected by the darkness of the subject matter inherent to *Millennium*. "I think that you always want to have hope, but what the show really did and pushed to the limits is that it did take a look at all of the underbelly of what goes on and the darkness in the world, and I think that's where the show triumphed—and also struggled, in a sense." In those infernal matters involving Butler, *Millennium*'s viewers were always left wanting more, as was Redmond herself. "You try your best to let it go, but I have to admit that most of the time what I took home was, 'Did I do it justice? Did I bring as much as I could have? Was I creative enough? Was the work there?' That's what I have a tendency to bring home more of. You always have a sense of watching it and thinking, 'Wow, there were so many more layers that I could've gone to,' but I think that's just human nature."

As it was, Redmond brought great skill, talent, and an incomparable presence to her performance as Lucy Butler and created some truly iconic moments with the character, few as chilling as when she dispenses her parting words to Frank Black from a hospital bed at the end of "Antipas." Her delivery is scornful and full of threat, her expression twisted and demonic—in her own words, "ugly" and "awful!" Redmond recalls preparing to film the scene. "I remember it was probably five-thirty in the morning at a coffee shop, and I was rehearsing. I really wanted to get into that scene and really get to the down and dirty of it, so I rehearsed with a coach of mine. Literally the only place we could meet was at a coffee shop at five-thirty in the morning, and it was quite a funny scenario. I think that was a really telling scene of the ugliness of that character."

In spite of the fact that Lucy Butler represents the very essence of evil, Redmond was never superstitious about taking on the role. "That doesn't bother me, because it's a character and it's fun. It was so fun. How does it get any better? That's a wonderful thing about the industry, the business, and about Chris Carter's writing, to bite into that and to play is just really exciting. It's playing something that you are not but that you're giving life to. I think the characters that I don't like playing are the characters that are real characters—a mom or a wife—that don't have any respect or dignity, that are victims. I think those are the characters that I find I really don't want to give a voice to."

In addition to Carter, Redmond also compliments the work of Frank Spotnitz, who co-wrote "Antipas" with the series creator. "The two of them worked very closely together on the show," Redmond remembers. More recently, they collaborated on *The X-Files: I Want to Believe* (2008), which saw her return to the Ten Thirteen fold. "When I first went in, there was a wonderful part in the film that ended up going to another actress, and then they offered me that role, the one that I played. And again, just being involved in it and getting a chance to work with Chris again, it's like family. And seeing David [Duchovny] and Gillian [Anderson] again was really fun. David's a funny guy!"

The actress is also effusive in her praise for *Millennium*'s lead actor: Lance Henriksen. "I can't say enough about Lance," she enthuses. "I remember it was one of the first roles that I really got to sink my teeth into and, up until then, studying and doing theater and coming fresh out of wanting to get into the industry, you have all sorts of excitement about it. And not to downplay the work before, but you just wonder, 'Wow, is this it?' Like maybe that excitement isn't there in television, maybe you can only get it in live theater."

Working alongside her two male co-stars in "Lamentation" was to quickly dispel such fears. "I remember the first day going to set I had an out-of-body experience, I was so scared. There was a scene with Lance and Terry [O'Quinn] and it was at Lucy's house. I basically had to walk circles around them, and I thought, 'Oh my God. Here's these two powerful actors and what have I done, really, and I've got to play cat and mouse with them.' It was just something with the character; it was something with how Chris wrote it. And I also think there's a real trap when you're playing a character like that if you play the intensity of it or if you play where the character is coming from. If you're trying to play that, it doesn't work. You have to find a real place to come from. So I just remember working with Lance, and I couldn't sleep for days. It was just so exciting. He was so playful; he's like a big kid. He's a kid in a grown-up's body, and he makes it so fun, and he's a very exciting actor."

Lucy Butler also encounters a formidable female foil, of course, in her Season Three appearance, a rival embodied by actress Klea Scott. "She's such a sweet woman. I can't say anything bad about her; she was wonderful. She was really sweet, open, generous, and very thoughtful. You could always see her thinking what the scene was about and what she was going to bring; she takes her work very seriously."

Sarah-Jane Redmond's performance across several unique episodes allowed *Millennium*'s ultimate evil to assume a veritable legion of forms and contexts, and it allowed the actress to truly explore the role. Would she like to see Lucy Butler return to the screen? The question is a no-brainer for Redmond. "Let's hope that we all get a chance to work together again. What a party that would be!" She is less eager to be drawn on what direction such a return might take for the character, leaving such decisions in the hands of the series creator. "I think I would be a fool to ever contemplate where Chris could or should [take her]."

Lucy Butler would relish the opportunity to face off against Frank Black once again, of course. "I know this for certain: playing with Lance would definitely be something that Lucy would enjoy and thrive upon. Getting back into the box with Frank Black, I know she'd jump at the chance."

Having inhabited the role of this mythic villainess so completely and so memorably, Redmond has a rather unique perspective on the character of Lucy Butler as well as the dramatic and moral limits to which she took her, which she sums up in her own words: "When in life do we have the opportunity to explore darkness, 'evil,' power? Most of us are kind, most of us operate from wanting to be good. I do believe that although we understand the instincts of wrongdoing, hatred, and spite, we rise above.

"Lucy Butler was the ultimate, the extreme, the furthest one could go into the dark. But she was not full of hatred, spite; she rejoiced in her rejection of 'God.' She rejoiced in her corruption of the mightiest. She rejoiced in her power over God's goodness in the world.

"Frank understood. That's why his struggle was so great, and that is why Lucy had to conquer him. Even in his dreams—in the motel room, in his bed—she came to Frank in the way he wanted her, letting him know she knew his thoughts: his demons. He could not escape. Her desire is to crush his will, to have him weep in her arms and surrender and be hers. They would have the battle of all time. He would see true evil and feel his soul cursed and devoured."

Regardless of what any future onscreen conflict holds for these two seemingly eternal nemeses, Redmond cherishes the time she spent on the series. "I shall always carry *Millennium* in my heart. I am forever grateful to Chris Carter and Lance Henriksen."

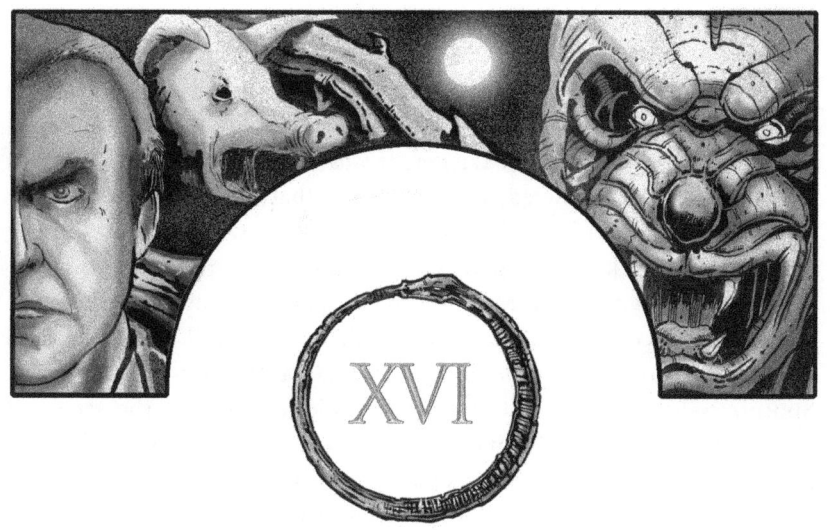

SEEING EVIL:
LUCY BUTLER AS LEGION THROUGH THE EYES OF FRANK BLACK

by Alexander Zelenyj

"'My name is Legion,' he replied, 'for we are many.'"

—Mark 5:8-10

Of the various overarching thematic concerns of the groundbreaking *Millennium* (1996-99) television series, one stands distinctly as the most prevalent: the nature of evil in the world in all of its manifestations. While that evil was often depicted as stemming from a distinctly human origin—particularly throughout the series' relentlessly grim first season, with its seemingly endless menagerie of serial killers and otherwise damaged human beings—an increasingly supernatural element began to infiltrate the stories and their inherent sense of fragile and tortured humanity, ultimately growing to encompass the world of *Millennium* and infusing it with an overwhelming apocalyptic gravity. This was epitomized in a story cycle which came to be known as the Legion myth-arc. At the heart of this mythology lies the great deceiver and nemesis of humankind: Lucifer. It was the beguiling incarnation of the fallen angel depicted in the series that struck a particularly significant chord with *Millennium* devotees. She was by turns alluring and seductive, deceiving and utterly enigmatic, and, at her most extreme, horrifyingly violent, inhumane, and governed by no moral law, acting according to her own selfish maxims and a perverse and emotionless logic. As *Millennium* writer and co-producer Frank Spotnitz says of creator Chris Carter's unique vision of the series, "I think Chris had the idea that evil as a concept had been degraded in our society by secularism, by science, and he still believed in evil as a real force. So, he wanted to make the scariest possible show he could, and that was what *Millennium* was" ("Order in Chaos").

In this sense, Lucy Butler, played by Sarah-Jane Redmond, epitomizes the antithesis of and a supreme adversary for series protagonist Frank Black. A former behavioral analyst and forensic profiler whose work for the Federal Bureau of Investigation brought about his nervous breakdown and subsequent retirement, Black's involvement as a candidate with the Millennium Group allows him to continue to use his inexplicable, gifted perceptions to enter the minds of the killers he investigates. Black's wide range of experience in the area of criminal behavioral science lends credibility to his evolving perspective of Butler, which quickly grows from a view rooted in psychology and behavioral pathology to encompass a tacit acceptance of her as embodying an omnipotent supernatural malevolence pervading the world at large.

Where Butler is selfish and motivated by the Dionysian desire to satisfy her overwhelming internal urges, Black is grounded by a moral center revolving around his devotion to both his family and his work, the latter of which sees him dedicated to ridding the world of evil through his efforts as a criminal profiler and consultant with the Millennium Group, an organization whose doctrines include the belief that the proliferation of violence throughout the world is symptomatic of the impending apocalypse.[1] More than any other "villain" seen throughout the *Millennium* canon, Butler parallels the enigmatic gift of

SEEING EVIL

Black with her own dark magic, although her powers appear to be rooted firmly in an altogether more supernatural place.

Spotnitz's explanation of Black's abilities sheds some light on the distinction between the two characters. "We never wanted to cross the line into the supernatural with any of that. It was more about an exquisite sensitivity to the way some people think, to the monstrous ways some people think" ("Order In Chaos"). Carter expands on this idea: "People get confused about Frank Black's gift, his ability, his facility, which is to get into the heads of violent criminals, to get into the heads of murderers or serial killers, to think like they think, and they confuse it with him being psychic or clairvoyant. I really see it as a perfection of technique as art" (Interview). This depiction of the hero and his abilities stands in stark contrast with Butler's depiction throughout the series, her uncanny ability to escape punishment for her violent crimes, and the fact that she continually thwarts the efforts of someone as professionally adept as Black to bring her to justice.

Lucy Butler made her debut in the compelling first season episode "Lamentation." The episode's opening sequence foreshadows not only the arrival of Butler's character into the life of Frank Black but also the subsequent personal awakening he would experience as a result of their interaction. This scene portrays convicted serial killer Dr. Ephraim Fabricant (Alex Diakun) being rescued, post-surgery, by a mysterious individual later revealed to be Butler herself. The violence and darkness of this opening sequence (both figurative and literal, steeped in atmospheric and deceptive shadow as it is) is juxtaposed with the episode's next scene as Black joins friend and colleague Lieutenant Bob Bletcher (Bill Smitrovich) in successfully attaining the summit of Mt. Baker in Washington state on a bright, clear afternoon with a grand vista of mountains spread before them. This represents a significant moment shared between the friends, conjuring the image of a heavenly place and ideals of pure achievement, their climb as spirited an ascension as ever seen throughout the series.

Bletcher's thoughts are insightful when he observes the geography of the mountains: "It feels like you're a million miles from… nowhere." Here, "nowhere" can be construed as suggesting the life of bleakness and futility the two friends have left behind—as epitomized through those things they witness daily in their work—for this place of purity.

At the episode's conclusion, Black brings his daughter Jordan to the selfsame site to share with her the experience he and Bletcher shared at

251

the beginning. Jordan is zealous regarding the breathtaking panorama before them. Her father comments, "It's the one thing in life that will never change." The scene depicts Black's constant efforts to return to peace, to keep his daughter and his family safe, as close to divine protection as he is able to provide. It symbolizes Black's initial embracing, whether conscious or not, of a divine potential in his life and, conversely, his slow-growing acceptance of Butler as representative of an evil more all-encompassing than the evils of humankind which he has faced so many times in his career previously. This nascent symbolism, pitting a greater spiritual good against its reflection of paramount evil, would grow to represent the overarching struggle at the heart of *Millennium*.

Butler's act of freeing a man as close to pure evil as Ephraim Fabricant reveals not only her own fearlessness when confronted by such evil but a greater embracing of it; her nurturing of the doctor represents the Devil's mission to nurture evil in the world at large. We see here the beginning of Butler's fixation with Frank Black himself, foreshadowing their ongoing relationship of criminal/investigative encounters which blooms into a more significant rapport encompassing the eternal struggle of good versus evil. In "Lamentation," an exchange between the two offers some insight into this deepening relationship. Butler acknowledges the similarity between Black and her husband, Fabricant, namely their mutual ability to comprehend the extremes of human behavior. Her seeming admiration for the connection between the two men, as well as her avid interest in Black, is clear. "The man you call your husband, he acts without conscience," Black tells her. Butler replies, "The soul expresses itself in so many amazing ways, especially when there's a comprehension of extremes. Ephraim said you and he share that ability."

We see Black's dawning perception of Butler's formidable powers as early as the episode's conclusion, when he admits to Detective Giebelhouse, "There's nothing she doesn't already know." This tacit acceptance of Butler's seemingly mystical powers infuses her character with an unsettlingly threatening aspect that grows to pervade the series more and more as her character recurs throughout, weaving her narrative inextricably within the greater tapestry of Black's saga. When Black encounters her for the first time, Butler is notably depicted not in epically malevolent terms but rather in exceedingly mundane trappings, answering the door in a housecoat, having been interrupted while in the midst of participating in an online chat. This illusory presentation of her character, as well as Black's initial perspective of her, would radically change by the conclusion of that very episode; Black's view of Butler would shift from that of an endangered, misled wife in need of protection from her inhumane husband, Fabricant, to the architect of an evil more far-reaching than that represented by the serial killer himself, a creature capable of the irrevocable act of violence which alters Black's worldview forevermore. The deceptive façade nurtured by Butler in successfully masking her overwhelmingly sadistic intentions and her dedication to chaos offers the first glimpse of her Luciferian nature. The inherent "freedom" offered by this dual persona, alternating at will from one extreme to the other, is a central trait of the Devil and is observable in various manifestations across literary, mythological, religious, and historical sources (Kephas 21).

"I'm not the person you think I am," she confirms for Black in the aftermath of Bletcher's murder. When this prompts Black to demand to know exactly who she is, Butler offers no response, only smiles enigmatically, until she eventually concedes in a mock-innocent tone that she is simply the widow of the late Dr. Ephraim Fabricant. Given the extreme and horrific nature of the murder itself—a murder which Black is certain Butler is responsible for—the cruel delight she displays during this exchange underlines her true, vindictive nature.

Another significant aspect of Frank Black's character that stands in contrast to that of Lucy Butler can be seen in his concept of "home." The Black residence is established early on as an oasis for Frank, Catherine, and Jordan, a place away from the world of violence and darkness that dominates his working life. In "Pilot," Black reveals his reasons for having relocated to Seattle following his retirement from the F.B.I.: "I'm here because I have a wife and a kid and I want them to live in a place where they can feel safe."

Symbolically, their house is painted yellow, the visual antithesis to the realm of darkness he knows via his work. Spotnitz, in discussing the importance of the Black family home, provides an illuminating perspective on the core ideology of the *Millennium* series, a philosophy that has specific implications for the relationship between Black and Butler as perpetual nemeses. "Most of us don't, in fact, want to look at any of the evil that goes on in the world around us," Spotnitz explains, "and *Millennium* was about that world versus the world inside the yellow house" ("Order In Chaos").

Carter further illuminates the dual nature of the series:

> I think that [*Millennium*] actually has a very, very bright center, a very bright hero. I think his dark is the world he lives in, works in. He is a person who has a tremendous amount of optimism and hope and I think if you look at what this man does, what his motivations are, they're very bright and noble and very interesting to me in that way. A yellow house, to me, represents happiness and I wanted that to be a very happy house, a sanctuary, a place where Frank could keep his family safe. He was, literally, by painting the house yellow, painting away the darkness, which I think is really what Frank's goal is, is to keep his family in the light, away from the darkness. (Interview)

Carter goes on to explain, "I guess you could say that this is, strangely, a family show, in the most perverse sense, in that it really is about a man trying to conduct two lives, his family life and his professional life, which he tries his best to separate but can't... We get killers and violent men and puppies and kids, all in the same package" (Commentary).

Notably, Lucy Butler represents a perfect opposite. Whereas Black is firmly rooted in a belief of home as haven, Butler is entirely nomadic in the way she perennially migrates from one location to another, resurfacing unexpectedly from time to time as a suspect in some new heinous crime. An example of her vision of "home" can be seen in the second season episode "A Room with No View," which depicts her overseeing a farmhouse which serves as a prison colony for a group of troubled youths whom she herself has abducted, a perverse inversion of the warm and loving Black family household. "Antipas" finds her attempting to usurp the household of a prominent family through the emotional manipulation of the daughter and sexual manipulation of the husband, and Butler deals with the dissenting wife in as viciously efficient a manner as is possible: murder. Where Black lives a twofold existence, attempting to balance the darkness of his professional life with the warmth and goodness of his home life, Butler displays only a single-minded adherence to spreading destruction wherever she goes.

Millennium director David Nutter offers insight into the driving force behind Black's personal beliefs and professional efforts, explaining, "As far as Frank Black was concerned, [he was a character] that's lived life and has seen Hell and has reached for Heaven but not often had it" ("Order In Chaos"). Lance Henriksen, the talented actor who played Frank Black with such intensity and pathos, offers a further illuminating perspective on the character's genesis, so far as Carter had envisioned him: "The fact that Frank Black is a stand-up guy, through all of this, is what makes him a hero" ("Order In Chaos"). Carter's vision for the character includes a basis in deep-seeded conflict: "He looks like he has the weight of the world on him, and I think that plays such an important part in what my ideas was, the idea of Frank Black, a person who was always suffering in a way"(Commentary).

The Legion myth-arc, outwardly a brief subplot within the greater series, has endured as a favorite among *Millennium* enthusiasts, and for good reason. Perhaps such outward appearances serve to belie a deeper conspiracy entrenched in the matrix of the series, much like the deceiving hand of Lucifer himself seeks always to conceal the magnitude of the evil rife in the world through which he moves. A more thorough examination of the core myth-arc stories reveals this hidden, though omnipresent, agenda, namely an allegorical depiction of Lucy Butler that symbolically places her within the very fabric of the *Millennium* universe, her archetype of pure evil implied to inhabit every serial killer and emotionally damaged character depicted in the series.

This raises a significant point regarding the illusory nature of the character's form. As Butler reappears throughout the series, she is repeatedly depicted as being able to alternate between several recurring figures, the most prevalent of which are commonly known as the "Long-Haired Man" and the demonic, winged "Gehenna" entity.[2] The appearances of these incarnations occur at pivotal times when the omnipresent nature of evil rampant in the world and related intimations of apocalypse, themes underlying the entire *Millennium* series, are evoked. Butler's shape-shifting nature is in accordance with historical depictions of Satan, who is often represented as having the ability to assume the guise of wild animals, "the most common of which are the bull, the cat, and above all, the goat" (Summers 134). Significantly, these alternate incarnations always appear to characters on the cusp of meeting their doom: Lt. Bletcher confronts the winged demon in "Lamentation"; young Divina encounters a serpent in the hedge labyrinth subsequent to her dream-death in "Antipas"; cult leader Ricardo Clement's demonic persona descends upon its victims in "Gehenna." Of course, these visions of alternating personas also appear to Frank Black (and, to a lesser extent, Jordan, who shares some aspects of his strange gift) when he is in the presence of Butler.

A striking parallel can be seen between Butler and Lilith, the famed character of Jewish mythology related to a class of malevolent female demons. Links between many aspects of Butler's personality can be drawn to various interpretations of the Lilith myth, suggesting that Butler is something of a gestalt creation. Lilith has traditionally been depicted as a seductress in sources such as the eighth-to-tenth century text *Alphabet of Ben-Sira*, the oldest story featuring the character, which depicts Lilith as Adam's first wife, preceding Eve, and portrays the female demon as the embodiment of lust who leads all men astray. This tale is paralleled repeatedly in Butler's story, such as during an intense conversation with Frank Black concerning the family for which she is serving as nanny in "Antipas." Here she claims of John Saxum (Art Hindle), "He wants me. And she knows it. He wants me like all men do."

An additional link between the Lilith demon and Butler is seen in her repeated efforts to seduce those around her, shown here and elsewhere throughout the series, often through characters that can readily be interpreted as representing incarnations of Legion. Specifically, Frank Black is repeatedly offered the opportunity to join an enigmatic "dark side" outside of and opposite to the Millennium Group. The Judge (Marshall Bell) from the episode of the same name displays a prescient understanding of Black's personal life and motivations—much as Black himself is able to understand the motivations of the killers he hunts—when he implores him, "Every man finds his own path to justice. You needn't commit yourself now. The offer's open. A month, a year... Many benefits. I know you're sometimes scared for your family, your wife. There's a child now, too, yes?"

The Dead Sea Scrolls (Songs of the Sage, Fragment One) also contain a reference to Lilith that effectively summarizes the seeming mandate of Butler's egoistic and destructive desire to bring chaos to the world:

> And I, the Instructor, proclaim His glorious splendour so as to frighten and to [terrify] all the spirits of the destroying angels, spirits of the bastards, demons, Lilith, howlers, and [desert dwellers]... and those which fall

> upon men without warning to lead them astray from a spirit of understanding and to make their heart and their... desolate during the present dominion of wickedness and predetermined time of humiliations for the sons of [light], by the guilt of the ages of [those] smitten by iniquity—not for eternal destruction, [but] for an era of humiliation for transgression. (4Q510-511)

This warning might very well serve as the archetype upon which Black's mission is founded, a mission to rid the world of Butler's pervasive evil and each of her own chaotic goals. Butler operates within an era so defined by its "wickedness" that it has necessitated the existence of the Millennium Group itself. Her dedication to "lead [men] astray from a spirit of understanding," rendering their hearts "desolate," speaks directly to her overt sexual manipulation of men. She is committed to the "humiliations of the sons of light," whether they be the manifestation of angels in the everyday world or individuals, like Black himself, who represent her moral and spiritual antithesis.

Another common characteristic of Jewish texts concerns Lilith being a child-murdering witch or demon. This sees a parallel with Butler's character, who was tried for (though found innocent of) the murder of her own son, who later seeks to desecrate the relationship between John and Una Saxum (Susan Hogan) and their daughter Divina (Rachel Victoria), in effect destroying their familial bond. It was revealed in "Lamentation" that during Butler and Fabricant's correspondence, the doctor expressed his desire to have a child, allegedly as an act of redemption. Butler herself expresses this same desire several times throughout her appearances. It is an unsettling wish considering her penchant for nurturing violence and conflict wherever she goes. More unsettling still is the fact, revealed in this episode, that the cause of death for her child was cyanide poisoning, the same method used to murder the federal judge who had tried Fabricant, a murder directly linked to Butler.

Debate continues as to whether the Lilith demon is referenced directly in the Bible, with one source cited as being closest to offering such an allusion. The Book of Isaiah 34:13-15 reads, "Wildcats shall meet with desert beasts, satyrs shall call to one another; there shall the lilith repose, and find for herself a place to rest." This is a notable source in relation to Butler as it draws comparisons between the demonic entity in question and "unclean animals" associated with demonic qualities. This conjures the images of serpents and dogs associated with Butler's manifestations, most notably in the third season episode "Antipas."

Greco-Roman mythology offers a further connection between the Lilith demon and Butler: in the Latin Vulgate Book of Isaiah 34:14, Lilith is translated to *Lamia*. Even the Lamia demon's physical description echoes the shape-shifting powers which enabled Butler to assume the guise of animals, such as the serpent, as well as various human forms. Known as the "child-killer," the Lamia demon was portrayed as having the upper body of a human being while being serpentine or "otherwise monstrous" from the waist down (Warner 7). Her malevolent origins saw her suffer the curse of the goddess Hera to have only stillborn children, an act of vengeance for the Lamia having slept with Hera's husband, Zeus. A variant of the myth tells that Hera's revenge took the form of murdering the Lamia's children, an act that filled the Lamia with a grief so profound that it likewise transformed her into a vengeful monster that abducted and devoured the children of others. The Lamia demon was consumed with an insatiable sexual appetite and was said to be a "vampiric spirit" who seduced men, murdering them by draining them of their blood. This role of seductress and murderess is paralleled in Lucy Butler's alluring and exceedingly violent personality, as seen juxtaposed to such startling effect in both "A Room with No View" and "Antipas."

Most significant was the gift bestowed upon the Lamia demon by Zeus. Known as the "mark of Sibyl," this constituted the gift of second sight, and it provides yet another parallel between Butler's character and her mysterious, seemingly visionary powers. A fascinating correlation between the two lies in that the Lamia was cursed with the inability to close its eyes so that it would forever see its dead children. Pitying the Lamia and her plight of everlasting woe, Zeus granted her the magical ability to remove and replace her eyes in her sockets whenever she wished. Not only does this scenario reflect Butler's overarching fixation with stealing children from others (as in "Antipas"), possibly as a means of avenging the loss of her son (as alluded to in "Lamentation"), but, more specifically, it sees an uncanny parallel in events depicted in "Saturn Dreaming of Mercury." Here, Jordan Black finds herself drawn to the Sanderson household. Outwardly, this is a compulsion stemming from her obsession with the family's young boy, Lucas. It is there, however, that she stumbles on a bizarre display cabinet housing a collection of artificial eyes—the same objects, allegedly "antiques," discovered earlier by the young son of a visiting neighbor, Mrs. Scranton, who perishes immediately afterwards in an automobile accident. While Jordan is examining one of the artificial eyes it is revealed that the eye itself "sees." Our view alternates between Jordan's perspective and the blurry, monochromatic, outward-gazing perspective of the artificial eye. Considering that Lucas Sanderson (Dillon Moen) is ultimately revealed to represent yet another incarnation of Legion—validated via a cameo from Butler—this scenario provides a startling connection between Butler and the Lamia demon mythology.

Like the Lamia, Butler has the metaphorical ability (and perhaps the psychological need) to remove and replace her eyes, referencing her own Lamia-like origins bound in a past haunted by grief over the mysterious death of her son. The possibility of this aspect to Butler—the exhibition of a maternal mourning at such a loss—would seem somewhat at odds with her malevolent character, until one considers the implications of her bringing a child into the world. This conjures images of the Empusae, the class of demons that the Lamia was said to have birthed and which would devour or frighten to death those whom they encountered. This aspect of the Lamia mythology is considered to have led to depictions of succubae or "lilim" in Medieval folkloric traditions, bringing full circle Butler's relation to each aspect of the malefic entity and demonstrating the epic scope of her influence. The image of an Empusae-like army of Butler's spawn running amok in the world certainly carries an apocalyptic dimension.

Interestingly, the designation bestowed upon the Lamia demon by Zeus to describe her ability of second sight (the "mark of Sibyl") sees a relevant parallel in Christian mythology which likewise relates to Butler's dark powers. The Sibyls were unique in Christian tradition because they were inherited directly from the pagan belief system and were related to demonesses, witches, and fairies. As time passed, Sibylline prophecies gained favor and were praised by thinkers such as Peter Abelard, who accepted them as portents of epic events ranging from extremes such as the coming of Christ to apocalyptic doom (Warner 70).[3] Franciscan poet Thomas of Celano expressed just such an apocalyptic perspective in his Mass of the Dead, which is sung to this very day: "The day of wrath, that day will dissolve the world into ashes, as David and the Sibyls testify." Similarly, Greek mythology depicts a Sybil's warning to Hecuba as prophesying the fall of Troy: "That future which we know was to come true" (Warner 67).

Biblical allusions recur throughout *Millennium* and serve as a clear point of reflection for Lucy Butler as the incarnation of Legion in the world. Butler's brief return in the follow-up to "Lamentation"— "Powers, Principalities, Thrones and Dominions" —provides a notable appearance in that it establishes with great clarity and startling effect her shape-shifting ability and its greater significance to the *Millennium* canon as it relates to the presentation of angels in the series. Outwardly, the story details Frank's encounter with the mysterious attorney Alistair Pepper (Richard Cox), a man who serves as legal representation for an alleged murderer whose victims include Millennium Group member and Frank Black's mentor, Mike Atkins (Robin Gammell). It is intimated throughout that Pepper represents another manifestation of Legion, and this culminates in a startling scene in which Frank, trailing Pepper through the crowded aisles of a supermarket, glimpses Pepper in several forms, including that of the Long-Haired Man and Lucy Butler herself.

Further evidence linking Pepper/Butler to a Luciferian origin in the eyes of Frank Black lies in his witnessing of an angelic figure seeking to smite Pepper in the supermarket parking lot. While Black witnesses a bolt of lightning exiting the angel's hand to strike Pepper, bystanders see a young man shooting the attorney with a handgun. The young man identifies himself by the name Sammael (Rodney Eastman), an angel in defiance of evil: "By Uriel and by Raziel, powers, principalities, thrones, and dominions, I bind and command you: stand!" He dispatches Pepper by proclaiming, "I, Sammael, bound by His will, command you: depart!"

Frank Black's subsequent conversation with Peter Watts (Terry O'Quinn) concerning Sammael is revelatory as it depicts his acceptance of the young man as representing a higher force of good, the divine antithesis to Lucy Butler. When asked about the young man's true identity Frank Black admits, "I don't know. Maybe he's part of something all of us are otherwise unaware of."

The depiction of Pepper is notable in that it hints at longstanding racial stereotypes equating the Jewish people to Satanic origins, including the notion that they are companions of the Devil (Wistrich 54) and "the incarnation of absolute evil" (Gerstenfeld 1). The physical traits of Jews were similarly demonized as they were depicted with

Satanic qualities, including horns, tails, and cloven hooves (Jensen 156). This portrayal parallels Pepper's character, as he is shown to shape-shift between a variety of forms or incarnations. In fact, Butler's multiplicity of incarnations can be identified with the controversial "serpent seed" (also known as "dual seed" and two-seedline) doctrine. This doctrine, traced to the Gnostic Gospel of Philip, was taught in different forms for thousands of years and held that the serpent in the Garden of Eden mated with Eve, and the offspring of their union was Cain. As Genesis 3:15 tells us, "And I will put enmity between thee and the woman, and between thy seed and her seed; it shall bruise thy head, and thou shalt bruise his heel." Although largely rejected by Christian theology, the doctrine is still upheld by certain groups such as devotees of Christian Identity, who believe that the Jewish people are descendants of Cain and are therefore likewise descended from the serpent. This doctrine offers an additional perspective when examining the depiction of Alistair Pepper and his motivations and purpose in the world.

Intriguingly, an angel by the name of Samiel (Eric Mabius) appears in another *Millennium* episode, "Borrowed Time," though the part is played by a different actor. The chosen name strongly suggests that Sammael and Samiel are in fact the same character, whose differing physical appearances can be explained in the same way as Butler's numerous incarnations are interpreted: *Millennium*'s angels of moral goodness have the selfsame shape-shifting abilities as Butler, and they manifest themselves to different individuals in different personas. Here, the angel Samiel does not battle manifestations of Legion as in his Sammael incarnation—rather, he murders seemingly innocent individuals in an effort to postpone the deaths of others, his own way of fulfilling God's plan. Biblically, the angel Samael is the angel of death, a role in accordance with the death-dealing actions of both Sammael and Samiel. Sammael is seen as the angel of death in Talmudic lore, a figure regarded as both good and evil, a representation that satisfies the dual representation of the character seen here, whose motivations appear nefarious to those not privy to or accepting of his divine mission.

The appearance of angels throughout the *Millennium* canon serves to offer a reflection of the perpetual presence of evil, both when they are operating to directly thwart Butler's schemes, as in "Powers, Principalities, Thrones and Dominions," and when they manifest elsewhere. The most notable example relates to Frank Black's partner, the forensic psychologist and Millennium Group candidate Lara Means (Kristen Cloke). Means possessed the lifelong gift of being able to witness the earthly manifestation of an angel, a divine being that appeared to her against her will and seemingly of its own volition. This spirit presence presaged imminent danger, serving as a guide of sorts for Means, which is in keeping with traditional roles of angels as protectors and guides. Again, this allowance for divine visitation in and interaction with the everyday world—in the Christian and Hebrew Bibles as well as the Quran, angels are considered, above all else, to be messengers of God—lends credibility to Black's perception of Butler as representing the opposing, tangible Satanic presence that is amok in the world.

Other appearances of angels, such as the messenger angel Simon (Gerry Currie) who speaks to Black in "Midnight of the Century," further validate the dual presence of a divine good and evil coexisting amid humanity in *Millennium*. Further, and perhaps most significantly, the presence of angelic figures as a fixture within the *Millennium* universe has a direct correlation with Biblical interpretations relating the manifestation of angels to the apocalypse. Both the angel Gabriel (God's messenger) and Michael (the holy fighter) are part of Daniel's apocalyptic visions and have come to be understood in relation to their evil, demonic counterparts. This idea has its origin "in the ancient Persian religious tradition of Zoroastrianism, which viewed the world as a battleground between forces of good and forces of evil, between light and darkness" (Coogan 5).

Lucy Butler's appearance in Season Two's stunning "A Room with No View" offers the definitive depiction of the vicious immorality that defines her prominent role in that battle. Here, Butler's allegiance to the state of chaos resonates throughout as she presides over a menagerie of teenage prisoners hidden in a lonely farmhouse in Waconda, Oregon, seeking to nurture them into automaton-like slaves to her will. She achieves this end by promising to accept their "ordinariness" in exchange for her love, claiming that she alone in the world loves them. This episode focuses on Butler's effective use of her sexuality to elicit what she desires from her victims, drawing a clear parallel with the demonic mythology of Lilith and its close associations with sexuality.

One of the more provocative developments in the Legion myth-arc occurs here, with Black and Watts's discovery of an inexplicable photograph of Lucy Butler amongst a collection of photographs and newspaper clippings displayed in a room at her farmhouse. The photograph is dated Monday, 18 September 1911, and in it Butler is wearing a Victorian-period dress. The attached clipping describes the recent disappearance of a schoolgirl named Annie Martin in Phoenix, Arizona. This artifact adds new depth to the mystery of Butler and leaves her origins deliciously open to speculation. Rather than detract from her character's unfolding history, it solidifies the notion that Butler is, more than anything else, beyond rationalization and comprehension. Did a young Butler, under a different name, encounter the same evil which she now represents, and was she corrupted by it? And if so, does that speak to the idea of a pervasive evil existing in the world? Or is this further evidence that Butler is the personification of that evil and existed then, in 1911, as she exists currently and has always existed?

Where other characters see Butler as merely a psychotic individual with a violent criminal background (witnessing her in any of her various incarnations), Black sees her on a deeper level, sees her for what she truly represents: a force far greater than so human a definition, one far superior to the summation of those disparate personas. He sees her as the pervasive malaise afflicting the world at large and which he and the Millennium Group—insofar as he initially understands their purpose—have dedicated themselves to combating. Butler's mysterious agelessness and strange shape-shifting powers reaffirm the notion that the nature of her evil is truly ubiquitous, offering further credence to the idea that this selfsame Luciferian malevolence resides within similarly violent and immoral individuals. This idea is most evident at the conclusion of "A Room with No View," during the brief but compelling exchange between Black and Watts in the aftermath of the F.B.I.'s release of the imprisoned teenagers from Butler's farmhouse, as they deliberate on her whereabouts. Watts asks, "So, where do we start to look for her?" Black answers, "Everywhere." Here again we witness Black's convictions regarding the far-reaching nature of Butler's powers, her aura of surreal mystery and mystical might all the more potent as fragments of her past continue to be pieced together. On one hand, Butler operates within the very tangible sphere of criminality, having, for example, a criminal record; yet, on the other hand, this aspect of her life, at first glance seemingly grounded in reality, is repeatedly tampered with, as if reality is not quite applicable to Lucy Butler.

In the Season Three episode "Antipas," when Black reveals to John and Una Saxum that the nanny they have employed to care for their daughter has a sordid past which includes having been tried for the murder of her own daughter, they share the following exchange:

> Black: "I know Lucy Butler. I had her investigated for the death of a Seattle police detective. And there were no two ways about it. And for the murder of her own child."
>
> Una Saxum: "The murder?"
>
> John Saxum: "Wait a minute. I have a staff that checks these things. Checks them thoroughly. If this woman had any kind of record, she wouldn't have been hired for this job. She would never have been considered."
>
> Black: "I checked her record, too. Somehow it was expunged."
>
> John Saxum: "There is no somehow with charges like those."
>
> Black: "You don't know what kind of person you're dealing with here."

It is in this inexplicable ability to operate perpetually above the law while engaging in immoral and criminal activity that elevates Butler beyond mere criminality, as seen in the countless characters Frank Black investigates throughout the series. Rather, a demonic magic seems to be at work, bending the reality known to the characters around her to her own twisted will.

The distinction between Butler's egoistic desires and chaotic nature and Black's selfless moral foundation is made clear in "A Room with No View's" closing scene, in which Black makes an emotional telephone call to his daughter immediately following the frustrating and unsettling conclusion to the case: "Hello, Jordan. This is your daddy. Ah, we keep missing each other. I was just calling to, um, I wanted to tell you, I needed to tell you how much I miss you, how much I love you. Very much. Bye." The sentiments expressed in this scene further establish that Black's character is the moral antithesis to Butler, and Butler's presence in Black's life has become the perennial threat which he has devoted his life to challenging.

SEEING EVIL

It would be in the third and final season of *Millennium* that Butler would next resurface. "Antipas" sees her character employed as a nanny for the wealthy Saxum family just as John Saxum, a state attorney general, is beginning a campaign for governor. Butler exerts her enigmatic influence on John Saxum's daughter, Divina, gaining her trust and devotion, while simultaneously using her bewitching sexual appeal to influence the girl's father. Acting on the impulse to connect with her arch-nemesis, Butler leaves anagram-based clues by which she communicates her whereabouts to Frank Black. This comes chiefly in the form of a Biblical reference left at a crime scene—the word "saint" handwritten over the letters "PA" (the abbreviation for the state of Pennsylvania on a Pittsburgh phonebook)—an allusion to Satan from the Book of Revelation. Specifically, this refers to the bishop Antipas, the martyr of Pergamos, one of the seven churches cited in Revelation. This Biblical name has apocalyptic associations, literally meaning "against all," and is derived from the term "Antipapas," which translates to "against the pope" or "opposed to the holy father." The term also evokes the name of Herod Antipas, the vain prince who faced Jesus Christ before his crucifixion. Black traces the Antipas reference to the Saxum residence, which is otherwise known by the name "Antipas Gardens."

One of the most memorable—and grisly—scenes in the episode is a foreboding, dream-like sequence in which Divina watches an immense serpent in a labyrinth of hedges, an obvious Biblical allusion to the nefarious nature of the snake. The child is held spellbound by the spectacle until the creature eventually swallows her. Notably, there are several scenes depicting brutal attacks on humans by dogs in "Antipas"—as when the Saxum's gardener is mauled by a pair of canines while the Long-Haired Man incarnation of Butler watches on—as well as throughout the series, such as in the second season installment "Beware of the Dog," in which German Shepherds are depicted as symbolic of an indomitable force of evil. This connotes a further connection between Satan and the bestial forms he is able to assume for his iniquitous purposes.

The episode is significant as it once again portrays Butler's fixation with conceiving a child, a theme first explored in "Lamentation." Here, her desire to conceive takes a perverse form as Butler appears to Black in a motel room during a surreal vision, essentially raping him. Later, she claims that their union resulted in her impregnation. As in

"Lamentation," Butler's fixation on bringing a child into the world mirrors her overarching desire to spread the seeds of chaos and disorder into the world at large.

An exchange takes place in the early portion of this episode between Black and Butler that is particularly significant as it offers the clearest example so far of Butler's wanton and destructive personality. "Leave these people be," Black demands, warning her away from the Saxum family. "I work for them," Butler replies. "That's not your little girl," Black retorts. Butler will not be deterred: "She is mine, Frank." We see also Butler's innate selfishness in the way she rebukes Black's admonishment of her attempts to "steal" the Saxum's daughter with a petulant and irate, "I don't like to share!"

This rebellious tone echoes the thirteenth-century folkloric writings of Rabbi Isaac ben Jacob ha-Cohen, in which the mythological character Lilith is said to have abandoned Adam after refusing to become subservient to him, refusing to return to the Garden of Eden following her union with the archangel Samael. Butler's anarchistic resolve to continually do what she pleases, outside of all moral law, is a reflection of this self-serving demonic persona.

Perhaps the most unsettling portion of the exchange is Butler's words of farewell, when she calls out to Frank and implores, "I just want us to be together." She perceives a perverse connection with Frank Black, and it reveals the overarching universal relationship of Good co-existing alongside its chaotic sibling, Evil. Whether this statement alludes to her forthcoming rape of Black and alleged resultant impregnation remains ambiguous.

The sexual assault itself is significant: Butler appears to Black first in a dream, from which he seemingly awakens to find that he and Butler are having sexual intercourse. Black's reaction—his initial shock, subsequent relinquishing to the spell-like pleasure of the experience, and ultimate revulsion and horror when Butler changes into her demonic persona mid-copulation—reveals the magically seductive power Butler wields, even over someone who feels as strong an aversion to her as Black. This portrayal of Butler's initial phantasm-like dream appearance, followed by the corporeal sexual union with Black, is a direct echo of the succubus myth, which dates back to Medieval times and describes the appearance of female demons to men, that they use their dark powers of seduction to charm and ultimately feed on their male lovers, murdering them in the act. This encounter, in which Black sees Butler's true demonic guise only after relinquishing himself to his desire for her—barely waking from his dream-vision and escaping her clutches as a result—holds direct echoes of the Lamia demon mythology in that the Lamia, and similar demons, were known to "turn into monsters unbeknownst to the heroes until it is—almost—too late" (Warner 7).

Similarly, Butler appears to Agent Emma Hollis (Klea Scott) in a whirlwind scene of alternating guises that include a serpent and Frank Black himself, who utters the sexually suggestive and violent threat, "What did you come looking for? What I gave the bitch?" before transforming into a pair of dogs and attacking her. This reversal of the succubus archetype, in which a male incubus figure appears to a woman in an overtly aggressive manner, is interesting as it further suggests the all-encompassing power of Butler to assume any form of her choosing in her corruption of man or woman.

The episode's penultimate scene is both startling and revelatory in how it portrays Black's now indisputable convictions regarding Butler. Here, Hollis and Black are vacating the scene of John Saxum's murder when their car strikes someone who appears to be the Long-Haired Man. When they exit the vehicle and examine the body they see it is Lucy Butler. Hollis and Frank's brief exchange is a telling one, illustrating Butler's exclusive status among the echelon of criminals Black has encountered. Hollis begins, "Frank, I think she's—" Black interrupts her coldly: "She's not. She never will be." It is unsettling to hear this admission from the hardened police veteran and preternaturally gifted criminal profiler for it openly confesses his new unequivocal worldview, established throughout three seasons of the series, in which forces beyond rational thought and outside of lawful endeavor operate in our midst.

The closing scene of "Antipas," wherein Black visits Butler in hospital, evokes with great effectiveness the same familial-based fear so effectively presented in other sources dealing with religious interpretations of evil, most notably William Peter Blatty's thematically similar *The Exorcist* (1971), in which the innocence and purity of a child is corrupted by the arcane evil of the demonic presence possessing her.[4] Here, Lucy Butler likewise invades Black's innermost realm of safety and security when she threatens that most sacrosanct and precious element of his life—the sole such element he has in a life otherwise preoccupied with the perpetual darkness embodied within his work—his daughter, Jordan. "Fear is what you want in us," Black tells Butler. "I came here to tell you I'm not afraid." Butler is quick in uttering the threatening reply, "Your daughter. Jordan. You're not afraid—for her?"

This scene reveals one of the great strengths of both the depiction of the relationship between Black and Butler as well as of the series generally. *Millennium* successfully and unflinchingly depicts what the characters peopling its internal universe—and perhaps the real society it so effectively mirrors—fear most: the bedlam plaguing the very world in which they live, wherein those things held most sacred are in perpetual danger of the chaos rampant in society. Despite this perennial threat to our inner and outer peace, we yet cling to hope via whatever means are available to us. It is the dichotomy of this willful determination to maintain moral goodness in response to a simultaneous resignation to the chaos of the world, epitomized by Black's and Butler's relationship, which allows *Millennium* to achieve its bittersweet, fearful yet hopeful narrative tone.

Butler was to make a final, fleeting, though defining appearance in Season Three's deeply unsettling "Saturn Dreaming of Mercury." Here again she is presented in her shape-altering guise, seen amid the chaos of death and destruction when Frank and Jordan Black witness her manifestation in the window of a burning house. The mysterious Lucas Sanderson—revealed in this scene to be responsible for the impending death of his father—changes fleetingly into Butler before being consumed by flames, blatantly mirroring the typical Christian fire-and-brimstone interpretation of Hell (Kephas 19-21). Lucas offers Black a taunt and challenge, an echo of Butler's defiant words in episodes past: "Who's stronger, Frank, me or you?"

Black's witnessing of this revelatory transformation alongside Jordan, who shares her father's gift of perception, serves the chilling purpose of uniting father and daughter in their knowledge of the chaos that is ever-rampant in the world outside of their family. It also offers a message of challenge from Butler herself as she defies Black's best efforts to rid the world of her pervasive presence. In effect, Butler's brief appearance serves to confirm in his mind the futility of seeking to vanquish the seed of chaos entrenched so permanently within the corrupted matrix of humanity while simultaneously giving him the reason he needs to continue upholding the righteousness he has upheld throughout his life—namely, to continue serving as protector of his daughter, the single reliable element of goodness he has left following the death of his wife.

Black and Butler's opposing roles and adversarial relationship reaffirm *Millennium*'s greater thematic concerns concisely, as noted by writer/producer Chip Johannessen: "There was always, like, on one hand mass murder and on the other hand redemption, so we were always wrestling with those two things" ("Turn of the Tide"). Further, by the conclusion of the series, the development of a parallel perspective becomes readily apparent. Black's perception of the nature of evil has grown to mirror that of his creator, Chris Carter. Carter set out to create a series grounded in the harsh reality of the everyday, rife with realistic evils, and his belief in the idea of evil as a "real force" unto itself, beyond the violence inherent in the personality and motivations of the damaged individual, led to the proliferation of that evil in an all-consuming, pandemic manner which would shroud the entire *Millennium* canon.

Frank Black's grounding in the grim reality of law enforcement grew to allow for an acceptance of evil existing on a far greater, spiritually pervasive scale, a belief nurtured most significantly through his relationship with his nemesis Lucy Butler. In fact, Carter maintained from the series' outset that the world of *Millennium* operated on a variety of levels, leaving room for expansion into much more epic narratives with a religious foundation beyond its original scope of a weekly " murder mystery" with "a millennial feel," explaining, "It really is an exploration of evil on the show, the now scientific approach to the explanation of evil, which is a psychological one, which says everyone is a victim of something. I was interested in the unscientific approach. The Bible plays an important role in the show. It's not a show about the Bible, yet you'll find a lot of these stories are in there and have been told before. It gives the show a nice foundation, it attempts to explain things on various levels, not just in the modern, scientific way" (Interview).

Lucy Butler is commonly credited as having made appearances in five episodes of *Millennium*. That's not exactly accurate. Really, Lucy Butler lives, and breathes, and operates within the very fabric of each and every episode of the series' three-year run—within the heart and mind of each serial killer and disturbed individual representative of the fast-approaching end times; within the deadly virus that devastates the country and changes the life of Frank Black forever; in the eye of the comet hanging perpetually in the heavens like an augury of Satan's descent to walk among us—summing up the series' purpose as much as she satisfies the purpose of Frank Black's existence in the world and the alleged reason for the founding of the Millennium Group.[5] This idea is driven home in episodes such as "Powers, Principalities, Thrones and Dominions" and "Saturn Dreaming of Mercury," in which Butler's persona appears only fleetingly amid a slew of other incarnations, in effect sending the message that she is omnipresent. She is, as Dr. Ephraim Fabricant reveals so succinctly to an increasingly lucid and vigilant Frank Black at the revelatory conclusion to Season One's poignant and disturbing "Lamentation" (Butler's ostensibly "first" appearance), "the base sum of all evil. The sleep of reason. The Devil's liege."

But perhaps the most illuminating revelation of Butler's iniquitous power and omnipresence comes from Butler herself in "Antipas," when she echoes Alistair Pepper's proposition that Frank Black join his ranks, here much more directly and in far more chilling a manner for the far-reaching and apocalyptic implications of her appeal: "We could rule the earth, Frank."

When we are immersed in the *Millennium* universe we, like the prescient Frank Black, witness the eternal Lucy Butler, because She is everywhere. Evil has many faces indeed, but each owns the same black and apocalyptic heart. Hope in the face of such eclipsing chaos, as represented by the virtue, purity, and acute perception of hero Frank Black, offers the single truest road to salvation in the face of that wanton evil.

NOTES

1. The term "Dionysian" is taken from Greek mythology, in which Dionysus, a son of Zeus, is the god of wine, ecstasy, and intoxication. Although Dionysus represents opposing traits to his brother Apollo, the god of the sun, dreams, and reason, the ancient Greeks did not view them as rivals. The Dionysian is often understood in terms of Nietzsche's definition of embracing the chaotic nature of one's experiences in order to feel a resultant godlike harmony. American humanities scholar Camille Paglia considers the Dionysian to be a force of chaos and destruction, which represents the alluring chaotic state of our wild nature.

2. In Christian, Jewish, and Islamic scripture, Gehenna is denoted as being the destination of wicked individuals and is widely understood to be synonymous with Hell as well as the metaphorical or literal site of the sacrifice of children.

3. Peter Abelard (1079-1142) was a pre-eminent medieval French philosopher, theologian, and logician. He was known as a great proponent of the use of reason in matters of faith and is widely considered the first person to utilize theology in its modern definition.

4. Blatty's sequel to *The Exorcist*—entitled *Legion* (1983)—tells the story of police detective Kinderman's investigations into a series of brutal murders. They lead him to make connections between events in the preceding novel (specifically, the exorcism of the twelve-year-old girl Regan) and the crimes of the notorious serial murderer known as the Gemini Killer. Blatty's depiction of the young girl's possession by Legion—as well as the ongoing influence of Legion haunting the lives of the first novel's characters—echoes the representation of Lucy Butler as an unending evil.

5. Prophetic signs of impending celestial apocalypse are found throughout the Bible, most prominently in the Book of Revelation 8: 10-13: "And the third angel sounded, and there fell a great star from heaven, burning as it were a lamp, and it fell upon the third part of the rivers, and upon the fountains of waters; And the name of the star is called Wormwood: and the third part of the waters became wormwood; and many men died of the waters, because they were made bitter. And the fourth angel sounded, and the third part of the sun was smitten, and the third part of the moon, and the third part of the stars; so as the third part of them was darkened, and the day shone not for a third part of it, and the night likewise; And I beheld, and heard an angel flying through the midst of heaven, saying with a loud voice, Woe, woe, woe, to the inhabiters of the earth by reason of the other voices of the trumpet of the three angels, which are yet to sound!"

WORKS CITED

Carter, Chris. Audio commentary. "Pilot." *Millennium: The Complete First Season*. Dir. David Nutter. Twentieth Century Fox Home Entertainment, 2004. DVD.

———. Interview. *Millennium Volume One: Pilot / Gehenna*. Twentieth Century Fox Home Entertainment (UK), 1998. VHS.

Coogan, Michael D. *A Brief Introduction to the Old Testament*. Cary, NC: Oxford UP, 2009. Print.

Gerstenfeld, Manfred. "Anti-Israelism and Anti-Semitism: Common Characteristics and Motifs." *Jewish Political Studies Review* 19:1-2 (Spring 2007): 2-3. Print.

The Holy Bible: King James Version. Uhrichsville, Ohio: Barbour Books, 2002. Print.

Jensen, Gary F. *The Path of the Devil: Early Modern Witch Hunts*. New York, NY: Rowman & Littlefield, 2006. Print.

Kephas, Aeolus. *The Lucid View*. Kempton, IL: Adventures Unlimited, 2004. Print.

"Order in Chaos." *Millennium: The Complete First Season*. Prod. John Mefford. Twentieth Century Fox Home Entertainment, 2004. DVD.

Summers, Montague. *The History of Witchcraft and Demonology*. Secaucus, NJ: Castle Books, 1992. Print.

"The Turn of the Tide" *Millennium: The Complete Second Season*. Prod. John Mefford. Twentieth Century Fox Home Entertainment, 2004. DVD.

Vermes, Geza. *The Complete Dead Sea Scrolls*. 7th ed. London: Penguin Classics, 2011. Print.

Warner, Marina. *From the Beast to the Blonde: On Fairy Tales and Their Tellers*. London: Random House, 1994. Print.

Wistrich, Robert S. *Demonizing the Other: Anti-Semitism, Racism and Xenophobia*. New York: Routledge, 1999. Print.

Alexander Zelenyj is the author of the short fiction collections *Experiments at 3 Billion A.M.* (2009) and *Songs for the Lost* (2012), published by Eibonvale Press, as well as the apocalyptic-themed short novel *Black Sunshine* (2005), published by Fourth Horseman Press. His fiction has appeared in many publications, including *Revelation, Euphony, Inscape, Front & Centre, Freefall, Blind Swimmer, Way Out West, Columbia & Britannia, Sex and Murder, Pulp Empire, Structo, Underground Voices*, and *The Medulla Review*. He lives in Windsor, Ontario, Canada, and blames the sleep of reason for his perpetual insomnia.

HEART OF DARKNESS:
A CONVERSATION WITH FRANK SPOTNITZ

Interview by James McLean & Troy L. Foreman
Written by Adam Chamberlain

Writer and producer Frank Spotnitz is well-known and deeply respected not just for his own work but also for his close collaborations with the creator of *Millennium* (1996-99) and *The X-Files* (1993-2002), Chris Carter. It is a long-standing partnership. "It's hard for me to believe but we've been writing together for over fifteen years," says Spotnitz, "and writing apart during that time as well."

He goes on to talk about their approach to working together and how much he values the relationship. "We've done it so many different ways over the years. Sometimes we would break the story together in the same room and then I would write half and he would write half, and then, especially in the early days, he was the rewriter—and still is, I have to say. Then other times, because he was so busy rewriting other scripts, I would simply break the entire story and then he would go and write the story I had broken. One time we sat in the same room and literally wrote every line of every page together around a computer.

"So, we've done it many, many different ways over the years, but the joy of it is that we do have a connection. There is an understanding between the two of us and a shorthand that makes it fun, and then there's just enough tension to just make it something that neither of us could've done separately, something that makes it better by having the two of us work on it together than it would've been if we'd done it alone. It's really been the great collaboration of my career."

Spotnitz had long held an ambition to work in show business in some capacity. "I always wanted to be in movies and television," he reveals. "From a very young age I was very obsessive about watching television and movies—I would go and see the same movie over and over again—but I didn't know what I wanted to do. I think for a long time I thought I might be an actor and then I finally chickened out right around college, and then I thought I would be a writer or director. But, honestly, I lost my nerve about that too and ended up being a journalist for seven years before I said, 'No, I've got to go back and do this.' So I moved back to Los Angeles, went to film school, and *The X-Files* was my first job. It was a good first job!"

And if he had to choose between the two mediums? "I love movies," he says, "but the movie business is just really so miserable, it kind of spoils it. Television is great because you make the deal and then—more or less—you get to go and do the work, and there is a lot less of the politics of actually trying to get something off the ground. I love them both, but I'd say that T.V. is really too much of a good thing. T.V. is great, but there is so much of it that the volume of it starts to become overwhelming. So I guess there are good and bad things to say about both."

Millennium's first year coincided with work for both the small and big screens on *The X-Files*, establishing an exceptional schedule for Spotnitz, a writer and executive producer on both properties. "It was really brutal, really punishing to do *Millennium* and *The X-Files* at the same time, and that was also the year that we wrote the script for the first *X-Files* feature, so it was just very, very tough. I was flattered on the one hand that Chris asked me to work on *Millennium* and *The X-Files*, but it was challenging, and I think *Millennium* was not an easy birth. I think the pilot is fantastic and is still probably my single favorite piece of writing that Chris has ever done—which is saying a lot, because I think he is such an amazing writer—but it was really tough, both with the writing staff and with the network, that first year to get *Millennium* off the ground. It was really pretty inhumane. I don't know what we were thinking! I think we hoped it would be easier than it was."

In addition to the shooting schedule for the series, the subject matter and themes of *Millennium* posed challenges of their own. Both Carter and Spotnitz conducted considerable research before embarking upon the series. "We read the John Douglas book [*Mindhunter*] and I think I read a dozen books that first summer. But the challenge to me was at first that you could have serial killers, that each had a different rationale, but then narratively that becomes repetitive pretty quickly, because then each episode becomes 'what's the rationale of the serial killer?' and that's not very interesting. So I think it wasn't too long into the series before research mattered less and it was more where could we take the idea of evil, less literally basing episodes on real serial killers and the things serial killers actually do."

Did working with such dark subject matter have any effect on the writer? "It changes the way you look at the world. I felt this way a number of times doing research, but especially with *Millennium* because you let this darkness into your head, like Frank Black. Once it's there it's never going away, and there are specific images I can remember seeing in books that I wish I had never seen, and things of cruelty that I have read people have done that are haunting and just stay with you forever.

"Actually, for my first job I was a wire service reporter in Indiana and I had to write a story about this crazy woman who broke into these people's rural home. It was a husband and wife and they had two small children and she held them hostage for a week, screaming about 'Yahweh' and murdered them all, one by one. It was just absolutely terrifying to me, the thought of being isolated like that and having it go on, witnessing the death of your family. It certainly does disturb you to think about what people are capable of."

Millennium's "Pilot" is an episode often cited as one of the darkest of them all, and Spotnitz recognized it as something very special from an early stage. "First, I read the script on Chris's computer before he had finished it, so he hadn't written the last six pages or something, and at that moment I thought it was incredible as a piece of writing. And then I remember watching the dailies—they'd come down from Vancouver every day—and they were fantastic.

"At the time the title *Millennium* had not cleared, and so they were calling it *2000*, which I was really disappointed about because I thought *Millennium* was far superior as a title. Chris was up in Vancouver the entire time with David Nutter, the director, and then he didn't let me watch any of the cuts of the show until it was almost done. So I didn't go through the normal process I would go through of seeing something get better and better, I just saw the finished product, and it was excellent.

"Then I got the pleasure of seeing it screened because, very unusually for a new series, Fox rented out movie theaters in a number of cities and screened it. So I got to see it on the big screen in Westwood, and it was fantastic. It held up beautifully on a big screen. I was just very, very excited about it."

It was only when the episode was first viewed by a wider audience that any concerns were raised over its content. "At the time of the pilot we heard no complaints about how dark it was. I think everyone recognized what a powerful piece of work it was, and they were really thrilled about it. Then they began testing it, and so we started hearing that the network and advertisers were concerned that the show was too dark. We were asked if we could lighten it up, if we could add some humor. And we thought about it—we certainly didn't want to ignore what they were telling us, and were mindful that it was for commercial television—but it did not seem appropriate to what we were doing, and so we didn't. I think the episode that focused on Megan Gallagher in the first season, ["The Well-Worn Lock,"] was an attempt to provide some release to the oppressiveness of Frank's work, but, as good as I think that was, I think we all felt the heart of the show was Frank Black and that darkness."

Spotnitz wrote two episodes for Season One himself. How does he approach penning a script? "It's the hardest question to answer. It's so mysterious to me where good ideas come from. One of the good things about writing for television is that the deadline pressure is so enormous that you're constantly thinking and digging for what you have to say, so sometimes images would come to me, or situations or ideas."

The first of the writer's episodes is "Weeds," in which a number of young men are abducted from their homes within a gated community and subjected to a series of unspeakable ordeals. "I think the idea of sons being punished for the sins of their fathers was what came to me first in that instance, and it all developed from there. I've had ideas come to me from reading cookbooks! Seriously, they come from the strangest places. It's like your subconscious mind makes connections and does the work for you."

"Weeds" stands as another particularly disturbing installment of the series, memorably featuring scenes in which the villain's captives are forced to consume his blood. "My interest in darkness is great," Spotnitz confesses. "I think there are some times where I go for it so relentlessly that it really is too much for a lot of people, both in that episode and there was an episode of *The X-Files* called '*Via Negativa*' where it is just so awful what's happening that you really have to like the darkness to stand it."

Spotnitz's second episode of *Millennium*, "Sacrament," develops a thread first suggested by Glen Morgan and James Wong in their first script for the series, "Dead Letters." It was a creative choice influenced by the type of story the writer was seeking to tell. "I was very eager in the second half of the first season to do a more emotional story and so I thought it would be interesting to pick up on that idea about Jordan and whether she would carry Frank's gift and curse. So I wanted to touch on that, and then I wanted to bring in Frank's brother and juxtapose his family against the other family, the Greens, and it all unfolded very naturally, actually.

"That was one of my most enjoyable writing experiences on anything. That episode came to me very fluidly because I felt connected to it emotionally. There were some producers who were against that episode and didn't want it made because of the very reason I wanted to make it—they thought we were personalizing the show too much and domesticating it too much, and I was really happy that Chris stood behind the idea."

Considering the input he received from other writers, Frank goes on to describe how the division of writing duties is typically determined between staff during a series' run. "It's sort of a healthy competition to see who can come up with the best ideas and get produced next. It usually starts out with an expectation that the senior writers will go first and then the junior writers and there will be a rotation until you run out of episodes, but it doesn't work out perfectly because sometimes senior writers are having a hard time breaking their stories and a younger writer might come up with a story sooner, or you realize that this writer's idea is good but it is too much like this idea that we're already doing and so it has to be pushed back. So it's very fluid, and sometimes scripts that you expect are going to work end up being set aside. It is mildly chaotic, I would say, in terms of who gets to write what over the course of a year."

"Sacrament" opens up the idea of evil targeting Frank Black and those close to him, suggesting there would be both challenges and great changes in the episodes ahead. "I remember Walon Green came on staff toward the end of the season and that was one of the episodes that he really responded to and thought was interesting," says Spotnitz. "But then the history of *Millennium* is so unusual, because at the end of the first season Chris decided it was just unfair to *Millennium* and *The X-Files* to continue the way we had, and he wanted to get somebody else to run *Millennium*." It was Spotnitz himself who was potentially in line to take up the reigns. "He approached me and asked if I wanted to leave *The X-Files* and just run *Millennium*," he explains, "and I thought about it for a couple of days, and then I came back and I felt like I was both too attached to *The X-Files* to leave it and too new to television to pretend I could do that job yet, because I'd only been doing television for three years."

The resulting rotation of producers led to a change in creative direction for the series and its emerging mythology. "We were able to persuade Morgan and Wong to come back, and it really became a different show in Season Two. All their brilliant ideas came to the show and took it in a different direction than I'm sure it would have gone in if it had continued the way it was with the same writing staff from Season One. And then they left again at the end of Season Two to go pursue their own things, and Season Three became something else entirely, so it's really like three different authors for each of the three seasons."

Morgan and Wong placed the Millennium Group center stage during the second season, a creative decision that Spotnitz endorses. "I think what they were trying to do—which I think was very smart—was elaborate on what this idea of 'millennium' meant, and what the Millennium Group was. They were trying to give it a mythology, I think that's true. But I think the nature of that mythology and conspiracy was radically different from *The X-Files*'s mythology, and the storytelling too was very different from the way that *The X-Files*'s mythology was told. I wouldn't second-guess them either, because they are such talented guys and they did things that I never would have thought to do that were great. It was a surprise to me but I think they did an amazing job overall, so I wouldn't begin to criticize it."

In attempting to identify a dominant mythology for *Millennium*, many followers of the series cite the looming presence of Legion, a veritable army of dark forces that seem to position themselves against Frank Black throughout the series. Is this perceived arc a mere fan creation? "It's something that is undoubtedly there," agrees Spotnitz, "but it was not mapped out in advance. It was something where we felt our way forward, because in the beginning we were very reluctant to have anything overtly supernatural, and yet Frank's identification with the mind of killers was so great that it in itself bordered on the supernatural.

"I think the inclination to expand upon evil and the nature of evil and to really embrace that as something real in this world grew stronger and stronger, so I think it became something that writers over time carried forward but without necessarily the producers of the show being the ones orchestrating that malign feeling. It was like all of us were sewing this quilt, a bunch of different weavers were working on it, and some of these threads got passed from different pairs of hands over the years."

Spotnitz clearly understands the appeal of the Legion mythology as he cites the demonic Lucy Butler, played by Sarah-Jane Redmond, as his favorite character from the series. "I thought she was just fantastic, and that's why we wrote 'Antipas' in Season Three, and she had a cameo in the last *X-Files* movie as well. I thought she was just great, and I loved every scene she had with Frank. I loved Klea [Scott as Emma Hollis] too, but she was just such a delicious villain."

Pressed to identify further favorites, Spotnitz turns the conversation toward the work of Glen Morgan's brother Darin, who also joined the team for *Millennium*'s second year, working as a Consulting Producer throughout and both scripting and directing two of the series' most distinctive and celebrated episodes: "Jose Chung's *Doomsday Defense*" and "Somehow, Satan Got Behind Me." These are among Spotnitz's favorite episodes of the series and he has much praise for Darin Morgan's body of work. "I loved both of his episodes. I thought they were fantastic. It was one of the challenges of *Millennium*. When Darin did an episode of *The X-Files* they were beloved by the fans. When he did those episodes of *Millennium* I thought they were fantastic and as good as anything he had done on *The X-Files*, but the ratings didn't support them. It was like it was too much of a curveball for the viewership that was tuning in, and I thought it was a shame because they were both so clever and beautifully crafted, like everything Darin does.

"He is such an interesting character. If you ever met him he's a very soft-spoken, kind of morose guy who is very self-deprecating, very funny, and just pours his heart and soul into everything he writes. He really suffers—it's like the stereotype of a suffering artist—and it takes so much out of him to write a script, and in the instance of *Millennium* he directed them as well. I think even if Glen and Jim had continued with the show for Season Three, I don't know if he could have taken it. I don't know if he could've stood another season because he was so drained from first doing *The X-Files* and then doing those two *Millennium* episodes. And I think he was a little disappointed that ratings wise they weren't better received, because the quality of the work was so great, and it didn't really get the ratings it deserved. I think they are some of the best."

Morgan and Wong's dramatic two-part finale to Season Two takes *Millennium* to further creative heights but also presented the incoming writers and producers with something of a challenge in terms of resuming the story at the start of Season Three. Was there an assumption that the series would not be returning for a third year? "No. What I remember is, actually, that I thought we were coming back for Season Three, but I had no idea how we were going to get out of the box that Season Two ended in. I thought we were coming back; I guess I was hoping Morgan and Wong were coming back so that they could get us out of the box that they had built!

"But when they didn't come back, it fell to Chip [Johannessen] and Ken Horton, and that's when Chris and I said we'd lend a hand and we committed ourselves to help, because we knew it was going to be a huge burden on those guys. My memory is that we did expect the show to come back for Season Three, but it was just, creatively, who was going to do the work? Who was going to be able to steer the ship? I thought those guys really rose to the occasion, and it was a heartbreaker when the show ended at the end of Season Three."

Millennium's cancellation came at a time when network television itself was undergoing a radical but somewhat imperceptible change. "I have to say, in retrospect now—and I can't even blame the network, because nobody really understood what was happening—but if you look at it now, it's clear that we were in the beginnings of the decline of network television viewership. Everything they put in that slot has just gotten smaller and smaller viewers. The same thing happened with *The Lone Gunmen* a little while later. It was like, 'We'll take it off and hopefully something else will get bigger ratings,' and then the next thing got smaller ratings still. It was an overall erosion of the network audience, so they didn't understand that *Millennium* was actually performing pretty well and canceled it, I think, way before they should have. I think you can see how they would have been tempted to roll the dice, maybe try to do a little better and maybe bring it up a ratings point or something, and they ended up killing the golden goose—or at least the bronze."

With the series ending in the lead-up to the millennium itself, it fell to Spotnitz to try to offer some closure to the character of Frank Black in a crossover installment of *The X-Files* named for its sister series. He is quick to acknowledge that the episode did not meet expectations. "Whilst 'Sacrament' was one of my best writing experiences ever, I'd say that 'Millennium' may have been my worst," admits Spotnitz, "because we were absolutely committed to bringing Frank Black back, and we knew we could do it through *The X-Files*. So we sort-of said, 'We're doing it,' and we set the machinery in motion to make the deal, and then we had to actually figure out a way to do it.

"It was much harder than we expected to make it an X-File with Mulder and Scully driving it and yet tie into Frank Black and his story and Jordan. It ended up, to me, not being really a great *Millennium* story or a great *X-Files* story and I was frustrated. We had the best of intentions but it wasn't the ending that *Millennium* needed. I didn't think it was bad but I didn't think it was great either, and it should have been. It should have been great. We would probably have been better if we'd just said, 'Okay, we're going to have a *Millennium* episode this week. We're just going to give Mulder and Scully the week off.' That probably would have been the better way to tackle it."

Had *Millennium* continued, might there have been the potential for further crossovers between the two series? "There probably was a way to do it, and I guess if *Millennium* had gone on long enough then we might have relaxed a little bit and been more open to it. But I think at the time we were so determined not to do anything that smacked of commercialism, and it just felt like a crossover was going to be a crass attempt to exploit one title for the benefit of another. So the only time we did a crossover was when *Millennium* had been canceled, so it could be of no benefit to that show whatsoever.

"They are very different. The storytelling is very different, the ideas of the shows are very different. I think initially we didn't want anything supernatural in *Millennium*, and then we came to embrace the supernatural role of evil in *Millennium*. But it is so different from the rules of *The X-Files*, and it was really one big arc even though we had three different authors, if you will, over the three seasons. It was one big arc and one mythology of evil, whereas *The X-Files* every week was a different monster and set of rules and all that. So it was a very different set of rules as a storyteller, but I could see overlap over time if *Millennium* had gone on longer."

Sadly, of course, the series did not enter a fourth year of production. Did Spotnitz have any plans for where to take the series next? "I didn't, but I know that Chip and Ken had it worked out. I don't know to what detail they had it worked out, but I know they certainly knew where they wanted to be early in Season Four and that Ken was lobbying very hard with the network to keep the show on the air. Ken had come from Fox and he knew them very well, so I was very hopeful that he would be able to prevail and keep it going and, like I said, I think the network was fighting against history, rolling the dice on something that might do better and only did worse."

Does the opportunity to write another outing for Frank Black interest Spotnitz? "It does, I just think the longer this goes on the harder it's going to be—both commercially and creatively—to do that. I know there has been interest to continue the story in other media, but so far Chris has not shown interest in doing that."

For the benefit of *Millennium*'s hero himself, however, Frank Spotnitz feels an enduring drive to return to the character and explore his dark world one last time. "Something that Chris has always said to me is, 'Writers want to get justice. They want justice in their work, because you can't get it in life.' And I kind of feel that way about Frank Black and *Millennium*. I want justice for these characters, and so that sense that the show was wronged makes me want to right it by finishing the show properly."

EVIL HAS MANY FACES:
THE DARKNESS IN THE WORLD OF *MILLENNIUM*

by Adam Chamberlain

At its heart, *Millennium* (1996-99) is an exploration of evil in the modern world, reflecting a growing sensibility that by the late twentieth century levels of criminality and other social ills had increased to the extent that they threatened the very fabric of our society. Across three disparate seasons and sixty-seven episodes of finely crafted television, the series portrays various manifestations of and potential explanations for such evils. From investigations into killers of every kind to hints of a conspiring legion of demonic forces, from personal crises to cult agendas and group dynamics by way of apocalyptic prophecy, the producers and writers would take Chris Carter's original idea and develop it in a host of directions that may not coalesce into a single definable perspective but that certainly reflect the complexity of its themes. "Evil has many faces," proclaimed early promotional material for the series alongside the defiant response that, in Frank Black, "Hope has just one."

The spark for the series and *Millennium*'s original concept were of course the creation of Chris Carter. As *The X-Files* (1993-2002) was becoming a hit show for Fox, Carter began discussing his ideas with the network for what would become *Millennium*:

> After the success of *The X-Files*, it was about the middle of Season Two when Fox came to me and asked me if I would do another series, and I'd told them subsequent to this that I'd had an idea rattling around in my head to do a show about the approaching millennium. It really is an exploration of evil on the show, the now scientific approach to the explanation of evil, which is a psychological one, which says everyone is a victim of something. I was interested in the unscientific approach. The Bible plays an important role in the show; it's not a show about the Bible yet you'll find a lot of these stories are in there and have been told before. It gives the show a nice foundation. It attempts to explain things on various levels, not just in the modern, scientific way. (Interview)

Immediately apparent from this interview excerpt is the dichotomy between the scientific and faith-based approaches to the subject matter that would resonate throughout the series' run and which indeed were also central themes of the more recent *The X-Files: I Want to Believe* (2008).

In fact, one particular installment of *The X-Files* was illustrative of the examination of human evil that Carter was interested in exploring further. For the Season Two episode "Irresistible" he had scripted a tale investigating the desecration of a grave that, in spite of an initial suspicion of alien involvement, turns out to have a more terrestrial providence. The perpetrator, Donnie Pfaster (Nick Chinlund), is a "death fetishist" who ultimately targets Dana Scully (Gillian Anderson).[1] Significantly, he is also glimpsed in the form of a demon during the course of the episode, a potentially supernatural angle which is never fully explained but which would become a common visual metaphor in *Millennium*. As Carter said of the episode,

EVIL HAS MANY FACES

> The original idea for *Millennium* actually took shape over time. Fox wanted to do another series and I'd done an episode of *The X-Files* which I liked a lot. It involved a serial killer; it didn't actually have a paranormal element. It had a kind of supernatural element, but it wasn't the paranormal. And it got me to thinking about the sort of monsters that surround us, the people that are in the supermarket checkout line with us, at the post office with us. You just never know about someone. ("Order in Chaos")

The character of Pfaster and the way he is presented in this installment of *The X-Files* are therefore something of a template for the kinds of human monsters that Carter wished to explore in this new series, territory that *The X-Files* allowed itself to explore on occasion throughout its run but which are arguably all the more terrifying in *Millennium* due to the series being more grounded in the real world.

Millennium's "Pilot" debuted in October 1996 to considerable fanfare and nearly eighteen million viewers. This finely crafted introduction to the world of Frank Black (Lance Henriksen) is an extremely dense and economical hour of television containing a number of strands, defining or hinting at themes and arcs that would resonate over the next three years.

The episode's central mystery is the investigation into the Frenchman (Paul Dillon), a punter so-called by the girls working at the Ruby Tip peep show club due to his propensity for reading French poetry to them as they perform. A man who commits some of the most horrific acts that *Millennium* would ever portray, he comes to the attention of the Seattle Police Department having targeted one of the girls from the club. Perhaps more significantly in relation to his underlying motives, however, he seeks out gay men in cruising areas and subjects them to a horrendous ordeal: he buries them alive in coffins having sewn their every orifice closed whilst he tests their blood for the HIV virus, then brutally murders those who test positive. His motive is in one respect psychosexual, as Frank details in the profile he delivers to a room of belligerent cops in a key scene. Confused and guilt-ridden regarding his sexuality, the Frenchman went to the peep show to try to feel something towards women and was fueled to murderous intent by finding himself affected by nothing but anger.

On another level, he is motivated by an inflated sense of righteousness distilled from his interpretations of apocalyptic literature. Enhanced recordings of the Frenchman's voice reveal him quoting from "The Second Coming" (1920) by William Butler Yeats, the Bible's Book of Revelation, and the writings of Nostradamus, concocting a twisted justification for his violent crimes as he perceives his fight being to quell what he has interpreted as "the great plague in the maritime city."

Directly following Frank's audience with the Seattle Police Department, Lt. Bob Bletcher (Bill Smitrovich) intercepts Frank as he is leaving the underground car park in what is another defining scene. He challenges Frank as to how he has such insight into the investigations on which he consults. Frank responds, "I see what the killer sees... I put myself in his head. I become the thing we fear the most... I become capability. I become the horror, what we know we can become only in our heart of darkness." Crucially, this is what the Frenchman has also become. He shares something of Frank's insights regarding the rising tide of evil, explicitly stating, "You can see it, just like I do." He is, then, something of a mirror image to our hero, personifying the moral and psychological depths into which the darkness to which they both bear witness can push a man. As such, he serves to emphasize the heroism of Frank Black as a man who also sees such horrors but is able to handle them, retain his humanity—notably through his family and the sanctity of his yellow house—and moreover to render his curse into a gift, a weapon against evil. The contrast between protagonist and antagonist here underlines Frank Black as the "very bright center" that Chris Carter had envisioned to shine out against the darkness that surrounds him (*Millennium Volume One*).

The Frenchman is in many ways the archetypal *Millennium* serial killer, as befits a pilot episode. This mix of psychopathology—a strong element of sexually motivated homicide, further twisted by an obsession with apocalyptic poetry and prophecy—is of a type that would become something of a model for *Millennium*'s first year. A composite of serial killer attributes merged with some other factor that serves the story and theme foremost without being identifiable to any single category of killer, it forms a device that is used often but successfully to dramatic effect. Far from representing a repetitive formula, the season presents great variety within the types of killers it portrays and the subjects they allow the series to explore as the embodiments of societal anxieties. As

Carter said in the same month that "Pilot" was aired, "I think people are imagining that *Millennium* is going to be a 'serial-killer-of-the-week' show, which it isn't. With this series I really want to explore the problems with culture and society, the nature of evil, the nature of goodness, heroism and spirituality" (Probst 47).

A few representative examples from *Millennium*'s first year illustrate this variety in both the creation of these human monsters and the issues they allow the series to explore. Early in the season, the Glen Morgan and James Wong-scripted "Dead Letters" features a killer of the type that reflects some common ill or sense of ennui endemic to modern society. In this instance it is an overwhelming sense of being inconsequential and desperately seeking any form of recognition. The episode's highly organized killer carefully stages the scenes of his crimes and leaves oblique messages for the police to assert a level of superiority over those investigating his murders, in stark opposition to his apparent sexual impotence. There is a long history to killers taunting police in one form or another—most commonly in letters—such as David "Son of Sam" Berkowitz, the Zodiac Killer, and even Jack the Ripper. What marks out this episode's antagonist as different is how obtusely his messages are communicated: etched upon a single human hair left at the crime scene in each instance. In communicating in this fashion, he targets his message specifically at the investigative team who would be examining such forensic evidence so closely, daring them to find it whilst also seeking to highlight his individuality and thus reflecting how he feels: "faceless, a dead letter." This aspect of his psychology informs Frank's profile of the killer as "angry that his life will go unnoticed, that he will have left nothing." That pervasive sense of personal worthlessness is pushed to its dramatic limit here, shining light into a dark corner of humanity in a way that the series often accomplishes so effectively.

In "Kingdom Come," written by Jorge Zamacona, the transformative power of personal loss is examined alongside a return to the central themes of religion and faith. Galen Calloway (Michael Zelniker) is an example of a seemingly good man turned evil, meting out brutal, ritualistic killings upon holy men. Calloway has suffered greatly in life, experiencing what Frank labels an "emotionally catastrophic event" when both his wife and daughter perished in a house fire several years prior. If anything, his homicides could be classified as revenge killings, crazed attempts to take vengeance on the representatives of a merciless God by singling out those clergy members who had administered significant ceremonies through the course of his life. As Father Schultz (Laurie Murdoch), a friend of Calloway's first victim, suggests to Frank when he asks the holy man if the killer's lack of conscience represents evil, "There's a disconnectedness out there and those desperate with that feeling expect faith to fill the void. And when it doesn't, they blame us." Frank ultimately intuits Calloway's true motive—a self-loathing because his faith persists in spite of all his suffering—which is expressed through extreme violence directed outwards. Ultimately, and most poignantly, this case gives Frank cause to consider his own more secular faith. When, during the episode's dramatic final confrontation, Calloway asks him if he believes in God, the script called for Frank to respond with a simple, "No," however Henriksen adlibbed the more considered line, "I haven't thought about it in a very long time" before going on to explain how his view is shaped by the evil he has seen wrought by one man upon another in the world. This is the central dramatic theme of the episode, reflected in the Black family dynamic and ending with a touching scene as Frank arrives home and discusses the subject with his wife Catherine (Megan Gallagher). Considering his insights regarding Calloway, Frank tells her, "I felt how human he was, so inundated by pain, fragmented by grief. It led him to surrender his humanity. We can't stop evil, but we can't lose our faith either." The personal tragedies of life are represented as potential ways into our lives for evil, threats that can only be combated by a stronger personal sense of purpose.

This theme is revisited in Chip Johannessen's "Blood Relatives," in which James Dickerson (Sean Six), a parentless delinquent, desperately attempts to reconnect with the world by insinuating himself into the lives of strangers at funerals. Catherine has a significant role in the episode as a Victim Services Department counselor and offers a commentary on the damage wrought upon Dickerson and others from his start in life, deploring, "How could anyone abandon a child? But millions of people do it. Millions. God, it's scary. We have home after home filled with kids like James. And we know they'll turn violent. How do I tell the survivors that no one saw it coming? They're out there, Frank... People full of holes." Dickerson displays various characteristics—such as the collecting of souvenirs from the families he has encountered—that lead us to believe he is indeed the killer behind the murders of some of the people he has met. In fact, it is the trustee of the halfway house in which he lives who is the true culprit. Seeking to retain control and power—two common and recurring motivators—over Dickerson through the killings, the very person who should be protecting the young man's interests reveals himself to be another damaged soul.

The serial killer would be utilized less often as *Millennium* entered its second and third years, as both storytelling and themes diversified, but perhaps the series' most celebrated and iconic killer is Avatar, as featured in Michael R. Perry's Season Two episode "The Mikado."[2] The highly organized Avatar has eluded Frank Black before, and the investigation into his crimes is confounded this time around by the fact that the location of his killings is unknown—they are broadcast live over the internet from an undisclosed location. As such an infamous and mysterious serial killer, having taunted the authorities for so long and yet eluding capture, Avatar attains mythological status, an escalation of sorts that seems fitting with the developing tone of Season Two. With his penchant for Gilbert and Sullivan's light operas, casting himself as none other than "The Lord High Executioner," Avatar not only presents the audience with a memorable adversary for Frank, he also provides a social commentary on the public's online voyeurism that precipitates the bloody culmination of each killing, making them complicit in Avatar's crimes.

Other episodes in *Millennium*'s first season present us with murderers and disturbed individuals who do not fit the category of the serial killer but nevertheless are driven to commit terrible acts of violence upon others, notably those closest to them. Chris Carter's "The Well-Worn Lock" once again places Catherine in the spotlight in a story that examines intra-familial sexual abuse, whilst "The Wild and the Innocent" portrays a murderous road trip centered upon a desperate young mother's attempt to contact her child, who has been sold to another couple by her own father. "Covenant" sees a sheriff admit to the murder of his entire family due to the guilt he carries at having committed adultery on his wife, the actual culprit, who blames her husband's adultery for inspiring her to such action in order to protect her children's innocence.[3] In each of these episodes, the disintegration of family life is the driving force behind acts of evil—as, by extension, is the lack of a strong moral and social foundation.

Another recurring theme in Season One of *Millennium* is the desecration of the sanctity of the home. Frank Spotnitz's "Weeds" sees the sins of the fathers visited upon their teenage children within a gated community, undermining the perception of security within its walls. "Wide Open" relates the story of a killer capitalizing upon real estate open house events to gain access to homes defended by security systems, then lying in wait for his victims and striking when they return home. Again, the security we feel within the apparent safety of our homes is revealed to be an illusion, and these episodes tap into a primal fear. Things take a more personal turn when Frank's sister-in-law is kidnapped in another Spotnitz-penned episode, "Sacrament," foreshadowing yet more terrifying events that were to descend upon the Black family later in the season and culminating in Catherine's abduction by the Polaroid Stalker in "Paper Dove," the dramatic season finale.

Viewed in isolation, many of the killers that Frank Black investigates in Season One of *Millennium* offer up a cracked mirror to the modern world in which we see damaged people resort to violent means. Focusing specifically on its serial killers as distinct from the more interpersonally motivated crimes, a significant common component is in their victimology. Whilst the vast majority of murders as a whole are committed by people know to the victim and for a relatively straightforward motive—revenge, passion, jealousy, anger—serial killers usually target strangers, albeit within a specific demographic. Herein lies one of the most fear-inducing aspects of these human monsters: we are all potential victims.

Effectively executing Carter's mandate for *Millennium*, Frank Black's intuition-led investigations into serial killers represent an ideal prism through which to define and scrutinize a rising tide of evil in the world. The serial killer is the stranger in the dark, the human monster who would, seemingly without rational motive, come unbidden into our homes to murder us and our loved ones. "Wait" and "worry" warn the opening credits to *Millennium*'s first year. This universal fear is represented by the sanctity of Frank's yellow house and the pervasive, ongoing threat to the Black family posed specifically by the Polaroid Stalker. The dominance and narrative use of serial killers throughout Season One and its ties between personal histories and society's ills as informing their motives speaks to its perspectives upon crime, criminality, and the very nature of evil. The serial killer is theorized to represent a horrendous perfect storm of abuse and neglect that compounds perverse fantasies and leads the individual to enter a career of unrestrained, primal violence. He is literally created by society. The very term "serial killer"—coined by Robert K. Ressler, F.B.I. agent and pioneer of psychological profiling—was in part chosen to reference the escalation in the actions of such a monster, an "improvement continuum" in which the killer seeks to perfect his method from one murder to the next. Ressler describes a comparison with "serial adventures" in which cliffhangers "increased, not lessened the tension," and, in a similar fashion, so the career of a single serial killer can itself be seen to mimic that wider sense of a rise of evil (33).

There is a commonly held perception that the serial killer is a relatively modern aberration in human behavior. Colin Wilson and Donald Seaman's *The Serial Killers: A Study in the Psychology of Violence* (1990) sums up this theory, placing societal changes as the primary cause of their genesis and positing a gloomy future:

> The serial killer is a virtually inevitable product of the evolution of our society... In the mid-twentieth century, the age of sex crime merged into a new age of self-esteem crime... In the late nineteenth century there were just as many frustrated, high-dominance working-class males in the world, but poor education and the gap between social classes kept them "in their place." By the mid-twentieth century increasing literacy and the erosion of class barriers meant that increasing numbers of these males were able to articulate their resentment. Some of these had the kind of traumatic childhood that seems typical of serial killers—lonely, physically abused, unwanted by parents, accident-prone (often suffering head injuries) and obsessed by sexual fantasies—and the result was bound to be, sooner or later, a sex crime explosion. This is what we have witnessed in the last four decades of the twentieth century, and there seems no reason to assume that the early decades of the twenty-first century will show any improvement—on the contrary, it seems inevitable that Europe will follow America into the age of serial murder... What this means, unfortunately, is that there is no simple short-term solution to the problem of the serial killer, any more than there has ever been a simple solution to the problem of crime and violence. (307-08)

There are, however, problems in the underlying assertion exemplified here that levels of serial murder are increasing. The proportion of crime that is actually recorded is well known to vary from actual crime rates and, moreover, for serial homicide the situation is much more complex. The victims of serial killers are invariably strangers to the murderer and, whilst there may be some correlation in features such as age, appearance, or perhaps the geographical location of the killings, there is little that otherwise obviously connects them. Added to this, a serial killer's victims are often those on the fringes of society and so potentially their disappearance may not be noticed, reported or investigated with the same vigor as other such cases.

Perhaps most significantly, before the advent of forensic psychology and scientific techniques, it has historically been very difficult to establish links between victims of serial homicide and therefore to attribute them to a single perpetrator. It has thus been a challenge to identify patterns that indicate the work of a serial killer, and it is possible that any number of unexplained disappearances or murders in the less recent past might have been the work of as yet unidentified killers. It was the very unit to which Frank Black once belonged that was to change that trend:

> Sex crime... was difficult to solve because in most cases there was only a causal connection between the criminal and the victim... The major breakthrough occurred in the mid-1970s with the setting up of the Behavioral Science Unit at the F.B.I. Academy in Quantico, Virginia... Equally important in the investigation of serial murder has been the use of computers... Computerization of fingerprinting has also been a major advance... Perhaps the most exciting advance of recent years has been the development of 'DNA fingerprinting.' (305–06)

It is, then, not really possible to accurately quantify this apparent rise in the frequency of serial homicide, as the modern specialty of forensic science, complemented by our understanding of human psychology—itself still a young discipline—has given rise to an increased ability to identify the perpetrators of such murders and to correlate their crimes. The notion that serial killers have proliferated over the past few generations has, however, certainly entered public consciousness such that it has defined a perception regarding the level of certain types of violent crime and therefore our fears in the social sphere—the very types of fears that are made manifest in the world of *Millennium*. These fears come to be of more significance to society's mood and preconceptions than does the obfuscated truth.

If the use of the serial killer as a storytelling and tone-setting device places the source of human evil as societal, then "Pilot" also hints at an entirely different root cause, one more in keeping with Chris Carter's stated interest in the "unscientific." Frank eventually tracks the Frenchman to a police laboratory via the blood samples he has taken from his victims, and this leads to a dramatic showdown. In his final moments the killer spouts warnings of the greater evil that is coming, a rising tide that hints at this very outset of the series towards something larger at work than the pathology of individual murderers operating in isolation. Once again, "Pilot" acts as a superbly crafted introduction to Carter's vision for *Millennium*, hinting at the different interpretations and manifestations of evil that the series would explore over three seasons and which viewers are still debating fifteen years later.

"Gehenna," the second episode of the series, also scripted by Carter, goes much further in opening up the dialogue on the nature of evil. It features an insidious apocalyptic cult that seeks to raise funds for terrorist activities via telemarketing sales, an idea that was envisioned to represent the invasiveness of modern communications. As Carter explained in an interview that accompanied the original U.K. video release of the episode, "The idea that evil could be carried out over the telephone is also a very scary idea, and one that I think is all too real and common these days. People can reach right into your homes in so many ways now, by fax, over the telephone, through your computer, and I think this is one of the ways that we're scared these days. This is something I was trying to communicate."

Significantly, the episode also introduces some new visual symbols to *Millennium*'s repertoire. Compounding speculation as to his facility's true nature, both at a crime scene and when faced with cult leader Ricardo Clement (Bob Wilde) after he is brought into custody, Frank's visions flash him images of an archetypal winged demon.[4] This could be interpreted as either a literal demonic entity, thus betraying Clements's true nature, or a visual metaphor for Frank's sense of some malign force exerting an influence over his behavior. In either eventuality, it represents *Millennium*'s first physical representation of some force at work above and beyond any inherent capacity for evil that resides within the individual. It is perhaps also significant that Frank sees these representations of demons in his mind's eye at this point in his personal history, having returned to work as a forensic psychologist after suffering a breakdown. His sanity is called into question a few times during the series, but it is usually implied that his understanding has deepened and become clearer now. In a sense, his arc reflects that of the psychiatrist Dr. M. Scott Peck. Peck's work is heavily informed by his personal religious beliefs, and some of his work concludes that the basis of evil lies within an extreme form of character disorder rooted in a denial of true human nature. Significantly, however, he sought to apply his theories of human evil to claims of demonic possession in order to understand them in more scientific terms. But as he delved deeper into the subject matter, he found himself reaching the contrasting conclusion that the Devil is real.

Also of note are some key scenes within the episode that compound Frank's perspective or have him question its implications. When one of the cult's members—known only by the name "Bob Smith" that all of its members use in the course of their telemarketing—is brought in for questioning, an oblique conversation between the two follows. Frank describes "the red rain falling in the face of the beast" that he saw at the crime scene and tries to convince Smith that he is safe from it, whilst he asserts back "no-one is safe from it." Throughout their conversation, it is unclear if Smith is referencing an evil entity from which he cannot be protected or if his rant is the product of the cult indoctrination to which he has fallen victim alongside the copious amounts of LSD he has consumed. Their conversation ends in dramatic fashion as he suffers a fatal seizure, causing Frank to ask his mentor, Group member Mike Atkins (Robin Gammell), "What could be so powerful that you couldn't escape it?" Atkins brings the dialogue on the subject matter back to more human origins, proclaiming, "I've seen the face of evil, Frank. I've looked into its eyes, seen it staring back at me. The face has always been a man's face, a human face. I've always believed that evil is born in a cold heart and a weak mind." This was Frank's previous understanding also, but now that belief has been shaken.

Two episodes later, "The Judge" returns to such territory with its tale of a vigilante who metes out his own deadly form of justice by directing readily influenced, violent young men to murder supposedly deserving individuals according to his will. Known simply as the Judge (Marshall Bell), he is eventually tracked via his latest disciple, Mike Bardale (John Hawkes), to his farmhouse base, where he states he has been expecting the police and, seemingly, Frank in particular. Back at police headquarters he is questioned in vain but Frank chooses to talk with him before he is released. The Judge asks for Frank in turn, referring to him as "the outsider," and here follows another intense exchange. When Frank asks him what he should call him he replies, "Judge is fine, or the name on the report. My name is Legion." The term references a Biblical passage from the Gospel According to Mark in which Jesus is said to have cast out demons from a man into a herd of swine.[5] Jesus asks the name of the "unclean spirit" inhabiting the man, and it responds, "My name is Legion, for we are many" (*Holy Bible*, Mark 5:9).

This single reference to Legion by name in *Millennium* was enough to inspire fans of the series to adopt the moniker in reference to the demonic forces that array themselves against Frank Black throughout the series. Certainly his meeting with the Judge also points to a larger threat of this nature and a considered plan. The Judge claims a common objective with Frank, promising, "I can show you an absolute justice, an unconstrained justice," as well as claiming control over the whole situation in adding, "You and your group of associates have never been as close to me as I've allowed this time. I wanted you to hear my offer, feel its truth, see my strength." Neither is the proposal a one-time deal, with his parting words to Frank indicating, "The offer's open. And if I'm hard to reach, well, don't make the usual assumptions."

Indeed, this temptation of Frank Black, to lure him away from his work, would be attempted on two other significant occasions in the series. Later in Season One, during the episode "Powers, Principalities, Thrones and Dominions," attorney Al Pepper approaches Frank almost as though by way of a continuation of this prior conversation with the Judge. And in Glen Morgan and James Wong's atmospheric Halloween installment early in Season Two, "The Curse of Frank Black," Frank is haunted by visions of the same demonic entity first glimpsed in "Gehenna" and is led to a meeting with the ghost of Mr. Crocell (Dean Winters). The offer given to Frank this time is framed a little differently than before, suggesting not a joining of forces but for Frank to give up his fight against evil and to seek to resume a normal family life. There is a further veiled threat too, as Crocell advises Frank to "secure you and your family's future, because the time is near and he will win. There's no way he can lose." Encouraging Frank to "give up the fight" equates to the maxim that "all that is necessary for the triumph of evil is that good men do nothing."[6] With Frank Black presented as our last and best hope against the rising tide of evil in the world, the implication is clear: if he sits out the fight, evil wins. The offer is never made again, and indeed the Black family suffers terribly in the months and years ahead. The curse of Frank Black is to be heroic and to suffer for that heroism.

This emerging mythology of evil in the series was to be blown wide open towards the end of *Millennium*'s first season, in Chris Carter's seminal and superb episode "Lamentation." Brought in to advise the Behavioral Science Unit on the escape of Dr. Ephraim Fabricant (Alex Diakun), Frank Black and Peter Watts identify Lucy Butler, a woman with whom the killer exchanged wedding vows whilst in prison. The duo trace her to and subsequently visit her at home, and there follows the first of a number of obtuse confrontations, with Sarah-Jane Redmond's perfectly judged performance infusing Butler with an intense mix of barely concealed menace and dangerously alluring sensuality. She knows of Frank, seemingly through Fabricant, and alludes that the two men share "a comprehension of extremes." Taunting biblical references directed at Frank—in an email sent to Butler, as well as in the staging of a murdered judge—again seek to undermine the scientific approach to understanding evil. The first, from the Book of Judges, "[is] about what we do in Behavioral Science, the arrogance of trying to learn the nature of evil and stop it by studying it," as Frank phrases it. This references that Fabricant has been kept alive as an object of study, and also suggests a folly in seeking to understand evil in such scientific terms. The second is from the Book of Ezekiel 19:10, thus denoting the Black family's home address of 1910 Ezekiel Drive and implying a considerable amount of forethought on the part of Carter. Whilst somewhat obtuse in its translation, Frank notes, "The killer is saying that evil begets itself." This is a powerful statement with far-reaching implications, inferring the potential for a contagion of evil.

Most significantly and memorably in the episode, the sanctity of the yellow house is well and truly broken as Butler enters the Black family home, terrifying Catherine, murdering Lt. Bletcher, and then somehow escaping unnoticed. Her supernatural identity is confirmed by her shape-shifting status here, a facet that marks each of her return appearances (including fleetingly in "Saturn Dreaming of Mercury") and hints at her status as more than a person. She appears to Catherine as the so-called Long-Haired Man and, in one of the most iconic moments of the series' entire run, shifts between this form, the winged demon, and Butler herself whilst Bletcher can only look on transfixed as she slowly descends the stairs to dispatch the veteran detective in brutal fashion. Moreover, she apparently leaves three sets of fingerprints behind, none of which are traceable to her, and walks free. From this point onwards, the stakes are raised. Given how violent and evil a killer Dr. Fabricant is characterized to be, it is chilling to see him rant from his hospital bed to Frank: "You had me commuted so you might learn the nature of evil." He goes on to warn Frank, "I can tell you now. You think I'm evil, Frank? You don't know what that is. It's greater than we are, you and me," and to describe Butler as "the base sum of all evil, the sleep of reason, the Devil's liege," before warning Frank that it knows him now, that it is feeding off his passion, and advising him to run from it. The stage is set between Frank and this entity, one that—whatever its true nature—is clearly more in form and power than just another human adversary.

The story is continued to some degree in the next episode, "Powers, Principalities, Thrones and Dominions," which significantly contains more evidence of the selfsame supernatural evil force. Connections are implied when the episode's killer, Martin (Guy Fauchon), confesses in court to Bletcher's murder—a link Frank had instinctively suspected—and via the aforementioned job offer from his lawyer, Al Pepper (Richard Cox). Furthermore, the phone calls that draw Frank and Watts to Mike Atkins's hotel room—where they find him mortally wounded from a brutal, ritualistic knife attack—appear to have come from a source capable of mimicking their voices to perfection. The episode's climactic scenes see Pepper transform into Martin and Butler, before Sammael (Rodney Eastman)—named for one of the angels alluded to in the episode's title—strikes him down with what appears to Frank to have been a bolt of energy. This confrontation between angel and demon is an overt representation of higher forces at work, and Frank's ensuing conversation with Sammael hints at a greater plan whilst still leaving him with many unanswered questions.

Lucy Butler herself was to make two more major appearances in *Millennium*. Season Two's "A Room with No View" is a lower key affair but exhibits powerful themes alluded to by its title's reference to the celebrated E. M. Forster novel *A Room with a View* (1908)—the protagonist of which, spookily, is named Lucy. Here, Butler is targeting young men of some non-conformist promise, abducting and imprisoning them in an isolated farmhouse where she drains them of their spirit through a mixture of psychological torture and outbursts of violent punishment. Her latest victim, Landon Bryce (Christopher Masterson), is shown to possess "an interesting mind" and an "intangibility of soul"—a piercing intellect and a free spirit, qualities that sometimes set him at odds with the norms and strictures of the educational system. As such, he is shown to be a very different type of target for Butler: not the heroic force for good represented by law enforcement but marked instead simply for his individuality and potential. She also compounds the mystery of her true nature by referring to her alter ego as a separate person, threatening Bryce, "If you even try to leave me, he will kill you." The male persona of the Long-Haired Man is the one who metes out violence whenever it becomes necessary to prevent her prisoners' attempts at escape, whilst Butler's power resides more in a sinister seduction, her each appearance in the episode finding her wearing fewer clothes than before, an insidious figure of stifling, domineering femininity. An old newspaper cutting found at her hideout shows Butler looking identical in 1911, implying that she may have been part of a similar cycle of abuse but moreover that she might be in some sense eternal.

Frank perceives Butler's involvement early on at Bryce's house and is moved to try calling his daughter Jordan (Brittany Tiplady) having felt the demonic presence there. Even as Watts attempts to dissuade him given the nature of the abductions, Frank is certain of her influence, that she is "selling the idea that the Devil is born again." It seems odd that the Millennium Group hasn't been investigating her more thoroughly, with their surveillance having been scaled back to the degree that a single Group member is assigned to submit monthly reports on her, reports that Butler is able to fake without detection after killing him. Perhaps this is evidence or foreshadowing of some infiltration of the Group by the force known as Legion, as would

EVIL HAS MANY FACES

become more overt in Season Three. Either way, and even after her operation is revealed, she once again evades capture.

Season Three's "Antipas" sees Lucy Butler's third and final major appearance, in a script from Carter and Spotnitz that evokes *The Omen* (1976) in its set-up and which finds her insinuating her way into the life of a State Attorney General and that of his daughter, who Frank later discovers has apparent connections to Butler's own supposedly dead child. She also seems intent on drawing Frank Black close to her once again, and as such her focus is squarely back upon him, as well as Agent Emma Hollis (Klea Scott). Dramatic developments in the episode see some mythology rich scenes set in a hedge maze on the grounds of the Attorney General's home, with dogs, a giant snake, and even a particularly disturbing moment in which Frank himself is presented as a manifestation of Lucy Butler's power. These events culminate in a potent and disturbing scene in which Butler materializes in Frank's motel room and proceeds to rape him, then accuses him of doing so to her, before finally professing to have conceived from their twisted union before losing the child! As she taunts Frank from her hospital bed in their final chilling meeting, "You came to me, Frank. All men come to me in time. The fruit of our union populates the Earth. We could rule the Earth, Frank." Frank counters, "You can corrupt men, but you cannot corrupt innocence." His words reflect a key theme of Season Three in relation to children as the guardians—or shepherds—of a future free from evil. Butler's parting shot is a direct threat aimed towards Jordan. If Frank will not align himself with the forces of evil, then the ongoing threats to him and those he loves is clear.

If anything, Butler's appearances after "Lamentation" suffer from a dearth of consistency or escalation to her purpose in comparison with her dramatic introduction. But perhaps for this selfsame reason—alongside Redmond's unforgettable and unerring performances in the role and her electric chemistry with Henriksen—many fans encourage her reappearance in any continuation for *Millennium*, so that her infernal dance with Frank Black might play itself out to a dramatic climax.

Butler is not, however, the sole supernatural personification of evil that the series offers. Season One also gives us Yaponchik (Levani), the antagonist of "Maranatha," reputedly a Russian bogeyman and presented as an invulnerable Antichrist figure modeled upon real life

Russian Mafia member Vyacheslav Ivankov, who was known by the same nickname. Season Two's "Siren" presents the mysterious Tamara Lee (Vivian Wu), a character related to the titular myth but whose charms Frank ultimately overcomes. And in Season Three's "Saturn Dreaming of Mercury"—an episode shot through with bizarre supernatural elements—Jordan senses evil in Lucas Sanderson (Dillon Moen), the child of a family new to the neighborhood, and ultimately her instincts are borne out. In the final moments of the episode, as he stands in the inferno of his home, Lucas momentarily transforms into Butler, indicating that the two are at the very least related in some way. The multiplicity of Legion is not overt in most instances, but here the existence of a host of evil forces is very apparent.

The characterization of such entities as Lucy Butler and the so-called Legion demon featuring in the world of *Millennium* embodies the "unscientific approach" that Carter had envisioned for the series. It also posits a quite different theory regarding the nature of evil than does the consensus of opinion regarding the social nature of serial killers. Philip Zimbardo's book *The Lucifer Effect* (2007) examines his famous Stanford Prison Experiment and is bookended by considerations as to the nature of evil and heroism.[7] He describes how the embodiment of evil can simplify the debate as to its nature and influence:

> The idea that an unbridgeable chasm separates good people from bad people is a source of comfort for at least two reasons. First, it creates a binary logic, in which Evil is essentialized. Most of us perceive Evil as an entity, a quality that is inherent in some people and not in others. Bad seeds ultimately produce bad fruits as their destinies unfold… Upholding a Good-Evil dichotomy also takes "good people" off the responsibility hook. They are freed from even considering their possible role in creating, sustaining, perpetuating, or conceding to the conditions that contribute to delinquency, crime, vandalism, teasing, bullying, rape, torture, terror, and violence. (6-7)

Such binary logic is at work in the development of the demon as part of the iconography of evil in established religion and folklore.

Demons entered the lexicon of many cultures in ancient times and can be represented as physical entities or unclean spirits capable of possession, thereby inducing sin in their helpless victims. They can be shown to possess the ability to change their form at will—exemplified in *Millennium* by Lucy Butler—whilst the visual representation of the red-skinned, horned, and winged beast, as seen at times in the series, owes much to the emergence of representations of the Devil in art. Such imagery only began to appear in the sixth century alongside the establishment of religious doctrine regarding the existence of the Devil, with depictions drawing upon the likes of the Greek god Pan, and developed further in the Middle Ages through the work of artists such as the German Gothic painter Stephan Lochner and the Italian Renaissance and Late Gothic styles of Carlo Crivelli. It is noteworthy at this juncture that the consideration and representations of such ancient religious concepts of evil alongside stories involving modern law enforcement in *Millennium* are not such unlikely bedfellows as they may at first appear; criminologists describe how the development of the constructs of law and order owes much to the origins of organized religion as a tool of social control over the masses, and thus likewise with its lexicon of iconography. In his analysis of such topics in *Problems at the Roots of Law* (2003), Joel Feinberg considers the purpose served by the Devil as a focal point. "Without the Devil, some writers fear, a strange moral complacency will take over the world, and the full horror of fiendish evil will not be properly appreciated. This nonchalant indifference to evil, some think, is itself a serious evil" (142).

More modern psychological interpretations of demons and demonic possession argue that such legends and folklore grew from a lack of scientific understanding of the human psyche and mental illness, that to characterize an internal drive as some kind of possession represents a dissociative disorder on the part of the "possessed." Most of the demonic manifestations presented in *Millennium* could be interpreted in either a literal or figurative context, but it can be informative to consider at least some of them as ciphers, representing an inner conflict or uncontrollable drive. Whilst Frank Black himself refers to evil as a force during the series, the demons in his visions could be interpreted as representing the personal demons afflicting the killers he seeks, with whom they may be engaged in their own internal battles of conscience. This interpretation blurs the boundaries of the good-evil dichotomy, inviting a more complex but perhaps more accurate perspective.

By considering evil to be a force rather than the manifestation of demonic beings, some of the most supernatural events in *Millennium* can be distilled to the simplest of themes: the temptation to not be heroic, as represented by Crocell's attempts to lure our hero from his chosen path in "The Curse of Frank Black," or the pressure to be ordinary, as per Lucy Butler in "A Room with No View." In the latter example, Butler embodies that definition of evil as a driving force that might stifle the will to be the best of one's self:

> Evil is in opposition to life. It is that which opposes the life force. It has, in short, to do with killing... I do not mean to restrict myself to corporeal murder. Evil is also that which kills spirit. There are various essential attributes of life—particularly human life—such as sentience, mobility, awareness, growth, autonomy, will. It is possible to kill or attempt to kill one of these attributes without actually destroying the body... Evil, then, for the moment, is that force, residing either inside or outside of human beings, that seeks to kill life or liveliness. And goodness is the opposite. Goodness is that which promotes life and liveliness. (Peck 46-7)

In "A Room with No View" we bear witness to Butler seeking to kill the spirit of Landon Bryce, telling him that he will be special only when he chooses to be ordinary, because "you will be working to be ordinary, unlike most others, who just are." This particular scene immediately follows that in which guidance counselor Teresa Roe (Maryangela Pino) describes the "despicable system of numbers" that fails students such as Bryce, those of a less measurable promise who might yet "affect the quality of our lives for the better." This is arguably the true evil in the episode: a construct of the educational system, to which Roe herself eventually surrendered. The implication is that without free and creative thinkers enriching the human experience, we risk allowing evil into our lives.

The most singular demonic manifestations in *Millennium*, however, deserve some consideration entirely in their own right. Darin Morgan's exquisite "Somehow, Satan Got Behind Me"—its title a play on Jesus's response to his temptation by the Devil—famously features four demons discussing their malevolent work overnight in the infamous Donut Hole. The most whimsical entry in the entire

EVIL HAS MANY FACES

Millennium canon—moreso still than Morgan's other superlative contribution as writer/director, "Jose Chung's *Doomsday Defense*"—the episode is segmented by each of the demon's stories. The first, Blurk (Bill Macy), describes how he encouraged a young man, Perry (Stephen Holmes), to seek to become the most prolific serial killer of all time by telling him little more than to "play the hand you've been dealt." Deterministic in its implications as to how evil surfaces in Perry, Blurk observes that, "We were so envious when man was given free will, but what has it brought them? The belief that their lives are determined by anything other than their own free will."

The other demons protest that they prefer not to work with serial killers because "the evil is too conspicuous" and therefore it might dangerously encourage self-reflection regarding the nature of evil, and the remaining segments of the episode concern themselves, for the most part, with more everyday situations and individuals. Another of the fiends, Abum (Dick Bakalyan), relates the story of a man driven to commit suicide through the relentless pointlessness and dullness of his own daily routine. Abum notes, "Mankind has progressed to a point in their dim-witted history where life has been drained of all its enchantment," and there is therefore no need for him to intervene beyond "minor irritations." The third segment is somewhat self-referential—and highly entertaining—in its deconstruction of a Broadcast Standards and Practices television censor, whilst the last tale is the most poignant. Toby (Wally Dalton) gets involved in a relationship with an aging stripper only to callously break her heart, which leads her to commit suicide. Outwardly, he expresses relief in being reminded from the experience "what ridiculous creatures [humans] are, to destroy themselves over something so fleeting as emotional attachments and biological needs," yet there is a flicker of insincerity and humanity to his demeanor that hints towards less of a division between him as a demon as opposed to a normal man plagued by internal demons. The episode ends with all four somewhat deflated from their conversation as they exit the Donut Hole.

Throughout the episode, these demons appear as elderly men to everyone save Frank Black, who unnerves the foursome by apparently discerning their true nature. Frank sees Blurk riding with Perry in his van at a crime scene, and the audience's scope for interpretation as to his true nature is distilled yet further by his indirectly narrated assertion that Perry's claims that he was an elderly hitchhiker were merely the figments of a personality disorder. Particularly telling is Frank's simple yet devastating observation to Toby at the scene of his lover's suicide: "You must be so lonely." Toby repeats the line to himself as he closes his anecdote, and it is clear that its meaning is a judgment upon his nature as opposed to his bereavement. Are all four really demons carrying out their work to lead mankind to eternal damnation? Are they four cynical old men plagued by their own demons, sharing their spite and malice with those whose paths they cross? Or are they merely figments and metaphors? Darin Morgan's script is brimming with ideas, philosophies, and tinder-dry wit—just what Ten Thirteen audiences had come to expect from him—and yet manages to render itself deliciously open to interpretation on the part of the viewer. At its heart, it offers a meditation upon the pettiness of lives lived in ignorant slavishness to numbing routine, its effect upon heart and soul, and how a propensity for evil can rise from the resulting and pervading sense of cynicism towards the world.

The Devil as allegory crops up elsewhere in *Millennium*. In the first season episode "Sacrament," for example, the threat to the Black family becomes very real as Frank's sister-in-law is abducted by Richard Green (Dylan Haggerty) from her son's christening. Clearly of a disturbed mind, Green is revealed to have been let down by institutional mental healthcare, released from hospital "with only a prescription bottle and a prayer." One of his doctors narrates how he was diagnosed as delusional since "he claimed Satan was forcing him to do evil. He thought he was protected as long as he stayed here, but the Devil would pull him back into evil when he got out." Ultimately, Green's own father is revealed to be the true culprit and the source of that evil, abusing his son and using him to procure victims. As Frank sums up, "He was the Devil that Green couldn't escape." The episode precedes "Lamentation," but the figure of Green's father looming at the top of the staircase as Helen Black is finally found—concealed behind a wall in the basement of his house—is eerily similar in its framing to the iconic visualization of Lucy Butler in Frank Black's own home before she descends upon Bletcher. In this instance, the Devil is a man, infecting his own son with his perverted appetites.

Furthermore, after taking Frank's gun and threatening Green on his doorstep, Tom Black (Philip Anglim) has an angry confrontation with his brother, blaming the whole situation upon his work. "This never would have happened if we hadn't come here to see you! You don't see it, do you, Frank? You bring it upon yourself. It's a sickness. You can't just keep it locked away in the basement." Indeed, it seems to be no accident that it is in the basement of 1910 Ezekiel Drive where Frank works on his cases, the only part of the house upon which he allows his career to encroach. In Gaston Bachelard's *The Poetics of Space* (1964)—which draws upon Jungian theory in terms of the house as a metaphor for the mind—the basement is described as "the dark entity of the house, the one that partakes of subterranean forces. When we dream there, we are in harmony with the irrationality of the depths" (18). Frank can be thought of as allowing evil to encroach upon this space. Bob Bletcher is murdered there, as is the Old Man in "Roosters." Those visceral scenes in the gloomy interior beneath the yellow house contrast with the clarity and open space of the breathtaking views of the Cascade Mountains that bookend "Lamentation," further reflecting the psychological metaphor for evil being represented.

It can be seen that not all representations of evil as a force or entity need necessarily lend themselves to a pure dichotomy of good and evil, and indeed *The Lucifer Effect* gives some consideration to this more nuanced interpretation:

> An alternative conception treats evil in incrementalist terms, as something of which we are all capable, depending on circumstances. People may at any time possess a particular attribute (say intelligence, pride, honesty, or evil) to a greater or lesser degree. Our nature can be changed, whether toward the good or the bad side of human nature. The incrementalist view implies an acquisition of qualities through experience or concentrated practice, or by means of an external intervention, such as being offered a special opportunity. In short, we can learn to become good or evil regardless of our genetic inheritance, personality, or family legacy. (Zimbardo 7)

Specifically, Zimbardo here presents a view that argues for the value of personal agency and strength of character over more deterministic factors, as well as recognizing that the seed of evil has the potential to rise in each and every one of us. This is a suggestion that is revisited a number of times throughout *Millennium*. A clear metaphor for such a view is found in "The Pest House," in which a nurse is leeching the violent impulses out of inmates in a psychiatric hospital only to find himself consumed by them. As Frank muses, "Maybe evil is like matter. [It] can't be destroyed, it only changes form. I believe he had good intentions, but we who hunt monsters, who touch evil, run the risk that evil will touch us. I think he figured out a way to take it out of them, but he couldn't take it out of himself." His dialogue here touches on the very dangers to which his work exposes him. The Season Three episode "Matryoshka" ploughs a similar furrow. Revisiting an F.B.I. investigation at the nuclear research base at Los Alamos in 1945, Frank and Emma discover that one of the scientists involved in developing the atom bomb was deeply affected by seeing that men who considered themselves good had created something "so obviously evil." He attempted further experiments to split off the part of himself that he considered evil, creating a demonic-type entity that then committed murder.

The incremental view also informs the nature versus nurture debate as to the origins of evil. The episode that perhaps best explores this subject matter is "Monster," in which Frank is sent to investigate claims of child abuse. Frank is initially confused as to why he is involved in the case, and he has unknowingly been set against fellow Group candidate Lara Means (Kristen Cloke). The two unite in their investigation and learn about Danielle Barbakow (Lauren Diewold), a young girl with violent impulses who engineers a scenario in which she can accuse Frank himself of violently abusing her. Means muses, "How can anyone know about, yet alone commit, murder at five years old? Has our culture bred this possibility? Is it violence on T.V.? Is she Damien? Is this girl some evolutionary mutation? And are there more of these kids, these people, coming?" By this point in the series, however, Frank seems certain from his experiences to date that evil is a force all of its own. His response to Means is to explain, "Recently I've seen, I've experienced evil. It feels like a force, like gravity, like the wind. It has blown across Cambodia, been a cyclone in Nazi Germany. It gusts throughout Los Angeles. Danielle Barbakow is a pre-storm, a breeze of an approaching hurricane." *Millennium* does not seek to answer such a fundamental question as to what might give rise to evil behavior in one so young but, whatever the cause, Frank senses that much worse is to come.

EVIL HAS MANY FACES

Perhaps the boldest statement that the propensity for evil might reside in each and every one of us is courted by the Season Two opener "The Beginning and the End." If the threat of evil might be seen to be circling the Black family when his sister-in-law is abducted in "Sacrament," then Frank's worst fears are made manifest in "Paper Dove" with the abduction of Catherine. Having briefly flirted with the notion that the Polaroid Man might direct other killers in the Season One finale, the second season opener focuses upon Frank's desperate hunt to track him down in order to rescue his wife. The Millennium Group ultimately reveals the identity of the stalker—memorably and grandiosely played by Doug Hutchison—to Frank and, upon locating him, he eschews Peter Watts's plea to wait for backup and seeks to rescue Catherine alone. In one sense, Frank is behaving in a similar fashion to Tom, the brother that he berates for such action in "Sacrament," yet Frank's position is certainly more dire and arguably more understandable: he knows the identity of the man he seeks for certain, a man who has taunted him for years, he cannot rely upon forces of law enforcement for immediate support, and he is a seasoned police veteran. A violent confrontation ensues, culminating in Frank repeatedly and fatally stabbing the Polaroid Man. The Millennium Group sees to it that no charges are brought, but the experience opens up a deep rift between Catherine—who witnesses the confrontation—and her husband, one that ultimately sees them separated. Back home, Catherine admits, "I don't know yet if it was wrong, what you did." "Neither do I," responds Frank. Catherine goes on, "But I feel like you lost something, sacrificed something for the safety of Jordan and me." Frank has made it clear to Watts earlier in the episode that he is prepared to sacrifice whatever he needs to in order to ensure Catherine is brought home safely, and the audience is also left to determine if his actions were entirely justifiable, and perhaps to muse upon how they might have reacted in the same circumstances. As Lance Henriksen commented regarding Season Two's developments at the time, "It isn't so much that my character has changed so much as that you are seeing more of him; more sides of him, rather than just dealing with an issue or a crime. You are seeing a human being" (Brooks 11). It is a stretch to say that Frank has behaved in an overtly evil way, but Glen Morgan and James Wong signal from their very first episode as executive producers that the perspectives upon right and wrong, and by extension the forces of good and evil, are to be redefined in shades of gray during their tenure.

The very next episode in Season Two builds upon this dramatic opening and adds further depth to the series' mythology of evil. "Beware of the Dog," also penned by the duo of Morgan and Wong, sees Frank dispatched to a remote town, Bucksnort, ostensibly to investigate a series of dog attacks. He first must meet with the mysterious Old Man (R. G. Armstrong), the Millennium Group's figurehead. The Old Man lectures, "Serial killers, spree killers, mass murderers: it's all just societal, genetic inevitability. You have no idea about true evil," and he goes on to posit, "Our role is to achieve equilibrium, and as we do that we must respect evil, and we must make evil respect us." He rejects the equation of crime with evil, reflecting Frank's own recent experience by suggesting, "Any of us would steal if we were hungry, and any of us might even kill if we were without hope." Frank's investigation into Bucksnort reveals a security-conscious new arrival who has upset this purported balance in what plays out as something of an abstract tale wherein the fear of individuals regarding their wider community is represented as blinding them to the world beyond their own four walls.

As well as pushing Frank Black to his limits in Season Two's opener and then exploring mysticism in the definition of evil through the wisdom of the Old Man, when Morgan and Wong were handed the reigns as executive producers during *Millennium*'s second year, they sought to elaborate upon the series' original concept and were especially interested in the dynamics of cults and secret societies. The two took bold steps to evolve the Millennium Group in this direction, portraying the organization as a divided, flawed entity with a sinister agenda. In "Pilot," Watts lurked in the darkness outside 1910 Ezekiel Drive, waiting to speak with Frank rather than intruding upon his family, but now such behavior is imbued with far more insidious and secretive subtext. In a sense, the Group takes the convictions regarding an imminent apocalypse that were the driving force for the Frenchman's actions in "Pilot" to a whole other level.

These malign developments regarding the true nature of the Group were disturbing to some—not least to Henriksen himself—in terms of the moral dereliction they seemed to represent relative to the more altruistic motives of the real-life Academy Group, upon which the Millennium Group was based. It is perhaps, therefore, more helpful to consider the Group as a perspective upon any faction granted a position of authority so convinced of the import and righteousness of its cause that it deems extreme actions to be justifiable and necessary. Perhaps this is what the Old Man seeks to caution Frank about when he speaks of respecting the equilibrium between good and evil. If all that is necessary for the triumph of evil is that good men do nothing, then perhaps the Millennium Group's development is a cautionary tale as to the evil that can be allowed to prosper when good men will stop at nothing.

The potential for the corrupting influence and the contagious nature of evil has been explored and described in academic terms as it relates to group dynamics, specifically in terms of specialized groups such as those in law enforcement:

> Firstly, the specialized group inevitably develops a group character that is self-reinforcing. Second, specialized groups are therefore particularly prone to narcissism— that is, to experiencing themselves as uniquely right and superior in relation to other homogenous groups. Finally, the society at large—partly through the self-selection process...—employs specific types of people to perform its specialized roles—as, for instance, it employs aggressive, conventional men to perform its police functions. (Peck 261)

Such fervent belief is represented by Peter Watts in the mythology-rich episode "The Hand of St. Sebastian," which shows a lengthy history to the Group and its maxims, as well as the fact that elements within the Group would kill to protect their purpose.

We also bear witness to the Millennium Group's fragmentation into two emergent and sparring factions—the titular "Owls" and "Roosters" of a spectacular mid-season two-part story—each of them certain of their righteousness in terms of contrasting beliefs as to the timing of the upcoming millennial event. Following on from Frank's uncomfortable interview with Group members at the outset of "Luminary," in these two episodes he goes head-to-head with Peter Watts. The performances of both Henriksen and O'Quinn make a confrontation between the two in "Owls" absolutely electric as Frank lets rip with his misgivings: "I respected Millennium. I respected you, and even came to respect myself. But then there's hints and intimations, passwords and candidacies, centuries old origins, end of world prophecies, secrets and lies." Later, when the Old Man seeks out Frank and Means, he bemoans how the Group is in ruins from its infighting, how it has descended into conflicts over "power and control."

"Owls" and "Roosters" are also notable in that they define the divisive religious dogma at the very heart of the Millennium Group. This seems an apt subject to include in the series' canon since it is undeniable that fervent religious belief has been the inspiration for many evil acts throughout human history, persisting to this day. "Anamnesis" is an episode that not only offers a very welcome center stage for Megan Gallagher, but also further explores the dynamics of such dogma. It tells the tale of Clare McKenna (Genele Templeton), a Seattle teenager who claims to see visions of Mary Magdalene and who turns out to be a descendant of a purported union between Magdalene and Jesus Christ. Catherine comes to understand more about the import and responsibilities of her husband's work, as well as the visions that plague Means. We also bear witness to how Clare is demonized by some devoutly Christian elements of her school and community. Here, as in the early church's sanctioning of belief in and representations of the Devil, the notion of evil can be seen as a societal construct established in order to assert righteousness, power, and control over others. The drives to exert power and control are strong and recurring motivators—for serial killers and for cult-like groups focused upon their own interests.

As well as being bound up in its concepts of the millennium and of good and evil, religion also informs other aspects of *Millennium*, such as the very belief in and definition of the apocalypse. It seems fitting, therefore, that Season Two would build towards such an event, and one inextricably tied to the Millennium Group. In the first part of the tumultuous two-part season finale, "The Fourth Horseman," Frank and Peter Watts are quarantined after it is discovered that they have been exposed to a pathogen at a crime scene. Frank senses from Watts's behavior that the Group knows more than they are letting on about the virus and, each solitarily confined to a cold clinical holding cell, they have another powerful confrontation, this time via telephone. Frank narrates how these events sum up his involvement with the Group in that, "I'm alone in a cell. I'm away from my family. I'm in a danger, but I don't know what it is. But you do." Watts claims that it is faith that has led him to resolve to continue his work with the Group, quoting scripture to Frank and thus highlighting the importance of religious belief to their purpose, but Frank counters, "Faith fills in the holes of uncertainty. Elements that are never meant to be known: God, death. The Group creates uncertainties with their secrets. That's not faith, that's control." He later goes on to describe the Group as an illusion and challenges Watts's involvement. Watts replies by explaining why he was drawn in by them and their purpose. "They came to me at a time in my life when evil—there's no other word for it—had lost all proportion with the rest of the world around me. I was witness to crimes that had no basis in human motivation. There has to be something more to it than just us. There has to be. It all has to lead in some inevitable direction, Frank. I believe that. Their answers touched on all my questions." It is clear that Watts subscribes to the existence of an evil that is more than a mere facet of the human condition and that it forms part of some greater purpose and narrative. The origins of Watts's involvement also point to the draw of cult-based organizations to those seeking some greater meaning to their lives and the world around them, and how this contributes to the potentially insidious influence of group dynamics.

Frank challenges Watts to question his faith in the Group by investigating them, and through such resistance he personifies the heroism of the individual who refuses to be drawn in by such a dynamic. As Peck describes:

> The plain fact of the matter is that any group will remain inevitably potentially conscienceless and evil until such time as each and every individual holds himself or herself directly responsible for the behavior of the whole group—the organism—of which he or she is a part (249-50).

In "The Time Is Now," the conclusion of the two-parter, the Group's lack of conscience is exemplified during a confrontation between Frank and sinister senior member Mr. Lott (Stephen Macht). Lott explicitly states that the Group is not concerned with the life of any individual, rather that the life of all mankind defines the "nature of our responsibility." Over the course of the episode there follows a struggle that sees a deadly outbreak of the Marburg virus and an initiation to the Millennium Group that consumes Lara Means's sanity as the truth and the extent of their knowledge is revealed to her. Frank ultimately faces a truly apocalyptic scenario of his own as a direct result of the outbreak: the death of his beloved wife, Catherine, a life-changing blow to the heart of the family he has fought for so long to keep safe.

For Season Three, *Millennium* found itself with a new production team led, for the most part, by Chip Johannessen and Chris Carter. The sheer scale of the ambitious storytelling in Season Two was eschewed for a return to what Carter felt were the themes at the heart of the series:

> This year we will continue to tell some of the mythology stories but go back to the stories that are about real human emotion. This isn't serial killer of the week, it's about what happens when bad things happen to good people. I felt the mythology moved away from that, in a way that kind of gave it a fictional distance. The reason that *Millennium* is even a show is because there were human monsters that you couldn't do on *The X-Files* that really were interesting to me as a storyteller. That's what makes the show scary—the monsters are all too real. (May 30)

In some sense, *Millennium*'s third season is something of a hybrid of the previous two. Frank is back at the F.B.I. with a new partner, Emma Hollis, allowing for a resumed focus upon investigations into certain types of serious human crimes. The threat of the Millennium Group remains and it looms large over proceedings, not least in Frank's unveiled mistrust and understandable hatred towards them—in particular directed at Peter Watts—which grows as they begin to manipulate Hollis and court her as a candidate and, ironically, is facilitated by Frank heeding Assistant Director Andy McLaren's (Stephen E. Miller) advice to keep a distance from her. There are still manifestations of demonic evil, complete with appearances by Lucy Butler, yet they are often more explicit and mysterious in nature, and there is a strong implication that these same forces might be at work within the Group itself.

But Season Three also boasts an emerging sense of hopefulness—exemplified in the central and aforementioned consideration of children in so many episodes—as the series looks to the approaching millennium and considers the future. Frank's voiceover in "Exegesis," at the end of the season's opening two-parter, speaks to this as he muses, "We can see the future in tantalizing glimpses that vanish as quickly as they appear. A premonition. Not what the future is, but that it is. Waiting for us. A reassuring thought. This sight is a burden for some... We sense the chaos. We worry. We wait. Who's going to see a different future?" Watts answers for the Group in "Skull and Bones," even as he attempts to defend the killings of forty-three people to assure the fulfillment of their veiled purpose. Ominously, he tells Hollis, "There are forces at work today that could easily tear this country apart. Terrible weapons being developed, with us as their target. Who, Agent Hollis, is prepared to do what is necessary to assure our future? You'll see. And then we'll talk." As Watts sees it, the Millennium Group is the entity that will stand up, face the difficult decisions at which most people would balk, and act to assure the future of mankind.

Some thematic threads begin to converge over the course of the season. A strong example can be found in the seminal "Seven and One," Carter and Spotnitz's final contribution to the series as credited writers. Frank finds himself once again the recipient of disturbing Polaroids, but this time they depict himself as a victim of drowning, drawing upon a fear that has haunted him since childhood. Frank suffers a nightmare in which a man enters his home and attacks Jordan only to wake and find the man truly is there, in the house, and he escapes without Frank being able to identify him. To the audience it is clear that this man is Mabius, a mysterious figure recurrent throughout the season and portrayed by actor Bob Wilde. Wilde bears a facial resemblance to Lance Henriksen and is often similarly clothed, such that he can be seen to represent the most evil kind of a person someone in Frank's position might become.

First glimpsed in "The Innocents" and identified then to be something of an assassin working for the Millennium Group, Mabius goes on to attempt to kill Frank in both "Exegesis" and "Skull and Bones" and threatens to do so again after dispatching several others in "Bardo Thodol." But it is "Seven and One" that offers his most revelatory appearance, in which he makes an attempt on Hollis's life in addition to invading the Black home. Throughout the episode Special Agent Del Boxer (Dean Norris) investigates Frank with fervor, seeking to prove his mental instability and therefore have the F.B.I. renege on his reinstatement. As Hollis seeks to defend Frank, Boxer describes him as someone "whom to be successful, has to live with the most base and horrible acts and the unthinkable human impulses that drive them. So horrible as to become unreal but, when reality itself becomes subjective, when the connection between who you are and what you know commingle and confuse to the point where the hunter so identifies with the hunted, he becomes him." In a pivotal scene Boxer visits the home of Dr. Luanne Chase (Judith McDowell), Frank's therapist. When she demands to know why he is there, he responds, "To show you Frank's fear is real, and that all your understanding and psychiatry are powerless against it." With this he transforms into Mabius before her eyes, then fatally stabs her. In this moment, if taken literally, the character is revealed to belong to the so-called Legion and demonstrates that such forces are at least a part of the Millennium Group itself as two strands of the series' mythology of evil merge. Viewed more allegorically, the Group's chosen path to combat evil has allowed that selfsame darkness to invade its mission and work and ultimately to undermine its purpose.

The episode also revisits the theme of science versus faith, in Boxer's words to Dr. Chase and also in Frank's struggle to confront his own mortality. The very fact that a therapist is murdered by what is apparently a liege of the Devil is a bold statement in this ongoing dialogue. In another key scene, Frank visits Father Yahger (Norman Armour), a Catholic priest at a church with former connections to Catherine. He admits to the priest, "I feel the presence of evil, but I don't know if it's real or if it's something—someone—playing with my fears." In seeking to help Frank, Hollis also visits the priest, who advises her, "Evil dwells where fear lives. In a heart without fear, evil can find no purchase." He goes on to explain, "It is those who feel the strongest that evil wants most." Frank is rendered vulnerable through his fear, a fear that the episode represents as being very real, but he also gains strength from facing and conquering it. Similarly, the Millennium Group has given in to its fears and is being consumed by them. The episode ends with another voiceover from Frank, one that reflects upon his famous dialogue with Bob Bletcher in "Pilot" at this point in the series. "I have been given the gift of insight," Frank states, "of seeing in the dark and seeing into the darkness of men's hearts and minds. I know what evil is. I've seen it, felt it, tasted it. Inhaled the demon breath of its ancient powers, the same powers that have been prophesied through history and which are now marshaling." Yet his experiences over the past three years have allowed him to reevaluate his ability, and in doing so to no longer also refer to it as a curse. "I have misjudged my gift," he concludes. "If I see in the darkness it's because there is light, and it is the light which guides me now, the light that will not go out, that will lead us out of the dark night if we let ourselves feel this too. It will protect me as it protects those around me, even as the ancient forces try to steal our breaths." Again, Frank and the series have moved towards a point of hopefulness in the fight against evil, even as its threat seems to grow.

Themes also converge or come full circle in the series' effective two-part finale, a story that revisits the type of investigation that might have featured in *Millennium*'s first year but with a fresh twist that again informs perspectives upon the nature of evil. After Frank witnesses the execution of Ed Cuffle—the killer referenced in "Pilot" as having inspired the Polaroid Stalker—what appears to be a copycat begins murdering with his same modus operandi. Representations of Roman numerals carved into or drawn upon surfaces at a crime scene lead Frank to suspect that they denote the Stations of the Cross and indicate that this new killer, Lucas Wayne Barr (Jeff Parise), suffers in the act.[8] Special Agent Barry Baldwin (Peter Outerbridge) makes a connection to a man who was acting strangely, reenacting one of the Stations of the Cross at a local church, where Frank and the priest subsequently discuss how the man believed he was "possessed, performing acts by someone else." As they consider this possibility, Marjorie David and Patrick Harbinson's shooting script for the episode describes "Frank and the Father accepting this on some level that leaves Baldwin feeling out of it." Frank's deeper level of understanding regarding the nature of evil and the behavior of those under its influence has detected something he has never before seen in such a killer, something that a man of God can understand too, but that eludes the understanding of the more pragmatic Baldwin.

The concept plays out in series finale "Goodbye to All That," in which it is revealed that Millennium Group scientists have learned how to switch back on the physiological process of learning and development in adults. Exploring similar territory to that inferred in Season Two's "Sense and Antisense" (albeit by different means), this also reflects the career of Jose Delgado, a neuroscientist who in the 1970s pioneered a brain chip by which he believed it would be possible to manipulate the mind. He envisioned a "psychocivilized society" in which members might control their own mental functions or—more insidiously—those of others. Delgado was able to induce emotions in his subjects that ranged from fear and rage to euphoria through his controversial work, and declared he was on the verge of "conquering the mind" and creating "a less cruel, happier and better man" (Horgan 71).

The Millennium Group's work is by all accounts more sophisticated and at the opposite end of the scale, since it becomes evident that it has used this groundbreaking scientific knowledge to "reincarnate" Ed Cuffle in the form of Lucas Barr. It could be a powerful tool in the arsenal against the rising tide of evil, yet the Group appears to have used this science to create a killer rather than deconstruct or negate one. The discovery also poses deep moral questions raised by the availability of such technology—the ability to alter brain biology and human impulses—and opens up debate as to the responsibility that comes with such knowledge and power. To what end the Group created Barr is uncertain—although Frank believes that the link to Cuffle means this act is aimed squarely at him—but one last meeting between Frank and Watts sees the two once again discuss their true intent. Watts claims that the Group is "choosing the future" and "attempting to preserve human values that are worth preserving." He goes on to claim that he has been protecting Frank by not being open and honest with him about the extent of their activities. Whilst the two never reconcile—and indeed their relationship is pushed to new limits in this finale—their conversation hints at the potential for redemption which Frank claimed he had to believe in during the episode "Bardo Thodol" just a few installments previously. "We are shepherds, Frank. All of us," Watts suggests to him, words that are echoed by Jordan later in the episode.

Frank tracks Barr to an address where he is living under a pseudonym and quite literally brings light to the darkness there when he breaks into the boarded-up house. After briefly threatening to harm his girlfriend with a power drill in order to protect himself and before instead ending his own life—apparently overwhelmed by the enormity of the knowledge he now has coursing through his brain—Barr implores Frank to tell him why "they" chose him for their experiment, suggesting, "I always had it in me, didn't I?" Crucially, Frank responds, "We do. We all do." The clear implication is that with the right trigger or influence, we are all capable of evil. This is the series' final statement on the nature and cause of evil, and it is a powerful and uncomfortable one.

Even if evil is an entity or force rather than a primal seed within the human spirit, then it can invade or grow within any of us based upon our circumstances, or moreover our ability to resist it. Frank's final dialogue, as he and Jordan flee in his iconic red Jeep Cherokee, finds him telling his daughter that he has seen the future "where the battle between good and evil that has raged for millennia is fought to conclusion." When Jordan asks who wins, he replies, "It's up to us." The responsibility is an individual one, implying the need for wider reflection and personal sacrifice, that can be faced only "by discarding the question that confuses us—what do I want—and asking what the world, what the universe wants and needs."

Chris Carter's vision for *Millennium* was to reflect upon evil in the modern world in its many guises, and in this regard it is an undeniable and unparalleled success. *Millennium* presents an often challenging viewing experience in the darker aspects of life that it explores, although crucially it never sanitizes its subject matter or the violent acts perpetrated within its stories, and above all it stands out due to its authenticity. As Carter described in an interview during the series' first year of transmission:

> The world is a very scary place. More and more, in most neighborhoods, you can't go out and walk around at night. I felt *Millennium* was a way to look at the world we live in, to ask the question, 'What is evil?' Where does it lie? Does it have a face, a presence—or is it in us? I wanted to deal with faith, and with hope, and with understanding ourselves and possibly finding meaning—not to sound crass—on how we conduct our lives. We're so overwhelmed by this kind of thing happening that we've become desensitized, hamstrung from speaking out or acting heroically. To me, *Millennium* is a response to the darkness and the times of the world that we live in. (Mauceri 47)

That response to evil is of course personified in Frank Black, a man who consistently resists situations and rises above the nature of his work to repel that darkness. He is the polar opposite of a man desensitized; he experiences the dark souls of the monsters he seeks more deeply than anyone yet resists the evil that lurks there and that seeks at times to subvert him. He is the very definition of heroism, as Zimbardo describes it in the concluding chapter of *The Lucifer Effect*:

> Heroism focuses us on what is right with human nature. We care about heroic stories because they serve as powerful reminders that people are capable of resisting evil, of not giving in to temptations, of rising above mediocrity, and of heeding the call to action and to service when others fail to act. (461)

Frank's work clearly affects him deeply, causing him to reevaluate his own beliefs at a fundamental level and challenging *Millennium*'s audience to do the same. Towards the end of "Gehenna," Catherine finds Frank lying in bed reading the Bible. She asks him if he is seeking answers from within its pages and if he wants to talk about what is clearly disturbing him. Frank explains, "I'm just confused about something I thought I understood about evil. What it is, exactly... It seems that the old biblical concept of the Devil's influence has lost any currency." Catherine's perspective is, "I just think the language has changed. I think science and psychology have given us a clearer idea of why people commit evil acts." Frank questions whether each and every one of us is therefore capable of evil, "Or is there something out there—a force or a presence—waiting until it can create another murder, another rape, another holocaust?" Catherine's response is simple: "I think it's something that everyone who looks deeply at life wonders." At its core, this unanswerable question is what *Millennium* explores, considering the evil that is manifest in the modern world more deeply than any other television series would dare to do either before or since. Recoil from the darkness in fear, it warns, and we merely allow it to permeate yet deeper. The series teaches us instead that evil exists and that it needs to be faced, respected, and hence ultimately resisted. In doing so, *Millennium* examines its subject matter from a number of different perspectives, diverse in its storytelling without ever patronizing its audience by serving up oversimplified answers.

Herein lies a strength of the series, a sign of maturity: it never seeks to trivialize its subject matter by honing in upon a single, narrow mythology within which to seek to define its main themes. It is a complex and unsettling perspective to which Peck's work also drew him:

> Human evil is too important for a one-sided understanding. And it is too large a reality to be grasped within a single frame of reference. Indeed, it is so basic as to be inherently and inevitably mysterious. The understanding of basic reality is never something we achieve; it is only something that can be approached. And, in fact, the closer we approach it the more we realize we do not understand—the more we stand in awe of its mystery. (42)

With its range of creative men and women contributing to the world of *Millennium* across three seasons and sixty-seven episodes, coupled with the elusive and nebulous nature of its subject matter, it is unsurprising that there is no readily definable overarching perspective on evil offered by the series when viewed as a whole. Evil has many faces, literal and figurative, framed through the eyes of a protagonist cursed or perhaps gifted with the ability to conjure in his mind's eye the darkest thoughts of his fellow man. In a world tainted by moral bankruptcy, tormented by eldritch evils, and teetering on the verge of apocalyptic meltdown, he offers our best line of defense. Through his unique ability he reminds us that, whether it originates from within or without, evil is a force that, unchecked, has the power to permeate every aspect of our lives and of our society. We are stronger if we live in that knowledge and, like Frank Black, risk staring deeply into the darkness so that we might come to know it well enough to be victorious over its dark influence.

NOTES

1. Donnie Pfaster was ultimately described as a "death fetishist"—a fictional term—in the episode as the Fox network deemed the original script's classification of his character as a "necrophiliac" to be inappropriate for transmission.

2. Avatar was based upon the real-life Zodiac Killer, an infamous serial killer who claimed responsibility for seventeen murders in San Francisco and northern California between 1966 and 1974 but has yet to be identified or brought to justice. In Michael R. Perry's original script, the killer was Zodiac himself. Network executives vetoed the notion of basing the character upon a real-life killer, however, and a subsequent draft that renamed him Omega was also rejected due to Lance Henriksen's endorsement contract with the watch manufacturer of the same name.

3. The first cut of "Covenant" ran to nearly one hour and twenty minutes, hence many scenes were excised in order to fit the required running time. Many of these scenes further highlight the stress suffered by wife Dolores Garry (Colleen Winton) whilst also drawing visual comparisons between her dead daughter and Jordan Black, adding further resonance to the case for Frank.

4. Bob Wilde played both Ricardo Clement in "Gehenna" and the shadowy Millennium Group member Mabius in Season Three. Whilst both characters could be linked to the loosely conveyed Legion arc, no other overt link was established between these two characters during the series' run.

5. The eponymous Judge states during this exchange, "When Jesus of Nazareth expelled demons from a herd of enchanted hogs, story has it that the demons told him their name was Legion." In fact, the Bible passage tells of the unclean spirits being cast out of the man into a herd of some two thousand pigs, who then run off a hillside or cliff into the sea, where they drown. The story is also referenced by the pigs that live on the Judge's farm, to whom Bardale ultimately serves up the Judge when he rebels against his influence.

6. Normally attributed to Eighteenth century Irish statesman and philosopher Edmund Burke, he in fact never phrased this assertion in quite this fashion. He did, however, write the slightly less pithy phrase, "When bad men combine, the good must associate; else they will fail, one by one, an unpitied sacrifice in a contemptible struggle" (Burke 106).

7. The Stanford Prison Experiment took place in 1971 and comprised a group of students randomly assigned guard or inmate status in a mock prison environment. Within a matter of days, the "guards" began to adopt increasingly violent and sadistic behavior towards the "inmates," who for their part exhibited pathological behavior in keeping with their prisoner status, such as passively accepting the abuse to which they were exposed or, by contrast, rebelling. Intended to run for two weeks, the experiment was abandoned after just six days out of concern for the wellbeing of its participants.

8. The Stations of the Cross are a series of artistic representations of Jesus Christ carrying the cross to his crucifixion and are often represented in Roman Catholic churches.

WORKS CITED

Bachelard, Gaston. *The Poetics of Space*. Boston: Beacon, 1994. Print.

Brooks, James E. "Black for Good." *Xposé* May 1998: 10-16. Print.

Burke, Edmund. *Thoughts on the Cause of the Present Discontents*. London: J. Dodsley, 1770. Print.

Carter, Chris. Interview. *Millennium Volume One: Pilot / Gehenna*. Twentieth Century Fox Home Entertainment (UK), 1998. VHS.

Feinberg, Joel. *Problems at the Root of Law*. New York: Oxford UP, 2003. Print.

The Holy Bible, King James Version. London: Cambridge UP, 1945. Print.

Horgan, John. "The Forgotten Era of Brain." *Scientific American* September 2005: 66-73. Print.

Mauceri, Joe. "Carter's Millennium." *Shivers* March 1997: 47-49. Print.

May, Caroline. "Group Therapy." *Xposé* October 1998: 28-31. Print.

"Order in Chaos." *Millennium: The Complete First Season*. Prod. John Mefford. Twentieth Century Fox Home Entertainment, 2004. DVD.

Peck, M. Scott. *People of the Lie*. London: Arrow, 1990. Print.

Probst, Christopher. "Mining the Macabre." *American Cinematographer* October 1996: 46-55. Print.

Ressler, Robert K. and Tom Shachtman. *Whoever Fights Monsters*. New York: St. Martin's, 1993. Print.

Wilson, Colin and Donald Seaman. *The Serial Killers: A Study in the Psychology of Violence*. Croydon: Virgin, 2007. Print.

Zimbardo, Philip. *The Lucifer Effect*. Reading: Rider, 2007. Print.

Adam Chamberlain is the Associate Publisher for Fourth Horseman Press and co-editor on a number of its publications, including *Columbia & Britannia* (2009), which was nominated for the 2010 Sidewise Award for Alternate History. He has also been a consultant for and contributor to the Back to Frank Black campaign for the past two years, and was inspired by Frank Black and *Millennium* to complete a degree in psychology and criminology. He lives in London.

AVATAR UNMASKED:
A CONVERSATION WITH MICHAEL R. PERRY

Interview by James McLean & Troy L. Foreman
Written by Adam Chamberlain & Brian A. Dixon

Michael R. Perry was so impressed by the first season of *Millennium* that he actively sought a role within Ten Thirteen Productions. "I was a viewer only, but loved it so much that I pressed to join the team. I asked my agency to send writing samples to Chris, with hopes of being considered for either of his two shows," he says. Ultimately, it was a crime novel he had written years previously that was to secure him a role as both writer and producer on the series. "*The Stranger Returns* landed me the interview on *Millennium*," he explains, "and they hired me in the summer of 1997."

The 1992 novel posits the escape from death row of real-life serial killer Ted Bundy. "I wrote that when I was very young and it was an awesome experience. It was trying to do a fictional sequel to a true crime story, and it has certain elements of meta-fiction, but it is a very straightforward crime procedural wherein the father of one of Bundy's victims starts seeing signs that he is still around and comes to believe that perhaps he is still out there. He is the exact worst person to have this happen to, because of course he's going to see that everyplace because it is the thing that turned his life around. He is the least credible person to advance this theory. He just happens to be right. It's a straight up crime procedural."

The experience of writing *The Stranger Returns* and its follow-up, *Skelter* (1994), is something that Perry cherishes to this day. "It was great to write a couple of crime novels before getting into T.V., because I loved writing. I loved sitting down and writing. A lot of people say that's their worst nightmare, even T.V. writers. There are T.V. writers who like all the stuff such as breaking stories and going to the set but the actual writing is like their punishment, and for me it's the opposite. Having started out writing—I wrote four books that got published, a bunch of magazine articles and stuff like that—I don't mind going to the set, I don't mind going to the editing room and stuff, but my refuge and retreat is sitting down at the keyboard. Or sometimes I'll even write longhand, so sitting down with pen and paper and writing stuff out."

Not only does Perry feel at home writing, the experience of crafting fiction was one upon which he would draw during his time on the series. "I think the discipline I got by starting in fiction really helped me a lot, and the research I did for that book really rolled into the *Millennium* stuff. But then the *Millennium* research went so much further, because we had such an incredible research on that show, being that we were able to talk to the Academy Group guys, and you see some of it in Lance's performance. Lance recognized the humanity and the intelligence in those guys and he was able to roll it into the Frank Black character."

Perry's writing career pre-dates *The Stranger Returns*. At the start, he was writing for an altogether different medium. "I started out actually making industrial films after I graduated from college, thinking that would lead to a career making movies. It didn't—you just talk to automakers all the time. So I stopped doing that, I took a temp job, and I started writing anything I could write.

"I wrote articles for music magazines, computer magazines, *The Hollywood Reporter*, and then I published some books. In all I published two novels that were paperback original crime novels for Simon & Schuster Pocketbooks, and then those tipped me into writing for television."

How did that transition take place? "At one point a man named Robert Ward, who is still a close friend, found out that I was writing crime novels and trying to get into T.V., and he said, 'We have a really difficult time breaking plots on this T.V. show called *New York Undercover*. Do you think you could do one?' I said, 'Yeah, I'd love to do that.' My first credit is actually on *New York Undercover*, which was two guys in New York—undercover cops—and Ice-T was the guest star! I was super-excited to have Ice-T as the guest star, and then it rolled from that to working for Sam Raimi on *American Gothic*, and then various other things."

In spite of his roundabout route into television writing, Perry stresses the importance of having a good portfolio. "It is always that you have your writing samples and people meet you. As you start a writing career, to get in the door you have to have good writing samples and then you have to come in with not one good idea but usually five, because the first four that you'll pitch they'll say, 'Well, we're already doing one similar,' or 'We vowed never to do a story about that.' You hear that a lot of times. So you have to constantly go out and come up with a new story for a television series, or whatever it happens to be."

Perry's first produced script for *Millennium* happens to be an enduring fan favorite, one of the most gripping crime thrillers the series ever produced. "The Mikado"—featuring the unforgettable Avatar, an ingenious serial killer who eluded Frank Black earlier in his career—aired mid-season during the second year of the series, a time of considerable change for *Millennium*. "Season Two was a wholly owned subsidiary of Morgan and Wong," recounts Perry, who was credited as an Executive Story Editor for the series' second year. "Those guys came in and I think their deal was, 'We get to do whatever we want,' and they actually physically moved to a different office a little way away, closer to the editing room than where the writers were. Glen and Jim took the second season and ran with it. It was very much their baby. They had a vision, they had the authority to pursue that vision, and they pursued it aggressively." Nevertheless, the writer describes his debut episode as "a bit of a throwback to Season One."

In "The Mikado," the infamous Avatar returns to torment Frank Black, the Millennium Group, and police across the country by presenting his sick crimes to the public during live internet broadcasts. As the investigators strive to track the killer, they find he is exploiting the law's inability to keep pace with technology. "The devil," as Frank Black suggests, "has a new playground." The episode was inspired by the emerging culture and technology of the online world. Perry explains that in 1996, "in the Pleistocene era of the internet, a young woman decided she would be on camera twenty-four seven, and thus was born Jennicam, the first webcam exhibitionist. She was just going to be on camera twenty-four hours a day and people were saying, 'She's going to be naked on camera!' That's what everybody was worried about, and I thought, 'What if a crime occurred?' I guess that's why I'm a crime writer, because of course she's going to be naked, but what if a crime occurred? Who are going to be the people who investigate it? It doesn't take place in any jurisdiction; it's not in a place. What if we don't even know it's Jenny, so we don't know who the person is who did it, we don't know where it happened, we don't know who the victim is. I just thought, 'That is a dynamite beginning for a mystery story.'"

This dramatic start lent itself to a number of related themes and subjects posed by the infancy of the internet, "when most people connected via dial-up lines and modems," as Perry notes. "The situation raised all kinds of knotty issues about when a spectator becomes an accomplice, the distancing aspects of mediated communication, the difficulty of law to keep pace with technology, and so on. Plus, it was just a straight-up creepy idea.

"Then I wanted to get into the themes of alienation that mediated communication creates, and we see that it has become a huge national problem. People say vicious things via email or Facebook that they never would say in person, and people are far crueler when they are in the middle of things than they ever would be. That tide was just starting to go, and it was already starting to show that people can be very callous when they think they are just part of an anonymous group. That was the sub-theme of the thing. Would people keep visiting a room knowing that the more clicks it gets the closer somebody is to dying? Nobody died making that episode, but absolutely I think the answer is that people would go click crazy!"

Perry also got to produce "The Mikado" and is quick to sing the praises of the executive producer alongside whom he worked on the episode. "I got to go to Vancouver with Jim Wong, who's a great guy and brilliant. A problem that would take you or me five minutes to figure out how to solve, the question is asked and Jim answers with the solution. That's what I want to be, that's how to do this.

"That same year he had just started his directing career, and I think he was nominated for an Emmy for directing an episode of *The X-Files* the previous year, ['Musings of a Cigarette Smoking Man']. He's a good director; he's a really brilliant editor too. So my limited involvement with those guys was fantastic, just seeing how Jim produces. Everybody produces in a different way, and the way that he produces is very much keeping the whole picture in his head. He was doing that and he'd be outlining an episode that is four episodes down [and also] rewriting one that they are going to do next week. He was keeping three or four things in his mind simultaneously, and just watching and thinking, 'Okay, this is how it's done,' was a real joy."

Perry also credits Chris Carter with his introduction to the role of producer. "I learned really to produce on *Millennium*," he explains. "They let me edit, they let me cast. That's a great gift that Chris Carter gives to his writers, to turn them into producers, just by saying, 'Look, you're going to do this, you will learn how to do this, you will mess things up and you will have to correct them in the editing room,' and that is the greatest lesson ever."

The role of producer often requires a flexible approach to scripting, as Perry learned prior to his work on *Millennium*. "The show I worked on the year before was *The Practice* and David Kelley would write a whole script, then the first day's dailies would come in, the footage that you had shot yesterday. He would watch it and he'd go, 'Look at that actress. She has incredible chemistry with the main character of our show.' We'd go, 'That's interesting, yeah. On film it looks that way,' even though it was written for a tiny little part. So then a rewrite would come out and suddenly she has thirty scenes.

"What he taught me is that you always have to react honestly to the footage, to the stuff that's right in front of you and what you planned on, what you hoped to have happen, what you thought might happen is all important, but nothing is authoritative until it has been filmed. So you watch the film as though you are not involved with the show at all. You watch this stuff and you go, 'What are the joys here that we hadn't anticipated?' and the stuff that you had hoped would come through that sometimes doesn't, you just go, 'Well, we can't play that anymore,' and it keeps you alive creatively. That is sort-of the essence of producing—problem solving—but it is also saying that you have to forget all of our plans and go with what's really before us, not getting too involved with what you hoped would happen but always being aware of what really is happening on the film, or on the digital video."

"The Mikado" is notable not only for its celebrated, Gilbert-and-Sullivan-loving, hooded antagonist Avatar but also for a story concept that was genuinely original for its time. "If I were doing a similar story [today] it'd be radically different, taking into account all the things that have happened since," Perry concedes, but the writer is able to admit, "It's been oft imitated, but the imitators never understand what is interesting about the subject matter." The online world exploited by Avatar has exploded since the episode first aired, and the social commentary in "The Mikado" has only become more relevant with each passing year.

Originality is essential to Perry's approach to storytelling. "Personally, if I've seen it before then I don't want to do it." Such a noble approach is not, however, always practical given the demands of network television. "When you're writing a television series, if it's a whole year, it's twenty-four episodes. Ideally, you want to never repeat anything. But people get exhausted! You've been locked together in this room, and it starts turning into Stockholm syndrome, where people will say or do anything to get another episode out. You sometimes see that on television series. I don't think that it's people deciding, 'Hey, let's go and repeat what other people have done.' I think it's more just, 'We have to have another episode and we could do a variation on that one.' And I've had many things I've written turn up on other people's series the year following. 'The Mikado' got knocked off by a variety of other T.V. series, it got knocked off by a movie, and it's always funny to get emails and phone calls from people saying, 'Hey, are you gonna sue those guys for taking your idea?' You could spend your whole life trying to track that stuff down."

Millennium's creative team had a novel resource upon which to call if they were ever stuck for inspiration. "We had the best way of coming up with stories ever," reveals Perry. "Our consultants were these people called the Academy Group, and it was the very agents who had created the behavioral profiling unit at the F.B.I., the unit that is fictionalized in *The Silence of the Lambs* and *Red Dragon*. These were the real guys, and they had gone around and talked to many, many serial killers and figured [profiles] out by looking at crime scene photos or by going to a crime scene. They could tell you, 'This guy was between this age and that age. He was probably employed, or not employed.' They could tell you tons of stuff just by looking at gory crime scene photos.

"I called them up all the time, and I would always say, 'What are you doing today?' I would never say, 'Tell me a story of something cool you did,' because they always think you want to hear something similar to what was on T.V. And they would say, 'Well, we're staking out at such-and-such a place where we think a guy's gonna come back,' or 'We're interrogating a suspect,' or whatever kind of thing. And I just constantly asked them, 'How do you do your work? How do you guys apprehend these really difficult-to-apprehend murderers?'

"When you talk to homicide detectives, about ninety percent of homicides are ridiculously easy to solve, because it's usually some guy who goes around for weeks or months saying, 'If I ever see that guy who slept with my wife, I'm going to kill him!' And then that guy winds up dead and everybody says, 'Hey, that guy said he was going to kill that guy if he saw him,' and they close it. But then there's that tiny pie slice of five or ten percent of murders that are not done for financial gain, they're not done to cover up a crime, they're not done for revenge. They're done for crazy reasons. And it used to be that was just chaos, nobody knew how to solve those things."

This changed through the F.B.I.'s pioneering work with profiling, as Perry explains. "The Behavioral Science Unit said, 'There're lots of sub-species of crazy. There're lots of different reasons. And crazy people have reasons, they're just crazy reasons, and we can go in and sort those out. We can figure out exactly how to do this kind of stuff.' The first thing they do is that they look at crime scene photos, do crime scene analysis, and decide what kind of person should the police be looking for.

"But they had tons of other stuff they did, too. One of them was that they would use their psychological insights to make people confess, by bonding with another person, by giving them an opportunity to say what they have always wanted to say. A lot of the kind of murderers that they would apprehend might have some part within them that wants to stop, that wants to tell everything and get it off their chest. I would ask them, 'How do you do that? A guy who's going to tell you that is going to go to jail forever,' and they would tell me story after story after story about that kind of stuff.

"So, for example, that's what Lance does so incredibly well in 'Nostalgia.' I really feel that 'Nostalgia' is an underrated episode. Lance and Klea's performances in there are straight out of all those conversations with those people. There's a five-minute scene between Lance and the character Jerry Nielson. That is straight out of the many conversations I would have with these very interesting and cool guys. On *Millennium* we had a lot of opportunities to do that kind of thing."

Though the Academy Group provided a mine of potential story ideas, the predicament facing the series' creative team at the start of Season Three was not easily resolved. "*Millennium* is such an interesting show, because the first year was run by one group of people, and the second year was run by a group of people who really had a totally different aesthetic approach to the people who did Season One, and then they destroyed all of the Earth's population in the final episode, and we were all convinced it was going to be canceled."

So certain was Perry that *Millennium*'s world had ended with the apocalyptic events of "The Fourth Horseman" that he began to actively seek other projects. "I would go interview on other T.V. series and they would say, 'But you're under contract to *Millennium*.' I would say, 'Look, I've read the final script, there's a plague, it kills several main characters and everybody on Earth.' And they would go, 'Oh, you're going to be canceled.' I was getting ready to try to get a job for the next season when I got a call and they said, 'Hey, guess what? *Millennium* is coming back for Season Three.' I said, 'But Earth's population is dead and they've lost Megan!' And they said, 'Yeah, well, you'll have to try to figure that out, won't you? So that's the work ahead of you!'" Perry thereby returned in the role of producer for the series' final season.

In a creative sense, does such a marked change in the aesthetic from one season to the next help keep a series fresh? "It does, but I did miss Megan Gallagher," Perry opines. "I thought she added a great counterpoint to some of the other characters in the show, and narratively we needed that humanity. In Season Three the person who filled it in was Brittany Tiplady. She brought heart to the show, brought a kind of humanity and softness. A lot of the scenes where you watch Lance and Brittany Tiplady, they just have this really great father-daughter chemistry, and you see Lance doing some of his best work with a little girl. And she was really good also. Anyway, I feel like we missed Megan. We made up for it by leaning a little more heavily on Brittany Tiplady, and she was certainly up to it."

The changes in character and setting were productive in terms of keeping the series fresh, but there remained challenges. For some fans, *Millennium*'s third year took far too long to address the climactic events of its second season finale. This lack of closure proved as frustrating for the professionals working on the series as it was for viewers. "At the beginning of Season Three we had another showrunner who didn't work out," explains Perry, "and Chip [Johannessen] was second in command. Chip had a lot of ideas, but the other guy who was brought in for whatever reason was not a good match for the show. So in a lot of the early episodes we had to duck and dodge to not establish anything that didn't feel right and try to do episodes that stayed in the reality of the show and didn't contradict things that had happened, but without answering everything. Once we got the command structure straightened out, then we could start approaching those sorts of things very directly."

Were *Millennium*'s writers told what not to write rather than given a more positive focus? "It wasn't that unusual. On most shows some amount of uncertainty exists as to what direction to take; that's why they need writers. I prefer a slightly chaotic atmosphere because you can have a real influence on the strategic decisions and more variety in storytelling. It's harder work, though, than being on a more rigid format like a typical procedural where a body shows up in the teaser and a perp is arrested in the final scene."

Though it took some time to address the Marburg virus outbreak and Catherine's death, the creative minds behind the scenes still found novel and captivating stories to tell. "I felt that we did a lot of original and bold material on Season Three of *Millennium*. I would say that's not one of the shows that I felt like we were re-hashing other people's stories."

Among such stories was "Collateral Damage." Perry goes on to describe his inspiration for the politically charged episode. "I read a lot of conspiracy theory literature, not because I believe many conspiracy theories but because I find it very interesting. I used to listen to Art Bell, and there was the whole Gulf War syndrome thing going on, and I wanted to do a whole thing about the conflict between personal conscience and duty. What happens when those two things get into radical conflict?

"We had [Eric Swan] played by James Marsters, who is such a brilliant actor that, even though I was a *Buffy* fan, when he came to audition to play the character he blew us away. That guy had the role the second he walked out of the door, and I didn't recognize him as Spike from *Buffy the Vampire Slayer* even though I had seen five or ten episodes of that. But in that, with duty versus conscience, we had a lot of different ways of going at it, and one of them was what happens when a solider is told to fire on his own troops for some corrupt reason. But then in present day, what happens when Peter Watts works for the Millennium Group and he knows that he could save his own daughter by selling out the Millennium Group? So it was a thing that happened in 1993 and a thing that's happened in present day, both all tied up together. So I guess story ideas come from talking to people, listening to people, reading things, stuff like that."

There was some negative reaction—notably from Lance Henriksen himself—to the frictions played out between the characters of Frank Black and Peter Watts, as well as between Frank and the wider Millennium Group. There was a certain inevitability in this new dynamic, however, as Perry explains. "I felt that Morgan and Wong had set up the Millennium Group as having a certain darker side, and Peter Watts being part of that. So we had to play that. We had to roll with that, because it was part of the official narrative of the show. Nothing for me is more disappointing than watching a show that just ignores stuff that happened in the past, and so you inherit a thing like that. It's a hand that you're dealt and you have to play it the best you can, and I loved Terry O'Quinn, particularly in 'Collateral Damage,' where I think we played it the most nakedly. He has a sparkly threat; he's charismatic and threatening at the same time. He keeps a lot of stuff inside and, of course, it played on a lot of the characteristics that he has personally in *Lost*. I was totally thrilled with how he came off in Season Three."

Ultimately, the clashes between these two commanding figures see them become all-out enemies, although the scenes they share in the series finale, "Goodbye to All That," hint at a complex and multifaceted relationship. "It pays off," says Perry, "and also the scenes with those two actors together have so much depth and history. It might be that because they are such good actors and both guys carry so much in their body, in their face, in the tiniest gesture, we could write away from that stuff and they wouldn't have to explain the relationship because they played it so clearly. So you could just have a few words here and there, and have a very powerful scene. You can't do that with very many people. Lance Henriksen would be number one, Terry O'Quinn would be number two, and I think there're very few people in that club that you just look at them and think you don't need to give them very much dialogue explaining the relationship because it's right there."

Perry outright rejects any suggestion that the mixed reaction to Season Three was a response to a lack of dedication on the part of the creative team working on the series. "There's no conspiracy. We really, honestly, every time are trying the best we can to make the best episodes we can given the circumstances. Sometimes what seems like a difficulty turns into a creative opportunity. I loved going onto a show where they go, 'Hey, they destroyed all of the Earth's population. What are you gonna do?' My favorite kind of thing is where people believe they've been painted into a corner and saying, 'No, we can do all kinds of great stuff with this.' Similarly, on a television series when—for whatever circumstance—sometimes, say, an actor might be sick. I think one of the best subplots [on *The X-Files*] came about because [Gillian Anderson] had to take maternity leave, and it turned into this incredible conspiracy involving aliens that they hadn't planned on, but they said, 'Look, we have this opportunity. We have to write around her, let's see what we can do.'"

Another of Perry's scripts for *Millennium*'s third season allowed him to rise to just such a challenge when he was handed the task of incorporating the rock band Kiss into the episode "Thirteen Years Later." How did the likes of Gene Simmons, Paul Stanley, Peter Criss, and Ace Frehley come to play a role in the ominous world inhabited by Frank Black? "Fox Television said, 'Put Kiss in an episode of *Millennium*,'" Perry explains. "Then they said, 'Make it the Halloween episode.' And they had to perform a song. Each of them needed a speaking role, out of make-up, and the kicker [was that] only two were real actors. This was non-negotiable. I know, because Ken Horton valiantly tried to get them to relent during several loud phone calls. How we got Kiss into *Millennium* was entirely our own business. At the time I was working on a more typical episode: basically, Frank visits a town where an old case is being made into a movie and sees telltale signs of the crime recurring. Chip and Ken came in to tell me how the episode I was partway through outlining had to change; mine was the only script that could be ready in time for a Halloween airdate. Very quickly, it had to be gutted and rebuilt to accommodate the Kabuki-faced kings of stadium rock."

The writer's solution was to embrace the implausibility inherent in the proposition. "It's such a crazy idea that I had to say, 'This is a crazy story. It's being told by a crazy man.' It seemed like an unnatural fit. How could you possibly have Kiss on *Millennium*? But [it was easier] once you go, 'No, we have to accept that; that's what's going to happen. They are going to be in that episode. It'll either be a good episode or a bad episode. Do the best you can with it.'

"It was like one of those games where you pull thirty random words out of a hat and make a poem. The words I pulled were: Halloween, Frank Black, a movie being made of an old murder case, and lots and lots of Kiss. Everyone around the office groused that there's no room for Kiss in the *Millennium* diegesis. In their complaints, I found a creative approach: Frank Black would encounter a film that was an intentional distortion of a real case, and he could be as appalled at the distortions in tone, style, etc. that were in the movie-in-the-episode as my officemates were at the very idea of a Kiss Halloween episode. A wee bit of deconstruction goes a long way. Here was an opportunity to put the usual complaints about our show into the mouths of characters and have Frank Black respond and defend his honor and worldview. The episode would contain its own critique. Jacques Derrida might've had a field day, if he ever watched.

"I am a connoisseur of 1970s and 1980s horror movies and decided to pack the episode with references to favorites such as *Halloween*, *Motel Hell*, *The Hitcher*, and so on. Many details of life on B-movie sets came from my wife's firsthand experiences. For example, it was she who told me that, whenever a nude scene was about to be filmed, producers would 'coincidentally' show up on the set to see how things were going. Tacky, funny, and true."

It was a collaborative suggestion from a fellow staff writer that inspired Perry to force Frank Black to face the monsters in some of his favorite horror movies. "After the outline was published, while I was writing the script, Kay Reindl and/or Erin Maher contributed a favorite detail: have Frank Black watch all these horror movies for the first time but use his profiling talents to intuit the end of the movie after seeing only one or two scenes. Impossible? Of course. But it's exactly the kind of boast the insane man who thinks he has become Frank Black would make. It's a great bit and Lance ran with it. After the first read of this script, Lance had a couple of questions—who wouldn't?—but once he bought into the conceptual break with the other episodes he was brilliant and brought many special nuances to his performance.

"As I wrote, the piece took on an unexpected vitality of its own. The point of the poetry game—thirty words out of a hat—is to reach strange, dark corners of the unconscious mind that might never otherwise surface. Similarly, 'Thirteen Years Later' may have begun as an obligatory assignment, but turned into a surprisingly personal and strange exploration of why I love horror movies, the pleasures and pain of low-budget filmmaking, as well as a civil answer to the people who didn't really 'get' our show and wished it were more like *Murder, She Wrote*."

Alongside Henriksen, Perry also credits the episode's director in rising to the challenge. "Tom Wright did a phenomenal job with the most physically demanding episode ever—including many, many stunts and a musical number—while still making the schedule. Many *Millennium* fans will still hate 'Thirteen Years Later' thirteen years later. That's their privilege. But it's a very fun and crazy episode."

The aforementioned "Nostalgia" is another of Perry's episodes on which he is quick to praise *Millennium*'s most prolific director. "Tom Wright knocked himself out on that show," he proclaims. "It has a totally different visual style than many of the other episodes. He went very close to people's faces. He had to use a special optical thing called a split-focus diopter in order to get some of those amazing compositions. Tom Wright started out as a storyboard artist for Alfred Hitchcock, so he thinks, 'These are the elements that need to be in the frame,' and then figures out how to get them in there.

The script for "Nostalgia" also provides Lance Henriksen's third season co-star with an opportunity to step forward and show her talent. "That episode has, I think, the best performance by Klea Scott in any episode that she is in. I think that she is a phenomenal actress. I'm shocked, honestly, that she hasn't gone on to be the lead on another show. But [she is at her best] in that episode when she's visiting her hometown, meeting kids she knew when she was a little girl, and now they are adults in this place that she had such fond memories of that turns out to be part of the real world. In that, it wasn't the place: it was the time. It was her childhood that was so innocent and pure, it wasn't South Mills, Pennsylvania that was so pure. The scenes that she gets with the sheriff of that town, Tommy, calling him on these little tiny mistakes that he made, these little tiny lies that he did to avert being embarrassed but that opened the door for a guy to kill a bunch of women, she does it with real humanity. She's not the condemning, typical T.V. cop; she's broken-hearted. It is such a rare and beautiful performance to see. She's so good in these episodes."

Perry subverted the typical approach to revealing the identity of the perpetrator in this installment, which in turn allowed him to explore some unusual territory. "It is in some ways a straightforward procedural, but I did a dirty trick. In the first five scenes we say, 'This is the guy who did it.' Because it's Frank Black and he realizes, 'This is the guy who did it,' we've taken the whodunit element off the table and now it becomes how are you going to bring this guy to justice, and what are the social elements? What is the culpability of the other people in this town, the people who knew this woman and let her death go unnoticed and let the fact that [in relation to] the very first victim, years ago, nobody even knew it was a murder? It was because she wasn't politically connected. She wasn't powerful. She was like a girl who hung around bars and everybody laid her, and nobody respected her, even in death. It becomes an episode about how—even though I'm not a person who says it is society's fault—it sometimes is a thing that serial killers learn they get away with it because they start preying on victims who aren't powerful people: sometimes prostitutes, sometimes just people who are not well connected."

As was often the case on *Millennium*, there are parallels between the story and high-profile real world serial killing cases. "That's how the Green River Killer got away with it for so long," Perry explains. "And in Los Angeles, in 2010, we had a guy who got picked up, and he had killed eight women in South Central Los Angeles during the Eighties and nobody looked very hard. They said it was drug crimes, it was crack whores, and it wasn't always… This guy knew, in this neighborhood, that he could get away with it. It was seeing in real life the same thing, so the message of that show was that you've got to investigate all of these things, everybody is valuable, and that in covering up their small embarrassments—everybody had had an affair with this girl years ago and it was a little crude so they hid her diaries—they let all of the subsequent victims get killed.

"Tom really brought that out beautifully, he did a fantastic job with that stuff. Lance's final interrogation is brilliant, and Klea in her scenes with this guy that she knew in third grade, and now she knows him and he's a local sheriff and she's an F.B.I. agent. I wanted to play that she's really gone places and he hasn't. There's still an affection between them but also she's disappointed in the compromises that he has made, and we see that these compromises that he made have allowed all of these other people to die. I just really loved that episode."

As well as some singular, standout episodes of *Millennium*, Perry wrote an unproduced script titled "Dirty Snowball." To this day, the episode-that-never-was is something of a celebrated fan legend. "I got hired on *Millennium* and was very excited," Perry recalls. "Morgan and Wong were going to develop a theme across the entire season of a comet that was bringing millennial changes. I think they were inspired by the thirty-nine members of the Heaven's Gate cult who committed suicide. These guys were down in a rich suburb of San Diego, California, and they had actually heard on Art Bell's T.V. series that behind this comet is a spaceship. Totally untrue, but nevertheless they believed it and they decided they were going to get on that spaceship by taking apple sauce laced with cyanide, that would somehow or other transport them up to the comet.

"I thought, 'Well, this is cool material. It's great, it's millennial, it's crime-related,' and my first pitch to Morgan and Wong was, 'Let's do a story centered in a group like that and have the Millennium Group investigating a group of people who are going to do what may be their right. They may have the right to kill themselves. The Millennium Group may have no standing; the F.B.I. may have no standing. How do you fit into a thing like that?' It was a great way to define the difference between the F.B.I.—which can only respond to crimes—and the Millennium Group, who are a sort of extra-legal, more powerful organization that is trying to avert some great disaster that is going to happen at Y2K, either because Y2K is going to change all of the world or simply because people believe that it will, and if enough people believe something is true it becomes like Nazi Germany. All the things that the Nazis believed were certainly not true, and yet because they all believed it they took some pretty heinous action. I wrote an outline, got notes on the outline, I wrote a script, gave them the script and that was it. They said, 'We're not going to do it.'"

Though the script was never produced, there is something enticing about the thought of this lost installment of *Millennium*. "The premise was that there was one group of people who had committed a group suicide like the ones in San Diego, and the Millennium Group—through Frank Black, largely—became convinced that it was going to happen again. In trying to infiltrate it they happened to cross paths with a woman who does a daily astronomy radio broadcast, who is the character Roedecker's favorite radio voice. He's in love with this mysterious voice. He sets out to meet her and they have this real chemistry. They are both people who have accepted their lot in life as loners and yet here they are; they have really found each other. It has this tragic love story that runs through it, because in the end it turns out that they are separated with extreme prejudice, so to speak. But it gave a human side to Roedecker and it gave Frank Black a chance to see the difference between the F.B.I. and the Millennium Group.

"It was a cool investigation and it was a fun episode, but [Morgan and Wong] just said, 'It's going into the bottom drawer, we're not going to do that. We're doing all that Owls and Roosters stuff, taking the show in a different direction.' This sort of stuff happens, but I thought, 'I am so fired,' because you don't want to do that as a television writer, to have somebody say, 'We're not going to make your episode.' The message to everybody all the way up the feeding chain is clear: 'This guy can't write this show.' So, although I love that script, [for] the people in the office—for whatever reason—just the times had changed in-between when I started writing it and when I finished the draft."

Fortunately, Perry is able to link his disappointing experience with the script for "Dirty Snowball" to what became his most celebrated episode of *Millennium*. "Part of the fear of what happened there [was that] I said to myself that my next episode, 'The Mikado'—although it wasn't called that yet—has to be good enough that if they do fire me I can hold up a script and say, 'I got fired after writing this.' It had to be good enough to stand up on its own. It had to be a barn-burner, one that if you read it you go, 'That's a rocking episode!' I just put a lot of stuff in there, so out of the ashes of 'Dirty Snowball'—which is an astronomer's description of a comet—came the fear that motivated me to write a very thought-provoking and scary procedural plus. That's what I think described what *Millennium* does best: procedural with a big, interesting theme. And so out of that came 'The Mikado', which people loved."

"Dirty Snowball" was destined never to make it to the screen but it has never been forgotten, by the fans or its writer. "I started writing a synopsis of it a year ago," Perry reveals. "It genuinely does exist. I could probably find paperwork because it had a production number and I got paid for it and all that kind of stuff, but it never got made and it is fan lore. I can't send the script around because it is owned by Fox. The strangest thing is that when a show is canceled, if they have outstanding episodes they finish them all, even if they won't be aired, because they think it might have an afterlife. Similarly, on a show that has ordered scripts that they know they are never going to shoot, they nevertheless have the writers go through every draft, they get notes from the network or from the studio who's paying the salary and then it goes into a drawer someplace, in case the thing ever comes back to life. I think *Star Trek* was the example of a show than got canceled—from low ratings or whatever reason that they canceled the original *Star Trek*—and then later it became the most valuable property in all of Paramount history."

As the interview nears its end, Perry reflects upon his time on the series. "It's impossible to compare working on *Millennium* to working on any other show because it was such an astonishing learning experience. Chris Carter makes a point of ensuring that new writers learn how to produce their own scripts. You learn rewriting, casting, working with the various departments like Props, Costumes, Locations, Production Design and so on, and work closely with the director. Later, you sit in the editing room with the editors and face the consequences of your decisions—after they've been irrevocably committed to film, and there's no one to blame for the problems except yourself—and it's up to you to fix them. Perhaps the most fun part [is when] you go over to Mark Snow's house and he plays all the music cues and solicits feedback."

Though he also served as Executive Story Editor for Season Two of *Millennium* and as a producer for Season Three, it is the writing from which Perry took the most enjoyment. "Writing is the engine that pulls all the other titles along behind it," he explains. "Without the writing, there is no story editing, there is no producing." He has particularly fond memories of working with Chip Johannessen and a deep appreciation for the type of following the series attracted. "It's a smart group of people. You read what people write about the show and you think, 'Wow, these are unique fans. These are people who get it, who look in.' The viewer that you imagine, the viewer that you hope for, that goes and dissects the thing, picks up all the sub-themes, understands the threads that connect one to another. And even when they are complaining and saying, 'This didn't quite work,' you think, 'Huh, we thought we got away with that!' It's nice to have somebody watching closely enough to pick up on all that stuff."

Michael R. Perry left his mark on *Millennium*, and *Millennium* has left its mark on him. "It was a great couple of years of hard work and creative challenges. It changed the way I write, the way I think about television production. That can only happen to you once."

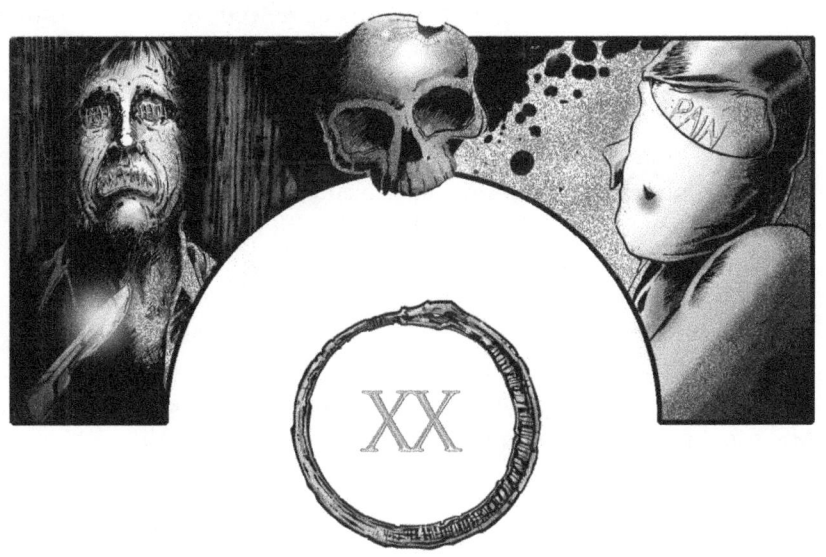

SECOND SIGHT:
PROFILING, PROPHECY, AND DEDUCTIVE REASONING IN CHRIS CARTER'S *MILLENNIUM*

by Brian A. Dixon

> "He makes, in silence, a host of observations and inferences. So, perhaps, do his companions; and the difference in the extent of the information obtained, lies not so much in the validity of the inference as in the quality of the observation. The necessary knowledge is that of what to observe."
>
> —Edgar Allan Poe
> "The Murders in the Rue Morgue" (1841)

When Frank Black (Lance Henriksen) buttons up his coat and bows beneath strands of police tape to stand beside the chalk outlines and blood stains of a gruesome crime scene, a knowing audience braces for the inevitable onslaught of sensory cues. There will be warm blood and hot fire, breaking bones and torn sinew, screams of agony and the din of a desperate struggle. *Millennium* (1996-99), created by Chris Carter, appropriates and ambitiously reinterprets the familiar signs, characters, and formula of the classical detective story by positioning the incomparable investigator at the heart of its drama against a seemingly insurmountable tide of violence, crime, and evil. Never before has a detective been challenged with overcoming ominous mysteries on such an apocalyptic scale. Frank Black must possess an extraordinary gift, and the cinematic style of *Millennium* represents a milestone in the evolution of the detective drama that left an indelible mark on the landscape of televisual crime.

The classical detective story originates most clearly in "The Murders in the Rue Morgue" (1841), a tale by Edgar Allan Poe that boasts a literary formula so effective that it would be adopted wholesale by countless writers and critics in the decades that would follow. It is a formula still satisfying audiences today and its influence is to be found in every modern day cozy, crime thriller, and police procedural on television. Poe's narrative invention proved to be so prescient it almost singlehandedly launched those genres that would come to dominate late nineteenth and twentieth century popular culture. On a number of levels, Poe can be viewed as a creative ancestor to Carter and this literary lineage is traceable in the development of *Millennium*.

"The Murders in the Rue Morgue" concerns the mysteries inherent to a crime scene as ghastly as any inspected by Frank Black but, in a move quite uncharacteristic of Poe's fiction, the narrative proper is prefaced by an abstract thesis on the subject of analytical thinking. "I am not now writing a treatise," Poe interjects rather defensively, "but simply prefacing a somewhat peculiar narrative by observations very much at random" (76). In spite of his protests, the author's commentary on the analytical powers certainly stands as a treatise, and his thoughts on the subject of those skills that allow players to triumph at games of strategy are hardly random. The author is declaring, more overtly than ever before, what he famously referred to as the "single effect" of the narrative, the sole dominant thought or emotion that must dictate each word and every turn of phrase in a unified short story. Analysis, analytical thinking, is the driving philosophy at work.

It is obvious from the very nature of the story's opening that Poe's ultimate purpose in composing "The Murders in the Rue Morgue" has less to do with invocations of terror than with the virtues expounded upon in the thesis. As he describes the means by which a player adept at the game of draughts might overcome his opponent, he is establishing the very talents that the detective hero will henceforth use to apprehend those wicked souls responsible for murder: "Deprived of ordinary resources, the analyst throws himself therewith, and not unfrequently sees thus, at a glance, the sole methods (sometimes indeed absurdly simple ones) by which he may seduce into error or hurry into miscalculation" (76). With the cruel murder of Madame L'Espanaye and her daughter Camille, Poe is outlining a new genre, and the driving ideal behind the detective tale is asserted from the story's opening epigraph from Sir Thomas Browne: "What song the Syrens sang, or what name Achilles assumed when he hid himself among women, although puzzling questions, are not beyond *all* conjecture" (75).

A close reading of the story suggests the reasons for Poe's overwrought attempt to spell-out this defining characteristic of the detective story, a notion that would go on to plague Chris Carter, Lance Henriksen, and *Millennium* more than a hundred and fifty years later. In his preface, Poe describes the character of the analytical thinker and those skills that endow him with a superior intellect. "He is fond of enigmas," Poe writes, describing the personality of countless future investigators, "of conundrums, hieroglyphics; exhibiting in his solution of each a degree of *acumen* which appears to the ordinary apprehension præternatural. His results, brought about by the very soul and essence of method, have, in truth, the whole air of intuition" (75). Here, the rational is placed in direct opposition to the "præternatural," and the emphasis is both vital and necessary. Indeed, "The Murders in the Rue Morgue" is littered with uses of the latter term. There is to be no confusion; Poe ensures that the audience does not mistake the analytical abilities of his hero for some preternatural perception. The end result of analytical thinking should be astonishing, especially in a well-crafted detective tale, but this is the merit of a gifted mind, not of some supernatural occurrence.

The hero of the "The Murders in the Rue Morgue" is C. Auguste Dupin, the first detective in fiction and the prototype of Sherlock Holmes, Frank Black, and all who would follow. Dupin is a withdrawn and eccentric figure, detached from society at large and given to sullen reveries. He is a man who prefers the darkness to the light and spends his nights engrossed in philosophical musings and quiet observation. Most remarkable of all is that fact that the hidden machinations of his analytical mind not only allow him to disentangle stimulating riddles, they offer him uncanny insight into the motives of his fellow man. As his anonymous companion, narrator of the tale, explains, "He boasted to me, with a low chuckling laugh, that most men, in respect to himself, wore windows in their bosoms, and was wont to follow up such assertions by direct and very startling proofs of his intimate knowledge of my own" (79). Dupin is the personification of those qualities exemplified by the story's thesis, the very archetype of a superior analyst. His intuitive skills not only enable him to connect and elucidate an array of complex clues but also to discern the innermost thoughts of any man's mind. His talents are wasted in his literary immersions and midnight wanderings until the occurrence of those appalling murders in the Rue Morgue when, following a whim born of boredom, Dupin sets his extraordinary mind at the challenge of solving a seemingly impossible crime.

The formulaic essentials of Poe's model were adapted and, indeed, significantly improved by Arthur Conan Doyle when he began to write a series of detective stories that would soon find their place as the most celebrated and beloved in all of literature. The locked rooms along the Seine in Paris are left behind as these stories embrace the rich character and atmosphere of the streets of London and, beyond, the English countryside. Gone is the anonymous first-person narrator, replaced by the caring and attentive Dr. John Watson. In the public eye, C. Auguste Dupin's taciturn analytics evolve into the wit and professional dedication of the world's first consulting detective, the incomparable Sherlock Holmes. Doyle's works would prove incalculably influential. There is something of Holmes in every detective hero to follow, and Frank Black is no exception.

Chapter Two of Doyle's *A Study in Scarlet* (1887), fittingly entitled "The Science of Deduction," begins with an introductory tour of the well-furnished rooms to be found at No. 221B Baker Street and swiftly initiates a skeptical Dr. Watson in the feats of deductive reasoning by which his newfound companion makes his living as a consulting detective. Holmes "claimed by a momentary expression, a twitch of a muscle or a glance of an eye, to fathom a man's innermost thoughts." Watson's reaction, as ever, parallels the reaction of the reader and expresses the same concern for credibility so evident in Poe's work: "So startling would his results appear to the uninitiated that until they learned the processes by which he had arrived at them they might well consider him as a necromancer" (14).[1] Our only insight into the inner workings of Holmes's mind is to be found in his improvisatory violin playing, which expresses "the thoughts which possessed him," an activity that obscurely symbolizes "the tantalizingly indecipherable inner workings of Doyle's 'calculating machine'" (Rzepka 125-26). The heroic potential of Holmes's talents is soon established as Watson learns that Holmes is interested only in applying his singular mind to the task of solving crimes, a task at which he is uniquely adept. "There is a strong family resemblance about misdeeds," Holmes confidently assures us, "and if you have all the details of a thousand at your finger ends, it is odd if you can't unravel the thousand and first" (Doyle 15). Sherlock Holmes would go on to demonstrate the truth of his mantra in a further three novels and fifty-six short stories.

    The traits exemplified by C. Auguste Dupin and Sherlock Holmes, traits that would become so exquisitely embodied in the form of Frank Black, are essential to our understanding of the appeal of the classical detective genre as a whole. Analytical thinking, deductive reasoning, or ratiocination resonate at the very heart of the detective tale. In John G. Cawelti's discerning study of genre, *Adventure, Mystery, and Romance: Formula Stories as Art and Popular Culture* (1976), the author emphasizes those qualities that drive the detective story as a popular genre and, in so doing, he repeatedly returns to the balance between detection and mystification, the difference between reassuring certainty and a worrying uncertainty. This balance is essential to the genre and to the satisfaction of a reader immersed in a detective story. Each clue offers the reader a tantalizing glimpse of truth, each dead end or red herring serves only to heighten an ever-mounting sense of stupefaction. The language of "The Murders in the Rue Morgue" suggests that, to the intelligent mind, an analytical puzzle is "a source of the liveliest enjoyment" (75). As Poe's prototype for the genre insists so emphatically, analytical thinking is not simply some quirky character trait or a gimmicky literary device to be employed in tying up a tangled mystery plot at its climax; the narrative, structure, and dominant effect of every detective story is inherently tied to its unique depiction of the deductive process.

    The link between the science of deduction as elucidated by Poe and Doyle and the real work of criminal detection is far stronger than one might expect. It is a connection openly acknowledged by renowned F.B.I. criminal profiler John Douglas. Founder of the Bureau's

Criminal Profiler Program and a onetime unit chief for the Investigative Support Unit at Quantico, Douglas spent his distinguished career studying some of history's most infamous killers—including Edmund Kemper, David Berkowitz, Ted Bundy, John Wayne Gacy, and Charles Manson—and was instrumental in the capture of countless other violent offenders. Douglas found validation in classic detective fiction. In turn, the skills and techniques developed and employed by the agent and his colleagues at the Federal Bureau of Investigation would later provide the basis for new fiction, inspiring a further development of the detective story. In Thomas Harris's *The Silence of the Lambs* (1988), the novel that popularized the serial killer thriller, the character of Jack Crawford is based on John Douglas.

In *Mindhunter* (1995), the first of several bestselling accounts outlining his career tracking serial killers, Douglas writes about the connection between detective fiction and behavioral profiling.

> ...though most of the books that dramatize and glorify what we do, such as Tom Harris's memorable *The Silence of the Lambs*, are somewhat fanciful and prone to dramatic license, our antecedents actually go back to crime fiction more than crime fact. C. August Dupin [*sic*], the amateur detective hero of Edgar Allan Poe's 1841 classic 'The Murders in the Rue Morgue,' may have been history's first behavioral profiler. This story may also represent the first use of a proactive technique by the profiler to flush out an unknown subject and vindicate an innocent man imprisoned for the killings. Like the men and women in my unit a hundred and fifty years later, Poe understood the value of profiling when forensic evidence alone isn't enough to solve a particularly brutal and seemingly motiveless crime. (19-20)

With the advent of behavioral profiling, the sort of analytical deductions wielded by fictional detectives were now being employed to understand, predict, and in some instances direct the behavior of society's most violent criminals, including serial killers. As fellow F.B.I. profiler Robert Ressler describes, the pioneering development of forensic profiling prompted these agents to adopt a new point of view, and their extensive interviews with inmates offered the means by which to see the world through another's eyes. "Formerly, I and everyone else looking into these matters had been on the outside of a killer's mind, looking in; now I was gaining a unique perspective, from the inside of that mind, looking out" (43-44).

The legacy of this fusion of fact and fiction, of detective lore and true crime, is realized in *Millennium*, a landmark television series that reinvents the detective story for the last days of the twentieth century. *Millennium* situates the detective as profiler in a world of deplorable crime and unspeakable horrors. Frank Black, his family, his allies in law enforcement, and his sadistic enemies assume pivotal roles in an increasingly complex and apocalyptic drama formed from the anxieties of the paranoid decade that preceded the turn of the third millennium. In *Millennium*, the detective hero is a self-sacrificing behavioral profiler and the murder suspect often takes the beastly form of evil incarnate; the series pushes its constituent narrative elements to their logical and mythological limits.

Creator Chris Carter's darkest drama, *Millennium* admittedly defies all traditional genre labels, simultaneously adapting and combining the stylistic elements of mystery, horror, police procedurals, scripture, crime thrillers, slasher films, mythic and apocalyptic fiction, and others. The series disrupts those lines that we imagine between genres, reinventing each in turn for its own creative purposes and ultimately defying any definitive attempt at classification. Nevertheless, as the profound mysteries explored in the series consistently originate with criminal investigations, the elements of the classical detective genre are apparent throughout, most visibly in the hero. Frank Black stands as the ultimate evolution of the detective, an epitome of deductive reasoning and empathic spirit, a stalwart figure strong enough to challenge the inconceivable forces sowing chaos in his world. Actor Lance Henriksen's performance in the role is at once powerful and moving, conveying a strength and sensitivity that renders the character real and vital.

From the first Fox network promotional trailers for *Millennium*, part of a $10 million advertising campaign that emphasized the unusual style and sensibilities of this bold new series from the creator of *The X-Files* (1993-2002), it was clear that the protagonist was to be unique.[2] Frank Black's origin is rooted in the investigative traditions of Sherlock Holmes but his own talents would extend well beyond the limits of deductive reasoning as it had been traditionally conceived. Carter explains that the way in which his hero sees the world was essential to his conception of the character and the series.

> The big idea for me was a guy who wants to have a normal life but sees the world differently than everyone else and can't ignore this ability. I think it's something that talented people do, geniuses often do; they see the world in a different way. I think it's something that artists aspire to do, scientists do; they're able to push our concepts of the world forward by looking at things and then communicating them in different and new ways. That was the kind of idea behind this character of Frank Black, somebody who doesn't necessarily have an inborn gift but something he has developed through his hard work with catching criminals, seeing how they operated, knowing them, and ultimately being able to see like them. (Commentary)

In the pilot episode of *Millennium*, Frank vividly describes his abilities in what may be the series' best-remembered monologue: "I see what the killer sees… I put myself in his head. I become the thing we fear the most… I become capability. I become the horror, what we know we can become only in our heart of darkness. It's my gift. It's my curse. It's why I retired." At the moment of his introduction, Frank has spent a distinguished career in law enforcement earning a reputation as a renowned investigator. Indeed, in a crossover with *The X-Files* he would later be described by his forerunner, Fox Mulder, as "the greatest criminal profiler that Quantico ever produced." Frank's insight is incomparable, his dedication unwavering. He possesses the same window into men's souls boasted by Dupin but he must use this gift to inhabit a disturbing psychological terrain the likes of which Poe's indifferent sleuth could not have fathomed.

It is not difficult to discern the links between scripts written by Chris Carter, Ted Mann, or Jorge Zamacona and the literary canon. Each episode of *Millennium*'s first season is preceded by an epigraph, stark upon the screen in decrepit text, a passage taken from verse or novel that presages the themes and subject matter of the drama about to unfold. *Millennium*'s opening quotations introduced many Friday night television viewers to the affecting words of Herman Melville, Jean-Paul Sartre, W. H. Auden, Ernest Renan, and George Eliot. Its investigations into murders and sexual assaults are laden with references to the works of writers such as William Butler Yeats, Anne Sexton, Joseph Conrad, and Jorge Luis Borges. The structure of early installments such as "The Judge" or "Weeds" has been described as "O. Henry by way of Flannery O'Connor" (Uhlich). Given the intricacies of their investigations, it is unsurprising that Frank Black and Peter Watts (Terry O'Quinn) are shown to be exceptionally well-read, their exacting and detail-oriented profession demanding an instant, comprehensive knowledge of religious lore and philosophical treatises. With unabashed erudition and an uncommon cultural awareness, *Millennium* firmly establishes its literacy. The effect is distinctive for a dramatic television series, situating these stories in a distinguished literary tradition.

Prevailing among *Millennium*'s literary nods are the formulaic conceits of the classical detective story, a genre which had been repeatedly reiterated and fractured throughout the twentieth century in "a seemingly endless sequence of… smaller and smaller generic denominations within the 'post-classical' world of detective fiction" (Rushing 18). Just as Doyle did during the anxious last days of the nineteenth century and the Victorian era, Carter inventively draws upon familiar tropes and figures, reimagining them for the tense cultural moment in which he is writing in order to establish a structure of narrative support for his protagonist. The comforting home base of the sleuth, represented so memorably by the sitting room at 221B Baker Street, takes on blatant domestic symbolism in the yellow house at 1910 Ezekiel Drive in Seattle. The Millennium Group's army of expert profilers, forensic psychologists, and medical examiners represents a collected, encyclopedic knowledge of the history of crime, a veritable living library of man's misdeeds. Most notably, the Seattle police for whom Frank regularly consults are dedicated and honest men but, by dramatic necessity, they lack the ingenuity necessary to solve such horrific cases. Lieutenant Bob Bletcher (Bill Smitrovich) and his colleagues serve as the modern day heirs to the Parisian Prefect of Police or Inspector Lestrade. They offer a counterpoint to the astonishing abilities possessed by the hero and evoke earlier iterations of the classical detective story in which "police appeared primarily as foils or straight-men to assorted amateur crime-fighter savants or private detectives" (von Mueller 97). None fill this role more obviously than Detective Bob Giebelhouse (Stephen J. Lang), the affable but so often clueless cop who rushes in with sidearm and handcuffs at the ready when it is at last time to apprehend a suspected serial killer. Giebelhouse's wit is purely comedic, but what he lacks in investigative insight he more than makes up for with his good humor and a bulldog-like tenacity.

Millennium only blatantly acknowledges its debts to classical or hardboiled detective formulas in its comedies, when it is freed from more solemn contemplations. Literary figures take center stage in "Jose Chung's *Doomsday Defense*," the first of two stand-out satirical installments written and directed by the acclaimed Darin Morgan.[3] The episode is, as television critic Matt Roush memorably described it, "written with the density of a *Simpsons* cartoon" and, in lampooning the traditional plots and trappings of *Millennium* in addition to launching a thinly veiled assault on Scientology, it features an uproarious, perhaps inevitable collision between the series' dedicated investigators and the sort of crime fiction clichés that once made for bestsellers. "Jose Chung's *Doomsday Defense*" is littered with books, many of them paperback pulps—such as *Dance on the Blood-Dimmed Tide*—the hardboiled detective thrillers of Juggernaut Onan Goopta. As "*Monsieur Noir*" immerses himself in a copy of Goopta's *The Hacked-Up Hack*—"It's investigative research. Don't be so dark."—he imagines himself as the outrageously upbeat Rocket McGrain, a "roving, freelance, forensic profiler" who has been twisted into an absurd caricature of the hardboiled private dick.

There is an equally knowing comedic critique about Michael R. Perry's Halloween-themed "Thirteen Years Later," a surprisingly meta-textual pastiche of slasher films that appropriates cinematic cues from *Psycho* (1960) and *Halloween* (1978). The episode's array of eccentric suspects, clues, and plot twists prompted Ken Tucker of *Entertainment Weekly* to write that "Thirteen Years Later" boasts "a good murder plot as solidly constructed as an old episode of *Columbo*." There is some humor to be found in drawing attention to the creative divide between the likes of *Millennium* and *Columbo* (1968-2003) but the comparison is stimulating nonetheless and, perhaps, in its invocation of genre, more telling than we might expect.[4]

The true nature of the relationship between *Millennium* and the canon of detective fiction can be found in far more subtle moments during those heart-breaking or pulse-pounding investigations that imbued the series with such a disquieting relevance. There is a revelatory moment in the Chip Johannessen-scripted "Blood Relatives" in which Frank, standing on the shore of a glistening lake, his thoughts dominated by the details of a hideous crime, takes a moment to slip off his coat and tosses it to the waiting Watts. The dedicated viewer knows just what will happen next. Before Bletcher can even cry out a protest, as he did during a similar scene in the pilot, the profiler steps forth and trudges determinedly into the water in search of the case's next clue. He finds it nearly a dozen feet from the shore, fishing with his arm beneath the surface of the water, fingers combing submerged sand and rocks in search of a reflection. He emerges from the lake soaking wet but grasping the evidence that will lead them onward in their search for a brutal killer. Here, as in "Pilot" and "Kingdom Come," water symbolically serves to illustrate a trait that is intrinsic to Frank Black as a character and essential to our understanding of his deductive talents.

If the meaning of the lakeside scene in "Blood Relatives" is lost on the viewer, it is reiterated just moments later as the investigators storm a halfway house that hides a suspected killer. As Bletcher, Giebelhouse, and Watts follow posted signs and spoken directions and head for the subject's bedroom on the second floor of the building, Frank dashes in an entirely different direction, moving underground, to the house's darkened basement, where he discovers that the suspect has escaped them via a cellar window. While the Seattle police search obvious or expected terrain, above the surface, Frank alone dares venture below.

The resolve that Frank demonstrates when he is faced with the barrier of a river, lake, or other body of water is what allows him to dip beneath the murky, seemingly impenetrable surface of the human psyche. Lieutenant Bletcher leads a police force possessed of pedestrian thinking and limited imagination; Frank Black is a man of wholly unconventional thinking with the courage to match it. As an investigator, he possesses both the ability and willingness to venture beyond the boundaries of the safe or the anticipated, that selfless inclination to immerse himself in darkest depths in search of an answer. When Frank follows his own deductive reasoning beyond all foreseen limitations he is allowing himself to be plunged below the surface of what is known into uncertain territory as uninviting as an icy river, as dark and foreboding as any abandoned basement. From a psychological perspective, his forays into the mind of the killer are no less bold.

Millennium is a television series that continually embraces alternate modes of perception, both stylistically and thematically, and it employs a variety of cinematic techniques to develop the themes of the detective genre. Through the eyes of its visionary heroes and its delusional villains, the series explores the way in which our memories, emotions, and instincts reveal themselves in the way that we see the world around us. Among the most captivating of these techniques is to be found in the show's preoccupation with spectatorship, the act of looking. Few thematic preoccupations are as dominant throughout the series.[5] There is an inherent power in the gaze, there is an undeniable threat in a stare, and these ideas are exemplified in the serial killers seen so frequently on the series. It is evident from that first blood-drenched peep show the Frenchman pays to see in the visually arresting "Pilot."

On *Millennium*, spectatorship inevitably gives way to the threat or menace of voyeurism, which inevitably gives way to sudden and brutal death. The only hope for security, in fact, is offered not by fences, locked gates, or burglar alarms—each repeatedly revealed, as in episodes such as "Wide Open" and "Weeds," to be utterly inadequate—but by the gaze of Frank Black. The lurking serial killer is not the only character possessed of a watchful eye. Opposing voyeurism with vigilance, the series shows us the power provided by our eyes and our imaginations and thereby reinforces the unique power of the protagonist. Frank is a hero whose might lies not in his lightning reflexes or his unrivaled strength but in his eyes and in his mind's eye, in his often astonishing capacity for observation. It is what Frank sees, what he chooses and is willing to see, that sets him apart.

One of many stunning stylistic elements that separate *Millennium* from earlier crime dramas is to be found in its attempt to offer a distinctive visual representation of the hero's deductive methods. As the early Fox network promotional trailers reveal, it was one of the show's trademark hooks, an attention-seizing spectacle that instantly distinguished this dark mystery from other detective dramas. Over time, *Millennium* has proven itself to be a landmark series, and this is evident in the breakthrough signified by the hero's visions. Frank Black's gift of perception as realized onscreen represents an innovative cinematic contrivance that served as the vanguard of a narrative device which, in the twenty-first century, would become a standard of the detective story on film and television. As a man possessed of an unrivalled facility for observation and deductive reasoning, Frank sees extraordinary things, and the innovative visual narrative of *Millennium* allows the viewer to experience the detective's mind at work. Never before has the audience's engagement with this essential conceit been so direct or affecting. Deductive reasoning drives the detective story and in *Millennium* the analytical powers are presented as a graphic display of an intensity equal to the horror of the crime. Ratiocination is rendered both visual and visceral, and the effect is groundbreaking.[6]

The impulse to visualize deductive reasoning, a purely abstract mental process, may be inherent to detective fiction. In his essay "A Philosophical View of the Detective Novel," Ernest Bloch observes that the detective story has a specific narrative form, "the form of a picture puzzle" (264). Much has been written of the interactive quality of detective fiction, and the puzzle provided by each story's plot pieces offers an invitation to imagine or, more specifically, envision a solution. The reader anticipates the climax that will accompany the story's revelatory deductions and, necessarily isolated from the thoughts and musings of the detective throughout the narrative, cannot help but attempt to envision the way in which the hero's brilliant mind might organize the array of available clues. Agatha Christie's classic *One, Two, Buckle My Shoe* (1940) provides a striking demonstration of this phenomenon. The moment in which the great detective Hercule Poirot at last solves the mystery linking a number of vexing deaths is described with a dizzying succession of visual cues that would, no doubt, incite a bout of *déjà vu* in Frank Black.

> *He saw it...* He was in a daze—a glorious daze where isolated facts spun wildly round before settling neatly into their appointed places. It was like a kaleidoscope—shoe buckles, size nine stockings, a damaged face, the low tastes in literature of Alfred the page boy, the activities of Mr. Amberiotis, and the part played by the late Mr. Morley, all rose up and whirled and settled themselves down into a coherent pattern. For the first time, Hercule Poirot was looking at the case *the right way up*." (141)

The pieces of the picture puzzle fall neatly into place before the mind's eye of the detective. Christie's language is mesmerizing, her word choice teasing, and the reader is left desperate to see the case as the hero does, "the right way up." On television, in the detective dramas of *Alfred Hitchcock Presents* (1955-65) or *The NBC Mystery Movie* (1971-77), the potential to depict this sort of imagery onscreen would repeatedly go unrealized.

The visions of Frank Black seen on *Millennium* at last provide an artfully constructed means of conveying the genius and horror of the intuitive revelation so essential to the narrative of the detective story. They allow the television audience fleeting, furtive glimpses of the astonishing knowledge possessed by the hero. "I see what the killer sees," Frank declares, and so can we in montages that are both captivating and undeniably frightening. There is reason for Cawleti to so luridly describe the talents of a detective hero as a "terrifying ability to expose hidden secrets," a "demonic power" to identify and project guilt, and that reason is wholly evident in the horror of these quick-cut sequences (95-96). That purely abstract process, the once cold and calculating mental art of ratiocination, is suddenly inseparable from the sensation and the horror, the desperation and the humanity of the crime itself. Blood and tissue samples found under the fingernails of a corpse prompt our hero to re-envision the events of an early killing; the expert analysis voiced by a pathologist induces a visualization of precisely how the newest victim was subdued. Each stylized flash of understanding provides an imaginative extrapolation of the evidence at hand prompted by clue or cue seen, heard, or felt by Frank Black—and, by extension, television audiences.

It would be easy to overlook these sequences or underestimate their significance given the fact that they are so ephemeral. The average vision that Frank experiences on *Millennium* bursts into frenzied life, thrashes in blood before us, and dies in no more than two seconds. The average first season episode contains no more than approximately twelve seconds of hallucinatory footage from the profiler's point of view in total. Based on the running time for an episode of the series, that amounts to 0.4% of the total screen time.

Temporality is a constant thematic concern in *Millennium*—as the show's title implies—and this is shown in its fleeting visions of death. In her studies of temporality and detection in postwar Italian cinema, Domietta Torlasco investigates the way in which films such as *Blow-Up* (1967) and *The Passenger* (1975) dilate time and obsess over the scene of the crime and its visuals, a phenomenon observable more recently in all screen adaptations of Steig Larsson's *The Girl with the Dragon Tattoo* (2005). Recalling the descriptive analysis of Bloch, Torlasco observes that, in many cases, it is "the puzzle in pieces, and not the process of its reassemblage" that exercises "the strongest attraction" in a detective story (78). *Millennium* acknowledges the attraction inherent to the sense of mystification achieved by incomplete or unclear images, frenziedly intercutting footage of fatal immolation and impromptu amputation. It blatantly defies any attempt to fully process them.

In a forty-five minute installment of *Millennium*, we are never permitted to obsess over the hideous imagery of the crime, even if it is everlasting in the mind of Frank Black. Torlasco argues that the investigator is safe, the story is structured, so long as he remains external to the investigation, in "a position of mastery... at the center of the visual field, yet external to it. He is endowed with the power to survey, measure, and evaluate" (80). *Millennium* uses its graphic visions to immerse both hero and audience in the horror of a murder. The profiler's visions take him, very specifically, internally—into the hearts of slaughtered victims, the minds of vicious killers, and the most labyrinthine depths of a criminal investigation.

The brevity of the grotesque spectacle is, of course, tactical as well. Thomas J. Wright, the most prolific of *Millennium*'s directors and the most identified with the series, explains that the strategy in these matters is one of sensitivity as well as dramatic tension. "I think it was sort of a device for the audience, particularly, because that show was so strong and such a tough show, a hard show, and a dark show," Wright suggests. "To actually hold on some of the images like you would like to, of course the network wouldn't let you. So, another way to get these images across to the audience would be these multiple quick cuts of the images, or pieces of them. You get the sense of it without really holding on it" ("Order in Chaos"). The visions end quickly because they must, allowing audiences no more than the briefest of glimpses into the troubling thoughts of Frank Black. We are spared the true horror of the profiler's experience and left desperate to learn, to see more, for it is a defining characteristic that "detective stories often delight in the macabre and exotic" (von Mueller 104). Slowed down, taken frame-by-frame, these lurid visions often reveal details of the crimes never otherwise shown or discussed on screen and thus act as a compelling representation of the complexities of the profiler's investigative thought process. They contain far more detail than could ever be properly absorbed by the audience during a traditional viewing, a veritable sensory overload, revealing just how much artistic effort was put into crafting these fleeting displays on film.

It was David Nutter, director of *Millennium*'s masterful pilot, and Peter Wunstorf, cinematographer, who were challenged with first realizing Frank's visions on film. Their inspired approach involved combining a variety of techniques used in commercial photography with lessons learned from the memorable visual storytelling of Oliver Stone's *JFK* (1991), a film that earned Academy Awards for Best Cinematography and Best Editing. "We actually had gone out early in the process and even spoken to Hank Corwin, who was a famous commercial editor who had cut *JFK*," Nutter explains. "Hank and I sat down and spoke about the work that [Robert Richardson] had done with him and the various techniques and so forth that were used to really create an organic mental picture as far as the characters were concerned" ("Order in Chaos"). Maintaining that sense of the organic would prove integral to realizing the innermost imaginings of *Millennium*'s visionary hero. As Nutter insists, "the camera should be a part of the character" (Probst 50).

Ten Thirteen's cinematographers were inspired to be innovative in crafting these trademark visuals, as Director of Photography Robert McLachlan suggests when he notes that they "came out of some experiments that we did" prior to filming. The end result of those experiments combined a variety of camera and lighting techniques typically employed only in commercial photography to produce imagery that looked entirely unlike anything else previously seen in television drama.[7] McLachlan explains:

> One of the camera rental houses has these strobe lights that are normally used to get super-sharp images of beer being poured or milk being poured and any kind of action and stuff of bubbles coming out of a pop bottle being opened but they give you a super, super sharp image because they fire at 50/1000s of a second. What we did was we combined lighting a scene of some of those images—some of those violent images from the killer's point of view—we lit that with a combination of those strobes and normal light and shot them at six frames a second, which is much slower than you normally film at, and then printed them back to normal, and what you got was an image that was both blurry and extremely sharp at the same time. And then, added to that, we played with the stop on the camera and turned the camera on and off. It was sort of a mixed bag of things all being done at once, and then we pulled most of the color out most of the

time. Maybe we'd leave just the red in if there was a lot of blood or whatever, or not. It created a really unique look. ("Order in Chaos")

The end result is a stimulating sensory experience. The deductive process written about so endlessly in literature, the ideal that provides the basis for all detective stories, is realized with startling intensity onscreen.

The idea of this abstract mental process rendered sensory was a core component of Carter's concept for his protagonist. "Frank sees things differently than the rest of us," the show's creator suggests in a commentary recorded to accompany the pilot. "He's able to make connections, which I guess is a mark of genius, the idea of seeing patterns and things that other people don't see." Such an understanding was fundamental to actor Lance Henriksen's performance in the role. "You know how a great chess player works, right?" Henriksen asks. "They study, they study, they study—they know all the moves of different great chess players. I always felt Frank Black had morphed into a person who put abstract loose ends together in his head in a way that other people couldn't." The profiler, Henriksen observes, possesses the unique ability to envision the whole of the narrative puzzle. "He could take threads of an idea and they would suddenly appear to him almost as a linear story. In other words, walking into a room he would see pieces of a puzzle like a great chess player and he would string them together" (Henriksen 230). In spite of obvious differences in narrative form and style, *Millennium*'s creator and star both observe that there is a connection between the appalling things seen with unfortunate regularity by Frank and those picture puzzles mentally assembled by detectives such as Hercule Poirot.

This sort of thinking has been honed to a science by Dr. Roger Depue, a veteran of the F.B.I.'s Behavioral Science Unit who founded the Academy Group in 1989 and thereby inspired the creation of its fictitious counterpart, the Millennium Group. When asked about the sort of scrutiny he applies to the clues found at a crime scene, Depue indicates that fantasy provides the link between killer, profiler, and, in the case of a Ten Thirteen television series, audience. "Fantasy is very important," Depue argues. "Many times in a crime you can see the fantasy of the perpetrator. Frank Black does this from time to time. He does it in a more dramatic way than we do it. He almost sees it. You see these splashes and flashes of what he's seeing." Though the experience conveyed in an episode of *Millennium* does not precisely match with that of Depue and his associates in the Academy Group, the end result is the same. "We do something similar to that. We look at the crime scene and we see the behavior there and we see the evidence of the fantasy and we say, 'I know what this guy is thinking. I've seen this before'" ("Chasing the Dragon"). Carter's premise has a firm basis in true methods of criminal detection.

An emphasis on the significance of evidentiary detail is also expressed by writer Chip Johannessen, who would become an executive producer on the series in its third and final season. His scripts for *Millennium* continually explored the profiler's gift in intriguing new ways. He explains, "For me, the Frank gift thing was like he would kind of get this accumulation of details or facts about something that would allow him to glimpse something almost physically, like it was inevitable then that the place where the next murder would happen will look like this or the place where the guy lives would look like this or the street the guy must have grown up on looked like this" ("Order in Chaos"). Johannessen's explanation implies a sort of transformative power, allowing patterns of data and information to manifest as recognizable images before Frank's eyes. It is unsurprising that Johannessen's "Walkabout," written with Tim Tankosic, is one of the few episodes to discuss Frank's facility in purely medical terms as he and Watts argue about epileptic seizures, neurological pharmacology, and temporal lobe anomalies.[8]

The terminological approach of "Walkabout" is strategic, perhaps, given its placement amid some of the formative first season's more dramatic shifts in tone and mythology. Though the intensity of *Millennium*'s visions is indisputable, the graphic nature of their contents undeniable, there has long been a struggle to define the precise nature or origin of these chaotic visuals in relation to the character of Frank Black. Indeed, the debate has been furthered in large part by the series' own oblique approach to any scene discussing the phenomenon. The conundrum surrounding the hero's gift persisted throughout the series—from "Walkabout" to "Midnight of the Century" to "Seven and One"—and has continued long after it aired its final episode. Truly, it remains one of *Millennium*'s most enduring enigmas.

"Pilot" introduces viewers to the visual device by presenting a string of gruesome, sometimes symbolic montages representing the unique perspectives of both the Frenchman and Frank Black. Whilst they often serve to illustrate the particulars of the crimes that have been committed, these visceral sequences are also undeniably surreal, immediately evoking the supernatural sensibilities already associated in the minds of the audience with the show's creator. As a result, the script for the episode defends Frank's so-called facility as purely intuitive or intellectual. In his famous exchange with Lieutenant Bletcher, Frank emphatically insists that there is nothing psychic about his deductive feats. Such assurances are not enough to keep Bletcher from later suggesting to his friend in "The Judge" that "five hundred years ago, you would have been burned as a witch." When Frank contends that none of the feats he performs should be misconstrued as magic, Bletcher is quick with a retort: "Yeah, a lot of people shouted just that from the middle of a bonfire." As Cawelti implied, there is something inherently "terrifying" and "demonic" in the detective's ability to divine guilt.

For many viewers—and, in particular, reviewers—*Millennium*'s filmic flourishes of violence and gore were at once associated with psychic phenomenon, the sort of extrasensory perception one might expect to see providing the plot for an episode of *The X-Files*. Oversimplified assessments of *Millennium*'s complex central conceits were abundant at the time of its debut, after the series had earned unprecedented public attention for Fox culminating in a record-shattering premiere watched by over seventeen million television viewers. Such was the case in a particularly scornful *MediaWeek* review that accused the series of being founded on "supernatural hogwash" that included the hero's "special occult power" (Grossberg 38), or in *TV Guide*'s assessment that the series' protagonist was "a former cop" with a "sixth sense that lets him visualize crimes" (Jarvis 11). Snarky television critics in search of gibes or a sarcastic punch line were granted their own gift in the form of Frank's ambiguous talents. In their mockery they would find other referents for the character—not in the likes of Dupin, Holmes, or Poirot but in members of the Addams family or "wealthy young man about town" Lamont Cranston, the radio crime-fighter known as the Shadow (Martin 20). Even those more nuanced critiques of the series evinced a preoccupation with this curious "metaphysical ability" (Barrymore 19). The question was ubiquitous and annoyingly persistent in the wake of *Millennium*'s debut: "Is it ESP?" (McConnell 19). Just as Poe and Doyle warned, the results of pure deductive reasoning are easily mistaken for the preternatural, and Frank Black was at once mistaken for a modern day necromancer.

Though the paranormal forces that inspired *The X-Files* played no role in the birth of *Millennium*'s remarkable hero, this oversimplified assessment from an uncertain viewing public is something Carter should have anticipated.[9] It is an assumption that has long beleaguered true behavioral profilers. Recounting his participation in the investigation of an attack on an elderly woman who was sexually assaulted and brutally beaten, John Douglas recalls delivering a highly detailed profile to police in Virginia. The response he received from law enforcement professionals was a combination of superstition and disbelief. "The chief and detectives wanted to know how, if I wasn't a psychic, I could come up with such a specific scenario," Douglas writes, noting that he emphatically denied possessing any psychic powers. He explained to the police, "What I try to do with a case is to take in all the evidence I have to work with—the case reports, the crime-scene photos and descriptions, the victim statements or autopsy protocols—and then put myself mentally and emotionally in the head of the offender. I try to think as he does… If there is psychic component to this, I won't run away from it, though I regard it more in the realm of creative thinking" (147). The profiler's description matches Frank Black's own attempt to explain his abilities.

Perhaps because of its reckless application in many less-than-considered reviews of *Millennium* following its debut, references to psychic phenomenon are abhorred by those who have devoted more serious consideration to the program and its themes. For the *Millennium* devotee, "psychic" is a dirty word. Co-Executive Producer John Peter Kousakis is characteristically firm in his response to such interpretations, echoing the sentiments of many in the cast and crew when he insists, "Frank Black was *not* a psychic." Kousakis suggests that it is the artistry of Frank's visions, in part, that causes confusion. "It's misconception on the audience's part and a lot of the critics because when Frank would investigate a crime… there would be flashes, and we used a device, a technical device, on film to try and manifest that and try to somehow interpret for the audience what he was going through" ("Order in Chaos"). It is the spiritual implications of the word itself—the suggestion that revelatory knowledge is imbued by outside forces, not by superior intellect or inner enlightenment—that render the term so inappropriate. For this reason, none dispute the preternaturality of the character's gift more emphatically than Henriksen, whose assessment of the situation blames forces outside the production for the descriptive predicament. "We never, ever used the term—'Frank was psychic.' That came from the outside" ("Order in Chaos"). The actor is adamant when he states, "the gift was intellect and intuition—not psychic" (Henriksen 230).

It is clear that the term "psychic," with all of the supernatural sensibilities it conveys, has little role to play in any committed attempt to decipher the enduring mysteries of *Millennium*. From the very start, however, there exists an undercurrent of the miraculous that troubles our understanding of Frank's extraordinary gift. At least two specific aspects of the pilot episode, our introduction to the character and our initiation into the mythology of the series, leave us wondering about the true extent of his mental talents. Firstly, there is his refusal to use his eyes as he repeatedly turns down opportunities to personally view the bodies of murder victims hidden by tarps or body bags. It is this quirk that prompts a coroner to glibly dub him "the man with the x-ray eyes." Then there is the Frenchman, who, in the midst of his ravings, insists that he shares a sort of prophetic power with the retired lawman who has proven able to track him: "You can see it, just like I do. You know the end is coming."

"Gehenna," the second installment of the series and a significant story that serves as a sort of secondary thesis for Carter, furthers our uncertainty in a tale that confronts the hero with the terrifying images of evil incarnate. When Frank imagines the face of cult leader Ricardo Clement, clenched teeth and unblinking night vision goggles are at once swapped for the gaping maw and doglike snout of a winged demon. Frank is witnessing a tantalizing glimpse of the snarling, bestial face of the demonic presence that would come to be known as Legion. His experience presages important future developments in *Millennium*'s explorations of perception. Though the investigative revelations of the hero in a classical detective story are meant to render "what had seemed chaotic and confused" as "clear and logical" (Cawelti 87), *Millennium*'s visions often serve only to deepen the metaphysical mysteries at hand.

The tensions associated with Frank's mysterious gift build to a startling climax in "Lamentation," an episode that represents a sudden turning point in the series and in the lives of its characters. "Lamentation" would forever change the status quo of *Millennium*. It is

Carter's bold mandate for the shifting mythology of the series. In her legendary first appearance, Lucy Butler (Sarah-Jane Redmond) introduces both Frank Black and an astounded audience to horrors of a depth and strangeness never before envisaged within the framework of the series. One of many remarkable aspects of this stunning story is the fact that it represents the first *Millennium* episode to completely reject Frank's visions as a storytelling device. The imperiled profiler doesn't experience so much as single flash of bright insight in the hunt for Dr. Ephraim Fabricant (Alex Diakun) and his devilish bride. The hellish revelation that Bob Bletcher experiences before his brutal murder more than compensates; the image of Lucy Butler lit by lightning as she flickers between forms atop the staircase arguably stands as the single most memorable visual in the whole of *Millennium*.

In place of Frank's trademark visions we are granted a number of weighty speeches, monologues in which he lectures to a room full of F.B.I. analysts on the nature of human evil, behavioral science, and aberrant psychology. In several key scenes, "Lamentation" strongly reinforces the idea that the profiler's talents are deductive, analytic, not preternatural. Ultimately, however, these scenes serve to provide a stark contrast with the occult evil embodied by Butler and to reinforce the gravity of those dark forces threatening the Black family. The mortified Fabricant, mocking Frank's psychological approach to criminal profiling, has the last word: "You think I'm evil, Frank? You don't know what that is! It's greater than we are." Fabricant now understands that Butler is "the devil's liege," that she represents "the sleep of reason." The deductive reasoning that Frank has spent a lifetime employing in the apprehension of violent offenders will not serve him in his efforts to capture her. "Lamentation" does nothing to temper a hastening inclination toward exploring the more uncanny aspects of the hero's exceptional gifts. In fact, the ill-boding events witnessed here inspired an immediate and quite intensive renewal of *Millennium*'s penchant for exploring modes of perception.

If Frank's visions stand as one of *Millennium*'s most enduring enigmas, it is the conceptual follow-up to "Lamentation" that represents one of the foremost keys to that great riddle. In "Powers, Principalities, Thrones and Dominions," the protagonal gift is reimagined in dramatic fashion. Given the flash-forward offered to us by the episode's uncharacteristic teaser sequence, the effect is startling and immediate. Carter and Henriksen may be justified in arguing that our heroic profiler was not a psychic but in the wake of this story it became impossible to suggest that the hero's visionary abilities were merely intuitive, the imaginings of a particularly skilled detective. Frank sees what the killer sees and, as the episode so dazzlingly demonstrates, he sees far more than most mortal men.

"Powers, Principalities, Thrones and Dominions" blatantly suggests that the hero is witnessing not simply sparks of the imagination, not insightful hallucinations, but experiences and events wholly inaccessible to others. When the angel Sammael confronts the sinister Alistair Pepper in the mundane setting of a grocery store parking lot, we are offered two distinctly different perspectives on the unfolding conflict— one earthly, the other incorporeal. To the layman bystander, the somber youth is dispatching the lawyer with bullets fired from a handgun; Frank alone witnesses Sammael execute his opponent with a bolt of celestial lightning that emanates from the palm of his hand. The profiler's subsequent conversation with the angel of death allows us to come to terms with the dramatic turn of events we have witnessed. "Lamentation" boldly asserts that there is more to the forces of good and evil than can be commonly calculated. "Powers, Principalities, Thrones and Dominions" reveals that Frank is able to glimpse behind the deceptive veneer of this reality, that his facility for observation has made him privy to the unseen elements that bind unearthly forces in never-ending conflict. Henriksen expresses his understanding of these developments when he considers those characteristics that define Frank Black, explaining, "I don't see him as a tortured soul so much as constantly in touch with a reality that other people are not seeing" (236). That bright and unexpected bolt of lightning proved irrefutably influential for *Millennium*, every bit as influential as Bletcher's deadly encounter with Butler. The events that unfold here are memorable and strange and, as later episodes reveal, they would forever change our understanding of the hero's gift and curse.

As the events of "Lamentation" and "Powers, Principalities, Thrones and Dominions" suggest, there is a dramatic necessity in embracing the more miraculous facets of Frank's extraordinary abilities, a necessity born of the increasing complexity of *Millennium*'s potent mythology. Asked in interviews to elaborate on his inspiration for the series, Carter expressed his desire to depart from society's increasingly scientific attempts to understand the nature and origins of evil: "It really is an exploration of evil on the show, the now scientific approach to the explanation of evil, which is a psychological one, which says everyone is a victim of something. I was interested in the unscientific approach." *Millennium*, Carter asserts, aims to "explain things on various levels, not just in the modern, scientific way" (Interview, *Millennium Volume One*). Ultimately, Frank's gift must be metaphysical to resolve the central paradox of Carter's premise for the series. As the modern descendent of Dupin, the personification of a century's worthy of psychoanalytical tradition, and the greatest behavioral profiler that the F.B.I. Academy at Quantico ever produced, Frank Black is introduced as the very embodiment of a forensic, scientific rationale. As passing days bring him ever closer to the end of the millennium, the final chapters of *Millennium*'s first season confront the profiler and his family with an unimaginable force of otherworldly evil. For the hero to confront this threat, for him to begin to understand and combat the efforts of Lucy Butler and Legion, he must evolve beyond the limitations of behavioral science and embrace the more uncanny aspects of the unparalleled perceptual gift he has spent his career honing. The mythology demands a developmental leap from *Millennium*'s hero, and it is a demand that would distinctly shape subsequent seasons of the series.

As writers, Glen Morgan and James Wong were among those most interested in exploring and expanding the hero's gift. Many of their first season episodes embrace the enigma inherent to his insights. "Dead Letters"—at its heart an episode about "bad dreams" which considers the nightmares that torment slumbering children and those grim truths that torment waking adults—adds a significant layer to the mythos building up around Frank's unusual flashes of insight by offering the first hints of a prophetic bond between father and daughter. "522666" internalizes the profiler's visions for the first time, using his mysterious gift for introspective purposes. Perhaps no installment in the first season embraces the show's preoccupation with modes of perception more fully than "The Thin White Line." The hero's remarkable inner eye is dilated as his trademark visions are supplemented with recurring nightmares, dreams in which he is forced to relive one of the most terrifying confrontations of his life. One of these dream sequences in particular, in which the present day Frank joins forces with his wide-eyed younger self in an effort to rewrite history, beautifully enacts the psychological struggle of the story. Morgan and Wong remain true to form with the script, forever aiming to more deeply explore Frank's unique way of seeing the world and to ensure that his visions contributed to the themes of the story rather than providing highly stylized distraction or plot loopholes. Dreams are undeniably key to understanding the series and the struggles of its characters and, under the direction of Morgan and Wong, dreams and visions would become an increasingly intrinsic element of *Millennium*'s deepening mythology.

When Morgan and Wong assumed a supervisory role and executive producer titles for *Millennium*'s second season, the hero's trademark visions were among those elements that were reimagined in an effort to provide the series with a more epic and mythic mandate. Morgan went on record to express his feeling that "those visions were a cheat" during certain first season installments. As a result, the creative team made an effort to redefine the very nature of the visions, integrating them as part of the archetypal hero's quest that awaited Frank in the ambitious second season. "What we were trying to do… was to elevate Frank's visions to a dream-like state, so he would have to interpret what he's seeing," Morgan explains. "There would be more mystical, symbolic imagery that might give him more of a sense of what's going on. I had wanted to strip away the gift for a long time and see if the show really played well without it. But we got back into that. The Old Man in 'Beware of the Dog' was trying to tell Frank, 'Your gift isn't gone; it's going to be different'" (Vitaris 20).

The difference was evident almost immediately as *Millennium* began to systematically replace images of fresh corpses and grisly evidence, the visuals of the crime scene, with the symbolism of religious prophecy. "Monster," the season's fourth installment, introduces Frank to Lara Means (Kristen Cloke), a forensic psychologist for the Millennium Group who regularly witnesses visions of a guardian angel in the presence of imminent danger. Morgan and Wong wanted the character to serve as a foil for the series' protagonist, "somebody with an incredible gift to counter Frank," a character who mirrored both the utility and the trials of his miraculous abilities. "Right from the beginning, the idea was to have Lara see these visions and know what the Millennium Group was saying was true. Knowing that would drive her crazy because if the world is ending, what's the point of going on?" (19). As Morgan's description of her character suggests, the decision to enact a shift from behavioral profiling to prophetic insight was not arbitrary, it was mandated by the apocalyptic themes of the season. Just as the advent of Lucy Butler and the escalating menace of Legion prompted a development of the profiler's talents, the imminence of the cataclysmic events witnessed in "The Fourth Horseman" and "The Time is Now" called for a study of apocalyptic prophecy. Means's very presence on *Millennium* aided in a push towards plots concerned with hallucination and divination, away from the gritty sights, sounds, and trappings of the police procedural.

In "A Single Blade of Grass," written by Erin Maher and Kay Reindl, the hero's visions are radically reimagined for the first time as he is confronted with a steady stream of surrealistic imagery taken from the myths and legends of the Mohawk, Seneca, Cherokee, Hopi, and Seminole—the symbols of Native American prophecy. Examining evidence obtained from a burial site turned crime scene, Frank is no longer confronted with the imagery of fierce, blood-soaked struggles of life and death. He is now seeing coyotes, waterfalls, a hissing snake, a mask in the shape of a grinning skull, the setting sun on the horizon, and the ethereal mists of a spirit road. "I see it," Frank tells a mystified anthropologist as he sifts his hands through soil taken from the burial site and sees crows fleeing an Iroquois longhouse. "That other plane? How you wished it were true? How you wanted it to be there? When I'm here, touching this earth, I sense it. I'm in that plane. I can't call it up, I can't control it, I can't understand it. I have an ability that I thought I'd lost. I was told that it would change in ways I wouldn't understand. It's happening now."

Frank's brilliant insights would no longer be constrained by the circumstances surrounding a crime, no longer restricted to the simple facts and evidence of a murder investigation. His deductive reasoning would now be employed to decipher and interpret the cryptic symbols of dreams and prophecy, half-understood observations of another plane of reality. In *Millennium*'s openly experimental second season, these surreal sequences combine the oppositional qualities of detection and mystification considered by Cawelti, offering hero and audience both understanding and confusion in a curious commingling of the qualities that drive the detective story. Frank's observations are as powerful as ever but, instead of delivering intellectual insight of the sort that handily resolves the plot of a mystery story at the height of its mounting tension, these visions require a degree of interpretation or exegesis befitting only the most spiritually aware of detective heroes.

Among those elements significantly developed during the course of *Millennium*'s second season is the character of Frank Black himself. The fateful events that unfold following the death of the Polaroid stalker and the loss of the yellow house allow us unprecedented insight into the character's personal life and personality. Specifically, the season's pair of holiday-themed installments flicker into black and white to depict those difficult formative years of the profiler's personal history. "The Curse of Frank Black," a celebration of Halloween, allows us to observe Frank when he was a timid five-year-old boy and suggests that even at the age of fourteen he possessed an uncannily mature understanding of those transgressions that torment the human soul. "Midnight of the Century," an emotional Christmas episode, further integrates the show's changing visions with character by drawing on mythological threads that began as subtle ambiguities first suggested at the start of the series. Frank Spotnitz explains, "Early on there was a Morgan and Wong episode, very effective, where it was hinted that Jordan had the same ability. And then it was expanded upon in an episode that I wrote... At least for me, and I think for Chris, we never wanted to cross the line into the supernatural with any of that. It was more about an exquisite sensitivity to the way some people think, to the monstrous ways some people think" ("Order in Chaos"). Episodes such as "Dead Letters," "Sacrament," and "Walkabout" establish that the "exquisite sensitivity" possessed by Frank has been passed on and there is an extraordinary inheritance possessed by the young Jordan Black (Brittany Tiplady).

In painful scenes that showcase the divide between Frank and his estranged father Henry, "Midnight of the Century" reveals that Frank, too, has inherited his gift, that apparitions of angels and flares of divine prophecy tormented his mother, Linda, from the moment her brother died on the beachhead at Normandy. Maher, who scripted the episode with writing partner Reindl, says, "We were thinking about Frank's visions and we thought if one of his parents had visions, that would mean something, since Frank's daughter Jordan has them. It's something that's passed from generation" (Vitaris 21). At the turn of the millennium, Frank and Jordan are re-enacting a struggle that has seemingly been played out throughout their troubled family history.[10] With its emphasis on family and heritage, "Midnight of the Century" is able to quietly reinforce the bond between this loving father and his beloved child, a connection that has resonated with viewers since Lance Henriksen and Brittany Tiplady first shared the screen. The bond that connects Frank to his exceptional daughter is the sort of bond that can exist only between two kindred souls who share the same gift, the same curse. Theirs is the relationship that proves to be the very core of *Millennium*'s unfolding mythology.

The changing nature of Frank's visions and what they depicted demanded new and different ways of realizing them on film. Sequences previously dominated by the sense-stirring makeup of Lindala Makeup Effects, Inc. and practical effects provided by Bob Comer and his special effects team were now often rendered using visual effects and animation from Justin Hammond or Glenn Campbell. The cinematic changes initiated by philosophical stories prompting the detective hero to embark on spirit quests would continue into *Millennium*'s tumultuous third season. Under the supervision of Carter, Johannessen, and Michael Duggan, the series would be dramatically reinvented yet again, departing from the religious mysticism of the Millennium Group's epic struggles to avert an impending Armageddon in favor of focusing a dark lens on the social ills, scientific aberrations, and government conspiracies afflicting contemporary America. In Frank's visions, the strobe-lit slaughters of the first season and the allegorical animations of the second were traded for enhanced stock footage creatively spliced to provide chilling historical context for the intrigues under investigation, reinforcing the unsettling realism imposed by the show's latest creative team.

As he tracks a disgruntled Army veteran afflicted with Gulf War syndrome in "Collateral Damage," Frank's gift of insight blasts him with black-and-white footage taken of the aerial bombardment of Iraq during Operation Desert Storm. The nuclear age enigmas of "Matryoshka" present persistent images of glowing mushroom clouds, the alarming pictures of atomic bomb tests. The hero still relies on his facility for deductive reasoning but these third season sequences marry the traits that were dominant during each previous season, allowing the hero's visions to assume an appearance that couples evidentiary exposition with the need for interpretation. Frank's considerable knowledge and keen deductive skills are put to good use in a series of mysteries haunted by the troubled history of the twentieth century, a century that changed detective fiction as it changed all art with its "apocalyptic implications… that history might soon end altogether with the annihilation of the human race" (Rzepka 218). In a commentary recorded for "Collateral Damage," Thomas J. Wright explains that the ephemeral nature of *Millennium*'s visions prompted him to reconsider his approach to filming them in the third season. "The flashbacks were so much and so fast, I didn't know what I was seeing... I would see an eye, or I would see blood, and it was over. Not that you necessarily had to see everything. So, in the third season we did start slowing the cuts and the flashbacks down a bit so we could see a little more of what was happening. " The shift towards a more measured approach to the typically frenetic visuals would accompany a significant shift in the role they would play in the series' mythology.

Millennium's third season embraces the inherent abnormality of its central characters as Frank and Jordan Black are thrust into a number of disturbing scenarios in which the dark forces closing in on them compel an acknowledgement of the true power of their gifts. "Saturn Dreaming of Mercury," written by Johannessen and Jordan Hawley, showcases startling developments in the evolution of Jordan's own astonishing abilities, developments that demonstrate in spectacular fashion that her unique perception of the ominous events unfolding around her will ultimately prove to be far more powerful than even her father's considerable talents. As the Sanderson home explodes into a blinding wall of fire in the episode's startling teaser sequence—and then, in one incomprehensible instant, temporally inverts itself and implodes into the shape of a typical two-story residence before the seven-year-old's eyes—we realize that Jordan is possessed of a powerful prescience, that she is able to portend future events, possibilities, and consequences. "Seven and One," the final episode of *Millennium* to be written by Carter and Spotnitz, initiates a corresponding renewal of her father's gift. As Frank contemplates the traumatizing tactics employed by the shadowy figure of Mabius in an attempt to unravel his sanity, his thoughts are conveyed in a monologue that serves to suggest a tentative yet hopeful renewal of the miraculous gift of understanding first discussed in the series pilot.

> I've been given the gift of insight, of seeing in the dark and seeing into the darkness of men's hearts and minds. I know what evil is. I've seen it, felt it, tasted it, inhaled the demon breath of its ancient powers, the same powers that have been prophesied throughout history and which are now marshaling. Who is witness to this? Have we stopped listening to the prophets, the seers and the sayers? I have

misjudged my gift. If I see in the darkness it's because there is light. And it is the light which guides me now.

These bright visions of insight, the gift of deductive reasoning intensified by a spiritual understanding, are defining for Frank Black. They serve to both stimulate and mirror momentous developments in his character, the continuation of the hero's quest that began with the invasion of the yellow house in Seattle. By the time of the sunset in "Goodbye to All That," the central creative conceit of *Millennium*, the effort to succinctly convey the innermost thoughts and observations of its perceptive and empathic protagonist through the use of evocative visuals, has accomplished far more than merely reinventing the *modus operandi* of the classical detective story.

The enduring efficacy of those televisual techniques that helped to define Carter's *Millennium* and its protagonist can be observed in the endless procession of forensic dramas that would arrive in the third millennium, crime series in which stylized visuals would play a decisive role. In the years following its cancellation by Fox in 1999, noted media critic John Kenneth Muir has suggested that *Millennium* may be "the most-often imitated show in TV history," and current television schedules add considerable credence to the bold claim. "Everybody has ripped it off," Muir declared in a recent interview. "They've dissected it. They took off the arms and made *Medium* and *Ghost Whisperer*. They ripped off the legs and made *CSI* and *Criminal Minds*. I don't think there's been a more influential show in the last decade." The visualization of deductive reasoning in particular, that flash of inspiration and intuition rendered vibrant and visual, has since become a pervasive component of the twenty-first century detective drama on film and television. The significance of that cinematic achievement accomplished through the filming of Frank Black's visions can be witnessed in *Millennium*'s countless conceptual progeny.[11]

The most visible of these stylized crime dramas, *CSI: Crime Scene Investigation* (2000-), has earned widespread critical attention thanks in large part to its enduring popularity with television audiences worldwide. *CSI* follows the exploits of a Las Vegas Police Department crime scene unit as they solve criminal cases amid the dazzlingly-lit hotels and casinos of Sin City. The series is well-known for its bright, vibrant, over-saturated visuals, which offer television viewers a seemingly omniscient view of Las Vegas crime scenes and the glamorous Clark County forensic laboratories. Like Frank Black before him, the character of forensic entomologist Gil Grissom (William Petersen) represents "an allusion to the concurrent talents and torments of Holmes" but the technology and techniques he employs to trace fingerprints, blood spatters, and D.N.A. ultimately "serve as the requiem for the police officer's intuition that was once the lynchpin of detective fiction" (Arntfield 89-90).[12] Extended sequences that make use of color-enhanced photography and computer-generated visual effects allow the camera to penetrate microscopic realms, entering the human body in search of the scientific evidence that will prove to be the solution to the week's mystery. As Corinna Kruse suggests in her analysis of the series and its impact on the public's understanding of forensic science, "*CSI* legitimizes its evidence not only by establishing CSI forensic science as valid science—that is, as in accordance with established non-fictional science and carried out by dedicated scientists…—but also by establishing the evidence itself as certain. It does so through an imagery of 'reconstructing' and 'visualizing' that creates the illusion that viewers can 'see for themselves'" (84). The impact of this technique on the audience's understanding of evidentiary procedure in criminal investigations has become so pervasive that it has earned a title—the "CSI effect," also known as "CSI syndrome." In its efforts to assign guilt, *CSI* privileges the lab machine, the computer as chief analyst, whereas *Millennium* emphasizes humanity and empathy.

CSI is so reliant upon stylized visuals to convey narrative exposition and analytical breakthroughs that it employs them in a variety of contexts, including that all-important dramatic moment of deductive revelation. On *CSI*, "crimes are almost always portrayed as flashbacks, often as imaginary reconstructions, hardly ever as prosaic realism, which continually disrupts the cause-effect logic that is common to visual narratives" (Gever 449). The resolution of each case is accompanied by a final flashback re-enactment that definitively depicts the events of the crime. By the time of the episode's fade-to-black and the appearance of the executive producer credit, the viewer has "seen the evidence confirmed as being truthful through the flashback's direct access to the crime," completely resolving any lingering tension between mystification and deduction. "This truth in turn is the prerequisite for the unerring justice that *CSI* delivers" (Kruse 85). The *CSI* flashbacks provide a shortcut to visual truth that definitively closes the case before the hour is up. *CSI* stands as the very model of a judgment declared by

Torlasco: "What defines the contemporary crime scene is often the display of forensic expertise, the demand that everything be made clear and explained in terms of cause and effect, chronological succession, and identifiable agents" (79). *Millennium* was rarely so absolute in its determinations, and the visions of Frank Black have left us with more questions than answers.

As *CSI* continues to lead its genre on CBS and cable, *Millennium*'s creator now considers the intricacies of the series to be among the reasons for its cancellation. "When I look back at *Millennium* now, I think, in a way, the concept was actually too complex," Carter states. "Especially when I look at shows that have become hits, like *CSI*, or other procedurals... They don't deal with ideas like the yellow house. They don't deal with things like family, necessarily" (Interview, Muir). Carter's work on *Millennium* embraced many of those elements associated with the postmodern detective story, including "the typically unrealized possibilities of an open-ended plot, undecidable conflicts in testimony, indecipherable clues, and impenetrable motives—in short, all the wayward possibilities of real life that the traditional detective story deliberately excludes from its highly rational, causally coherent universe" (Rzepka 233). The sheer complexity of *Millennium*'s approach to stories of profound mystery and equally profound evil may be enough to explain why it never boasted the mass audience of *CSI*. The influence of *Millennium*'s artistic innovations, however, remains readily apparent.

Hyperactive, highly stylized visuals employed to convey the deductive reasoning of an unrivaled genius have also become a staple of modern screen adaptations of Arthur Conan Doyle's works. The BBC's *Sherlock* (2010-), created by Steven Moffat and Mark Gatiss, defies cinematic tradition by boldly reimagining Doyle's stories for the contemporary moment, placing Holmes, Watson, and the arch-villain Moriarty in modern London. *Sherlock*'s critically acclaimed stories are ruled by its pop culture sensitivities and its relentless dry wit, qualities which carry through to its stylized depiction of Holmes's famously eccentric thought process. Whereas *Millennium*'s filmmakers endeavored to imbue Frank Black's visions with a sense of the organic, the internalized analytics observed on *Sherlock* are wholly technological. Holmes's observations of the world around him are replete with textual tags, computer-rendered signs that suggest the world's greatest detective processes information in the same way that he would engage with a mobile phone, touch screens, or augmented reality. As is the case on *CSI*, the speed and organization of modern technology has proven irrefutably influential for the visual devices of the series. With his focus ultimately on the digital age, Brendan Riley observes that "both classical and hard-boiled detective stories function as narrative allegories for the act of rational thought in the literate age" (920). *Sherlock*'s stories function as a narrative allegory for the act of rational thought in an age of exponentially increasing digital literacy.

At the cineplex, Robert Downey, Jr. is Holmes and Jude Law is Dr. Watson in a series of gritty action films inspired by the celebrated formula of the classical detective story. Guy Ritchie's *Sherlock Holmes* (2009) offers a fresh perspective on Doyle's consulting detective by unabashedly embracing the potential for choreographed violence, risqué humor, and epic set pieces latent in his adventures. The Holmes depicted by Ritchie is a street brawler whose lightning wit is perhaps best demonstrated in those action sequences in which he is threatened with grievous bodily harm. The films embrace the dilation of time and crime studied by Torlasco, allowing the audience to follow the hero's staggeringly complex thought process, step-by-step, through the use of radically decelerated photography. Again, the analytical process of the detective is continually represented through an onscreen deployment of stylized cinematography, but while Frank Black's visions were tantalizingly brief, the time-warped imaginings of Downey, Jr.'s Holmes are unhurried, allowing us to experience the thrill of each strategic countermeasure and the impact of every physical blow. The playfulness in the presentation of this process escalates with each occurrence and reaches its peak at the arresting climax of *Sherlock Holmes: A Game of Shadows* (2011), in which the opposing intellects of both Holmes and Moriarty clash on the theater screen and a life or death struggle is enacted almost solely within the minds of its combatants high above Reichenbach Falls. With Moffat's *Sherlock* and Ritchie's *Sherlock Holmes* breathing fresh life into the most popular detective in all of fiction and digital photography and computer generated imagery continually providing new and exciting ways of realizing abstract thought processes onscreen, the visual representation of Holmes's deductive talents has seemingly become a requisite element in any screen adaptation of Doyle's work. It would be truly surprising if CBS's forthcoming *Elementary* (2012), in which yet another modern reimagining of Holmes will be relocated to New York City, were to prove resistant to the trend.

The detective continues to triumph on television, at the box office, and in fiction, and the archetypal analytical thinker has seemingly gained relevance with each passing decade. From Frank Black to Gil Grissom to the latest reincarnation of Sherlock Holmes, it is the detective's gift of deductive reasoning that imbues such enticement, and it is the visualization of this device in series such as *Millennium* that has renewed the efficacy of the detective genre and its derivatives on film and in new media. Today, the legacy of the visionary profiler's extraordinary gift flashes like a strobe throughout countless detective dramas. The formula established in Poe's "The Murders in the Rue Morgue" continues to prove popular and effective and, as Cawelti suggests in his in-depth analysis of the genre, it continues to invoke certain psychological themes that resonated at the heart of Poe's works. Eschewing external conflicts, the writer's representation of characters such as Roderick Usher in "The Fall of the House of Usher" (1839) "internalized conflict between the reasoning and ordered consciousness and the hidden dynamism and anarchy in the depths of the mind" (102). This psychological struggle would prove imperative to the development of the postmodern detective story and to the complex and compelling storytelling of *Millennium*.

Media critic Andy Lane once wrote that "*Millennium* is so realistic it tears away the last vestiges of the lies we try to tell ourselves about the way the world works" (75). Though the series is founded on the enduring formulas of the classical detective story, its hero cannot offer us the detachment and mediation we might demand or anticipate, that aspect of the formula that effectively transforms "human situations of death and horror into problems perceived by a more or less detached investigator" and allows the audience to "understand aspects of life that may be too painful or disturbing to confront without this mediating structure" (Cawelti 131). Traditional detective stories delight and comfort us by depicting "the triumph of law, order, and rationality over crime, chaos, and the irrational" (Rushing 118), but the ancient order that is the Millennium Group remains alarmingly at large, and the coalescing darkness known as Legion represents an eternal, immortal influence upon mankind. Frank Black's investigations into frightful, obscene mysteries initiate us in the true horrors of the world, compelling us to confront the most abhorrent of sins. His gift to us is the virtue of his own intuitive talents, that miraculous gift for embracing and ultimately understanding the most disturbing truths of the world we live in. It is the gift of understanding, the gift of empathy, that proves the most powerful of all.

If the detective is driven "to uncover secret terrors of the human soul without being overpowered by the dark tides of unreason, despair, and anguish" (Cawelti 131), Frank Black stands as the epitome of the form, an exquisite embodiment of the enduring ideals of analytical thinking, deductive reasoning, and an empathic spirit. His presence throughout Chris Carter's apocalyptic masterpiece inspires, challenges, and empowers us to confront the most hideous and unspeakable of all evils.

NOTES

1. Amusingly, Holmes is rude and dismissive in regard to his investigative forerunner, commenting that "Dupin was a very inferior fellow... He had some analytical genius, no doubt; but he was by no means such a phenomenon as Poe appeared to imagine" (16). We can only imagine what the mighty Sherlock Holmes would make of the intuitive gift possessed by Frank Black.

2. *Millennium* made its debut on Fox at 9:00 pm on the night of 25 October 1996, nearly a month after the premiere of NBC's *Profiler* (1996-2000) on 21 September. *Millennium* and *Profiler* are all-but identical in premise but extraordinarily dissimilar in execution. Each series follows the ongoing investigations of a gifted forensic profiler who, desperate to protect family, tracks serial killers whilst being threatened by an unknown stalker. At the time, there was considerable commentary from the media concerning the similarities between the two series and their near simultaneous debuts. Cynthia Saunder, creator of *Profiler*, has repeatedly denied any intentional similarities to Carter's *Millennium*, as have those producers and executives who were responsible for the show (Braxton).

3. Darin Morgan's "Jose Chung's *Doomsday Defense*" offers its own wry summation of those specialized skills involved in behavioral profiling and the qualities that distinguish *Millennium*'s hero. In the episode, Chung writes: "Like television weathermen, giving information one could gather simply by looking out the window, forensic profilers provide little of practical value. Mr. Blork, however, not only intuits specific details, but to better comprehend a particular pathology, he's willing to submit himself to that very madness."

4. Partly because of the nature of its storytelling—the transformation of "whodunit?" into "howcatchem?" in a famed inversion of the structure of the classical detective story—*Columbo*, created by William Link and Richard Levinson, possesses a number of minor features that can be tentatively linked to Carter's *Millennium*. After all, Frank Black and Peter Watts are often seen devising proactive means of capturing a killer the audience has been familiar with since the teaser sequence. Like *Millennium*, *Columbo* sometimes evinces a cinematic preoccupation with the eyes in a display of those themes that dominate its genre. A particularly striking example of *Columbo*'s use of experimental cinematography to explore its themes can be found in one of the series' earliest and most artistically ambitious installments, "Death Lends a Hand" (1971), in which the wide-lens glasses worn by guest star Robert Culp offer a morbid window into the actions and motives of the murderer. The deductive reasoning of the deceptively disheveled Lieutenant Columbo, of course, remains delightfully ambiguous, expressed onscreen only in the contortions of Peter Falk's face.

5. From the night vision gear worn by Ricardo Clement in "Gehenna" to the glowing goggles donned by Lucas Wayne Barr in "Goodbye to All That," symbolic representations of the human eye abound in *Millennium*. Ocular imagery plays an important thematic role in the series. The third season, in particular, seems at times as if it is compiled from an endless chain of optical symbolism. The remnants of Project Grillflame, the secret C.I.A. initiative in remote viewing central to the plot of "Exegesis," are marked at the Stanton Research Institute by the painted emblem of an eye. The same glyph appears throughout "Skull and Bones," adopted as a signature by the paranoid observer Ed. The Sandersons of "Saturn Dreaming of Mercury" collect glass eyes and, oddly, exhibit them in display cases in their home. Psychiatric patient Cassie Doyle obsesses over Darwin's theories of ocular evolution as she scrawls associated imagery on the wall of her hospital room in the appropriately titled "Darwin's Eye." When Emma Hollis unfolds an origami palm in the same story she finds herself staring into a photograph of her sister's right eye. *Millennium* offers countless examples, each inherently tied to its dominant thematic preoccupations.

6. Possible precedents for the innovative visual device used on *Millennium* are evident in other film genres, specifically horror. John Kenneth Muir suggests an example in the alien visions of *Species* (1995), a science fiction horror film directed by Roger Donaldson. The bizarre and unsettling sequences seen in *Species*, however, dominated by the artistic designs of H. R. Giger, serve as representations of the unconscious mind repressed by the alien-human hybrid Sil (Natasha Henstridge). Hellish, graphic, quick-cut hallucinatory visuals

would, of course, become more dominant in horror cinema following the premiere of *Millennium*, as in Paul W. S. Anderson's *Event Horizon* (1997).

7. In filming *Millennium*'s pilot, Director of Photography Peter Wunstorf devised a means of photographically distinguishing the perception of apocalyptic visions from the standard visual narrative of the series. Wunstorf employed a 16mm Arriflex SR camera using Eastman 7249 and 7259 Ektachrome color reversal stock to film each violent, hallucinatory vision and "visually distinguish it from the main narrative material," which was conversely shot on 35mm film with "an Arriflex 535A for A-camera coverage, BL 4s for B-camera angles... and a Moviecam Compact for Steadicam shots" (Probst 49).

8. "Walkabout," written by Chip Johannessen and Tim Tankosic, directed by Cliff Bole, features a number of firsts for *Millennium*. Though the stylistic device offering the audience a visualization of the investigative process had been a key part of the series from its start, this is the first episode that is fundamentally about the hero's gift. It also marks the first occasion on which Frank Black's visions—typically saturated with bold, expressive colors—are presented in black and white. The cinematic tactic is employed here for a familiar purpose, as a means of representing the fleeting, blurred memories of the amnesiac hero.

9. Robert Cettl's encyclopedic *Serial Killer Cinema* (2003) cites a number of films that feature "a split profiler figure in the form of an expert criminologist and an intuitive psychic" (115), films that include *Dead on Sight* (1994), *Fear* (1990), and Wes Craven's *Night Visions* (1990). As Cettl suggests, with the debut of *Millennium* "the dynamics of the serial killer film entered the living room" (1) and the phenomenon of the visionary profiler, as well as stories featuring psychic links, would become increasingly prevalent after its advent.

10. *Millennium*'s second season hints at numerous details suggesting origins for Frank Black's prophetic inheritance. This includes an offhand and oft-neglected reference made in "A Single Blade of Grass," an episode rooted in Native American culture and mythology, to the fact that his grandmother's mother was of Crow Indian descent. The allusion would be unremarkable but for the fact that it is made during a scene in which Frank is undertaking the forensic equivalent of a Native American vision quest.

11. A number of television dramas dominating the airwaves in the years following *Millennium*'s cancellation evince its influence. *Criminal Minds* (2005-), for instance, depicts serial killing cases investigated by the F.B.I.'s Behavioral Science Unit at Quantico. A significant portion of these series rely

on stylized visuals to depict mystic foresight or the intricacies of an intellectual process. Joss Whedon's *Angel* (1999-2004), a modern reinvention of the hardboiled detective story featuring a cast of supernatural characters, occasionally depicts the titular vampire experiencing Delphic visions from "The Powers that Be," visions that help him to solve cases. CBS's *Ghost Whisperer* (2005-10), a supernatural drama series with mystery elements, regularly explores alternate modes of perception in its saga of a compassionate woman who is able to see and communicate with the spirits of the dead. *Numb3rs* (2005-10) employs stylized transitions and C.G.I. sequences to illustrate the complex mathematical theories and equations applied by hero Charlie Eppes (David Krumholtz) to critical criminal investigations. Indeed, presenting a comprehensive list of those twenty-first century crime dramas that evince similarities to the style and themes of *Millennium* would require a separate, dedicated volume.

12. Even that casting of *CSI* calls to mind the precedent of *Millennium*. Prior to taking the role of the night-shift supervisor for the L.V.P.D.'s Clark County Crime Scene Investigation unit, actor William Petersen inhabited a persona similar to Frank Black. Petersen starred as retired F.B.I. profiler Will Graham in *Manhunter* (1986), written and directed by Michael Mann, the first big screen adaptation of Thomas Harris's *Red Dragon* (1981).

WORKS CITED

Arntfield, Michael. "TVPD: The Generational Diegetics of the Police Procedural on American Television." *Canadian Review of American Studies* 2011: 25-95. Print.

Barrymore, John. "*Millennium*." *Xposè* February 1998: 19. Print.

Bloch, Ernest. *The Utopian Function of Art and Literature*. Trans. Jack Zipes and Frank Mecklenburg. Cambridge, MA: M.I.T., 1988. Print.

Braxton, Greg. "The Case of Double Vision for NBC and Fox." *Los Angeles Times*. Los Angeles Times, 27 July 1996. Web. 14 August 2012.

Carter, Chris. Audio commentary. "Pilot." *Millennium: The Complete First Season*. Dir. David Nutter. Twentieth Century Fox Home Entertainment, 2004. DVD.

———. Interview. *Millennium Volume One: Pilot / Gehenna.* Twentieth Century Fox Home Entertainment, 1996. VHS.

———. Interview by John Kenneth Muir. *Reflections on Cult Movies and Classic Television.* John Kenneth Muir, 15 December 2009. Web. 14 August 2012.

Cawelti, John G. *Adventure, Mystery, and Romance: Formula Stories as Art and Popular Culture.* Chicago: U of Chicago P, 1976. Print.

Cettl, Robert. *Serial Killer Cinema: An Analytical Filmography.* Jefferson, NC: McFarland & Co., 2003. Print.

"Chasing the Dragon: A Conversation with the Academy Group." *Millennium: The Complete First Season.* Prod. Jon Mefford. Twentieth Century Fox Home Entertainment, 2004. DVD.

Christie, Agatha. *An Overdose of Death* [*One, Two, Buckle My Shoe*]. New York: Dell, 1972. Print.

Douglas, John and Mark Olshaker. *Mindhunter.* New York: Pocket Books, 1996. Print.

Doyle, Sir Arthur Conan. *Sherlock Holmes: The Complete Novels and Stories.* New York: Bantam, 1986. Print.

Gever, Martha. "The Spectacle of Crime, Digitized." *European Journal of Cultural Studies.* November 2005: 445-463. Print.

Grossberg, Lewis. "Dead Man Acting." *MediaWeek* December 1996: 38. Print.

Henriksen, Lance and Joseph Maddrey. *Not Bad for a Human: The Life and Films of Lance Henriksen.* Los Angeles: Bloody Pulp Books, 2011. Print.

Jarvis, Jeff. "*Millennium.*" *TV Guide* 16 November 1996: 11. Print.

Kruse, Corinna. "Producing Absolute Truth: *CSI* Science as Wishful Thinking." *American Anthropologist* March 2010: 79-91. Print.

Lane, Andy. "*Millennium Vol. 4.*" *Dreamwatch* April 1998: 75. Print.

McConnell, Frank. "A Killer Serial: Chris Carter's *Millennium.*" *Commonweal* 18 July 1997: 19-20. Print.

Martin, James. "*Millennium*, Math, and Money." *America* 16 November 1996: 20. Print.

Muir, John Kenneth. Interview by James McLean and Troy L. Foreman. *The Millennium Group Sessions*. Back to Frank Black, 6 February 2010. Web. 14 August 2012.

"Order in Chaos." *Millennium: The Complete First Season*. Prod. John Mefford. Twentieth Century Fox Home Entertainment, 2004. DVD.

Poe, Edgar Allan. *The Tell-Tale Heart and Other Writings*. New York: Bantam, 1982. Print.

Probst, Christopher. "Mining the Macabre." *American Cinematographer* October 1996: 46-55. Print.

Ressler, Robert K. and Tom Shachtman. *Whoever Fights Monsters*. New York: St. Martin's, 1993. Print.

Riley, Brendan. "From Sherlock to Angel: The Twenty-First Century Detective." *Journal of Popular Culture* October 2009: 908-922. Print.

Roush, Matt. "Jose Chung's *Doomsday Defense*." *USA Today* 20 November 1997. Print.

Rushing, Robert A. *Resisting Arrest: Detective Fiction and Popular Culture*. New York: Other Press, 2007. Print.

Rzepka, Charles J. *Detective Fiction*. Malden, MA: Polity, 2005. Print.

"*The Turn of the Tide.*" *Millennium: The Complete Second Season*. Prod. John Mefford. Twentieth Century Fox Home Entertainment, 2004. DVD.

Torlasco, Domietta. "Undoing the Scene of the Crime: Perspective and the Vanishing of the Spectator." *Camera Obscura* January 2007: 76-111. Print.

Tucker, Ken. "Super Freaks." *Entertainment Weekly*. Entertainment Weekly, 13 November 1998. Web. 14 August 2012.

Uhlich, Keith. "*Millennium: The Complete First Season*." *Slant Magazine*. Slant, 20 July 2004. Web. 14 August 2012.

von Mueller, Eddy. "The Police Procedural in Literature and on Television." *The Cambridge Companion to American Crime Fiction.* Ed. Catherine Ross Nickerson. Cambridge: Cambridge UP, 2010. 96-109. Print.

Vitaris, Paula. "*Millennium*: TV's Best Kept Secret Improves in its Sophomore Season." *Cinefantastique* October 1998: 18-22, 125. Print.

Wright, Thomas J. Audio commentary. "Collateral Damage." *Millennium: The Complete Third Season.* Dir. Thomas J. Wright. Twentieth Century Fox Home Entertainment, 2005. DVD.

Brian A. Dixon, Ph.D., is a writer, publisher, and independent scholar who has taught writing, literature, and film. His previous works include studies concerning college writing centers, nineteenth-century American literature, ethnic humor in British sitcoms, the works of Ian Fleming, and the James Bond films. Dixon has served as the Assistant Editor of *ATQ: The American Transcendental Quarterly* and, with Adam Chamberlain, edited the Sidewise Award-nominated *Columbia & Britannia* (2009). He is also the curator of *The Millennial Abyss*, widely regarded as one of the foremost websites dedicated to celebrating Chris Carter's *Millennium*.

OUT OF THE MASTER'S SHADOW:
A CONVERSATION WITH THOMAS J. WRIGHT

Interview by James McLean & Troy L. Foreman
Written by Adam Chamberlain

In order to gain entry to the Directors Guild of America, three established directors are required to sponsor any given candidate as being in good standing. The three names on Thomas J. Wright's card show all one need know about the caliber of the veteran director. "One was Robert Wise, one was Mark Robson, and the other was Alfred Hitchcock," Wright tells us before adding, "That's a nice piece of paper hanging on my wall!" It was his work with Hitchcock, he says, that secured his membership. "I did three movies with him. That's actually how I got into the Directors Guild. There was quite a bit of second unit work on the last movie we did together, enough to warrant getting into the Directors Guild, so his was the first signature." The movies in question include *Topaz* (1969) and *Family Plot* (1976). Wright was to collaborate with Wise, an Academy Award winner, on *The Andromeda Strain* (1971). "Robert Wise was the second signature and Mark Robson was the third. That was at a time when Robert Wise was President of the D.G.A., and he said that he wanted me in there whilst he was President because he wanted to sign my application also. So it was pretty good."

Wright served Hitchcock primarily as a storyboard artist, developing artistic skills that continue to play a vital role in his work as a director. "Actually, I started out as an actor and got into the art end of it because I was an artist," he says, his typically gruff voice a pleasing growl. "It did very well by me. I used to plan a lot of prep work with directors on big movies. Every movie I've worked on I've done the storyboards on, whether it's a movie I'm directing or a movie I'm just working on as the storyboard artist and second unit director. I did all the action sequences in *Beverly Hills Cop*, for example, *Terms of Endearment*—movies like this. But it was a big, big boost for me to get into directing because I was able to do my art to meet and work with a lot of well-known directors on big projects. You just keep constantly knocking on the door for somebody to give you a break. Somebody's putting a book together on *Jaws* that has a lot of my stuff in it. There was so much stuff I had to get rid of some of it, but usually when I do a show now either cast or crew members will ask for my script. So whoever asks for it usually gets it, unless it's one I especially want to keep. That's what I usually do. It really helped me tremendously. I still do it now. Every show I do, I storyboard as well. I never will show up without having storyboarded a show."

What advantages does storyboarding grant to a director? "It affords you some time to think about what you would like to do once you've found the locations, read the scenes, and thought about it. It affords you some time to really think about it and maybe do something a little different than if you had just showed up on the set to start your day, which is really not the way to do it. Some directors make their notes or whatever you want to call them—they're like my notes, except mine are pictures."

Film is a visual medium and the sketching out of ideas in the margins of shooting scripts, Wright explains, offers him a sort of prescient glimpse at the finished episode prior to shooting. "It gives me a lot of visual thought when I start the show, and I pretty much know, once I've done the storyboard for the show, basically what I want to do. It changes continually as you're doing the scene, because then you get involved with the actors and the story, and people are inputting. You start finding maybe another way to do something that maybe you like a little better. But you still have a very definite visual track of where you want to go and what you want that scene to look like. It looks pretty close, usually, by the time I'm through. I usually get out of it what I want and a little more. It's a lot of work, but it pays off very well. I try to have every script done before I start shooting. There's a lot of work involved, because you're involved in casting, scouting for locations, meetings, and script meetings. So all of this is going on and you're also trying to get your storyboards done too, in between. It's paid off for me tremendously because I attribute a lot to the visual end of it. I try to make my shows a little different, visually, and do things that they don't normally do—at least in a few places. That's another reason I've been pretty lucky. People hire me a lot because of the way my shows look."

Wright explains that "being visual" and a disciplined approach to prep work are key to achieving the distinctive visual style that has earned him such a reputation. "There are moments in the scene were you do the normal stuff because you have to do it to tell the story, but how I get into the scene, how I get out of the scene, what my transitions are, what I want it to look like light-wise, all this is considered very, very carefully before I show up to shoot. It works, however you plan it. You don't have to be able to draw to do it. It's a big plus as far as I'm concerned, a big plus because you're very visual to start with. I can see a location once and I can remember it exactly. So being visual is a big, big plus."

Both technical and instinctive traits feed into his direction, but Wright emphasizes the latter as being of particular significance. "It's instinct, a lot of it," he affirms. "When I do the storyboards I act the scenes out in my head before I put them down, so once I know what the set is and the location, by the time I'm through with it I have a really good, solid idea of how I want to approach this scene. I don't have to worry about shooting it anymore. I just walk in and start dealing with the actors, and we work out what we want to do from the acting end. I don't worry about what the shots are going to be because I already know what they are, basically. They'll change, but overall I would say eighty percent of them stay the same. When I finish a scene I pretty much have it shot the way I've laid it out."

Given Wright's background—his work in art departments, visual effects, editing, and the director's chair—which aspect of the process thrills him the most? "Shooting it," he answers without hesitation. "You're heavy duty into it from the word go, but once you walk onto the stage you've done a lot of work on it and you're ready to start there. Once I get into it there and I've got the actors and all the crew, that's my most enjoyable part of it. But then you show up in the edit a week later and you start the process all over again and that becomes very enjoyable, actually seeing everything go together—and hopefully well. But it's shooting for me, actually being on the stage with the actors and the crew. Running into those problems and finding out it's not quite working how you want it. What are you going to do? Let's fix it."

It was the creative duo that went on to become executive producers during *Millennium*'s second year who were responsible for bringing Thomas J. Wright to the series, a move that would prove fateful for its future development. "Jim Wong and Glen Morgan wrote a script for *Millennium* and put my name in to Chris Carter to do the show," he remembers. "I got the show and that started it. They were trying to get me in on *The X-Files* early on, and the shows that he was involved with—because of Jim and Glen—but I was always busy. Finally this one broke, and I went in to do it. Chris kept calling me to do *The X-Files*, but then he'd come back and have another *Millennium* and go, 'No, I'd rather you do *Millennium*.'"

As he tallied more and more episodes, Wright's name became synonymous with the series, earning the director a credit as producer. "When I started producing *Millennium* it was basically because Chris said, 'You're Mr. Millennium, Tom, so you should take it and do whatever you want, and call me whenever you want or have to, and go from there.'" Wright did just that, ensuring that Carter remained close to the series and that his creative vision was maintained. "Chris was really good to me, and we discussed a lot of things even when he wasn't actually heavily involved in doing the show. I still kept in close touch with him, on the scripts and so forth."

With the role as producer came more work for Wright, although he did not mind one bit. "It takes you time, but I loved that series so much," he glows. "It's one of my all-time favorites, and you're so involved in everything that you don't really think about it. It's just another thing you do because you're involved in it and you want to see things happen. I just loved it. I prepped, shot, cut, prepped, shot, cut, prepped, shot, cut. That's what I did, basically, because I did quite a few of the episodes and was involved in some of the others I didn't actually direct, of course. But I loved the show. Chris said, 'Here' and left me alone, totally, and it was great. When Jim and Glen came in, of course, I knew them from earlier and it was the same."

The single most prolific director working on the series, Wright would helm a total of twenty-six episodes of *Millennium*—well over a third of its entire run—across all three seasons. The first of these was the aforementioned Morgan and Wong-scripted installment, "Dead Letters." Does Wright recall anything from his debut directorial assignment on the show? "Well, I've looked at it a couple of times over the years and I thought it was a very good episode," he considers. "I really worked myself to do a terrific episode because I liked the script a lot. There's a lot of detail and I do that on a lot of shows I do, whether it's *Millennium* or something else—*N.C.I.S.* is another show I do a lot of material on. 'Dead Letters' was a very dark show, which I like and I have fun with them. It's storytelling, and how do you tell it really well and hopefully better than anybody else tells it. Anytime you move into a new show, your first one or two episodes, you really bear down anyway, because it's a whole different group of people—new storylines, the characters, the actors. So you're learning a lot very quickly. You've got to adjust really quickly. James Morrison is a good friend and he's terrific—he was fantastic in that. We had a good time and it was hard, hard work. As time went on, of course, I got to know Lance better and better, and now we're really good friends. It was a good deal."

Another visually striking episode from Season One directed by Wright and written by Morgan and Wong is "The Thin White Line." The director recalls how some of the key set pieces—staged in an abandoned building—were filmed. "That was really visual because we found this building they were renovating. With the production designer, Mark Freeborn, we came up with an idea how it was going to be done with the hanging sheets of plastic and the water running through and dripping. That was one of my favorite episodes."

Wright often speaks about *Millennium* in terms of favorites, which is significant given the sheer length of his resume. What is it about the series that inspires him to regard it with such high esteem? "Well, I am really interested in serial killers, for instance," he ventures. "I like

Seven—that's one of my favorite movies. It's a grotesque subject, of course, very terrifying, but I think if you're doing entertainment and you get those type of stories to do, for myself it was terrific because I can get really visual with them and create a whole other world—a very scary world. It's all in what size shots you use, what the angles are and the lighting, all of that. I liked it because it was dark. That may sound a little weird but it's true, because I could do a lot of things with it visually and from the acting standpoint that really helped scare people and tell the story. It is a really interesting topic."

Considering the themes of Season One, Wright suggests the early stories depict "Frank Black and his demons." The inner turmoil afflicting the profiler is, Wright believes, what rendered the series so immediately engaging. "That's why he got out of it in the beginning, and it kept drawing him back. There was a lot of conflict there, that and then with his family, how to protect his family. He was always worried. There were so many elements to that show, particularly the first season. I think the first season was the best. There were so many elements to deal with, and that's what made it really interesting. It wasn't just the scary murder thing or the bodies you find. It was how Frank Black was dealing with his life."

The director is one of the key crew members to have worked consistently on *Millennium* throughout a variety of creative changes from season to season, allowing him a unique perspective on the forever shifting mythology of the series. Were the changes instituted by executive producers Glen Morgan and James Wong evident from the very start of development on Season Two? "Totally," he affirms. "When Jim and Glen came in, of course, things change dramatically. There was a whole different take on *Millennium*." This in turn affected his perspective on each episode in the season, although his overall method remained the same. "I looked at how I would approach what they were dealing with, because you had this whole thing between Peter Watts and Frank Black, all the stuff with the Millennium Group going on. It was a big switch. Again, each show that I do I look at and decide what kind of style I am going to give it. I approach pretty much every script, no matter what the series is, on its own, and I don't think about the series and does it have to have some kind of continuity or anything. I don't think about that. I just take that episode and approach how I want it to look, what I want it to feel like and what do I want it to be. That's how I approach every show I do, no matter what the series is. It was pretty cool there because Jim and Glen were doing it and it was like, 'Here, Tom. Here. Here. See ya!' They are really talented guys. They really know what they're doing and when they hire somebody to do the job, they expect them to do it. That's a big part of the job—once it's been handed over to you, filling the bucket the way they would like it filled."

Describing this task in a little more detail, Wright outlines the director's role in interpreting the contents of a script. "Your job is to take that, of course, and tell that story the best way you can. But it's still that story. I try to be as lean and mean with the writer's stuff as I am with anything, because it's their story, they've picked me to do it and I want to tell it their way—really tell it the way they see it. It does change, of course, but still, I want the writers to be happy with it by the time I'm through with it. You don't just shuck it—it's your job."

Millennium could, at various times, be ambiguous in its exposition or epic in its scope. The onscreen realization of those descriptions that appear on the page of a shooting script can pose quite the challenge. When he is unable to draw upon his own experiences to envision a scene, where does Wright start? "You've got to understand the story. I figure when I read scripts I actually understand them, or at least most of them. You understand them and then, at this point in my life considered a creative person, you can put yourself—at least in your mind, if nothing else—in certain situations. There's a certain mood you want to create and a certain feeling. As you make the show you have a lot of things at your disposal, such as sound, and a lot of things you can do after you have shot the scene that help lift it, so there's all of that to consider. There's a lot there when you show up on the set, but you've got to be thinking about this. When I'm doing a sequence, before we ever even shoot it, a lot of this is in my head. I know what I want it to feel like, what the mood is like, so you have a plan and sometimes you hit it, sometimes you don't. That's a situation where you've seen enough of this sort of tragedy on the news or whatever that there is a certain feeling and you just try to capture it."

The director, of course, is not alone in the task of filming, as Wright suggests when he recalls his collaborations with one of the other talents who helped to define *Millennium*'s distinctive visuals. "Sometimes you had a few problems, but I had a great working relationship with the director of photography, Rob McLachlan. We really hit it off and we talked about the vision and the shots and so forth, and he would hit it pretty much every time. It got almost like shorthand between Rob and myself, because we did so many of them together that I could just drop an image to him or show him something or we would discuss something and the direction that particular episode would go. Each time I did an episode I would try to approach it differently, from a lighting standpoint, from a shooting standpoint, anything to boost it and make it really different, but he was great in that sense. You did run into problems. Sometimes you couldn't quite get it the way you wanted it because you ran out of time, or it's too involved so you had to make a few compromises, but overall I would say that the ones I did basically came out pretty much the way I wanted them. I thought some of the scripts were better than others, but that's a whole other thing. No matter what you think about them, once you get them, you take them and you go for them all out."

In addition to valuing his collaborations with McLachlan, Wright has high praise for the instincts of his leading man on *Millennium*. "Lance is just a great guy," he says. "He's a very good friend, and he's an actor I like because he's from the gut. He does a scene the way he feels about it. You'll get take to take and never are two alike because it comes out different every time he does it. He's just a really interesting guy. He's got a lot to draw from and he's terrific. When he's into it, he's terrific and I would say to him, 'I'm sitting here watching the movie as you're doing it. This is a great job.' He's just right from the bootstraps. There's nothing protracted from him. It's just, 'What do I feel as I'm saying it?'"

Speaking to some of the challenges presented during filming, one episode that enters the conversation is "The Innocents." The focal point of the season three premiere is the investigation of a plane crash, and the episode features a shockingly realistic representation of such a scene. "That was very difficult to shoot," Wright admits. "We were up on the side of a mountain with all this plane wreckage and helicopters and no time to do it. It was really an interesting script and that was Klea [Scott]'s first adventure into the show. She was great. She was one of my favorites. It was hard to do, but it was a really good show, I thought. The plane wreckage stuff was interesting because I wanted to create this almost unreal atmosphere. What's really going on and how do you create it in two hours, for Christ's sake! There's never any time, but I thought we did a good job."

Another Season Three installment directed by Wright is the memorable Halloween episode "Thirteen Years Later," famous for featuring Kiss. The inclusion of the rock band's founding members was an intriguing element, Wright notes, in spite of their lack of acting experience. "I hadn't really done anything with rock stars before, so we met these guys and they were all fantastic. It was like they would come up to everybody or their buddies and say, 'This guy's the director and you do exactly what he tells you to do, period.'" Marking a rare opportunity for cross-promotion on *Millennium*, "Thirteen Years Later" features a climactic chase sequence set against a performance of "Psycho Circus," the title track from Kiss's 1998 comeback album. "It was so much fun and with their number that they were doing in the show we ended up actually shooting a little video of it, the whole thing all the way through. They loved it—they were really blown away by it. It took us about four hours for the whole scene that they were in, and that included shooting the whole thing as a music video besides, and they loved it." Unfortunately, in spite of the band's enthusiasm, the performance shot by Wright on the set of *Millennium* was prevented from becoming the official music video for the song. "Fox and Chris Carter said, 'No, they can't use it because Fox owns it,' and so they wouldn't let them use it to put it out as a music video. What was interesting was that they had just done a music video of their own that they had paid for, and they said they were so much more pleased with this one and they would have used it. It was better than the one they bought! They were great, though. Anything you wanted them to do they would do, and we had a really good time. It was wild."

Though the finished episode is entertainingly eclectic and undeniably unique, Wright's first reaction to Michael R. Perry's script for "Thirteen Years Later" was one of consternation: "How the hell are we going to do this?! It was a huge script. The biggest problem I had with it was in the editing, as it was ten or twelve minutes over. That's an act and a half right there, so a lot of stuff ended up getting cut out of it, which was too bad in a way because it was so much fun stuff. Besides being crazy and full of people getting their throats cut at every corner, it was just a lot of tongue-in-cheek stuff too. I just said, 'I'm going to go for it and I'm going to do whatever works.' You keep a certain line and there are certain things you won't do, but it opened it up quite a bit. For instance, the scene where Lance and Klea are watching movies and they've got popcorn, when we were doing that scene we had a really great time and they were right into it. It was like sitting in your living room, of course, but it was a total kick. It was just crazy."

Guest star Jeff Yagher puts in an unforgettable performance as Mark Bianco, an actor portraying Frank Black for a movie based upon one of his cases. The role allowed Yagher the once-in-a-lifetime opportunity to deliver an uproarious caricature of star Lance Henriksen. The episode also boasts a twist in the reveal that the entire story is nothing more than a figment of Bianco's crazed imagination. "I think it did have two edges to it," says Wright. "It had the *Millennium* edge and then the Halloween influence, but you had Frank Black as Frank Black and everybody else was crazy, so I think that kept you seated there." He points to Henriksen's reactions to Bianco's parody of Frank as a highlight of the episode. "Lance is great at that stuff. I have given other interviews where I have talked about Lance's reactions to things. They are just so spot on, and sometimes they take you totally off guard, they are so wild—without him saying anything. It's just a school in itself."

The make-believe nature of the narrative also helped to push the envelope in terms of the episode's comedic tone. "I think it needed that too," agrees Wright. "I think that really helped it. I think if you tried to do it totally straight it would have probably died, but just because of the nature of it, what it was, what it involved and what was going on—like the shadow character of Frank Black—you needed to lift it up a little bit and give it its own special *Millennium* show. Jeff Yagher ended up marrying Megan [Gallagher] and I thought that was interesting! He was great too. We had a ball doing it. We were laughing more than anything—that I do remember. It was one of those special ones, because none of the other episodes in three years were anything like that, or at least the ones I did. There were a couple that were really out of left field, but the *Millennium* stuff was usually what it was, and for me when this one came along it gave me a chance to have a lot of fun—more fun than usual. One of my favorite episodes because of all the different elements, and it just went up street a little bit off from what *Millennium* usually is."

In addition to the length of the first cut, the other challenge in the editing process was to tone down the gore. The episode sought to mimic slasher movies, but this brought some challenges from Fox. "The only thing was too much blood—the usual—but they had kind of given up on us by then. They knew what to expect. We had all reached a level where we knew exactly what we could do, but that was always the main thing: 'It's too gory. It's too bloody. You've got to be careful.' I did have some scenes in there that we did trim back and take back because I had blood all over the walls and everything! You go around the corner and there would be somebody hanging there, or somebody lying on the floor with their head cut off or something. But it was also in the vein of being a Halloween show, like *Nightmare on Elm Street* and all those kind of movies. So we pushed it as far as we could, still keeping it a little tongue-in-cheek and also having that *Millennium* edge, so I think it worked pretty well. It was totally off the wall, though, from what a *Millennium* show was."

Wright was eager to ensure that the film set which acts as a backdrop for the episode was represented with authenticity. "I didn't want to get what you usually see in movies", he explains. "One of my pet peeves about when you see movies or a T.V. show is that during the filming business it really is kind of hokey. I've never seen one I've been really happy with, although the movie *The Player* was a pretty good depiction of the film business, in a way. It really drives me crazy—unless it's a total comedy, then you go with whatever—when they are portraying it as a real movie set or something. One of my favorites of all time is *Living in Oblivion*, with Steve Buscemi as the director, about making a small, independent movie. It's one of my all-time favorite movies about making a movie. Every time I look at it I go, 'That's my life every day. That's exactly what happens to me every day.' You've got these special effects guys with a rolled-up script in their back pocket that they're trying to sell, and you've got the business going on with the two main actors. It's a good movie. It's just a riot because it's so true." Authenticity was important to the director in general for his work on the series. "You've got to try to keep it real, especially with *Millennium*, on the edge. Procedural-wise, we tried to stay true to form and everything. It's when you get into the crime scenes and the autopsy, of course, you have little flairs and ways you do certain things for those scenes, but we try to stay pretty much on clock when we're doing those things. We had people there that if you have a question you will ask it, but then you'll say, 'Never mind, I'm going to do it this way anyway,' but you try to stay pretty much on."

Visually—in terms of the lighting and color palette—"Thirteen Years Later" features noticeable deviations from *Millennium*'s trademark look for the movie set scenes. "I hope you notice something like that," says Wright. "When we were shooting that scene, we did change the lighting and the look a bit from what the on-camera crew was doing compared to what we really do, because when we shot *Millennium* it was a dark but very real look that we were going for, and I do remember that when we were doing that sequence we purposefully juiced it up a little bit with more color than we normally do just to give it a change when you're looking at it—so you can tell the difference right away—but it was subtle. Sometimes you do certain things for a reason."

As someone who has worked extensively in both mediums, does the director perceive any distinct differences between working in film and television? "No," he states simply. "There's a whole perception that there is, but there isn't. You approach a movie the same way you approach a T.V. show. It's just you've got a hell of a lot more time and money to do it, but it's exactly the same way, because I've done some movies. It's all the hierarchy of 'I'm better than you!' or whatever it might be, but of course that's changed a lot now because a lot of people that do a movie are from T.V. Where did all these people come from, basically? Some just walked into movies, but a lot of them, when you check up on them, passed through T.V. at some point in their life. But we approach it exactly the same way: you still have to cast it, you still have to find the locations, you still have to have the script, you still have to shoot it. It's the same way exactly."

Wright believes that television itself is becoming more cinematic in its scope and that *Millennium* stands as an early example of the trend. "I think that a lot of T.V. shows are better than most movies I see. They're done better. They look better. I go to movies now—I'm a huge movie fan—and I walk out disappointed most of the time. I'll go to a movie and really try to watch it and enjoy it, and a lot of movies I do, but I'm just a fan so I just have to let myself go. I think I've changed in that respect a bit where I will just sit there and watch it. If I start cringing then my wife hits me and I go back to watching it again!

"There has been a change, though, and of course they want a one-hour episode to look like a fifty million dollar movie. You go in with that in mind because this is what they want, and it's hard to do. Sometimes you do a really pretty good job and sometimes you do just okay, but there are a lot of things that happen during this that dictate how things may go and may not go. If you have a shot at it and you can do it then you go all out, but it's approached exactly the same way, I don't care what they say."

OUT OF THE MASTER'S SHADOW

Having been involved throughout the run of the series, did Wright feel that, had it continued, *Millennium* still had places to explore that would have enabled him to keep on taking a fresh approach to the subject matter as a director? "I felt that way," he affirms. "I was going for five years myself. I just found each episode was its own thing and I didn't go back to two before and say, 'I did this. I never do that.' Each scene presents itself and there's a lot of ways you look at it, and I try not to think about what I did two shows ago, or on the last show. Each script is fresh. It's new—it gives you a whole new perspective. That's part of the fun of it—for me, anyway."

Even with a substantial list of credits to his name, Thomas J. Wright still emphasizes *Millennium* as one of the highlights of his career. "*Millennium* is one of the shows that I have worked on in my career that I've been really proud of. *N.C.I.S.* is another one. *The Wire* is another. *Space: Above and Beyond* was a huge amount of fun, and it did get me rolling with Glen and Jim because it was the first thing I had done with them. I came down and started doing them, they really liked me and kept giving me more of them to do, and that started a great relationship. Another show I enjoyed doing was an episode in the miniseries *Taken* because I was reunited with a really good friend of mine, Matt Frewer. We did *Max Headroom* together, and that was another series I really loved doing. Another show I'm doing right now which I'm finding out is a lot of fun—and I'm enjoying it tremendously—is *Castle*. I like the people on it tremendously, and I have worked with Nathan Fillion on *Firefly*, and a lot of the crew are *X-Files* crew guys. So when I went over to do that show I knew a lot of the faces and it became really fun, so I'm enjoying that."

In closing, the conversation inevitably returns to *Millennium*. "We loved doing *Millennium*. The crew, the actors, everybody: this was just a great series for us." The memories of his work on the series remain with him, even thirteen years later. "We still talk about it to this day. I was just up in Vancouver doing a new series, and I had a lot of my old *Millennium* crew working with me. We did nothing but talk about *Millennium* for weeks and tell stories. It was great having them again and seeing them, and just a really good time, but all we did was talk about *Millennium*."

THE PAINTER OF LIGHT:
A CONVERSATION WITH ROBERT McLACHLAN

Interview by Adam Chamberlain
Written by Brian A. Dixon

The interplay between darkness and light defines *Millennium* (1996-99). This is a literal truth when we consider the distinctive visual style artfully achieved for the series by cinematographer Robert McLachlan, A.S.C. Lighting is the essence of visual storytelling and, as the director of photography explains, it is our window into the soul of Frank Black that imbues *Millennium* with essential glimmers of brilliance and light. "As much as possible, we tried to see the world through Frank's eyes. Here is something about the lighting: one of the reasons we could get away with so little is that Lance has these amazing eyes and they catch even the tiniest bit of light there is. It meant we could use very little, but you would always have life in his eyes."

Robert McLachlan has long been captivated by visual storytelling. "I have always loved movies and photography," he says. This is evident in his personal remembrances, which include childhood memories of his father developing home movies on 8mm film. McLachlan began to imagine himself in the role of cinematographer as early as tenth grade, when an English teacher offered him the choice of submitting a creative project in lieu of simply writing an essay. He joined forces with fellow classmates to create a film, and the resulting Super 8 reel earned him the first A he had ever received in English.

McLachlan went on to study at the Simon Fraser University Film Workshop—offering a production-oriented curriculum that emphasized educational filmmaking and became the foundation of the university's film program—and got his start shooting industrial films and commercials. "I started a film company in 1979 because people would hire me to make little documentaries and commercials when I couldn't get work as a cameraman," says McLachlan, recalling the early days of his career. "The company is OMNIFilm Productions and now it is huge, with over twenty-five employees. They make a lot of series for Discovery Channel. I sold my share to my partner ten years ago."

A remake of the classic adventure series *Sea Hunt* (1987-88) produced for MGM and shot primarily in Victoria, British Columbia, provided him with what he considers his "big break," initiating him in the television industry. Soon McLachlan was working behind the camera on primetime series such as *MacGyver* (1985-92) and Stephen J. Cannell's *The Commish* (1991-96). It was his work on the short-lived Fox series *Strange Luck* (1995-96), starring D. B. Sweeney as uncannily unlucky photographer Chance Harper, that would usher him toward the darkest corners of the Ten Thirteen universe. *Strange Luck* shared Friday nights on Fox with *The X-Files* (1993-2002) and the standout cinematography in the earlier series quickly caught the attention of Chris Carter.

In 1996, after director David Nutter and cinematographer Peter Wunstorf had produced a pilot for the series, Carter contacted McLachlan about lending his distinguished eye to filming the highly anticipated *Millennium*. "Chris Carter approached me shortly after the pilot was done," McLachlan recalls. "Actually, they had asked me to take over on *The X-Files* Season Three, but I was out of town and didn't respond quick enough. Chris had seen my work on a quirky show called *Strange Luck* and liked the photography. From there I was teamed up with the pilot director, David Nutter, on the initial episodes to establish the look."

THE PAINTER OF LIGHT

McLachlan was impressed by the style of *Millennium*'s inaugural installment, an episode shot with the skill and flare of a major motion picture, and he was excited by the prospect of helping to create the dark world to be braved by Frank Black and the Millennium Group. "The pilot was just amazing, and with Chris Carter in charge it meant the show would go to air the way *we* wanted it to look, not some lowest common denominator-thinking studio exec. I could see I'd have the kind of support and control normally a director of photography only gets in features, and often not even then."

During filming on the visually stunning first season of *Millennium*, Lance Henriksen referred to the show's talented D.P. as a "painter of light," evoking a moniker associated with famed Romantic landscape painter J. M. W. Turner. The title is apt for the discerning use of color and light were integral to establishing the mood and narrative tone of the series. "With the subject matter being so dark and having permission to go there from Chris, it meant you had to be careful to draw the viewer's eye to where you wanted it to go." Resurrecting the classic techniques of those filmmakers who defined cinema during the Golden Age of Hollywood, *Millennium* was a television series shot in a distinctive black-and-white style, one that offered harsh back lights and hard edges. "I realized because we were the first to really start desaturating the image a lot that, in order for the picture to not go flat and muddy, I needed to start to light it the way one would if you were shooting real traditional black and white." The end result, McLachlan says, "was really satisfying."

The deepest colors of those scenes set far from the sanctity of the yellow house were pulled out of the film in post-production to create a distinctly desaturated look. It was a technique that proved to be groundbreaking for television, appearing in countless other primetime dramas following *Millennium*'s high-profile premiere. "I had a genius color timer named Philip Azenzer, who also was instrumental in the look of *The X-Files*. We worked together on the desaturation degrees, but otherwise it was all in camera and on set." At the end of each day's shooting, there was little for the post-production team to manipulate. Results had to be achieved on set or on location. "No C.G. back then," McLachlan points out.

The city of Vancouver, British Columbia, famous for offering picturesque locales ranging from fog-filled forests to unspoiled beaches, chameleonic locales ideal for film production, proved to be a great asset to McLachlan as he attempted to capture just the right light for Frank Black's weekly forays into woodlands and abandoned warehouses alike. "Vancouver's often overcast skies provided perfect soft light that one could then make darker or brighter," McLachlan observes. Indeed, the diverse coastal city was undeniably a key player in the drama of both *The X-Files* and *Millennium*. "The subdued tones of the city—other than the ubiquitous vibrant green, which we toned down—worked too."

Location shooting, however, is rife with challenges inevitably compounded by the unforgiving shooting schedule imposed by network television production. McLachlan admits that his efforts were complicated by those instances in which he was unable to scout a location far in advance of shooting there. "Lack of prep made it hard but having done so much documentary work early in my career and a *lot* of episodic work, I am pretty good at improvising." The setting must dictate the lighting, McLachlan explains, not some preconceived pictorial palette. "We tried to keep the lighting appropriate to the subject and setting. Any good film lighting does this. As soon as you try to impose a look on a location that doesn't warrant it, you lose."

Filming *Millennium* presented the cinematographer with many challenges but the dominant vision of the show's creator and the standard style established by McLachlan and his crew were maintained in spite of occasional bouts of creative resistance. "The best thing about the show was, again, Chris Carter," McLachlan insists. It was the sheer strength of Carter's creative vision, he argues, that carried *Millennium* through creative turmoil. "We had a hard and fast style laid down for the show and if any director tried to deviate from it they got reined in very fast by the producers. One time in Season Two, when Glen Morgan and James Wong were running the series while Carter did *The X-Files* movie and series, we had a guy who had only done *NYPD Blue* in that long-lens, follow-the-action, off-axis proscenium style. He had no clue how to block a scene traditionally. He was giving me a lot of grief and not doing *our* show. Glen Morgan was on a plane the very next day to Vancouver and sorted him out in no uncertain terms. It then just meant the operator and I ran the set rather more than usual. Glen and Carter had some differences over the years but he and Jim Wong's dedication to maintaining the look and feel of Chris Carter's show was absolute. They did a great job, I think."

THE PAINTER OF LIGHT

Millennium distinguishes itself from other television series largely through its unique approach to the art and science of cinematography. McLachlan confides that, although lighting was key to establishing mood and setting, it was a unique approach to photographing the action and drama of the series that truly set it apart. "For many people the style of the show came from the lighting, but I think the real style of the show was in the fact we almost never, ever used zoom lenses, always fixed prime lenses. We also only used the same set of lenses all the time in similar circumstances." Again, the pace and quality of the approach harked back to a bygone era of filmmaking. "Almost no one does that anymore because they think it's too slow. But we were really fast—often knocking out up eighty set ups a day of very, very solid work."

The series, McLachlan explains, was shot on 35mm film, primarily Kodak 5298. Capturing Frank Black's dynamic visions of death and destruction, however, necessitated a shift to 16mm in order to achieve rapid, expressive visuals unlike anything else seen in T.V. drama. "This was something we invented and I still love it," McLachlan beams, recognizing that the profiler's visions were "very, very unique." As he describes it, the technical devices employed in realizing these sequences on film remain fascinating. "First we shot on 16mm to make it grainier. Then we ran 'off speed,' usually at six or twelve frames per second. This gives, if played back normally, a very fast motion effect, but we would transfer the film to tape at the same speeds so, while it was normal speed, there was only a half or quarter as much information there and because the shutter was going much slower there was a lot of motion blur as compared to twenty-four frames per second, which is normal. Then we added another element while shooting. We used these strobe lights from Clairmont Camera which flash once each time a frame is exposed for 1/50,000th of a second. This means whatever they light is very, very sharp if it's moving fast. We would light part of the subject with those and the rest normally so what you got was a violent-motion, blurry image that was both blurry and razor sharp at the same time."

From shadowy portraits of Vancouver's dense forests to razor-sharp showreels capturing murderous rage, Robert McLachlan's outstanding work on *Millennium* captivated the show's viewers and was well-recognized within the industry. McLachlan was nominated for three American Society of Cinematographers Awards as a result of his contributions to *Millennium* and for three consecutive years his work on the series received a Canadian Society of Cinematographers Award for Best Cinematography in a Television Series. The accolades are well earned considering the widespread creative impact of his unique approach to filming the series. "The show was hugely influential," McLachlan admits. Few of its imitators, however, can truly capture its striking style. "After Season Two, that desaturated look broke out like the plague, but most of them didn't do it right because they lit as if it was color, but really it was closer to black and white, which is a much more disciplined style."

Today, McLachlan continues to deliver outstanding visuals, his time for digressions such as interviews necessarily constrained by strict shooting schedules for the likes of HBO's Emmy-winning *Game of Thrones* (2011-). Asked if there are any who serve to inspire him in creating compositions of light and shadow on the screen, McLachlan considers that his cinematic work is inspired by the artists of many mediums, primarily those painters recognized for their chiaroscuro style. "Many people inspire. Architects inspire, painters from the Dutch genre schools, George de la Tour, the pre-Raphaelites, Andrew Wyeth... All sorts."

The brilliance of these influences shines through in McLachlan's work and is reflected in his advice to those interested in pursuing a career in cinematography. "My first advice is you'd better really, really love it, because breaking in and then putting up with the hours and the egos and the irregular schedule is very, very hard. You really need to love it. That, and don't go to film school. Study fine art and do photography on your own. Also, I tell them to shoot everything they possibly can get their hands on: mattress commercials, documentaries, you name it."

After serving as *Millennium*'s dedicated director of photography across three disparate seasons as the style of the series shifted to meet the demands of its production and the themes of its mythology, is there any episode that stands out as McLachlan's favorite? "I love 'Gehenna,' which David Nutter directed. Also 'The Sound of Snow' by Paul Shapiro, and 'Borrowed Time,' the one about the girl trapped in the sinking train, by Dwight Little. Also 'The Wild and the Innocent,' the one by Tom Wright about the hillbilly looking for her child." Clearly, it is difficult for him to pick just one. "I'm sure there are others!"

Thanks to Robert McLachlan's vision as a cinematographer, Frank Black's investigations were imbued with a palpable sense of oppressive darkness and hopeful radiance, and McLachlan wants to be there when television's greatest criminal profiler steps forth from the shadows once more. "Man, would I love to revisit that subject," McLachlan exclaims, and the cinematographer has put considerable thought into his approach to a twenty-first century take on *Millennium*. "I know today we would likely shoot on digital, which is fine. I still like shooting on fixed lenses. You know the approach always. It always starts with what's on the page. And what was on the pages of a *Millennium* script was often fantastic."

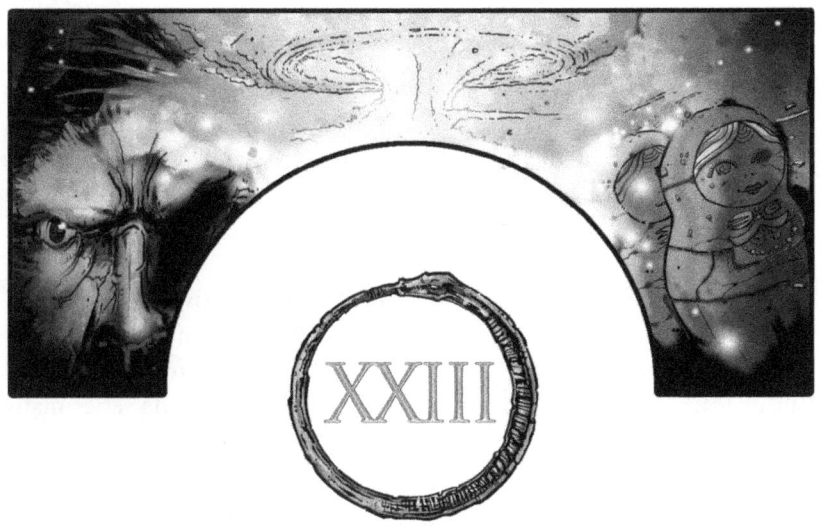

BARDO THODOL:
THE THIRD SEASON AND A NEW, UNIFIED THEORY OF *MILLENNIUM*

by John Kenneth Muir

Chris Carter's series *Millennium* (1996-99) was broadcast for three seasons on Fox, airing sixty-seven hour-long episodes, and during that span the series developed three very distinctive but nonetheless connected formats to depict the ongoing story of criminal profiler Frank Black (Lance Henriksen) and his family.

For many fans and academicians, the frequent alterations in format on *Millennium* proved almost vexing. Did each season exist in a separate, independent universe? If the seasons did connect meaningfully and tonally to one another, what were viewers to make of such U-turns in approach and narrative? How did a T.V. series that presented grounded tales of harsh reality, such as "The Well-Worn Lock," also dramatize such outré narratives as "Somehow, Satan Got Behind Me"? In Carter's *Millennium*, were viewers actually witnessing the tale of one man—our heroic anchor, Frank—told through three very separate and distinct storytelling lenses? Or was there a different, more substantial, and purposeful aesthetic at work, dictating the shape of such changes? In short, many *Millennium* scholars have meaningfully sought in this remarkable, technological work of art a brand of "unifying theory," one that accounts for all the permutations, changes, and developments in Frank Black's world over the series' three seasons, one that presents a single overarching explanation for them and a way of understanding the series as a whole.

Such a unifying theory has remained notably elusive, however, and yet that very fact also remains a perpetual delight of the series. There is a feeling encoded in many of the episodes that a big answer exists just out of reach, just beyond our grasp. One can return to the series many times and glean an amorphous sense—an aura—of a truth half-glimpsed, of a meaningful verity half-understood. *Millennium* delights for the very reason that it spoon-feeds the viewer virtually nothing. Few easy answers are to be found. Few explanations are offered. In developing its overarching tale in this ambiguous, multifaceted way, *Millennium* remains wonderfully available to individual interpretation and insight and asks the viewer to truly, actively, *persistently* engage with the provocative material.

Film director Nicholas Meyer once opined that examples of true art provide only some of the answers that observers seek in it. They thus leave the percipient's psyche to fill in the remaining mysteries with his or her sensibilities or even belief system. *Millennium* admirably adheres to this noble philosophy and this definition of art. And in the gaps between seasons and tones, it forges an even deeper sense of mystery and meaning.

I am among those who return to *Millennium* frequently in search of this elusive "unified theory." I have often felt, since writing extensively about the first and second season for my blog in 2008, that I was still missing some critical aspect of understanding in regards to the series. Although I have always enjoyed and appreciated the third season more than many fans, I simultaneously felt that I could not quite get a handle on what it was attempting to convey overall, even after several viewings of its installments.

If I did not fully grasp the meaning of this work of art's last act, what intelligent conclusions about the series could I possibly reach? The third season remained, for me, so irrevocably opaque, I felt there was no way I could approach *Millennium* as a meaningful whole. And that is very much how I wanted to approach such an initiative: as a complete and fulfilling work of art.

And then, finally, on a recent marathon of the third season, my "Eureka" moment arrived.

In examining the third season segments, I began to ponder the admittedly strange idea that *Millennium* as a series was actually some strange expression of the Bardo Thodol, a Tibetan funerary text conceived and written in the eighth century by a man named Padmasambhava.

In very broad terms, the Bardo Thodol stresses our human ways of *knowing* things. In particular, the passages concern what Carl Jung once termed a "spiritual way of knowing" (Shelburn 26) and a focus on the human consciousness in three important stages: before death, during death, and in the process of rebirth. Those three stages of human consciousness suddenly struck me as vital in a total understanding of *Millennium*. I wondered: is it possible to gaze at the three very different seasons of *Millennium* as Consciousness Before Death (First), Consciousness at Death (Second) and Consciousness in the Process of Rebirth (Third)?

Although I boast no hubristic illusion that this was the precise or even imprecise "plan" of creative talents such as Chris Carter, Frank Spotnitz, Glen Morgan, James Wong, Chip Johannesen, and others, it nonetheless became plain to me that viewers can indeed interpret the three seasons in such a fashion and, by doing so, gain a new perspective on Frank Black's tale and his character arc. In other words, I found a way—I hoped—to fill in the gaps in *Millennium*'s storytelling equation with a unique theory, as well as my own mindset and belief system.

By many accounts, that interpretation fulfills the very definition of art.

THE FIRST SEASON:
CONSCIOUSNESS BEFORE DEATH

In the first season of *Millennium,* Frank often dealt with depraved serial killers who reflected some pertinent aspect of American society in the 1990s. When Frank saw "what the killer sees" in those gritty, violent, dark first season episodes, he was also viewing American culture up-close, as well as the foibles it faced as the nation neared the projected apocalypse of the end of the century, a kind of societal death.

From various serial killers, Frank learned why the world was ending. He witnessed hypocrisy ("Weeds"), sexual dysfunction and lack of intimacy ("Loin like a Hunting Flame"), and even lost children, symbolic of a sacrificed tomorrow ("Blood Relatives" and "The Well-Worn Lock"). He saw good men and families torn asunder in "Dead Letters" and the law itself grown corrupt and monstrous in "The Judge."

Frank's overall view, then, was of a society crumbling before the inevitable end. This viewpoint is roughly analogous to the first stage of the Bardo Thodol as I described it above: consciousness before death. In the first season, Frank Black is aware of the encroaching darkness, of the gloom that seems to be settling upon the modern world. Man's very moral compass seems to be sliding towards inevitable entropy.

THE SECOND SEASON: CONSCIOUSNESS AT DEATH

During the second season of *Millennium*, Frank loses his clarity of vision or insight and must deal with death as it pertains not just to society but to the most important people in his life.

In the second season catalogue, he witnesses the death of his marriage ("The Beginning and the End"), the death of his father ("The Fourth Horseman"), the death of his partner, Lara Means ("The Time Is Now"), and then, finally, the death of Catherine, his wife ("The Time is Now"). And then, in the last moments of the season, death comes to claim the world itself.

In witnessing so many deaths up close, Frank finally comprehends that the Millennium Group has "forced the end" in an apparent apocalypse and he no longer wishes to be involved with them. As the season closes, Frank's death also seems inevitable in that remote cabin in the woods, and thus the path of the entire season becomes clear. This second sortie concerns—at least from one perspective—human consciousness (and therefore knowledge) at the time of death. This is the second phase of the Bardo Thodol.

THE THIRD SEASON: REBIRTH

By the advent of *Millennium*'s third and final season, Frank looks very much like a broken man. His hair has grayed considerably and he appears older and more world-weary. In early episodes such as "The Innocents," his insights are often wrong because his mind is now consumed with rage, revenge, and anger. He has not found a way to "be" yet in this new world. He remains dead inside because of the loss of Catherine.

And yet this valedictory season is not about further decline and decay, but rather about Frank's conscious in the third state of being dictated by the Bardo Thodol, the stage of "spiritual understanding" and "rebirth" after death.

Accordingly, the third season frequently sees Frank encountering people who, like him, boast singular and unique ways of "seeing" life. Importantly, these figures are generally not the sick madmen of the first season but rather gifted individuals who contribute to Frank's sense of spiritual understanding about himself and the universe. As much as Frank may feel he is alone and dead inside due to the loss of Catherine, this is not the case. Throughout the season, he frequently meets analogs for *himself*, outsiders with different perspectives on existence. In many ways, even his daughter, Jordan, fits this definition.

In "The Innocents" and "Exegesis," Frank encounters a family of female oracles, so-called "remote viewers" who bear direct knowledge of the future and have learned to "think" on a very different level from normal human beings. Frank learns from them how deeply they are committed to the survival of their family and how zealously they plot to win the future and a safe harbor or sanctuary for those like them.

In "Skull and Bones," Frank encounters Ed (Arye Gross), another prophet who sees not the future but the hidden connections in life and therefore the truth of human existence—and the Millennium Group. Ed has hand-written an ad-hoc history of the Group's corruption in a series of notebooks, documenting, essentially, an alternate history of the past. In Ed, Frank hopes, he has an ally, one who sees the world differently but quite powerfully and quite accurately. Each man boasts an insight and different ways of harnessing it.

In "Borrowed Time," Frank crosses the path of the fearsome personification of Death, an immortal figure who views the world not on human terms but rather via some kind of radically different (cosmic?) time scale, one that measures the death of individuals according to some invisible plan. Again, Frank is forced to see the world from the perspective of another individual. His sight and spiritual wisdom is, in this case, harrowingly widened.

In perhaps the season's most haunting and memorable episode, "The Sound of Snow," Frank is forced to "see" differently himself once more, this time through a strange hallucination-inducing audiotape. Through this mysterious technological auspice, however, Frank finds not the death and despair of other "victims" but closure in his relationship with Catherine. This is a necessary step towards his spiritual understanding of self and his eventual rebirth as a wise, knowing soul. "The Sound of Snow" is the third season's turning point in many significant ways, with Catherine appearing as a "ghost" (or guide) to absolve Frank of guilt and to let him return to the mortal world in every sense, with the past truly and finally behind him.

Another significant third season episode about "seeing" and "spiritual understanding" is the deeply disturbing "Saturn Dreaming of Mercury." In this almost diabolical segment, Frank is confronted with a strange evil that seems to inhabit, creepily, a small wooden case of "antique" glass eyeballs. Some twenty-four eyeballs are displayed in the home of a mysterious, possibly sinister neighbor, Will Sanderson, and each of these orbs appears to boast the capacity to see and bloodily affect others. Clearly, the good-hearted Frank would never adopt this evil manner of seeing, but he is exposed, again, to a different vision of the world, one that enhances his wisdom.

Eyes, naturally, are the medium through which all creatures see and, accordingly, "Saturn Dreaming of Mercury" is dominated by references and allusions to the process of sight. "No one sees everything," Frank stresses at one point.

"Do you see it?" a frightened Jordan (Brittany Tiplady) asks her father in regard to a demonic visage in an upstairs window. "Yeah, I see it," he responds. What they speak of is something undetectable to those at different stages of spiritual consciousness. They boast an insight those others lack.

Even Agent Emma Hollis (Klea Scott) obsesses on the act of seeing in this particular third season episode. She notes, "I'm so tired of stumbling through this, not seeing." Frank's response is the initially cryptic, "I see what I was allowed to see." But perhaps what Frank is really noting here is that he and Emma occupy different points in their spiritual journey on the path of the Bardo Thodol, and he thus "sees" the world quite differently. Emma has not yet reached Frank's stage of development, his place beyond spiritual death and towards a spiritual rebirth.

The episode "Bardo Thodol" is another critical episode in understanding the nature of *Millennium*'s third season and Frank's series-long spiritual quest. Here, the profiler becomes involved with Tibetan monks who are caring for an injured, rogue member of the Millennium Group, Dr. Steven Takahashi (Tzi Ma). The monks at the temple tend to Dr. Takahashi and read to him passages and sermons from their funerary text. Importantly, Frank is present for many of these moral and spiritual lessons. In this episode, Frank's journey finally shifts from one of "seeing" to one, essentially, of "starting over." The lead monk (James Hong) speaks of "listening without distraction" and "setting aside perceptions." He suggests "everything you experience is but a projection of the mind." Again, another way of interpreting reality is presented at Frank's feet.

Karma is discussed meaningfully as well in "Bardo Thodol," providing Frank a framework for understanding his experiences pre-"death" (Season One), during "spiritual" death (Season Two), and, finally, after-death (Season Three).

Importantly, Hollis herself makes strides "seeing" in this episode. After discovering for herself evidence of Peter Watts's (Terry O'Quinn) deception and "evil," she tells her mentor, "I saw them, Frank. For just one moment, I saw them clearly." It very much appears that Emma is now where Frank once was, a season or a season-and-a-half-earlier, perhaps.

Even non-arc third season episodes such as "Thirteen Years Later" and the significantly titled "Darwin's Eye" concern the act of seeing and Frank's insight into how others see themselves and the world. In "Thirteen Years Later," Frank is forced (quite unwillingly) to countenance the world through the filter of post-modernism, where things don't actually have meaning, only the meaning we accord them. In "Darwin's Eye," he is forced to see into the beautiful and compelling madness of a woman named Cassie Doyle (Tracy Middendorf). Once more, these "ways of knowing" are not Frank's but they show him alternate paths.

Keeping all of these examples in mind, more than a mere handful of episodes in Season Three meaningfully involve Frank's path to spiritual wholeness and rebirth following the loss of so many he loves. The characters he encounters—from the healing wood nymphs in "Omerta" to phantasms of his wife in "The Sound of Snow"—teach him about how to see the world with new, wiser eyes.

The overall implication is that Frank's ultimate role in this mortal coil is also as a "seer," one who can provide wisdom and knowledge to others, including his gifted daughter. Unfortunately, Frank's spiritual daughter, Emma—despite her ability, briefly, to see the Millennium Group for what it is—becomes lost. Her "karmic fate," it is strongly suggested, is to "come upon a bad end," one she has made herself by accepting a deal with the Millennium Group—with the Devil.

In *Millennium*'s final episode, "Goodbye to All That," a wiser Frank—one who has traced the three stages of consciousness from the Bardo Thodol—takes young Jordan in hand and heads off to an unknown future. He does so, significantly, with the spiritual understanding that his strange experiences have brought him. He is thus a changed man, having traveled through the gauntlet of death and despair and come out on the other side, with a rebirth of knowledge and wisdom.

If a unifying theory of *Millennium* exists, I submit it rests in this connection to the Tibetan Bardo Thodol, the belief that, according to Jung, "spiritual understanding" can only come from a man who acquires the "special training" to understand it. *Millennium* is therefore about Frank Black getting that training and then applying it to the times that can and do try his very soul. By the end of the series, Frank not only has seen "what the killer sees," he has seen the mysteries of life and the weight of individual insight from multitudinous points of view.

If we are "all shepherds," then Frank's next mission will surely be to share this wisdom with his daughter and anyone else willing to listen.

WORKS CITED

Shelburn, Walter A. *Mythos and Logos in the Thought of Carl Jung: The Theory of the Collective Unconscious in Scientific Perspective.* Albany: State University of New York, 1988. Print.

The Tibetan Book of the Dead (Bardo Thödol). Trans. Lama Kazi Dawa-Samdup. Ed. W. Y. Evans-Wentz. London: Oxford University UP, 1949. Print.

John Kenneth Muir is the author of over two-dozen books of film and T.V. reference, including award-winners *Terror Television* (2008), *Horror Films of the 1970s* (2007), and *The Encyclopedia of Superheroes on Film and Television* (2008). His popular blog, *Reflections on Cult Movies and Classic Television*, was selected one of the "100 Top Film Study" sites on the net in 2010. He is also the creator of the independent web series *The House Between* (2007-09). In 2009, Muir appeared in the documentary *Nightmares in Red, White and Blue: The Evolution of the American Horror Film* along with John Carpenter, Larry Cohen, Joe Dante, and voiceover narrator Lance Henriksen. Muir's most recent books are *Horror Films of the 1990s* (McFarland; 2011) and *Purple Rain: Music on Film* (Limelight Editions; 2012). He lives in Charlotte, North Carolina, with his beautiful wife and young son.

RUSHING TOWARD AN APOCALYPSE:
A CONVERSATION WITH CHIP JOHANNESSEN

Interview by James McLean & Troy L. Foreman
Written by Brian A. Dixon

As a television drama with an eclectic and oftentimes disturbing focus, *Millennium* offers its spellbound viewers its share of bizarre and frightening visions. Some of the most unusual of these sprang forth from the depths of the creative mind of Chip Johannessen. Insanity-inducing drug trials, a man in an iron lung, a drowning on dry land, an imaginary friend who pushes and bites, a cooler filled with living hands—none of these nightmares would have troubled Frank Black but for the fevered imagination of Johannessen, one of *Millennium*'s most inventive writers and the man who would guide the series through its third and final year on television.

Johannessen's contributions to *Millennium* represent a creative leap in a writing career that began with scripts for episodes of *Married with Children* (1987-97) and *Beverly Hills, 90210* (1990-2000)—shows that helped to establish and define the Fox network amid the modern television landscape—and continues today with his award-winning work on acclaimed series including Showtime's *Dexter* (2006-) and *Homeland* (2011-). When it came to finding a place on the writing staff of *The X-Files* (1993-2002), an unexpected hit for Fox from creator Chris Carter, Johannessen's stint was over before it began. "Some time before *Millennium*, my agent got me a meeting with Chris Carter to talk about working on *The X-Files*," Johannessen recalls. "I went in without story ideas and with only the vaguest understanding of the show. Not only did nothing come of it, but Chris clearly thought I was wasting his time."

It was the captivating pilot for *Millennium* that convinced him to face Carter again. "Maybe a year later, I saw the *Millennium* pilot at the Directors Guild and was utterly blown away. It was the most amazing thing I'd ever seen, by far, and I really wanted to work on it." Fortunately, the show's creator proved himself to be a man who believes in second chances. "Despite the bad meeting on *The X-Files*, Chris was willing to try again because he was already hiring a friend of mine, Ted Mann, and Ted was suggesting that he give me a second chance."

Johannessen was better prepared for his next meeting at Ten Thirteen Productions. "Not wanting to blow it again, I spent a lot of time thinking up stories, and when I went in to talk to Chris I had a lot of material to present. But Chris always surprises. He said he didn't want to hear material. He just said, 'I like Ted and Ted likes you. Let's do this.'"

The somber "Blood Relatives," Johannessen's first script for *Millennium*, perfectly captures the themes and formula of the show's first season. A serial killer mystery complete with foreboding set pieces and an unexpected twist, the episode features plotlines for both Frank and Catherine and openly confronts the iniquities of a society that has lost the capacity to care for its emotional orphans, children abandoned by families and starved of love. Though the strength of the screenplay speaks to Johannessen's talents, "Blood Relatives" would prove to be an uncharacteristically straightforward script from a writer whose stories would delve brazenly into more labyrinthine depths of occult symbolism, warped perception, and weird science. *Millennium* offered writers the opportunity to explore eclectic subject matter and, as its mythology became deeper and stranger with each passing season, Johannessen's scripts often led the charge into unknown territory. "I was going to say I wrote the exact same kind of thing all three seasons but that's not really true," he considers, reflecting on the stories he contributed across three remarkably disparate seasons of the show. "Things got more and more magical, and conspiratorial, and complicated, not necessarily in a good way."

By the time of the third season, in classic installments such as "Skull and Bones" and "Saturn Dreaming of Mercury," sinister conspiracies drawn by unearthly forces had become a staple of the series. "Probably we were all feeling the pull of *The X-Files*. I'm not sure. But I'm pretty sure we got away from Chris's original concept for the show, which was to stay based in reality, unlike *The X-Files*, while imagining and depicting the different ways the world might be experienced by certain evil people."

Experiencing the world in new and unexpected ways would seem to be one of the mandates of *Millennium*, and it is a concern that distinguishes its hero. From "Walkabout" to "Exegesis," Johannessen's episodes are among those that endeavor to explore the true depth of Frank Black's gift. Though the debate concerning the nature and origin of these visions continues to this day, Johannessen's interpretation remains firm. "These images of the world, which Frank Black was tuned to, were not supposed to be objective reality. They were highly subjective. In fact, in script the shots were labeled 'His Internal P.O.V.' or 'His Subjective P.O.V.'" Did the exploration of Frank's gift in such episodes hasten the inclination toward embracing the uncanny on the series? "Already in the first season there were some speculative episodes that were terrific but keeping a lid on this would probably have been a good idea."

Millennium's willingness to embrace surreal spiritual concerns is, in fact, what consistently set it apart from other series. Metaphysical concerns distinguish the spiritual quest of "Luminary," perhaps the most celebrated of Johannessen's contributions to *Millennium*. It is an episode that still evokes pride in the writer: "'Luminary' has a lot of influences and makes my short list of favorite episodes."

The story of Frank Black's search for the missing Alex Glaser is based on the real life events chronicled in Jon Krakauer's *Into the Wild* (1996), an account of the Alaskan journey of self-discovery famously undertaken by Christopher McCandless, a quest that resulted in the teen's tragic death in 1992. "At the time, I was working on a pilot called *Vanishing Point* with John Hulme and Mike Wexler," Johannessen explains. "It was based on a series of radio plays they had done about an odd dropout culture hidden in plain sight. Our 'bibles' were books like *Blue Highways* and *Into the Wild*, which at that point was relatively unknown… [Alex Glaser] was a seeker, abandoning material possessions, looking for a more magical existence. Ken Horton suggested this kind of guy could be the basis for a cool episode. That was the foundation."

One of the second season's most unique and memorable installments, "Luminary" explores many ideas and evinces many influences. Johannessen reveals that his script was shaped by input from *Millennium*'s charismatic leading lady as well as his fellow second season scribes. "I had dinner with Megan Gallagher, who turned me on to the whole astrology convergence theme. She asked if I could possibly fit it in somewhere and, as it turned out, it was just what I was looking for. Other elements are taken from an organization I belonged to in college, the *Harvard Lampoon*. Also, Darin Morgan gave me the younger brother with the telescope, and for some reason insisted that when the plane flies off with the injured boy at the end, that Frank had to squat at lake's edge. Finally, I was reading some book at the time whose title I've forgotten, but I'm pretty sure that the idea of the stars matching to houselights on earth came from that.

"So there were a lot of thoughts floating around and I was up in Vancouver on a location scout for some other episode, and I was obsessing on that kid, and when I stepped off the bus I thought of those lines he says toward the end about what you should do with your life."

In the episode, Alex Glaser—rechristened Alex Ventoux—poses serious existential questions in the writings of his journal: "Imagine, for one second, you could drop in on a past life. What would you like to find yourself doing there? What would charm you? Make you proud? Ask yourself that and the question what to do in this life becomes so simple it's terrifying."

"When that thought appeared," Johannessen continues, "it was time to start writing. The production was mainly charmed, though Lance can tell you the water was crazy cold. The weather forecast said storms but when it came time to land the seaplane there were beautiful, sunny skies." Johannessen even had a hand in selecting the evocative soundtrack for the finished episode. "Normally, I leave Mark Snow to his own devices, but I was listening to a Finnish women's vocal group at the time, which felt perfect for the piece. He graciously adapted it for the score."

Johannessen served as a consulting producer on the second season of *Millennium* as he continued to contribute his unique brand of multifaceted mysteries in episodes such as "Sense and Antisense" and "In Arcadia Ego." When Executive Producers Glen Morgan and James Wong departed *Millennium* in the wake of their cataclysmic climax to the season, he found himself facing more daunting creative challenges and a host of newfound responsibilities. He would serve as showrunner for the third season, guiding *Millennium* and its apocalyptic mythology to the fateful series finale. "Running *Millennium* was a vastly bigger deal than my second year involvement, which was writing a few scripts," he admits. "Shortly after we started the third season I rented an apartment a block from the studio because I was leaving so late every night, then coming back early the next morning. For a while there, I never really got home. That said, the nature of the work didn't really change because of the unusual way that Chris runs shows. Unlike most shows, he really encourages writers to step up as producers. If you're willing to be as obsessive about quality as he is, he gives you a lot of freedom. So by the time I was executive producer I already had experience with most aspects of making T.V. thanks to Chris."

As he took charge of a relentless production schedule, Johannessen's family proved to be equally supportive during times of stress and creative upheaval. On "Bardo Thodol," an inscrutable third season installment that significantly deepens the mythology of the Millennium Group, Johannessen was joined by a co-writer, Virginia Stock, whose name was new to the credits of *Millennium*. "Virginia Stock is my wife of twenty-plus years," Johannessen explains. "We have a daughter, named Martine. One of her first words was ouroboros! 'Bardo Thodol' started with an image Virginia had: the tiny hands discovered in a cargo hold. She contributed to many other episodes, but I think that's the only one with her name on it."

Charting Frank Black's third season journey proved difficult, particularly in the aftermath of the apocalyptic events that had ended the previous season. Confronted with these trials and with the task of reinventing the series yet again, Johannessen admits to feeling overwhelmed. "We'd had a bad start at the beginning of Season Three, with some personnel changes that put us behind schedule. Also, I was mad at Jim and Glen for having burned the house down with their pandemic, but in retrospect it would have been smarter to have honored where they left us off instead of trying to work around it. In any case, Season Three had been a scramble and by the end we were kind of tired. Ken Horton and I were basically partners running the show at that point." The third season's development was demanding, but Horton and Johannessen had hope for the future and *Millennium*'s unrealized fourth season. "We felt like we'd had some hits and some misses but were excited about getting a good start into a more coherent fourth season. We were really trying to make sense of what it all meant, especially as we were now heading toward the actual millennium."

Would some of Johannessen's more baffling mysteries have been resolved had *Millennium* been renewed for its millennial fourth season? "I wrote a ten-point manifesto for the Millennium Group, which I no longer have, but I remember the first point was, 'We are rushing toward an apocalypse of our own creation.' I don't remember the rest exactly, but it tried to honor Chris's original idea that the various forms of evil present on this earth are connected and that they were coming to a boil. In this the Millennium Group saw itself as a vanguard, the only people who could see a clear path to the future. Since the Group's goal was basically the protection of humanity that might justify practically any means."

In spite of his grand plans for the show's story arc, the path from the past is always clearer than the path to the future, and Johannessen has had time to consider what could have been done differently on the series. "What would probably have made more sense would have been to get rid of the Millennium Group mythology entirely and do a heightened, sometimes speculative crime show. That would probably have been closer to what Chris had originally envisioned and, who knows, it might still be on today."

Today, more than a decade since "Goodbye to All That" brought an abrupt end to the mysterious mythology of *Millennium*, the series has gained a renewed relevance and dedicated viewers and critics alike continue to clamor for closure. Chip Johannessen has high expectations for Frank Black's eventual return: "Anything that Chris writes and Lance is in would be awesome."

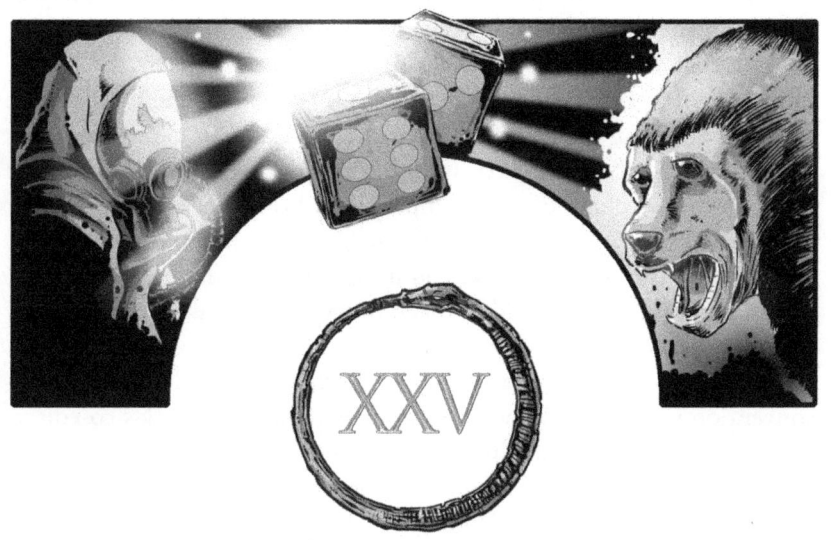

HARD GRAFT:
A HISTORY OF THE BACK TO FRANK BLACK CAMPAIGN

by James McLean

There is no doubt that this book in your hands is little more and certainly little less than a compendium of dedicated thought on the complex subject matter found in a scary little show called *Millennium* (1996-99). It can therefore be safely argued that a chapter within that compendium that doesn't deal with the subject matter of the book, rather the compendium itself, could be described as having "black sheep syndrome." In the midst of this tome's collective of enthused critical love for a television show that was tragically born before its time—and, equally, killed before its time—a chapter surrounding a small bunch of determined enthusiasts and their aspirations to bring a concept they rather enjoyed back onto our screens feels akin to a small child looking for a comfortable seat at a giant's tea party.

I'm sure you can appreciate a certain insecurity that this chapter doesn't inherently feel like a sore thumb, but it is the very core of this book, for all you read here derives from the work done by the people featured within this chapter. My purpose is not to sing their praises but to sing praises to all who have been involved and to assure you that nearly all who have spoken to us, all who have let us use their comments on behalf of the campaign to bring back the world of *Millennium*, have done so with cordiality, generosity, and enthusiasm. This chapter will hopefully give you insight into all who have supported this campaign and provide a reminder that quality art has no boundaries to its appreciation.

June 2012. I was fortunate to catch Lance Henriksen at a convention in Milton Keynes, England, alongside this book's co-editor, Adam Chamberlain. At the Friday night party, we were standing outside, having watched *Superman*'s Brandon Routh fail to tame the electronic bucking bronco. Lance turned to the pair of us, a forgotten glass of wine in one hand, a cigarette smoking in the other, and said, "Remember, we are Tribe." It's a comment he's made many times before. If you've followed Lance on Facebook, you'll have heard him refer to those who enjoy his page "the Tribe" as he feels the term breaks down the hierarchy between "fan" and "star." We are equals in his eyes and, hopefully, in your own. His comment on this occasion, however, was far reaching, referring to the three of us standing there and to all of you reading this book right now. In deep thought, I drove home from the convention, a flurry of cars probably left spinning in my wake, the point of the Tribe having hit home, realizing it was really the very axiom of the campaign. This campaign has not been a one-sided affair. It's not been the quarry of enthusiasts. This has been a movement from all sides.

If we were to be technical, the campaign was born in the summer of 2008. 24 July is a better date than any, and born a better term than any, for a campaign is born and it grows, organically. As parents to a campaign, we have to shape it—and, as with all parents, at the start, we hadn't got a clue how to do that. But back to that date—it was indeed when the campaign started, but, as with any data presented in black and white, this fails to distinguish those vital shades that sit in between. First and foremost, if a campaign is born on a date, when was the illicit midnight squidgy meeting of event and idea that sired it?

The best answer for this starts with me—not out of any measure of self-importance but simply because it's a path I can offer that dovetails the key ingredients to the campaign.

I won't pretend I'm *Millennium*'s biggest fan. I'll let the publisher of this book, Brian A. Dixon, pretend that—and he has far more credentials to prove it. My love of *Millennium* is fairly recent. I recollect the promotions for the show that splashed themselves across the pages of various science fiction publications back in the 1990s. With the internet little more than a tadpole to the ugly frog we someday will turn into something a little more handsome than it currently presents itself as, we relied on magazines for our information. For those a little younger than myself, we used to read magazines without a mouse or a login name. You can "lol" now.

The magazine articles painted a fascinating show, surfing the wave of popularity conjured by Chris Carter's iconic sensation *The X-Files* (1993-2002). What sold it to me, however, wasn't the legacy of Ten Thirteen Productions or even the crime or mythology angles but the family unit. That seemed different and refreshing and I was certain I wouldn't be missing a single week of this new show. Britain's main independent television channel, ITV, had other ideas, buying the show as an alternative to their rival channel's hit *The X-Files* before taking up the anchor and letting it drift on a sea of turbulent midnight scheduling. I didn't fully get in-between the sheets with *Millennium* until nearly a decade later, in 2007, when my thrifty pocket found the season DVD box sets at a bargain price.

I remember having finished the third and, sadly, final season of the box sets thinking how I'd like to have met Lance Henriksen. I'd never seen that many films with him in, but his work on *Millennium* had wrought the deepest admiration. Lo and behold, he was appearing within a month's time at a Collectormania event at the G-Mex Centre in Manchester on Saturday 17 and Sunday 18 November 2007.

Something Lance has always found fascinating about the campaign is the nature of accumulation; one event sparks another event which sparks another, a snowball starting an avalanche, "a wave becoming tidal," as he says during the current intro narration for the campaign's podcast. I was not some major *Millennium* enthusiast—television scheduling had put a sharp end to that prospect—but the timing between finishing the box sets and Lance's visit to Manchester was a major catalyst for my involvement.

423

At Manchester, Lance was to intimate Frank Black was returning soon.

That event offered great insight into the man behind Frank Black. Anyone who has been to a convention might have noted how curious autograph signings are. I once commented that, as a "fan," wandering past autograph tables was like wandering around a dog shelter—some dogs had lots of people poking and cooing over them, others sat alone in an awkward corner, and as the visitor you'd do your best not to catch the gaze of the lonely dog in the fear of giving it false hope. This was rather a crass suggestion that demeans the whole nature of these events. They are far more considered than that but for me personally, my initial observation marked an interest in the nature and stresses of autograph queues. For the queue, there is a hunt for that perfect moment, meeting a face from your intimate living room and wanting to connect with a person you feel you know so well, yet you don't know at all. For the signer, there is the pressure of the moment, trying to make each encounter special for that lady or gentleman who has come all this way to see you. There is the strain of conscience in not letting the queues become desensitized. For you, your meeting is one in hundreds. For the person coming to meet you—a person you don't know from Adam, most likely, but they feel they know you like an uncle—it's very hard to keep the moment true.

After I'd got my signature from Lance—upon a photo no one will ever be allowed to see, so as not to disgrace whatever god watches over aesthetic beauty—I kept an eye on him from afar, watching how he handled the task of autograph signing. By five o'clock he looked no different to how he had looked at ten in the morning. He gave his one hundred percent to each fan. Such dedication and willingness to embrace the moment, to make the day special for each person he encountered, propelled my interest in *Millennium* even further. If Lance had been standoffish or disinterested in the people around him, that could very much have cooled me to the show and certainly ended any future campaign before it was launched.

The news of Lance's comments regarding *Millennium*'s future spread during the following week. I'd been casually but progressively slipping into *Millennium*'s internet fandom, first through the aforementioned Brian A. Dixon's discontinued website *The Millennial Abyss*, from which I absorbed information on a daily basis while watching the show, and then to the *This is Who We Are* (*TIWWA*) community forums. When the news of Lance's suggestion was discussed in one particular thread, it led to a lot of excitement. On the Sunday, Lance had said that he'd been told by Chris Carter to avoid mentioning Frank Black in regards to the upcoming *The X-Files 2*. That got people—myself included—very excited as we wondered just how Lance could appear.

The campaign didn't start there. Why should it? With *The X-Files 2* coming in the summer of the following year, we were all waiting for something more concrete to pop out of the woody woodwork. Indeed, it did, but not as we expected. On 2 March 2008, at the Scandinavian Sci-Fi, Game, and Film Convention in Sweden, Lance said he had heard from Chris Carter and that his next project following the untitled *X-Files* sequel would, indeed, be the *Millennium* motion picture (Smith).

On March 26, Chris Carter mentioned *Millennium* at the William S. Paley Television Festival in Hollywood. Of the project he said, "We've talked about that over the years. Lance would love to do it. I don't know if it would ever get done. It's a long shot. It would be fun. I have ideas about how to do it" (Lee).

And so, people waited with bated breath, wondering whether there was a definite possibility that Chris Carter and Frank Spotnitz were keen to do another *Millennium* project, uncertain whether these comments meant that Lance was definitely not cameoing in *The X-Files 2*.

Those who are very astute, and more astute than most, including myself, will note that the date I gave for the birth of the campaign was 24 July 2008, the very same date on which *The X-Files: I Want to Believe* received its U.K. première (with the United States première held on the 25 July). It should now be clear why all this past data is so relevant. By the week of the film's première, we knew that Frank Black would not feature in *The X-Files 2*. We'd waited on a vain hope that *Millennium*'s hero would make the cut, but he hadn't. As that knowledge sunk in, the need to do something about it intensified. In fact, on Sunday 20 July 2008, as the press coverage for *The X-Files* increased, Frank Spotnitz discussed *Millennium* in an interview with Moviehole.net. "It's funny, Chris and I have done a lot of appearances over the last seven months, and we're always—*always!*—asked about a *Millennium* movie," he was quoted as saying. "Funnily enough, there doesn't seem to be any interest on the part of the studio... It's

425

something we would definitely be interested in, but it's going to take a massive appeal by fans to get it up" (Morris).

This comment—the final sentence in particular—was pivotal, a direct slice of advice to supporters of *Millennium*. A whole group of *Millennium* enthusiasts began to swap ideas on the *TIWWA* forums. I was one of them—which is why I certainly won't take credit for there being a campaign, solely for being the person who was willing to run it. Being a fathead with a loud mouth atop a skinny body, I was more than open to giving my opinions on how a campaign should be run, but from the get-go I didn't want to run it. I could foresee the workload. My key concern was that we needed a name. "Legion of Black" was my first suggestion, playing on the Biblical reference to the devil as "Legion" that pops up in the show—though, on reflection, this was better suited for a thirteen-year-old's first attempt at a self-indulgent garage band. My second concern was that we'd need a website and the question of, well, who the hell we'd be contacting.

I'm glad now that I didn't take my own advice, but I was wary of the workload. This would need to be more than an internet fan petition. A month after Frank Spotnitz's *Moviehole* interview, I'd talked so much I think I'd talked myself into running the whole thing.

By chance I'd read a few books on fan campaigns, particularly around *Star Trek*'s (1966-69) revival in the Seventies. I'd seen the hard work that had gone into such a plan. I was also acutely aware of the disposable nature of an internet voice; the internet offered an easy means to self-expression but it is not easy for one to be heard. So often, recent campaigns from fans would rely on an internet petition, something I believed—and still believe—is next to worthless. If you want to lobby a studio to bring a product back—and bear in mind that favorite show of yours is a product, first and foremost—you need to convince them that rationale is profitable. As strange as it seems to many fans, any studio representative worth his salt might want a little more than an internet petition when he is being asked to invest millions of dollars in a project the studio has, more often not, decided recently wasn't worth investing millions of more dollars in. Anyone can waste twenty seconds in adding his or her name to a screen. It shows no measure of incentive or certainty that individual truly represents market interest. Even in this digital age—in fact, especially in this digital age—a piece of paper stuffed in an envelope, stamped, and sent direct to the studio carries far more weight for that person has invested time and some small amount of money. There is conviction behind that individual that suggests the show is worth the effort. They are more than likely to watch and please advertisers, or even to buy advertised products for home use.

Looking at my comments from July to September 2008, these key plans could be associated into a rather unwelcome bundle codenamed "Hard Graft." It was going to be hard work, the matter of reaching out to everyone: the press, websites, actors, and even fans who we couldn't rely upon looking in the right direction and spotting our stubby little soapbox. It was important that our website was easy to navigate for all parties—less about being flashy, more about getting that message across as effectively as possible to the widest audience. One final consideration at this early stage that wouldn't be fleshed out for nine months or so was a podcast, the newfangled means of online broadcasting that everyone was talking about.

The bottom line was we couldn't simply rely on people to help; we had to go and look for help. We had to beg, plead, wine, dine, seduce, and canoodle our way to gaining attention. There was just one key factor in this regard that I was keen to stress, that any attempts to gain interest were through positive rather than negative means. I insisted that if any negative publicity tactics were employed in the name of this unnamed campaign, I would no longer run it and we'd shut down. That included silliness, like snarky videos directed at Fox or letters inappropriately directed to anyone in any arm of the Fox family of companies. This wasn't a pressure campaign, it was a platform—a podium—for people who would not be heard as an individual voice but might be heard in a conglomerate of many. Given that Graham Smith, the host of the forums we were plotting in, had given his technical support as a host for any site or services we required, it was important that any campaign didn't tarnish that trust. Graham had spent many years building up his *Millennium* forums and website, and I certainly didn't want to be the one to bring them into disrepute.

This was the birth of the campaign to bring back Frank Black. I had become the campaign's coordinator and manager (I even picked out a tie for work and a top floor office with a panoramic view of my garden), Graham Smith, the owner of *This is Who We Are*, became a silent partner, and Mark Hayden, one of his staffers on the forum, would run as an intermediary between Graham and myself. It may all sound horribly officious, but it is important to put structure into any plan, no matter how trivial it may sound.

On 4 September 2008 we got a little nearer to a name as the website was being planned and a domain name needed to be selected. Two options I offered on that date were "Bring Frank Black Back" (it rolls off the tongue!) or "Back to Black" (a little more innocuous but possibly more catchy). The first did get used on a supporting news blog, the latter was dropped when common sense, neatly cellotaped to a breezeblock nailed to the front of a rocket-propelled four-by-four, hit me square on the head: "Back to Black" was the name of a rather catchy song of yesteryear. If it weren't bad enough *our* Frank Black shared his name with the lead singer of the Pixies, having to share our domain name with an Amy Winehouse song and album would have been a rather weak way to confront the nearest search engine. Back to Frank Black was the next best thing—though I don't think I've been part of a single interview wherein that name hasn't ambled, tripped, and finally mangled the tongue on at least one attempt to say it.

Appeals to the network had to be written. That was key in my eyes. We could run an online petition—which we did, for a time—but the focus was back to basics: letters, letters, letters.

So it began, with a large forum team. I coordinated the campaign, built the website, and started work on publicity. Graham Smith granted us server space and even purchased the domain name backtofrankblack.com. And Mark Hayden filled the gaps in between. We had a whole team working on translating the website into different languages including Russian, Spanish, Finnish, and French (as *Millennium* had a global fan base and net translators were still simple beasts back in 2008). Others began the wander around other fan sites and forums, looking for people to engage.

The website design was simple. Black background, naturally, with four Polaroid images that would lead you to four different areas on mouseover: "Write to Fox," "Who is Frank Black?," "Why Bring Frank Black Back?," and "Online Petition." It was a naïve site, really. The design, while simple and effective as desired, didn't allow our child to grow. The use of image slices to construct the pages made the format very rigid. The campaign website grew and grew quickly. Soon enough we needed pages for translations, flyers, posters, conduct, games, and, of course, current news.

The Back to Frank Black website has changed a great deal over four years. In part to keep it interesting, in part to allow it to expand with more fluidity, and in part because the nature of social media keeps changing. The internet is far from static. In 2008 we had a host of fans working on translating the site. Today we have a simple menu switch that will translate any page into as many languages as it would take to turn a protocol droid prissy. So much has changed, and what has been key to this campaign is to adapt and utilize as much of the growing technological changes in social media as possible. From MySpace to Facebook, from Facebook to iTunes, from podcasting to mobile phone applications, it's all about growing with the times and leaping on every slice of techno-evolution that comes our way. We're very lucky to have had a campaign kick-start in the middle of such media expansion. It has given campaigns new avenues and fanbases to explore.

There is a problem, however. As social media becomes more accessible, its worth in offering support for a product wanes. A good example of this can be found in the internet petition, an "e-sign" on a list that can then be printed out by the list owner and presented as an example of support. Before Back to Frank Black, a talented *Millennium* fan named Sue Myatt ran her own internet petition to campaign for *Millennium*'s return. She researched the reasons to justify a return to the series and started a simple online petition. By the time Back to Frank Black had appeared, the vogue of net petitions—particularly in the entertainment culture—was waning, and I'd argue rightly so. If you're trying to prove support for any ideology or product to another source—in this case, Fox Broadcasting—you need to show that your fans are fully behind the ideal. Any Frank, Dick, or Harry can drop a name onto a computer screen in five seconds—this doesn't really show a commitment. If they send a paper letter directly to the company in question, that shows they care enough to write, post, and pay to have their message delivered. When we started the campaign, we put the internet petition aside to go back to basics and do as the *Star Trek* campaigners had done so many moons ago. We wrote fan letters.

The letter campaign has been a staple component of Back to Frank Black since 2008. We've seen a response from it too, from several divisions of Fox, including FX, a leading cable channel that has been considered a good prospect for any future television series featuring Frank Black. That's not to say that all of our letter campaigns have been fruitful, but we have earned notice—the campaigners were noticed—

and more for the old-style practices than the new ones. The campaign was keen not to simply to embrace new technologies in spite of the old. We wanted to push in all directions.

As with all campaigns, it's not about what you use but how you use it and understanding your relevance, your gains, and your obstacles. Against us, we were readily aware that *Millennium* doesn't have the media interest or fan base of its sister show, *The X-Files*. We also had to confront the fact that it had been nearly a decade since *Millennium* had ended, which would mean a potentially smaller fan base and a less curious media. At the same time, there was an argument that time and distance can be favorable for a revival. One of the positives we had with Back to Frank Black, which we were to soon discover, was the enduring legacy of the show. As a high-quality and memorable series, *Millennium* had found allies across the world in a wide range of people—people who enjoy intelligent and groundbreaking drama. *Millennium* inspired many in the film industry through its unique vision and smart production. In fact, in shows following *Millennium,* it was easy to see where some had paid homage or built upon the foundation that Chris Carter had laid out. This in itself gave the campaign an advantage. It was easy to cite references in shows made since that carried themes or styles akin to *Millennium* and that had been commercial successes.

But perhaps the biggest weapon in our arsenal was provided by the people from within the show itself. Very quickly we found that we would be hard pushed to find a single actor, writer, or crewmember who hadn't been touched by their time on *Millennium*. They would be there behind us, supporting a revival in whatever form. None stood out more prominently than the show's iconic star himself, Lance Henriksen.

Our first venture to contact the cast and crew came during the first month of the campaign. The contact was nervous and possibly a little uncertain. As I recall, Mark Hayden and myself split the list and tried to contact some of the people who had been involved in the show, looking to gain written interviews. We weren't sure what the response would be, whether people would give their time freely, or whether they would want to be involved with such an obscure fan campaign.

There were early successes, including several figures from Season Three of *Millennium*: Stephen E. Miller, who had played Frank's boss Andy McClaren, was a very encouraging early score, as was computer expert Doug Scaife actor Trevor White.

My first encounter with Lance for Back to Frank Black was fairly nerve wracking. Having located his agency representation through no more sleuthing than a search engine, I gave them a call. This in itself can be uncomfortable for an Englishman such as myself. Though Americans and the English speak the same language, on a crackly trans-Atlantic telephone line it can be very off-putting trying to get yourself heard correctly—particularly when one offers the rather unusual notion of contacting a noted actor in regards to a campaign managed by internet fans in the hopes of reviving a show he starred in a decade ago. This was not an easy conversation to put out there—at least, not at the beginning, when I was very much uncertain whether this was how I should be doing things.

It was, however, how I should have been doing things and the response came via an email from Lance offering his words of support.

```
Fri 03 OCT 2008 8:36 PM. James, Thank
you for spearheading such an outburst of
fan-based desire to have "Frank Black"
return. It is a part of me, after the
time I spent working on the show. You
have my gratitude. Lance.
```

I remember my reply went through several drafts. I did not want to sound too eager and weird, but not so timid that I didn't take advantage of the response. From the message I wasn't too sure whether or not I could get an interview with him, which was something I knew we really needed. The response went back and that was it for a month or so. But when the confirmation for an interview came, I knew that the campaign had a chance.

The interview with Lance occurred sometime in November. In fact, it was Thanksgiving, 2008. The campaign had been running for a couple of months. I hadn't mastered any sort of digital recorder so I got out my old analogue four-track recording machine from my days in music and rigged it up to a mic that hung over the speaker. It was a bizarre hybrid born of pure ingenuity and a blatant lack of digital accomplishment. The call came and went so very fast but those forty-five minutes were fascinating. Lance was intelligent, smart, and dry. The dialogue shifted from *Millennium* to the recent success of Barack Obama. He was enthusiastic about the show and his achievements and very open about the state of the world and how he felt there was potential to see that world through Frank Black's eyes. Once the interview was over, to place the proverbial sweet cherry on the top of aforementioned lack of digital accomplishment, I began transcribing the whole interview. A month later, that interview was released as a three-part event. For me, it was a breakthrough, a way of showing the ever-skeptical *Millennium* fan community that we could accomplish something. If we could get Lance Henriksen to speak to us, maybe we could do more.

The following year saw a second big change in both the campaign and the interviews we were conducting. While Mark Hayden continued his written interviews, I took part in an online podcast, *Tha Dark Side Vibe*, speaking about the campaign with *Millennium* fan Troy Foreman.

The podcast went well. We enjoyed the banter we had, being as close to chalk and cheese as oil alludes to being to water, and Troy came on board to work on running a campaign podcast. The idea of a podcast had been mooted previously but, as with so much, time and technological experience had hindered the project. With Troy we began *The Millennium Group Sessions*, which would provide a mixture of chat featuring ourselves and fans as well as the cast and crew of *Millennium* and professionals relevant to the campaign.

Troy had worked on other campaigns previously, most notably a rather successful drive dedicated to the television series *Brimstone* (1998-99). While the show wasn't revived, they did manage to get the remaining episodes aired. With his tenacious attitude and knack for securing interviews, Troy's part in the campaign grew.

The podcast itself, named last minute as *The Millennium Group Sessions,* carried a sharp learning curve. Our first interview was with "The Judge" from the episode of the same title, played by veteran actor Marshall Bell. The interview itself was replete with technical problems that required several re-recordings. All the time Marshall was both as gracious and professional as we were humble and bumbling. It taught us a lot about the podcasting medium and gave us our first taste of the human face of *Millennium*'s cast and crew—a gesture that has never faltered in all our podcasts, especially when the recordings themselves have faltered. Twice interviewing Frank Spotnitz there have been technical difficulties on my end that have led me either to the profound conclusion that some digitally devious deity likes to jinx my important interviews out of spite or, alternately, a sober realization that I was using a rather naff internet service provider.

As for the shows themselves, the approach was to keep it relaxed. The laid-back style to the podcast was deliberate. I'd tend to write up a "funny" intro (that would occasionally stun everyone into an awkward silence) and questions were largely *ad hoc*. Some research was done prior to the recording, but the interview style would attempt to resonate from the questions rather than a prepared list. As a whole, the whimsical, light-hearted, and "of the moment" style was, in my mind, the best way to get professionals to feel that they were being treated like the humans they were rather than idols or simply conduits to the characters they may have played.

By the end of 2009 we'd had a host of cast and crew on the podcast. If I had to pick a favorite—which, thanks to the mix of great interviews and a failing, hazy memory, is hard—I'd have to suggest our chat with the wonderful Jon Polito, who starred in the Season Three episode "Omerta." Jon serves as a perfect example of how I had totally misjudged the love these actors and filmmakers had for *Millennium*. I had always been wary—as had Troy—of the fact that so many "fan interviews" would use their guests simply as cyphers for their own geeky interests. An interview with an actor appearing on *Star Trek* would be more about the show and the character than the artist behind the role. We wanted to make sure that the artists on *Millennium Group Sessions* felt they were being interviewed for who they were, not being treated as a teat from which the fan could suckle more information about their favorite television show. Myself and Troy would research our guests as heavily as we could and make sure that seventy-five percent of the interview would be focused around their world and not one show. Jon Polito serves as a memorable example of a man who defied this approach—he came on to talk about *Millennium*. He *wanted* to talk about *Millennium*. Indeed, at one point, he asks to go back to talking about *Millennium*! *Millennium* was a show that had a profound impact on many of the artists involved, even those who came on for a single episode. It's easy to underestimate the show's influence in pursuit of the goal to serve as an objective and balanced interviewer. It may be different for other series, but with *Millennium*, we've always found the guest has drawn us back to *Millennium* far more than we would have anticipated. I would encourage you to root out the Jon Polito interview as it offers an incredible bout of honesty from Jon about his highs and lows in acting, and how *Millennium* and Lance Henriksen will always represent a milestone in his career.

The Chris Carter interview recorded in 2009 was—rather understandably—a nerve-nippy affair. This was not simply because we were speaking to the creator of *Millennium*—not for me anyway, I can confess bravely—but because the outcome of the interview would mean a great deal for the campaign. His people were very gracious in setting up the interview and Chris himself was very easy to talk to. The only difficulty in the whole affair was the telephone connection. Chris has a very gentle, calm voice and the telephone line had very loud, tempestuous static on both ends. On top of that, for my part rather than Troy's, there's the whole English/American accent thing that is exasperated on a bad line, making asking questions a far more nerve-racking experience. As you can probably tell, if I was ever given the job of Santa Claus, the family homes of Mr. Accountable Internet Service Provider and Mr. Questionable Telephonic Connection would rarely be visited by anything more than a brick through their metaphorical windows on snowy Christmas Eves.

Chris's response to the idea of *Millennium*'s return wasn't a gate-closing "no," thankfully, but he couldn't yet see a likely opportunity for it. He did admit that he had ideas for a follow-up to the show that he wasn't ready to announce just yet. In later years, that perspective would continue to shift toward something even more encouraging for the campaign.

By the end of 2009, our first full year, more changes were afoot for the campaign. If we return to the analogy of a campaign being like a growing offspring, by 2010 the campaign was more a teen than a child. It had learned to walk, it had educated itself in ways to nurture itself and grow stronger. By 2010 it was starting to walk by itself; it moved away from the parent servers at the *This is Who We Are* website to stand on its own. Several of its nannies had moved on. Mark Hayden had dropped out of the campaign at the start of the year as did many of the founding staff. This was to be expected. Life is about change, and nothing is constant. As people grow, their priorities and interests alter. This isn't always a bad thing. On Shakespeare's stage, to use a rather crassly above-our-station example, the characters remain the same but the players change, bringing new perspectives and color to the roles. In 2010 we evolved a new core group which included Lance Henriksen himself, making that particular year an important one for Back to Frank Black as it moved from what was largely a *Millennium* fan site and letter writing service to something far more industry focused.

It would be misleading or untruthful to suggest that Back to Frank Black has had the approval of the entirety of *Millennium* fandom. That is a statement that might surprise some who are less acquainted with fan ilk, though it might not seem overtly rum when one considers it further. I doubt you'll find a single football team, sewing group, chess club, or circle of lingerie admirers that don't have occasional splits in ideology or perspective. The term "fan" derives from fanatic, and fanatics are by nature territorial. Sometimes your most critical agent comes from within a group you'd expect to offer your most avid supporters. There's nothing new there, but it is a pity we don't all get along. As Lance says, we are "Tribe," equals in the pursuit of the same goal or love. We shouldn't exist in any other mode than that, ideally. Sadly, it's never the case.

So, what have been the issues with the campaign? What possible issues could a *Millennium* fan have with bringing Frank Black back? By and large, whatever the issues are, they have very rarely proven a practical problem. It would be fair to say there are two types of problems: personal and territorial. There is a type of fan who will automatically baulk at the idea of investing hope in a future Frank Black event because to invest hope requires, by nature, an element of risk. You hope, you lose, you feel down—so why hope at all? Best to say it cannot be done. There is another type of fan who simply has a territorial instinct—one could even suggest a green eye, perhaps. This is the *ultimate* fan, and for anyone else to be making waves without them—positive or otherwise—is considered uncomfortable. Either category would not necessarily seek to hinder the campaign, but it is a genuine surprise when you find people denouncing the effort or suggesting that it will fail. It has also struck me that it is far more difficult to be negative about a campaign than to ignore it. If you're positive, you have nothing to lose and everything to gain, but that's not an ideology in which everyone can invest. This is a perpetual frustration given the fact that a niche fandom needs every hand it can muster.

One of the most common negative responses we see—and I imagine it is one that a fair few book browsers are at this moment considering—is a simple question: "Okay, where's the movie then?" In a world of growing consumer demand where everything is delivered as fast as a digital device can toss its impetuous binary zero or one upon your lap, people don't expect to wait. Unfortunately, anyone with experience in film or television can—and most likely will—tell you that getting any show green-lit takes time. When I began on this campaign I was under no illusions it would be a fast run. My primary concern was how a campaign could keep up the pace over a long tenure, how to keep the word out there.

One of the greatest purveyors of patience and positivity has been Lance Henriksen—Frank Black himself. A man with decades of experience in the industry from all angles and walks, from productions of all sizes, he knows the value of and the need for patience and he knows enough not to let that patience dampen enthusiasm. As human beings we exist to adapt, and what once was sparking and exciting dulls with time. In this light, patience, the effort to never lose our desire for what we want, is a constant battle against the wane in the need to fight for what we want. Lance has never given up, and we've always said on staff that as soon as Lance says there's no hope—through his insight and understanding of the entertainment industry waltz—we will step back off the dance floor ourselves.

2010 was the year that Lance Henriksen fought for Back to Frank Black. Lance was—and is—an idea man. Some of his ideas are big, some are small, but all are charged with enthusiasm and hope. Some of those ideas we used, some we didn't or were unable to. We looked at a script-writing competition, an effort to get writers to create a *Millennium* movie treatment that would be read by relevant actors. We explored the possibility of producing a Lance Henriksen-starring, Tom Wright-directed mock *Millennium* film trailer. We even considered a full-blown *Millennium* convention. These high-concept ideas have not, to date, materialized, but other ideas have helped further energize the campaign. Back to Frank Black hosted a movie poster competition judged by a *Millennium* panel featuring Lance, Klea Scott, and Mark Snow. The campaign auctioned *Millennium* memorabilia in support of Children of the Night, a charity dedicating to helping the sufferers of child prostitution. Lance lent his voice to sound bites, videos, and even the *Millennium Group Sessions* intro. We managed to get some radio airtime with myself, Troy, and Lance. We pushed and we pulled. And as Lance worked with us, he was working on his own book, *Not Bad For A Human* (2011), written with the wonderful Joe Maddrey. The autobiography would help to promote the subject of *Millennium* and even drew some of its sources from the campaign.

Alongside Lance's heavy involvement, two other individuals came onto the team as consultants. One man in particular carried great relevance. Brian A. Dixon has been involved in *Millennium* internet fandom dating back almost to the premiere of the show itself. (In fact, there is a character named after him in "The Time is Now.") His iconic *Millennial Abyss* website was my first introduction to *Millennium* on the internet. What gave us some rather wonderful symmetry was the fact that while the *Millennial Abyss* had introduced me to *Millennium* fandom, Back to Frank Black brought the now-retired Brian back into fandom. He came onboard as a consultant with his long-term friend and collaborator Adam Chamberlain. Both have proven their worth to Back to Frank Black, and this book itself is a testament. Alongside Brian and Adam, for a great deal of the year we had input from *X-Files* fan Joselyn Rojas, a doctor and a fantastic videographer, as well as a very pleasant lady who has since devoted a fair bit of radio time to the campaign, Christina Nicholls. Staff meetings between myself, Troy, Adam, Brian, Lance, Christina, and Joselyn were certainly interesting. If the campaign was growing into a mature and considered entity, the humor in those meetings was decidedly moving in the opposite direction. If you wanted to pin a "Wanted" sign on the culprit, I'd point you in Lance's direction. These were fun, silly times.

The end of 2010 is perhaps the perfect time to illustrate why Back to Frank Black has become more than an attempt to return Frank Black to our screens. In any journey, the path is often as important—or sometimes more important—than the destination, and I'm very proud of some of the moments we've had on this continuing voyage. At the end of 2010, in a fairly short span of time, we managed to reunite the Black family. This was Troy's moment of glory, and he coordinated the busy-bee schedules of Lance Henriksen, Megan Gallagher, and Brittany Tiplady to arrange for them to meet in one digital room for the first time since the show had ended production. We'd spoken to Lance and Megan before, but getting Brittany to return to the *Millennium* fold was exciting—doubly so for the fact that we were present for their first meeting in over a decade. I think that for Lance, especially, it was a sensation to have little Brittany, the child, now talking to him as an adult. It was all thanks to the wonders of digital technology. As with any interview, I had prepared a brief narrative introduction to frame this unique moment, but there was no need. If you listen, it's not an interview—it's a conversation between three old friends. Neither Troy nor James were required. This was a humbling honor amid a moment of mild voyeurism, listening to their personal conversation. It was the reunion of three old colleagues that proved so special.

Other highlights we're equally proud of include our interview with Klea Scott, none other than Emma Hollis from Season Three, who'd taken a step back from the world of *Millennium* having had the dubious pleasure of reading some rather unpleasant internet responses to her character and performance not long after the third season's premiere. Klea has been a supporter of *Millennium* and the campaign ever since that interview. It was a moment in which we had the opportunity to show someone who'd lost faith in fans just how wonderful they can be, that the loud few on the internet do not represent the feelings or character of the majority. Similarly, Glen Morgan and James Wong had stepped back from *Millennium*. Their absence on the *Millennium* DVD box set special features is conspicuous given how much they gave to the show both as writers and producers. Glen and James came across the campaign via the non-profit t-shirts that we sold, many created by British artist Barry Renshaw, each offering subtle nods to the show's content and in-jokes. I recall Glen saying the link between the humorous shirt designs and his own personality convinced him we were worth reaching out to. Both he and James Wong granted us some great interviews and have supported the campaign's efforts ever since. And we have, in turn, done our best to return the favor, as on the occasion of the recent release of *Space: Above and Beyond* (1995-96) on Region 2 DVD.

It's worth noting that none of our guests have been compensated for their time and efforts, so promotion and help offered in aid of their current, future, or personal projects is the best payment we can offer. But the guests never hold us to that offer, really. They do the interviews for the love of *Millennium* rather than any "we scratch your back, you scratch ours" ideology. It's the spirit of Lance's Tribe. We're all human beings. Working together, helping each other, is integral to any respectful relationship. It's a great feeling when you can extend your hand beyond the confines of the campaign and touch something beyond it.

The journey is far, far, far more important than the destination for me.

Other campaign successes we've had might not be as direct but are no less accomplished. Each fan campaign generates ripples within its sphere of influence. Bringing Brian out of "retirement" from

Millennium fandom was one. For Troy and myself, he was the quintessential godfather of the fans, given we'd both nurtured our way into *Millennium* appreciation through his site. It was gratifying to see Jason Morris, who had produced an independent web film entitled *Millennium Apocalypse* (2006), postulating a future for the young Jordan Black as a young woman, come forward and do a second season. (Troy even earned a cameo!) Jason has also done some wonderful promotional work for the campaign and this book. Jason once acknowledged that Back to Frank Black had some influence on his decision to return to *Millennium Apocalypse* and launch a second season. The acclaimed *Millennium* Virtual Seasons, full scripts written by fans perpetuating the Frank Black storyline, have continued into a sixth season being crafted alongside the campaign. In each of these cases, the campaign is in no way responsible for the talent, but I'm proud that it has managed to support other *Millennium* fans and their creations. For any negativity one might find in fandom, you don't have to search far to find a positive.

2011 opened with one of our greatest feats. We dubbed it "Make or Break." To us, this really was such a moment. We'd managed to secure an audio interview with series creator Chris Carter, writer and producer Frank Spotnitz, and Frank Black himself, Lance Henriksen. It genuinely felt like a point in the campaign that could either propel it further or finish it utterly. If Chris Carter was coming on the show to tell us he really wasn't interested in doing *Millennium* it was, as the great scholar Private Hudson one decried, "Game over, man." Lance was not interested in pushing for a return to *Millennium* without Chris—if, indeed, that was possible at all. What made it all the more tense was the fact that Chris was so interested in coming onto the show—he wasn't coerced. In fact, having been unable to make the scheduled date, he was more than happy to reschedule a few days later. We knew that he was genuinely interested in appearing, the question was just what it was he wanted to say on the subject of *Millennium*. He wanted more? He felt it was creatively complete? Either way, I'd be happy with the outcome. If this was the end, we'd taken it as far as we could. If the creator said no, I could respect that decision and call my taxi. If it was yes, super stuff. Either way I was comfortable, although inevitably I preferred a positive outcome.

A few horrific technical hitches aside (one of which lost me the first five minutes of the conversation, during which Chris indicated he was interested in *Millennium*'s return—if you don't believe me, go ask Lance or Frank) the interview was very enjoyable and very positive. Frank, I recall, was particularly enthused. They all agreed that a return to *Millennium* required a step in a bigger, bolder direction so as not to result in simply another chapter of what had been done for three seasons a decade ago. There is a lovely little moment wherein Chris accepts Lance's offer to meet and "spill his guts" on the show, on the proviso Lance moves somewhere really cool to hang. Lance nominates Hawaii, given he'd been learning Chris's golden pastime: surfing. It was a very genuine little moment, something I think that we've had in every podcast we've done for the *Millennium Group Sessions*. What you hear is the real deal, the real people behind an amazing show.

All in all, the podcast was a wonderful accumulation of what we'd been working for: to have Lance, Chris, and Frank all on the same level and all very open to *Millennium*'s return. It was indeed one of the benchmarks in the campaign.

These benchmarks are wonderful, but ultimately they carry their own burden. An ongoing campaign and its continued successes generate a problem that compounds annually. How do you top the previous year? For 2009, the *Millennium Group Sessions* was key. We started by getting some great names involved. By 2010, we had charity auctions, more interviews, responses to our letter campaigns, radio interviews, and the "Christmas with the Black Family" podcast. 2011 was a worry because "Make or Break" was released in February. How do you top that? The answer came midway through the year when it was decided we'd follow in Lance's footsteps and work on a Back to Frank Black book.

To be fair, a book had long been discussed as a dream, but with Brian and Adam already publishing books at Fourth Horseman Press—and with their latest, *Columbia & Britannia* (2009), nominated for the Sidewise Award for Alternate History—it seemed the time to try and push the campaign in a new direction. We felt that a book might serve as a testament to *Millennium*, the campaign, and the fans of the show. I won't harp on too much about the book given I'm sure you'll have found time to, at the very least, read this page of it, but suffice to say what we envisaged is very much what it became. In some respects, you could say it became all it could be: an intelligent compendium of responses to a mature and well-crafted television series.

The book would, in some sense, become yet another "Make or Break." At best, it might prove to be a key instigator in furthering the campaign. At worst, it will stand as a monument to what the Tribe can achieve if they put their collective mind to it. That word pops up again, and it is so very fitting. This book is not a testament to people who own DVDs, the type you'd commonly call "a fan"; this book features journalists, filmmakers, actors, writers, and artists. It is the epitome of what Lance calls the Tribe: a group of individuals, each as vital as the other, coming together to celebrate the past and potential future of a timeless work of art.

While we planned this book, Lance had published and was promoting his own. Alongside his co-writer, Joe Maddrey, he had been taking part in events all over the United States. *Not Bad for a Human* is a truly wonderful book, and there is no doubt that the energy and enthusiasm Lance and Joe demonstrated gave us the kick-start to bind these very pages. I was fortunate enough to catch up with Lance, Joe, and Troy in Atlanta at the back-end of Summer 2011 for Dragon-Con. It was inspiring to see the queues for Lance, all eager to lap up his time, book, and silver squiggle. What was more interesting were the Q&As Lance participated in. I saw those held on both Saturday and Sunday and they were quite different in many ways, but *Millennium* came up in each session. (On Saturday, it did get a prompt from yours truly after I'd slipped into the question queue. Troy's idea!) On the Sunday, *Millennium* featured in the very first question, posed by the host: would Frank Black be coming back? There was a roar of approval from the audience and, as Lance will tell you, that roar is heard worldwide. People want Frank Black. Lance wants Frank Black. Sometimes when you're staring at websites, emails, and audio files, it's easy to become self-conscious as to whether what you're doing is worth it, whether it truly resonates out there beyond the confines of the digital ether. It does, and it's wonderful to get the opportunity to witness that.

2011 ended, like a cliffhanger for a season finale, on a rather interesting note. The campaign was unusual enough to attract the attention of British journalist Patrick Munn. Patrick had covered fan campaigns before, having previously looked into *X-FilesNews.com*, a website featuring a campaign that I would refer to as our "Big Sister" and proudly carrying a far more buxom fan base than Back to Frank Black can boast. (The campaign is run by the fairer sex; I won't pretend my monikers are coined by anything but shallow observation.) What fascinated Patrick was the talent associated with Back to Frank Black. We weren't the largest fan campaign, and we certainly weren't pitching for the return of a character or series that was a current media hot topic, but while there have been fan campaigns for television shows endorsed by crew members, the close association on Back to Frank Black from key artists, on a show over a decade old, seemed unusual. Most campaigns kick off after a cancellation, hot off the press, filled with energy and frustration at the recent show's demise. Back to Frank Black began in 2008, fighting for the return of a show that ended in 1999. That was rather odd as campaigns go.

Patrick's curiosity had him flexing his journalistic muscles, feeling out into the industry for any quantifiable answers to the campaign's questions. The initial answers we got were absolutely of no surprise. If you were believing that Fox was gearing up for a major *Millennium* investment in 2011 you were, to be frank, probably confusing *Millennium* with some other show. However, there was never a "no" uttered in response to these queries, which is important in this industry. If a door is closed, they will tell you. The door isn't closed and—as of this writing, in 2012—it remains still wide. Lance Henriksen recently made mention of *Millennium* at an unrelated roundtable press event promoting *Tron: Uprising* (2012). His remarks were picked up by several major news outlets and resonated throughout the entertainment industry. Just days ago, the *Fox All Access* website ran Lance's comments on the return of *Millennium*. There is no end in sight and hope has yet to be extinguished. Beginning with a small website back in 2008, this campaign has continued to endure and has grown in size and relevance, slowly but surely. I find it quite amazing that the decision to launch a fan campaign has brought you this book, a year in the making.

In some respects, it would have been fitting for this chapter to end with the end of the campaign. I can't do as is done on television and simply tie up the loose ends and deliver you a fully concluded story. All I can offer is a summary in two parts. The first is whether this campaign brings *Millennium* back is, to a large part, academic. If you put your mind to it, you can accomplish anything. In 2008, I never expected that a small, frivolous suggestion for a campaign called Back to Frank Black would produce a volume such as this. Regardless of whether *Millennium* returns, that is amazing to me. Furthermore, this campaign has given me such insight into the world of *Millennium*, the people who created it, and the people who adore it. That, to me, is what has made Back to Frank Black so special and, by reading this book's pages, we impart that same journey and appreciation to you, dear reader.

Which brings me to the final point of my two-part summary. This book is a collaboration that brings together many walks of life as well as the many eyes reading this page. We are all so different, so unique, but we can be quantified by what unites us equally: Frank Black. This campaign has been very much about that. Coming together as a whole, not to deify a show or its artists, but to join hands and shout for the same thing in unity. We are Back to Frank Black. We are Tribe.

This is who we are.

WORKS CITED

Lee, Patrick. "Carter Offers *X-Files* Spoiler." *Scifi.com*. Sci-Fi Channel, 27 March 2008. Web. 27 March 2008.

Morris, Clint. "Exclusive Interview: Frank Spotnitz." *Moviehole*. Moviehole, 20 July 2008. Web. 20 June 2012.

Smith, Graham P. "Lance Henriksen Speaks Again on *Millennium* Movie." *Millennium: This is Who We Are*. TIWWA, 8 March 2008. Web. 20 June 2012.

James McLean is the founder of the Back to Frank Black campaign. A commercial artist by day, McLean produces artwork for video games, advertising, and magazines. He has supplied artwork for franchises such as *Star Wars*, *Doctor Who*, and *High School Musical*. Occasionally he dabs his quill in digital ink, smearing words across reviews, interviews, and articles. He has written for *Showreel Magazine* as well as being a regular contributor for *Kasterborous.com* and *Toonzone.net*.

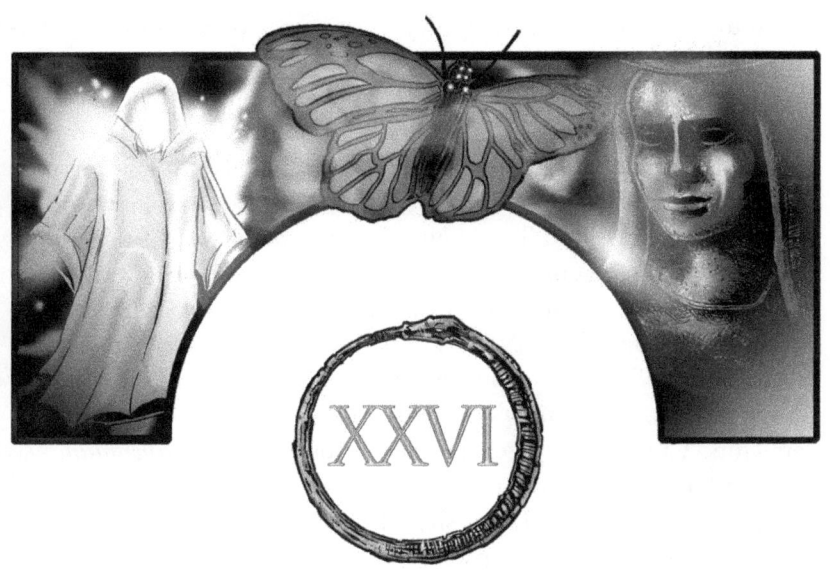

THE END OF INNOCENCE:
A CONVERSATION WITH KLEA SCOTT

Interview by James McLean & Troy L. Foreman
Written by Troy L. Foreman

No other character from *Millennium* has divided a fandom like Special Agent Emma Hollis. Her character arc is a highlight of Season Three, as is actress Klea Scott's portrayal. From her first appearance in the season opener, "The Innocents," to the life-changing decision she makes in the series finale, "Goodbye to All That," over twenty-two episodes we are able to watch Hollis evolve from a green F.B.I. agent to a more assured and independent investigator.

Klea's relationship with her work on the series had, until recently, been impacted by that divided reaction. Even her introduction to the series back in 1998 was not without controversy or challenge. "There's quite an interesting story behind my auditioning for *Millennium*," she teases. "Because Season Two had ended with the viral outbreak that looked like the end of the world, it was up to the writers of Season

Three to really figure out how they were going to explain that fuzzy-snow ending to the second season."

It must have been difficult for Klea Scott to come into the world of *Millennium*. Not only had the series already been on the air for two full seasons, those two years had been markedly different from one another. Season One was criticized in some quarters for a serial-killer-of-the-week format. In Season Two, control of the show was given to Glen Morgan and James Wong, and the two had their own idea of where the show should go creatively. Morgan and Wong decided to concentrate on the evolution of the Millennium Group over investigations into killers. Season Two boasts some great episodes but, like the character of Emma Hollis, *Millennium*'s second year has its fans as well as its detractors. Chris Carter became more involved when *Millennium* was renewed for a third season and, along with the rest of the writing staff, he was handed a very different show from that seen in Season One. A terrible viral outbreak had apparently destroyed much of the population and Frank's wife, Catherine, had been killed off. This put the writing staff in a creative corner when it came time to plan an overall arc for Season Three.

With the death of Catherine, the series lacked a female lead. Lara Means was also a casualty of "The Time is Now," and the evil seductress Lucy Butler was certainly not the sort of character who could fill this dramatic void. In stepped Scott as Emma Hollis.

"The idea was that the outbreak had only happened in the Pacific Northwest and Frank Black was returning to D.C. as a consultant to the F.B.I. and there was going to be a partner," Klea explains. "It was working on *The X-Files* to have a young woman, so they were going to get a woman to be the young, neophyte agent who was impressionable, curious, and rather rebellious in her respect for Frank Black as a rogue interpreter of things, so they were auditioning."

The auditions for *Millennium* were to be quite different from anything Klea had experienced previously. "The process of auditioning for the first show I ever did out of school that wasn't theatre was *Brooklyn South*. The Bochco/Milch power duo really had control over their casting and production in a way that, because I was new to it, I had no reference for. They did not have to pass through a lot of the network testing and the anonymous, business-degreed suits that sign off on who is on a television show and who is not, and so they just got to audition and hand pick you and you got the part, and I didn't know that wasn't the way it was done."

Klea's agent revealed the full story behind her casting on *Millennium* only after the process was complete. "He didn't want to freak me out before the auditions, but he submitted me for the call and he was unable to get me an audition for the role. He pursued it with the casting director and the casting director said, finally, after a push, 'Look, they're not looking for an actress of color for this part.' He said, 'How do you know that?' and she said, 'I just know.' And he said, 'Well, why don't you see Klea and let the producers decide?' She said no, and he said, 'Why don't you just audition her.' And she said no, and he said, 'Well, how about this. I will never submit another client to you again if you see her and she's terrible.' And he put his job and, somewhat, his reputation on the line—something I did not know—and she relented."

Her opportunity secured, Klea attended the audition. "So I went in and, as a result of them not looking for an actress of color, I was the only actress of color in the room. I didn't know any of this, I just went in to read for Chip Johannessen and it may have been Frank Spotnitz— I know Chris [Carter] wasn't there at this point—and I auditioned and it went well. I don't know if I had a call back or if the next thing was going to network and studio tests, and because Fox is both a network and a studio you have to go through these rounds of auditioning. This was all new to me but very regular par for the course in terms of pilot season for any show, so I was now getting the experience I didn't get during the lead-up to *Brooklyn South*."

The next round of auditions was to involve the series creator himself. "I went back to the studio and I think the next time I came and auditioned it was for Frank and Chris Carter and I was at the Ten Thirteen offices, and I just remember it was very moody lighting, a lot of venetian blinds. Then I was to proceed to the next level, which was the network test, I think.

"The next level was not just the creators of the show but all the suits and all the people coming in, so at that point there's usually only five people going in to read for the role, and you sign your contract before you audition. It's very bizarre. So everybody signs their contracts, and I guess that's a part of the choosing you process—how much you cost—because everybody has a different quote per episode that's in the contract. Then they have the power to either choose you or release you from the contract, but you are now theirs if they want you."

In spite of her competition, Klea stood out in the process. "At this point, of the five of us there were three blondes, a redhead, and me, and just out of my logic I decided, 'Well, they either want a black actress—they're going to do something really unusual—or I'm here to appease the N.A.A.C.P. [National Association for the Advancement of Colored People] quotas for auditioning people,' because it was a thing at the time. There was an outcry from the N.A.A.C.P. that there weren't enough black faces on network television and people were somewhat scrambling to add black characters to T.V. shows. So I thought, 'Okay, they're just doing this to appease them and say [they] auditioned them, or they actually are really interested in me.'

"I believe I did that audition twice, probably once with network and then, the next time—the next day or later that afternoon—I had to go to the studio across the parking lot on the Fox lot, and again the same five girls, and some of them have changed their outfits because their agents have called them in between and said, 'They don't like the pants!' So I went back again, and everybody's very nice to you, and at this point really it is out of the creators' hands, so if they love you they can coach you and tell you what they like, but they don't know what the suits are going to say, so they just say, 'Good luck!' and you can tell they are rooting for you but they're not going to be able to do anything about it. And I went into the room, and it was the fourth or fifth time I had done the scenes that were chosen, and I believe they were from Episode One of Season Three with the plane crash, and I auditioned and then we left."

Klea had to juggle her audition with other commitments on the day of this final audition. "I was late—I was in a play that night—so I was trying to make my half hour call for the show and I was running across the parking lot." This was the momentous moment that she was to learn that she had been cast as Emma Hollis, though the actress did not have the time to celebrate her victory. "Some woman who I don't really know was coming out of the same meeting and yelled at me, 'You got the part!' So I went, 'Woo-hoo!' and then I went running off to do the show. And then, I have to say, Chip [Johannessen] came to see me in the play as well, which I was really impressed by."

Her casting had proved to be a controversial decision at Fox. "I heard, after the fact, that there was something of an argument in the room about me because it was declared that the male Fox television audience who watched *Millennium* on Friday nights—the very desirable demographic of eighteen to thirty-five year olds—weren't black. They didn't want a black actress in the show, and there was a little argument there. I don't know who was on what side, but I'm pretty sure that the producers and writers wanted me and they were the ones gunning for me, and I got the part."

Filming for *Millennium* based Klea in Vancouver, somewhat familiar territory for the actress. She had grown up in Canada after her family relocated there when was still an infant and enjoys dual citizenship. "I was born in Panama," she explains, "but my parents moved to Ottawa, Canada, when I was about two years old and I was nationalized as a Canadian citizen there with my whole family. So I'm Canadian American and Panamanian."

Klea has enjoyed a lengthy career, having aspired to be an actress as a child. "It started very young. I was a professional kid actor at one point... Blame it on *The Wizard of Oz*. I was about six years old when I saw that, and then I demanded dance classes. At about ten or eleven, in the midst of a dance competition, I was crushingly told by a judge that I was an actress, not a dancer, and then launched myself into that whole-heartedly and kept up with the dance until my twenties. I was teaching by the end."

Her subsequent television debut was about as different in tone from *Millennium* as is imaginable. "I actually auditioned for a children's television series. It was called *You Can't Do That on Television* and it was early days of Nickelodeon out of Boston, so strangely enough we were a huge hit in the United States, but in Canada nobody watched us. The show had even been on for a number of years before I joined it, but I auditioned for what were ostensibly improvised sketch comedy drama classes run by the producers of that show, and then they would call from that group the kids that they would put on the show."

In a literal sense, Klea outgrew her part on *You Can't Do That on Television* and her time on the comedy series came to a natural end. "I think I was about eleven, twelve, or thirteen and I grew too tall for the show. There was a height limitation, so you got taller than the host and you were out of there! And I quickly got pretty tall, but during those years there was quite a rigorous course of improv sketch classes that went along with the actual work, which was weekends in a studio taping and filming and weekdays after school of rehearsals. So that was all the beginnings of it and I was always in some kind of drama class."

Klea's development as an actress continued after her time at Nickelodeon. "I outgrew that experience and jumped into my first actual sci-fi experience that I could list, which was *UFO Kidnapped*. Then I pretty much finished up high school and I was dancing and teaching, then I moved to Toronto and decided I was going to break into the business, because there was quite a bit of American television coming up at this time. It was the Eighties and it was the time that I guess Toronto became the stand-in for New York, so a lot of people were coming up there to shoot stuff. I somehow managed to get myself an agent. I think I had a lot of fantasies that happily led me to forge into areas I never should have gone into."

It was the advice that Klea received during her time in Toronto that prompted her to trade the imitation for the real thing. "While I was there I was doing a lot of extra work, and I happened into a film acting class with a great teacher from New York City who said, 'If you're serious about this business, you've got to go to New York.' Because I had the dual citizenship, I didn't think twice about it. I jumped on a plane and I auditioned for a musical theater school in New York City, which I really shouldn't have been in, but it got me to New York!"

Like dance, however, musical theater was not quite Klea's groove. "I lasted about a year there and realized I didn't want to be in the chorus of any musical that was running; although I could sing, I certainly was still better at acting. They weren't teaching the things I wanted anyway, so I jumped to just taking classes in New York, and I somehow got myself an agent and a manager and started doing off-off-Broadway at whatever theater I could find. Eventually I landed myself in Shakespeare in the Park for a great summer in the ensemble and understudying for the major roles, and then I got a summer in a place called Williamstown, which is a theatre festival in Massachusetts."

As with her *Millennium* audition, here Klea stood out from the rest. "It's dominated by Yale school drama and Juilliard and I was the kid who was waiting on tables in New York and the street element of our ensemble, but I got incredible casting and was double-timing the rest of my ensemble's work with looking up words like 'scansion' that I didn't understand at all because I hadn't gone to conservatory school. So at the end of that summer I decided I should go back to college, and I auditioned for actually only two schools. I got into both, but I chose North Carolina School of the Arts because it was a cheap state to live in and far away from New York, which had a lot of distractions for me at this point in my life. I returned to college at the ripe old age of twenty-four and got my undergrad Bachelor of Fine Arts there. Whilst I was there—because I still had an agent—every summer I returned to New York City and would audition for theatre, whatever I could get my hands on."

It was during one of these summers that Klea landed a role that would see her return to television. "I came back and got a very short-lived little guest star part on *Cosby*. This was the *Cosby* show in its later incarnation, with Madeline Kahn, and he had one grown daughter, and that led to a little extra attention from Mr. Cosby. I like to say he took a mentor attitude towards me, because that's the way I like to remember it, and he took me under his wing. I was auditioning for the part of his daughter and he said, 'I'm not going to give you that part, but I'm going to give you another role as a guest star part and I want you to observe Madeline Kahn.'" It was to prove a formative experience for the actress. "He had me sitting behind the camera, watching everything and wanting me to just absorb everything I could about the industry. It was a wonderful experience, and then, of course, I went back to school; I think I had two more years at that point.

The young actress' fleeting television roles had shaped her significantly. In Klea's senior year, she began to seek further television work in earnest. "My agent had me starting to audition in the January/February/March pilot season—the old pilot season that used to exist in New York and L.A.—while I was graduating in the spring." The result was a career breakthrough. "He had me putting myself on tape down in North Carolina for projects that I would be able to participate in once I graduated and I fatefully landed my first series regular role, on Steven Bocho and David Milch's *Brooklyn South*. That was in my senior year, so I went and shot the pilot and then went back to school and finished, did another play, then graduated and moved to Los Angeles.

"And so that was the start of the L.A. chapter of my life. That was my first recurring role and I met my husband at school—he was a director in the year ahead of me—and the two of us moved to Los Angeles. I did a play when that show got cancelled after a full season and, while doing the play, I auditioned for *Millennium*."

Having secured the role of Emma Hollis after a lengthy audition process and flown to Vancouver to commence filming in her first leading role, Klea's introduction to *Millennium* accompanied a significant period of change for the series. From the first moments of "The Innocents," it is clear that this season is going to be a different from what had gone before. The audience first meets Special Agent Emma Hollis at a crime scene where a plane has crashed, killing everyone onboard. Agent Barry Baldwin asks if she is alright, given she has never experienced a scene quite like this. Enter Frank Black, flown in to offer his own expert observations.

Emma and Frank's first interaction is an interesting one. Hollis is seemingly in awe of him and she is eager to impress him with her knowledge both of the scene and his background. Although there is a significant age difference between the two leads—the veteran F.B.I. profiler and the up-and-coming rookie with a thirst for knowledge—their partnership works. It is a dynamic seen before on television but one handled particularly well by *Millennium*'s writers. There were some inevitable comparisons drawn to the team of Mulder and Scully from flagship Ten Thirteen series *The X-Files*, but there are few true similarities. The casting of Klea Scott proved to be a standout factor which helped to establish the series as forward-looking.

"I've always felt that series was ahead of its time anyway," Klea agrees. "It was just on the precipice of us in this country entering the Bush years and I think today, with the president we have, it wouldn't be that ground-breaking to cast me, but at that moment it was, and it was a fight just to audition for the show. I felt we were a little further along back then than we were."

The initial reaction to Hollis was certainly mixed, as Klea recalls. It was the sheer negativity in some of the feedback she encountered that gave Klea cause to distance herself from *Millennium* fandom. "Some of the things that I have read about myself on the internet or my casting on that show, sometimes they were so awful that I thought, 'Is this about me being black or is this actually about my work on the show?' I wasn't sure and I actually don't want to assume that anyone's opinion is not valid or is based on something that justifies me being a sucky actress, but I know how hard we worked on that show and Lance and I really had an excellent actor-to-actor relationship.

"It was long hours and it was hard work and I'm not sure if there was some truth to the fact that some of the audience members weren't ready for that kind of a partnership, and it was too much ahead of its time. Ultimately, the show getting cancelled in 1999 was just, to me, such shortsightedness on the part of the network as well. I just felt like there was a lack of vision. Fox Television isn't exactly known for its liberal, progressive programming, so I just think we were ahead of our time in many ways, and the partnership and the casting of me was just another of those things that was pushing an envelope for people not ready to open it, I think."

In addition to the upheavals on the series following Catherine's death, the nature of Hollis's role in the dynamic of the series offered its own challenges in terms of the character's reception. "You can only do what the writing gives you," Klea notes, "and I was definitely in a student-mentor relationship with Frank. So I can imagine [it was frustrating] having to listen to Emma Hollis ask for the umpteenth time, 'What do you mean by that? I'm sorry, I don't understand,' this kind of constant questioning of your lead as opposed to being the wife or being the crazed psychic sidekick."

Klea was never involved in discussions regarding the development of Hollis, and the extraordinary demands upon the creative minds shaping the direction of series meant that their attentions were, by necessity, divided. "I was never invited, really, into the arc; I was handed scripts. It was difficult too, because at the time *The X-Files* had just moved to Los Angeles and we were still in Vancouver. *The X-Files* was at the height of its popularity and we felt like *Millennium* was sort of the bastard child of Chris Carter. We were always wondering where our father was and making long distance calls to see what things meant and not really getting [answers]. I think I saw Chris at Christmas and at the end of the show, after I got the part."

In spite of such developmental challenges, *Millennium*'s third season began to take shape. In "Closure," the fourth episode, some backstory is finally revealed for Hollis, significantly that she once had a sister who was murdered when she was a child. This event has haunted Emma ever since. The tragedy prompts her father to obsess over the loss of his child, and we begin to explore the intriguing relationship between Emma and James Hollis, a relationship that is explored more deeply over the course of the season. Until this point, Frank has kept his distance from Hollis, but in "Closure" he seems to take her under his wing, not only helping to solve the troubling case they are working on but also helping her to deal with the death of her sister. This is the first time an emotional attachment is established between the two characters.

It is an installment that Klea very much appreciated. "I liked 'Closure.' That was the first time I got a backstory, and I thought [guest star] Garret Dillahunt was really scary. That was the first time I felt like I got to sink some acting chops into some work, and it was very subtle too."

In episodes like "Closure," it was *Millennium*'s technical and stylistic details that helped to characterize the series and added a further dimension to the drama, drawing out the subtlety of the performances. "I was learning to work in extreme close-up in that television show. It was a style of shooting that Tom Wright used, and since he directed every second episode that season it was something I became very used to. Stylistically, I think they decided that this was the look of the show, so I was learning things like how to act with a piece of tape on a mat box, because they were in such tight close-up you couldn't even look at the actor you were talking to; you had to act with a piece of tape that was right next to the camera lens.

"For me there was a great triumph of a subtlety of emotion in conjunction with the power of your imagination in some cases… There's a sequence in particular, which has a beautiful piece of music composed by Mark Snow. [It consists of] flashbacks, and there's just me and a computer screen and I just felt like I was able to communicate things without language in close-up. It was a triumph for me in terms of what Lance was calling 'real thought.'"

Of all her experiences on *Millennium*, Klea speaks most passionately and positively about working alongside Lance Henriksen. "It was fantastic. Just going into it I was so reverent of his abilities, and then getting to work with him. He's a fascinating human being, and just the subtleties of his craft I felt he very generously shared with me. I'm not sure what it was, why the two of us hit it off so well, but I felt I had to earn his respect—it wasn't something he just handed out to everyone. But once he felt, as an actor, that you were really talking and listening, he was the greatest ally you could have."

The mentor dynamic between Frank and Hollis was in many ways mirrored in the relationship between Lance and Klea on-set. "He taught me many, many things. The whole experience, because it was my first lead on a television show, was really formative in my working with a camera and he could not have been more generous with tips. I always remember him saying, 'The camera reads two things: adrenalin and real thought. That's what the camera picks up.' He would give me just amazing [advice], and this was the guy who was in *Dog Day Afternoon*!"

Lance also shared experiences and time with Klea beyond their work together on the series. "He would tell me stories about New York and his early days. He was just so generous, and his wife at the time also—the two of them. I had been married two months and then I moved to Vancouver for ten months by myself, in the rain, working on a serial killer show, fourteen-hour days, and they were so kind to me in terms of personal support and moral support and opening up their home to me, and then the little acting gems and jewels.

"Some of it you just pick up from watching, and I did; I'm a sponge, I'll absorb anything. At some point, I don't want to speak for him, but I felt like I gained his trust, and then we were really locked in, we were a really great pair. I felt like we were communicating that and it was really interesting."

Their contrasts added to the singular nature of their onscreen partnership. "I was black; he was white. He was a good twenty to thirty years older than me. He was the professional; I was the naïve newcomer. There were so many interesting dichotomies to even what we visually looked like. Nobody looked like that on T.V., no two people stood beside each other with this kind of trust. It's funny because he's a Taurus and I'm a Capricorn and, even though I'm not a horoscope junkie, I always have this image of a bull and a goat standing next to each other—these two horned animals, known for their stubborn nature and their doggedness, gnawing on the bone and refusing to let it go until they get to the truth."

There was also some clear common ground between the two as actors. "I think there were probably some similarities in terms of how we approach the craft too," Klea explains. "I was coming not too long out of acting school, which couldn't be more about the craft and listening, and he had perfected that. So it was fantastic to get to work with somebody who had such respect for the craft. I just think he's so talented. I know people focus on his face and how amazing it is to look at his face. I always say he has a great mug. But there are subtleties of vulnerability with his daughter on the show, [played by] Brittany [Tiplady], just lovely, emotional things, and he was always a hundred percent working on those things."

Henriksen also had a crystal clear perspective on how those affected by the events depicted onscreen should be treated. "He always had respect for the victims on our show. He always told me, 'We can never take for granted the violence of these crimes we are talking about. We can never disrespect the dignity of the victims on this show.'"

That same respect also extended to the other artists with whom the duo worked. "Another thing he taught me, and I'll never forget it, was that he said, 'When you are the leads on a show and there are only two of you and it's an hour-long drama, you work really long hours. When the guest stars come in and the day players come in, they are dropping in to your world. You are the host and hostess. It is your responsibility to make them feel as comfortable and as trusting as they can so they can do their best work. It's not a game of egos or possessive ownership of something that gets to intimidate the person who is only there for a day. You have to make them feel completely welcome and safe and then they can do their best work, so you can do your best work.' That's really important and I've taken it to everything I have worked on since and have been lucky enough to have a lead role on. Don't be threatened by the good-looking blonde who is guest starring this week. You open your arms to them and create a world in which they feel like they can soar, and then you're flying along with them and then the show takes off. Amazing lessons like that. I can't thank him enough."

The lessons Klea took from Lance Henriksen also extended to his other pursuits. "He's such a craftsperson too. Even his ceramics, the things he does in his life that are outside of his acting that make him a whole person. He was very careful to teach me the lessons of not just being an actor who focuses on only the next television role, but be a whole human being, have a life, love your time off, fill it with people you love."

Family plays a significant role in the development of Emma Hollis. In addition to one sister having been killed when she was a child, "Human Essence" reveals that Emma has a half-sister living in Canada who struggles as a drug addict. After she receives a package in the mail containing tainted drugs and a plea for help and it is intercepted by the F.B.I., Hollis is temporarily suspended. The Emma Hollis we met at the start of the season would have reached out to Frank Black, told him what was going on, asked for guidance. Now, more confident and independent, she chooses to deal with the problem on her own. Again, we see a more assertive Hollis taking charge, an agent who, over the course of the season, has increasingly had to rely upon her instincts and judgments.

THE END OF INNOCENCE

Central to the Hollis family dynamic in Season Three is, of course, the relationship between Emma and her father, James. This was another collaboration that Klea very much enjoyed. "Everything with the character who played my father, John Beasley—an extraordinary actor—at the end of the season, having to commit him to the nursing home, finding him, getting attacked by him in the middle of the night... Everything that we did was so rich for me, emotionally, to have them give me a relationship outside of work. This was a living, breathing human being playing my father that I got to work with constantly. John and I remained really good friends as well. It was fantastic casting and we had an immediate connection, [such] that I always felt like when I watched the two of us on screen together I believed we were related to one another, and I was very proud of that connection that we had. I think it was the last three or four episodes that really built on that relationship for me that I was very proud of."

The third major recurring actor in the season was Terry O'Quinn, continuing his role as Peter Watts, although he and Hollis shared precious little screen time. "I wish I had got to work with him more often," laments Klea. "He was not around as much and kind of dropped in for the guest-starring parts. He was usually engaged with Frank Black and I was catching a glimpse because I was sniffing out the Millennium Group and then realizing it was for real. I believe I called him a 'bald man!' They gave me that line and I think we had a giggle about that, but I didn't get to talk to him ever as much as I wanted to. And he was fascinating too, because he clearly had this rich life; he was always flying in from Virginia and had a guitar in his room and a great family that he was always flying away from to come to rainy Vancouver.

"But I did run into him two years ago in Monaco at a television festival. He was there for *Lost* and I was there for *Intelligence*. It was an international T.V. festival, so they were honoring actors from all over the world, and we ended up in a shuttle van back from the convention center to the hotel together, and I finally got to tell him that I really like his work as well. I'm a huge fan of *Lost* and of Terry O'Quinn. I just think he's an exceptional actor, so I mostly have been feeling 'thank God for *Lost* and his part on it' because I feel like he's gotten his due. People really know how amazing he is. I just got to tell him how happy I was for all the success in his career, because he certainly deserved it. There were just really good actors on that show. Steven E. Miller was awesome, and a Canadian, actually. It was a great time, and really wonderful actors, such as Sarah-Jane Redmond—incredible artists that I got to work with, amazing people. Some of them, I got to figure out how amazing they were in the years since, but I just value that time and that show because it taught me so much. It taught me never to go on the internet and Google your own name!"

Terry O'Quinn's diminished role in the season is largely driven by ongoing developments regarding the Millennium Group. By Season Three, Frank Black has a profound distrust of the Group, although he seems to be the only one who questions their motives. This belief is expressed to Hollis and significantly emphasized in "Skull and Bones." Emma begins to realize that Frank may not be off-base as far as the Millennium Group is concerned. Frank and Peter continually compete for her loyalty and this places Hollis in a very awkward situation, one that will come to have a major impact. At this point, Hollis has become a more confident agent, still relying on Frank to a degree but able to think and work independently from him. Meanwhile, her father is suffering from Alzheimer's and the disease is worsening.

If the themes, situations, and storytelling of the third season were dark in tone, there were lighter moments on set. "There wasn't a lot of time to pull jokes, but we would certainly burst out laughing in situations where the tension had just gotten too high. I cannot think of pranks that we pulled, and I was definitely being a good student quite a lot of the time and not tinkering [with] things. I would have left it up to Lance to pull the jokes. I feel like Terry O'Quinn might have done something funny. I probably said a ton of funny things while waving a severed finger, but I can't remember them!

"We weren't so serious all the time, but we were serious about what we were doing. I remember one time I had an episode where I got beat up in an elevator shaft ["Human Essence"] and I was taking it a little seriously, I think. I was jogging on the spot and running around to keep my breath up; I'm kind of a physical actress anyway, with all the dance in my background. So I was taking it very seriously and the stunt seriously, the whole thing, and keeping it going between takes in a way that was pretty exhausting. The director, Tom Wright—who directed every other episode and was another huge part of what I think was a pretty steep learning curve for myself on that show—grabbed me by the shoulders and stopped me from doing jumping jacks and said, 'Klea, it's only a T.V. show!' And then I kept going and saying, 'It's only a

T.V. show! It's only a T.V. show!' I always remember that, having to be reminded."

Occasionally, the script itself would allow the cast and crew to lighten the mood, most notably in "Thirteen Years Later." Klea remembers, "That was our opportunity to have a little fun. In some ways it was a campy spoof of a lot of things, of the genre itself. I felt like I didn't get enough of it, but I got to infuse a little comedy into my work on that show. I don't think I smiled at all in that entire season! It was funny, and very tongue-in-cheek in a sly way too. I think they tried to make a big deal out of the original airing of it and time it up with Halloween, but I just thought that, for the show we were doing, it was funny." One of the most memorable scenes in the episode sees Hollis and Frank sit through a number of horror movies on video, profiling the likes of *Halloween* and *A Nightmare on Elm Street*. "Eating popcorn! Oh, we had a blast. That was us getting to have some fun together for sure."

Filming was mostly a demanding process, though. Recalling her biggest challenges on the series, Klea says, "Physically, it was probably the stunt things. Because Chris was so clear on how he wanted the characters to look, I was in pointy-toed heels the whole season. The Greater Vancouver Regional District Forest—in which we filmed a lot of things—is quite mushy and filled with roots and weeds, and hilly, and it's an intense physical process to be getting up and down those hills. You're filming through the night, it's five on a Saturday morning and you've been working since two in the afternoon on the Friday… The physical tests of endurance came all the time, quite literally. It's cold. I think I had to, at one point, leap over a chain link fence and land, and by the end of the season I thought, 'I can do anything in heels! I can leap, I can run!'

"That was a constant, and I was surprised at first and then kind of buckled down and was very proud of my ability with just the constant scripts coming in and the lines, because one of the things that happened in the course of that season is that it became apparent that I could memorize lines, and I got more and more of them as the season went on, in terms of just having to handle the exposition of the plot. I think Frank got to do some more of the action and the figuring out and I ended up having these monologues of explanations for things that would keep the audience abreast of what was happening. So just the fact of, 'Can I handle this much dialogue when I just worked fourteen hours on a whole other script, and can I memorize this in time for tomorrow? We're shooting ten pages tomorrow!' Lance would always say, 'Wouldn't it be nice to do a movie and have one page per day instead of ten to twelve?!' And I hadn't done any movies so I said, 'I don't know! I thought this was the way it is!' I was memorizing it, and he would say, 'Be careful. If you get good at this, they're gonna give you more!' And it happened, gradually, so I just felt like the physical endurance was something that went on for the whole season."

What of the more emotional challenges offered by the series? "I never phoned anything in on that show," Klea states proudly. "I was always searching for truth and emotional motivations for even the driest of expository dialogue. I really felt like what was the most satisfying was that relationship with my father that I got to really ground something in towards the end of the season. I would say that was the greatest. It's weird in acting, because the things that break your heart are the things that you ultimately feel most triumphant about when you manage to do that on camera, in those magic seconds. My relationship with my father in that show broke my heart, so that's what went on my reel. That's what was my greatest challenge. Is it a challenge or is it the reason why you're doing this, ultimately?"

Season Three is marked by a tendency for somewhat ambiguous storytelling. Whenever the script was unclear in some respect, Klea would seek out relevant source material. "The kind of research that I would do would often give me more information than it did Emma Hollis, just to know what is being referenced. Even if my character didn't know, I wanted to know, 'What world are we in?' I always made an attempt to understand. There were times when you couldn't, and some of it is also being able to hold onto a mystery in the sense of a plot unfolding in that you can't know certain things. You may be shooting things out of order but you can't know this yet because it doesn't make sense, so you're playing out of time and sequence with your own sense of discovery, which is a mind fuck! In the watching of *Millennium*, that's what I enjoyed, so I like knowing that stuff and I'm a big reader too so that stuff is fun for me to know about. It doesn't necessarily inform exactly what your character does, but for me it helps build a world."

The many mysteries of the season and Emma Hollis's personal story arc lead to a major decision. Throughout there are hints that her father's condition is progressing at a rapid pace. He does not recognize

Emma one moment but is coherent and loving in the next. These emotional scenes serve to illustrate some one of the most horrific aspects of Alzheimer's disease. In one outstanding scene between the two, James Hollis puts a gun to his daughter's face while she is sleeping and attacks her. Klea Scott and John Beasley are stunning in their performances.

The Millennium Group—in particular, Peter Watts—sees an opportunity to offer Emma a cure for her father's disease and, in the process, arrange for a permanent ally within the F.B.I. Herein lies the moral dilemma that Hollis faces. Frank Black has repeatedly insisted that the Millennium Group cannot be trusted. Emma has the opportunity to save her father by accepting help from the Group, but she will then be indebted to them. What might the younger, less experienced Emma Hollis of "The Innocents" or "Closure" have made of this decision? Might her loyalty to Frank have prompted her to refuse the bargain? Or might she have forgone that allegiance and accepted the Group's offer? What we do know is that the Emma Hollis of "Goodbye to All That" does accept the offer, and her father is cured. Her actions precipitate Frank Black's dismissal from the F.B.I. and disappoint her father, leaving Emma in a very bad place at the end of the series. Her final scene sees her looking upon an ouroboros displayed on her computer screen, a confirmation that she is now a member of the Millennium Group.

As dark a trajectory as this was for the character, Klea was pleased with how her arc played out. "I think they figured out, by the end, where to take it, and unfortunately that's when we got canceled, but I really think that putting Emma Hollis into the position of having to choose between the health of her father through the Millennium Group and her loyalties to Frank was really interesting."

The series' cancellation meant that the next stage in Hollis's storyline was destined to remain unexplored. Klea gave her character's future a lot of thought at the time, though, imagining a tantalizing possibility as to what might have happened next. "Lance and I had a million ideas for the next season," she elaborates. "We had this whole thing that we were going to come back and Emma's on the inside. You're going to think she's total Millennium Group and they're going to be meeting and she's just trying to break them down from the inside, she's just posing for the Millennium Group.

"I just didn't feel like she could be that completely disloyal to Frank, ultimately. That's too strong a relationship for her to just jump wholeheartedly into, and I thought she was too smart as well. I thought 'she's going to figure out a way to work this system,' and that would have been a really rewarding moment of revelation, to assume they were adversaries and then suddenly realize they're on the same side again. And who knows how long her father would have lived? Perhaps his demise would have released her from any contract she felt too.

"We had all these ideas, as actors, where this could go, and unfortunately we were cut off at the knees! I think by the end that giving Emma that struggle was really interesting and gave her a momentum that wasn't just a surrogate to Frank's experiences but gave her her own motivations for things."

Klea was working elsewhere when she heard that *Millennium* would not be returning for a fourth season. "It was June and I was on location filming a little film in Charlotte, North Carolina, and I just got a phone call from Chris [Carter]. He just said, 'I really loved working with you, thank you so much, but the show's canceled.' He was already deep into *Harsh Realm* that was replacing us. I don't know if it was as unceremonious as it was because of *Harsh Realm*, which was at that point the hottest pilot in town; it was written in invisible ink and everybody was up for a part in it. It was crazy, so I think they had great hopes for that."

Both at the time and looking back now, Klea shares the views of so many others when it comes to *Millennium*'s cancellation mere months before the turn of the millennium, seeing it as a missed opportunity. "It was just so timely, the idea that it was called *Millennium* was so wonderful. I just felt like they had it all there in their hands. I don't know if it was the level of popularity of *The X-Files* that just made it seem that it wasn't as valuable a project for some reason, because it wasn't achieving those numbers. I don't know what it was that made them lose faith, because it was such a strong and loyal fan base. It was as though they didn't want the medium numbers because they wanted a shot at the big gold hoop. To me it seemed like a Fox network moneymaking decision that just had no vision."

She also considered the possibility of a *Millennium* movie long before there was an active campaign for such a project. "I really just thought there were a million things too that could have been done at the point of cancellation," she ponders. "I thought that was the point to make a feature film, to actually coincide with the millennium. Even me, as a layperson in the business of it, could've come up with a million ways to tie up the end of the show in a far more interesting way. They had a rather lame episode where they attempted to address, at the turning of the millennium, our storyline on *The X-Files*. They had Lance appear, but it was secondary to watching Mulder and Scully kiss and I just thought, 'Really? That's what you gave us?' The millennium was actually turning, everybody was all freaked out about the Y2K stuff and it was just a lack of vision somehow. I don't know where the breakdown was. Then I thought, 'It's still the millennium, now we're into the Aughts. Let's try a movie, or a T.V. movie or just something to satisfy the story,' because I'm a story whore! I really am, I love great stories. I still feel like I'm hanging on that one."

Asked if she would approach Hollis differently if she were playing her today, Klea says, "I don't think so." Is her process as an actor still the same? "I hope it's matured and evolved, but I don't think it has changed drastically in any direction. I hope that, if anything, it's a more relaxed and confident approach to things instead of trying to be a good student, which actually, I think, dovetailed nicely with Emma Hollis's character anyway, but certainly as you get older in this business you stop trying to do things 'right' as much and start trying to be truer to your artistic needs and truth, I think."

In terms of the fan reaction, Season Three has benefited from the passage of time. "I think the show itself is quite fascinating," considers Klea, "because every single season there were different writers at the helm, and they took it in a completely different way. So maybe the best idea would have been to give it a Season Four with a whole new writing team and take it in another direction and never let the audience get complacent about what the show was about and where it was going. Because I just think the supernatural bent in the second season versus the first season's gritty crime show reality was what there was an attempt to return to in the third season, but because of the approach of the millennium it did get more apocalyptic in its perspective on crime and the criminal and the nature of evil. And we were just about to enter into these Bush years of having an actual Axis of Evil and that question of, 'Does evil exist?' I just wish that it had gotten a chance to play itself out in the minds of the writers with all the potential it had built. Nobody knew where it was going, and I have to admit that was some of the fun of being on the show."

Certain themes key to *Millennium* were present in 2008's *The X-Files: I Want to Believe*, which had an air of familiarity to Klea. "It's interesting, because they shot the F.B.I. headquarters in the movie where it was actually my office on the T.V. show *Intelligence* that I had just finished in Vancouver. It had been canceled and *The X-Files* movie bought our set to use for their movie, so I watched Mulder and Scully walk into my office and have a whole conversation in my office! It was very weird and there were all these overlapping actors and things like that, so I felt so bizarrely connected, and Frank Spotnitz has remained in my life too as a friend."

Watching the progression of Emma Hollis throughout Season Three was one of the most engaging aspects of *Millennium*'s final year. Many fans of the series were not receptive to the character at first, but it is clear that by the time the season was done, Klea Scott's portrayal of Special Agent Emma Hollis had converted a great many viewers.

This is a sentiment that is not lost on Klea, who remarks on it as we near the end of her interview. "It really meant a lot to me that you were really respectful of the work, because regardless of how you received it—if you liked it or not—I worked my ass off on that show and I'm proud of it, so I really appreciate that there are people out there who received what I was trying to give. This is a nice reintroduction to a world of fans and people who support your work, that it can be a nice place to visit." And of the many questions that linger concerning Emma Hollis and her predicament at the end of the series, Klea believes that this only adds to the expectation of a return, both for the character and for *Millennium*. "If you end on a hanging note, people will be hopefully waiting for you to finish that song."

Troy L. Foreman is the co-project coordinator for the Back to Frank Black campaign. He joined the campaign in 2009 after inviting James McLean to be a guest on his podcast *Tha Darkside Vibe*. He subsequently launched the *Millennium Group Sessions* podcast, which he edits and produces. Foreman has been a fan of *Millennium* since it first aired. He lives in Arlington, Virginia, and works as a network engineer for a real estate company. In his spare time, he works on several other projects, including two more podcasts—*Voice of the Verse* and *The Pop Culture Principle*—and several other entertainment-related blogs.

BACK TO FRANK BLACK:
A NEW *MILLENNIUM*

Interviews by James McLean & Troy L. Foreman
Written by Adam Chamberlain & Brian A. Dixon

Our final image of Frank Black is a lasting one. Sensing imminent danger, the desperate profiler bursts into his daughter's school. Taking young Jordan by the hand, the two flee the nightmare of their lives, desperate to escape the forces of evil conspiring against them. They have no allies, no safe haven, but they do have a solace in each other and in their hope for the future. The long-suffering Frank remains defiant, undaunted, a force for empathy and conviction in a world teetering on the brink of chaos. As the hero's Jeep Cherokee speeds toward a distant horizon and the sun sets on a landscape of lengthening shadows, the future remains uncertain, at once tantalizing and terrifying.

BACK TO FRANK BLACK

Millennium (1996-99) is unique in the annals of television crime drama and Frank Black represents a singular prism through which audiences are invited to examine the conflicts and depravity of modern society. Given his profound abilities, he reflects something primal in us all—an instinctual awareness of the looming, ever-present darkness forever encroaching upon the world. Contemporary examinations of this milestone series and the creative process that inspired its affecting stories ultimately serve to impart an emergent truth: we need Frank Black.

Central to any pending finale to his story are the visionary creators, writers, producers, actors, and crew, all of who contributed to a seminal body of work. Time and again, each have stated their enduring belief in and appreciation for *Millennium* and their desire to return to its unquiet world one final time. In 2011, the Back to Frank Black campaign brought together three leading alumni from *Millennium* for a landmark interview. Creator and executive producer Chris Carter, co-executive producer Frank Spotnitz, and Frank Black himself, actor Lance Henriksen, spoke together for the first time in over a decade. In the resulting conversation, the three discuss their interest in the return of *Millennium* and consider the possible creative approaches to this long-awaited project.

Of the countless roles he has so memorably portrayed across a prolific career, Frank Black is the character that Henriksen would most like to reprise, as he explains to Carter. "I've never let it go because the restraint you imposed upon that character was so rewarding. I've never stopped really liking that character so much." Carter affirms that Henriksen's is a performance that will continue to endure: "You've entered the pantheon for sure."

Spotnitz credits the actor's singular performance as one of the primary reasons for the show's lasting impact. "I think that's why it still holds up," he reasons, "and why people are still so passionate about it. Lance, I can't give you enough credit for what you brought to the role and how much depth you brought to the character. You brought such gravitas, and you felt the character's decency and suffering throughout, and [the viewer] just wanted to follow you through all three years of the show. But it also was a show that was about something and made you think, and so it endures in a way that a lot of other shows won't, because with a lot of other series there's a thinness to them that *Millennium* never had. It's not for everybody—it was certainly way too intense for a lot of people—but that's why I think people are so passionate about it. And I think that depth that you had then has only gotten deeper over time, so I think it would be very exciting. I would be excited to do it."

Millennium's creator recognizes the series to be distinct against the canvas of popular crime procedurals currently on television. "I look at these crime shows on T.V. now which are so popular—*Criminal Minds* and *CSI* and the kind of procedural shows—I think that what we tried to do was give *Millennium* a depth beyond these procedurals." Summing up the enduring appeal of the critically acclaimed series, Spotnitz adds, "*Millennium* was about the darkness in the world, the darkness that Frank Black was trying to protect his family from, but that was inside of him as well. And the world now, since *Millennium* went off the air, has become so much more overtly dark and evil and frightening. The mood and ideas that were in *Millennium* have become more real and vivid to everyone, sadly. So, I do think it's even more in keeping with the times in which we live."

In these early days of the twenty-first century, Frank Black could not be needed more urgently, Henriksen insists. "Most of the films that are being made dealing with all these kinds of thing are more of a personality versus principles. They're more egocentric: do battle, kill, murder, fight back with a gun rather than with the mind. I would love it if we pursued this, it would be a tremendous gift, because there's a dignity in it that I almost feel like the world—or the country, certainly—needs. I just think there is a place for us that is so poignant now. It's much more poignant now than ever."

For three years on Fox, *Millennium* ardently pushed the conceptual and artistic boundaries of television production. Its characters are peerless, its themes universal, its mythology epic in scope. The possibilities for a film based on the series are tantalizing. Carter shares his vision. "I think that if there were a faithful movie, it would certainly have to be on a grander scale than the television series. I think if there's any reason to do it then it needs to be more than the sixty-eighth episode. It would need to be a reconceiving of the original idea. It would have to be a refocusing on the series." Creatively, Henriksen is very much on the same page, underscoring the need to both honor the integrity of the series whilst also placing its hero in a contemporary context. "That sounds really good, Chris, because a lot has happened to us all since *Millennium*." Carter continues, "Well, a lot has happened to the world as well. Who knew 2001 would be such a dark time for the world. Definitely, the world feels sick right now."

Henriksen, a man who lived as Frank Black during his time on the series, shares specific thoughts on how the character might be represented for his return, stressing the opportunities for visual storytelling offered by technological advances in filmmaking. "There's a claustrophobic kind of nature to language," Henriksen suggests, "and I've been thinking about the advent of C.G.I. and 'green screen.' It could do for us what we tried to do with the flashbacks at certain moments, where you can almost get a streaming effect of Frank Black's thinking in different ways." One of *Millennium*'s trademark devices, the visionary gift of the profiler, served to inspire countless crime dramas on television and in film. Henriksen believes that a new production based on the series could revolutionize cinema's approach to the visual representation of abstract ideas yet again. "It would be new and different. I've been lit up about it forever, every time something new comes in."

The actor is also adamant that he would love to see Brittany Tiplady reprise her role as Jordan Black, returning alongside her onscreen father. "I've seen a picture of Brittany. I've spoken to her. She's absolutely beautiful but has the same eyes. She's a great kid. She's almost the same age as my daughter."

Film and television, of course, are an industry, one that is driven by billion dollar box office returns and ruthless competition. In addition to the rich creative opportunities still offered by *Millennium*, there are business concerns that must be weighed as well. Simply put, Frank Black's return would need to be commercially viable. "The difficult thing with *Millennium* and *The X-Files* or any of these things is that they are owned by a big studio," Spotnitz points out. "They have a business model. It's not just about our passion—which I think you can hear is there—it's about the business and whether they are willing to support the passion that we clearly still have. But I think Chris's thought about doing it as a movie for television is realistically the way this could happen.

"It would be an event on television. It's a tough sell in the movie business. I don't think they look at the Ten Thirteen fan base; I don't think they look at it that way. But I think if you could say this would be an event you could promote and you'd get a lot of those people who did watch the show—which was a significant number, especially in today's T.V. landscape—I think there's a compelling commercial and creative argument to be made." Carter agrees, noting that the series maintained respectable audience figures throughout its run: "With network viewership being the way it is now, *Millennium* would be a giant hit still on Fox. We were cancelled with ratings that far exceed most T.V. shows now."

Spotnitz wisely cautions against indulging in pure nostalgia, noting that every film production must possess its own *raison d'être*. "The thing that I also think about is that nostalgia is a double-edged sword, and I think if we did a new *Millennium*, if it didn't have integrity and a reason for being on its own, aside from revisiting people's love for the old series, it would be disappointing." Inspired by these conditions, Carter offers a hint of his imaginings for the film. "It would need to have that integrity from the original idea, but it needs to be a rethinking. I've had random thoughts about this and one was to use a character like Doggett [as played by Robert Patrick] and do a cross-pollination with *The X-Files*." Such a move would ensure further interest from fans of *The X-Files* and also offer the potential to continue the story for some of that series' popular supporting characters.

"It's almost like you have to re-introduce the show," Carter continues. "It would have to be exciting to people beyond the original show. I'm sure it could be done, if the story were good enough. We've got all the other elements, including Lance, in place. They are interesting characters to resurrect, and it would be nice to shoot it in Vancouver if we ever did it, and bring back Rob McLachlan, who won so many awards for his great cinematography." Indeed, McLachlan is another talent who has expressed his desire to return to *Millennium*. "None of these guys have ever let it go," Henriksen can attest. "As difficult as it was for everybody—it's a lot of work—nobody ever let it go. I think it drove the spear in deeper."

"I know," says Carter. "It was a real labor of love. It blows all of us away that there is this continued interest, because everyone moves on but the television show lives on."

As far as Spotnitz is concerned, his devotion to the series has been repaid. "I know I speak for Chris and Lance too, but I can't say how much I appreciate the support and loyalty and passion and intelligence of the people who support *Millennium* and—for Chris and me—*The X-Files* and all the Ten Thirteen shows I was blessed to be a part of. I am honored by all of these people. That's the ultimate compliment paid to

Millennium—the caliber of the people who are devoted to it. It tells you a lot about the caliber of the show."

Speaking more recently, Henriksen reaffirmed his belief that Frank Black will return, invoking those qualities that continue to inspire him. "I love the idea of a non-judgmental character like Frank Black. He wants to know why and how all these things happened, but he knows that judging someone for what they've done would just get in the way of finding out things. Imagine that kind of morality and focus, like a master chess player. There are beads on a string, and suddenly you've got a necklace. When you trap a guy like Frank Black, who has that kind of imagination, and you put him in a world like Bulgaria, where everything is in Cyrillic and he can't communicate actively with a lot of people, he has to do it in another way. You just keep moving the pressure in on him about, say, a terrorist plot. The pressure keeps building and building and building until you realize that that pressure gives him all the answers he needs. You would be gasping for air to wonder what is going to happen to this guy.

"If *Millennium* were made today with those characters, it would be a far more interesting show than the limited palette they had with serial killers. I think it's going to happen, I really do. It's crazy that you wouldn't give it a shot. It doesn't have to be a $30 million movie either. There are a lot of fans out there—in sixty-five countries. I can't go into any other country without them wondering when the movie is going to be made."

Other key figures from the series have joined Henriksen, Carter, and Spotnitz in expressing their desire to see *Millennium* return. Writer and producer Michael R. Perry offers his own perspective on the matter, considering the self-sacrificing protagonist's core qualities as vital to the series' enduring appeal and relevance. "I think Frank Black is a man of enormous empathy and tragedy who has a superior intelligence but also an emotional intelligence, and his ability to empathize and to intuit what is inside another person is great when he is around good people, but because of the nature of his job it takes him to some dark places sometimes. That, to me, is fascinating—I love that. I would use the Frank Black character always to do the two things. It has two great qualities. One is a thriller pacing and really interesting mystery cases, in the oldest Agatha Christie sense, but then incredibly modern themes, getting into the bigger questions of what it is to live in the twenty-first century, now. That was, for me, what was brilliant about *Millennium*, and I think that would play perfectly right now. I think it would play on television so much more, to get into the human side of things. I think some procedural shows have a tendency to get into the technical evidence-gathering stuff and to be a little broader than what we were going for. What you could do with *Millennium* is to bring real specificity and lots of human detail to that kind of thing while not losing any of the mystery pacing. You need Chris Carter, though."

Should such a return to this world of grim mysteries and malign forces ever be realized, veteran director Thomas J. Wright wants to be at Carter's side. "Well, of course I would be interested," declares Wright. "Lance and I talk about this a lot, because Lance would still love to do the big screen version of *Millennium*. The big screen version would, of course, give you a lot more areas to explore, because you don't have the time limit that crunches you so much during a one-hour episode. You'd have more time to explore the characters, and it's just a bigger venue, and you can do a lot more."

Actress Klea Scott reflected upon the creative possibilities for the franchise after attending a screening of *The X-Files: I Want to Believe* (2008). "It's interesting," she says, "because I went and saw the second *X-Files* movie and I see that's living on and it's in the film world and at the behest of, really, its fan base as well, and I know that the *Millennium* fan base is probably smaller than *The X-Files*, but I just think it's an easier job to write something for *Millennium*."

Turning to *Millennium*'s focus on confronting issues of violence and abuse, Scott addresses a recent spate of shootings in the United States, reflecting on deplorable attacks in Aurora, Colorado, and Oak Creek, Wisconsin. "There are bad people in the world. I wish Frank Black could tuck me in at night and remind me that he's there—in between me and the chaos. Perhaps, these thirteen years later, having a child of my own makes me more aware of danger. I have always been so proud to have been included in the story-circle of *Millennium*. I know, I'm supposed to call it a T.V. series, but it seems to have been more than that. When writers, designers, actors, and crews are coming together to tell big stories on big themes and doing it at one in the morning, in the rain, in the forest, in high heels, you just can't help but feel like you are telling a bigger story."

After years of avoiding the sometimes vicious critiques of internet fandom, Scott credits the Back to Frank Black campaign with uniting cast and crew in addition to the many enduring fans of the series. "The day I was first contacted by Back to Frank Black was the day I made a friend," she says. "The intelligent interest in work I thought had been foolishly cancelled in its prime, work that I thought deserved an audience, had an audience all along. A dedicated, funny, supportive fan base with an insane work ethic—and such nice manners! It has always been a pleasure to talk with anyone from the campaign, but Back to Frank Black has also put me in touch again with dear friends that were missing me too.

"I often think that the simple hunger for good storytelling is what unites us most clearly. *Millennium* told a great story, and Back to Frank Black has always been a great audience. I do think it's interesting that you could come back at any point and address a lot of these things, because it's going to be—for a couple of years more at least—the millennium. We're going to be in the new millennium a while, so it is out there to be explored, and I believe the character of Frank Black is one you could easily come back to and have aged the characters and still be able to pick up the storyline quite easily. It would be fascinating, I think. If, as we did, you end on a hanging note, people will be waiting for you to finish that song."

Troy Foreman, one of the guiding personalities behind the campaign to return Frank Black to the screen, writes to provide a perspective from within this remarkable movement itself. "Should *Millennium* come back as a feature film? This book answers that question. Everyone who has participated in this project has one thing in common: their love for *Millennium* and for Frank Black. *Millennium* was definitely ahead of its time and, with recent events, the character of Frank Black is more relevant now than ever—a man who can try to make sense of what is going on in the world. Frank Black has had a lasting effect on me and thousands of people from all over the world—from seventy-five countries, based on those who listen to the campaign's podcasts and visit the website. Frank Black is a universal character representing universal themes. More than anything, I think that should be enough to make the studio take another look at *Millennium*, and to give it the film it so deserves."

There are poignant dramatic possibilities yet to be explored. Quite aside from his singular perspective on the evils of the modern world, Frank Black would now be approaching old age. He would be forced to contemplate that, soon, he will no longer be able to protect his daughter from such evils. Jordan must find her own place and make her own way in the world, drawing upon the strength of her own unique intuitions. In the years since we last saw him, Frank will most likely have raised Jordan to adulthood as a single parent, and she will have grown into womanhood without her beloved mother to guide her. The two may have grown closer as a result, but it will not have been easy. Frank doubtless continues to bear the guilt that his involvement with the Millennium Group led to the death of his wife, Catherine. He is likely still wounded by the inescapable void in his family that can never be filled. Spoken or unspoken, Jordan may carry some resentment at having had to endure her teenage years without a mother by her side. She may have come to understand the circumstances that led to this more deeply and, on some level, to blame her father in turn. Their situation, these tensions, and how they reflect wider concerns about the state of the world, a world in which Jordan must now begin to find her way and become her own person, are powerful themes. Against the background of the escalating evils of the modern world, the unfolding saga of these characters allows for a unique perspective that is at once deeply personal and utterly universal.

Millennium possesses the potential to prompt us to acknowledge the unpleasant truths of the modern world—singularly so through the veteran perceptions of Frank Black. In a new millennium that has wrought mass murders upon the world in the name of terrorism, extremist ideology, and mental disturbance—inflicted by organized groups and lone wolf offenders alike—evil can be construed as a force that continues to conspire, and Frank Black maintains a place in the midst of such fateful events that has the potential to prove deeply resonant, powerful, and revelatory.

In a world in which evil has many faces, hope has just one: Frank Black. Forensic profiler, devoted father, visionary hero. He stood alone against the rising tide of evil during the dark final days of the last century, braving a world of deplorable crime and unspeakable horrors. In the uncertain early days of a new millennium, we need him more than ever.

APPENDIX
EPISODE GUIDE

SEASON ONE

"Pilot"   MLM-100

Written by Chris Carter   Production #4C79
Directed by David Nutter   Aired 25 October 1996
Edited by Stephen Mark   Nielsen Rating 11.9

Renowned criminal profiler Frank Black retires with his family to Seattle, where he joins the mysterious Millennium Group in an effort to track a serial killer whose viciously slain victims include an exotic dancer.

"Gehenna"   MLM-101

Written by Chris Carter   Production #4C01
Directed by David Nutter   Aired 1 November 1996
Edited by Stephen Mark   Nielsen Rating 8.1

The discovery of human ashes in a flowerbed brings Frank Black to San Francisco, where the Millennium Group investigates a controlling cult linked to a telemarketing firm.

"Dead Letters" MLM-102

Written by Glen Morgan & James Wong Production #4C02
Directed by Thomas J. Wright Aired 8 November 1996
Edited by Chris Willingham, A.C.E. Nielsen Rating 8.1

On a serial murder case in Portland, Oregon, Frank Black is uneasily teamed with a troubled Millennium Group candidate who proves ill-suited to handle the horrors of the case.

"The Judge" MLM-104

Written by Ted Mann Production #4C04
Directed by Randy Zisk Aired 15 November 1996
Edited by Stephen Mark Nielsen Rating 7.6

Dismembered remains provide Frank Black with a lead to the Judge, a vigilante who persuades aimless ex-cons to enforce a code of murderous personal justice.

"522666" MLM-105

Written by Glen Morgan & James Wong Production #4C05
Directed by David Nutter Aired 22 November 1996
Edited by Chris Willingham, A.C.E. Nielsen Rating 7.6

A deadly explosion in a crowded Washington, D.C., pub is traced to a serial bomber who subsequently toys with Frank Black and the authorities as he plots to strike again.

"Kingdom Come" MLM-103

Written by Jorge Zamacona Production #4C03
Directed by Winrich Kolbe Aired 29 November 1996
Edited by George R. Potter Nielsen Rating 7.2

A crisis of faith figures in the motive for the slayings of clerics by a grief-stricken killer tracked by Frank Black and the Millennium Group.

APPENDIX

"Blood Relatives" — MLM-106

Written by Chip Johannessen
Directed by James Charleston
Edited by George R. Potter

Production #4C06
Aired 6 December 1996
Nielsen Rating 7.5

In her role as a clinical social worker, Catherine Black lends her expertise to a heinous case: the slayings of the recently bereaved.

"The Well-Worn Lock" — MLM-107

Written by Chris Carter
Directed by Ralph Hemecker
Edited by Stephen Mark

Production #4C07
Aired 20 December 1996
Nielsen Rating 6.8

Accusations of incest draw Catherine Black to the plight of a troubled woman who has kept a terrible secret for twenty-three years: she was sexually abused by her well-respected father.

"Wide Open" — MLM-108

Written by Charles D. Holland
Directed by James Charleston
Edited by Chris Willingham, A.C.E.

Production #4C08
Aired 3 January 1997
Nielsen Rating 6.7

A shadowy killer uses real estate open houses to commit heinous murders and terrorize a child whose traumatic experiences may prove to be the key to his capture.

"The Wild and the Innocent" — MLM-110

Written by Jorge Zamacona
Directed by Thomas J. Wright
Edited by Stephen Mark

Production #4C10
Aired 10 January 1997
Nielsen Rating 7.1

A murder case takes Frank Black to Missouri, where he begins the pursuit of a killer traveling cross-country with a mysterious young woman on a desperate quest.

"Weeds"   MLM-109

Written by Frank Spotnitz   Production #4C09
Directed by Michael Pattinson   Aired 24 January 1997
Edited by George Richard Potter   Nielsen Rating 7.6

In a private gated community, the kidnapping and brutalization of teenage boys leads Frank Black to investigate the secret sins of their fathers.

"Loin Like a Hunting Flame"   MLM-111

Written by Ted Mann   Production #4C11
Directed by David Nutter   Aired 31 January 1997
Edited by Chris Willingham, A.C.E.   Nielsen Rating 8.0

In Colorado, Frank Black and an associate track a killer who is driven by sexual neuroses and who uses mood-altering drugs to gain control of the couples he kills.

"Force Majeure"   MLM-112

Written by Chip Johannessen   Production #4C12
Directed by Winrich Kolbe   Aired 7 February 1997
Edited by G. Richard Potter   Nielsen Rating 7.1

An enigmatic character haunts Frank Black and the Millennium Group during a strange case involving planetary alignment, genetic cloning, and a man in an iron lung.

"The Thin White Line"   MLM-113

Written by Glen Morgan & James Wong   Production #4C13
Directed by Thomas J. Wright   Aired 14 February 1997
Edited by Stephen Mark   Nielsen Rating 6.8

Frank Black is forced to confront his past when startling similarities in serial slayings twenty years apart indicate that the man imprisoned for the earlier crimes molded the current killer.

APPENDIX

"Sacrament" — MLM-114

Written by Frank Spotnitz
Directed by Michael Watkins
Edited by Chris Willingham, A.C.E.

Production #4C14
Aired 21 February 1997
Nielsen Rating 6.4

The abduction of his sister-in-law embroils Frank Black in an intensely personal case linked to a vicious sex offender recently released from an asylum.

"Covenant" — MLM-116

Written by Robert Moresco
Directed by Roderick J. Pridy
Edited by Stephen Mark

Production #4C16
Aired 21 March 1997
Nielsen Rating 6.9

In Utah, Frank Black is hired to offer expert testimony against a confessed killer in support a death sentence but soon comes to believe the accused is innocent of the crimes.

"Walkabout" — MLM-115

Written by Chip Johannessen & Tim Tankosic
Directed by Cliff Bole
Edited by George Potter

Production #4C15
Aired 28 March 1997
Nielsen Rating 6.3

An online connection to a disturbed doctor leads Frank Black to become personally entangled in a murder case linked to an experimental drug that drastically heightens anxiety.

"Lamentation" — MLM-117

Written by Chris Carter
Directed by Winrich Kolbe
Edited by Chris Willingham, A.C.E.

Production #4C17
Aired 18 April 1997
Nielsen Rating 6.7

The grisly fate of an infamous serial murderer introduces Frank Black to Lucy Butler, an infernal figure who initiates terrifying events at the Black household.

"Powers, Principalities, Thrones and Dominions" MLM-118

Written by Ted Mann & Harold Rosenthal Production #4C18
Directed by Thomas J. Wright Aired 25 April 1997
Edited by George Potter Nielsen Rating 6.7

Still reeling from a tragic loss, Frank Black is swept into a bizarre case of ritualistic slayings that involves an inscrutable lawyer and a conflict of seemingly unearthly origins.

"Broken World" MLM-119

Written by Robert Moresco & Patrick Harbinson Production #4C19
Directed by Winrich Kolbe Aired 2 May 1997
Edited by Stephen Mark Nielsen Rating 6.8

Evidence in the malicious slayings of domesticated horses across North Dakota leads Frank Black to fear the genesis of a psychosexual killer who will soon prey upon humans.

"Maranatha" MLM-120

Written by Chip Johannessen Production #4C20
Directed by Peter Markle Aired 9 May 1997
Edited by Chris Willingham, A.C.E. Nielsen Rating 6.7

In Brighton Beach, Frank Black joins forces with a Moscow cop to investigate gruesome slayings linked to the Chernobyl disaster and a man the Russian people believe to be the antichrist.

"Paper Dove" MLM-121

Written by Walon Green & Ted Mann Production #4C21
Directed by Thomas J. Wright Aired 16 May 1997
Edited by George Potter Nielsen Rating 6.6

Vacationing in Washington, D.C., Frank Black agrees to try to clear an admiral's son of murder in a case that appears to be the work of a serial killer.

APPENDIX

SEASON TWO

"The Beginning and the End" — MLM-201

Written by Glen Morgan
& James Wong
Directed by Thomas J. Wright
Edited by Chris Willingham, ACE

Production #5C01
Aired 19 September 1997
Nielsen Rating 7.3

Frank Black launches into a desperate search for Catherine, who has been abducted by the elusive psychopath who has long stalked his family by taking Polaroid photographs.

"Beware of the Dog" — MLM-202

Written by Glen Morgan & James Wong
Directed by Allen Coulter
Edited by George R. Potter

Production #5C02
Aired 26 September 1997
Nielsen Rating 6.5

The Millennium Group prompts Frank Black to investigate a pack of vicious dogs that are terrorizing a rural town in attacks seemingly understood by a mysterious old man.

"Sense and Antisense" — MLM-203

Written by Chip Johannessen
Directed by Thomas J. Wright
Edited by James Coblentz

Production #5C03
Aired 3 October 1997
Nielsen Rating 6.7

Frank Black is tasked with locating and identifying patient zero in a case involving a biomedical behavioral-control project and a conspiratorial cover-up.

"Monster" — MLM-204

Written by Glen Morgan & James Wong
Directed by Perry Lang
Edited by Chris Willingham, A.C.E.

Production #5C04
Aired 17 October 1997
Nielsen Rating 6.0

In rural Arkansas, Frank Black and forensic psychologist Lara Means investigate a young boy's death, which they alarmingly link to a five-year-old girl.

"A Single Blade of Grass" MLM-205

Written by Erin Maher & Kay Reindl
Directed by Rodman Flender
Edited by George R. Potter

Production #5C05
Aired 24 October 1997
Nielsen Rating 6.7

Frank Black joins an anthropologist to investigate a lost tribe of Native Americans gathering in Manhattan to commit bizarre, ritualistic slayings in an effort to fulfill apocalyptic prophecy.

"The Curse of Frank Black" MLM-207

Written by Glen Morgan & James Wong
Directed by Ralph Hemecker
Edited by Chris Willingham, A.C.E.

Production #5C07
Aired 31 October 1997
Nielsen Rating 5.7

On Halloween, Frank Black experiences a number of unsettling coincidences that spark flashbacks to his youth and lead to a fateful encounter with a tragic figure from his past.

"19:19" MLM-206

Written by Glen Morgan & James Wong
Directed by Thomas J. Wright
Edited by James Coblentz

Production #5C06
Aired 7 November 1997
Nielsen Rating 6.1

In southeastern Oklahoma, Frank Black, Peter Watts, and Lara Means must race against time to locate a busload of abducted children entombed in an abandoned quarry by a crazed visionary.

"The Hand of St. Sebastian" MLM-208

Written by Glen Morgan & James Wong
Directed by Thomas J. Wright
Edited by George R. Potter

Production #5C08
Aired 14 November 1997
Nielsen Rating 6.7

Frank Black and a driven Peter Watts travel to Germany in search of a religious artifact relating to the Millennium Group's secret history, which is steeped in dark intrigue dating to the first millennium.

APPENDIX

"Jose Chung's *Doomsday Defense*" MLM-209

Written by Darin Morgan
Directed by Darin Morgan
Edited by James Coblentz

Production #5C09
Aired 21 November 1997
Nielsen Rating 5.6

When Jose Chung becomes the target of a religious group known as Selfosophy, Frank Black teams with the flamboyant writer to investigate a string of bizarre murders.

"Midnight of the Century" MLM-211

Written by Erin Maher & Kay Reindl
Directed by Dwight Little
Edited by George R. Potter

Production #5C11
Aired 19 December 1997
Nielsen Rating 5.6

Unnerving visions that haunt Frank Black at Christmastime hark back to his troubled youth and lead to a fateful reunion with his estranged father, Henry.

"Goodbye Charlie" MLM-210

Written by Richard Whitley
Directed by Ken Fink
Edited by Chris Willingham, A.C.E.

Production #5C10
Aired 9 January 1998
Nielsen Rating 5.6

Murders in the guise of assisted suicides bewilder Frank Black and Lara Means, whose primary suspect is a charismatic nurse convinced he is ministering to the terminally ill.

"Luminary" MLM-212

Written by Chip Johannessen
Directed by Thomas J. Wright
Edited by James Coblentz

Production #5C12
Aired 23 January 1998
Nielsen Rating 5.7

In defiance of the Millennium Group, Frank Black sets off on his own into the Alaskan wilderness to search for a missing teen who has risked his life in a search for enlightenment.

"The Mikado" MLM-213

Written by Michael R. Perry Production #5C13
Directed by Roderick J. Pridy Aired 6 February 1998
Edited by Chris Willingham, A.C.E. Nielsen Rating 5.4

A killer screens his elaborately planned crimes over the internet in a case that Frank Black links to Avatar, an ingenious serial killer who eluded capture in the 1970s.

"The Pest House" MLM-215

Written by Glen Morgan & James Wong Production #5C15
Directed by Allen Coulter Aired 27 February 1998
Edited by James Coblentz Nielsen Rating 5.7

A series of gruesome slayings are committed near a psychiatric hospital, where Frank Black and Peter Watts conduct an investigation that yields multiple suspects.

"Owls" MLM-214

Written by Glen Morgan & James Wong Production #5C14
Directed by Thomas J. Wright Aired 6 March 1998
Edited by George R. Potter Nielsen Rating 5.5

Covert operations and assassinations surround the search for a piece of the cross of the crucifixion that sparks infighting among the Millennium Group's two opposing factions: the Owls and the Roosters.

"Roosters" MLM-216

Written by Glen Morgan & James Wong Production #5C16
Directed by Thomas J. Wright Aired 13 March 1998
Edited by Chris Willingham, A.C.E. Nielsen Rating 5.4

The Millennium Group's Old Man links the schism within the organization to the actions of ODESSA, an underground network of Nazis bent on obtaining the cross of the crucifixion.

APPENDIX

"Siren" — MLM-217

Written by Glen Morgan & James Wong
Directed by Allen Coulter
Edited by George R. Potter

Production #5C17
Aired 20 March 1998
Nielsen Rating 5.8

The seizure of a ship smuggling Chinese immigrants draws Frank Black into the deadly mystery surrounding another passenger: an enigmatic seductress.

"In Arcadia Ego" — MLM-218

Written by Chip Johannessen
Directed by Thomas J. Wright
Edited by James Coblentz

Production #5C18
Aired 3 April 1998
Nielsen Rating 5.5

In Idaho, Frank Black tracks two escaped female prisoners: a troubled killer and her pregnant cellmate, who believes her pregnancy to be an immaculate conception.

"Anamnesis" — MLM-219

Written by Erin Maher & Kay Reindl
Directed by John Peter Kousakis
Edited by Chris Willingham, A.C.E.

Production #5C19
Aired 17 April 1998
Nielsen Rating 5.3

Catherine Black and Lara Means clash as they independently investigate a sensitive high-school girl who claims to be experiencing religious visions.

"A Room with No View" — MLM-220

Written by Ken Horton
Directed by Thomas J. Wright
Edited by George R. Potter

Production #5C20
Aired 24 April 1998
Nielsen Rating 4.8

Clues in the disappearance of a bright and outgoing teenage boy point to Frank Black's nemesis: the unearthly, seductive Lucy Butler.

"Somehow, Satan Got Behind Me" — MLM-221

Written by Darin Morgan
Directed by Darin Morgan
Edited by James Coblentz

Production #5C21
Aired 1 May 1998
Nielsen Rating 5.7

Four demons assemble in the predawn at a doughnut shop and reflect on the havoc they have wreaked in their efforts to lead humanity into damnation.

"The Fourth Horseman" — MLM-222

Written by Glen Morgan & James Wong
Directed by Dwight Little
Edited by Jim Thomson

Production #5C22
Aired 8 May 1998
Nielsen Rating 4.7

Frank Black takes a stand against the Millennium Group over its secrecy and its apparent involvement with a virulent contagion to which he and Peter Watts have been exposed.

"The Time is Now" — MLM-223

Written by Glen Morgan & James Wong
Directed by Thomas J. Wright
Edited by George R. Potter

Production #5C23
Aired 15 May 1998
Nielsen Rating 4.9

The spread of a deadly virus and the mysterious undertakings of the Millennium Group precipitate a crisis of apocalyptic proportions that will forever change the Black family.

APPENDIX

SEASON THREE

"The Innocents"   MLM-301

Written by Michael Duggan   Production #6C01
Directed by Thomas J. Wright   Aired 2 October 1998
Edited by Chris Willingham, ACE   Nielsen Rating 5.2

Frank Black teams up with intuitive young F.B.I. agent Emma Hollis to probe a plane crash linked to a family of seemingly identical women who are being systematically murdered.

"Exegesis"   MLM-302

Written by Chip Johannessen   Production #6C02
Directed by Ralph Hemecker   Aired 9 October 1998
Edited by James Coblentz   Nielsen Rating 4.5

Frank Black and Emma Hollis follow a trail of assassination leading to a gifted psychic who is on the run from the murderous Millennium Group.

"TEOTWAWKI"   MLM-303

Written by Chris Carter & Frank Spotnitz   Production #6C03
Directed by Thomas J. Wright   Aired 16 October 1998
Edited by Peter B. Ellis   Nielsen Rating 4.8

Frank Black's investigation into a deadly shooting spree at a high school is tied to an influential group of private citizens setting its own agenda for the year 2000.

"Closure"   MLM-304

Written by Larry Andries   Production #6C04
Directed by Daniel Sackheim   Aired 23 October 1998
Edited by Chris Willingham, A.C.E.   Nielsen Rating 5.1

The pursuit of a remorseless spree killer troubles Emma Hollis, whose fierce resolve to capture the madman is tied to a violent incident that scarred her emotionally as a child.

"Thirteen Years Later" — MLM-305

Written by Michael R. Perry
Directed by Thomas J. Wright
Edited by James Coblentz

Production #6C05
Aired 30 October 1998
Nielsen Rating 5.4

Bizarre murders disrupt the filming of a movie based on a grisly case from Frank Black's past as he and Emma Hollis visit the set—and encounter the rock band Kiss.

"Skull and Bones" — MLM-306

Written by Chip Johannessen & Ken Horton
Directed by Paul Shapiro
Edited by Peter B. Ellis

Production #6C06
Aired 6 November 1998
Nielsen Rating 5.1

The discovery of skeletal remains secretly buried at a construction site leads Frank Black and Emma Hollis to suspect the conspiratorial maneuverings of the Millennium Group.

"Through a Glass, Darkly" — MLM-307

Written by Patrick Harbinson
Directed by Thomas J. Wright
Edited by Chris Willingham, A.C.E.

Production #6C07
Aired 13 November 1998
Nielsen Rating 5.1

When a ten-year-old girl goes missing in rural Oregon, Frank Black and Emma Hollis join an unsettling case that involves a convicted child molester out on parole.

"Human Essence" — MLM-309

Written by Michael Duggan
Directed by Thomas J. Wright
Edited by Peter B. Ellis

Production #6C09
Aired 11 December 1998
Nielsen Rating 4.4

In Vancouver, British Columbia, Emma Hollis takes on a drug case involving her half-sister, an addict who claims that new heroin on the street is turning users into monsters.

APPENDIX

"Omerta" — MLM-308

Written by Michael R. Perry — Production #6C08
Directed by Paul Shapiro — Aired 18 December 1998
Edited by James Coblentz — Nielsen Rating 4.8

On a Christmas holiday in Vermont, Frank and Jordan Black become involved in the plight of a resurrected mobster and two ethereal women with miraculous healing powers.

"Borrowed Time" — MLM-310

Written by Chip Johannessen — Production #6C10
Directed by Dwight Little — Aired 15 January 1999
Edited by Chris Willingham, A.C.E. — Nielsen Rating 5.3

Strange fevers endanger the life of Jordan Black, whom her father believes is being stalked by a sinister man obsessed with near-death experiences.

"Collateral Damage" — MLM-311

Written by Michael R. Perry — Production #6C11
Directed by Thomas J. Wright — Aired 22 January 1999
Edited by James Coblentz — Nielsen Rating 5.8

Tensions resurface between Frank Black and his former ally during the search for Peter Watts's daughter, who has been abducted by an Army veteran with a grudge against the Millennium Group.

"The Sound of Snow" — MLM-312

Written by Patrick Harbinson — Production #6C12
Directed by Paul Shapiro — Aired 5 February 1999
Edited by Peter B. Ellis — Nielsen Rating 4.7

Mysterious audio tapes containing white noise trigger deadly hallucinations in the Seattle area, where Frank Black's investigation induces visions of the deceased Catherine.

"Antipas" MLM-313

Written by Chris Carter & Frank Spotnitz   Production #6C13
Directed by Thomas J. Wright   Aired 12 February 1999
Edited by Chris Willingham, A.C.E.   Nielsen Rating 4.6

Frank Black's nemesis, the evil Lucy Butler, resurfaces as the prime suspect in a murder case that involves Wisconsin's attorney general and the demonic corruption of a young girl.

"Matryoshka" MLM-314

Written by Erin Maher & Kay Reindl   Production #6C14
Directed by Arthur Forney   Aired 19 February 1999
Edited by James Coblentz   Nielsen Rating 4.6

The suicide of a former F.B.I. agent leads Frank Black into an investigation that uncovers dark secrets and Bureau intrigue at Los Alamos during the dawn of the atomic age.

"Forcing the End" MLM-315

Written by Marjorie David   Production #6C15
Directed by Thomas J. Wright   Aired 19 March 1999
Edited by Peter B. Ellis   Nielsen Rating 4.1

Leads in the abduction of a pregnant woman from Brooklyn steer Frank Black and Emma Hollis to a plot hatched by a fanatical cult driven by Hebrew prophecy.

"Saturn Dreaming of Mercury" MLM-316

Written by Jordan Hawley & Chip Johannessen   Production #6C16
Directed by Paul Shapiro   Aired 9 April 1999
Edited by Chris Willingham, A.C.E.   Nielsen Rating 4.2

Mystery surrounds Frank Black's new neighbors, a couple and their preteen son whose arrival coincides with erratic, often violent behavior from Jordan.

APPENDIX

"Darwin's Eye"   MLM-318

Written by Patrick Harbinson   Production #6C18
Directed by Ken Fink   Aired 16 April 1999
Edited by Peter B. Ellis   Nielsen Rating 3.7

Frank Black and Emma Hollis are perplexed by inconsistencies relating to an escaped mental patient with a violent past who has taken an apparently compliant hostage.

"Bardo Thodol"   MLM-317

Written by Virginia Stock & Chip Johannessen   Production #6C17
Directed by Thomas J. Wright   Aired 23 April 1999
Edited by James Coblentz   Nielsen Rating 3.8

Eerie discoveries haunt Frank Black and Emma Hollis on a case involving Buddhist mysticism, Millennium Group secrets, and incredible advances in biotechnology.

"Seven and One"   MLM-319

Written by Chris Carter & Frank Spotnitz   Production #6C19
Directed by Peter Markle   Aired 30 April 1999
Edited by Lauren Schaffer   Nielsen Rating 3.7

An ominous stalker uses intimidations inspired by a childhood trauma to prey upon Frank Black, who is also beset by an F.B.I. official who believes Frank is experiencing a mental breakdown.

"Nostalgia"   MLM-320

Written by Michael R. Perry   Production #6C20
Directed by Thomas J. Wright   Aired 7 May 1999
Edited by James Coblentz   Nielsen Rating 4.5

A journey back to the town where she grew up is anything but sentimental for Emma Hollis, who investigates unsolved serial murders with a sheriff she knew as a child.

"Via Dolorosa" MLM-321

Written by Marjorie David & Patrick Harbinson Production #6C21
Directed by Paul Shapiro Aired 14 May 1999
Edited by Casey O. Rohrs Nielsen Rating 5.0

On the trail of a copycat killer, Frank Black is haunted by his memories of the original while Emma Hollis is distracted by the deterioration of her father, an Alzheimer's patient.

"Goodbye to All That" MLM-322

Written by Ken Horton & Chip Johannessen Production #6C22
Directed by Thomas J. Wright Aired 21 May 1999
Edited by James Coblentz Nielsen Rating 4.5

The ongoing search for a serial killer is marked by bizarre occurrences and revelations concerning the Millennium Group's experimentation with radical brain surgery.

INDEX

48 Hours, 50

"A Whiter Shade of Pale," 212
A&M Records, 224
ABC, 102, 128, 236
Abelard, Peter, 259, 271
Abum, 303
Academy Awards, 26, 356
Academy Group, The, 30, 62, 72, 133-34, 138, 143, 147, 152, 154, 308, 324, 328, 330, 357
Aerotech International, 147-49
Alan Partridge, 123
Alaska, 145
Alfred Hitchcock Presents, 353
Alien, 167
Aliens, 32, 95
All the President's Men, 26
Allen, Irwin, 53
Allworth, John, 52-53
Alpert, Herb, 224
Alphabet of Ben-Sira, 256
American (band), 226
American Beauty, 120
American Doll, 105
American Gothic, 325
American Museum of Ceramic Art, 57
America Online, 175
American Revolution, 149
American Society of Cinematographers, 401
Anderson, Gillian, 46, 284, 333
Anderson, Paul W. S., 377
Andrews, Cheryl, 142, 155
Andromeda Strain, The, 384

Andy Griffith Show, The, 236
Angel (series), 378
Anglim, Philip, 130, 304
Annie Hall, 110
Antichrist, 299
Antipapas, 265
Antipas of Pergamum, 265
Antipas, Herod, 265
Antonioni, Michelangelo, 231
Apocrypha, 184
Arkansas, 136, 483
Armageddon, 122, 368
Armour, Norman, 314
Armstrong, R. G., 196, 227, 308
Arriflex, 377
"Artificial Flowers," 222
Atkins, Mike, 132, 260, 294, 297
Atlanta, Georgia, 441
Atlantic Records, 202
Auden, W. H., 348
Aurora Borealis, 83
Aurora, Colorado, 471
Avatar, 289, 320, 325, 328, 486
Axmann, Rudolph, 148
Azenzer, Philip, 399

Bacharach, Burt, 224
Bachelard, Gaston, 305
Bakalyan, Dick, 303
Baldwin, Barry, 315, 452
Barbakow, Danielle, 306
Bardale, Mike, 295
Bardo Thödol, 407-12
Barnum, Doug, 31, 34

495

Barr, Lucas Wayne, 85, 226, 315-16, 376
Bass, Teddy, 151
Battlestar Galactica, 198
BBC, 123, 372
Beach Boys, The, 237
Beaman, C. Philip, 216
Beasley, John, 457, 461
Beatlemania, 111
Beatles, The, 202
Bee Gees, The, 202, 237
Beedle, Ellsworth, 220
Behavioral Science Unit, 133, 292, 296, 329, 357, 377
Behold a Pale Horse, 27
Bell, Art, 331, 337
Bell, Marshall, 256, 295, 432
Bends, The, 227
Berkowitz, David, 218, 236, 287, 346
Beverly Hills Cop, 384
Beverly Hills, 90210, 416
"Beyond the Sea," 219, 222
Bianco, Mark, 392
Bilderberg Group, The, 114, 147
Billboard Hot 100, 224-25
Bishop, 32, 95
Black Christmas, 168
Black, Catherine, 18-19, 41, 44, 49, 78-80, 82, 84, 89-90, 93, 95-99, 117, 121, 128, 131-38, 140, 143-45, 147-51, 153-54, 157-58, 163, 170, 183, 186, 220, 222, 227, 232, 253, 288-90, 297, 307, 310, 312, 314, 318, 331, 408-10, 416, 446, 453, 473, 479, 483, 487, 491
Black, Frank, 15-16, 18-19, 22, 25-26, 29-35, 41-49, 51, 58-68, 71-90, 96-99, 106-12, 116-17, 121, 124, 126, 128, 133, 137, 140, 143, 158, 160, 163-64, 170, 171, 173, 179, 180, 183, 195-98, 206, 208, 211, 217, 222, 234, 244-46, 248, 250-56, 260-61, 264-70, 275-86, 289-90, 292, 295-96, 299, 301, 303-04, 308, 318-19, 324-25, 332-34, 336, 338, 341-45, 347-66, 370-78, 388, 392, 397, 399-02, 405-08, 412, 415, 417, 419-20, 424-43, 446, 452, 457-58, 461, 465-68, 470, 471-73, 477-94
Black, Helen, 304

Black, Henry, 152, 179-80, 367, 485
Black, Jordan, 19, 44, 63, 72, 79-80, 82, 93, 95, 101-02, 104, 106, 128, 131-32, 135, 140, 143, 146, 152-53, 155, 157-60, 181, 251, 253, 256, 258, 264, 268, 277, 281, 298-300, 307, 313, 316-17, 320, 367, 369, 409, 410, 412, 439, 465, 468, 473, 491-92
Black, Thomas, 130, 304
Blatty, William Peter, 267, 271
Bletcher, Robert, 79, 102, 132, 241, 251, 253, 255, 286, 297, 304-05, 314, 349, 351, 359, 362-63
Bloch, Ernest, 353-54
Blork, Frederick, 375
Blow-Up, 231, 354
Blue Highways, 418
Blue Velvet, 236
"Blue Velvet," 236
Blur (band), 231
Blurk, 303
Bobbitt, Lorena, 27
Bochco, Steven, 446
Boggs, Luther Lee, 219
Bonanno family, 150
Bond, James, 75
Borges, Jorge Luis, 349
Boston Theater Company, 75
Boston, Massachusetts, 75, 449
Boxer, Del, 313
Bracco, Lorraine, 137
Bradley, Barbra, 121
Brady Bunch, The, 128, 213
Brando, Marlon, 141
Brasco, Donnie, (see Pistone, Joseph Dominick)
Brasi, Luca, 148
Brel, Jacques, 237
Brimstone, 432
British Columbia, 399, 490
Broadway, 75, 91-93, 203, 237, 450
Brooklyn South, 446-47, 451
Brudos, Jerome, 28
Bruford, Bill, 238
Brunelli, Max, 84
Bryce, Landon, 225, 298, 302
Bucksnort, 125, 135, 196-97, 308
Buffalo Springfield, 202
Buffy the Vampire Slayer, 332
Bundy, Ted, 50, 323, 346

INDEX

Burke, Edmund, 320
Buscemi, Steve, 393
Bush, George H. W., 27
Butler, Lucy, 42, 44, 67-68, 132, 197, 225-26, 234, 241-71, 279, 296-302, 304, 312, 362-65, 446, 481, 487, 492

Caan, James, 141
Cagney & Lacey, 30, 203
Cain, 261
Cal State Northridge, 176-77
California, 57, 97, 176, 202-03, 320, 337
Calloway, Galen, 287
Campbell, Glenn, 368
Canadian Society of Cinematographers, 402
Cannell, Stephen J., 111, 398
Capaldi, Jim, 233
Capone, Al, 141
Carpenter, Karen, 237
Carpenter, Richard, 224, 237
Carr, James, 232
Carter, Chris, 15, 17, 21-22, 25-35, 39-49, 51, 58, 60, 62, 65, 73-74, 76, 89-90, 96, 106, 111, 116, 128, 132-34, 138, 154, 185, 204-06, 241, 243, 246, 248, 250-51, 254-55, 269, 273, 275, 283-87, 289-90, 293, 296, 299-300, 312-13, 317, 327, 339, 342-43, 347-49, 357-58, 360-63, 368-70, 372, 375-76, 386, 391, 398-400, 405, 407, 416, 423, 425, 430, 434, 439, 446-47, 453, 462, 466-67, 469, 470-71, 477, 479, 481, 489, 492-93
Cascade Mountains, 305
Cash, Johnny, 179
Cassatto, Robert Walden, (see Darin, Bobby)
Castle, 395
Castro, Fidel, 138
Catholicism, 198, 314, 321
Cawelti, John G., 345, 359, 366, 374,
CBS, 372-73, 378
CCH Pounder, 142
Celano, Thomas of, 259
Celtic, 196, 206
Central Intelligence Agency, 138, 376

Chamberlain, Adam, 39, 89, 107, 163, 175, 201, 241, 273, 283, 323, 383, 397, 422, 437, 440, 465
Chamberlain, Richard, 224
Chambers, Hank, 32, 34
Chaplin, Charlie, 108
Charlotte, North Carolina, 462
Chase, Luanne, 314
Cheers, 166
Cherokee, 366
Chig, 124
Children of the Night, 61, 436
Chinen, Allan, 81-82
Chinlund, Nick, 284
Christianity, 28, 33, 141, 147, 179, 185, 198-99, 259, 261-62, 268, 271, 310
Christie, Agatha, 353, 470
Christmas, 105-06, 143, 170, 179, 181, 191, 238, 244, 367, 434, 440, 453, 491
Chung, Jose, 69, 110, 116-17, 126, 207, 279, 303, 350, 375, 485
Clairmont Camera, 401
Clapton, Eric, 202
Clark, Josh, 218
Clark, Paul, 77
Clement, Ricardo, 255, 293, 320, 361, 376
Clinton, Bill, 27, 50, 54
Cloke, Kristen, 98, 112, 136, 163-73, 262, 306, 365
"Close to You," 223-24
Collective Unconscious, 81
Collectormania, 76, 423
Columbia & Britannia, 440
Columbo, 350, 376
Comer, Bob, 368
Commish, The, 111, 398
"Confide in Me," 238
Connecticut, 92, 144
Conrad, Joseph, 349
Conway, Jimmy, 142
Cooper, Alice, 202
Cooper, William, 27
Coppola, Francis Ford, 129
Copycat, 50
Corleone family, 137, 142, 152
Corleone, Michael, 113, 129, 143, 150, 152
Corleone, Vito, 141, 148

497

Corwin, Hank, 356
Cosa Nostra, (see Mafia)
Cosby, 451
Cosby, Bill, 451
Coscarelli, Don, 32
Cour, Pierre, 225
Cox, Richard, 260, 297
Crane, Frasier, 166
Cranston, Lamont, 359
Craven, Wes, 377
Crawford, Jack, 346
Cream (band), 202
Creative Artists Agency, 111
Criminal Minds, 370, 377, 467
Criminal Profiler Program, 346
Criss, Peter, 231, 333
Crivelli, Carlo, 301
Crocell, Mr., 140, 234-35, 295, 302
Cross of the Crucifixion, 146, 153, 227-28, 321, 486
Crow, 377
CSI: Crime Scene Investigation, 41, 370, 371-73, 378, 467
Cuffle, Ed, 226, 315-16
Culp, Robert, 376
Cult of the Black Virgin, The, 185
Currie, Gerry, 262
Curtis, Tony, 237
Cypress Hill, 218
Cyprus, Greece, 242
Cyrillic, 75, 470
Cyrus, 65

Da Vinci Code, The, 169
Dahmer, Jeffrey, 27, 50, 52
Dallas, Texas, 50
Dalton, Wally, 303
Dance on the Blood-Dimmed Tide, 350
Darin, Bobby, 219, 221-23
"Dark End of the Street, The" 232
Dark Knight, The, 45, 74
Dark Side Vibe, Tha, 432
Darkroom, 33
Dateline, 50
David, Hal, 224
David, Marjorie, 315, 492, 494
Dawson, Bob, 148, 226
de la Tour, George, 402
De Niro, Robert, 141-42
De Palma, Brian, 141
Dead Calm, 165

Dead on Sight, 377
Dead Sea Scrolls, 256
Declaration of Independence, 149
Deep Masculine, 81, 83-84
Delaney & Bonnie, 202
Delgado, Jose, 315
Demme, Jonathan, 26
Denver, John, 242
Depp, Johnny, 244
Depue, Roger L., 133, 357
Derrida, Jacques, 334
Detroit Rock City, 231
Devil, 28, 42, 67, 140, 196, 234-35, 241, 252-53, 260, 270, 294, 297-98, 301-02, 304, 310, 314, 318, 412
DeVito, Tommy, 141
Dexter, 22, 116, 416
di Bernardo, Giuliano, 129, 131, 145-47, 149, 158, 160
Diakun, Alex, 251, 296, 362
DiCaprio, Leonardo, 189
Dickerson, James, 288
"Die Moritat von Mackie Messer," 222
Diewold, Lauren, 306
Dillahunt, Garret, 454
Dillon, Paul, 285
Dionysus, 270
Directors Guild of America, 383, 416
"Dirty Snowball," 337, 338, 339
Discovery Channel, 398
Dixon, Brian A., 57, 107, 241, 323, 341, 397, 415, 423-24, 437-38, 440, 465
Dog Day Afternoon, 455
Doggett, John, 469
Doherty, Joe, 231
Donaldson, Roger, 376
Donnie Brasco, 150
Donut Hole, The, 302, 303
Douglas, John, 73, 116, 275, 345, 360
Douglas, Kirk, 69
Dove, Gary, 151
Downey Jr., Robert, 373
Doyle, Arthur Conan, 29, 344-45, 349, 372-73
Doyle, Cassie, 231, 376, 411
Dracula, 26
Dragon-Con, 441
"Dream Lover," 222

INDEX

du Maurier, George, 26
Duchovny, David, 42, 123, 247
Duggan, Michael, 154, 187, 368, 489-90
Dunfermline, Scotland, 233
Dupin, C. Auguste, 343-46, 348, 359, 364, 375
Duvall, Robert, 135
Dynasty, 203

Easter, 180
Eastman, Rodney, 260, 297
Ebola virus, 121
Eden, 261, 266
Edmundson, Mark, 26, 27
Ektachrome, 377
El Cajon Valley High School, 110
Elder, The, 150-51
Elementary, 373
Eliot, George, 348
Emmy Awards, 327, 402
Empusae, 259
Entertainment Weekly, 350
Eppes, Charlie, 378
Ertegün, Ahmet, 202
E.T.: The Extra-Terrestrial, 210
Evans, Rick, 238
Event Horizon, 377
Everley Brothers, The, 233
Exorcist, The, 267, 271
Ezekiel Drive, 49, 79, 86, 107, 241, 296, 305, 308, 349

Fabricant, Ephraim, 251-53, 257, 270, 296-97, 362
Falco, Edie, 143
Falco, Richard David, (see Berkowitz, David)
Falk, Peter, 376
"Fall of the House of Usher, The," 374
Family Plot, 120, 384
Fauchon, Guy, 297
Faulkner, William, 25
F.B.I. Academy, 133, 292, 364
Fear, 377
Federal Bureau of Investigation, 22, 30, 39, 44, 66, 73, 133, 144, 147, 150, 152, 154-57, 188, 230, 234, 250, 253, 263, 291-92, 306, 312-13, 328-29, 337-38, 345-46, 357, 362, 364, 377-78, 445-46, 452, 457, 461, 464, 489, 492-93
Feinberg, Joel, 301
Ferdinand, Franz, 148
Few Good Men, A, 92
Fields, W. C., 94
Fife, Barney, 236
Fillion, Nathan, 395
Final Destination, 110, 125
Firefly, 395
First Mafia War, 142
Florida, 50
Foreman, Troy L., 39, 57, 89, 107, 163, 175, 201, 241, 273, 323, 383, 415, 432, 445, 465, 472
Forrest Gump, 29
Forster, E. M., 298
Four Horsemen of the Apocalypse, 199
Fourth Horseman Press, 440
Fox, 17, 32, 40, 44, 50, 59, 90-91, 97, 101-03, 105, 109, 111, 113, 117, 118, 122, 124, 169, 187, 205, 276, 282, 284-85, 319, 333, 339, 347, 352, 359, 370, 375, 391-92, 398, 405, 416, 427-29, 447-48, 453, 463, 467, 469
Fox All Access, 442
Fox Broadcasting, 429
Fox Studios, 62
Frankenstein, 28
Franklin, Aretha, 202
Freeborn, Mark, 110, 188, 387
Freemasonry, 134, 145, 147, 152
Frehley, Ace, 231, 333
Frenchman, The, 42, 217, 285-86, 293, 308, 352, 359, 361
Fresno, California, 176
Freud, Sigmund, 81
Frewer, Matt, 395
Fringe, 213
Fugitive, The, 208
FX, 125, 429

Gabriel, Peter, 191
Gallagher, Megan, 19, 41, 49, 79, 89-99, 102, 128, 170, 276, 288, 310, 330, 392, 418, 437
Galloway, JoAnne, 92
Game of Thrones, 402
Gammell, Robin, 132, 260, 294

499

Gandolfini, James, 129
Garry, Dolores, 320
Gatiss, Mark, 372
Gemini Killer, 271
Ghost Whisperer, 370, 378
Giacchino, Michael, 213
Gibbons, Beth, 220, 235
Giebelhouse, Robert, 157, 252, 349, 351
Giger, H. R., 376
Gilbert & Sullivan, 289
Gilbert, Richard, 152-53
Gilligan, Vince, 116
Gilmore, Gary, 117
Gingrich, Newt, 54
Girl with the Dragon Tattoo, The, 354
Glaser, Alex, 69, 83, 417-18
G-Mex Centre, 423
Gnosticism, 189, 198, 261
God, 21, 33-34, 60, 63-64, 86, 125, 176, 180, 189, 228, 247-48, 261-62, 288, 311, 315, 458
Godfather, The, 113, 135, 141-43, 146, 148-49, 152, 155
Godfather: Part II, The, 129, 137, 150, 157
Golden Globe Awards, 59
Goodbye Charlie, 222, 237
"Goodbye Charlie," 221-23, 237
Goodfellas, 137, 140, 141-43, 149-50, 160
Goopta, Juggernaut Onan, 350
Gordon, Howard, 117
Gospel of Philip, 261
Gothic, 26-29, 34, 301
Graham, Will, 378
Grammer, Kelsey, 90, 166
Grateful Dead, The, 202
Greater Vancouver Regional District, 99, 459
Green River Killer, 336
Green, Richard, 304
Green, Walon, 278, 482
Greenwood, Bruce, 91
Grissom, Gil, 371, 374
Gross, Arye, 155, 409
Gulf War, 331, 368
Gunsche, Helmut, 148-49, 226
Guthrie Theater, 75

ha-Cohen, Isaac ben Jacob, 266

Hagen, Tom, 135
Haggerty, Dylan, 304
"Hair of the Dog," 233
Halloween, 104, 109, 124, 180, 235, 295, 333-34, 367, 391-93, 459, 484
Halloween, 334, 350
Hammond, Justin, 368
Hance, Richard Alan, 237
Harbinson, Patrick, 315, 482, 490-91, 493-94
Hard Target, 65
Harding, Tonya, 27
Harper, Chance, 398
Harris, Thomas, 346, 378
Harsh Realm, 44, 462
Hart to Hart, 203
Harvard Lampoon, The, 418
Hatton, Ricky, 59
Hawaii, 22, 108, 183, 440
Hawkes, John, 295
Hawley, Jordan, 369, 492
Hayden, Mark, 427-28, 430, 432, 434
HBO, 74, 125, 129, 143, 156, 402
"Head Like a Hole," 217
Heaven, 254, 337
Hebrew, 118, 262, 492
Hecuba, 260
Heindl, Scott, 237, 245
Hell, 154, 254, 268, 271
Hemmings, David, 231
Henriksen, Lance, 15-16, 19, 29-35, 42-43, 49, 57-86, 90, 95, 102, 114, 123, 128, 130, 134-35, 158-59, 170, 182-83, 195, 217, 247-48, 255, 285, 288, 299, 307-09, 313, 320, 332-33, 335, 341, 343, 347, 357, 361-63, 367, 392, 399, 405, 422-23, 430, 432-34, 436-37, 439, 442, 454, 456, 466-70
Henry, Deanne, 221
Henry, O., 349
Henstridge, Natasha, 376
Hepburn, Katharine, 91-92
Hera, 258
High School of Music and Art, 203
Hill, Henry, 137, 139, 142-43, 150, 156
Hill, Karen, 137
Hindle, Art, 256

INDEX

Hitcher, The, 334
Hitler, Adolf, 149, 227
"Hits from the Bong," 218
Hogan, Susan, 257
Hollis, Emma, 35, 86, 138, 154-55, 158-59, 230, 232-33, 267, 279, 299, 306, 312-14, 376, 410-12, 438, 445-46, 448, 452-53, 455-64, 489-90, 492-94
Hollis, James, 453, 461
Hollywood, 64, 66, 96, 104, 399, 425
Hollywood Reporter, The, 324
Holmes, Sherlock, 29-30, 343-45, 347, 359, 371-75
Holmes, Stephen, 303
Holy Bible, 199, 295
Holy Blood and the Holy Grail, The, 185
Holy Grail, 228
Home Alone, 209
Home, Pennsylvania, 219
Homeland, 416
Hong, James, 411
Hoover, J. Edgar, 147, 188
Hopi, 366
Horner, James, 210
"Horse with No Name," 226-27
"Horses," (see "Land")
Horton, Ken, 280, 333, 418, 420, 487, 490, 494
"How Deep is Your Love?", 237
"How I Could Just Kill a Man," 218
Howard, James Newton, 208, 210
Howard, Ron, 237
Hudson, William, 439
Hulme, John, 418
Hutchison, Doug, 97, 307
Hyde, Henry, 54
I Love Lucy, 203
"I Wanna Get High," 218

Ice-T, 325
"In the Year 2525," 228, 238
Indiana, 275
Inner Feminine, 81, 83-84
"Insane in the Brain," 218
Intelligence (series), 457, 464
Into the Wild, 71, 417
Investigative Support Unit, 346
Invitation, The, 67
Iroquois, 366

Isaiah, Book of, 257-58
Islam, 271
ITV, 423
Ivankov, Vyacheslav, 300

Jack the Ripper, 287
Jacks, Terry, 220, 237
Jaws, 384
Jeep Cherokee, 234, 317, 465
Jefferson Airplane, 202
Jennicam, 326
Jennifer Eight, 31
Jesus, 85, 184, 259, 265, 295, 302, 310, 320-21, 390
JFK, 356
Johannessen, Chip, 69, 71, 115, 154, 187, 190, 269, 280, 288, 312, 331, 340, 350, 358, 368-69, 377, 415-20, 447-48, 479-83, 485, 487, 489, 490-94
John Paul II, 27
Johnston, Gordon, 148-49, 226
Joplin, Janis, 202
Judaism, 228, 256-57, 260, 271
Judge, The, 256, 295, 320, 432, 478
Judgment Day, 167, 228
Juilliard School, 201, 203, 207, 450
Jung, Carl, 81, 305, 407, 412

Kahn, Madeline, 451
Kamen, Michael, 201-02
Kelley, David E., 327
Kemper, Edmund, 346
Kevorkian, Jack, 220
K.G.B., 152
King Crimson, 238
Kingsley, Ben, 151
Kingsley, Hank, 89
Kiss (band), 231, 333-34, 391, 490
Kitano, Takeshi, 150
Knight, Clear, 148
Knights Templar, 134, 147
Knotts, Don, 236
Kodak, 401
Kolchak: The Night Stalker, 27
Konoval, Karin, 109
Kousakis, John Peter, 360, 487
Krakauer, John, 71, 417
Krumholtz, David, 378
Kruse, Corinna, 371

501

Lake District, England, 242
La-La Land Records, 207
Lamia, 258-59, 267
"Land," 120, 171, 229, 239
"Land of a Thousand Dances," 229-30
Land of the Giants, 53
Lane, Andy, 374
Lang, Stephen J., 349
Lanyard, Michael, 157
Larry Sanders Show, The, 89
Larsson, Steig, 354
Las Vegas Police Department, 370
Las Vegas, Nevada, 370
Law & Order, 187
Law, Jude, 373
Lawrence Welk Show, The, 218, 236
"*Le Moribond*," 237
Leave it to Beaver, 127
Ledger, Heath, 74
Lee, Tamara, 300
Legion, 28, 249-50, 255-56, 259-62, 279, 295, 298, 300, 314, 320, 361, 364-65, 374, 426
Legion (novel), 271
Lenart, Ernest, 148
Lestrade, Inspector G., 349
Levani, 299
"Life During Wartime," 220
Lilith, 256-58, 262, 266
Lincoln Center, 203
Lindala Makeup Effects, Inc., 368
Liotta, Ray, 137
"Little Demon," 234-35
Little, Dwight, 170, 402, 485, 488, 491
Living in Oblivion, 393
Livingston, Bob, 54
Lochner, Stephan, 301
Logan, Don, 151
London Symphony Orchestra, 211
London Symphony Chorus, 211
London, England, 211, 242, 344, 372
Lone Gunmen, The, 281
Long Beach Comic Con, 76
Long Beach, California, 76
Long Wharf Theatre, 92
Long-Haired Man, The, 245, 255, 260, 265, 267, 297, 298
Los Alamos, New Mexico, 187-89, 306, 492

Los Angeles, California, 44, 61, 142, 274, 306, 336, 451-53
Lost (series), 190, 213, 332, 457-58
Lost in Space, 127
Lott, Mr., 154, 311
"Love and Marriage," 216, 225
"Love Hurts," 232-33
"Love is Blue," 225-26
Loyola Marymount University, 110-11, 120
Lucas, George, 210
Lucifer, 250, 255, 300, 305, 318
Lynch, David, 219, 236

Ma, Tzi, 84, 411
Mabius, 155, 313, 320, 369
Mabius, Eric, 261
MacCleister, Tom, 84
MacGyver, 398
Macht, Stephen, 154, 311
"Mack the Knife," 222
MacLeod, Frank, 33
Macy, Bill, 303
Maddrey, Joseph, 25, 77-78, 134, 144, 154, 436, 441
Mafia, 128-29, 135, 137-46, 148, 150-52, 154-56, 211, 300
Magdalene, Mary, 184-85, 310
Maher, Erin, 175-93, 334, 366-67, 484-85, 487, 492
Mailer, Norman, 117
Majestic, 27
Mamet, David, 141
Manassas, Virginia, 62
Manhattan, New York, 197, 203, 484
Manhunter, 378
Mann, Michael, 378
Mann, Ted, 64, 348, 416, 478, 480, 482
Manners, Kim, 219
Mannix, 121
Manson, Charles, 346
Marburg virus, 121, 154, 199, 229, 311, 331
Married with Children, 216, 416
Marsters, James, 331
Martin, Annie, 263
Martin, Quinn, 121
Mass of the Dead, 259
Massachusetts, 450
Masterson, Christopher, 225, 298

INDEX

Mathis, Johnny, 219
Mauriat, Paul, 225
Max Headroom, 395
Mayberry, North Carolina, 236
McCafferty, Dan, 233
McCandless, Christopher, 418
McClaren, Andy, 154, 430
McDowell, Judith, 314
McGavin, Darren, 179, 180
McGrain, Rocket, 69, 350
McKenna, Clare, 310
McKuen, Rod, 237
McLachlan, Robert, 110, 120, 356, 389-90, 397-03, 469
McLaren, Andy, 155-56, 312
McLean, James, 39, 57, 89, 107, 163, 175, 201, 241, 273, 323, 383, 415, 421, 445, 465
McMartin, Virginia, 28
McShane, Ian, 151
McVeigh, Timothy, 27, 50
Means, Lara, 86, 98, 118, 120, 136, 139, 163, 167-68, 170-73, 186, 227, 229, 262, 306, 311, 365, 408, 446, 483-85, 487
MediaWeek, 359
Medium, 370
Megaville, 165
Melville, Herman, 348
Menendez brothers, 27
Metesky, George, 28
Meyer, Nicholas, 406
MGM, 398
Middendorf, Tracy, 231, 411
Middle Ages, 196, 301
Milch, David, 451
Millennial Abyss, The, 424, 437
Millennium
 "19:19," 140, 484
 "522666," 28, 34, 117, 364, 478
 "Anamnesis," 98, 146, 170, 183-84, 189, 191-92, 310, 487
 "Antipas," 244-46, 254-56, 258, 263, 265, 267, 270, 279, 299, 492
 "Bardo Thodol," 84, 155, 313, 316, 408, 419, 493
 "Beginning and the End, The," 97, 131, 133-35, 196, 307, 408, 483
 "Beware of the Dog," 82, 135, 188, 196-97, 199, 223, 265, 308, 365, 483
 "Blood Relatives," 34, 288, 350-51, 408, 416, 479
 "Borrowed Time," 261, 402, 409, 491
 "Broken World," 482
 "Closure," 453-54, 461, 489
 "Collateral Damage," 156, 331-32, 368, 491
 "Covenant," 54, 289, 320, 481
 "Curse of Frank Black, The," 34, 113, 119, 124, 140, 180, 234-35, 295, 302, 367, 484
 "Dead Letters," 34, 112, 117, 277, 287, 364, 367, 387, 408, 478
 "Exegesis," 154, 313, 376, 409, 417, 489
 "*Force Majeure*," 28, 480
 "Forcing the End," 492
 "Fourth Horseman, The," 120, 139, 152, 171, 197, 199, 200, 228, 310, 330, 366, 408, 488
 "Gehenna," 117, 132, 218, 255, 271, 293, 295, 318, 320, 361, 376, 402, 477
 "Goodbye Charlie," 221-23, 237, 485
 "Goodbye to All That," 72, 85, 158, 315, 332, 370, 376, 412, 420, 445, 461, 494
 "Hand of St. Sebastian, The," 134, 141-42, 145, 148, 155, 197-99, 309, 484
 "Human Essence," 456, 458, 490
 "In Arcadia Ego," 419, 487
 "Innocents, The," 313, 390, 409, 445, 452, 461, 489
 "Jose Chung's *Doomsday Defense*," 69, 110, 116, 118, 126, 207, 279, 303, 350, 375, 485
 "Judge, The," 64, 256, 294-95, 349, 359, 408, 432, 478
 "Kingdom Come," 33, 130, 287, 351, 478
 "Lamentation," 28, 42, 132, 197, 241, 245, 247, 251-52, 255, 257-58, 260, 265, 270, 296, 299, 304-05, 361-63, 481
 "Loin Like a Hunting Flame," 28, 480
 "Luminary," 33-34, 69-71, 81-83, 143, 145, 309, 417-18, 485
 "Maranatha," 299, 482
 "Matryoshka," 147, 157-58, 177, 187-88, 306, 368, 492
 "Midnight of the Century," 143, 170, 179, 180, 188, 191, 238, 262, 358, 367, 485

503

"Mikado, The," 28, 289, 325-26, 328, 338, 486
"Monster," 28, 136-38, 221, 306, 365, 483
"Nostalgia," 329, 335, 493
"Omerta," 138, 211, 412, 433, 491
"Owls," 118, 134, 146-49, 151-52, 169, 186, 198-99, 226, 309-10, 338, 486
"Paper Dove," 79, 290, 307, 482
"Pest House, The," 306, 486
"Pilot," 40, 42, 94, 129, 206, 217, 253, 275, 285, 287, 293, 308, 314-15, 351-52, 358, 477
"Powers, Principalities, Thrones and Dominions," 132, 260-61, 270, 295, 297, 362-63, 482
"Room with No View, A," 225-26, 234, 244-45, 254, 258, 262-64, 298, 302, 487
"Roosters," 118, 134, 146, 148-49, 150-52, 169, 186, 198-99, 228, 305, 309-10, 338, 486
"Sacrament," 130, 277-78, 281, 290, 304, 307, 367, 481
"Saturn Dreaming of Mercury," 258, 268, 270, 297, 300, 369, 376, 410, 417, 492
"Sense and Antisense," 136, 315, 419, 483
"Seven and One," 313, 358, 369, 493
"Single Blade of Grass, A," 177, 181-82, 191, 197, 199, 366, 377, 484
"Siren," 300, 487
"Skull and Bones," 155, 232, 313, 376, 409, 417, 458, 490
"Somehow, Satan Got Behind Me," 110, 124, 183-84, 207, 279, 302, 405, 488
"Sound of Snow, The," 99, 157, 232, 402, 410, 412, 491
"TEOTWAWKI," 489
"Thin White Line, The," 117, 143, 226, 237, 364, 387, 480
"Thirteen Years Later," 98, 231, 333, 335, 350, 391, 393, 411, 459, 490
"Time is Now, The," 44, 86, 120-22, 124, 153, 171, 197, 200, 228, 366, 408, 437, 446, 488
"*Via Dolorosa*," 158, 494
"Walkabout," 358, 367, 377, 417, 481
"Weeds," 53-54, 218-19, 276-77, 289, 349, 352, 408, 480

"Well-Worn Lock, The," 54, 276, 289, 405, 408, 479
"Wide Open," 49, 51-53, 96, 290, 352, 479
"Wild and the Innocent, The," 54, 218, 289, 402, 479
Millennium Apocalypse, 439
Millennium Group Sessions, The, 432-33, 436, 440
Millennium Group, The, 30, 35, 40, 70, 83-84, 86, 110, 114, 128, 130-41, 143-49, 151-56, 158-60, 164, 171, 188-89, 195-99, 220, 226, 233, 250, 256-57, 260, 262-63, 270, 278, 298, 307-16, 320, 325, 332, 337-38, 349, 357, 365, 368, 374, 388, 399, 408-09, 411-12, 419-20, 432, 436, 440, 446, 457-58, 461-62, 473, 477-78, 480, 483-86, 488-91, 493-94
Miller, Stephen E., 155, 312, 430
Mills Brothers, The, 188
Milton Keynes, England, 76, 422
Milwaukee, Wisconsin, 50
Mindhunter, 73, 275, 346
Minogue, Kylie, 238
Modern Family, 128
Moen, Dillon, 259, 300
Moffat, Steven, 372
Mohawk, 366
Montana, Lenny, 148
Monti Sabatini, Italy, 141
Monty Python, 202
Moon Over Miami, 111
Moore, Mary Tyler, 91
Moore, Ronald D., 198
Morgan, Darin, 43, 69, 110, 116, 122, 169, 222, 279, 302, 304, 350, 375, 418, 485, 488
Morgan, Glen, 43, 68, 82, 98, 107-26, 132-34, 143, 147, 149, 154, 166, 168-69, 173, 175, 178, 180, 182-83, 186, 189-91, 195, 219-20, 222, 224, 226, 230, 277-80, 287, 295, 303, 307-08, 325, 332, 337-38, 364-65, 367, 386-88, 400, 407, 419, 438, 446, 478, 480, 483-84, 486-88
Moriarty, Professor James, 372-73
Morning Edition, 121
Morris, Jason, 439
Morrison, James, 112, 387

INDEX

Morshower, Glenn, 152
Moses, 60
Mossad, 152
Motel Hell, 334
Moviecam Compact, 377
Moviehole, 425-26
Mt. Baker, 251
Mt. Ventoux, 81
MTV, 230
Muir, Edwin, 77
Muir, John Kenneth, 49, 195, 370, 376, 405
Mulder, Fox, 21, 26, 32, 35, 39, 45, 109, 205, 281, 348, 452, 463-64
Munn, Patrick, 441-42
Murder, She Wrote, 335
"Murders in the Rue Morgue, The," 341-43, 345-46, 374
Murdoch, Laurie, 288
Museum of Jurassic Technology, 112
Music Box Theatre, 92
Mussolini, Benito, 148
Muzak Holdings Corporation, 237
Myatt, Sue, 429

National Association for the Advancement of Colored People, 448
Nazareth (band), 232-33, 320
Nazi, 147-49, 228, 306, 337
NBC, 122, 353, 375
NBC Mystery Movie, The, 353
N.C.I.S., 387, 395
Nebraska, 228
New Haven, Connecticut, 92
New York Rock & Roll Ensemble, 201-03
New York Times, The, 59, 93
New York Undercover, 325
New York University, 212
New York, New York, 197, 236, 374, 450-51
Nicholls, Christina, 437
Nickelodeon, 449-50
Nietzsche, Friedrich, 270
Night Gallery, 120
Night Visions, 377
Nightmare on Elm Street, A, 393, 459
Nine Inch Nails, 217
Nixon, Richard, 26
No Escape, 32

Normandy, France, 367
Norris, Dean, 313
North Carolina, 236, 451
North Carolina School of the Arts, 451
Nostradamus, 42, 286
Not Bad for a Human, 30, 77, 80, 82, 134, 158, 441
Notorious Seven, The, 113
Nowhere Man, 91
NPR, 121
Numb3rs, 378
Nutter, David, 19, 89-90, 125, 206, 243, 254, 276, 355, 398, 402, 477-78, 480
NYPD Blue, 400

O'Connor, Flannery, 349
O'Quinn, Terry, 19, 71, 131, 171, 198, 247, 260, 309, 332-33, 349, 411, 457-58
Oak Creek, Wisconsin, 22, 471
ODESSA, 147-49, 151-52, 228, 486
Ogden, Utah, 54
Oklahoma City, Oklahoma, 50
Old Man, The, 135, 151, 196, 227, 308, 365
Oliver Oliver, 92
Omega, 320
Omen, The, 299
OMNIFilm Productions, 398
One, Two, Buckle My Shoe, 353
Operation Desert Storm, 368
Orbison, Roy, 233
Oregon, 91, 490
Osborn, Paul, 92
Others, The, 122
Ottawa, Canada, 449
Ouroboros, 198
Outer Limits, The, 27
Outerbridge, Peter, 315
Outrage, 150
Owls, 118, 146, 149, 151-52, 169, 186, 198-99, 338, 486

Pacific Northwest, 446
Pacino, Al, 129
Pacquiao, Manny, 59
Padmasambhava, 407
Paglia, Camille, 270
Parallax View, The, 26

Paramount, 90, 339
Paris, France, 344
Parise, Jeff, 85, 315
Parsifal, 152, 227-28
Passenger, The, 354
Patrick, Robert, 469
PBS, 236
Peacock family, 108-09, 219, 223
Peck, M. Scott, 294
People's Choice Awards, 64-65
Pepper, Alistair, 260, 270, 295, 297, 363
Perry, Michael R., 116, 134, 208, 289, 320, 323-340, 350, 391, 470, 486, 490-91, 493
Pesci, Joe, 141
Petersen, William, 371, 378
Petey, Edward, 218
Pettey, Homer B., 233
Pfaster, Donnie, 18, 284-85, 319
Phoenix, Arizona, 263
Picket Fences, 91
Pileggi, Nicholas, 151
Pino, Maryangela, 302
Pirates of the Caribbean, 208, 244
Pistone, Joseph Dominick, 150
Player, The, 393
Poe, Edgar Allen, 341-46, 348, 359, 374-75
Poirot, Hercule, 353, 357, 359
Polaroid, 97, 115, 131, 134-35, 220, 290, 307, 315, 367, 428, 483
Polaroid Man, The, 131, 134-35, 220, 307, 367
Polito, Jon, 433
Pomona, California, 57
Popp, André, 225
Portishead, 217, 220, 235
Portland, Oregon, 478
Portsmouth Naval Prison, 80
Potter, George, 121, 478-88
Powder, 31, 34
Practice, The, 327
Pre-Raphaelites, 402
Previn, Dory, 222
Princip, Gavrilo, 148
Profiler (series), 375
Prohibition, 142, 147
Project Grillflame, 376
Psycho, 231, 350, 391
Psycho Circus, 231, 391

"Psycho Circus," 231
Puzo, Mario, 142

Quantico, Virginia, 30, 133, 292, 346, 348, 364, 377
Quran, 262

Radiohead, 227
Raimi, Sam, 325
Rashomon, 35
Raziel, 260
Red Dragon, 328, 378
Redgrave, Vanessa, 231
Redmond, Sarah-Jane, 19, 42, 67-68, 241-48, 250, 279, 296, 299, 362, 458
Reichenbach Falls, 373
Reilly, Charles Nelson, 110, 126
Reindl, Kay, 175-93, 334, 366-67, 484-85, 487, 492
Renan, Ernest, 348
Renshaw, Barry, 438
Ressler, Robert, 291, 346
Revelation, Book of, 121, 171, 265, 271, 286
Reynolds, Debbie, 237
Rhode Island, 50
Rich, Frank, 92, 93
"Ride of the Valkyries," 223
Riley, Brendan, 373
Ripley, Ellen, 167
Ritchie, Guy, 373
Road, The, 123
"Roads," 217
Roberts, Gordon, 127
Roberts, Jeremy, 237
Robson, Mark, 383
Rock & Shock, 76
Roddenberry, Gene, 51
Roe, Teresa, 302
Roedecker, Brian, 110, 338
Rojas, Joselyn, 437
Rookies, The, 203
Room with a View, A, 298
Roosters, 118, 146-47, 149, 151-52, 169, 186, 199, 228, 338, 486
Ross, Freddy, 31
Roswell, New Mexico, 27
Roth, Hyman, 150, 157
Roth, Peter, 91, 109, 111
Roush, Matt, 350

INDEX

Route 509, 220
Routh, Brandon, 422
Rowland, Rodney, 112
Royal Air Force, 242

Sabrina the Teenage Witch, 102
Sacks, Oliver, 216, 225
Samael, 261, 266
Samiel, 261
Sammael, 260-61, 297, 363
San Diego, California, 110-11, 337-38
San Diego Chargers, 122
Sanderson, Lucas, 259, 268, 300
Sandy Howard Productions, 111
Sartre, Jean-Paul, 348
Satan, 28, 198, 255, 265, 270, 304
Saunder, Cynthia, 375
Saxum, Divina, 255, 257, 265
Saxum, John, 256, 264-65, 267
Saxum, Una, 257, 263-64
Scaife, Doug, 430
Scandinavian Sci-Fi, Game, and Film Convention, 425
Schutzstaffel (SS), 147
Scientology, 350
Scorsese, Martin, 137
Scott, Klea, 19, 138, 154, 230, 247, 267, 279, 299, 330, 335-36, 390-91, 410, 436, 438, 445-64, 471
Screen Actors Guild, 165
Scully, Dana, 21, 26, 39, 45, 219, 281, 284, 452, 463-64
Sea Hunt, 398
Seaman, Donald, 291
"Seasons in the Sun," 220-21, 237
Seattle Police Department, 285-86
Seattle Victim Services, 288
Seattle, Washington, 39, 50, 229, 232, 253, 264, 285-86, 310, 349, 351, 370, 477, 491
"Second Coming, The" 286
Second Mafia War, 142
Seminole, 366
Seneca, 366
Serling, Rod, 120
Seven (film), 40, 50, 96, 388
Severin, Alice, 232
Sexton, Anne, 349
Sexy Beast, 151
Shadow, The, 359

Shakespeare in the Park, 450
Shakespeare, William, 434, 450
Shapiro, Paul, 402, 490-92, 494
Shelley, Mary, 28
Sherlock (series), 372-73
Sherlock Holmes (film), 373
Sherlock Holmes: A Game of Shadows, 373
Shima-Tsumo, Linda, 124, 183-84
Showtime, 116, 125, 416
Sibyl, 258-59
Sil, 376
Silence of the Lambs, The (novel), 30, 328, 346
Silence of the Lambs, The (film), 26
Simmons, Gene, 231, 333
Simmons, Peter, 231
Simon & Schuster, 325
Simon (angel), 262
Simon Fraser University Film Workshop, 398
Simon, Don, 93
Simpson, Homer, 224
Simpson, O. J., 27, 50
Simpsons, The, 224, 350
Sinatra, Frank, 216
Six, Sean, 288
Skelter, 324
Skull and Bones (society), 139
Sledge, Percy, 232
Sly and the Family Stone, 202
Smallwood, Tucker, 112, 220
Smith, Graham, 427-28
Smith, Patti, 120-21, 171, 192, 229
Smitrovich, Bill, 19, 102, 132, 251, 286, 349
Snow, Mark, 19, 159, 191, 201-13, 217, 227, 235, 238-39, 419, 436, 454
Son of Sam, (see Berkowitz, David)
Soprano, Carmela, 143
Soprano, Tony, 129, 156
Sopranos, The, 63, 129, 141, 143, 156
Sorkin, Aaron, 92
South Mills, Pennsylvania, 335
Soviet Union, 27
Space: Above and Beyond, 111-13, 121-22, 124-25, 166-69, 173, 395, 438
"Who Monitors the Birds," 121
Species, 376

507

Spelling, Aaron, 203
Spice Girls, The, 102
Spielberg, Steven, 206, 210
"Splish Splash," 222
Spotnitz, Frank, 17, 45, 53, 73, 246, 250-51, 253, 273-82, 289, 299, 313, 367, 369, 407, 425-26, 432, 439, 447, 464, 466-70, 480-81, 489, 492, 493
St. Andrew, 196-97
Standards and Practices, 124, 183-84, 303
Stanford Prison Experiment, 300, 320
Stanley, Paul, 231, 333
Stanton Research Institute, 376
Stanwyck, Barbara, 167
Star Chamber, The, 143
Star Trek, 51, 213, 339, 426, 429, 433
Stations of the Cross, 315, 321
Steadicam, 377
Stevenson, Robert Louis, 26, 187
Stewart, Malcolm, 148, 226
Stock, Virginia, 419, 493
Stoker, Bram, 26
Stone, Randy, 125
Stone Cold, 65
Stone, Oliver, 356
Stop Making Sense, 220
Story and the Fable, The, 77
Strange Case of Dr. Jekyll and Mr. Hyde, The, 26
Strange Luck, 398
Stranger Returns, The, 323-24
Strasberg, Lee, 150
Streiber, Whitley, 27
Stringfellow, William, 79
Study in Scarlet, A, 344
Super Bowl, 122
Superman Returns, 422
Survival Quest, 32, 34
Susan Smith Agency, 164
Swan, Eric, 331
Sweeney, D. B., 398

Takahashi, Steven, 84-85, 411
Taken (series), 395
Talking Heads, 220
Talmud, 261
Tangari, Joe, 215
Tankosic, Tim, 358, 377, 481

Taylor, Andy, 219, 236
Templeton, Genele, 310
Ten Thirteen Productions, 44, 47, 109, 111, 126, 168, 203, 206, 243, 246, 304, 323, 356-57, 398, 416, 423, 447, 452, 468-69
Ten Years After (band), 202
Terms of Endearment, 384
TGIF, 102
Thanksgiving, 179, 431
This is Who We Are, 424, 426
Three Days of the Condor, 26
Threepenny Opera, The, 222
Tibetan Book of the Dead, The, (see *Bardo Thödol*)
"Till Then," 188
Tiplady, Brittany, 63-64, 79, 93, 95, 101-06, 128, 298, 330, 367, 410, 437, 456, 468
Topaz, 384
Torlasco, Domietta, 354-55, 372-73
Toronto, Canada, 450
Traffic (band), 233
Trilby, 26
"Trimm Trabb," 231
"Trio," 238
Tron: Uprising, 442
Trust, The, 152-53
Tuck, Jessica, 232
Tucker, Ken, 350
Turner, J. M. W., 399
TV Guide, 34, 103, 359
Twilight Zone, The, 27
Tyler, Jacob, 237

U2, 177
U.F.O., 27-28
UFO Kidnapped, 450
Universal Pictures, 176
University of Reading, 216
Untouchables, The, 141
Uriel, 260
U.S. Marshals, 156
U.S. Naval Intelligence, 138
U.S. Senate, 152
Usher, Roderick, 374

Valachi, Joseph, 152
Vancouver, British Columbia, 22, 42, 44, 91, 93, 95, 115, 124, 179, 243, 275-76, 326, 395, 399, 400-01,

INDEX

418, 449, 452-53, 455, 457, 464, 469, 490
Vanishing Point, 418
Vansen, Shane, 166-67
Ventoux, Alex, (see Glaser, Alex)
Victoria, British Columbia, 398
Victoria, Rachel, 257
Vinton, Bobby, 236
Virgin Mary, 185
von Sydow, Max, 59

Waco, Texas, 50
Waconda, Oregon, 262
Wagner, Richard, 152, 223, 227-28
Walt Disney Studios, 39
Ward, Robert, 325
Warwick, Dionne, 224, 229
Washington (state), 251
Washington, D.C., 44, 230, 478, 482
Washington, George, 149
Watson, John, 344, 372-73
Watts, Peter, 22, 35, 71-72, 83, 131, 139, 154, 156-58, 186, 198, 227, 260, 262-63, 296-98, 307-13, 316, 332, 349, 351, 358, 376, 388, 411, 457, 461, 484, 486, 488, 491
Watts, Taylor, 156-57
"We Three Kings," 238
Wegner, D. M., 216
Weill, Kurt, 222
Welk, Lawrence, 236
Wexler, Mike, 418
Whedon, Joss, 378
Whitcher, Patricia, 111
White, Trevor, 430
Whitehead, Robert, 92
Whitley, Richard, 223, 485
Wilde, Bob, 155, 293, 313, 320
Willard, 110
William S. Paley Television Festival, 425
Williams, John, 206, 209-10
Williams, Tennessee, 92
Williams, Tim I., 216
Williamstown, Massachusetts, 450
Wilson, Colin, 291
Winehouse, Amy, 428
Winstone, Ray, 151
Winters, Dean, 140, 234, 295
Winton, Colleen, 320
Wire, The, 395

Wise, Robert, 120, 383
Witness Protection Program, 156
Wiz, The, 111
Wizard of the Oz, The, 449
"Wonderful! Wonderful!," 119, 219, 223
Wong, James, 43, 68, 82, 98, 107-26, 132-34, 143, 147, 149, 154, 166, 168-69, 178, 180-82, 187, 189-91, 195, 219-20, 222, 224, 226, 277-78, 280, 287, 295, 307-08, 325-26, 332, 337-38, 364-65, 367, 386-88, 400, 407, 419, 438, 446, 478, 480, 483-84, 486-88
Worcester, Massachusetts, 76
World War I, 148
World War II, 138, 147
World Wrestling Federation, 231
Wormwood, 271
Wright, Thomas J., 22, 120, 167, 171, 227, 335, 355, 368, 383-95, 402, 436, 454, 459, 471, 478-80, 482-94
Wrinch, Mike, 120
Writers Guild of America, 115
Wu, Vivian, 300
Wunstorf, Peter, 355, 377, 398
Wyeth, Andrew, 402

X-Files, The, 17-21, 25-28, 30, 32, 35, 39, 40, 42-47, 50, 62-63, 90, 107-13, 116-19, 125, 143, 168, 172, 175, 179, 201, 203-04, 206-09, 212, 219, 222-23, 243, 246, 273-74, 277-82, 284-85, 312, 327, 333, 347-48, 359-60, 386, 395, 398-400, 416-17, 423, 425, 430, 437, 441, 446, 452-53, 462-64, 468-69, 471
"*Die Hand Die Verlezt*," 117
"Field Where I Died, The" 168, 172, 175
"Home," 108, 109, 219, 220, 236
"Humbug," 116
"Irresistible," 18, 284
"Musings of a Cigarette Smoking Man," 327
"Squeeze," 111
"*Unruhe*," 50
"*Via Negativa*," 277
X-Files: I Want to Believe, The, 45-46, 246, 284, 425, 464, 471

X-Files News, 441

Y2K, 21, 49, 199, 337, 463
Yagher, Jeff, 98, 392
Yale University, 139, 155, 212, 450
Yaponchik, 299
Yardbirds, The, 231
Yeats, William Butler, 286, 349
Yellow House, 15, 19, 31, 41, 49, 62, 64, 78-80, 82, 84, 94, 107, 130, 135, 153, 159, 229, 232, 234, 253-54, 286, 290, 296, 305, 349, 367, 370, 372, 399
You Can't Do That on Television, 449
Young Artist Awards, 104

Zager & Evans, 228
Zager E-Z Play, 238
Zager, Denny, 228, 238
Zamacona, Jorge, 33, 287, 348, 478, 479
Zane, Billy, 165
Zelenyj, Alexander, 249
Zelniker, Michael, 287
Zeus, 258-59, 270
Zimbardo, Philip, 300
Zimmer, Hans, 208, 210
Zodiac Killer, 28, 287, 320
Zoroastrianism, 262

"I made this!"

www.ingramcontent.com/pod-product-compliance
Lightning Source LLC
Chambersburg PA
CBHW030411100426
42812CB00028B/2921/J